ALPHA KAPPA ALPHA SORORITY, INC.®

THE HISTORY OF CENTRAL REGION

Pledged to Remember

A Tradition of Timeless Service

LOANN JULIA HONESTY KING

Third Edition

Pledged to Remember

*The History of Central Region
Alpha Kappa Alpha Sorority, Inc.®*

THIRD EDITION. ©2014 BY LOANN JULIA HONESTY KING.
ALL RIGHTS RESERVED. ALPHA KAPPA ALPHA SORORITY, INC.® IS A REGISTERED
TRADEMARK OF ALPHA KAPPA ALPHA SORORITY, INCORPORATED.

DESIGN BY DANIELGRAPHICS. PRINTING BY STELLAR GRAPHICS.
PRINTED IN USA.

ISBN 978-1-4951-0046-8

About the Author

Loann Julia Honesty King was educated in the Chicago Public Schools and received her B.Ed. degree from Chicago Teachers College (Chicago State University) and her M.A. degree in Inner City Studies from Northeastern Illinois University with post graduate work at DePaul and Roosevelt Universities.

She is a retired educator and administrator with over forty years of experience in the public and private sectors at the city, state and federal levels. When she retired in 2003 as Vice President of Student Services and Enrollment Management at Kennedy-King, College City Colleges of Chicago, a Congratulatory Retirement Proclamation was issued by the State of Illinois' House of Representatives, Ninety-Third General Assembly.

She was initiated in Beta Chapter, Chicago IL, in 1959 and has been an active financial member since the day of her initiation. Transferring to Theta Omega Chapter, Chicago, IL in 1963 where she currently serves on the Basilei Council, Graduate Advisor's Council and member of the Theta Omega Chapter/AKArama Foundation, Inc. Executive Committee.

Her record of sorority service has included almost every aspect of membership participation and leadership. She served as Basileus of both Beta and Theta Omega Chapters; was elected, as an undergraduate, to the National Nominating Committee; served as Supreme Tamiouchos (1976-1980); was an Incorporator and the first Treasurer of the Educational Advancement Foundation; a consultant to the Corporate Office; Chairperson of the National Finance Committee and National Economic Development Sub-Committee; chaired the sorority's first Economic Development Conference; served as the 21st Central Regional Director (1986-1990); and as the Centennial International Program Committee Chairman (2006-2010).

Following her tenure as the 21st Central Regional Director, she authored the 1st edition of the History of Central Region—*Pledged to Remember*, in 1997 and in 2006 authored an extension of that work in a second edition. This third edition of the history is an extension of those works.

A Golden Soror she is also is a life member, charter member of the Heritage Club, a member of the Capital Improvement Project (CIP) Loraine Green Club, and a charter life contributor to the Educational Advancement Foundation. In recognition of her outstanding service Soror King was the recipient of the sorority's highest honor for sorors the Founders' Graduate Service Award at the Centennial Boule in 2008.

Her volunteer and community service is not limited to the sorority and she has received many notable recognitions and awards for her community and professional service. Soror King has extensive nonprofit board experience. She has served as President of the Parkway Community House Board of Directors, and served on the boards of Jane Addams Hull House and HRDI (Human Resources Development Institute) and currently serves as a founding member of the African American Legacy Board of the Chicago Community Trust and the Advisory Board for Urban Prep Academies.

She and her husband of 52 years established the Loann and Paul King Philanthropic Fund, in 2001, with the Chicago Community Trust, becoming the Trust's first family donor advised fund established by African Americans. They have two adult sons, Paul J. King III and Timothy Jay King.

Dear Sorors,

It my pleasure and an honor to present to you the 3rd edition of our Central Region History Book, *Pledged to Remember*. Central Region holds a special place in the history of Alpha Kappa Alpha. It is the birthplace of our Founder, Soror Ethel Hedgeman Lyle. Central Region is the home of our Corporate Office and home to the second and third oldest undergraduate chapters in Alpha Kappa Alpha. Five Former Supreme Basilei, have called Central Region their home. In July of 2014, Central Region will have a sixth soror who will serve as the Supreme Basileus of Alpha Kappa Alpha — Soror Dorothy Buckhanan Wilson. Twenty-eight dynamic women have served us well as Regional Directors who have helped to keep our region on the cutting edge with their progressive thinking and dedicated service. Ours is a proud history that we want told.

I thank our Central Region Historian, Soror Loann Julia Honesty King, 21st Central Regional Director and Former Supreme Tamiouchos, for taking on the task, again, of updating our history book. Soror Loann's commitment to preserving Central Region's history has given us three comprehensive and well-documented editions. Finally, I thank you for your support of this endeavor. You will find that our Central Region History Book is a valuable addition to your Alpha Kappa Alpha library. Enjoy!

Yours in Sisterhood and Service,

Gisele M. Casanova

Soror Giselé M. Casanova
28TH CENTRAL REGIONAL DIRECTOR

For the many Sorors whose unselfish service, dedication, commitment and friendship taught me the true meaning of sisterhood! And to my family whose love and support continues to sustain me.

Table of Contents

Preface IX
Acknowledgements X
AKA International Timeless Histories Historical Perspective XIII
Central Region's Timeless Histories Historical Perspective XV

PART I — THE FIRST QUARTER OF THE CENTURY 1
Beta Chapter 5
Gamma Chapter 11
Pauline Kigh Reed 17
Kappa Chapter 18
Mu Graduate/Gamma Omega 20
Xi Graduate/Eta Omega 29
Theta Omega Chapter 35
Eta Chapter 45
Lambda Omega 46
Tau Chapter 47

PART II — THE SECOND QUARTER OF THE CENTURY 53
Alpha Eta Omega 57
Alpha Mu Omega Chapter 61
Beta Delta Chapter 65
Beta Zeta Chapter 68
Beta Epsilon Chapter 70
Beta Gamma Omega 72
Alice E. McGhee Smart 76
Beta Rho Omega Chapter 77
Arlene Washington 79
Beta Upsilon Omega Chapter 80
Beta Omega Omega Chapter 84
Blanche Patterson Williams 86
Gamma Kappa Omega Chapter 87
Maenell Hamlin Newsome 90
Gamma Psi Omega Chapter 91
Delta Delta Omega Chapter 100
Lucille Wilkins 107
Delta Phi Omega Chapter 108
Delta Chi Omega Chapter 111
Epsilon Epsilon Omega Chapter 115
Epsilon Kappa Omega Chapter 118
Epsilon Lambda Omega Chapter 122

PART III — THE THIRD QUARTER OF THE CENTURY 125
Evelyn Roberts 128
Beta Iota Chapter 129
Delta Beta Chapter 130
Zeta Zeta Omega Chapter 134
Maude Lillian Mann 137
Annetta Moten Lawson 138
Delta Omicron Chapter 139
Eta Kappa Omega Chapter 142
Eta Mu Omega Chapter 146

Lee Anna Shelburne 150
Ordie Amelia Roberts 151
Epsilon Delta Chapter 152
Theta Rho Omega Chapter 153
Epsilon Zeta Chapter 158
Gamma Chi Chapter 160
Epsilon Eta Chapter 162
Epsilon Iota Chapter 163
Beta Phi Chapter 165
Epsilon Xi Chapter 169
Epsilon Rho Chapter 173
Johnetta Randolph Haley 176
Zeta Zeta Chapter 178
Zeta Iota Chapter 179
Zeta Nu Chapter 180
Zeta Phi Chapter 182
Eta Alpha Chapter 184
Eta Gamma Chapter 185
Eta Rho Chapter 186
Iota Chi Omega Chapter 188
Theta Omicron Chapter 190
Kappa Epsilon Omega Chapter 191
Iota Delta Chapter 194

PART IV — THE FINAL QUARTER OF THE CENTURY 195
Gloria E. Smith Bond 198
Iota Epsilon Chapter 200
Iota Sigma Chapter 201
Kappa Mu Omega Chapter 202
Kappa Tau Omega Chapter 205
Kappa Psi Omega Chapter 208
Lambda Alpha Omega Chapter 211
Lambda Mu Omega Chapter 215
Lambda Xi Chapter 218
Lambda Nu Omega Chapter 222
Lambda Psi Chapter 225
Lambda Tau Omega Chapter 227
Mu Beta Chapter 234
Mu Delta Omega Chapter 236
Peggy Lewis LeCompte 239
Mu Rho Chapter 242
Nu Lambda Chapter 244
Nu Omicron Omega Chapter 247
Nu Pi Omega Chapter 250
Nu Sigma Chapter 253
Xi Epsilon Chapter 254
Xi Zeta Chapter 255
Xi Eta Omega Chapter 256
Xi Nu Omega Chapter 261
Xi Kappa Chapter 268
Mabel Evans Cason 271
Omicron Delta Omega Chapter 273
Omicron Eta Omega Chapter 275
Omicron Theta Omega Chapter 280

Omicron Sigma Omega Chapter..287
Omicron Phi Omega Chapter 292
Pi Gamma Omega Chapter 296
Omicron Alpha Chapter...302
Pi Lambda Omega Chapter...303
Loann Julia Honesty King 311
Omicron Xi Chapter...313
Sigma Phi Omega Chapter 316
Yvonne Perkins 325
Pi Lambda Chapter 327
Tau Gamma Omega Chapter 331
Pi Nu Chapter 334
Martha Levingston Perine Beard...337
Rho Lambda Chapter 339
Upsilon Mu Omega Chapter..340
Upsilon Phi Omega Chapter 343
Nadine C. Bonds..346
Phi Epsilon Omega Chapter...347

PART V — THE NEW CENTURY 353
Phi Kappa Omega Chapter 357
Sigma Gamma Chapter 369
Sigma Eta Chapter..371
Chi Alpha Omega Chapter...372
Dorothy W. Buckhanan..378
Chi Xi Omega Chapter..380
Chi Sigma Omega Chapter...381
Chi Phi Omrga Chapter..385
Chi Chi Omega Chapter...387
Chi Omega Omega Chapter 392
Pamela Bates Porch..399
Giselé M. Casanova 402
Tau Iota Chapter 405
Tau Mu Chapter...410
Tau Rho Chapter..412

PART VI — A TRADITION OF SERVICE 415
Loraine Richardson Green..417
Maudelle Brown Bousfield 419
Maude Brown Porter 421
Linda Marie White...422
Barbara A. McKinzie 424
Officers & Appointments 426

PART VII — CENTRAL REGIONAL CONFERENCES................437
A Pictorial View..440

APPENDIX I: Chapter Listing/Charter Dates.......................................516

APPENDIX II: Selected Resources 524

INDEX 526

Preface

A bit of history lies in how The History of Central Region, *Pledged to Remember,* came about. While I was serving as Central Regional Director Soror Loraine Richardson Green suggested on many occasions that I should document the many contributions of the chapters and sorors of Central Region. So at the 55th Central Regional Conference in 1989 I appointed a Central Region History Committee chaired by the late Anne Mitchem Davis, former Executive Director and Sorority Archivist. For several reasons including Soror Davis' move to Washington, D.C. deferred the writing of the Region's history.

Encouraged by Soror Green to pursue this "noble" endeavor, I requested of my successor, Soror Yvonne Perkins, 22nd Central Regional Director the appointment of another regional history committee and volunteered to serve as chairman. She responded positively and the first meeting of the committee was held at the 57th Central Regional Conference in 1991 and continued into the administration of the 23rd Central Regional Director, Soror Martha Perine Beard and was published in 1997.

I shall forever cherish the personal note received from the 15th Supreme Basileus, Soror Marjorie Holloman Parker, Ph.D. after receiving a copy of the first edition in which she stated that "It is beautiful and beautifully done." And her public accolades at the general session of the 58th Boule in Chicago, Illinois. Six years later, the 26th Central Regional Director, Soror Dorothy Wilson Buckhanan commissioned the writing of the 2nd edition.

This third edition of the History of Central Region *Pledged to Remember* is an expanded version of these two edition's story of one region's contribution to the history of Alpha Kappa Alpha Sorority, Inc. I am extremely grateful for the support and vision of these fellow Former Central Regional Directors for the opportunity to document Central Region's extraordinary history. My heartfelt thanks to Soror Giselé M. Casanova for officially appointing me Central Region's Historian and her confidence in me to write this 3rd edition in response to the Timeless History project.

The preparation of this edition involved extensive research, revisiting numerous sorority documents and publications, non-sorority historical documents, and incorporating updated information submitted by chapters. In addition the history of the region is tied to the history of the struggle of African Americans to gain human dignity and equal rights. Although the task was great and many hours have been spent to produce a quality comprehensive product. Much has been learned from the experience.

As with the first and second edition, this edition also moves from the sorority's beginning to the establishment of chapters and the formation of the region. Each Chapter's history is listed following the description of the tenure of the Regional Director that chartered the chapter. Pictures of the Regional Directors' and other national officers are from the period of their tenure.

Information on Central Regional Conferences which provided a forum for interpretation and fulfillment of national policies and programs, reports on chapter and individual participation in national activities, and an opportunity for region fellowship is presented in chronological order. Statistical information and conference highlights are recorded for each conference, where records were available, starting with the first Central Regional Conference on May 23, 1931 in Indianapolis, IN to the 79th, April 4-7, 2013 also in Indianapolis, IN.

As a whole, the sorors of Central Region have never failed to rise to the occasion or answer the call, and often go beyond the expected. Sorors serving on National/International Committees is also documented and future histories will continue to document the exemplary contributions of the region and its members. "So let it be written—so let it be done."

– *Loann Julia Honesty King*

Acknowledgements

My appreciation is extended to those chapter historians and other sorors who aided in gathering information, and writing and updating chapter histories. Words are inadequate to express my sincere gratitude to Regional Editor Chairman and Co-Chairman, Soror Melody R. Waller and Soror Phyllis Gray both members of Chi Omega Omega Chapter. Their help, support, expert editing skills, conscientious oversight and assistance to chapters in the writing of their individual chapter Timeless History submissions was invaluable. Without them it could not have been done.

Thanks to Sorors Patricia A. Watkins, Corporate Office Membership Director, Charita Callaway, Membership Department, Barbara Sutton, EAF Executive Director, Erika Everett, EAF, Finance Director and Crystal Kelly, EAF Executive Assistant for providing information. Thanks also to Sorors Melody R. Waller, Phyllis Gray, Janae LeFlore, Kara Holloway, Veletta L. Bell and Sheila Solomon for the final editing review. Thanks also to Michelle Paramore, Michelle R. Willis and Edna Shanklin.

A very special thanks to my fellow former Theta Omega Chapter Basilei: Sorors Essie Blaylock, Mae R. Carr, Frances Carroll, Audrey Cooper-Stanton, Deborah Dangerfield and Deborah Underwood who provided me with source documents and research information. I am also extremely grateful to my son Tim for his expert input, my husband Paul, son Paul III and "BFF" Soror Judith Daylie Armstead, for just being there.

History Chapter Contacts and Contributors

Gamma Omega	Frederica Coleman
Eta Omega	Shirley Fuqua-Jackson
Theta Omega	Kara Holloway
Alpha Eta Omega	Tasha Tyler Roberts
Alpha Mu Omega	Joyce Rand
Beta Gamma Omega	
Beta Rho Omega	Betty Baker-Wharton
Beta Upsilon Omega	Anitra Williams
Beta Omega Omega	Aubrey B. Lee
	Ruby G. Tolliver
Gamma Kappa Omega	Faith Y. Miller
Gamma Psi Omega	Joyce Price
	Penny Cochran
Delta Delta Omega	Juanita Brown
Delta Phi Omega	Lisa M. Tittle
Delta Chi Omega	Adrianne Hayward
Epsilon Epsilon Omega	Tamara Hoff
Epsilon Kappa Omega	Dara Atandare
	Brenda Thompson
Epsilon Lambda Omega	Laverna Thomas
Zeta Zeta Omega	Vicki White
Eta Kappa Omega	Schundra Hubbard
Eta Mu Omega	Giovanna Edwards
Theta Rho Omega	Linda Bailey
Iota Chi Omega	
Kappa Mu Omega	Lita Holmes

Kappa Tau Omega	
Kappa Psi Omega	Barbara Nichols
Lambda Alpha Omega	Osie Davenport
Lambda Mu Omega	Joy Pilcher
Lambda Nu Omega	Cherise Hall
Lambda Tau Omega	Judy Rush
Mu Delta Omega	Lucretia Starnes Young
Nu Omicron Omega	Belinda J. Carr
Nu Pi Omega	Davina Sharee Frazier
Xi Eta Omega	Brenda Hanes
Xi Nu Omega	Latrice Eggleston
Omicron Delta Omega	Jennifer Palmer
Omicron Eta Omega	Taina Charleston
Omicron Theta Omega	Nina Caldwell
Omicron Sigma Omega	Barbara Pollock
	Anna Senter
Omicron Phi Omega	Sharon Grier
Pi Gamma Omega	Joyce D. Higgins
	Coleen Williams
Pi Lambda Omega	Janice Hodge
Sigma Phi Omega	Lezie Thompson
Tau Gamma Omega	Valerie Leon Brown
Upsilon Mu Omega	Victoria Pryor
Upsilon Phi Omega	Carolyn Jason
Phi Epsilon Omega	Daneen Edmonda
Phi Kappa Omega	Debra Crump
Chi Alpha Omega	Sandra Lane
Chi Xi Omega	Latrina Denson
Chi Sigma Omega	Sherri Hale
Chi Phi Omega	Yava Jones
Chi Chi Omega	Aimee Laramore
Chi Omega Omega	Tracey McGhee

UNDERGRADUATE CHAPTERS

Beta	Beta 100 Celebration Committee
Gamma	Tamara Hoff, Epsilon Epsilon Omega
Kappa	
Tau	Paris Rogers-Thomas
	Paige Wells, Graduate Advisor
	Cyrielle Jordan, Graduate Advisor
Beta Delta	Melanie Gatewood
	De-Andrea Blaylock, Graduate Advisor
	Candance Nance, Graduate Advisor
Beta Epsilon	Alexis Leavell
Beta Phi	Briana Lemon
Beta Zeta	Anita Williams, Graduate Chapter
Gamma Chi	Melissa Brown
Delta Beta	Brittany Greathouse
	Deborah McCoy, Graduate Advisor

Delta Omicron	Patricia Smith, Graduate Advisor
Epsilon Delta	Jessica Watkins
Epsilon Zeta	
Epsilon Eta	
Epsilon Iota	
Epsilon Xi	Tasha Tyler Roberts, Graduate Advisor
Epsilon Rho	Marissa Lyles
Zeta Iota	
Zeta Nu	Pam Black, Graduate Advisor
	Marlene Johnson, Asst. Graduate Advisor
Zeta Phi	
Zeta Zeta	Ruby Toliver, Graduate Advisor
Eta Rho	Eugenia Johnson-Smith, Graduate Advisor
Iota Delta	
Iota Sigma	
Lambda Xi	Colleen Taylor
Lambda Psi	Bobbie Bates, Graduate Advisor
Mu Beta	Regina Dixon-Reeves
Mu Rho	Merone Melekin
	Peggye Mellie, Graduate Advisor
Nu Lambda	Ge' Tina williams
Xi Kappa	Cristal L. Clay
Omicron Alpha	Barbara Wade, Graduate Advisor
	Lili Savage, Asst. Graduate Advisor
Omicron Xi	Clara Keal, Graduate Advisor
Pi Lambda	
Pi Nu	
Sigma Gamma	Cherise Hall
Sigma Eta	
Tau Iota	Arielle Austin
Tau Mu	Yoko Ihaza, Tiffany Seay, Graduate Advisor
Tau Rho	Chelsea Brown

Alpha Kappa Alpha Sorority, Incorporated
A Legacy of Sisterhood and Timeless Service

Confined to what she called "a small circumscribed life" in the segregated and male-dominated milieu that characterized the early 1900s, Howard University co-ed Ethel Hedgeman dreamed of creating a support network for women with like minds coming together for mutual uplift, and coalescing their talents and strengths for the benefit of others. In 1908, her vision crystallized as Alpha Kappa Alpha, the first Negro Greek-letter sorority. Five years later (1913), lead incorporator Nellie Quander ensured Alpha Kappa Alpha's perpetuity through incorporation in the District of Columbia.

Together with eight other coeds at the mecca for Negro education, Hedgeman crafted a design that not only fostered interaction, stimulation, and ethical growth among members; but also provided hope for the masses. From the core group of nine at Howard, AKA has grown into a force of more than 265,000 collegiate members and alumnae, constituting 972 chapters in 42 states, the District of Columbia, the US Virgin Islands, the Bahamas, Germany, South Korea, Japan, Liberia, and Canada.

Because they believed that Negro college women represented "the highest—more education, more enlightenment, and more of almost everything that the great mass of Negroes never had—Hedgeman and her cohorts worked to honor what she called "an everlasting debt to raise them (Negroes) up and to make them better." For more than a century, the Alpha Kappa Alpha Sisterhood has fulfilled that obligation by becoming an indomitable force for good in their communities, state, nation, and the world.

The Alpha Kappa Alpha program today still reflects the communal consciousness steeped in the AKA tradition and embodied in AKA's credo, "To be supreme in service to all mankind." Cultural awareness and social advocacy marked Alpha Kappa Alpha's infancy, but within one year (1914) of acquiring corporate status, AKA had also made its mark on education, establishing a scholarship award. The programming was a prelude to the thousands of pioneering and enduring initiatives that eventually defined the Alpha Kappa Alpha brand.

Through the years, Alpha Kappa Alpha has used the Sisterhood as a grand lever to raise the status of African Americans, particularly girls and women. AKA has enriched minds and encouraged life-long learning; provided aid for the poor, the sick, and underserved; initiated social action to advance human and civil rights; worked collaboratively with other groups to maximize outreach on progressive endeavors; and continually produced leaders to continue its credo of service.

Guided by twenty-eight international presidents from Nellie M. Quander (1913-1919) to Carolyn House Stewart (2010-2014), with reinforcement from a professional headquarters staff since 1949; AKA's corps of volunteers has instituted groundbreaking social action initiatives and social service programs that have timelessly transformed communities for the better—continually emitting progress in cities, states, the nation, and the world.

Signal Program Initiatives

2000s—Launched Emerging Young Leaders, a bold move to prepare 10,000 girls in grades 6-8 to excel as young leaders equipped to respond to the challenges of the 21st century; initiated homage for civil rights milestones by honoring the Little Rock Nine's 1957 desegregation of Central High (Little Rock, AR) following the Supreme Court's 1954 decision declaring segregated schools unconstitutional; donated $1 million to Howard University to fund scholarships and preserve Black culture (2008); strengthened the reading skills of 16,000 children through a $1.5 million after school demonstration project in low-performing, economically deprived, inner city schools (2002); and improved the quality of life for people of African descent through continuation of aid to African countries.

1990s—Built 10 schools in South Africa (1998); added the largest number of minorities to the National Bone Marrow Registry (1996); Became first civilian organization to create memorial to World War II unsung hero Dorie Miller (1991).

1980s—Adopted more than 27 African villages, earning Africare's 1986 Distinguished Service Award; encouraged awareness of and participation in the nation's affairs, registering more than 350,000 new voters; and established the Alpha Kappa Alpha Educational Advancement Foundation (1981), a multi-million dollar entity that annually awards more than $100,000 in scholarships, grants, and fellowships.

1970s—Was only sorority to be named an inaugural member of Operation Big Vote (1979); completed pledge of one-half million to the United Negro College Fund (1976); and purchased Dr. Martin Luther King's boyhood home for the MLK Center for Social Change (1972).

1960s—Sponsored inaugural Domestic Travel Tour, a one-week cultural excursion for 30 high school students (1969); launched a "Heritage Series" on African American achievers (1965); and emerged as the first women's group to win a grant to operate a federal job corps center (1965), preparing youth 16-21 to function in a highly competitive economy.

1950s—Promoted investing in Black businesses by depositing initial $38,000 for AKA Investment Fund with the first and only Negro firm on Wall Street (1958). Spurred Sickle Cell Disease research and education with grants to Howard Hospital and publication of The Sickle Cell Story (1958).

1940s—Invited other Greek-letter organizations to come together to establish the American Council on Human Rights to empower racial uplift and economic development (1948); Acquired observer status from the United Nations (1946); and challenged the absence of people of color from pictorial images used by the government to portray Americans (1944).

1930s—Became first organization to take out NAACP life membership (1939); Created nation's first Congressional lobby that impacted legislation on issues ranging from decent living conditions and jobs to lynching (1938); and established the nation's first mobile health clinic, providing relief to 15,000 Negroes plagued by famine and disease in the Mississippi Delta (1935).

1920s—Worked to dispel notions that Negroes were unfit for certain professions, and guided Negroes in avoiding career mistakes (1923); pushed anti-lynching legislation (1921).

1900s—Promoted Negro culture and encouraged social action through presentation of Negro artists and social justice advocates, including elocutionist Nathaniel Guy, Hull House founder Jane Addams, and U. S. Congressman Martin Madden (1908-1915). Established the first organizational scholarship at Howard University (1914).

—Earnestine Green McNealey, Ph.D., AKA Historian
August 2013

Alpha Kappa Alpha Sorority, Incorporated
The History of Central Region
"Pledged to Remember"

A Tradition of Timeless Service

It takes only one drop of water to start a waterfall and so it was with the building of the organizational structure of Alpha Kappa Alpha Sorority, Incorporated. Thus, the idea of one molded by nine, nurtured by sixteen, and incorporated by three spawned the evolution of this great sisterhood.

Following the sorority's incorporation in 1913 and the election of the first Supreme Basileus, Nellie Quander the sorority began its expansion beyond Howard University. Quander appointed the first national organizer, Founder Beulah Elizabeth Burke to help with the expansion. Founder Burke moved swiftly in her task and chartered Beta Chapter in Chicago, IL on October 8, 1913 giving Beta Chapter the distinction of being the first chapter chartered following the sorority's incorporation. Beta Chapter's chartering was soon followed by the chartering of Gamma Chapter at the University of Illinois Urbana-Champaign on February 12, 1914 (the first chapter chartered on a predominately White campus). The chartering of these two chapters was the beginning of the legacy of Central Region and its members roles and contributions to the growth and development of Alpha Kappa Alpha Sorority, Incorporated.

During the sorority's early years, chapters were not designated according to regions however, a regional structure was inevitable. The first indication of this was the addition of geographic designations to the titles of the National Organizers (the first title of Regional Directors) which occurred following the 2nd Boule when a Central, Western, and Eastern Organizer were appointed. Six years later, at the eighth Boule in 1925, the title Regional Director was officially adopted and seven regions were established: Northeastern, Eastern, Southeastern, Central, Southern, Central Western and Western. Central Region was comprised of the states of Ohio, Michigan, Wisconsin, Illinois, and Indiana. At the ninth Boule in 1926 Central Region's name would be changed to the North Central Region and Kentucky would briefly become a part of the North Central Region. The sorority once again reorganized the chapters of Alpha Kappa Alpha at the 11th Boule in 1928 and North Central Region would again become Central Region and Minnesota would return to the Region.

Many changes have occurred in the name designation of regions and the states comprising those regions. The exact date of the current composition of Central Region (Illinois, Indiana, Kentucky, Minnesota, St. Louis and Cape Girardeau, Missouri, Wisconsin, and North and South Dakota) could not be pinpointed. However, Gamma Omega in St. Louis became a part of Central Region with the election of Blanche Hayes Clark as Central Regional Director due to the requirement adopted by the Boule in 1930 that the Regional Director must reside in the region from which she is elected. The state of Kentucky rejoined Central Region by 1956 and North and South Dakota joined in 1964; and Cape Girardeau, Missouri joined the region with the chartering of Nu Sigma Chapter, Southeastern Missouri State University, on March 22, 1981.

Historically, leading the way has been the hallmark of Central Region beginning with the election of the second Supreme Basileus of the sorority Loraine Richardson Green in 1919 at the 2nd Boule in Chicago, IL. Also elected at that Boule were Pauline Kigh Reed, Central and Western Organizer, and from Indianapolis, Indiana, Murray B. Atkins, Assistant Grammateus, Phyllis Wheatley Waters, Supreme Epistoleus and Myrtle Johnson, Assistant Epistoleus.

During her term as Supreme Basileus 1920-1923 Loraine Green presided at four Boules and the sorority's operational structure began to take shape. The Constitution of the Boule of Alpha Kappa Alpha Sorority (the original name of the document) was adopted; membership and other official forms were created; the first *Ivy Leaf* was published; the Coat of Arms designed by Phyllis Wheatley Waters of Indianapolis, IN was adopted; and the annual National Founders' Day observance was established. In 1926 Alpha Eta Omega Chapter charter member Evangeline Harris Merriweather wrote the words and music to the Ivy Hymn and according to historical papers housed in the Virgo County Public Library, Terre Haute, IN she also wrote the words to the Initiation Hymn.

The regional structure of the sorority has served to help with the administration of chapters and program implementation. Organizing chapters and oversight of chapter operations and programs were under the jurisdiction of National Organizers until 1925. Pauline Kigh Reed, December 1919 – December 1922, Fredericka Brown December 1922 – December 1923, and Carolynne Payne, December 1923 – December 1925 served as Central Organizers. Murray B. Atkins was the first soror to be elected with the title Central Regional Director. She served from December 1925 – December 1927 followed by Althea M. Simmons December 1927 – December 1930.

Since the first Central Regional Conference in 1931, the Region has grown from nine chapters (five Undergraduate and four Graduate Chapters) and approximately 100 recorded members in 1931 to in 2013 ninety chapters (53 Graduate Chapters and 37 Undergraduate Chapters) with an active membership of 3,899 (3,509 Graduate members and 390 Undergraduate members). And has been expertly led by twenty-three Directors who have presided over 79 Central Regional Conferences: Blanche Hayes Clark, December 1930 – December 1934; Alice McGhee Smart, December 1934 – December 1937; Arlene J. Washington, December 1937 – December 1940; Blanche L. Patterson McWilliams, December 1940 – December 1943; Maenell Hamlin Newsome, December 1943 – August 1946; Lucille Wilkins, August 1946 – December 1950; Evelyn Roberts, December 1950 – December 1954; Maude L. Mann, December 1954 – August 1958; Annetta M. Lawson, August 1958 – December 1962; Lee Anna Shelburne, December 1962 – August 1966; Ordie Amelia Roberts, August 1966 – August 1970; Johnetta Randolph Haley, August 1970 – August 1974; Gloria E. Smith Bond, August 1974 – July 1978; Peggy Jean Lewis LeCompte, July 1978 – July 1982; Mable Evans Cason, July 1982 – July 1986; Loann J. Honesty King, July 1986 – July 1990; Yvonne Perkins, July 1990 – July 1994; Martha Levingston Perine, July 1994 – 1997; Peggy Lewis LeCompte, 1997-1998; Nadine Bonds, 1998-2002; Dorothy Wilson Buckhanan, 2002-2006; Pamela Bates Porch, 2006-2010; and Giselé M. Casanova, 2010–2014.

Central Region is proud of its history over the past ten decades and the service rendered by its members who have served at every level in Alpha Kappa Alpha Sorority. Four have served as Supreme Basileus: Loraine Richardson Green (2nd), 1918-1923; Maudelle Brown Bousfield (6th), 1929-1931; Maude Brown Porter (7th), 1931-1933; Linda Marie White (26th) and Dorothy Buckhanan Wilson will become the 29th Supreme Basileus in 2014.

Six members have served as First Supreme Anti-Basileus: Zelma Watson, Carolynne Payne, Maudelle Brown Bousfield, Maude Brown Porter, Lucile Robinson Wilkins, Linda Marie White and currently Dorothy Buckhanan Wilson; two have been elected Second Supreme Anti-Basileus; Frances E. Smith, Nan Arrington Peete; three Undergraduate Members-at-Large: Erica S. Horton, Delta Springer Irby, Anita L. McCollum (Irby and McCollum were attending schools outside of the region when elected); nine as Supreme Grammateus: Irma Frazier Clarke, Elizabeth Johnson, Carolyn S. Blanton, Murray B, Atkins (Walls), Evelyn H. Roberts, Lauretta Naylor Thompson, Peggy Lewis LeCompte, Linda Marie White and Dorothy Buckhanan Wilson; eight as Supreme Tamiouchos: Irma Frazier Clarke, Gladys Buffin Johnson, Helen Cromer Cooper, Loann J. Honesty King, Yvonne Perkins (two terms), Martha Levingston Perine and Barbara A. McKinzie; five Supreme Parliamentarians: Lucille B. Wilkins, Gladys Chapman Gordon, Helen Cromer Cooper, Johnetta Randolph Haley and Constance Kinard Holland; one International Regional Director: Nadine Bonds.

The 48th Boule established the current size and composition of the Directorate in July 1978. This action abolished several offices from the Directorate structure. Also, the Boule dissolved the executive committee and the public relations committee and enlarged the constitution committee and program committee to include representation from each region. Central Region members who served in these positions were: Supreme Anti-Grammateus, Murray B. Atkins; Supreme Epistoleus: Phyllis Waters, Alice McGhee Smart, and Irma Frazier Clarke; Financial Director: Helen Cromer Cooper and Lauretta Naylor Thompson; Editor-in-Chief of the *Ivy Leaf*: Helen Kathleen Perry (1st), Althea Merchant Simmons and C. Elizabeth Johnson; Director of Publicity: Bertha Moseley Lewis and Pauline Kigh Reed; Undergraduate Program Advisor: Hazel Ross Bolan; and Graduate Member-at-Large: Lauretta Naylor Thompson.

National/International Standing Committees have been chaired by: Constitution: Helen Cromer Cooper, Constance Kinard Holland and Johnetta R. Haley; Finance: Helen Cromer Cooper, Lauretta Naylor Thompson, Loann J. Honesty King, Barbara A. McKinzie, Martha Perine Beard and Yvonne Perkins; Program: Marian J. Warring and Loann J. Honesty King; Nominating (elected): Beatrice Lafferty Murphy, Constance Kinard Holland and Giselé Casanova; Building and Properties: Alison Harris Alexander and Carey Preston; Personnel/Human Resources (1990) Nan E. McGehee, Helen Cromer Cooper, Evelyn Freeman Walker, Gloria E. Bond, and Deborah Hill Burroughs; Membership: Peggy Lewis LeCompte and Alana M. Broady; Standards: Leola Madison, Johnetta Randolph Haley and Yvonne Perkins; Honorary Members and Rewards: Mae Ruth Carr; and Technology: Brenda Ladipo.

In addition, to chairing standing committees Central Region Members have provided extraordinary service as members of these committees as well as on other committees with at least twenty having served in multiple elected or appointed positions. It should also be noted that the position of Supreme Tamiouchos was held by Central Region members for sixteen consecutive years 1986-2002.

Several Central Region members have also served in special appointed capacities. In 1990 Alana M. Broady and Linda M. White were appointed the first Protocol Liaisons and Larnell Burks Bagley also served in the position. Barbara A. McKinzie chaired the first Business Roundtable Committee and Loann J. Honesty King; Chairman of the Economic Development Sub-Committee chaired the sorority's first Economic Development Conference in 1983, Washington, D.C. Mae Ruth Carr was personal escort to Honorary Member Madame Leah Tutu at the 52nd Boule in 1986.

The Centennial Traveling Exhibit was conceptualized and developed by June Mustifield and Audrey Cooper-Stanton has led the Leadership Fellows Program as Chairman of the committee from 2006 – 2014. Essie Blaylock (2002-2006) and Ericka V. Everett (2006-2009) served as Executive Assistant to the Supreme Basileus. Other Central Region members who received Special Chairman Appointments were Rita Wilson, Corporate Partnership/Marketing; Peggy Lewis LeCompte, Central Region Heritage Committee; Melody McDowell, Communications Committee and Yvonne Perkins, Graduate/Undergraduate Concerns.

Nine Central Region members have received The Founders' Graduate Service Award (the sorority's highest honor given to a member) for their outstanding record of service to Alpha Kappa Alpha and the community. They are Helen Cromer Cooper, Delta Chi Omega; Winona Lee Fletcher, Kappa Tau Omega; Constance Kinard Holland, Kappa Tau Omega; Frances Brock Starms, Epsilon Kappa Omega; Johnetta Randolph Haley, Omicron Theta Omega; Nadine C. Bonds, Alpha Mu Omega; Loann J. Honesty King, Theta Omega; Peggy Lewis LeCompte, Delta Delta Omega and Audrey Cooper-Stanton, Theta Omega. The region is also home to eight honorary members including the sorority's first honorary member, Chicago's Hull House founder Jane Addams.

Central Region can boast of being the home to the sorority's Corporate Office and its members have served in advisory and volunteer roles from the opening of the first office on October 8, 1949 in Chicago, IL to the purchase of the first property at 5211 South Greenwood in 1951 to the multimillion dollar facility at 5656 S. Stony Island Avenue. Four of the ten Executive Directors have come from Central Region: Carey B. Maddox Preston, Barbara A. McKinzie, Alison A. Harris Alexander and Deborah L. Dangerfield. The street in front of the Corporate Office bears the honorary name of Loraine Richardson Green Drive because of the efforts of member Doris Powell.

The Corporate Office also houses the Educational Advancement Foundation (EAF) created in 1980 to ensure perpetual support for its commitment to education. Central Region's Constance Kinard Holland, Kappa Tau Omega Chapter was the visionary and conceptual drafter of EAF, drafted the articles of incorporation and served as a Member-at-Large on the 1st elected Board of Directors. Peggy Lewis LeCompte, Delta Delta Omega Chapter served as Secretary and Challis M. Lowe, Theta Omega Chapter as Member-at-Large also served on the 1st elected Board of Directors; Loann J. Honesty King, Theta Omega Chapter, was an incorporator and the first Treasurer. Doris Parker, Alpha Mu Omega, was appointed the EAF's first Executive Secretary and Central Region members Deborah Dangerfield and Barbara Sutton both from Theta Omega Chapter served as Executive Director.

Central Region has also hosted:
- Eleven Boules including the second in 1919, Silver Anniversary Boule, 1944 and the last Boule of the twentieth century, 1998
- Four Leadership Conferences: 1981 in Indianapolis, and 1983, 1985, and 1991 in Chicago, IL
- The first national reading experience workshop in Chicago, with Theta Omega Chapter as organizers.
- The first Leadership Fellows program in Spencer, IN near Bloomington at the McCormick Creek State Park in 1976.
- The 17th and 18th Leadership Fellows program in Minneapolis, MN in 1997 and 1998 respectively at the Sheraton Minneapolis Metro dome in partnership with Pillsbury.

Commitment, dedication, and loyalty to the sisterhood are continually exhibited by Central Region members. As a whole, the members of the Central Region have never failed to rise to the occasion or answer the call, and often go beyond the expected. As we look to the future the Confident Central Region members remain prepared to continue to carry and pass on the torch in "Service to All Mankind."

– Loann Julia Honesty King, Central Region Historian
September 2013

Part I

The First Quarter of the Century

1900 – 1925

The First Quarter of the Century

The year was 1907. The civil war had freed the Negro from slavery, but it had hardly won them full citizenship. Scores of Negroes were still being lynched each year. It had been 11 years since the Supreme Court turned Congressional reconstruction upside down with the 1896 Plessy v. Ferguson decision. Four years had passed since W.E. B. DuBois published his notable work: "The Souls of Black Folk." The social constraints of "Jim Crow" confronting Negroes had caused many to rethink the conservative philosophy of Booker T. Washington and search for alternate ways out of their difficult situation.

Alpha Phi Alpha had been founded on the campus of Cornell University the previous year, and the fraternity was debating the establishment of a second chapter at Howard University. George Lyle, suitor of Ethel Hedgeman, was among the young men being considered as a potential charter member of this second chapter.

Whether or not these bits of history had any influence on the series of events that would lead to the formation of Alpha Kappa Alpha Sorority is unclear. But, one thing is certain: Ethel Hedgeman, a scholarship student at Howard University, would go home to St. Louis, for summer vacation, just as she had done before and the idea of starting a sorority would be born in the fertile matter of her brilliant mind.

Ethel Hedgeman would return to Howard University and her dormitory room in Minor Hall in the fall of 1907, exuberant and ardent to share her idea to form a sorority. She began to discuss her thoughts with fellow classmates and associates. Intrigued with the idea of forming a sorority, eight of her associates joined with Ethel Hedgeman and began to work on the group's formation.

In January 1908, these young women successfully petitioned the officers of Howard University for permission to function as a recognized campus group. One month later, the initial nine invited seven sophomores to join them. The sorority recognizes this group of sixteen women as the Founders of Alpha Kappa Alpha. Thus, the idea of one, molded by nine, and nurtured by sixteen, spawned Alpha Kappa Alpha Sorority.

From 1908 to 1913, Alpha Kappa Alpha existed exclusively on the campus of Howard University and was comprised solely of women matriculating at the university. Membership increased slowly with subsequent initiations, of small numbers in 1909, 1910, 1911 and 1912. During this period, Negroes, representing approximately 11 percent of the total population in the United States had been completely disenfranchised. Race riots continued to occur in both the South and North. The race riot that shook the entire country in Springfield, IL spawned the formation of the National Association for the Advancement of Colored People (NAACP) in 1909.

Social and economic conditions of the Negro were being deliberated in churches, in Congress, in public forums and in homes across the country. Perhaps it was this overall frustration that influenced certain chapter members at Howard University, in the fall of 1912, to decide to change the name, motto, colors and symbol of the sorority. Whatever the reason for the decision of these members to suggest this change, it was not supported.

Nellie Quander who had just graduated in June and was the immediate past president of Alpha Chapter would have no part of it. To preserve the name and what was distinctive to Alpha Kappa Alpha, Nellie Quander took action to incorporate the organization. On January 29, 1913, Alpha Kappa Alpha Sorority was incorporated under the laws of the District of Columbia. In accordance with the rules of the incorporation, the first Directorate with Nellie Quander as the Supreme Basileus was established. Her plan for development was to "expand to every nook and corner of our land."

Word of Alpha Kappa Alpha's existence had already begun to spread beyond Howard University, primarily by the founding sixteen who, during this period, had earned their respective degrees and moved on to continue their contributions to society in the broader community. Most of these outstanding young women remained on the East Coast, except Ethel Hedgeman Lyle who went to teach in Oklahoma. Marie Woolfolk-Taylor attended graduate school in Cleveland and Beulah Elizabeth Burke taught for one year in Georgia and then moved to Kansas City. Supreme Basileus Quander contacted Founder Beulah Elizabeth Burke to help her in this task. Beulah Elizabeth Burke agreed to help and became the sorority's First National Organizer.

In a segregated environment poisoned with racial and gender discrimination, Beulah Elizabeth Burke moved swiftly to fulfill her promise. In 1913, she chartered the second chapter of Alpha Kappa Alpha Sorority: Beta Chapter in Chicago, Illinois. In 1914, she chartered the third chapter of the sorority: Gamma Chapter at the University of Illinois in Champlain-Urbana, the first chapter to be established on a predominately white campus.

August 1914 marked the beginning of World War I, with its additional hardships. The war preoccupied Alpha Kappa Alpha Sorority members, like the rest of the nation. In addition, the nation was experiencing one of the most important social and economic phenomena: the migration of hundreds of blacks out of the South.

From 1914 – 1919 there would be no additional chapters chartered in the designated states that currently comprise Central Region. In fact, only three undergraduate chapters would be chartered in the sorority during this period.

In 1918, one month after the end of World War I, Alpha Kappa Alpha women (primarily members of Alpha Chapter) would convene the sorority's first Boule on the campus of Howard University in Washington, D.C. Events of this first meeting led to plans for a second Boule.

Alpha Kappa Alpha Sorority held its second Boule at the War Camp Community Center in Chicago, Illinois, in December of 1919. The members assembled, though small in number, laid the foundation for the sorority to begin functioning as an effective national organization. Loraine Richardson Green, Basileus of Beta Chapter was elected the sorority's second Supreme Basileus; Pauline Kigh Reed was elected Central and Western Organizer. This milestone in the history of the sorority takes on even greater significance because it was accomplished during the year that United States' history marked as the "Red Year," a fitting title because of the bloody race riots and the "Red Scare." Race riots began in April, erupting in 25 cities during that year and white mobs were assaulting Negroes around the city of Chicago. Across the country Negro homes in white neighborhoods were burned and documented lynchings went from 38 in 1917 to 83 in 1919.

Yet, Alpha Kappa Alpha Sorority, Incorporated strengthened its resolve, under the leadership of Central Region's own Loraine Richardson Green, to carryout programs of service designed to raise the social stature of the race. The principle of service was formally articulated by the 1922 Boule's edict that "each chapter give to the community where it is located at least one piece of Christian, social or civil service and an annual affair for the aesthetic development of the public."

The Constitution of the Boule of Alpha Kappa Alpha Sorority, the original name of the document, established the election of National Organizers for the Eastern, Central and Western sections of the country. This was the first indication that the sorority would eventually organize the chapters of Alpha Kappa Alpha Sorority, Inc., according to geographical locations.

Little change had occurred in the Negroes' social and civil condition during the war years. The vague hope that the war's end would cause new opportunity to advance the cause of democracy rapidly diminished. Despite severe discrimination and post war recession, Alpha Kappa Alpha continued to build.

In 1920, the first Graduate Chapter, in a state which now comprises Central Region was established. Mu Graduate/Gamma Omega Chapter in St. Louis, Missouri, the third graduate chapter of the sorority. Also, at the 3rd Boule in December 1920, the sorority's coat of arms designed by Phyllis Waters, a chartering member of Kappa Chapter (which had just been chartered in February of that year) at Butler University in Indianapolis, Indiana was adopted.

During this period, women would struggle for the right to vote and Alpha Kappa Alpha women were a part of that fight. However, full participation in the voting process for Negroes was still deterred by state laws. Competition for jobs and housing continued to heighten racial tension. America was busy escalating the "Red Scare" and the Ku Klux Klan was fiercely building its membership. The largest Ku Klux Klan rally recorded was held in a small town in Indiana on July 4, 1923.

However, these political and social conditions did not deter the women of Alpha Kappa Alpha. Motivated by Supreme Basileus Greens' watchword: "FORWARD" and the motto: "ORGANIZATION AND EXPANSION," Directorate members chartered a total of thirty-six chapters of Alpha Kappa Alpha between 1920 and 1925.

Seven of these chapters are currently in the geographic area designated as Central Region including: Kappa City Chapter (1920), Indianapolis, IN; Mu Graduate Chapter (1920)/Gamma Omega (1922), St. Louis, MO; Xi Graduate Chapter (1921)/Eta Omega Chapter (1922), Louisville, KY; Theta Omega Chapter (1922), Chicago, IL; Lambda Omega (1922), Indianapolis, IN; Eta Chapter (1922) University of Minnesota in St. Paul, MN; and Tau Chapter (1922)Indiana University, Bloomington, IN.

The 5th Annual Boule of Alpha Kappa Alpha Sorority, Inc. was held in Kansas City Missouri on December 1922. The meetings were held at the Lincoln High School. The number of chapters chartered during the period 1920 - 1922 would point out the necessity of having both a Central and Western Organizer. In addition, a bylaw change would allow for the appointment of Deputy Organizers. The sorority's system for naming graduate chapters with the appendage "Omega" would also be adopted at this Boule.

FREDERIKA BROWN was elected Central Organizer and served in this office from December 1922 to December 1923. She was initiated in Kappa Chapter (Butler University, Indianapolis), and received her A.B. degree in 1917 from Lawrence College in Appleton, Wisconsin. She was an instructor of English and History at Wiley University and served as YWCA Secretary at Indianapolis.

The 6th Boule, held in Baltimore in December1923 would again impact on the development of chapters in the central section. The position of Northeastern Organizer would be added to the list of officers and Standing Deputy Organizers would be appointed by the Supreme Basileus. In addition, the Boule would formally establish the separation of undergraduate and graduate chapters: "That in a city where there are five or more graduates and five or more undergraduates of Alpha Kappa Alpha; the regional organizer of the district is notified; that she makes investigations with the view of establishing a graduate chapter in that city."

Murray B. Adkins, who would be elected Central Regional Director in 1925, was elected Supreme Grammateus. Blanche L. Patterson, who would be elected Central Regional Director in 1940, was reelected Western Organizer.

CAROLYNNE PAYNE (pictured at left) was elected Central Organizer in 1923 and served until December 1925. She was initiated in Zeta Chapter, Wilberforce University, and received her B.S. degree in 1920. She was a teacher of Physical Education in the Wilberforce school system.

This 1923 Boule would for the first time address the issue of a sorority house for Gamma Chapter: "that the question of helping Gamma chapter purchase or rent a desirable piece of property is tabled. We recommend, however, that the Alumni of the University of Illinois who are Alpha Kappa Alpha and that the sorority chapters of Alpha Kappa Alpha assist in helping Gamma to establish a Sorority house." Note: See History of Gamma Chapter.

Beta Chapter

City Chapter
Chicago, Illinois
October 8, 1913

Beta Chapter Members 1918, Charter Members: Eva Overton, Top Row—Third from the Left; Geraldyne Hodges, Top Row—Second from Right; Bertha Moseley, Second Row—Second From Right. Soror Loraine Richardson Green, Chapter Basileus, Seated Third from Left.

Charter Members

GERALDYNE HODGES (MAJOR) BEATRICE LEE
VIRGINIA GAINES (THOMAS) BERTHA MOSELEY (LEWIS)
                          EVA OVERTON (LEWIS)

Founder Beulah Elizabeth Burke, the sorority's First National Organizer, chartered Beta Chapter on October 8, 1913. Giving Beta Chapter the distinction of being the first chapter established under the laws of incorporation.

Five young female scholars attending the University of Chicago and actively involved in causes to advance the race were selected to become charter members of Beta Chapter. They were Beatrice Lee, Bertha Moseley (Lewis), Virginia Gaines (Thomas), Eva Overton (Lewis), and Geraldyne Hodges (Major).

As the second chapter organized in Alpha Kappa Alpha Sorority, Inc., great accomplishments were expected of Beta Chapter. After all, it was the second chapter of the sorority in the second largest city in the United States. Added to the expectation for great accomplishments and self-affirmation was the challenge of maintaining high scholastic and ethical standards while encouraging other women with the same values to join them.

Indoctrinated with the high ideals and standards of the sorority, the five charter members moved unfaltering to meet these challenges and to live up to these expectations. They were the cream of the crop scholastically, socially and professionally. Beatrice Lee was a straight "A" student and achieved the highest GPA among the entire sophomore class in 1914; Bertha Moseley Lewis received her Bachelor of Philosophy from the University of Chicago in 1914 and did graduate study in the Theater Arts at Northwestern University.

Eva Overton Lewis was the daughter of the founder of Overton Hygiene Company, the Douglas National Bank, Chicago Bee Newspaper and the Victory Insurance Company and who following her graduation centered her professional life on her father's businesses; Virginia Gaines (Thomas), prominent socialite and scholar; and Geraldyne Hodges (Major) following her graduation from the University of Chicago in 1914 became Society Editor of Jet Magazine and on the staff of Ebony Magazine.

Between 1913 and 1918 an additional thirty-nine women, some college graduates and others undergraduates from various universities from Evanston, Illinois to Gary, Indiana, were added to the chapter's membership roster. These women collectively invested themselves in showing society that they belonged and could celebrate achievement in spite of racial discrimination. During these first six years of the chapter's existence sorors became YWCA group leaders; volunteers for the United Charities; solicitors in the financial lives of the Urban League and the NAACP; volunteer efforts with the Red Cross and other groups actively involved in the War efforts; and sponsors of cultural and social events.

Many notable women were among those initiated into the chapter within this period and are listed among the many firsts in both the local and international community. Following are just a few:

- Loraine Richardson Green, the first Black woman to receive a master's degree in Sociology from the University of Chicago.
- Mary Elizabeth Link, the first Black woman awarded the Gertrude Seltz Scholarship for the highest average among first-year women at the University of Chicago (1917).
- Maudelle Brown Bousfield, Phi Beta Kappa and the first Black woman to graduate from the University of Illinois (1906).
- Ida Taylor, the first Black woman appointed to teach in a Chicago Public High School.

Following the first Boule in December, 1918, Alpha Kappa Alpha a second Boule was planned for Chicago, IL. Sessions were held in the World War I War Camp Community Center and Beta's Basileus, Loraine Richardson Green was elected the second Supreme Basileus. She presided over four Boules from 1920-1923. During her terms as Supreme Basileus, the sorority's operational structure began to form; the first *Ivy Leaf* was published; the sorority badge and Coat of Arms design was adopted; and the annual National Founders' Day observance were established. During this period Beta members continued to achieve academic excellence:

- Georgiana Simpson became the first Black woman to receive a doctoral degree from the University of Chicago (1921).
- Maudelle Brown Bousfield became the first Black Dean of Girls at the Wendell Phillips Academy High School in 1921 and was appointed the first Black public high school principal in 1927.
- Mercedes Rojas becomes the second Black woman to attain recognition by the University of Chicago's chapter of Phi Beta Kappa in 1926 preceded only by her sorority sister Mary Link who was the first.

Beginning in the mid-1920s and lasting into the 1950s black Chicago experienced a cultural renaissance. Beta Chapter presented cultural programs as a means of raising money to help improve social and economic conditions through community service programs and to provide scholarships for high school students. Beta Chapter again dared to be first by breaking barriers and believing there were no boundaries. On June 5, 1926 the fourth annual Beta Chapter Musical Comedy "Marrying Marian" was rendered to a sell-out crowd at the Goodman Memorial Theater used for the first time by blacks.

Beta Chapter had for nine years since its chartering in 1913 maintained a solitary existence with a membership comprised of graduate members from Chicago and the surrounding cities and Border States and undergraduates from various universities in the Greater Chicago area. Under the leadership of Loraine Richardson Green, Beta Chapter received a partner with the chartering of Theta Omega Chapter on November 3, 1922. The first Graduate Chapter to be chartered in Chicago and the eighth

Graduate chapter of the sorority. Geraldyne Hodges Major, Bertha Moseley Lewis and Eva Overton Lewis charter members of Beta became charter members of Theta Omega Chapter and Bertha Moseley Lewis was elected the first Basileus of Theta Omega Chapter. To-date 21 members initiated in Beta Chapter have served as Basileus of Theta Omega Chapter and six have served as Basileus of both Chapters.

On November 18, 1929 Beta worked with Theta Omega to bring Marian Anderson for the first time to a Chicago audience in recital at Orchestra Hall. And in 1933 presented The First Negro Ballet ever danced "Sojourn in Mars" at the Artists' Ball held at the Stevens Hotel.

The decade of the thirties with the Great Depression would find the nation in economic chaos and escalate the problems of the race. In spite of these conditions Beta Chapter continued her involvement in community-building by creating progressive programs through service initiatives relating to education, family, health, and economics. Members also continued to achieve through independent initiatives.

Beta Chapter's legacy is rich with collective efforts of many working and striving together in the accomplishment of great deeds. Beta Chapter members attended the First Central Regional Conference May 23, 1931 in Indianapolis, Indiana and along with Theta Omega Chapter achieved the status as "hostess with the mostess" as they were affectionately dubbed when they co-hosted the Alpha Kappa Alpha Silver Anniversary Boule in 1933 and the first Central Regional Conference held in Chicago, IL in 1929.

During the Great Migration members assisted the Travelers Aid Society and other groups, to help southern blacks adjust to Northern society, find housing and navigate around the city. The Second World War brought its own set of problems and resulted in a more aggressive fight for equality and justice. During the war years programs had been somewhat curtailed but Beta Chapter had continued activities to uplift the spirits of its members and to enrich the lives of others.

Following a 3 year hiatus to keep the sorority strong and alive during the war crisis and to plan for the future execution of its programs an Emergency Business Boule was convened in Chicago during the weekend of February 18-20, 1944. Bethesda Baptist Church was selected as the meeting site and Beta and Theta Omega Chapters once again rose to the occasion as hostesses.

Throughout the decades of the fifties, sixties and seventies members sponsored health forums, vocational guidance, job training, reading enrichment and youth programs; supported the Cleveland Job Corps, DuSable Museum, Provident Hospital and the NAACP. Beta was also there in 1952 for the dedication of the sorority's first National Office building at 5211 South Greenwood and for the 5656 South Stony Island Corporate Office groundbreaking in 1982.

Through the years, Beta Chapter and its members have earned many awards for service and scholastic achievement. Beta initiate Barbara Spears received the first AKA National Scholarship at the 1952 Boule; the chapter was the recipient of Central Region's first Undergraduate Achievement Award in 1956; and Nan Arrington was elected Second Supreme Anti-Basileus in 1958.

The Boule would return to Chicago in 1961 and Beta and Theta Omega Chapters with Chicago style would provide opportunities for the attendees to visit the National Office Building and tour some of the businesses owned by blacks. Loann Julia Honesty was elected to the National Nominating Committee and Alana Kathleen Moss was the first recipient of the sorority's Foreign Travel Grant from Central Region in 1968.

Throughout the eighties, nineties and into the 21st Century Beta Chapter provided after school mentoring programs, celebrated Black History Week, and adopted an African Village, participated in voter registration activities, Red Cross Blood Drives, Salvation Army Tag Days, food bank donations and visits to nursing homes. In 1983 Beta Chapter was one of the hostess chapters for the Golden Anniversary Regional Conference and was the recipient of the Undergraduate Achievement Award for City Chapters six times during the 1980's. The chapter again jointly hosted the Central Regional

Conference in 1997. And fittingly the membership would return to Chicago in 1998 to close out the century with the fifty-eighth Boule.

The 21st Century saw both progress and regresses for black Chicagoans. Racial issues still flared and housing, education, health and employment issues were still on the forefront. Voter registration and affirmative action laws were also being challenged. Beta Chapter addressed many of these issues through sponsorship of educational and social activities on various college campuses throughout the city to draw awareness to these issues. In 2001 the chapter presented Political Activist Sister Souljah and sponsored programs to address health related issues such as AIDS, breast cancer, physical fitness and obesity.

On October 13, 2003, Beta Chapter celebrated its 90th anniversary. Approximately 250 Sorors from across the country were in attendance for a weekend celebration. In commemoration of this exciting event, each soror in attendance received a Beta anniversary pin. The weekend included a reception at Ida Noyes Hall, a Beta mixer, a banquet, and an Ecumenical Service at The University of Chicago's Rockefeller Chapel.

The Chapter responded to the call for help in fall 2005 after Hurricane Katrina by contributing money to the disaster relief fund and helped get out the vote for the 2008 Presidential election all while celebrating the sorority's centennial year and what a grand year it was! One hundred years of service to mankind has witnessed Beta Chapter's involvement in the Chicago Community and Alpha Kappa Alpha's National/International Programs from Vocational Guidance launched in 1924 to Global Leadership through Timeless Service.

Beta initiates have also gone forward to serve the sorority as National/International officers and chaired National/International committees. Soror Loraine Richardson Green and Maudelle Brown Bousfield rose through the ranks to become Supreme Basilei, the second and sixth, respectively. Sorors Lucille Robinson Wilkins (11th), Maude L. Mann (13th) and Loann J. Honesty King (21st) served as Central Regional Directors. Soror Wilkins also, served as Supreme Parliamentarian and First Supreme Anti-Basileus and Soror Loann J. Honesty King served as Supreme Tamiouchos, Incorporator and first Treasurer and of the Educational Advancement Foundation, International Program Chairman from 2006-2010, authored three editions of the History of Central Region "Pledged to Remember" and was appointed Central Region Historian in 2010. Soror Lauretta Naylor Thompson served as Graduate Member-at-Large, Supreme Grammateus and Financial Director. Soror Alana Moss Broady served as Chairman of the International Membership Committee; Judith Daylie Armstead served as Conference Planning Consultant for the Corporate Office; Rita Wilson was appointed Chairman of Corporate Partnerships/Marketing and Essie T. Blaylock served as Executive Assistant to the Supreme Basileus from 2002-2006.

To honor the chapter's 100 years of service and sisterhood sorors initiated in Beta Chapter, other sorors, friends and family gathered in Chicago, Illinois on October 10-13, 2013 for a weekend of celebration, rededication and reconnecting. More than 400 individuals enjoyed the camaraderie and festivities of the "Welcome to Beta Boulevard" reception at the Theta Omega Chapter/AKArama Foundation, Inc. Community Service Center; the "Memory Lane Luncheon," "Beta Journey Gala" and the "Until We Meet Again" Rededication Brunch held at the Hyatt Regency Chicago Hotel. This extraordinary celebration of the second chapter of Alpha Kappa Alpha to reach 100 years can best be summed up in the words of Beautiful Beta 1991: "Take Pride in How Far We Have Come. Continue To Have Faith In How Far We Can Go!"

Beta is proud of the chapter's part in making the world outside remember, cherish and appreciate the ideals for which Alpha Kappa Alpha stands and the chapter's contribution to the Chicago and international community. The Chapter's 100 years existence stands as testimonial to the fact that each Beta member left her imprint on the memories of those left behind and that those who went before realized that their tomorrow and the tomorrow of many whom they would never know would be determined by the actions in which they participated.

Chapter Members Who Have Held International/National Office or Been Elected to the International/National Nominating Committee

Loraine Richardson Green	Supreme Basileus	1919 – 1923
Ida L. Scott	Second Supreme Anti-Basileus	1946 – 1949
Nan Arrington	Second Supreme Anti-Basileus	1958 – 1959
Loann Honesty (King)	Nominating Committee	1961 – 1962

Beta Chapter Basilei

Bertha L. Mosley	1913
Virginia Gaines	1914
Beatrice Lee	1916
Maudell Bousfield	1917
Loraine Richardson Green	1918
C. Vivian Carter	1919
Alice McGhee	1921
Elizabeth Neeley	1922
Lucille Wilkins	1923
Wilhelmina Harrison	1924
Ruth Thomas	1925
Maudelle Bousfield	1930
Genevieve Nichols	1931
Julia Jackson	1932
Pauline Redmond	1933
Nelmatilda Ritchie	1934
Sarah Ozella	1937
Alice Lew	1938
Dorothy Giles	1940
Eunice Randall	1941
Mary Ruth Ridley	1944
Ida Scott	1948
Orphah Shands	1949
Pauline Redmond	1950
Carolyn Scott	1951
Angela Batteast	1952
Leslie Johnson	1953
Marian French	1954
Florence Lester	1955
Theresa Williams	1956
Mary Ellen Robertson	1957
Nan Arrington	1958
Raymonda Greene	1959
Gloria Greene	1960
Loann Honesty	1961
Rhonda Davis	1962
Sandra Sneed	1963
Deveree Starks	1964
Trina Govia	1965
Barbara Harrold	1966
Marion Spillman	1967
Jacquette Cosey	1968
Arletha Gardner	1969
Mary Montgomery	1970

Josephine Welch	1970
Gail Bledscoe	1971
Scherelle Pryor	1972
Tyna Widerman	1972
Benna Lou White	1973
Vennalu Whyte	1973
Pamela Bates	1974
Phyllis Latham	1974
Donna Pittman	1975
Gernell Austin	1976
Esther Cobb	1978
Diane Giles	1979
Machio Readus	1980
Cheryl Denton	1981
Nila Barnes	1982
Ora Williams	1983
Jetaun Short	1984
Carolyn Booth	1985
Rita Wilson	1987
Ethel Hall	1988
Stephanie R. Sherrer	1989
Carla M. Norfleet	1991
Lisa M. Kendall	1992
Tresa Dunbar	1993
Chantle Hays-Carsons	1994
Marlyn Evans	1996
Kamaca Pierce	1997
Lauren Cutrone	1998
Mokneque Clark	1999
Tamisha Causey	2000
Lena Henderson	2001
Janice Riddle	2002
Jamari Trent	2003
Erin Gilmore	2004
Marceia Hawkins	2005
Krystal Hudson	2006
Constance Brasher	2007
Michelle Walker	2008
Ashley Brooks	2010
Cherrell Evans	2010
Diamon Lockett	2011
Jevita Brister	2012
Alexandria Passmore	2013
Jasmine Marshall	2014

PART I: THE FIRST QUARTER OF THE CENTURY

Gamma Chapter

UNIVERSITY OF ILLINOIS
URBANA-CHAMPAIGN
FEBRUARY 12, 1914

Left to Right Front Row: Ivorine McAllister, Louise Laura Lewis, Frances Irene Ellis, Helen Gordon Stevens
Second Row: Emma Matilda Ballinger, Edith Hasseltine Stevens, Clara Vesta Lewis, Martha Selma Beck

CHARTER MEMBERS

MARTHA SELMA BECK
EMMA MATILDA BALLINGER
FRANCES IRENE ELLIS
LOUISE LAURA LEWIS

CLARA VESTA LEWIS
IVORINE MCALLISTER
EDITH HASSELTINE STEVENS
HELEN GORDON STEVENS

Gamma Chapter grew out of the Delta Phi Eta Club, which was organized by a group of women at the University for the purpose of fostering a more friendly relationship among the students. With the help of Founder Beulah Burke, these eight women became the charter members of Gamma Chapter. Three of them—the Stevens sisters and Ivorine McAllister—were from Founder Ethel Hedgeman Lyle's hometown of St. Louis.

As the first sorority for Black women at the University, Gamma chapter members were obliged to live with families in town. There was no campus housing in the early 1900s for Black women attending the University of Illinois. Students had to find living quarters in the local community. Black residents in the Champaign community were supportive of AKA endeavors and opened their homes to Gamma Girls.

GAMMA HOUSE: Gamma Girls began addressing the issue of housing for Black women as early as 1919. They lived together as a chapter at 506 East Stoughton Street in Champaign. In 1922, the first "chapter" house, a boarding house operated by Mrs. Penny, was purchased by the "Patronesses," a local group of women from the Urbana-Champaign community who gave the Gamma Girls both moral and financial support—inviting the girls into their homes for meals, fellowship, and relief from home sickness—while furnishing the house with such extras as a piano, a record player, draperies, and the like, which their rent could not provide.

In those days, the house was considered to be an organized place for Black women to live, not strictly a sorority house. Many of the girls who lived in the house were not members of AKA, but after living with the sorors, most of them soon decided to pledge.

Gamma House was a safe haven for the sorors and other young women that lived there. The $25.00 monthly charge covered room rent and meals: Lunch and dinner on weekdays, Sunday dinner and a breadline consisting of sandwiches, cookies, soft drinks and other snacks just after curfew. Monday nights were reserved for chapter meetings at which sorority affairs were addressed. The chapter room was sacred, but on Friday, Saturday, and Sunday nights—date nights—it was reserved for the sorors and their company.

Coming in after the 10:30 p.m. curfew on weeknights and Sundays or after 1:00 a.m. on Fridays and Saturdays was frowned upon, although it did happen. It was not easy for the guilty one to face the housemother, and for someone inside to open the door for a latecomer was definitely out of order.

After many years at Mrs. Penny's, the members of the sorority moved to 1010½ Main Street. The housemother was "Mother" McCrosky. Each girl took turns cooking, cleaning and assisting with other house duties. After living with Mrs. McCrosky for several years, many girls moved from one rooming house to another or lived in private homes. The next house was at 904 Stoughton Street, which was leased from Mrs. E. H. Scott. Soror Alice McGhee Smart, a former "Gamma Girl" and who would later serve the sorority as Supreme Epistoleus and Central Regional Director, worked steadfastly to secure an official house for Gamma Chapter.

Gamma Chapter's housing issue was addressed at the sixth Boule in Baltimore held in 1923. According to the Boule minutes the matter was postponed: "That the question of helping Gamma Chapter purchase or rent a desirable piece of property be tabled. We recommend, however, that the alumni of the U of I who are AKA and that the chapters of AKA assist in helping Gamma to purchase a house."

An organization of patrons from the local community solicited funds to assist with the housing acquisition and on June 1, 1928, the Chapter purchased the property for Gamma House at 1201 West Stoughton. Later that same year at the 11th Boule, held in Nashville, TN Gamma Sorors requested that they be allowed to incorporate. For reasons related to the legality of that action, the Boule postponed a response to the request.

A student residence and campus activities center, Gamma House was a collaborative effort between AKA and other chapters in the Central Region. It was the Sorority's first "chapter house" and served as the foundation for AKA sorority houses at the University of Kansas (Delta Chapter) and Indiana University (Tau Chapter).

During the 1935 Boule in Detroit, $1,000 was advanced to the Chapter to obtain the deed for Gamma House. The Gamma Alumni Association was organized in 1935 by UI graduates to relieve the chapter of its administrative duties by forming a senior administrative committee in Chicago and similar groups in nearby cities, including St. Louis and Indianapolis. Beta and Theta Omega chapters secured additional funds for this endeavor. In addition to repaying the loan, various chapters made other contributions to Gamma House. In lieu of hosting a Central Regional Conference in 1935, the chapters in the region voted to donate the funds designated for the conference to the Gamma House Project. Repayment of the loan was divided among 10 chapters in the Central Region over a period of five years, beginning monthly in 1936. Graduate chapters paid $30.00 and undergraduate chapters paid $16.00. The Boston Boule in 1939 yielded an additional $1,000 for repairs.

According to an article in the December 1940 *Ivy Leaf* magazine, "The decision of the Boule was indeed gratifying to students who have attended Illinois and who know how difficult it is to secure adequate and comfortable living facilities for Blacks at the University of Illinois, and especially to sorors who initiated this project and who made great sacrifices to maintain the house." The Sorority's national Undergraduate Housing Program was formally established in 1949 and in 1952; Alpha Kappa Alpha took responsibility for Gamma House.

University expansion forced the closing of the Stoughton house in 1958, but it reopened the next year in larger and nicer quarters at 1106 West Oregon Street in Urbana. However, after only five years, the house again fell victim to expansion when the University purchased the property to build the Krannert Center for the Performing Arts.

Gamma House Association, Inc. was created in 1965 under the inspirational leadership of Soror Ordie Roberts and incorporated in 1966 by Sorors Roberts, Beatrice Lafferty Murphy, Jean Pierce Durades, Judy Earley Upshaw, Carolyn Jones Boone, Carey B. Preston and Marie L. Johnson to "give financial and moral support to Gamma House for future operation." Other hard-working members of the early days included Sorors I. Roberta Bell, Ruth Louise Montrose and Rachelle Burch.

In July 1966, Gamma House Association purchased two new buildings — "Gamma House III" at 105 East Daniel to be used as living quarters and an apartment building on an adjoining lot. By the late 1960s and early 1970s, Gamma House grew increasingly difficult to maintain due to various factors—university housing became equally available to all students, interest had dwindled in living in the house, there were problems collecting room and board payments and difficulties hiring reasonable and dependable help. It was finally sold on June 24, 1971. An offer from a campus fraternity led to the sale of the apartment building.

In the years since the sale of the house, fundraising continued with the hope that one day Gamma House would be on the campus of the University once again. Gamma House Association remained in existence until 1976. In August 1977, a group of Gamma alumnae met to discuss reviving the efforts of Gamma House Association in exploring the possibility of a Gamma House IV—with a twist.

Rather than the traditional sorority house, the group considered building or purchasing a facility that could serve as a permanent site for meetings and social events and to provide a place for storage of records. Despite their efforts, raising funds proved to be an insurmountable task and eventually the group dissolved.

Throughout the years of joys and struggles with the affairs of Gamma House, one person served as the inspiration to continue the tradition—Soror Clara Vesta Lewis Caldwell, a charter member whom members of Gamma House Association saw on a regular basis. Many credit Soror Ordie Roberts as the driving force, as one soror put it: "She was Gamma House Association."

GAMMA CHAPTER: As the third link in the Alpha Kappa Alpha chain, Gamma Chapter played an integral role in the young sorority's national expansion. Gamma sorors, proudly known as "Gamma Girls," blazed a path of excellence in the earliest decades of the Chapter's existence.

Historically, Gamma Chapter has been committed to providing quality programs throughout the campus and Urbana-Champaign communities. Gamma was instrumental in expanding the cultural events that were open to black students. Its members have consistently been among the vanguard of campus leadership.

In 1919, merely five years after the Chapter was chartered, AKA had the highest grade point average among UI sororities, which helped the members establish an academic presence on campus. During the 1920s, sorors sought to improve race relations and focused on scholastic achievement.

In 1940, Gamma hosted a performance by Soror Marian Anderson at Foellinger Auditorium, the first black act to be presented by the campus productions and promotions organization. As the war effort mounted, Gamma hosted many activities to boost the morale of troops stationed at Chanute Air Force Base in nearby Rantoul. On campus, Gamma focused on enlightening the student body about the "Negro intelligentsia" by sponsoring a series of lectures presented by black professors from other institutions. Famed poet Langston Hughes presented the lecture "Poems of Negro Life" in 1945.

In 1949, Gamma, the mixed chapter, became Gamma the undergraduate chapter and Epsilon Epsilon Omega, the graduate chapter. The association between the two chapters is designed to continue as both chapters being a part of one whole. The difference in age and focus does not negate the shared aim to be supreme in service to all mankind.

Soror Clarice Davis made history in 1954 as the first Black woman elected homecoming queen at a Big Ten university by what was then the largest popular vote on record. Soror Charlynn Chamberlin, a 1968 initiate, also holds the honor of being elected a homecoming queen.

Alpha Kappa Alpha Sorority and Alpha Phi Alpha Fraternity were the first Black student organizations to participate in the All-University Spring Carnival in 1953. The Chapter hosted its first Miss Fashionetta® Pageant in 1955.

Gamma Chapter's commitment to innovative programs has spanned decades, from reading to blind students in the 1960s to hosting orientation sessions in the 1970s and holding the annual AKAlympics, a friendly competition between Greek-letter organizations and the student body, in the 1980s.

The tradition of new trails continues today. During Founders Week, the Chapter has hosted the "Mr. Gamma Gorgeous" contest to benefit local charities. Other past programs have included "S.T.A.R.S. (Sorors Teaching about Real Sisterhood)," mentoring sessions, "AKAdemics First" study halls, AKAerobics, and various seminars. Gamma Chapter has also sponsored campus-wide book, coat, clothing and toiletry drives for local shelters and community organizations.

Gamma Girls have proudly served the Sorority in regional and national capacities since Alpha Kappa Alpha's earliest years:

- Charter members Sorors Martha Selma Beck Harry and Clara Vesta Lewis Caldwell organized other chapters in the Central Region. Soror Beck Harry chartered Kappa Chapter in Indianapolis and Soror Lewis Caldwell became a charter member of Theta Omega Chapter.
- Sorors Althea Merchant Simmons, Marie Felicia Stevens Alexander, Clara Mosby and Edith Stevens Rhetta were charter members of Mu Graduate Chapter, which existed from 1920 to 1922 becoming Gamma Omega Chapter in 1922. Soror Alexander and Soror Rhetta were also charter members of Gamma Omega.
- Soror Althea Merchant Simmons was editor-in-chief of the *Ivy Leaf* magazine and the fifth Central Regional Director.
- Soror Alice McGhee Smart, the seventh Central Regional Director, also served as Supreme Epistoleus.
- Soror Ordie Amelia Roberts, the sixteenth Central Regional Director, worked to ensure the perpetuity of Gamma House for decades, even donating the proceeds from sorority paraphernalia sales to the Chapter.
- Soror Marian Johnson Waring received the Founders' Graduate Service Award in 1964. Soror Waring, who also chaired the National Program Committee, received the Sorority's highest honor, the Anna Eleanor Roosevelt Medal of Honor, in 1968.
- Soror Henrietta Seames Pelkey was the 17th Basileus of Theta Omega and a member of the National Standards Commission's evaluation team for 10 years.
- Soror Leadie Mae Clark and Soror Archalene Amos Martin served as Far Western Regional Directors.
- Soror Raven Hill was on the International Archives Committee from 2006-2010 and the North Atlantic Region's Undergraduate Transition Committee from 2010-2012.
- Soror Tiffany Gholston served as the Central Region Technology Chairman from 2006-2010.

Gamma Chapter was suspended in 2006 and remained inactive until 2013. On November 17, 2013 the chapter was reactivated with 31 new initiates. Their legacy of love, loyalty and labor has spanned 100 years and in the spirit of sisterhood, they continue knowing that "greater laurels…greater tasks" await them.

GAMMA CHAPTER BASILEI

Clara Vesta Lewis	Spring 1914
Martha Selma Beck	1914 – 1915
Vivian Hicks	1921
Margaret Wilkins	1922 – 1924
Gladys Lucas	Fall 1924
Lucille Armstead – Helen Cantrell	1925
Alynn McRoberts	1926
Martha Ann Roberts	1927
Viola Neely	1928 – 1930
Arlene Jackson	1930 – 1931
Lucille Sanders	1932
Dorothy Moore	1933
Audrey Benton	1934 – 1935
Maxine Carter — Gladys Laden	1936
Marian Singleton	1937 – 1938
Geraldine George	1938 – 1939
Mary Grace Jordan	1940 – 1941
Ruth Wilson	1942 – 1943
Dorothy Tate	1943
Eleanor Caldwell — Gwendolynn Duncan	1944
Martha Louise Harry	1945
Helen Anderson	1946 – 1947
Zephrynn Simms	Fall 1947
Faye Johnson	1948 – 1949
Odessa Cooper	Spring 1950
Erlene Collins	1950 – 1951
Cynthia Supples	1952
Jean Ann Pierce	1953
Joan Tyler	1954
Joanne Miller	1955
Harriette E. Dawson	1956
Jacqulyn Pruitt	1956
Antoinette Twine	1957
Clotilde Phelps	1958 – 1959
Barbara Turnipseed	1959 – 1960
Nathalia Payne	1961
Leatrice Y. Edwards — Marvinia Randolph	1962
Marilyn Warren	1963
Veronica Williams	1964
Robbery Tipton	1964
Barbara Holt	1965
Sondra Lawson	1966
Barbara English	1967 – 1968
Brenda Gaines	1968 – 1969
Charlynn Chamberlin	1969 – 1970
Wanda Young	1970 – 1971
Karen Bagley	1972 – 1973
Paula Payne	1974
Joycelyn Gardner — Debbie Eaves	1975
Judith Bradley	1976 – 1977
Cecilia Potter	1977 – 1978

Carolyn Kidd	1978 – 1979
Robynece Scott	1979
Camille Willis — Rhea Steele — Robin Gay	1980
Laura Willis	1981 – 1982
Lolita Smith	1982 – 1984
Nancy Stinson	Fall 1984
Pat Owens	Spring 1985
Elizabeth R. Franklin	1985 – 1986
Dominique M. Collins	Fall 1986
Sadira Muhammed	Spring 1987
Danielle Agee	1987 – 1989
Angela Hurley	1989 – 1990
Terrilyne Cole	1992
LaTacia Morgan	1993
Bridgette Williams	1994
Ontisar Patton — Toi Walker	1995
Torry Bennett	1997
Rachel Ivy	1998 – 1999
Staaraha Abernathy	Fall 1999
Arlecia Taylor	2000
Meredith Stone	2001
Tiffany Hale	Spring 2002
Tiffany Smith	2002 – 2003
Nehanda Loiseau	2003 – 2004
Tamara Hoff	Fall 2004
Tahani Cooper	Spring 2005
Mia Layne	Fall 2005
Inactive 2006 – Fall 2013	
Bria Purdiman	2013

Pauline Kigh Reed

1ST CENTRAL AND WESTERN ORGANIZER
DECEMBER 1919 – DECEMBER 1922

Pauline Kigh Reed was the first Central and Western Organizer. The geographical sections under her supervision included: Illinois, Iowa, Kansas, Kentucky, Michigan, Ohio, Wisconsin, Missouri and Minnesota.

She was initiated into Zeta Chapter at Wilberforce University in 1916 were she received her B.S. Degree in 1917 and later served as Registrar. After attending the University of Chicago Graduate School of Social Work, Pauline became a Social Worker for United Charities from 1921-1961. She simultaneously became an "activist" who fought for changes in the social welfare system. Pauline's keen intellect and adventurous spirit kept her on the vanguard of change. She became an active force in the emerging black intellectual, social and cultural circles of her day. Her life personified the pledge she made when she was initiated "to be supreme in service to all mankind." She became the Co-Founder of the South Side Community Art Center, the Chicago Chapter of the National Council of Negro Women and the Chicago Chapter of the Links. She was also a member of the NAACP, the Urban League and many other organizations.

Her contribution to the south side community of Chicago was recognized in 1941 when she was presented a citation for her work as a Co-Founder of the South Side Community Art Center during dedication ceremonies by Mrs. Eleanor Roosevelt. Pauline was also cited by the Chicago Committee of 100 for cultural contributions to the community during that same year.

Pauline was very proud of her 75 years as an Alpha Kappa Alpha member. She served as Basileus of Zeta Chapter in 1916; Basileus of Theta Omega Chapter in 1930; received a Central Region Award for Service as a National Leader, in 1977 and 1980; the recipient of a Boule Certificate of Merit in 1978 and 1980. She became a loyal member of the Heritage Club in 1982. Pauline Kigh Reed remained an active member of Theta Omega Chapter for more than fifty years and in the later years was a member of TOCS (Theta Omega Chapter Seniors) and established the Pauline Kigh Reed Scholarship Fund. She became an Ivy Beyond the Wall on May 3, 1991.

Kappa Chapter

City Chapter
Indianapolis, Indiana
February 14, 1920

Charter Members

HAZEL ALEXANDER
MURRAY ATKINS
SELMA BECK (BARRY)
EUGENIA DENT (BURBRIDGE)
HENRIETTA HEROD
FANNIE HYDE (SYKES)

JOYCE THOMPSON STEWART
MERLE STOKES (DUNSTON)
GOLDIE THOMPSON (SCOTT)
PHYLLIS WHEATLEY WATERS
ADA HOSKINS WHEELER
MERCY WOLFOLK (SMITH)

Kappa Chapter was founded February 14, 1920 on the campus of Butler University. At the time, the chapter's charter included: Butler University, Indiana University — Purdue University Indianapolis, Franklin College, Marian College, and the University of Indianapolis.

Many of the charter members of Kappa Chapter played important roles in the growth and development of Alpha Kappa Alpha Sorority, Inc.

- Murray Atkins was elected Central Regional Director while a member of Kappa Chapter. She was the first soror elected to the position with the title designation Central Regional Director
- Phyllis Wheatley Waters designed the sorority's coat of arms
- Hazel Alexander and Selma Beck where charter members of Lambda Omega Chapter
- Hazel Alexander would also become a charter member of Alpha Mu Omega as well as Eugenia Dent (Burbridge) and Fannie Hyde

Kappa Chapter has always been energetic, enthusiastic and ambitious. The chapter has tried in every way to promote the onward march of Alpha Kappa Alpha.

It was standing room only at the Meridian Street United Methodist Church in March of 1970 when Kappa Chapter in observance of their 50th Anniversary hosted Miss Angie Elizabeth Brooks;

President of the United Nation's 24th General Assembly addressed those assembled. Another memorable experience was when Kappa Chapter members hosted Coretta Scott King's visit to Ball State University. A beautiful silver tray was presented to Mrs. King to mark the occasion.

Kappa Chapter has a tradition of providing service to the Indianapolis community by focusing on the sorority's international targets. Some of the chapter's community service projects have included:

Emily Hunt Walk — 5K walk in honor of little girl with spinal dystrophy

Dayspring Center — making donations to homeless shelter

AKA Coat Day — collect coats that are donated to shelter housing

Woman to Woman — spiritual discussion for collegiate women

Mu Graduate/Gamma Omega Chapter

St. Louis, Missouri
December 2, 1920

Mu Graduate Charter Members
(1920-1922)

HAZEL B. MCDANIEL
INITIATED — DELTA CHAPTER

FELICIA STEVEN
INITIATED — GAMMA CHAPTER

HELEN E. MCWORTER
INITIATED — BETA CHAPTER

CLARA MOSBY
INITIATED — GAMMA CHAPTER

ALTHEA MERCHANT
INITIATED — GAMMA CHAPTER

EDITH RHETTA
INITIATED — GAMMA CHAPTER

Gamma Omega Charter Members
(1922)

Left to Right, Felicia Stevens (Alexander), Helen McWorter (Simpson), Edith Stevens (Rhetta). Hazel McDaniel (Teabeau), Dawn Casey (Slaughter), Clara Scaffner (Mosby).

FELICIA STEVENS (ALEXANDER)
DAWN CASEY (SLAUGHTER)
EDITH STEVENS (RHETTA)

HAZEL MCDANIEL (TEABEAU)
HELEN MCWORTER (SIMPSON)
CLARA SCAFFNER (MOSBY)

Gamma Omega Chapter formerly Mu Graduate (1920-1922), was chartered December 2, 1920, in St. Louis, Missouri, during Soror Loraine R. Green's term as Second Supreme Basileus (1919-1923).

These loyal A.K.A. women, determined to perpetuate the name and work of the Alpha Kappa Alpha Sorority, organized for the purpose of assisting deserving girls to obtain a college education. To these end two scholarships of fifty dollars each were given every year, one to the ranking pupil in the high school class, and the other to the ranking pupil in the normal (Junior College) class of Sumner High School. They also sought to influence Sumner High School girls to take training beyond the Junior College by giving them vocational information.

The chapter held nine meetings each year during the school months. Each meeting was designated as either social, study or art needlework.

By 1921 membership in the chapter had grown to eleven. In 1922 the chapter name was changed to Gamma Omega Chapter and Soror Helen McWhorter Simpson was the first Basileus.

Gamma Omega Chapter, the third oldest graduate chapter, has a rich heritage of service to the community. Since her chartering, Gamma Omega Chapter has been involved in and sponsored numerous activities for the benefit of the community.

Gamma Omega and Beta Delta, the city-wide undergraduate chapter sponsored by Gamma Omega, sorors actively participated in promoting civil rights in the late 1950s and early 1960s. During the 1963 the Jefferson Bank demonstration attracted national attention. During this time many Gamma Omega sorors became civil rights pioneers.

Some sorors were arrested and jailed along with many others. Gamma Omega led the movement to raise money for the release of jailed demonstrators. In one day the chapter raised $10,000 by soliciting financial contributions from sorors and the community at-large. In the 1960s, Gamma Omega was the first organization to charter the entire SS Admiral Excursion Riverboat, which not allowed African Americans prior to integration.

Gamma Omega programs consistently address every aspect of the sorority's international programs; most notably are the Literacy Center, the Food Pantry Project, Fashionetta®, HBCU Fair and tours, Health Fair and the Black Family.

VITA (VOLUNTEER INCOME TAX ASSISTANCE) an annual tax assistance program, initiated in the 1960s. Sorors continue to assist senior citizens and low income families in filing their state and federal income taxes from January through April 15th.

THE ANNUAL PIMS (PARTNERSHIP IN MATH AND SCIENCE) BOWL sponsored by the chapter continues to be a recognized and vital program in the St. Louis community. Area elementary and middle school students are invited to participate as teams in this competitive activity. A day of learning, fun and awards has been provided for students for many years and is traditionally held at the St. Louis Science Center.

SANTA'S WORKSHOP, held the first week in December, continued to grow with attendance reaching five hundred (500) elementary students for a day of crafts, storytelling, fun and pictures with Santa. Admission to this activity is a canned good. The food items are donated to area missions or food pantries.

MENTORING AND TUTORING STUDENTS continued to be an important component to the educational programs provided by Gamma Omega Chapter. Sorors mentored and tutored students weekly at the Cote Brilliante Elementary School, designated as the chapter's IVY AKAdemy.

LITERACY CENTER — The Alpha Kappa Alpha Sorority, Gamma Omega Chapter Literacy Center opened its doors on May 30, 1989 at the All Saints Episcopal Church in St. Louis, an area with a predominantly minority population. The Literacy Center provides assistance and instruction in reading, writing, and mathematics for area residents. The center houses a computer and a library where books can be borrowed. In addition, the Center provides professional training in effective teaching of reading and language arts for the Literacy Council of Greater St. Louis and the tutors who staff the Literacy Center. The center is operated two evenings a week for two and a half hours each evening.

The AKA Literacy Center is a collaborative effort of Gamma Omega Chapter, All Saints Episcopal Church, The Literacy Council of Greater St. Louis and the Adult Basic Education Council of St. Louis. Gamma Omega Chapter has won numerous awards for the Literacy Center and the work being done there.

LITERACY — The Patricia McKissack Reading Club, named for children's author and Soror Patricia McKissack, was founded in 2002 with students from five elementary schools. The club meets twice a year for special programs to promote reading and to encourage book club members to read the literature of African American authors.

In 2005, the Patricia McKissack Reading Clubs expanded to eight elementary schools with approximately 300 selected students in grades 3-6 participating. The program impacted students in three St. Louis area school districts: Ferguson-Florissant School District, Normandy School District, and St. Louis Public Schools. McKissack's books were used to teach diversity, celebrate African American culture, and make students aware of African Americans authors. Students were also encouraged to read books authored by other African Americans. To further promote literacy, a partnership was formed with the Black Repertory Theater. Its casting crew traveled to the participating school and performed plays on-site.

HBCU COLLEGE FAIR — In October 1989, Gamma Omega Chapter sponsored its first annual Black College Fair and Greek Showcase. This event has been held every year at the River Roads Shopping Mall except 1992 when the fair was moved to Jamestown Mall while River Roads was being renovated. Area students in grades eight through twelve are invited to participate in a day of workshops and information gathering. Approximately 250 students have participated each year.

HBCU COLLEGE TOURS — From 2004 – 2007, the chapter, through its Foundation, Ethel Hedgeman Lyle, sponsored four Black College Bus Tours to predominately HBCU's. Youth in grades eight through eleven were encouraged to participate. The tours included visits to HBCUs and to African American tour sites along the routes. A tour is being planned for 2013.

FASHIONETTA® COTILLION — Gamma Omega Chapter presented its first Fashionetta® Cotillion in 1984. Two thousand dollars in scholarships were given to debutantes that year. By the 1990's, more than 200 young ladies from the St. Louis area have been presented in a most elegant affair with more than $100,000 in scholarships awarded. A scholarship in the amount of $1,000 named for Gamma Omega Chapter charter member Felicia Alexander, is awarded to the debutante with the highest grade point average.

Fashionetta® continues to be a signature event for Gamma Omega Chapter in the St. Louis Community. In 2011, Gamma Omega Chapter's Fashionetta® Cotillion was highlighted in the New York Times Sunday Magazine. The participants are involved in community service projects and self-development, educational and cultural events for seven months prior to the cotillion. Attendance at the cotillion has ranged from 800 to 1,000 guests each year. From 2005 to 2012, 140 young ladies have been presented with over $300,000 presented in scholarships. The twenty-fifth anniversary year of the cotillion celebrated with the presentation of thirty-three debutantes; highest number of debutantes ever presented.

HEALTH — As a community outreach project, Gamma Omega was the first St. Louis sorority to establish health fairs in the shopping malls. The first was held in October 1991. The chapter also partnered with local agencies and practitioners to sponsor the Women's Cardiovascular Health Workshop. The goal was through speakers and screenings to promote awareness and aid in the prevention of cardiovascular disease. The Senior Health Issues Forum is another partnership with local agencies to sponsor a forum for senior citizens at a senior apartment facility to raise awareness and increase the potential for access to services. It assists the seniors with understanding, preventing and managing medical problems, safety and aging well.

In 2005 Gamma Omega collaborated with the other St. Louis metropolitan chapters to hold their first Metropolitan Chapters Team Walk in the Susan G. Komen Race for the Cure, which is ongoing.

Through another collaborative effort with the metropolitan chapters, each August Gamma Omega co-sponsors a Metropolitan Health Fair at the Monsanto YMCA. Health checks and screenings are provided by local health agencies. The screenings includes mammograms, prostate testing, and diabetes, blood pressure, and cholesterol checks. School supplies are also distributed. Gamma Omega also partnered with the CHIPS Health and Wellness Center to sponsor the Greek Walk during its community health festival. The chapter has an ongoing project to donate school supplies to various St. Louis area schools. Also participated in the local ESP 1908 global Centennial Walk that occurred simultaneously around the world in June of 2008 and in the Million Pound Challenge that encouraged sorors to exercise and eat healthy. Sorors weighed in at each chapter meeting. We sponsored an All Greek Walk-A-Thon that highlighted health issues that primarily affect African Americans. Since 2012, the chapter sponsors health related Public Service Announcements on a local radio station every Tuesday at noon.

FOOD PANTRY — Gamma Omega Chapter became involved with the St. Louis area Food Pantry Association in January 1991, in an effort to help feed the hungry. The chapter adopted the Hamilton Place Food Pantry which operates by referral from other agencies. Many social workers use the pantry when they have emergency needs for a client. The pantry is listed in the United Way Food Service Book.

The chapter held two canned food drives and gave donations for purchasing bulk perishables to help begin stocking the pantry. Sorors participated in the "Walk for Hunger" and raised $3,000 for the pantry. In addition to purchasing food, the money helped to purchase a refrigerator and repair the delivery van.

The food pantry operates an outreach program that distributes food weekly to senior citizens living in homes for the elderly. Residents are allowed to shop for many of the food items they need. The Hamilton Food Pantry received a Certificate of Merit from President George Bush for the community service it provides. Recognition was received from the Food Pantry Association for being the most improved pantry and for one soror raising $1,000 on her own for the pantry during the "Walk for Hunger."

Gamma Omega has continued its involvement with the St. Louis area food pantry. For 2011-2012 sorors were challenged to donate two (2) tons of canned goods. Each month the sorority provides canned goods for a local church's food pantry, and once a month sorors assist in the Feed the Hungry Program at Central Baptist Hospital.

YOUTH FINANCIAL LITERACY PROGRAM — For middle school students in the after school program at Girls' Inc. was implemented. This six-week program covered topics such as budgeting, spending, credit cards and entrepreneurship. Students were able to earn AKA dollars in the program and cash them in for valuable prizes at the end of the program. The program was continued and expanded in 2005 to include high school students from three St. Louis area high schools.

BLACK FAMILY — Continuing to contribute to the growth of the Black family, Gamma Omega Chapter donated "Baskets of Love' to women in the YWCA transitional housing. Large baskets were filled with toiletry items donated by sorors.

Hundreds of coats were donated for "AKA Coat Day" and given to a church mission. Sorors, family and friends worked at Operaation Food Search, an area food pantry, sorting food items and coats. They also painted two rooms at the Salvation Army Harbor Lights facility for homeoless men on "National Family Volunteer Day." Sorors painted and decorated a room for a teen mother and her baby at a facility that provides housing for pregnant and young mothers who are not able to live at home with family. The chapter purchased items of furniture, bedding and toys. The room that had an institutional look at first became a warm and pretty living space.

In 2007, the chapter adopted three families with mostly male children and provided education about community resources to assist them with budgeting that would lead to their becoming financially independent. Throughout the time of their training, home visits were made and some material assistance was offered to enable the family heads to stay on track. Sorors involved in another tutoring project, provided tutoring to some of the students in the families. The families were invited to and attended various events sponsored by the chapter such as the health fairs, back to school and holiday events.

SHOEMAN WATER PROJECT COLLABORATION — Gamma Omega under the Global Poverty Initiative launched a massive service project—a shoe drive from January 2011 through December 2012. This drive was in collaboration with the Shoeman Water Projects, which was originally established to bring water rigs to Kenya, Africa. Haiti became a focus after its 2010 massive earthquake. Gamma Omega's goal of collecting 10,000 pairs of shoes by the end of 2012 has been met and will enable the purchase of a $12,000 purification system. This system will provide Haitians with affordable access to clean water. Exporters purchase the shoes and distribute them in countries where people do not have and cannot afford to buy shoes. The proceeds are used to purchase water systems and to train Haitian residents on maintaining the systems. Sorors recruited family and friends to participate in the project. To stimulate donations, the committee implemented a friendly competition among chapter members' churches.

SCHOLARSHIP — is an ongoing major focus of the chapter. Many projects are promoted to raise funds: concerts, annual dances and Jazz and Blues Brunches.

THE TRADITION CONTINUES — The years 1993-1994 brought the first chapter sponsored Senior Resource Day. Health issues and concerns of Senior Citizens were addressed. Beyond becoming a life member of the Urban League, Gamma Omega Chapter also took out a second life membership in the NAACP. Notably contributing to the St. Louis Public schools, the sorors actively mentored students enrolled in a dropout prevention program and hosted a candidates' forum for the school board election. The first black mayor of St. Louis received his first plaque, while in office, from Gamma Omega that was then prominently displayed in his office.

75TH ANNIVERSARY OBSERVANCE — In December of 1995, "High Tea" was served at Charles Sumner High School to begin the weekend chapter observance of the chartering of Gamma Omega Chapter. The first activity of this observance was held at this venue because Alpha Kappa Alpha founder, Soror Ethel Hedgeman Lyle graduated from Sumner High School. The culminating activity was the Diamond Achievers Awards Reception where 14 community leaders were award recipients. Soror Eva L. Evans, 24th Supreme Basileus, was the Guest Speaker.

COLLABORATIONS, PARTNERSHIPS AND COMMUNITY RECOGNITIONS — A number of women's national organizations celebrated major birthdays in 1995: National Council of Jewish Women, 100 years; Junior League, 80; League of Women Voters, 75; Gamma Omega Chapter and the "Scholarship Foundation, 75; Church Women United, 60; and Women of Achievement, 40. Collectively their service totaled 595 years. The groups produced a video, "When Women Lead the Way," which was shown on KMOV-TV, the local CBS affiliate. A St. Louis history curriculum for 4th to 9th graders was also developed highlighting contributions of women through their service and volunteer activities.

During 1995-1996, Gamma Omega continued to collaborate with other organizations. Consumer Winter Wonderland was an activity co-sponsored with St. Louis Public Schools that emphasized Consumer Education. Sorors of Gamma Omega were both participants and exhibitors at the 1st Minority Scientist Showcase in St. Louis, which was held at the St. Louis Science Center. A number of awards were bestowed upon the chapter such as the "It Makes a Difference" Award from the Annie Malone Children's Home.

Gamma Omega continues to collaborate and partner with organizations in the St. Louis area:
- In 1999, partnered and collaborated with the Gateway Classic Foundation that sponsored the Gateway Classic Football game and parade. We participated in the parade and sold food at a concession booth at the Edward Jones Dome. An outgrowth of the partnership was the Jazz and Blues Brunch, which began in 1999 under the administration of Soror Patricia Perryman (1999-

2000). The major goal of the brunch was to raise scholarship money and to provide a venue for out of town, inactive, active sorors, and the general public to socialize prior to the Gateway Classic Football game with Gamma Omega sorors in promoting our community scholarship effort.

- To promote economic success an Earn Save Prosper Kids Club was established with a selected class of students at Langston Middle School. In partnership with United Missouri Bank, Hamilton Realty, and a Junior Achievement developed curriculum, sorors conducted classes in which students learned about earning, spending, saving, budgeting and investing money. The project terminated with all students opening college saving accounts at UMB Bank and were presented with Certificates of Completion of Coursework
- In partnership with Junior Achievement, an elementary curriculum on financial literacy was brought into the program. Students learned about earning, spending, budgeting, saving money, and credit. Through the diligence of soror volunteers, students at one school, Baden Elementary, planned and operated a school store. At the end of the session, proceeds were distributed to students on an equal basis and savings accounts were opened at the local branch of Bank of America.
- Anthony Bonner, former NBA basketball player, partnered with Gamma Omega to work with the boys' basketball team at Vashon High School. In partnership with GMAC Financial Services and Junior Achievement, the young men first studied the problems facing and the unsavory statistics of Black males in our society. The class moved on to a study of the basics of economic literacy. They learned the rudiments of establishing and operating a business, profit and loss, and buying and redeeming shares, etc. Students sold shares for the business they established, decided on a product to put on the market, elected officers and learned how to purchase and redeem shares.
- In late fall of 2008, Gamma Omega partnered with the Griot Museum of Black History in St. Louis to present the Centennial traveling exhibit for public viewing. The chapter sponsored an Opening Night Reception for all attendees. The museum was very grateful for the increased business the exhibit brought. The Fashionetta participants also used the exhibit as a cultural enrichment opportunity.
- In 2009 Gamma Omega forged a partnership with the 22nd Judicial Circuit of Missouri Family Court — Juvenile Division and Juvenile Judge Jimmie Edwards when he opened the groundbreaking Innovative Concept Academy as an alternative school for serious juvenile offenders. This afforded Gamma Omega a place to implement its ESP programs of service in the areas of financial literacy and the uplifting of families through mentoring and providing food and clothing. Gamma Omega was given office space and began holding monthly meetings at the school.
- Salvation Army partnered with the chapter to collect can goods for St. Louis food pantries and to donate Christmas baskets to the homeless.
- Gear Up and University of Missouri St. Louis — Through the program we serviced students in four school districts in the St. Louis metropolitan area.
- During the 2010 Boule in St. Louis, Gamma Omega along with the metropolitan St. Louis chapters partnered with the Griot Museum of Black History to provide a tour at the museum to view the sorority's traveling history exhibit.
- Additional partnerships include Women Against Hardship, Women's Safe House and Imagine School Environmental Science and Math.

CHAPTER AWARDS: During 1993-1994, Gamma Omega Chapter received the most awards in the history of the chapter at the Regional Conference. This included first place in Education, Health and Chapter Exhibit. Also, during this time, the chapter became a 100% member of EAF. Gamma Omega Chapter continues to win awards for their programs of service in all program areas, including the prestigious Overall Chapter Achievement Award; the 2008 Boule Award for our Youth Entrepreneur Program that incorporated into the Fashionetta® program; 2009 Heritage Award,

Platform I and Platform III Runner-up; 2010 Overall Achievement Award; and 2010 All Platform Awards.

COMMUNITY RECOGNITIONS — Gamma Omega chapter hosted the ribbon-cutting reception for the unveiling of the "BLACK AMERICANS IN FLIGHT" mural that is displayed at the St. Louis Lambert International Airport. The painted mural showcases and honors the history of the Tuskegee Airmen and highlights African American aviators and their contributions from 1917 to the space age. The mural was completed in 1990.

Sisterhood and sisterly relations are vital to the growth and welfare of the chapter and operates under the Membership Committee. Some activities have included the Pink and Green Gala and Senior Soror Round-Up to promote retention and reactivation; Recognition of the accomplishments and service given by a soror; monthly Sisterly Acts of Kindness recognition that recognizes a soror for outstanding service to the chapter or another soror with the honoree being nominated by another soror and presented a bouquet of pink tea roses at chapter meeting.

Since 2005 the Membership Committee has promoted sisterly lunches. Cultural and social activities such as game nights, movie and theater events and the annual Christmas Party are sponsored through the committee. To reclaim and retain sorors, socials for inactive sorors are held. Sisterly activities are a part of each chapter meeting, which promotes participation and togetherness.

FIRST INTERNATIONAL FOUNDERS' DAY CELEBRATION — The 1st International Founders' Day, hosted by Gamma Omega Chapter, was held in St. Louis, Missouri, on January 18, 2003, at the Marriott Airport Hotel. Supreme Basileus, Linda Marie White, was the guest speaker. V. Gale Hardeman was Chapter Basileus and Minnie C. Perry served as Chairman for the Founders' Day Luncheon and the weekend of related activities.

85TH ANNIVERSARY CELEBRATION — During the tenure of Basileus Soror Andriette Jordan-Fields (2005-2006) on December 3, 2005, Gamma Omega Chapter celebrated 85 years of service to the St. Louis Community with a gala celebration: "Continuing to Climb Like the Ivy Vine: 85 Years of Service to All Mankind." The elegant event was held at the Airport Marriott Hotel in Saint Louis and highlights included an 85 years anniversary toast by special guest, Central Regional Director, Dorothy W. Buckhanan and a slide presentation featuring the Basilei of Gamma Omega remarking on chapter accomplishments during their tenure. Other special guests included dignitaries from the St. Louis community, the 17th Central Regional Director, Johnetta Randolph Haley (former Basileus of Gamma Omega), 21st Central Regional Director, Loann J. Honesty King and sorors representing several chapters from throughout the region. Soror Andriette Jordan-Fields was Basileus.

90TH ANNIVERSARY CELEBRATION — Gamma Omega celebrated "Continuing the Legacy: 90 Years of Service to all Mankind" at the Doubletree Hotel St. Louis at Westport on Saturday, December 4, 2010. Central Regional Director Soror Gisele M. Casanova, PhD. and First International Vice-President, Soror Dorothy Buckhanan Wilson, extended greetings.

Chapter Highlights

- Gamma Omega has had the distinct honor of having four diamond sorors: Sorors Berenice Owsley Colbert, Basileus (1944-1945), Alberta Everett Gantt, Gladavelle Bell, and Maurine Flipper. Soror Gantt was recognized and presented with a diamond heart necklace by Central Region's 26th Regional Director Soror Dorothy Buckhanan. The Soror Alberta Gantt Scholarship Fund was established under the leadership of Basileus Andriette Jordan-Fields at the request of its namesake, Diamond Soror Alberta Gantt. An EAF Endowment was established in Soror Gantt's name upon her death.

- Reba Schinault Mosby was among the first scholarship recipients of the Alpha Kappa Alpha Sorority Scholarship. She attended Stowe Teachers College, where she became an Alpha Kappa Alpha member and later Basileus of Gamma Omega Chapter (1936-1938).

- Patricia McKissack has won numerous Coretta Scott King Book Awards for her books targeted for children and young adults. Her book, *The Dark Thirty: Southern Tales of the Supernatural* was a 1993 Newbery Honor Award book.
- Unforgettable, Unsung Sorors Of the Civil Rights Movement: Three Gamma Omega Chapter sorors were highlighted at the 2012 Boule in the Unforgettable, Unsung Sorors of the Civil Rights Movement exhibit: Minnie Perry, and Alice Parham
- Sandra Murdock was installed as the 88th president of the MSMA Alliance. She was the first African American to hold the position. She is a former educator, volunteers with many youth programs that expose student to science, and serves as a NAACP Youth Council Advisor. She also started the NAACP Youth Council Scholarship Program. She is co-chairman of the Gamma Omega Chapter's Health Initiative and makes weekly public service announcements on the radio.
- Gamma Omega Chapter has hosted two Boules and fourteen Central Regional Conferences.
- In this 21st century, Gamma Omega continues to be a vital force in the areas of Education, Health, the Black Family, Economics and the Arts; implementing the international program.

Gamma Omega Has Advised Beta Delta Chapter Since 1932.

Chapter Members Who Have Held International/National Office or Been Elected to the International/National Nominating Committee

Blanche Hayes Clark	Central Regional Director	1930 – 1934
Alice McGhee Smart	Supreme Epistoleus	1931 – 1933
	Central Regional Director	1934 – 1937
Blanche Patterson	Central Regional Director	1940 – 1943
Gladys Chapman Gordon	Supreme Parliamentarian	1950
Evelyn H. Roberts	Central Regional Director	1950 – 1954
	Supreme Grammateus	1954 – 1958
Clarice Dreer Davis	Nominating Committee	1950's
Vivian Dreer	Nominating Committee	1950's
Johnetta Randolph Haley	Central Regional Director	1970 – 1974
	Supreme Parliamentarian	1990 – 1994
Martha Levingston Perine	Supreme Tamiouchos	1990 – 1994
	Central Regional Director	1994 – 1997
Cheryl Cole Young	Nominating Committee	2000 – 2002

Gamma Omega Chapter Basilei

Helen McWorter Simpson	1922 – 1923
Anna (nee Annie) Mendel Blair	1923 – 1924
Vemba Brown Inge	1924 – 1925
Hazel McDaniel Teabeau	1925 – 1926
Nathella Sawyer Bledsoe	1926 – 1927

Anne E. Crosthwaite Simms	1927 – 1928
Althea Merchant Simmons	1928 – 1929
Ruth Miriam Harris	1929 – 1931
Alice McGhee Smart	1931 – 1932
Blanche L. Patterson McWilliams	1932 – 1933
Elizabeth Roberts Pruitt	1933 – 1934
Inabel Burns Lindsay	1934 – 1936
Reba Schinault Mosby	1936 – 1937
Lillian Witten Mosee	1938 – 1939
Cleo Hall Tucker Liggett	1940 – 1942
Blanche Hayes Clark	1942 – 1943
Mildred Jenkins	1943 – 1944
Berenice Owsley Colbert	1944 – 1945
Evelyn Hoard Roberts	1946 – 1948
Margaret Emory Simms	1948 – 1950
Alese Logan Morris	1950 – 1952
Gladys Chapman Gordon	1952 – 1954
Vivian E. Dreer McField	1954 – 1956
Thelma Smith Sutton	1956 – 1958
Gladys Elretta Coates Blaine	1958 – 1960
Vallateen V. Dudley Abbington	1960 – 1961
Phyllis Smallwood	1962 – 1963
Marian Waring	1964 – 1966
Johnetta Randolph Haley	1967 – 1970
Pearlie I. Evans	1970 – 1974
Marguerite S. Taylor	1975 – 1976
Virginia M. Gilbert	1977 – 1978
Dorothy Louise Jones	1979 – 1980
Mary (Mikki) Brewster	1981 – 1982
Sara Ingram Scroggins	1983 – 1984
Irene Forbes Schell	1985 – 1986
Ruth Alexander Pippins	1987 – 1988
Martha Levingston Perine Beard	1989 – 1990
Janice Orea Mosby	1991 – 1992
Cheryl Denise Cole Young	1993 – 1994
Minnie Calvert Perry	1995 – 1996
M. Denise Thomas	1997 – 1998
Patricia L. Perryman	1999 – 2000
Linda Johnson Huggins	2001 – 2002
V. Gale Greene Hardeman	2003 – 2004
Andriette Jordan Fields	2005 – 2006
Vera LeBlanc Atkinson	2007 – 2008
Leonor Shelton Buchanan	2009 – 2010
Teri Denise Bascom	2011 – 2012
Villajean Marie Jones	2013 –

Xi Graduate/Eta Omega Chapter

LOUISVILLE, KENTUCKY
1921/MAY 6, 1922

XI GRADUATE CHAPTER CHARTER MEMBERS
(1921)

MAUDE E. BROWN
IRENE BOWMAN CATALAN

HAZEL CRICE
M. ETHEL JACKSON
BESSIE BAKER WILLIS

ETA OMEGA CHARTER MEMBERS
(MAY 6, 1922)

MAUDE E. BROWN (PORTER)
MARINDA BUCKNER ROBINSON
HAZEL CRICE

M. ETHEL JACKSON (COFFMAN)
MARGUERITE PARKS (NORELL)
BESSIE BAKER WILLIS

In 1921, six women became the charter members of Xi Graduate Chapter. The chapter was organized at the residence of Soror Bessie Willis by Soror Phyllis Waters, Supreme Epistoleus, with the assistance of Soror Hazel Alexander, charter member of Kappa Chapter. Both women resided in Indianapolis, Indiana. Three of the chapter's charter members were already members of Alpha Kappa Alpha Sorority: Bessie Baker Willis, Northwestern University, Beta Chapter, Maude Brown and Hazel Crice; Howard University, Alpha Chapter. Irene Bowman Catalan was also a graduate of Howard University and M. Ethel Jackson had graduated from Fisk University. Two other women: Miranda Buckner Robinson and Marguerite Parks (Norell) were invited to join the newly formed chapter. On May 6, 1922 the chapter was renamed Eta Omega. Soror Loraine Richardson Green was the 2nd Supreme Basileus at that time.

The first chapter officers were elected May 14, 1922. They were: Basileus, Maude Brown; Anti-Basileus, Bessie Willis; Epistoleus, Ethel Jackson; Grammateus, Hazel Crice; Tamiouchos, Marguerite Parks; and Hodegos, Marinda Robinson. The first initiation after the organization of the chapter was held November 4, 1922. Sorors Carolyn Blanton, Augusta Cox, and Estelle Kennedy were initiated.

Chapter members' first attendance to a Boule was at the 4th Boule held December 27-30, 1922 in Kansas City, Missouri. The focus was on Community Service. Soror Ethel Jackson represented the chapter as a delegate at her own expense. Upon her return, she informed chapter members that the *Ivy Leaf*, the official publication of the sorority, would be published after the Boule. She also reported that Founders' Day would be celebrated during the third week of January. During that time, the work of Alpha Kappa Alpha Sorority was to be brought before the public either by meetings or through the press. Eta Omega Chapter of Alpha Kappa Alpha Sorority has prevailed through the years, leaving many footprints in the sands of time. Since its inception, the chapter has had an impact on the local community through many service projects and signature events.

THE PLYMOUTH RAFFLE — Was hailed as the greatest contribution to Race Relations when Eta Omega awarded a car (Plymouth) to a Caucasian in direct opposition to the Kiwanis Club's refusal to award a Negro the Cadillac he won in a raffle in Ahoskie, N.C.

During the decade of the forties, Eta Omega entertained soldiers at the USO and presented in recital Louise Burgee, Paul Robeson, the Charloteers, and Duke Ellington at the Memorial Auditorium. The chapter also presented three plays: "A Photographer's Trouble," "The Valiant One," "The Molluse," and two minstrels. The productions, arranged and directed by talented sorors of the chapter were well received by the public.

In 1946, Eta Omega hosted the South Eastern Regional, and in 1947 celebrated its Twenty-fifth Anniversary. Between 1951 and the mid 60's the chapter presented Fashionettas, debutante balls and luncheons. These events made an outstanding social and civic contribution to the community. They served as the highlight of educational, social, and cultural stimuli to all young women participating and as a source of joy in achievement to the sorors of Eta Omega. Eta Omega presented Billie Eckstein and George Shearing in 1951 and Leon Bibb in 1960. In 1972, the chapter celebrated its Fiftieth Anniversary and presented the "Best of Broadway Series."

In 1958, Eta Omega hosted the 24th Central Regional Conference and in 1965 hosted the 31st Central Regional Conference along with Beta Epsilon at the Sheraton Hotel. In 1996, Eta Omega Chapter was the prime hostess for the 62nd Central Regional Conference held at the Galt House East Hotel in Louisville, Kentucky. There were more than 1,000 sorors in attendance. The city was alive with pink and green. The banner announcing the conference was prominently displayed on the pedway between the Galt House Hotels. To demonstrate Eta Omega Chapter's commitment to the community, a $1,000 donation was made to the Dare To Care Food Bank of Louisville.

LITTLE MISS AKA COTILLION — This program was first implemented during the decade of the eighties and has become an annual event. Eta Omega Chapter is committed to working with and empowering the youth of our community. The Little Miss AKA Cotillion is not a beauty pageant, but a program that builds self-esteem and character; promotes self-respect and discipline; and encourages the improvement of scholastic achievement for young girls. Life skills are taught through charm school classes and the culminating activity is the Cotillion.

MINORITY EDUCATORS SYMPOSIUM — Eta Omega Chapter collaborated with the University of Louisville and the Jefferson County Public Schools to implement this symposium. The symposium was developed to address the issues of minority educators. The goals were to increase enrollment of minority students in the universities' schools of education; to acquaint junior and senior students with careers and opportunities in teaching; to develop positive attitudes toward teaching as a career; and to provide support services through a public forum addressing the concerns of the minority educator.

K.E.R.A. (KENTUCKY EDUCATION REFORM ACT) PARENT FORUM — Initiated in 1992, the purpose of the Educational Committee was to create A Comfort Zone of understanding for parents that empowered them to be more effective partners in the educational process of their children. Too often, African American parents feel intimidated when asked to visit their child's school. One of the chapter's goals was to bridge the gap between home and school by building confidence through parenting skills. Kentucky was undergoing new changes in education during this period.

ANNUAL DERBY SCHOLARSHIP BRUNCH — Eta Omega has always considered scholarships an important focus of the chapter's program. Scholarships are made possible through funds from the Hortense B. Perry Foundation and the estate of Henrietta Johnson (two deceased sorors). For the past 32 years, the amounts of the awards have increased due to the proceeds of the chapter's Annual Derby Brunch. Eta Omega is now able to award approximately $35,000 each year. The scholarships are awarded annually on Derby Day at the brunch to deserving African American females who have graduated from local high schools.

Eta Omega Chapter approached and entered into the 21st century with the same spirit of service that the original founders established almost one hundred years ago through initiatives such as the following:.

AKA DAY AT THE CAPITOL — During the legislative session of the general assembly of the State of Kentucky, sorors of Eta Omega Chapter travel to Frankfort, Kentucky to meet with legislative representatives and the Governor to talk with them about issues of concern in the African American community. This event has grown to the point that sorors from surrounding chapters throughout counties in Kentucky share a bus with Eta Omega sorors to travel to the capitol. Sorors dress to identify themselves as women of AKA

CONNECTION ACTIVITIES — The Connection Committee and Eta Omega were partners for the 2010 Census. They provided speakers to address sorors about proposed bills and the 2010 Census. The Connection representatives received certificates in the Health Disparities Training from the Louisville Health Department. The committee conducts Voter Education and Voter Registration at community fairs, local high schools, colleges, stores, beauty shops and barber shops; coordinates chapter involvement in the annual AKA Day at the Capitol; participates in the Martin Luther King Day of Service; requests written support of legislative bills; informed sorors about the Affordable Health Care Law; recognized women on the local Metro Council and the female Judge serving on the Kentucky Supreme Court; and conducted Issue Surveys so sorors could select issues to research, address, and share with community and elected/appointed officials. The Connection Committee also partnered with the NAACP, the Louisville Urban League, and the League of Women Voters to sponsor Candidate Forums and Get Out the Vote in the community. Among awards received, Eta Omega Chapter was awarded the 2009 Yvonne Perkins Graduate Connection Award and the 2009 Central Region Graduate Connection Award for the outstanding work of the Connection Committee.

HEALTH AWARENESS — Eta Omega is committed to improving the health of the local community. The chapter has hosted and participated in annual local community Health Fairs that address HIV/AIDS screening, blood pressure screening, nutritional information and other health issues. The chapter partners with and collaborates with organizations such as the American Cancer Society, which sponsors the Relay for Life; the American Heart Assocation which sponsors the Go Red for a Day program; and the Breast Cancer, Race for the Cure Walk.

MARTIN LUTHER KING JR. BIRTHDAY CELEBRATION — In recognition of this national holiday, Eta Omega Chapter sorors have participated in the Day of Service campaign by volunteering time at the charity of their choice. This activity has built awareness of the number of service hours that Eta Omega sorors give to the community and has increased the regular volunteer hours given in tutoring children in the public schools and churches.

AKA COAT DAY — Eta Omega Chapter instituted AKA Coat Day to support the Black Family. Each October the chapter collects coats for men, women, and children for donation to local homeless shelters in the community. Since 2000, this effort has provided more than 2000 coats to those in need.

AFRICAN AMERICAN READ-IN PROGRAM — In celebration of Black History Month, Eta Omega Chapter has sponsored the African American Read-In program. The program is designed to introduce preschool to high school youngsters the concept of how important reading is to success in life. Local celebrities, government officials, and other citizens choose a book that is important to them to read and discuss the book with the young people. The event is held at the Western Branch Library, the oldest library for African Americans in the country, and the participants come from the local daycare center, the nearby elementary school and the local high school.

A REMEMBRANCE OF MARIAN ANDERSON — Marian Anderson, the renowned opera singer, who was refused permission to sing in the D.A.R. Hall in Washington, D.C., performed in Louisville, KY in the 1930's. Eta Omega Chapter in collaboration with the Kentucky Humanities Council presented the story of Marian Anderson's life and her songs to commemorate this historic event. The program was presented at the Broadway Temple C.M.E. Church, which was designed by a Black architect in the 19th Century. The event increased awareness among the young people in the community on the contributions Marian Anderson made to American music.

BROTHERS OF PEACE — Eta Omega initiated this project from 2007-2010 targeting Black males in grades 4-8. The committee created proactive strategies and activities to address the current problems young black males are facing. The young men decided to claim the name of "Brothers of Peace." They met monthly and enjoyed the many activities and gifts awarded to them for their participation. The brothers of Kappa Alpha Psi fraternity served as mentors for the young men. Some of the activities that the young men were involved in included: acting workshops facilitated by staff from Actor's Theatre of Louisville, financial workshops, a golf outing and instruction, a trip to Huber Farm, horseback riding, various speakers such as judges, authors, police officers, etc. The young men also rendered service at a nursing home and had participated in an annual Black History Bowl.

EMERGING YOUNG LEADERS — Eta Omega implemented this signature program during the years of 2010-2011, 2011-2012, and 2012-2013. Each year 18-20 middle school girls in grades 6-8 participated in leadership development, educational enrichment, civic engagement and character building activities. The program is designed to help girls develop skills and talents with potential for becoming leaders within their local communities, as well as in other venues. Monthly meetings were held at a local church in the community. The girls participated in various activities such as service projects, field trips to cultural events and college tours, practiced public speaking, learned about nutrition and exercise, and personal grooming and body image.

AN EVENING SHOWCASE OF ARTISTS AND AUTHORS — This event was held in the fall of 2007 at a local restaurant. Ed Hamilton was the featured sculptor and artist of national acclaim. Four other artists and seven authors were also present. An artists' and authors' forum was held to acquaint the audience with the participants. Five sorors had an opportunity to present their books and their art. The Forum was hosted by Ms. Tiffany White, Assistant Editor of Today's Woman Magazine. Music was provided by Mr. Frankie Raymore, and a vocalist. The Showcase of Artists and Authors was inspired by Platform I (Entrepreneurship) & II (the Economic Keys to Success, to afford some African American Artists and Authors who are self-publishers an opportunity to share their works. Over 100 persons attended the event.

PRECIOUS PEARLS PROGRAM — This program was designed for 9th-12th grade girls. It focused on building self esteem, confidence building, academic excellence, development of social skills, and community service. Sorors served as mentors; providing bi-weekly group sessions and activities for the girls. The 12th grade girls were recognized at graduation time with a special program that included all program participants. The graduating seniors received special gifts and flowers. The other participants received certificates.

BLACK ACHIEVERS COLLEGE AND CAREER FAIR — Eta Omega Chapter has participated in this annual event with the Black Achievers Program, a national program that mentors young African American youth from 8th-12th grade. The program focuses on career preparation, academic success, and self-actualization. Eta Omega sorors spoke with the students about college life and the integration of Greek life in college. A special display of sorority history books, the *Ivy Leaf* publication, and other informative materials were made available for the students to review and discuss with the sorors.

This is just a summary of the kind of service the sorors of Eta Omega have been involved in during the past century and into the 21st century. To keep our footsteps entrenched in the sands of time, we will strive to continue to strengthen the Black Family, uplift our community, save our youth and render service to all mankind.

Eta Omega Has Been the Supervising Graduate Chapter for Beta Epsilon (University of Louisville) Since 1933 and for Sigma Eta (Northern KY University) Since 2001.

CHAPTER MEMBERS WHO HAVE HELD INTERNATIONAL/NATIONAL OFFICE OR BEEN ELECTED TO THE INTERNATIONAL/NATIONAL NOMINATING COMMITTEE

Maude Brown Porter	7th Supreme Basileus	1931–1933
	First Supreme Anti-Basileus	1929–1931
	Southeastern Regional Director	1927–1929
	South Central Regional Director	1925–1927
Carolynn S. Blanton	Supreme Grammateus	1949–1951
	Anti-Supreme Grammateus	1946–1949
	Southern Regional Director	1934–1935
	Southeastern Regional Director	1929–1931
	Associate Editor, *Ivy Leaf*	
C. Elizabeth Johnson	Supreme Grammateus	1946–1949
	Editor, *Ivy Leaf*	1937–1939
Hazel Ross Bolan	Undergraduate Program Advisor	1954–1958
Lee Anna Shelburne	Central Regional Director	1962–1966

ETA OMEGA CHAPTER BASILEI

Maude E. Brown	1922
Bessie Willis	1924
Carolyn Blanton	1926
Estella M. Kennedy	1928
Maude E. Brown	1930
Willie Carrington	1932
Gladys J. Spain	1933
Helen Y. Kuykendall	1935
Rose Ellen Goodloe	1937
Gertrude S. Wilson	1939
Yolanda Barnett	1940
Virginia Winlock Harris	1942
Hazel R. Bolan	1944
Alyne Martin	1946
Lee Anna Shelburne	1947
Evelyn R. Jackson	1949

Elizabeth W. Collins	1955
Eleanor Y. Guillard	1957
Lucy P. Larke	1959
Ima Farthing	1961
Rosamary Bell	1963
Margaret Woodson	1965
Barbara W. Stringer	1967
Gertrude Lively	1969
Anna Chandler	1971
Mary Gant	1973
Sara McPherson	1975
Cleopatra Gregory	1977
Mattie Clay	1979
Barbara W. Stringer	1981
Irene E. Smith	1982
Janis N. Brown	1984
O. Gloria Teague	1986
Anita H. Donaldson	1988
Janice Williams	1991
Rose Marie Stanley	1994
Ruby Fitzgerald	1996
Frances Sandifer-Cotton	1998
Naomi Christian	1999
Denise Jackson	2002
Shirley Fuqua-Jackson	2004
Verna Cahoon	2006
Stephanie D. Slates	2008
Chantelle Atkins	2010
Sherrie L. Bethea	2012

Theta Omega Chapter

CHICAGO, ILLINOIS
NOVEMBER 5, 1922

Left to Right: Ida Taylor Jones, Eva Overton Lewis, Helen Kathleen Lewis, Bertha Mosely Lewis
Not Pictured: Clara Vesta Lewis Caldwell and Geraldine Hodges Major

CHARTER MEMBERS

CLARA VESTA LEWIS CALDWELL
GERALDYNE HODGES MAJOR
IDA TAYLOR JONES

BERTHA MOSELEY LEWIS
EVA OVERTON LEWIS
HELEN KATHLEEN PERRY

In line with the philosophy of the founding sorors of Alpha Kappa Alpha Sorority, six visionary and dedicated women gathered on November 5, 1922, at 5200 South Wabash, Chicago, Illinois, under Supreme Basileus Loraine Richardson Green, to establish the eighth graduate chapter of the sorority. This was the beginning of an illustrious history.

It has been noted that the life of an individual is marked by well-defined stages, starting with infancy and its survival tasks—on through the establishment of identity and toward the final achievement of adulthood, hopefully maturity, and distinguished Golden, Diamond and Centennial years.

STAGE I—THE FORMATIVE YEARS

Soror Bertha Moseley Lewis was founder of both Beta and Theta Omega Chapters. As the first Basileus of Theta Omega Chapter, Soror Lewis's goals were to increase membership and formulate programs. Through initiation and reactivation the membership grew to 12.

This was a period of survival, tentative exploration and rapid growth. The infant chapter was nourished during its first 10 years under the leadership of Basilei: Helen Kathleen Perry (charter member); Maudelle Brown Bousfield (6th Supreme Basileus); Annabel Carey Prescott and through its individual and group participation in educational, community and cultural pursuits.

The chapter held luncheon meetings at the Ideal Tea Room, 3218 South Michigan Avenue. Highlights of these years included the awarding of scholarships to outstanding high school graduates; the presentation of lyceum programs utilizing the talents of local artists; and the initiation of a model Vocational Guidance Project that eventually became a national program.

The chapter also sponsored a recital featuring Soror Marian Anderson, her first appearance in Chicago, in 1929 at Orchestra Hall. This fundraising event was the cultural affair of the season. Beta Chapter cooperated with this effort, contributing to its great success.

Stage II—The Growing Up Years

The decade of the thirties reaffirmed the chapter's commitment to a program directed toward the needs of young people and active participation in community affairs under the guidance of Basilei: Pauline Kigh Reed (1st Central and Western Organizer and former Director of Publicity); Irma Frazier Clarke (former Supreme Grammatues and Supreme Epistoleus); Clara Mosby Wilson, Lucille Robinson Wilkins, Patricia Ferguson Harewood, Mary Gaines Mayo and Wilhelmina Harrison Alexander.

The vocational guidance program was extended to a week of activities, culminating in a mass meeting at the Good Shepard Congressional Church and exhibits at Hall Branch Library and DuSable and Phillips High Schools.

In 1930 the Christmas Day Breakfast Dance was started to raise scholarship funds. This event along with bridge parties in subsequent years allowed the chapter to expand its level of giving to include the YWCA, FEPC, NAACP, Urban League, NCNW, Provident Hospital, Parkway Community Center, Defender Charities and the Cancer Fund.

Activities in the community continued to add to the growing prestige of the young chapter. Membership increased to more than 75 members making it the largest chapter in the sorority. In 1931, the chapter hosted the 6th Central Regional Conference (1st to be held in Chicago) and received a gold cup for raising the largest amount of money for the establishment of a community house on the South Side of Chicago.

During the early months of 1933, the chapter was busily planning for the sorority's sixteenth Boule. It was the Silver Anniversary of Alpha Kappa Alpha Sorority and sorors throughout the country were looking forward to coming to Chicago. The Metropolitan Community Center was selected for the Boule Headquarters. The University of Chicago's International House was chosen for the Public Meeting and the formal dance. Chapter members were busy contacting relatives and friends for housing for the four hundred plus visiting sorors. Their tenacious planning efforts did not go in vain. Theta Omega sorors were declared to be "the hostesses with the mostest."

Membership had increased to more than seventy-five members through transfers and initiations making it impossible to continue to meet in private homes. Chapter meetings were moved to the South Side Art Center.

In addition to local projects, the chapter continued to support the Mississippi Health Project and the new Non-Partisan Council, both national projects. The chapter's Glee Club was born in 1937 and made its first appearance at a Pan Hellenic Tea.

Stage III — Young Adulthood

During the decade of the forties with Basilei: Edna Conner Hudson, Lucille Robinson Wilkins, Theolene Lewis Simpson, Dorothy Giles Wimby, and Henrietta Seames Pelkey at the helm, Theta Omega's participation in community undertakings grew by leaps and bounds. More than $4,200 was donated in scholarships during this period. Vocational guidance was continued with chapter members assisting high school graduating seniors in preparing for various careers. There were essay contests for high school girls to keep the community informed on the progress of the Nonpartisan Council. Concerns for human rights were expressed by the chapter's initiation of a Pan-American interest group that distributed literature on the Latin American Republic. Contributions were made to the Civil Liberties Union, Restrictive Covenants' Council and the Chicago Council against Racial and Religious Discrimination.

Due to World War II travel restrictions, the annual Boule had to be canceled for two years. The Supreme Basileus felt an urgent need to meet some business obligations and requested Theta Omega Chapter to host a streamlined business Boule. The 25th Boule was held at Bethesda Church in February 1944. In 1947, Theta Omega hosted the 12th Central Regional Conference.

STAGE IV — ADULTHOOD AND MATURITY

The fifties witnessed the progress of Theta Omega to even greater and more glorious achievements with Basilei: Maude Lillian Mann, Besshart Williams Cole, Nona Davis Webb and Ordie Amelia Roberts. Added to the now well-established programs of scholarship awards and financial contributions to community organizations was a Mental Health Program for adolescents and physical examinations for entering elementary school children. The chapter also convened a public meeting in the form of a panel discussion, Avenues to Equality, and sponsored programs on African and Negro culture.

During the mid-fifties, the suffix "rama" was very popular. Thus, the term AKArama was designated as the name for Theta Omega Chapter's annual fund raiser. As the principal fundraising mechanism, AKArama began November 30, 1956. The first AKArama in 1956 raised $2,000. This was a large sum at the time.

The year, 1961 was an exciting and busy year for Theta Omega Chapter. Not only did the chapter co-host the 27th Central Regional Conference with Delta Chi Omega and Beta Chapters held at the Georgian Hotel in Evanston, Illinois but, four months later, in August of that same year, hosted the 39th Boule with Beta Chapter at the Sheraton Chicago Hotel. The second International Regional Conference was held as part of this Boule. In 1966, Theta Omega would join Beta, Delta Phi Omega, Delta Omicron, Delta Chi Omega and Epsilon Kappa Omega as hostesses for the 32nd Central Regional Conference at the Hilton Inn in Milwaukee, Wisconsin.

A primary thrust of the chapter's program activities during the sixties under the leadership of Basilei: Lauretta Naylor Thompson; Maxine Hall Kirkwood; Rachelle King Burch, Nadine Ramona Ware, and Beatrice Lafferty Murphy was more active effort directed toward increasing sensitivity of sorors to the problems of the Black community. Seminars on the Black Revolution were conducted—covering education, the arts and politics.

Theta Omega's longstanding concern for the physical and mental health of the community and sorors found expression in the dissemination of information about sickle cell anemia, counseling services for unwed mothers and blood donations to the hemophilia fund (the first Black organization to do so).

STAGE V — SELF ACTUALIZATION — THE GOLDEN YEARS

The seventies and the introduction to the Golden Age of Theta Omega witnessed an even greater spirit in involvement and enthusiasm. During the span of the administrations of Basilei: Carrie Lou Payne, Loann J. Honesty King, Jessie Shaw, Alana Moss Broady, and Marva Jean Lee an unprecedented two-year educational program on Sickle Cell Anemia was enacted in the Chicago Public Schools, local colleges, and churches and in the community.

The chapter's vocational guidance thrust took the form of job recruitment. This project had as its objectives the securing of jobs for high school students and the counseling of high school graduates for consideration of careers not previously known about. Major businesses, school principals, counselors, and sorors worked together. The climax was a Job Fair attended by more than 100 students. Another project during this time was a Juvenile Court Volunteer Program wherein a soror became a "big sister" to a ward of the court.

In 1971, the Central Regional Conference would return to Chicago with Theta Omega as one of the hostess chapters. The conference was held at the Sheraton Chicago, site of the 39th Boule.

In 1972, the vocational guidance project was expanded to include career opportunities. A Job Opportunities Fair was held with more than four hundred high school seniors in attendance.

Additional initiatives during this period were a program to address some of the problems existing in the correctional system through volunteer service. A new Black Cultural Activities program was coordinated and climaxed by the showing of the movie, "The Life of Angela Davis."

Theta Omega Chapter's Golden Anniversary Celebration began with an event honoring outstanding members of the community on Sunday, November 5, 1973 at Greater Bethesda Baptist Church. Recipients of the Community Service "Torch Bearer" Awards were Muriel Beadle, Lerone Bennett, Jr., Gwendolyn Brooks, Margaret Burroughs, Manford Byrd, Jr., Clarence Henry Cobbs, Johnnie Coleman, Leon M. Despres, Jessie Louis Jackson, George E. Johnson, John H. Johnson, Jewel Stradford Lafontant, John W. Moutoussamy (who would later be the architect for the Alpha Kappa Alpha Sorority National Headquarters), and Charlemae Hill Rollins.

The Fiftieth Anniversary Celebration culminated the following weekend at the Hyatt Regency-Rosemont beginning with a chapter meeting on Friday, November 10, 1973 followed by a beautiful poolside rededication ceremony. On Saturday Theta Omega Chapter members were joined by more than 800 family members, friends, sorors and special guests at The Golden Anniversary Dinner Dance. Soror Johnetta R. Haley, 17th Central Regional Director, Soror Mattelia B. Grays, Supreme Basileus, and former Supreme Basileus (2nd), Soror Loraine Richardson Green were among the honored quests.

During 1974-1975 fifteen new sorors were initiated and Congresswomen Cardiss Collins was recommended and received honorary membership. In recognition of the International Women of the Year, plaques were awarded to Soror Loraine Richardson Green, Former Supreme Basileus; Mrs. Gertrude Johnson Williams, mother and Mrs. Eunice Johnson, wife of Mr. John M. Johnson, Publisher. Soror Carey B. Preston, Executive Secretary was saluted at the 1974 Founder's Day Celebration and in 1976 the chapter co-hosted the 42nd Central Regional conference at the Hyatt Regency O'Hare in Rosemont, Illinois.

Toward the close of the decade of the seventies, Theta Omega turned its attention inward. A Graduate Advisors' Council was established to assist the Graduate Advisors for Beta and Delta Omicron. And to address the problem of rising dues for retired sorors, on fixed incomes, who wanted to participate in a moderate chapter program of daytime activities, TOCS (Theta Omega Chapter Seniors) was formed.

A chapter emergency telephone chain was established and individual birthday greeting cards were sent to foster greater warmth, love and sisterliness among the sorors. This period also witnessed several other notable events.

- The chapter volunteered services and furnished a room at Provident Hospital
- Host chapter for the National Reading Program Seminar
- Implemented and supported three Reading Is Fundamental (R.I.F.) Programs
- Conducted two tutoring programs at the Urban Progress Center and the Woodson Regional Library
- Sponsored with four other Black National Women's organizations the Harsh
- African American Art Exhibit at the Chicago Public Library
- Sponsored the Mary M. Bethune Exhibit at the Carter G. Woodson Regional Library
- Trained sorors as special voter registrars and poll watchers
- Founder's Day in 1978 was a joint venture with thirteen chapters in the Chicago Metropolitan
- Soror Loann J. Honesty King was elected Supreme Tamiouchos at the 48th Boule in Houston, Texas.

STAGE VI — MOVING TOWARD THE DIAMOND YEARS

The eighties and into the nineties under the administrations of Linda Marie White, Essie Blaylock, Mae Ruth Carr, Rita Wilson and Judith Daylie Armstead represented a period of rededication of Theta

Omega Chapter to her mission of making Alpha Kappa Alpha Sorority, Incorporated, Supreme In Service. Several new programs were initiated and a decision was made to create a chapter foundation.

Since 1956, the chapter's major annual fund raising activity has been titled "AKArama." Thus on October 14, 1981, the chapter established the AKArama Foundation as a separate legal entity with a nonprofit 501(c) (3) status. Since 1981 more than $2,000,000 has been raised to support sorority and chapter programs and scholarships.

Theta Omega Chapter's Decade 80's Leaders Program was implemented in 1982 to formulate a Career Assistance Initiative, which included a Leadership Development Program of Service for young people. One aspect of the program is known throughout the Chicago Public School System as the Alpha Kappa Alpha Sorority's "Adopt-A-School Program."

Theta Omega's involvement helped to motivate students to develop a positive mental attitude, increase their basic skills, maintain good attendance, and commit themselves to fulfilling both their job and their academic responsibilities.

A Black Women's Conference was attended by more than 400 women to address issues of concern to Black Women. It was a collaborative project with six other influential Black women's organizations.

The membership committee sponsored a gala reactivation roundup entitled Put AKA Back into Your Heart. This project won the Central Region and National Outstanding Program Awards. The 1986-1990 International Membership Committee used this project as the format for its four-year program.

In 1983, Theta Omega Chapter was the prime hostess chapter for Central Regions 50th anniversary conference. This golden anniversary conference was held at the Hyatt Regency Chicago with a record breaking attendance of more than 1,100 sorors.

From 1986 – 1987, Theta Omega Chapter enhanced its participation in the arts, education and economic development. Soror Loann J. Honesty King was elected the 21st Central Regional Director in 1986. The formal observance of Dr. Martin Luther King's Birthday was celebrated with programs of music, speech and drama designed to keep Dr. King's dream alive for children and adults. Elementary children and their parents from throughout the Chicago Metropolitan area were invited to participate in these programs. The chapter also participated in public arts events, the development of the first city-wide cultural plan and the "Cultural College" exhibit in the Daley Plaza, and "Hands across America." In addition, chapter members attended the sorority's first International Conference held in Montego Bay, Jamaica.

The Teens Perspective Project was developed in 1988 to implement a program that would address the problems of teenagers. Activities, workshops and seminars were conducted in area high schools. A highlight of the program was its Annual Teen Leadership Conference including follow-up activities. Financing for the Teen Leadership Conferences and follow-up activities was partially funded through grants from the State of Illinois and The Chicago Chapter of the Links, Inc.

In 1989 the chapter held its first scholarship luncheon to honor the chapter's scholarship recipients and their families. The scholarship luncheon has remained the venue for awarding scholarships since that time. In 1990 Theta Omega Chapter co-hosted the 56th Central Regional Conference at the Hyatt Regency Hotel in Oakbrook, Illinois.

Basilei: Deborah Dangerfield, June Mustiful, Barbara A. McKinzie, Drema Lee Wolman, and Audrey Cooper-Stanton lead the chapter through the nineties. From 1990 – 1999, Theta Omega Chapter continued its service to the community. Collaborating with other organizations, the chapter assisted Chicagoans in completing census forms; political issues were addressed through letter-writing campaigns and voter registration campaigns. Chapter members became Deputy Registrars; served as volunteers for UNCF's Lou Rawls Parade of Stars and coordinated the Chicago Metropolitan UNCF Walk-a-Thon.

Program activities also included the "Caring and Sharing" food drive for the homeless as a component of the chapter's annual Holiday Affair Brunch. More than 1,400 sorors and guests donated canned goods and other non-perishable items that were given to three local food pantries. Theta Omega connected with our international Chapter in Freeport, Bahamas through the donation of over 350 books for the Freeport Children's library.

In 1994, the AKArama Foundation initiated an after-school program, F.A.M.E. (Families as Mentoring Entities) for eighteen fifth-grade students at a local elementary school. The students met after school, four days a week for three hours a day. The after-school schedule included tutoring and cultural and enrichment activities provided by volunteer tutors and chapter members and coordinated by a paid Project Director and a chapter liaison. A family activity was held once a month for the children in the program and their families and enrichment activities were provided by the Arts, Black Family and Health Committees. The program's success and significance has been recognized by several community organizations. In addition, the program was awarded enhancement grants from the Springboard Foundation for four consecutive years. F.A.M.E. was the AKArama Foundation's signature program activity for more than ten years and impacted more than 600 families.

The year 1997 was a year of tremendous excitement for Theta Omega Chapter. For the first time the annual fundraiser, AKArama, profited six figures, $123,500. Additionally, on November 22, 1997, members joyously celebrated the "Diamond" Anniversary of the chapter reflecting on 75 years of service to the community with a White Diamond Gala at the Westin Hotel. The black tie and white formal affair featured a video presentation of former Basilei with highlights of their administrations and culminated with a lavish dinner dance.

STAGE VII—BEYOND THE DIAMOND YEARS

Service to the community continued and expanded with the chapter's sponsorship of a Historically Black College and University tour and a Math and Science camp. Along with thirteen other organizations the chapter sponsored a Community Health Fair. Other first time service programs included registration of original projects for battered women and donating infant care products and diaper bags to a local DCF office with the National "Make a Difference Day" Foundation. The chapter also participated in an outreach program to enroll needy children in the Child Health Insurance Program (CHIPS) and operated a summer Music/Arts Camp for students 6 to 16 years old.

Theta Omega Chapter sponsored four high school students for the Regional PIMS Olympiad competition in 1997 with each receiving silver medals and sponsored the high school team in 1998 that received Gold medals at the Regional level and placed second at the 1998 Boule.

The 1998 Boule marked another milestone for Theta Omega Chapter. After 37 years, the Boule (58th) would return to Chicago, Illinois with Theta Omega Chapter as the prime hostess chapter and two of Theta Omega's former Basilei would be elected to an International Office: Linda Marie White, First Supreme Anti-Basileus and Barbara A. McKinzie, Supreme Tamiouchos.

This time frame also saw the implementation of the chapter's first automated voice delivery system to improve communication between the sorors and the Basileus. The Basileus used the system to inform sorors of emergency matters and to remind sorors of chapter activities in a timely manner.

Theta Omega voted to conduct a membership intake. One hundred and forty nine new sorors were inducted into our noble sisterhood on November 21, 1999. This induction of new members made Theta Omega the largest graduate chapter in the sorority, at that time. The weekend of activities culminated with a luncheon attended by over 300 sorors and their guests.

During 1999 the Economic Development Committee had been involved in the acquisition of property to house the foundation's programs, hold chapter/ foundation meetings, and other activities. The initial thrust of the committee was to look at available properties for rehab. But, after conversations with Senator Emil Jones regarding the potential availability of Illinois First Funds and also with Alderman Arenda Troutman on land owned by the city in the Woodlawn community, for building a facility; information was presented to the chapter in December 1999. Excited with the prospect of this undertaking the chapter voted to move forward with this project.

STAGE VIII — THE NEW CENTURY

The first twelve years of the new millennium saw the election of Theta Omega Chapter Basilei: Daisy T. Dailey, Bette J. Reid, Gladys L. Lloyd, Frances Carroll, Deborah A. Underwood, Essie L. Morris Kelly, and Tresa Dunbar Garrett, respectively.

At the beginning of the new century, the sorors of Theta Omega Chapter/AKArama Foundation, Inc. were aggressively involved in the building of a community service center. Work had also begun on the creation of a separate legal entity that would manage the construction project and the property once it was completed. The Theta Omega Foundation was established for this purpose.

The acquisition of the land needed to be finalized and a method of financing the project developed. Following numerous meetings with city and state officials, city agencies, approval of an assessment of the membership and the completion and submission of required documents things began to come together.

Eight parcels of land valued at $450,000 comprising 52,089 square feet of space were donated by the city for $1.00 per parcel and five-hundred thousand dollars in Illinois First Funds was secured from the State. Theta Omega Chapter/AKArama Foundation will be eternally grateful to the Honorable Emil Jones, Jr. President Illinois Senate and the Honorable Arenda Troutman, Alderman, Twentieth Ward — City of Chicago for their support and help in acquiring funding and the land for the Community Service Center. Additional, fundraising strategies for the project were developed by the Theta Omega Foundation including the "Builders of the Dream" Campaign.

On September 17, 2002 a ceremonial groundbreaking ceremony was held on the land site. Several city and state officials, community representatives and the 26th Supreme Basileus, Linda Marie White were present to extend congratulatory remarks.

Theta Omega Chapter/AKArama Foundation continues to focus on and implement programs that reflect the heart of our sisterhood and address the critical issues that face the local and broader community. Programs designed to enhance the overall quality of life for those to whom we provide service are carried forward through collaborations, partnerships, scholarships to high school graduates, grants and awards to local service organizations, health fairs, economics, black family and youth programs.

In 2003, Theta Omega was selected as one of the nine Ivy Reading Academy sites for the national programmatic initiative of the SPIRIT Program funded by the U.S. Department of Education to improve reading in the elementary grades in African American communities. Theta Omega Soror Peggy Lubin was hired as the National Ivy Reading AKAdemy Director and Willie Gray was appointed site Coordinator.

Internally, Theta Omega Chapter has continually embraced the use of technology as new formats have become available. The practice has helped to ensure that Chapter members are aware, engaged and informed about sisterly concerns and programming details in a timely manner. In 2004 the chapter newsletter became available on-line. In 2010 the chapter website was re-tooled, and in 2012 a membership portal with access for shared and stored documents was established.

These first few years of the 21st century were exciting and extremely rewarding for Theta Omega Chapter/AKArama Foundation, Inc. Not only did the Central Regional Conference (72nd) return to "Sweet Home Chicago" with Theta Omega as the prime hostess chapter but, the 2004 and 2005 AKArama Fundraisers both netted $125,000.00.

Most significantly, Theta Omega Chapter/AKArama Foundation, Inc. opened the doors to its multi-million dollar Community Service Center in 2007. The occasion was marked with a ribbon cutting ceremony and celebratory program attended by the 27th Supreme Basileus, Soror Barbara

McKinzie, government officials, sorors, family and friends.

The facility is primarily used for community programs for the Woodlawn and broader community and chapter and committee meetings are held at the facility. The property quickly became a destination place through opportunities such as health fairs, arts events, Black History programs, voter registration training and activities, candidate forums, community discussions, and an even a Presidential inaugural gala in the fall of 2008.

Chapter members also participated in the national festivities marking the Centennial Celebration of Alpha Kappa Alpha Sorority, Incorporated. The local ESP 1908 Global Centennial Walk in partnership with State Farm launched from the Theta Omega Chapter/AKArama Foundation, Inc. Community Service Center. Participants included Soror Pamela Porch, Central Regional Director, other area AKA chapter members, other fraternity and sorority members, family and friends.

Since that time, on-going programs for the community have included the Internet Café which provides online access and instruction for area seniors as well as adults conducting a job search, Legal Assistance which provides free consultation for those with a legal concern and a lecture series in collaboration with the University of Chicago.

Strong programming has always been and remains the core of Theta Omega Chapter. The positive feedback from the community has been abundant. The chapter regularly receives letters, cards and messages of gratitude, particularly regarding the annual Health Fair, Scholarship Awards, Emerging Young Leaders, Teen Pearls and Martin Luther King, Jr. Day programs.

Theta Omega Chapter celebrated its 90th anniversary in 2012 and her members remain committed as ever to provide service to all mankind. Over the past ninety-one years, Theta Omega Chapter has championed many causes within the local and broader communities. The chapters' distinguished record of service to has been recognized by the sorority, the community and local and national organizations through numerous awards for its programs.

Theta Omega Chapter has come a long way from the founding six. The chapter roster of more than 300 members reads like a "Who's Who" in the sorority and the broader community. Two members were elected Supreme Basilei: Maudelle Brown Bousfield (1929 – 1933) and Soror Linda Marie White (2002 – 2006). Theta Omega Chapter is best described by the words of the 2nd Supreme Basileus, Soror Loraine Richardson Green: "Theta Omega women in their individual careers and service in the sorority have played a significant role in the education and development of our people and have made a major contribution to the history of Chicago."

Theta Omega Chapter always has been and continues to be "Supreme in Service to All Mankind."

Theta Omega Advises Beta Chapter and Advised Delta Omicron Chapter From 1960-1982.

Chapter Members Who Have Held International/National Office or Been Elected to the International/ National Nominating Committee

Loraine Richardson Green	2nd Supreme Basileus	1919 – 1922
Pauline Kigh Reed	Central &Western Organizer (1st)	1919 – 1922
Helen Kathleen Perry	Editor of the *Ivy Leaf* (1st)	1923 – 1923
Zelma Watson	First Anti-Basileus	1925 – 1927
Bertha Mosley Lewis	Publicity Chairman	1927
Maudelle Brown Bousefield	First Anti-Basileus	1927 – 1929

	6th Supreme Basileus	1929 – 1931
Irma Frazier Clarke	Supreme Epistoleus	1937 – 1939
	Supreme Grammateus	1939 – 1946
	Supreme Tamiouchos	1946 – 1953
Lucille Robinson Wilkins	Supreme Parliamentarian	1951 – 1953
	Central Regional Director	1946 – 1949
	First Anti-Basileus	1934 – 1935
Althea M. Simmons	Editor-In-Chief, *Ivy Leaf*	1935 – 1938
Arlene Jackson Washington	Central Regional Director	1937 – 1940
Maude Mann	Central Regional Director	1954 – 1958
Ordie A. Roberts	Central Regional Director	1966 – 1970
Lauretta Naylor Thompson	Supreme Grammateus	1966 – 1970
	Financial Director	1970 – 1974
	Graduate Member-at-Large	1958 – 1962
Loann J. Honesty King	Supreme Tamiouchos	1978 – 1982
	Central Regional Director	1986 – 1990
Linda M. White	Supreme Grammateus	1994 – 1998
	First Supreme Anti-Basileus	1998 – 2002
	Supreme Basileus (26th)	2002 – 2006
Barbara A. McKinzie	Supreme Tamiouchos	1998 – 2002
Deborah Underwood	Nominating Committee	2010 – 2014

THETA OMEGA CHAPTER BASILEI

Bertha Mosley Lewis	1922 – 1924
Helen Kathleen Perry	1925 – 1926
Maudelle Brown Bousefield	1927 – 1928
Annabel Carey Prescott	1928 – 1929
Pauline Kigh Reed	1930 – 1931
Irma Frazier Clark	1931 – 1932
Clara Mosby Wilson	1932 – 1933
Lucille Robinson Wilkins	1933 – 1934
Patricia Ferguson Harewood	1934 – 1935
Irma Frazier Clark	1935 – 1936
Mary Gaines Mayo	1937 – 1938
Wilhemina H. Alexander	1939 – 1940
Edna Connor Hudson	1941 – 1942
Lucille Robinson Wilkins	1943 – 1944
Theolene Lewis Simpson	1945 – 1946
Dorothy Giles Wimby	1947 – 1948
Henrietta Seames Pelkey	1949 – 1951
Maude Lillian Mann	1951 – 1953
Besshart Williams Cole	1953 – 1955
Nona Davis Webb	1955 – 1957
Ordie Amelia Roberts	1957 – 1959
Lauretta Naylor Thompson	1960 – 1961
Maxine Hall Kirkwood	1962 – 1963

Rachelle King Burch	1964 – 1965
Nadine Ramona Ware	1966 – 1967
Beatrice Lafferty Murphy	1968 – 1969
Carrie Lou Payne	1970 – 1971
Loann J. Honesty King	1972 – 1973
Jessie Shaw	1974 – 1975
Alana Moss Broady	1976 – 1977
Marva Jean Lee	1978 – 1979
Linda Marie White	1980 – 1981
Essie Blaylock	1982 – 1983
Mae Ruth Carr	1984 – 1985
Rita Diane Wilson	1986 – 1987
Judith D. Armstead	1988 – 1989
Deborah Dangerfield	1990 – 1991
June Mustiful	1992 – 1993
Barbara McKinzie	1994 – 1995
Drema Lee Wolman	1996 – 1997
Audrey Cooper-Stanton	1998 – 1999
Daisy T. Dailey	2000 – 2001
Bettie Reid	2002 – 2003
Gladys Lloyd	2004 – 2005
Frances Carroll	2006 – 2007
Deborah A. Underwood	2008 – 2009
Essie L. Morris Kelly	2010 – 2011
Tresa Dunbar Garrett	2012 – 2013
Ethel J. Collier	2014 –

Eta Chapter

University Of Minnesota
St. Paul, Minnesota
December 12, 1922 – August 1964

Charter Members

RACHEL GOOD
ANTOINETTE C. MCFARLAND
KATHERYN TANDY
BELLA T. TAYLOR
FRANCES SMITH

During the spring of 1921 a small group of young women at the University of Minnesota began to dream of having a sorority. One of these young ladies, Kathryn Tandy, spent her summer vacation in Chicago and there met Alpha Kappa Alpha visitors from all over the country. She returned to Minnesota and fired the small group with enthusiasm, which developed into a determination to immediately take steps to make the dream come true.

In September, Mrs. Inez Wood Fairfax, the Eastern Organizer, en route to her home in Cleveland, stopped in Minnesota and organized this group into the University of Minnesota Ivy Leaf Club. On December 12, 1922, Mrs. Loraine R. Green, Supreme Basileus, came to Minnesota and established Eta Chapter. Eta Chapter struggled with membership for most of its existence. The chapter was dissolved at the 41st Boule in Philadelphia, PA, August 1964. The designated chapter name, Eta, was assigned to the undergraduate chapter at Bowie State College in Bowie Maryland in 1969.

Lambda Omega Chapter

INDIANAPOLIS, INDIANA
DECEMBER 15, 1922 – 1928

Seated: Selma Harris, Phyllis Waters, Hazel Alexander;
Standing: Tranquillia Riley, Eugenia D. Burbridge, Pauline Morton-Finney.

Charter Members

HAZEL ALEXANDER	PAULINE MORTON-FINNEY
EUGENIA D. BURBRIDGE	TRANQUILLIA RILEY
SELMA HARRIS (BECK)	PHYLLIS WATERS

Lambda Omega Chapter was the first Graduate Chapter to be established in Indiana. The chapter was established on December 15, 1922, in Indianapolis, Indiana. Soror Hattie Virginia Feger, First Supreme Anti-Basileus officiated at the chartering. The chartering ceremony was held at the home of Soror Eugenia Dent Burbridge. Following the ceremony an eight course dinner was served. The following evening the newly chartered chapter held a card party in honor of Soror Feger.

The following officers were elected: Phyllis W. Waters, Basileus; Eugenia D. Burbridge, Anti-Basileus; Tranquillia Riley, Grammateus; Pauline R. Morton-Finney, Epistoleus; and Hazel Alexander, Philacter.

On January 14, 1923, Lambda Omega observed it's first Founders' Day a special sermon by Reverend Father Louis H. Berry of St. Philip's Episcopal Church and an afternoon tea at the home of Soror Burbridge.

Two new members were added during the first year: Mary Rose Reeves and Spaulding Pritchett. All of the members of the chapter were school teachers. Though small in numbers the chapter carried out several activities including: awarded a full one year tuition scholarship to a Soror attending Indiana University; work with a Flanner House (a Negro Social Settlement Center); and read stories to children at the Negro Orphanage.

The chapter existed from 1922 – 1928. It is reported that the chapter was dissolved by the Regional Director for not operating within the policies of Alpha Kappa Alpha Sorority, Inc.

Lambda Omega Chapter Basilei

Phyllis W. Waters	1922 – 1926
Eugenia Burbridge	1926 – 1928

Tau Chapter

INDIANA UNIVERSITY
BLOOMINGTON, INDIANA
DECEMBER 16, 1922

Seated Center: Mabelle Lee Alexander; Standing Left to Right: Aletha Sylvester Mills

CHARTER MEMBERS

MABELLE LEE ALEXANDER
ETHEL V. HAMETT
ETHEL REED MARSHALL

ALETHA SYLVESTER MILLS
DAISY ARAMENTIA PAYNE
MATTIE MAE SELLOWS

In 1921, the Alpha Gamma Club was formed at Indiana University by a group of women interested in becoming an official chapter of Alpha Kappa Alpha Sorority, Inc. The aspirations of these women were guided by Soror Phyllis Waters, Supreme Epistoleus.

Information regarding these young women's interest was forwarded to the Supreme Basileus, Soror Loraine Richardson Green. Approval was given by Soror Green to move ahead with the chartering. And on December 16, 1922, the Alpha Gamma Club became Tau Chapter.

Tau Chapter has historically paid tribute to its chapter's charter members and the founders of Alpha Kappa Alpha Sorority, Inc. The first Tau Founders Day observance was held on February 16, 1924, and was the prelude to what would become "Tau Week."

TAU WEEK is held annually during the second week of February. The week-long activities are designed to celebrate the founding of the chapter and the Chapter's founders. Tau Week begins on a Sunday and ends on the following Sunday. The week's activities are scheduled as follows:

Sunday — The chapter members hold a rededication ceremony. The sorors rededicate themselves to Alpha Kappa Alpha and all that the Sorority stands for.

Monday — Included in the day's activities is a panel discussion on various topics. Some of the topics discussed in the past have been, "Black Women in White America," "The Misunderstood Black

Man" and "Greek Life."

Tuesday — Tuesday is set aside for public service programs. Some of thet programs in which the chapter has participated are, Citizens against Crime, and a Safe Sex Seminar sponsored by the Indiana University Health Center.

Wednesday — Contributions are solicited, on the campus, by the sorors and donated to a variety of local charities. Some of the recipients of these donations have been the Hoosier Hills Food Bank and the Salvation Army.

Thursday — Thursday of the week is the kickoff of the chapter's social activities. The original kickoff activity was a rendition of the television show, The Dating Game, where prizes were given, including restaurant coupons and free hair styling.

Friday — The night of the formal Tau Ball, when sorors "dress to impress" for Black Greek organizations biggest event.

Saturday — The night is set aside for an informal party. The chapter sponsored either a step show or a contest for the students.

Sunday — On Sunday the weeks' culminating activity was a Fashion Show. The show was a non-for-profit event that provided the Indiana University students, faculty, and the Bloomington community a glimpse of the new spring fashions. The fashions for the show were provided by local merchants.

THE "EVENING OF THANKS" is held during the week of Thanksgiving and Easter. It is an evening set aside for students, faculty and the Bloomington community to give thanks for the many blessings received each day. It is an evening of spirituality, joy and prayer to uplift the soul and ease the troubled mind. The program includes guest speakers, performances from church choirs (local and abroad), and individuals' testimonials of God's blessings.

This evening is not only for giving thanks, but for the support of and active participation in addressing the needs of the community. Sorors and the evening's participants contribute funds to support special causes and organizations. In addition, food and clothing are collected and distributed to local charities, such as Hoosier Hills Food Bank and Second Baptist Church.

THE BLACK FAMILY WEEKEND kicks off the first of many activities held during Unity and Diversity weeks. The weekend provides the opportunity for the African American students and their families, and members of the faculty to meet each other. Students exhibit their talents through artwork, singing, and dance.

In 1992, during Black Family Weekend, the Boys Choir of Harlem, The Voices of Hope Choir, and members of Indiana University Soul Review performed. In addition, the Indiana University Fine Arts Museum displayed "Celebration of Black Art" and offered tours.

Tau Chapter awarded one $250 scholarship and two $50 scholarships to the winners of an essay contest entitled, "What Are the Problems Facing Black Women Today and What Are Some Solutions?"

OTHER TAU CHAPTER EVENTS HAVE INCLUDED:

- "Beautifying Yourself inside and Out" — Program to promote building a positive self-image and sense of self-worth. Co-sponsored with a representative from Mary Kay.
- Bingo Night — A Tau program that brings students together for a fun evening of games, food, and prizes, while raising money for a good cause.
- Black History Challenge — Program to promote knowledge of Black History and kick off Black History Month celebrations.
- Black Male Appreciation Banquet — Evening to honor our Black men — special recognition is given to those who have excelled in academics, athletics, and in relationships. Awards are also given to the "Most Spiritually Uplifted" and the "Greek Man of the Year."

- Book Talks — African American authors are chosen to encourage reading and discussion of important issues.
- Business Etiquette Program — Informs students of the "how-tos" of landing a job — including interview and dining advice.
- Campus Awareness Initiatives — Programs discussing pertinent issues such as domestic violence, rape, healthy living, AIDS, and drunk driving.
- Carnival for Charity — Fun and games for all ages! All proceeds are donated to Homes for Black Children.
- A Closer Look at Indiana University — Used to acquaint new students with the many services, organizations, and activities IU has to offer.
- Coat Drives — Donated winter coats and spring jackets are collected from the IU campus and distributed throughout the Bloomington community.
- Elementary School Tutors — Reading tutors to students at Fairview Elementary and Bloomington Prep school.
- Evening of Thanks and Praise — Gospel extravaganza that features various musical and interpretive groups from the area.
- Harlem Renaissance: The Renaissance Revisited — An evening of poetry, jazz, dance, and the history of the Harlem Renaissance revisited.
- Heritage Environmental Learning Project (HELP!) — Mentor and discuss modern-day issues with the African American students of Bloomington North High School with the Men of Alpha Phi Alpha Fraternity, Inc.
- Higher Education Beyond the Undergraduate Level — Informs students of important and necessary information for graduate school.
- Midnight Buffet — An evening to taste a variety of foods well engaging in fellowship.
- Pop-A-Penny — Proceeds are collected throughout the Bloomington community and distributed to various causes such as the fights for Breast Cancer and Sickle Cell Anemia.
- Scholarship Essay Competitions — Book scholarships are given to top three winners — essay range in topics.
- Shaping Leaders for the Community — Encouraged and promoted strong leadership skills. Also, provided information on the many ways to get involved as a leader in the community.
- Sistah's Night Out — An evening for the women of IU to come together, relax, and meet new friends — toys are also collected and donated to the Middle Way House.
- Stress Management/Study Skills Workshop — Teaches tips on how to successfully cope with school and final exams.
- Tau Ball — Since 1969, this has been an elegant affair filled with dinner, dancing, and surprises.
- Trick-Or-Treat So Others Can Eat — Canned goods are collected and combined with turkeys or hams and distributed throughout the Bloomington community at Thanksgiving and Christmas.
- Women's Conference — Featured Rev. Joney Clark of Bethel AME Church and the acclaimed film "No More Sheets," by Juanita Bynum.

TAU CHAPTER ACHIEVEMENTS

Several of Tau Chapter community and campus service programs have been recognized by the university including:
- IU-NPHC Chapter of the Year, 1998
- IU-NPHC Sorority Fall Semester Highest GPA, 1998
- IU-NPHC Sorority Fall Semester Most Improved GPA, 1998

- IU-NPHC Chapter of the Year, 2000
- IU-NPHC Outstanding Service Project of the Year, 2000
- IU-NPHC Sorority Spring Semester Highest GPA, 2000
- Black Knowledge Bowl, First Place, 2000
- Winners of Black Student Union "Urban Challenge," 2001
- IU-NPHC Greek Collaboration Award w/ Kappa Delta, 2002
- IU-NPHC Outstanding Service Project of the Year, 2002
- IU-NPHC Chapter of the Year, 1st Runner UP, 2002

Also, chapter activities and programs have been cited in the local and campus newspapers:
- Tau Chapter's work with the Zeta Beta Tau campus incident, 1997
- Award of Excellence for Tau Chapter's "Trick-or-Treat So Other's Can Eat," 1998
- Tau Chapter's Honors at Greek Awards, 2002
- Tau Chapter's Annual Fashion show 2001
- Tau Chapter's 4th Annual AKA Book Talk, 2002
- Tau Chapter's 3rd Annual Carnival for Charity, 2001
- Tau Chapter AIDS Awareness Program, 2002

In addition, the local news had this to say: "Ivy Reading AKAdemy in Full Swing! Every Wednesday, the Ladies of Tau Chapter read and facilitate activities and discussion about manners, friendship, self-esteem, and diversity at The Rise."
- IU — NPHC Woman of The Year Award Tau Chapter's Aleah Bouie, 2011
- IU — NPHC Distinguished Scholar Award Tau Chapter's Paige Patterson, 2012
- IU — NPHC Chapter Advisor of the Year Tau Chapter's Jerrie Hayes, 2012
- IU — Greek Awards, Chapter of Excellence, 2012
- IU — NPHC Highest Chapter GPA, 2012
- IU — NPHC Intellectual Development Award, 2013
- IU — NPHC Values Integration Award, 2013

REGIONAL RECOGNITION

- Attendance Award — Most Sorors Present, 2002
- Assault on Literacy Award — Outstanding Program of the Year, 2001
- Attack on Literacy Award — Outstanding Program of the Year, 2000
- Dr. Michael Gordon — Trailblazer Award, 2000
- Overall Chapter Achievement, 1999
- 1999 Outstanding Program of the Year, in the Arts, Economics, Education, Black Family and Health Targets
- Outstanding Scrap Book Award, 1998
- Outstanding Program Award, 1998
- ESP Platform V Award — Health Resource Management, 2010
- ESP Platform II Award — Economic Keys to Success, 2010
- ESP Platform IV Award — Technology Signature Program, 2010
- Undergraduate Chapter Scrapbook Award, 2010
- Attendance Award — Greatest Percentage of Sorors Present, 2011
- ESP Platform I — Non-Traditional Entrepreneur Award, 2011
- ESP Platform V — Health Resource Managemant and Economics, 2011

- ESP Platform II — Economic Keys to Success, 2011
- Campus Overall Chapter Achievement Award, 2011
- Certificate of Commendation — Future Educator Runner-Up Tau Chapter Jasmine Porter, 2011
- Economic Security Award — GLTTS Initiative, 2012
- Emerging Young Leaders Award — GLTTS Initiative, 2012
- Health Award — GLTTS Initiative, 2012
- Global Poverty Award — GLTTS Initiative, 2012
- Campus Overall Chapter Achievement Award, 2012
- Social Justice and Human Rights Initiative Runner-Up, 2012
- Certificate of Achievement Runner-Up — Assault on Illiteracy Award, 2012
- Campus Overall Chapter Achievement Award, 2013
- Emerging Young Leaders Award — GLTTS Initiative, 2013
- Economic Security Award — GLTTS Initiative, 2013
- Health Award — GLTTS Initiative, 2013
- Global Poverty Initiative Runner-Up, 2013
- Outstanding Graduate Advisor Runner-Up — Jerrie Hayes, 2013
- Chapter Scrapbook Runner-Up, 2013
- Overall Chapter Achievement Runner-Up, 2013

Tau Chapter Basilei

Wilma Harry	1954 – 1955
Frances E. Smith	1955 – 1956
Gwen Hamm	1968 – 1969
Judy Jackson	1971
Peggy Smith	1972
Constance Ruppert	1973
Branita Griffen	1978
Mary Bacon	1979
Jean Poole — DeAnna Bates	1982
Debra Hurst — Elizabeth Gardner	1984
Debra Hurst	1985
Josefe — Marie Verna — Jennifer Jackson	1986
Kimberly Barlow	1987
Renee Conley — Sherri Smith	1988
Alicia Fair	1989 – 1990
Kimberly Lee	1991
Eleanor Anderson	1992
Yolanda Barnhill	1993
Stacy Hampton	1994
Vickie Parker	1995
Kiahna Woodard	1997
Natasha Frison	1998
Carla Leveringston	1999
Rochelle Leavell	2000
Meisha (Walker) Wide	2002
Vanessa Barnes	2003

Part II

The Second Quarter of the Century

1926 – 1950

The Second Quarter of the Century

The Second Quarter of the Century saw the peak of what is called the "Harlem Renaissance" and the "New Negro Movement." This was a time when many Negroes expressed their feelings through the written word, music and drama. Self-expression and self-revelation of the Negro in American life would have its impact on America's racial policies. The Negro would achieve a new position.

The author pauses here to pay tribute to a Central Region soror who would not necessarily be included in a history of the region. However, her accomplishments as an actress, singer, and philanthropist are worthy of note. ETTA MOTEN BARNETT (pictured at left), November 5, 1901 – January 2004, turned a blind eye to the overt racism and discrimination of the day and would not be deterred. She was a devoted wife and mother and the consummate Alpha Kappa Alpha woman who shared her talents with sorors and chapters throughout the sorority.

In appreciation for the support and courtesies extended to her by the sorors on her many concert tours, in 1937 at the Boule in New Orleans, Louisiana, she established the Etta Moten Scholarship to encourage undergraduates in the field of music. The first $100.00 scholarship was awarded at the 1938 Boule in Detroit, Michigan.

She was the first to break the stereotypical portrayal of Negroes in the movies with her role as a widowed housewife in "Golddiggers" in 1933. Her first screen credit was "Flying Down to Rio" where she played a Brazilian singing "The Carioca" while Fred Astaire and Ginger Rogers danced. She was the first Black Woman to sing at the White House in 1934 at President Franklin D. Roosevelt's birthday celebration. In 1942, she starred as "Bess" in the Broadway production of Porgy and Bess and toured in that production until 1945.

Her many distinctions include honorary degrees from Spelman College, Lincoln University and the University of Illinois. She received an award for her contributions to American music by Atlanta University and a scholarship for minority students was established in her name at the Chicago Academy for the Performing Arts. Her 100th Birthday Celebration in Chicago was attended by more than 400 guests. Her daughters, other family members and friends including Harry Belafonte and Studs Terkel paid tribute to her life and historic career.

In December 1925, Alpha Kappa Alpha returned to the site of her inception, Howard University, for the 8th Boule of the Sorority. At this Boule a report was presented for approval by the Committee on Regional Directors and Conferences, chaired by Althea Merchant, Editor-In-Chief of the *Ivy Leaf*, who would be elected Central Regional Director in 1927.

The committee would make four recommendations: (1) that the name of Regional Directors be used instead of Organizers, and (2) that there be seven regions as follows: NORTHEAST- New England States through New Jersey; EAST CENTRAL-Pennsylvania, Delaware and Maryland; SOUTHEAST-The Virginias, along the South Coast through Florida; CENTRAL-Ohio, Michigan, Wisconsin, Illinois and Indiana; MIDWEST-Kansas, Colorado, Nebraska, Iowa, Missouri and Oklahoma; SOUTHERN-Kentucky, Tennessee, Texas, Alabama, Louisiana and Arkansas; FAR WEST, Far Western States. (3) Set out the duties of the Regional Director including holding a regional conference in April, if possible, and (4) the appointment of an Assistant Regional Director, from a different section, whom would have the power of Regional Director if she was unable to function.

Following debate of the committee's report, the following action was taken: Recommendation (1) passed and the title of the office of Organizer was changed to Regional Director; Recommendation (2) passed with changes as follows: There would be seven regions but, they would be titled Northeastern instead of Northeast, Eastern instead of East Central, Southeastern instead of Southeast, Central Western instead of Midwest, and Western instead of Far West; Recommendations (3) and (4) did not pass.

Debate regarding the names of regions as well as the designation of the states within those regions would continue for several years. The acceptance of the recommendation that the name of Regional Organizer be changed to Regional Director would stand as the permanent designation for those elected to the position.

MURRAY B. ADKINS (pictured at left) of Kappa Chapter, Indianapolis, Indiana was elected the 4th Central Regional Director, and holds the distinction of being the first soror to be elected with that title. She would serve from December 1925 to December 1927. L. PEARL MITCHELL, Past Supreme Basileus (3rd), residing in Cleveland, Ohio, at the time, was appointed Central Deputy Organizer.

The delegates attending the ninth Boule in Columbus, Ohio in December 1926 were presented a second report by the Committee on Regional Directors and Conferences regarding the naming of regions and the states comprising those Regions. All four of the recommendations submitted by the committee passed.

Central Region would become the North Central Region comprised of the following states: Ohio, Michigan, Wisconsin, Illinois, Indiana and Kentucky. A regional conference would be held in April of each year, if possible, and an Assistant Regional Director would be deputized in each region, but from a different section. L. PEARL MITCHELL, serving as Central Deputy Organizer was elected North Central Regional Director.

For five years (1923-1927) there were no additional chapters chartered in Central/North Central Region. ALTHEA MERCHANT SIMMONS (pictured at left), a member of Gamma Omega Chapter, St. Louis, Missouri was elected Central Regional Director (5th) in December 1927 and served until 1930. St. Louis, Missouri was not a part of Central Region at the time of her election. The sorority's bylaws did not require that a candidate for the position of Regional Director reside in that region. This requirement was not approved by the Boule until1930. She chartered one chapter, Alpha Eta Omega in Terre Haute, Indiana.

Several actions taken at the 11th Boule in December 1928, held in Nashville, Tennessee would have a direct impact on Central Region:

1. The issue of the composition of the regions would again be debated. This time, the Boule would establish regions based on the location of existing chapters. Regions would be designated as the North Atlantic, South Atlantic, Southern, Great Lakes, Central, Midwest and Far West. Beta and Theta Omega (Chicago, Illinois), Gamma (Urbana, Illinois), Kappa (Butler College, Indianapolis, Indiana), Tau (Indiana University, Bloomington, Indiana), Lambda Omega (Indianapolis, Indiana), Eta Chapter (St. Paul, Minnesota) and Alpha Eta Omega (Terre Haute, Indiana) would comprise Central Region. Gamma Omega (St. Louis, Missouri), would be under the province of the Mid-West Region and Eta Omega (Louisville, Kentucky), would go to the Southern Region.
2. Lambda Omega Chapter, in Indianapolis, Indiana, was dissolved, and a new graduate chapter in the city would be proposed. Ironically, the next name in line for a graduate chapter was Alpha Lambda Omega. The petitioning members of the new Indianapolis group, two of whom were charter members of Lambda Omega, had concerns regarding the similarity of the name. They voiced these concerns to the Boule. Following debate on the issue, the Boule voted to assign the next name in line, Alpha Mu Omega, to the new graduate chapter being organized in Indianapolis.

3. Gamma Chapter requested that they be allowed to incorporate to purchase a sorority house. For reasons relating to the legality of that action, the Boule again postponed a response to the request.

Another significant event in the history of Alpha Kappa Alpha Sorority occurred at the 12th Boule held December 1929, in St. Louis. Delegates who gathered at the Peoples Finance Building would consider the following recommendations presented by the Boule Recommendations Committee: (1) "We with the view of increasing success of A.K.A. consider sanely and audaciously the wisdom of holding a biennial meeting of the Boule with Regional Meetings held in the odd years;" (2) "that the Boule take place in the summer." The committee further recommended that these matters be presented to the various chapters and a vote taken at the 1930 Boule.

The 1930 Boule held at Wiley College in Marshall, Texas, would pass both of the Boule recommendations presented in 1929, thus the birth of the Regional Conference and the Summer Boule. This Boule would also amend the bylaws to require that the Regional Director reside in the region that she represented.

BLANCHE L. HAYES CLARK (pictured at left), who had been elected Central Regional Director (6th) at the 1929 Boule was a member of Gamma Omega Chapter, St. Louis, MO at the time of her election. Therefore, with the residency requirement passed at the 1930 Boule, Gamma Omega Chapter joined Central Region.

Soror Clark served as Central Regional Director from 1930-1934, and convened the First Central Regional Conference of Alpha Kappa Alpha Sorority, Inc. on May 23-24, 1931, in Indianapolis, Indiana. Forty-three members attended the conference and addressed the social issues of the time.

The only Central Region chapter chartered during her administration was, Beta Delta, St. Louis, Missouri in 1932. Beta Epsilon, University of Louisville, Beta Zeta, Kentucky State University were chartered in 1933 and Beta Gamma Omega, Lexington, Kentucky in 1934. None of these chapters were designated as a part of Central Region at that time.

The decade of the thirties, with the Great Depression, would find the nation in economic chaos and escalate the problems of the Negro. However, the women of Alpha Kappa Alpha would aggressively support the sorority's national programs and alliances including: support of the Costigan-Warner Anti-Lynching Bill, the Mississippi Health Project, and Joint Committee on National Recovery to mention a few.

Chapter growth, in the geographical areas now comprising Central Region, would be slow during 1930 and 1934. The addition of Beta Delta, Beta Epsilon and Beta Zeta in 1932 seemingly was an indication that there was potential for undergraduate chapter growth. However, the undergraduate chapters in Central Region were experiencing difficulty with housing, finance, scholarship and chapter growth. Two of the undergraduate chapters, Eta and Tau, had at one time during the year only one undergraduate member--the others were graduate members.

The Second World War brought its own set of problems and conditions. Central Region chapters heightened their cooperation and financial support to organizations working to improve the social, educational, health, economic and civic conditions of the Negro. Still segregated and discriminated against, many events during these twenty-five years would create an awakening.

A political shift from the party of Lincoln (Republican Party) to the Democratic Party created a regeneration of the Negro in politics. World War II would result in a more aggressive fight for a larger share of every aspect of American life. Many Negro organizations would lead the way in this continuous fight. Alpha Kappa Alpha Sorority, Inc. was one of these organizations

Alpha Eta Omega Chapter

TERRA HAUTE, INDIANA
JUNE 16, 1928

*Left to Right, Top Row: Pearl Johnson, Evangeline Harris Merriweather, Eura M. Dawkins
Bottom Row: Myrtle Ann Smith, Jane D. Shackelford*

CHARTER MEMBERS

EURA M. DAWKINS
PEARL JOHNSON
EVANGELINE HARRIS MERRIWEATHER
JANE D. SHACKLEFORD
MYRTLE ANN SMITH

Twenty years after the founding of Alpha Kappa Alpha Sorority, Inc., five talented young ladies, impressed with the underlying philosophy and purpose of the organization, met at the home of Soror Evangeline Harris (Merriweather) on June 16, 1928, and organized Alpha Eta Omega Chapter in Terre Haute, Indiana. Participants in the establishment of the Chapter were Sorors Evangeline Harris (Merriweather) whose interest and leadership stimulated the Chapter's organization, Eura Dawkins, Pearl Johnson, Myrtle Smith, and Jane Dabney Shackelford. Soror Murray B. Atkins of Indianapolis, Central Regional Director, officiated at the meeting.

In September, 1928, Sorors Lena B. Lydia and Elva Martin Smith became the first 'neophytes' of Alpha Eta Omega Chapter. Some of the other dedicated members attracted to Alpha Eta Omega Chapter during the early period of growth were: Sorors Clara Parks Barnett, Ruth Hood Battle, Edith Hodge Bingham, Edna L. Edwards, Elena Cabell Hillman, Minnie Hoover, Catherine Sims Jones, Lena B. Lyda, Margaret J. Parks, Lottie Offett Robinson, Alibe Simpson Smith, Elva Martin Smith, Marguerite Taylor, and Celia Upthegrove Jones.

The role of Alpha Eta Omega Chapter has changed frequently during the past Seventy-plus years. Prior to the chartering of their Evansville Chapter, Zeta Zeta Omega in 1954, several sorors from Evansville met with the chapter for a period of time and shared program responsibilities and enjoyed sisterly cooperation. This loyal group included Ada Chester, Elfrieda Churchill, Allouise Jaxson, Agnes Mann, Jacqueline Neal, Alberta Stevenson, Lillian Syler, Willie Effie Thomas (past Basileus of Alpha Eta Omega Chapter, 1950-1951), Mary Coleman, Carolyn Wilson, and others.

During the year 1959, Alpha Eta Omega became a mixed chapter with the induction of a group of Indiana State University undergraduates. On December 6, 1969, the undergraduate sorors formed their own chapter with the chartering of Epsilon Xi on the campus of ISU. A Graduate Advisor from

Alpha Eta Omega Chapter has worked with the undergraduate chapter since that time, and sisterly cooperation between undergraduate and graduate sorors continues today.

Alpha Eta Omega Chapter, with its comparatively small membership over the years, is justifiably proud of the support they have given to the national program targets throughout their history. A few of the local services have involved the awarding of Scholarships, presenting cultural and social programs, remembering needy families at Thanksgiving and Christmas, contributing to the United Way, the American the Red Cross, various day care centers, providing Girl Scout camperships and sending Christmas gifts to patients at Logansport State Hospital for the mentally ill.

On the national level, the chapter has supported the Ethel Hedgeman Lyle Endowment Fund, the Cleveland Job Corps Center, and the United Negro College Fund, contributed to the NAACP Project Freedom Fund by purchasing an NAACP Life Membership in 1970, and cooperated with several other national program activities.

During the summer of 1977, a small group of sorors accepted the challenge of a recent national program and implemented "Reading: A Right, A Responsibility" by conducting a reading improvement workshop for children. During the late 1990's and early 2000's the chapter worked with a number of elementary girls and boys in the "On Track" national program. Currently, they are demonstrating the "Sprit of AKA" via an annual "Sharing and Caring" luncheon wherein the admission fee is a useful gift or monetary donation for a specific community service agency selected for assistance.

Among the many pleasant memories associated with Alpha Eta Omega's history, two special events are outstanding. One occasion was the Central Regional Conference of Alpha Kappa Alpha Sorority which convened in Terre Haute at the YWCA (then located on 7th Street, just North of Wabash Avenue), May 8-10, 1953. Alpha Eta Omega was the Prime Hostess Chapter and was assisted by three other Chapters: Tau, Indiana University, Kappa, Indianapolis, and Alpha Mu Omega, Indianapolis. The conference theme was "Equal Opportunity — Equal Responsibility." Soror Evelyn Roberts of St. Louis, Mo., was the Regional Director and Soror Jane Shackleford was chapter Basileus. The other notable event was the Founders' Day Program on January 15, 1966. It was held at Indiana State University with two national officers as chapter guests: Supreme Basileus, Soror Julia Purnell, Baton Rouge, Louisiana, was the guest speaker, and Regional Director, Soror LeeAnna Shelburne of Louisville, Kentucky, led the rededication service.

During the years 1986 – 1987, Alpha Eta Omega Chapter experienced difficulties which lead to its inactive status. Following a ten year hiatus, on a blustery winter evening, December 12, 1997 in Bloomington Indiana, in the presence of supportive sorors from Alpha Mu Omega and Kappa Tau Omega Chapters, Soror Peggy LeCompte, officially reinstated the Alpha Eta Omega Chapter of Alpha Kappa Alpha Sorority, Inc. The four Alpha Eta Omega officers present to receive their charge from Regional Director LeCompte were Soror Bernice Bass de Martinez, Basileus; Soror Valarie Bailey, Grammateus; Soror Mary Session, Tamiouchos; and Soror Tasha Roberts-Bolden, Graduate Advisor. They were honored with many congratulatory good wishes and even better fellowship. The sisterly good will was heartfelt and most encouraging for this "new beginning." Other Alpha Eta Omega members who pledged their commitment to reactivating the chapter were: Sorors Carolyn Tyler Roberts, Toni Baker, Nicole Dunham-Fykes, and Tamara Franklin.

In February of 1998, Alpha Eta Omega began a tradition of hosting high tea, the first commemorating the Chapter's reactivation held at the Swope Art Museum sparked a rich tradition that still continues today. Known as the "Most High Tea" this tea is first and only one of its kind in the Wabash Valley. This event has grown in popularity and attendance, and now must be hosted at an event facility. Ladies gather, discuss health, social and empowerment issues, and a community-wide service project is conducted during the time leading up to the tea, with Sorors and the community gathering necessities for community centers serving at-risk youth, foster children of incarcerated parents in support of social justice and human rights, and Vigo County School Corporation student weekend meal assistance and winter clothing programs addressing health and poverty.

Alpha Kappa Alpha Sorority's Centennial celebration marked Alpha Eta Omega's 80th year and Sorors continue to share rewarding contributions to our community for those who have shared in its gracious offerings of sisterhood and service to all mankind.

Since reactivation the Chapter has been working harder than ever, membership has increased, program goals have been exceeded and the "Home of the Ivy Hymn" has purchased a heifer from Heifer, International in support of reducing global poverty in Kenya.

In 2010 they introduced the GeniRevolution an on-line math/financial literacy video game to middle and high school students to provide educational and mentoring empowerment by African American male math teachers and college students majoring in math. Several entrepreneurial Sorors share business strategies and consulting for new and existing businesses and pro-bono marketing services through the Apple GreenBacks economic security and small business initiative.

2010 marked an exceptional year of stellar growth and activity for Alpha Eta Omega, as Regional Director Soror Giselé M. Casanova keeping her campaign pledge to engage and call upon Chapters to serve the sisterhood, October 2011 Alpha Eta Omega hosted the Cluster III Annual Retreat in Terre Haute, IN. Numerous committee and committee chairmanships appointments have been bestowed upon our membership. The chapter is honored to have had its member's present workshops and serve on the Regional Luncheon Committee at 2012 Boule'. The Chapter is humbled and will continue to serve the Classy, Competent, Central Regional and Alpha Kappa Alpha Sorority, Incorporated.

Plans are underway to re-vitalize the Artist and Model Ball, originated in the 1940's as a signature event preceding Alpha Eta Omega's 85th Anniversary on June 16, 2013. The past 85 years of Alpha Eta Omega Chapter's history as a part of Alpha Kappa Alpha Sorority, Inc. have provided gateway experiences through which its members have passed to preview future challenges of greater service to all mankind.   The torch of ideals lighted by our Founders in 1908, and passed to our charter members in 1928, still offers a challenge to present and future sorors. We are challenged to build on the foundation of our past, so that the strong bonds of sisterhood will ensure to ourselves and to our posterity the enduing charge to "Capture a Vision Fair," as we honor our past and propel towards our future.

SPECIAL NOTE: The AKA official songbook lists Soror Evangeline Harris Merriweather, one of the Charter Members of Alpha Eta Omega, as the author of both words and music of the AKA Ivy Hymn. According to historical papers located in the Vigo County Public Library, she also wrote the words to the Initiation Hymn.

Alpha Eta Omega Chapter Advised Epsilon Xi Chapter From 1969 – 1987 and Again in 1999 to the Present

Chapter Members Who Have Held International/National Office or Been Elected to the International/National Nominating Committee

Elizabeth Schmoke Randolph   Supreme Parliamentarian   1974 – 1978

Alpha Eta Omega Chapter Basilei

Evangeline Harris Merriweather	1928 – 1930
Myrtle A. Smith	1931 – 1932
Eura Dawkins	1933 – 1934
Pearl Johnson	1935 – 1936
Lena B. Lyda	1937 – 1938
Elena Cabell Hillman	1939 – 1940
Elva Martin Smith	1941 – 1942

Edith Hodge Bigham	1943 – 1944
Evangeline Harris Merriweather	1945 – 1946
Alibe Simpson Smith	1947 – 1948
Hattie J. Edwards	1949 – 1950
Willie Effie Thomas	1951 – 1952
Jane D. Shackelford	1953 – 1954
Leora E. Taylor	1955 – 1956
Katherine Sims Jones	1957 – 1959
Bertha Watt Romby	1960 – 1962
Nell Taylor	1963 – 1964
Millie H. Lyda	1964 – 1965
Alibe Hayes	1966 – 1967
Jessie Brown	1968 – 1969
Edith Hodge Bigham	1970 – 1971
SaRetta Brown	1972 – 1973
Adelaide Shelton	1974 – 1975
Jessie Brown	1976 – 1977
Adelaide Shelton	1978 – 1979
Deborah Rasberry	1980 – 1981
Karen Walden	1982
Deborah Raspberry	1983 – 1985
Ivonne Jones	1986
Barbara Seeney	1987
INACTIVE	1987 – 1997
Bernice Bass de Martinez	1997 – 1998
Valarie A. Bailey	1999 – 2000
Tamara Ramey Carter	2001 – 2003
W. Diane Cargile	2004 – 2006
Tamara Ramey Carter	2007
Tasha M. Tyler-Roberts	2008 – 2012
Naketa Young	2012
Pamela Hood	2012 –

Alpha Mu Omega Chapter

Indianapolis, Indiana
February 16, 1929

Two of Alpha Mu Omega Chapter Charter Members at Founders' Day

Charter Members

HAZEL J. ALEXANDER	MARY A. JOHNSON
HELEN HUMMONS ANDERSON	ETHEL KUYKENDALL
EUGENIA D. BURBRIDGE ASBURY	LILLIAN LEMON
SPAULDING PRITCHETT BERRY	HENRIETTA H. MACMILLIAN
VELMA PRITCHETT CAGE	PAULINE MORTON-FINNEY
ANNA M. HALL COURTNEY	EDITH M. OVERTON
IVA R. MARSHALL DAVIS	MERCY SMITH
GLADYS LUCAS DOYLE	FRANCES STOUT
HATTIE P. JONES EDWARDS	HARRIET TAYLOR
SELMA B. HARRY	LILLIAN TAYLOR
RUTH HAYNES	LORENE T. COOK TURNER
MARTHA HORNER	MURRAY B. ATKINS WALLS
FANNIE HYDE	PHYLLIS WATERS
THELMA JACKSON	A. LOUISE MOSS WEBB

Lambda Omega was the first Chapter of Alpha Kappa Alpha Sorority in Indianapolis. It was dissolved by the 11th Boule held in Nashville, Tennessee in December 1928. A new graduate chapter was proposed. Ironically, the next name in line for a graduate chapter was Alpha Lambda Omega. The petitioning members of the new Indianapolis group, two of whom were charter members of Lambda Omega, had concerns regarding the similarity of the name. They voiced these concerns to the Boule. After debate on the issue, the Boule voted to assign the next name in line, Alpha Mu Omega, to the new graduate chapter being organized in Indianapolis. The charter was granted and the authorization was given and the new chapter was chartered on February 16, 1929.

The Chapter was officially organized in March, 1929, Soror Maude Brown Porter, Regional Director officiated. Soror Mary A. Johnson, Dean of Girls at Crispus Attucks High School was the first Basileus. The last of the 28 charter members, Soror Frances Stout became an Ivy Beyond the Wall in January 2004.

Two chapter members made outstanding contributions in the early years of the national organization. Soror Murray B. Atkins Walls served as Supreme Grammateus of Alpha Kappa Alpha and Soror Phyllis Waters designed the coat of arms for the national organization.

Programs and Projects of the Chapter

Alpha Mu Omega has given leadership and vigorous support to national programs such as the Foreign Scholarship Fund, the Mississippi Health Project, Sickle Cell Anemia Project, the Cleveland Job Corps, the project to purchase Martin Luther King, Jr. birthplace and the Educational Advancement Foundation. The Chapter supports the Educational Advancement Foundation with its annual membership dues and has funded an endowed gift from Soror Vera Forte McCain.

Education continues to be the primary focus of the chapter. Alpha Mu Omega incorporated its scholarship fund in 1979. Soror Ruby Woodson, who conceived the idea, provided leadership to Scholarship Fund for more than 25 years. During those years nearly a half million dollars has been awarded to young women in the Indianapolis community. The Fund, a separate entity, changed its name to Ivy Endowment, Inc. in 2007 and operates as the scholarship committee of the Chapter. During World War II Alpha Mu Omega sorors provided comfort and support to the Negro soldiers stationed at Fort Harrison and Camp Atterbury, both Indiana military installations. Alpha Mu Omega has provided arts, entertainment, lectures and forums as social and educational opportunities for the local community. Among those personalities presented by the Chapter were news reporter and commentator, Carl Rowan, the Ramsey Lewis Trio, and Soror Angie Brooks, President of United Nations.

In recent years the Chapter has raised funds and gained community support by hosting debutante cotillions. The debutante cotillion began in 1986 with Kappa Chapter, the local undergraduate chapter, presenting twelve young ladies to the Indianapolis community. In 1987, Alpha Mu Omega and Kappa chapter jointly presented thirty-seven young women.

Debutantes are students in the eleventh and twelfth grades of metropolitan school systems throughout the greater Indianapolis area. Participants are engaged in a rigorous program for a designated period of time to prepare them for the cotillion. Scholarships are awarded to the participants. Alpha Mu Omega sorors who have provided leadership to the cotillion are: Grace Dowe, Geneva Murphy, Clarrean Anthony, Delores Casey, Mildred Smith, Marcella Taylor, Larnell Burks Bagley, Diane Pillow Cargile, Bruceil Mays, Kelly Blanchard, Jarnell Burks Craig, Nadine Bonds, Sherry Curry, Lauretta Holloway, Gloria Williams, Marvis Fulford, Tamiko Crayton, Heloise Archie, Marie Rahman, Margie Forte, Karen Dailey, Esther Bowman, Ruth Woods, Stephanie Young Moss, Alicia Gordy, Marcy Gordy, Thomanisa Ash, Rhonda Williams, Angela Henry, Angela Miller and Nichole Wilson.

Leadership, Service and Honors

Alpha Mu Omega proudly claims four past Central Regional Director as chapter members. They are Sorors: Maenell Hamlin Newsome, Annette Lawson, Yvonne Perkins, and Nadine Bonds. Soror Yvonne Perkins served as Supreme Tamiouchos from 1986 – 1990 and was reelected to serve in that office for a second time in 1994. Soror Nadine Bonds was appointed International Regional Director, by Supreme Basileus, Linda White for period 2002 to 2006. Soror Doris Parker has the distinction of serving as the first full time Executive Secretary of the Educational Advancement Foundation. She retired from that position in 1998. Alpha Mu Omega members are recipients of numerous awards such as the Freedom Foundation Award and listings in various publications of Who's Who.

Each year Alpha Mu Omega Chapter honors sorors with awards for outstanding service and achievements. These awards are Soror through the Years, presented to the soror who has contributed greatly to the chapter and the community over the years and Soror of the Year, presented to the soror who has demonstrated outstanding service to the chapter in a given year.

One of the most memorable services for Alpha Kappa Alpha Sorority, Inc. occurred in July 1994, when Alpha Mu Omega Chapter hosted the 56th Boule. Soror Jarnell Burks Craig served as General Chairman and Soror Sherry Curry as Co-Chairman. Using the theme "A Race to Indy," the Chapter presented a rousing invitation to the 56th Boule at the 55th Boule in New Orleans in 1992. Over 7,500 sorors accepted the invitation to attend "A Race to Indy." in 1994. Supreme Basileus, Soror Mary Shy Scott expressed her appreciation to Soror Jarnell Craig for her leadership and the Chapter for its dedication to make her last Boule a memorable event.

Alpha Mu Omega Advises Kappa, Tau, Beta Phi and Pi Lambda Chapters and Advised Epsilon Rho and Epsilon Xi Prior to Their Being Advised by Gamma Psi Omega and Alpha Eta Omega, Respectively.

CHAPTER MEMBERS WHO HAVE HELD INTERNATIONAL/NATIONAL OFFICE OR BEEN ELECTED TO THE INTERNATIONAL/ NATIONAL NOMINATING COMMITTEE

Murray Atkins Walls	Supreme Grammateus	1922 – 1923
Maenell Newsome	Regional Director	1944 – 1946
Annetta Moten Lawson	Regional Director	1958 – 1962
Yvonne Perkins	Supreme Tamiouchous	1986 – 1990
	Regional Director	1990 – 1994
	Supreme Tamiouchos	1994 – 1996
Victoria Clark	National Nominating Committee	1983 – 1985
Sherry Curry	National Nominating Committee	1994 – 1998
Nadine C. Bonds	Central Regional Director	1998 – 2002
	International Regional Director	2002 – 2006

ALPHA MU OMEGA CHAPTER BASILEI

Mary A. Johnson	1929 – 1931
Hattie Jones Edwards	1931
Pauline Morton-Finney	1932 – 1935
Thelma Jackson	1935
Eugenia Asbury	1935 – 1937
Artie German Price	1937 – 1938
Phyllis Waters	1938 – 1940
Mary A. Johnson	1940 – 1942
Maenell Newsome	1942 – 1944
Ethel Kuykendall	1944 – 1946
Stella Woodall	1946 – 1947
Ruby Woodson	1947 – 1949
Emma Mae Allison	1949 – 1951
Lois D. Bynum	1951 – 1952
Leslye Henderson	1952 – 1953
Ethel Kuykendall	1953 – 1954
Norma Wood Slaughter	1954 – 1955
Annetta Moten Lawson	1956 – 1957
Ruby Woodson	1958 – 1959

Gloria Ann Morton-Finney	1960 – 1961
Jeannette B. Greene	1962 – 1964
Hazel S. Moore	1964 – 1968
Wilma Battey	1968 – 1970
Marilyn Strayhorn Bradley	1970 – 1972
Yvonne Perkins	1972 – 1975
Marilyn Strayhorn Bradley	1975 – 1979
Diane Pillow	1980 – 1983
Zoearline G. Davis	1983 – 1985
Nadine C. Bonds	1986 – 1989
Sherry Crawford Curry	1989 – 1991
Zoearline G. Davis	1991 – 1993
Martha C. Mitchell	1993 – 1997
Jarnell Burks Craig	1997 – 1999
Esther Long Bowman	1999 – 2003
Stacia Gray	2003 – 2005
Victoria L. Clark	2006 – 2009
Pamela Miller Hatcher	2010 – 2011
Mariatu A. Swayne	2012 –

Beta Delta Chapter Basilei

NO RECORD	1932-1981
Denise Young	1982-1983
Lisa Boyd	1983-1984
Lori Johnson	1985-1986
Delores Bentley	1989
Marquita Gandy	1990
Kathy Porter	1991
DeCarla Albright	1992
Chandra Bell	1992
Pamela Whiteside	1993
LaTanya Reese	1996
Ruby Grady	1997
Onye Ejei	1998
Shavon McGowan Johnson	1998-1999
Stephanie Baker	1999
Michelle Purdy	2000
Olivia Coleman	2001
De-Andrea Blaylock-Johnson	2002-2003
Amber Spencer	2003
Tracey Randall	2004
Regina Taylor	2005
Ryan Day	2006-2007
Chelesa Phillips	2007
Monet Harrell	2008
Caitlin Parker Ladd	2008-2009
Jehan Rehaman	2009
Reva Broussard	2009-2010
Rebekah Shebazz	2010
Portia Britt	2011
Mahdiah Atkins	2012-2013
Melanie Gatewood	2013-

Beta Zeta Chapter

Kentucky State (College) University
Frankfort, Kentucky
February 25, 1933

Charter Members

HATTIE BIBBS	RUTH GARNER	EVELYN SHIELDS
ELVIRA BOWLES	ELEANOR HARROLD	VIRGINIA SMOTHERS
LENA COLEMAN	ODESSA MAJOR	RUTH TANDY
GEORGE MAE EVANS	VIRGIL PERRY	ALMA TERRY
LORRAINE FRANCIS	EMMA RICE	ANNA MAE WHITTAKER
		MARY WILLIAMS

On February 25, 1933, sixteen coeds of Kentucky State College claimed the salmon pink and apple green and made it dear to their hearts. They made it their own and were proud to wear the colors and to wear the significant pins over their hearts. It was the first Greek-letter organization for women on the campus.

On the cold evening in February, the Supreme Basileus, Maude E. Brown, and Regional Director, Carolyn Blanton, set up the Beta Zeta undergraduate chapter of Alpha Kappa Alpha Sorority at Kentucky State College in Frankfort, Kentucky. The sixteen members, whose lives would be guided by its ideals, are deeply moved, have waited patiently, and have these moments deeply engraved upon their hearts. They exhibited the essence of womanhood, character, intellect, style and grace. Under the guidance of Lucille Jewell and E. B. Lewis, their hopes are realized and all their hard work has come to fruition.

Before the end of the day chapter officers would be elected: President, Anna Whittaker; Vice-President, Elvira Bowles; Secretary, Lorraine Francis; Corresponding Secretary, Ruth Garner; Treasurer, Virgil Perry; and Dean of Pledges, E.B. Lewis. Sorors in attendance who witnessed the initiation were National President M.E. Brown; Regional Director C. Blanton both of Louisville; Miss Angie McNeal and Laticia May of Cincinnati; Miss Myrtle Hammons, Ollie Davis, Zelma Fuller and Alberta Robinson of Lexington, Kentucky; and Carrie King of Georgetown.

Through the years, various activities and programs have been implemented by Beta Zeta Chapter. Beta Zeta has planned and implemented programs concerning civic engagement, leadership, etiquette, and self-image. Additionally, they have collaborated with Beta Upsilon Omega in executing The Jewel Program for young girls and the EYL Program. Both programs focus on offering various programs and workshops on leadership, awareness of higher educational opportunities in math and science and leadership.

Chapter Members Who Have Held International/National Office or Been Elected to the International/National Nominating Committee

Anita McCullom Shelton   Undergraduate Member at Large   1982-1984

Beta Zeta Chapter Basilei

1933	Anna Mae Whittaker
1948	Edna Garvin
1949	Lottie Matthews
1950	Alice Gillespie
1954	Hattie Brittenum
1955	Bessie Lasley
1956	Myrtle Gillispie
1957	Maxine Gregory
1959	Bernice Mimms
1963	Margaret Parker
1964 Spring-1965	Joyce Dishman Owens
1966	Reba Wilson
1967	Delois King
1968	Rosaland Bishop
1969	Margaret Terry
1970	Freddie Williams
1971	Patricia Matillar
1972	Peggy Hattiex Penn
1973	Patricia Whorton
1974	Patricia Taylor
1975	Marsha Smith
1977	Portia Mumphrey
1978 Summer-1980	Francene L. Botts
1987	Yolanda Curlin Penn
1994	Tracey Bush
1999	Taneesha D. Seay
2007	Shonte Long
2008	Angelica Parnell
2009-2010	Erika Harrell
2011	Amber Rankins
2012 Spring	Marshawn Thomas
2012 Fall-Present	Tonyica Boykin

Beta Epsilon Chapter

UNIVERSITY OF LOUISVILLE
(LOUISVILLE MUNICIPAL COLLEGE)
LOUISVILLE, KENTUCKY
NOVEMBER 6, 1933

Beta Epsilon members in the mid thirties.

CHARTER MEMBERS

DOROTHY MAE ALLEN
MARGARET DURHAM
EVA MAE GLASS

LETTIE LOUISE HARRIS
JOEL PRENTICE POPE
RUTH ELLA TATE

Beta Epsilon Chapter of Alpha Kappa Alpha Sorority, Incorporated was the first undergraduate extension of the Sorority in the state of Kentucky. It was charted November 6, 1933 at Louisville Municipal College, Louisville, KY. This prestigious Chapter was chartered by six forward-thinking women: Sorors, Ruth Ella Tate, Eva Mae Glass, Margaret Ruth Durham, Lettie Louise Harris, Dorothy Mae Allen, and Joel Pernice Pope.

Beta Epsilon honors itself on successful programming. In the Fall of 2011, Beta Epsilon presented to the campus our "Service to ALL Mankind" Week. Some of the programs that we hosted were:

- M.A.D.D. (Mothers Against Drunk Driving)
- Community Service at Wayside Christian Mission Church with Delta Zeta Sorority
- In Spring of 2012, we taught the campus how to stay pretty with our "Protect Your Pretty Week"
  The following programs were used to Preserve Spiritual, Intellectual, and Physical Beauty:
- "Protect the Future with The Game of Life," which was teaching students how to dress for success, while preparing them for future job interviews.
- "Protect the health with AKAerobics Belly Dancing," which was an alternative way to exercise and stay healthy.

- "Protect the Mind with Pillow Talk," which is where we discussed issues relating to relationships, school, and more.

Signature programs of Beta Epsilon are:

- "For the Love of Harriett Breast Cancer Awareness Luncheon and Remembrance Walk." This is where Beta Epsilon provides the campus with a guest speaker to inform us on how to prevent Breast Cancer. As for the Remembrance Walk, this is where Beta Epsilon, along with other members of our campus, comes together and walks through the entire campus carrying pink balloons, while making short stops to read facts about breast cancer in Remembrance of Harriett B. Porter. She was a well-known African American woman who made a huge impact on the University of Louisville's campus and ended up dying from breast cancer.
- "Too Blessed to Be Stressed" This gives students an opportunity to relax before finals with encouraging words.

In 2011 Beta Epsilon donated one cow to the Heifer Foundation under the Global Poverty Initiative. The cow was equivalent to $500 donated.

Within this prestigious Beta Epsilon Chapter, we have many outstanding Sorors that have made many individual achievements. For instance, Soror Cassandra Webb was the President of Society of Porter Scholars, Soror Cortney Evans was the Vice President of USHR (Undergraduate Students Helping to Recruit), Soror Alexis Leavell is the President of ELT (Empowering Ladies Together), Soror Shanice Brown is the President of ESSENCE, and Soror Kaelin Gatewood is the 1st Vice President of NPHC (National PanHellenic Council). Soror Shanee Lassiter was Miss Black Diamond Choir, Soror Taryn Moran held the position as Miss Collegiate, Soror Jasmine Shadding was Miss Black U of L, and Soror Cheraye Durr was awarded with the Roberta Kniffley African American Psychology Scholarship.

Last but not least, Soror Marcela Moore was awarded with the highest GPA in the Central Region, and Beta Epsilon as a Chapter was awarded with the highest GPA of all sororities for the past two years.

Beta Gamma Omega Chapter

LEXINGTON, KENTUCKY
MARCH 30, 1934

CHARTER MEMBERS

IRENE HAWKINS	OLLIE DAVIS MILLER
MYRTLE HUMMONS JONES	ALBERTA ROBINSON
ZELMA FULLER WEAVER	

Don't you like stories that begin with "Once upon a time?" Well, once upon a time, there was sister Expecting-To-Be who had great expectations of chartering an Alpha Kappa Alpha chapter in the heart of the Blue Grass Region in Lexington, Kentucky.

As the time approached for the delivery, Sister Expecting-To-Be, who had the utmost faith in mid-wifery, would have no other than Soror Carolyn Blanton, our past Regional Director, who lived in Louisville, Kentucky. Our Supreme Basileus at that time was Soror Ida L. Jackson.

So on a beautiful evening, March 30, 1934, there was a great commotion at the old Dunbar High School Annex, which was a very, very old building that had once housed white orphans (that site is the present location of the Russell Elementary School). How surprised was Soror Carolyn Blanton to bring forth not only one cute little sister but four sisters! They were as follows: Alberta Robinson, a plump one who became Basileus. She really possessed executive ability and taught English at Douglas High School. Ollie Davis Miller was then as skinny as a canary bird and had such a beautiful powerful soprano voice. She was a social worker and was our Anti-Basileus. Myrtle Hummons Jones was the Grammateus. Perhaps she held that office because she had to write legibly for her first, second and third graders at the old Booker T. Washington School. Irene Hawkins, our Tamiouchos, was a quiet one who taught at Russell School. Zelma Fuller Weaver, the chapter reporter, was then another skinny one who taught many things at the old Russell School on Fourth Street and at Dunbar.

Soror Blanton stated that Beta Gamma Omega would be the beautiful name of Alpha Kappa Alpha's new chapter in Lexington. Lydia White Holly was our first initiate into Beta Gamma Omega and Evelyn Bailey Sallee was the second one. I'm trying to think of some of our projects in those early years. Jewel McNari and her dolls from Louisville, Kentucky danced their way into our hearts. Etta Moten, the beautiful singer, appeared on stage at our invitation. Marva Louis, Joe Louis's first wife, was presented in a style show at the Lyric Theater, located on the corner of Deweese and Third Street.

In the December 1940 *Ivy Leaf*, there was this bit of news. Beta Gamma Omega ended the year by awarding their sixth annual scholarship of fifty dollars to Miss Helen Porter, a 1940 graduate of Dunbar High School. Miss Porter has matriculated at West Virginia State College.

The chapter supplied milk to each of the five black elementary schools for the children of our community. Beta Gamma Omega operated a kindergarten for several years at the old 2nd Street YMCA, and completely furnished a room at the old YMCA Branch for the community's, as well as for the chapter's use.

Contributions were made to the following: The Mound Bayou Health Project in Mississippi, NAACP, United Negro College Fund, Urban League, March of Dimes, International Book Project, Cardinal Hill Hospital, Women's Neighborly Organization and others. The Hamilton Vogue and Ebony Fashion Shows and other distinguished artists have also been a source of raising funds for scholarships for some worthy high school girl.

The sorors of Beta Gamma Omega organized chapters of Alpha Kappa Alpha at the University of Kentucky (Iota Sigma), Soror Katye Jenkins, Graduate Advisor; Eastern Kentucky University (Zeta Nu), Soror Emma Butler, Graduate Advisor; and Morehead State University (Eta Rho), Soror Mary

Murray, Graduate Advisor.

Soror Teresa Searcy continued to stress the importance of a reading program upon becoming Basileus in 1980. The major fundraiser during this time was a fashion show featuring the "Hamilton Vogue Model" from Chicago. This event took place at the Opera House. The scholarship award went to Angela Parks. In 1982, Soror Pauline Gould-Gay was next in line to serve as Basileus. Soror Gould-Gay was the 1stAfrican American to hold office as President of the Lexington Ballet.

Under the leadership of Soror Finch and her supportive forty-three sorors the chapter implemented a tutorial program for students in kindergarten to twelfth grade. The goal was to offer tutorial services in the areas of Reading and Math. Soror Rose Perry played a vital role in formalizing the program. Soror Rose was instrumental in obtaining a computer for usage at the reading clinic. A matching grant from IBM made it possible to get the computer. Additional assistance came with the cooperation of the Fayette County School system with aid of Soror Edythe Hayes, Deputy Superintendent.

In 1985, Soror Yvonne Fluker became Basileus, completing the last part of the 1985 term. During her tenure more exciting events occurred. Soror Fluker contacted Soror Barbara Phillips, the 21st Supreme Basileus, to serve as our Founders' Day speaker. The event was held at the Spindletop Hall, Lexington, KY. What an exhilarating time to be held with the sorors!

The Fashions Unlimited fashion show was held at the Hyatt Regency. Five-hundred dollars was donated to the Morton House promoting culture through the arts. Soror Mildred Striders' husband, Maurice held an Art Showing at the Morton House.

Soror Fluker also had the opportunity to pin a tea rose corsage on Soror Corretta Scott King, when she was in Lexington, KY at the dedication of the opening of Martin Luther King Boulevard. Sorors MaryAnn Adams and Pauline Gould Gay were selected by the chapter to be honored at the Sixth Annual Women of Achievement Awards Program at the Hyatt Regency. The following year, Soror Harriet Haskins was selected. Ms. Wilma Rudolph, Olympic track star, was the honored speaker. Sorors Haskins and Fluker were photographed with the renowned track star.

The fundraising chairperson Soror Jesse Wilson and Co-Chairperson Juanita Peterson were responsible for bringing the Theater Workshop of Louisville to town. The play "Don't Bother Me I Can't Cope" was performed beautifully on stage at Haggin Auditorium located on the Transylvania University campus.

Our humanitarian project went to the Tabitha Foster Fund in support of the Little Tabitha Severe Birth Defect. Fayette Urban County Government Council on Art donated $2,500 to boost our project. A $500 grant was also received from the Kentucky Arts Council. This seed money and the hard work of the sorors generated $10,152.00 in revenue. A proclamation by Governor Wilkinson was presented to Tabitha's parents.

As the chapter continued to grow and serve the Lexington community, Soror Doris Brown was elected to serve as Basileus (1988-1989). Sorors worked diligently to plan and hosted a Fashion Show at the Hyatt Regency. The chapter also held a Champaign Brunch Fashion Show as a part of its fundraising efforts as well. In addition, Soror Donna George became the first African American Principal for a high school in the state of Kentucky.

The next in line to serve as Basileus for 1990-1991, was Soror Joyce Owens. During her tenure, the chapter conducted a Sisterhood Workshop, promoted "Black Dollar Day," which was chaired by Soror Veronica Gaines. The annual Cluster Area Retreat was hosted in Lexington by Beta Gamma Omega. In December1992, a Pink Ice Ball, a semi-formal event, was held with proceeds going to the scholarship fund. Soror Valeria Cummings Swope took the helm in 1992. The major fundraising efforts that took place during this time included the Fashion Show and Beautillion. Beta Gamma Omega also participated in Founder's Day activities and program held in Lexington, KY.

For the 2001-2002 term of office, Soror Zelia Wiley Holloway was elected Basileus. Under her leadership, Beta Gamma Omega hosted the 2001 Area Cluster Retreat for Clusters 6 & 7 that fall at the Kentucky Inn, Lexington, KY. The largest fundraising venture was the Fashion Show featuring the Uniqueness Modeling Troop.

Beta Gamma Omega's black family projects included participating in the Buckle Up for Safety program at the old Booker T. Washington School in which sorors assisted with car seat distributions. Sorors also participated in serving lunch monthly at the Salvation Army. At Christmas a joint project was completed with members of Delta Sigma Theta's Lexington Graduate Chapter. Members of each organization collected toiletry items for gift baskets to be donated for a local women's shelter. Another highlight of the chapter was hosting the Annual Roots & Heritage Arts reception.

Soror Eugenia Johnson-Smith was excited to take over as Basileus in 2003. Soror Eugenia's positive energy brought to the chapter monthly "Power Positive Moments" in which she used to share words of encouragement and motivation to members of the chapter. Soror Pamela Clayton worked very hard to institute the Ivy Reading AKAdemy. Soror Clayton was also responsible to for taking the initiative to prepare the "Partners in Youth" grant proposal. The chapter received $700 to help fund projects for the Ivy Reading AKAdemy.

The chapter continued to hold two fundraising Fashion Shows during Soror Smith's term. Each show was held in December at the Holiday Inn North, Lexington and featured the Uniqueness Modeling Troop. Each Soror sold tickets that included a delicious brunch, fashion show and the opportunity to win a number of various door prizes. Members of the chapter participated in and raised monies for the American Heart Association's Heart Walk, the March of Dimes, Walk America and the American Cancer Society's relay for Life. In 2004, chapter members "Leaped for Life" and collected nearly $1,200 in donations for the American Cancer Society.

In November 2003, Soror Dana Branham organized activities for the National Family Volunteer Day. A room at the Coleman House, a home for displaced children named after Soror Grace Coleman, was decorated in pink and green and new paint, bedding, posters were provided. In the spring of 2004 a second room at the Coleman House was decorated. Members of the chapter also gathered to serve as ushers at the local Martin Luther King, Jr. Celebration held at Lexington Heritage Hall. Beta Gamma Omega also continued to serve as hostess for the annual Roots & Heritage Arts Reception in 2003 and 2004.

In honor of Breast Cancer Awareness Month, members of Beta Gamma Omega participated in a joint project on October 30, 2004 to collect donations and wigs (specifically for women of color or of grey color) to be given to the American Cancer Foundation's wig bank. Members from Delta Sigma Theta Sorority, Zeta Phi Beta Sorority, Sigma Gamma Rho Sorority, the Frankfort — Links Inc. and the National Council of Negro Women-Lexington Central Kentucky Section came out to participate despite the rainy start to the day. That day 85 wigs were collected for the American Cancer Society's wig bank. In addition many hats (12), bandanas (21), turbans (4) were collected. $180.00 to go toward the purchase of new wigs and a $10.00 donation to the ACS was also collected at that time.

Give me the strength to make me kinder
To my sister's fault be blinder
Let me think less of myself and what's my due
Send me strength to smile at sorrow
Doubt not; fear not, for the morrow.
To the best that is within, O keep me true

Help me to raise my fallen neighbor
Spare not cheer, nor that or labor
If I smooth the path of only just a few
For this old world will be brighter
If we keep our thoughts from me
And think of you.

— Soror Agnes Berry, *Ivy Leaf,* 1930

Note: Portions of Beta Gamma's Hisory through 1980 was written by Soror Zelma Smith Weaver, Charter Member is as it appeared in Beta Gamma Omega's 50th Anniversary Luncheon souvenir program book, March 24, 1984.

Chapter Members Who Have Held International/National Office or Been Elected to the International/National Nominating Committee

Yvonne Fluker   Nominating Committee   1988 – 1989

Beta Gamma Omega Chapter Basilei

Alberta Robinson
Susan Garr
Ethel Payton
Marietta Hunter
Sally Moore
Grace Harris
Lillian Delaney
Janice Didlick
Grace Coleman
Mae L. Cleveland
Dorothy Bottoms
Doris Borwn
Katye Jenkins
Emma Butler
Charles Jones
Doris Brown
Katherine Rollins
Anna Conner
Teresa Searcy
Pauline Gould-Gay   1983 – 1984
Ida Nell Finch   1985 – 1986
Yvonne Fluker   1986 – 1988
Doris Brown   1989 — 1990
Joyce Owens   1991 — 1992
Valeria Swope   1993 – 1994
Mae L. Cleveland   1995 – 1996
Yvonne Fluker   1997 – 1998
Joyce Owens   1999 – 2000
Zelia Wiley Holloway   2001 – 2002
Eugenia Johnson Smith   2003 – 2004
Francene Botts-Butler   2005 – 2006

Alice E. McGhee Smart

7TH CENTRAL REGIONAL DIRECTOR
DECEMBER 1934 – DECEMBER 1937

Initiated into Gamma Chapter, at the University of Illinois during the spring of 1922, Soror Alice E. McGhee Smart made an impressive record at the university. She was elected to Pi Gamma Mu Honorary Social Science Club and was a member of the women's basketball team. She received the degree of A.B. from the University of Illinois in June 1924 and a M.A. degree from the University of Chicago. At the graduate level, she affiliated with Gamma Omega and Delta Omega Chapters.

Soror McGhee's career objectives were to be a worthy and acceptable member of society and to improve the position of Blacks in general. She was the first Dean of Women at Lincoln University; Principal of the Teacher Training School of Petersburg, Virginia; Assistant Professor, Department of Geography, Stowe Teachers College; and a teacher of social science at Vashon High School in St. Louis, Missouri.

Soror McGhee was elected Supreme Epistoleus at the 1931 Boule and was reelected in 1933 to a third term. During her first year in office as Central Regional Director, she visited all of the chapters in Central Region with the exception of Alpha Mu Omega and Kappa Chapters. Geography and travel were here passions. She traveled extensively abroad and for Alpha Kappa Alpha.

Soror McGhee's attention was always focused on the undergraduates and the housing problems of Black students at white northern universities. She often addressed this subject at Boules and worked to help secure a sorority residence for Gamma Chapter at the University of Illinois/Urbana, her alma mater.

A Central Regional Conference was not held during Soror McGhee's first year in office because there had been difficulty in securing a hostess chapter for the conference. The funds designated to be used for the 1935 conference were instead donated to the Gamma House Project.

Soror McGhee presided over the 3rd (1936) and 4th (1937) Central Regional Conferences and initiated the first Central Region awards to stimulate and encourage civic and community interest and scholarship among undergraduates.

Beta Rho Omega Chapter

HOPKINSVILLE, KENTUCKY
FEBRUARY 14, 1937

CHARTER MEMBERS

JENNIE BAKER	ANNIE MAE MOORE
ALMA CAMPBELL	EMMA SNORTON
ODESSA CHESTINE	RUTH B. TANDY (ASSOCIATE MEMBER)
ALMA LEWIS	BERNICE BROOKS THOMPSON
	GEORGIE M. WHITNEY

Hopkinsville, Kentucky. The chartering was held at the Freeman Chapel C.M.E. Church. Beta Rho Omega Chapter is a small chapter but conscientious and productive. The charter members of Beta Rho Omega were: Emma Snorton, Alma Lewis, Bernice Brooks Thompson, Annie Mae Moore, Georgia Whitney, Alma Campbell, Odessa Chestine, Jennie K. Baker, and Ruth B. Tandy, an associate member.

The first additions to the chapter included women from Hopkinsville, Bowling Green, Russellville, and Clarksville, TN. Since there were no other Alpha Kappa Alpha chapters in the area at the time, the Hopkinsville Chapter included members from surrounding areas.

One major objective of Beta Rho Omega was to establish an undergraduate chapter at Western Kentucky University in Bowling Green. During the terms of Claudia Greene as President (Basileus), the undergraduate chapter, Epsilon Zeta, was chartered. Beta Rho Omega advised Epsilon Zeta from 1968-1985.

Two chapters Of Alpha Kappa Alpha Sorority, Inc. were spawned from Beta Rho Omega's membership. Chapter members residing in Tennessee decided to form a chapter of their own. Austin Peay State College was located in Clarksville Tennessee, and to establish an undergraduate chapter there; a graduate chapter would have to exist locally. Clarksville members pulled out and formed Nu Kappa Omega Chapter under the direction of the Southeastern Regional Director. Later, the Bowling Green membership had grown sufficiently to form a chapter, Omicron Sigma Omega. A close bond of sisterhood is felt for both of these chapters. Beta Rho Omega's membership continues to include individuals from the surrounding areas.

Throughout the years, Beta Rho Omega has provided services to this community in a number of ways, both individually as well as in collaboration with other organizations. Beta Rho Omega's programs of service are guided by the International Program as it is tailored to meet the needs of the community. The chapter's participation in the Alpha Kappa Alpha Domestic Travel Grant Program produced two recipients of an all-expense paid trip to major cities in the United States. The first recipient was Marcia Means (Johnson) in 1969, followed by Angela Bradshaw in 1988.

In 1986, Beta Rho Omega, under the direction of Soror Ali Maxwell Taylor, produced a musical drama, "Searching for the Rainbow." This production, written by Soror Taylor, included approximately seventy-five interracial cast members and stage crew comprised of individuals from our community. An encore production was also given.

Beta Rho Omega has always awarded scholarships to deserving high school graduates each year. Beta Rho Omega hosts a Fashion Show which is widely supported by the community to fund the scholarship program. In addition Beta Rho Omega provides aid to families and children in foster care at Thanksgiving and Christmas.

Other service projects are varied and many:
- Clothing to school children in Kingston, Jamaica

- School supplies to children in Africa
- School supplies to local elementary schools
- Family Resource Center Donations
- Voter Registration Drives
- Health Fairs
- Nursing Home Activities
- Community Centers participation
- NAACP Martin Luther King, Jr. Birthday Celebration
- Activities for children in the Big Brothers/Big Sisters Program
- Human Relations Commission History Trivia Bowl
- Financial Support for Orphan Children in Port Au Prince, Haiti
- Coat Drive for Sanctuary House residents
- Financial Support for Sickle Cell Anemia Foundation
- Beta Rho Omega sponsored "Believe, Achieve, Succeed" Beautillion Program which exposed young African American males to the "world of business" through workshops and local entrepreneurs.
- Two signature programs that Beta Rho Omega is very proud of are the Precious Pearls Rite of Passage and the Emerging Young Leaders Program. Both programs provide training and mentoring for young ladies to assist them in their intellectual, emotional, and social development. They participate in workshops, activities, trips and presentations by various members of the community on a variety of topics. Each of these programs is at least a year-long program, culminating in some finishing activity or graduation ceremony.

BETA RHO OMEGA CHAPTER BASILEI

Annie Mae Moore	1937
Odessa Chestine	
Edith Brooks	
Claudia Greene	
Margaret Peterson	
Bernice Stephens	
Mary Thompkins	
Faye Smalley	
Elizabeth Dorsey	
Ersa Austin	
Shirley Malone	
Marsha Holloway	1985-1986
Ruth Lynch	1987-1988
Marcia Johnson	1989-1990
Betty A. Pettus	1991-1992
Allene Gold	1993-1994
Marcia A. Johnson	1995-1999
Betty A. Pettus	2000-2001
Teresa G. Moss	2002-2003
Sarah Newman	2004-2005
Marcia A. Johnson	2006-2010
Beverlyn Perry	2011-present

Arlene Jackson Washington

8th Central Regional Director
January 1938 – December 1940

Arlene Jackson Washington was elected in December 1937 at the 20th Boiule in New Orleans, Louisiana held at Dillard University and served from January 1938 – December 1940

Soror Washington presided over the 5th, 6th and 7th Central Regional Conferences. Also, during her term of office, in 1939 the deed to Gamma House was transferred to the national body.

Beta Upsilon Omega Chapter, in Frankfort, Kentucky, was chartered in 1938 and Beta Omega Omega Chapter, in Paducah, Kentucky, was chartered in 1939. These current Central Region chapters were under the province of the Southeastern Region at the time.

Beta Upsilon Omega Chapter

FRANKFORT, KENTUCKY
MARCH 5, 1938

Left to Right, First Row: Bessie T. Russell Stone, Carolyn Glover Utz, Laura Fife Lovelace, Mabel Campbell Atwood. Second Row Seated: Louella Bush, Jewell Miller Rabb, Ann Jackson Heartwell Hunter, Arletta McGoodwin Graves. Third Row Standing: Charlottee Wilson Black, Clarice Jones Michaels, Grace Sullivan Morton, Elizabeth Lindsey Barker, Winifred L. Gay, Dorothy G. Wilson, Ludye Anderson.

BETA UPSILON OMEGA CHARTER MEMBERS

LUDYE ANDERSON	ELIZABETH LINDSAY
MABEL CAMBELL ATWOOD	CLARICE JONES MICHAELS
LOUELLA BUSH	GRACE SULLIVAN MORTON
LAURA FIFE (ASSOCIATE MEMBER)	ARLETTA MCGOODWIN
WINIFRED L. GAY	JEWEL MILLER RABB
CAROLYN GLOVER	BESSIE T. RUSSELL
ANN JACKSON HEARTWELL	CHARLOTTE WILSON
	DOROTHY G. WILSON

On Saturday evening, March 5, 1938, a new chapter in the history of Alpha Kappa Alpha Sorority, Incorporated began. The event was the establishment of Beta Upsilon Omega Chapter, the first graduate Greek letter organization on the campus of the Kentucky State Industrial College in Frankfort, Kentucky.

Soror Maude Brown, assisted by Soror Rose Ellen Goodloe, was authorized by Soror Portia Trenholm, South Eastern Regional Director, to organize the chapter. The charter members represented some of the leading colleges and universities in the country, such as the University of Chicago, Columbia, Fisk, University of Illinois, Ithaca Conservatory, Iowa State, Kentucky State, Louisville Municipal, Ohio University, and West Virginia State.

A formal banquet at the home of Soror Mabel C. Atwood was the occasion for introducing the new chapter. The banquet was the loveliest in the history of the college. The beauty of the occasion was enhanced by a crystal candelabra and numerous bowls of pink sweet peas, while at the other end of the room the lighted insignia and cathedral candle cast soft light over the group. The chapter was presented to the national body by Soror Ann Jackson Heartwell and accepted by Soror Maude Brown. Sorors from sister chapters in the state were guests at the banquet. The Basileus from each chapter welcomed Beta Upsilon Omega and extended best wishes for a long life of worthwhile achievements and service to the local district.

Since its establishment, Beta Upsilon Omega has lived up to the expectations extended in the best wishes expressed the night of the chapter's chartering. The chapter has had an illustrious record of achievement and of caring, sharing, and serving the Frankfort/ Franklin County community. Following are some of the chapter's earliest community service projects: Salvation Army Camp Fund, Senior Citizen's Center, Green Hill Cemetery Fund, Scholarships and Tuition Assistance, Tutoring Services, and Financial Literacy Workshops. In addition, the chapter has sponsored community workshops on Techniques for Working Women, Voter Registration, and Parliamentary Procedures.

Governor Wallace G. Wilkinson, Mayor Michael A. Mills, Supreme Basileus Janet Ballard, and the Central Regional Director Loann J. Honesty King recognized the accomplishments of Beta Upsilon Omega on the occasion of the chapter's 50th anniversary celebration, held on February 20, 1988.

As the twenty-first century fast approached the ladies of Beta Upsilon Omega extended service to the Frankfort community by sponsoring and implementing many additional service projects such as: providing aid to various "Black Families," giving donations to the Building Blitz with Habitat for Humanity, providing tutorial services at the King Center, volunteering and providing aid to the Simon House, created a partnership with two local Girl Scout Troops, helped sponsor City and County Back to School Festivals, partnered with Kentucky State University's Extension Office, Franklin County Health Department, and the AIDS Volunteer of Lexington to bring about AIDS awareness.

The Sorors of Beta Upsilon Omega continue to provide service to all mankind in the new millennium and is a driving force among sororities within the state of Kentucky. The chapter participates in many service projects in Frankfort and surrounding communities. The distinguished ladies have made health a priority target for the twenty-first century focusing their energies on such projects such as: the Frankfort/Lexington Links Walk-A-Thon, collaborating with the Kings Center to sponsor a health fair, entering a team in the Franklin County American Cancer Relay for Life, and participating in "Great Strides Walk-A- thon for Cystic Fibrosis," just to name a few.

The organization also targeted many other national programs by taking part in the shoebox program (donations) for under privileged students in Africa, speaking with students and holding a back-to-school drive for school supplies called "Ready-fest", and partners with other community agencies to provide coats to the needy by way of the Alpha Kappa Alpha coat drive each year.

Not only has Beta Upsilon Omega touched the community through service projects, the organization has also left their mark by presenting many cultural awareness and history activities. Little girls from all over Frankfort flock to the annual and much anticipated African American History Workshop.

One of the highlights to-date for the group was the celebration of Blacks in the military. Sorors worked with the Kentucky History Museum to present "African Americans a View in Time: Experiencing Military Stories" and "Joining the Ranks: African Americans in the Military" panel discussion and reception.

The chapter has had an illustrious record of achievement and of caring, sharing and serving the Frankfort community for 75 years. The ladies of Beta Upsilon Omega have extended service to the community by sponsoring service projects such as: providing aid to various families, Habitat for Humanity, providing tutorial services at the King Center, volunteering and providing aid to the Simon House, sponsoring and leading Girl Scout troops, sponsoring City and County Back to School Festivals, and providing aid to the Sunshine Center.

Health has been a target through the years within the Sorority and the chapter has focused our energies on such health projects such as partnering with AVOL — AIDS Volunteers of Lexington to bring about AIDS awareness; the Frankfort/Lexington Links Walk A Thon, sponsoring health fairs in the community, participating in the American Cancer Society Relay for Life, Great Strides Walk A

Thon for Cystic Fibrosis, and the American Diabetes Association Walk for a Cure. In 2009, the chapter secured a Center for Disease Control grant from the Kentucky Department for Public Health-Cabinet for Health and Family Services to promote awareness of HIV/AIDS in the African American communities in Franklin County. Our chapter hosted health fairs in three communities in Frankfort to highlight and discuss AIDS/HIV prevention and awareness.

Not only has Beta Upsilon Omega touched the community through service projects, the organization has also left its mark by presenting cultural awareness and history activities. Little girls from the Frankfort community flock to the chapters annual and much anticipated African American History Workshop. Many young ladies have participated in our Little Jewels program which was a mentoring and awareness program for young girls and adolescents. Many of the young ladies in our Little Jewels program have participated in our Little Miss AKA pageant which was held in conjunction with our annual fashion show.

The chapter has sponsored Frankfort's Youth Summer Dance Camp for over four years. Spotlighting our commitment in helping develop well-rounded youth, community service to the camp fosters an appreciate for health awareness and physical activity for kids K-12. As well, in line with our EYL initiative, service to the camp helps to build self-esteem and positive moral for minority middle school girls.

Beta Upsilon Omega partners with the Franklin County Women's Shelter providing dinners, mentoring and assistance with the use of technology. The Chapter purchased a computer and computer desk for women and minor children living in the transitional housing. In 2011-2012 the Franklin County Women's Shelter provided shelter to an estimated 185 women and children. The Frankfort Women's Shelter operates a transitional living center (TLC) that houses 7 women at a time each of whom can stay up to one year. The shelter assesses each woman's situation and develops goals and objectives to help her move towards self-sufficiency. They also administer an emergency housing program through 30-day shelter beds and short-term hotel stays for women. In the past year, over 450 community members called the hotline and received assistance in one form or the other. Beta Upsilon Omega remains steadfast partnering with the Women's Shelter of Franklin County providing various resources throughout the year such as hot meals, clothing, personal care necessities, in addition to fitness and heart health information.

Currently our chapter is sponsoring young women in our Emerging Young Leaders (EYL) signature program initiative for middle school girls. Beta Upsilon Omega launched its Emerging Young Leader's "Jewel AKAdemy" program in September 2012. Emerging Young Leader's," (EYL) is the 2010-2014 signature program initiative of Alpha Kappa Alpha Sorority, Inc. for middle school girls. Consisting of four "AKAdemies, the program is designed to extend the vision of the sorority by cultivating and encouraging high scholastic achievement through: 1) Leadership Development, 2) Civic Engagement, 3) Educational Enrichment, and 4) Character Building. Session topics have included: goal setting, etiquette training, social media dos and don'ts, public speaking, and career and educational interest. The participants have also visited the Underground Railroad Freedom Center museum in celebration of Black History month. The EYL Jewel AKAdemy focuses on developing skills and talents of middle school girls with potential for becoming leaders within their community and schools.

We are proud of our 75 years of service in the Frankfort community, and our Sorority's 105 years of service to all mankind. We are honored to serve, and hope that we can continue to effectively serve the Sorority and the community for many decades to come.

In addition to all of their hard work to the community, Beta Upsilon Omega continues to advise the undergraduate chapter on Kentucky State University's campus, Beta Zeta.

Beta Upsilon Omega Advises Beta Zeta Chapter.

Chapter Members Who Have Held International/National Office or Been Elected to the International/National Nominating Committee

Laura Fife Lovelace   Supreme Parliamentarian   1939 – 1941
                       Supreme Basileus *   1949 – 1953

Soror Lovelace was not a member of Beta Upsilon Omega at the time of her election.

Beta Upsilon Omega Chapter Basilei

Ann Jackson Heartwell	1938
Laura T. Fife Lovelace	1939 – 1940
Mabel C. Atwood	1945 – 1946
Catherine O. Vaughn	1947 – 1949
Catherine Nash	1950 – 1951
Charlotte Wilson	1952 – 1953
Pauline Gould	1954 – 1955
Cathyne Moody Russell	1955 – 1956
Dorothy G. Wilson	1957 – 1958
Susie Ruth Jones	1959 – 1960
Helen Cousins Exum	1960 – 1962
Winona l. Fletcher	1963 – 1965
Lee Charles Harris	1966 – 1968
Leola Madison Travis	1969 – 1974
Cornieth York Russell	1975 – 1976
Betty Gibson	1977 – 1978
Ramona Bearden Griffin	1979 – 1984
Joawana Bowles	1985 – 1986
Karen Johnson	1987 – 1988
Ramona Bearden Griffin	1989 – 1992
Marianne Tichenor Hanley	1993 – 1997
Natalie Turner	1998 – 2001
Sheila Stuckey	2002 – 2003
Betty Gibson	2004 – 2007
Vada Shelton	2008 – 2011
Dionna McDonald	2012 –

Beta Omega Omega Chapter

PADUCAH KENTUCKY
FEBRUARY 18, 1939

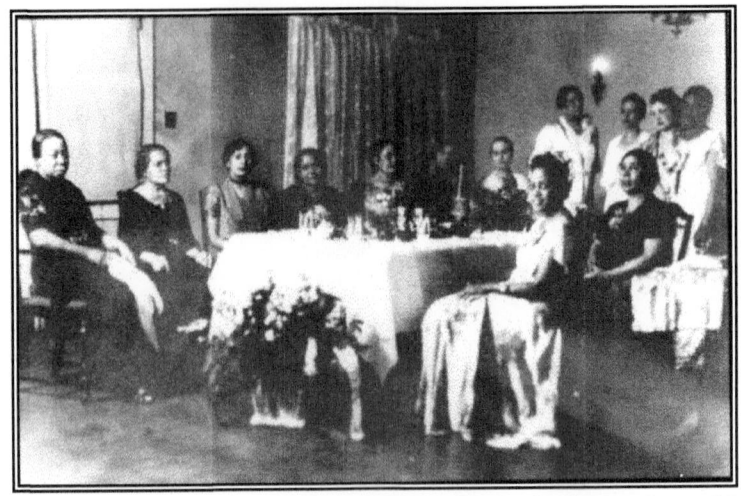

Left to Right: Maude Brown, Seventh Supreme Basileus and former Southeastern Regional Director, Margaret McGill, Helen Yancy, Henrietta Woodson, Beatrice Dawson, Alice Weston, Bettie Coulter, Mattie Strauss, Elizabeth Coulter, Genevie Griffin, Mayme Egester, Minnie Hall, and Marthenia Peyton

CHARTER MEMBERS

BETTIE COULTER COX
BEATRICE DAWSON
MAMIE J. EGESTER
GENEVIE GRIFFIN
MINNIE B. HALL

MARGURITE MCGILL
MARTHENIA PEYTON
ELIZABETH COULTER STORY
MATTIE O. STRAUSS
ALICE V. WESTON
HENRIETTA WOODSON

The charter members of Beta Omega Omega Chapter represented the best of Paducah having received their highest degrees from several notable colleges and universities: Elizabeth Coulter Story and Bettie Coulter, University of Michigan; Beatrice Dawson, Chicago School of Music; Mayme J. Egester, Fisk University; Margurite McGill, Michigan State University; Minnie B. Hall, Alice V. Weston, and Mattie O. Strauss, Kentucky State University; Genevie Griffin, Alabama State University; Henrietta Woodson, Indiana State University, and Marthenia Peyton, Lincoln University.

The chartering services were held on February 18, 1939 in the library of West Kentucky Vocational School at 14th and Thompson Avenues, Paducah, Kentucky with the seventh Supreme Basileus and former Southeastern Regional Director Soror Maude Brown Porter presiding. Soror Mayme J. Egester was the first Basileus of Beta Omega Omega.

SERVICE PROGRAMS: Beta Omega Omega Chapter's is proud of its service to the community. The chapter's programs have primarily focused on the youth of Paducah. One of Beta Omega Omega's earliest foci was and continues to be celebrating and encouraging scholastic achievement. The chapter sponsors city schools through financial gifts to provide clothing, scholarships, tutoring, and mentoring to students through a variety of programs. The chapter has hosted an annual graduate tea for community high school graduates. Sorors tutor students at local schools and churches and participate in a school help hotline.

For more than thirty years, Beta Omega Omega has supported the Oscar Boys and Girls Club financially and with hours of service and has participated in the organization's annual sing-a-thon. The Knights of Distinction is the chapter's newest program. Men of honorable character who are making contributions to the Paducah community are recognized for their service.

The Martin Luther King Day of Service has become not only "A Day On" of service but weeks of service. The activities began weeks ahead with the preparation for the MLK essay contest that is administered through the area schools for grades four through six. Sorors judge essays and prepare for the essay contest. The MLK luncheon is held on the official holiday. A youth forum and freedom march take place over the MLK weekend celebration. These activities are in partnership with the Paducah Branch of the NAACP and other area businesses and individuals. The chapter maintains 100% membership in the NAACP each year.

Little Miss AKA pageant — In the late 1960's the chapter sponsored its first Little Miss AKA pageant. In 1985 the program's activities were expanded to include six to nine months of activities for girls ages four through seven. The project culminates with the crowning of Little Miss AKA. The pageant serves as the chapter's annual fundraiser.

Beta Omega Omega Chapter Advises Zeta Zeta Chapter.

BETA OMEGA OMEGA CHAPTER BASILEI

Mamie J. Egester	1939 – 1940
Elizabeth B. Coulter	1941 – 1942
Information not available	1943 – 1946
Marie Davis	1947 – 1948
Information not available	1949 – 1953
Rhea D. Wilson	1954 – 1955
Catherine M. Means	1956 – 1957
Mary B. Miller	1958 – 1958
Claudia Milburn	1959 – 1959
Mary F. Bates	1962 – 1964
Hattie L. Stewart	1965 – 1966
Marguerite P. Branham	1967 – 1968
Mattie C. Massie	1969 – 1970
Bettie C. Cox	1971 – 1972
Anita N. Glore	1973 – 1973
Davene Wilson	1973 – 1974
Faye Clemons	1975 – 1976
Shirley Massie	1977 – 1979
Cheryl Brown	1980 – 1981
Carol Young	1982 – 1983
Donna K. Massie	1984 – 1985
Celeste F. Emerson	1986 – 1987
Cynthia Alston	1988 – 1989
Joyce Corn	1990 – 1991
Ruby G. Toliver	1992 – 1993
Robbin R. Massie	1994 – 1995
Carol Young	1996 – 1997
Shirley Massie	1998 – 2001
Erna F. Boykin	2002 – 2003
Ruby G. Toliver	2004 – 2005
Celestine F. Emerson	2006 2009
Shirley Massie	2010 2011
Varetta Hurt	2012

Blanche Lynn Patterson
9TH CENTRAL REGIONAL DIRECTOR
1940 – 1943

Soror Patterson wasa member of Gamma Omega Chapter when she was elected Central Regional Director at the 23rd Boule in Kansas City, Kansas, in December of 1940.

One chapter in Central Region was chartered during her term in office, Gamma Kappa Omega Chapter in Carbondale, Illinois. Following her term, Soror Patterson chartered Delta Delta Omega chapter, East St. Louis, Illinois, at the request of the then-incumbent Central Regional Director, Soror Maenell Newsom.

The conditions of World War II would cause the cancellation of the Boule in 1942. As a result, Soror Patterson would serve as Central Regional Director until 1943. She presided over three regional conferences; each of these conferences had themes that addressed defense issues emanating from the War.

Gamma Kappa Omega Chapter

CARBONDALE, ILLINOIS
MARCH 15, 1941

MEMBERS

Lucille Walker, Thelma Gibbs, Jenola McBride, Versa Hayes, Helen Bass, Helen Adams, Jennie L. Young, Grace Perkins, Gwendolyn Chambliss and Lovia Penn.

CHARTER MEMBERS

GWENDOLYN CHAMBLISS	LUELLA MCCALL (DAVIS)
VERSA HAYES (WHITE)	LOVIA BELL PENN
JENOLAR E. HILLSMAN (MCBRIDE)	DORENDA TAYLOR
MILDRED KEDLEY	LUCILLE WALKER
GRACE PERKINS KELLEY	THELMA GIBBS WALKER
	VELMA C. WOODS

On March 15, 1941, Gamma Kappa Omega Chapter of Alpha Kappa Alpha Sorority, Incorporated, was chartered in Carbondale, Illinois. Eleven courageous and visionary young women, Gwendolyn Chambliss, Luella McCall Davis, Mildred Kedley, Grace Perkins Kelley, Jenolar Hillsman McBride, Lovia Bell Penn, Dorenda Taylor, Lucille Walker, Thelma Gibbs Walker, Versa Hayes White, and Velma Woods, were moved to join the ranks of Alpha Kappa Alpha, and support the legacy and enhance the rich history of this dynamic sisterhood that was spreading all over the country.

Gamma Kappa Omega is the sponsoring chapter for Delta Beta Chapter. In 1952, Delta Beta was organized on the campus of Southern Illinois University at Carbondale, by Jenolar Hillsman McBride and Lucille Walker. Presently, the chapter still holds its active status and for several times over the years, has carried the highest GPA of the Greek-letter organizations on campus. They volunteer frequently at the Boys and Girls Club, various activities on and off campus and are diligent in numerous community service efforts.

Gamma Kappa Omega continues to bring new dimensions and excitement to the local community through innovative and creative efforts in the arts, education, economics, family, and health. Sorority members are focused on improving life, fostering education, and opening doors for the traditionally underserved local population. By partnering with various local agencies and networking with other Greek-letter organizations, outreach into the community is maximized.

Locally, a highly successful "Get-Out-the-Vote-Campaign" was realized from a collaborative effort with Alpha Kappa Alpha, Delta Sigma Theta, and Zeta Phi Beta sororities, Alpha Phi Alpha fraternity and the Carbondale Branch of the NAACP. This dialogue began in 2001, as an All-Greek-Round-Up that Alpha Kappa Alpha spearheaded, but became more of a chore to keep the momentum going. To date, the Greeks within the community have participated in efforts to get voters registered and registrar training with a member from each organization participating for the 2012 election.

An on-going partnership with Shryock Auditorium, on the campus of Southern Illinois University, has enabled Gamma Kappa Omega to co-sponsor several high profile events of its Celebrity Series. This partnership has increased the cultural enhancement for many elementary, middle, and high school youth who could not have benefited otherwise. From 1980-1995, the chapter hosted the Ebony Fashion Fair which contributed substantial funds for scholarship.

The chapter co-sponsored the renowned Boys Choir of Harlem In 1997; "Having Our Say," a story of the first 100 years of two Delaney sisters in New York, in 1998; the Preservation Hall Jazz Band in 1999; in 2000, the Urban Bush Women; in 2001, Mavis Staples: a Tribute to Mahalia Jackson; in 2002, Three Mo' Tenors; and in 2005, the return of the Boys Choir of Harlem. While the focus of the chapter has shifted in co-sponsoring events, we still support the programs as individual members and have not diminished in enthusiasm for the future possibilities of pursuing co-sponsorship.

Since 1983, 50 college-bound high school seniors have received more than $30,000 in annual scholarships from Gamma Kappa Omega. They have either distinguished themselves in their respective career choices, or are excelling in academic pursuits in various institutions of higher learning. In March 2003, for the 20th anniversary of the chapter's scholarship fund, and in commemoration of the chapter's 62nd Founders' Day, its annual scholarship was renamed to honor Thelma Gibbs Walker. She gave untiringly to the community as an educator, a civic leader, and a businesswoman, and has always been held in highest esteem. She was a lifetime member and the last surviving charter member of Gamma Kappa Omega. Even though in failing health and temporarily in a skilled care facility, she still became energized over the mention of Alpha Kappa Alpha. At the 2012 Founders' Day Observance, Soror Walker was honored with a permanent plaque that was placed on the grounds of the Carbondale Middle School. This moving program was highlighted by stories via a video and live tribute from former students (from the former Attucks School where she taught writing/penmanship), colleagues, family members, friends and former Gamma Kappa Omega chapter members and a dedication ceremony.

In 2002, Gamma Kappa Omega Chapter was featured as WSIL-News TV3's "Unsung Hero" for the work with the young Ladies of Elegance, a group of young African American girls. The girls were exposed to many different careers through hands-on activities.

In November 2003, to emphasize the focus on education and family, an initiative called Goal-Oriented Ladies Determined to Excel Notoriously (G.o.l.d.e.n G.i.r.l.s) was created. The name was later changed to Future Pearls, but the program's focus remained the same. School administrators recommend prospective participants from varying economic, ethnic, and racial backgrounds. After screenings, these young ladies, ages 13 to 17, are involved in workshops and social engagements, focusing on many issues and challenges that teenagers encounter. Efforts are designed to improve social graces, to ensure academic success, to improve attitudes, to encourage community service, to development leadership, staging fundraisers, creating teamwork, and attending educational, cultural and recreational activities as a group. We maintain a roster of 15 to 20 girls and keep a waiting list. Several other after school tutorials and mentoring-type projects have dissolved.

Gamma Kappa Omega participates in and promotes the local Relay for Life Cancer Walk, the Buckle Up America Month, the AKA's Coat Drive, SIDS Mother's Day Cards, MLK Day of Service, the American Heart Association Drive, Breast Cancer Awareness, the Women's Health Conference, and conducts various other initiatives, based on the needs of the community. It is so exhilarating to provide service to others in the SPIRIT of Alpha Kappa Alpha. As the size and scope of the graduate and undergraduate chapters fluctuates, sometimes, we find that both chapters can combine forces and accomplish more.

The 65th anniversary of Gamma Kappa Omega was a milestone in the history of the chapter. As one of the highlights of this anniversary, the chapter compiled a cookbook. This masterpiece included favorite and unique recipes of sorors, relatives, and friends from all over the world. The celebration also included an evening of jazz music, performed by a local artist. As year 72 approaches, Gamma Kappa Omega continues to work with youth in the community through the Global Leadership through Timeless Service (GLTTS) Initiatives and the Emerging Young Leaders Program. The chapter has supported local health initiatives by participating in the American Heart Associations' Heart Walk, Diabetes Awareness Days, and support the Southern Illinois Women's Teen Conference, and provide monetary and volunteer support for Back to School Night at a local elementary school as well as the after school program, "I Can Read." Since funding is limited for this program, the local graduate Greek Chapters ("Divine 9") have provided donations monthly for snack items. It is such a joy to honor our Founders, our Charter members and to live by example for the observant young women and girls, who are watching us, and to preserve and protect our membership in this beloved sisterhood.

Gamma Kappa Omega Advises Delta Beta Chapter.

GAMMA KAPPA OMEGA CHAPTER BASILEI

Lovia Bell Penn	1941 – 1944
Lucille Walker	1945 – 1953
Lovia Bell Penn	1954 – 1960
Lucille Walker	1961 – 1968
Sandra Warren	1969 – 1973
Sondra Jean Greer	1974 – 1979
Norma Jean Ewing	1980 – 1981
Valerie Epps	1981 – 1982
Geraldine Bowie	1983 – 1984
Joyce Hayes	1985 – 1988
Harriet Wilson Barlow	1989 – 1995
Deborah Walton McCoy	1996 – 1999
Vernola E. Sumner	2000 – 2001
Deborah Walton McCoy	2002 – 2003
Ann Marie Shepherd	2004 – 2005
Marilyn Haywood	2006 – 2007
Elizabeth Lewin	2008 – 2009
Faith Miller	2010 –

Maenell Hamlin Newsome

10TH CENTRAL REGIONAL DIRECTOR
DECEMBER 1943 — AUGUST 1946

Regional Conferences and Boule's were not held regularly during the war years of the forties, so the Directorate carried on the business of Alpha Kappa Alpha and appointed four Regional Directors in December of 1943, for terms of two years. Soror Newsome was one of those appointed.

Soror Newsome recalls: "The privilege of serving as Central Regional Director of Alpha Kappa Alpha Sorority was an interesting, enriching experience for me. I was somewhat handicapped by not receiving the benefits coming from an immediate meeting with the Directorate and the Regional Directors' Council. However, the former Central Regional Director, Soror Blanche Patterson, graciously offered her assistance and explained as well as one can possibly do so by mail, the duties, responsibilities and problems of the office as well as the strong and weak points of the six graduate chapters and the six undergraduate chapters of Central Region. Also, other members of the Directorate were very helpful.

All chapters, with few exceptions, cooperated splendidly and did much to make the work as pleasant as possible. I had the pleasure of being the Founders' Day speaker for Tau, Gamma, Gamma Omega, Beta Delta, Alpha Mu Omega, Kappa, and Alpha Eta Omega Chapters.

I visited the Dean of Women at Indiana State Teacher's College, at her request, to discuss the possibilities of establishing an undergraduate chapter of Alpha Kappa Alpha Sorority on that campus and was a luncheon guest of Alpha Eta Omega Chapter while there. In addition, I visited Eta Chapter at the University of Minnesota at their request to help them solve some chapter problems.

All chapters observed Founders' Day regularly as well as chapter anniversaries, Negro History Week, Clean-Up Week, Health Week, and Vocational Guidance and cooperated financially and programmatically with the sorority's national and community programs. Gamma and Tau alumnae were very busy assisting their chapters.

I was privileged to make all preparations for the chartering of Delta Delta Omega in East St. Louis, although Soror Blanche Patterson carried out the ceremony because I had transportation difficulties due to heavy troop movements and an unexpected railroad strike at the time."

During Soror Newsome's time in office she stressed the following:

1. Improvement of scholarship (grades) on college campuses
2. Improvement of sisterly relations everywhere
3. Better program planning to include interest of all age groups in Graduate chapters, and consideration of having auxiliary groups in graduate chapters
4. Greater assistance of retiring officers for newly elected officers
5. Realization of Graduate Advisors of their authority and responsibility for the undergraduate chapter's business and social activities and procedures
6. More publicity of chapter activities and achievements of the chapter and individual sorors

Gamma Psi Omega Chapter

Gary, Indiana
October 28, 1944

Top Row Standing: Kathleen Bingham, Clareon Hinkson, Ruth Battle, Joyce Morgan, Ferne Browne, Evangeline Morse. Second Row Seated: Mabel Haywood, Margaret Graham, Clemette Armstrong, Regional Director Maynell Newsome, Frances Renfroe, Alice Butts, Genevieve Gray — Third Row on Floor: Jane Schell, Bennie Collins, Johnnie Upshaw. Photograph Taken By: Charter Member Katherine Beckman (not pictured)

Charter Members

CLEMETTE ARMSTRONG	GENEVIEVE H. GARY
RUTH H. BATTLE	CLAREON HINKSON
KATHERINE F. BECKMAN	MABEL HAYWOOD
KATHLEEN BINGHAM	JOYCE T. MORGAN
FERNE BROWNE	EVANGELINE MORSE
ALICE BUTTS	FRANCES RENFROE
BENNIE N. COLLINS	JANE L. SCHELL
MARGARET GRAHAM	JOHNNIE UPSHAW

Gamma Psi Omega Chapter of Alpha Kappa Alpha Sorority, Inc. was founded in 1944 by sixteen of Gary's most illustrious women. Their talents and their training varied. Their careers included the fields of teaching and social work. One of the sixteen was a former librarian who had become a full-time homemaker.

Because the nearest graduate chapter of Alpha Kappa Alpha was located in Chicago, the need and possibility for a Gary chapter were considered. It was apparent by 1944 that Gary could accommodate its own local sorority chapter. Procedures were begun, and in the autumn of 1944, Gamma Psi Omega Chapter became a reality. Soror Beulah T. Whitby was the Supreme Basileus and Soror Maenell Newsome was the Central Regional Director.

In the autumn of 1945, the group received its first three initiates, YJean S. Chambers, Gladys H. Johnson, and Thelma A. Uzzell. These three sorors zealously guard this historic fact.

The history of our chapter has two components. It is the story of women who guided its destiny, and the story of the many other women who carried out the various aspects of an ever-widening program of service to Gary's community. The history of Gamma Psi Omega Chapter is the story of those who never forgot that they were Alpha Kappa Alpha women and of those who have rededicated themselves to active participation consistently through the years.

The first five Basilei were among the founders. Each brought a certain unique personality trait to her office. When examined in retrospect, the sequence of their selection seems to have come from a higher wisdom.

THE FIFTIES

In January 1954, the first Basileus in a long line of those elected from outside the charter group was Hattie Leonard. The chapter had grown too large for private homes; so the meetings were moved to the New Barber Youth Center on 20th and Massachusetts Street. The chapter members can't forget that Soror Leonard was the first Basileus to be sent to a Boule. We were able to have her represent us in August of 1955 at the 35th Boule in San Francisco. This said a great deal about the chapter's growth and financial solvency.

Also during the fifties the chapter expanded a number of community service projects and began to write and produce our own fashion shows. Sorors served as models. YJean Chambers was encouraged to write and narrate "Thematic Scripts." This style of programming fashion shows were a hit with the community and has never been successfully copied.

Gladys Johnson brought method and efficiency to the administration of the total sorority program. One of the highlights of Soror Johnson's administration was our purchase of an incubator for Gary Methodist Hospital. Soror Johnson's talents in administration and her attention to reporting procedures propelled her into national office. She became our National Tamiouchos and served from 1954 – 1958 under the 14th Supreme Basileus Arnetta G. Wallace. Thus, she remains our first and only Gamma Psi Omega soror to ever hold a national office.

The late fifties brought fiscal responsibility to the chapter. A practical form for planning the annual budget was instituted and the chapter began its first savings program. Also during this period, the chapter, under the efforts of Soror Juanita Grant, successfully negotiated a franchise for the chapter to sponsor the Ebony Fashion Fair.

THE SIXTIES

In the sixties the spirit of sisterliness and spirit was revitalized. The chapter turned its focus from many small service activities to one large family-centered project. The scholarship focus was placed on completing the education of one young woman rather than augmenting the college careers of different students. A comprehensive newsletter was established, an Indiana University Interest Group was organized, and the 29th Central Regional Conference was hosted in 1963. This time, the chapter used the Hotel Gary's facilities and recorded a first for Negro women.

Activities were expanded to include the younger sorors and a balance was achieved between the revolutionary ideas of the youth of the mid-sixties and the Alpha Kappa Alpha women who were products of a different past. The chapter wrestled with the problems of a sorority in transition. It was necessary that the chapter change with the changing times. The chapter's financial structure had to be completely overhauled. The annual formal had to be moved from Marquette Park to Chicago. This was truly a period of vast change.

The Miss Fashionetta Contest as an adjunct to the Ebony Fashion Fair was re-instituted. The chapter moved their meetings back into the warmer atmosphere of home meetings and re-taught the lesson inherent in the meaning "let him who would be first be the servant of the rest."

THE SEVENTIES

The chapter began the seventies with the establishment of Gamma Psi Omega's first undergraduate chapter, Zeta Phi of Indiana University Northwest. A bus was purchased for the children of Gary's oldest nursery school, the Steward Settlement House. In 1972, all of the chapter's energies were directed toward hosting the 39th Central Regional Conference. In 1974 the chapter celebrated the anniversary of the founding of Gamma Psi Omega Chapter.

The chapter's thirtieth year saw the appointment of a Community Services Project Committee. The committee assessed the needs of the Gary community and set priorities. Tutoring, political action, cleanup, hospital volunteer services, the YWCA, and child-care were established as our targets. Reactivation of sorors was given priority. Meetings were moved to the new Gary Neighborhood Facilities.

During the summer of 1977, the chapter instituted a reading program at Douglass School. More than 350 volunteer hours were donated to the project, twenty-five area children were enrolled for four weeks. The highest amount for a year was donated to scholarships, $6,000.

The pediatric unit of Gary Methodist Hospital was given a supply of books and clothing; thus another service "first" went into the thirty-four-year record of Gamma Psi Omega. Other activities during the seventies included a pre-Easter dinner for senior citizens; National History Week for famous Black Americans; and a joint concert with Eta Kappa Omega of East Chicago, featuring Delphine and Romaine, the only Black concert pianist duo in the nation.

THE EIGHTIES

The American Dream was fading and our nation had entered a period of economic and social confusion. Gamma Psi Omega moved on with its recognition of Black History Month, with a memorable showing of The Great Kings of Africa at the W.E.B. DuBois Library. Other activities included the second piano concert featuring Delphine and Romaine, the pre-Easter dinner for senior citizens, the annual Smarty Party, the chapter's annual dinner-dance, summer reading program, and annual card party. Miss Fashionetta was again reactivated and the Ebony Fashion Fair continued to be a social success.

The National Program Target—Economic Development was emphasized through "Buy-in-Gary Day." Sixteen honor students received $8,000 in scholarship money to attend college. For the first time ever, Gamma Psi Omega honored its "Golden Sorors," with dinner, gifts and tributes at a Christmas celebration.

THE NINETIES

Gamma Psi Omega continues to be visible in the community by participating in the Village Service Club Days. Sorors distributed Black history posters and biographical flyers of famous Black Americans and a salute to Historical Black Colleges and Universities, with pictures of sorors who attended these HBCU's. The chapter held a "Fantasy in Pink" Tea Dance and its annual Smarty Party. The summer reading program continues as well as annual scholarship donations.

Following the 1990 Boule, Gamma Psi Omega sorors returned to implement the new international program targets. Personal care packages were given to senior citizens at various nursing homes, canned goods and staples were provided for Thanksgiving baskets, and sorors volunteered for the Methodist Hospital Children's Health Fair.

Gamma Psi Omega's annual projects and activities were continued with much success. In 1991, the chapter began the sponsorship of a little league baseball team. Reading materials were donated to Concord Library Center. Monetary contributions were given to the Thelma Marshall Children's Home to help renovate their present site, the Marion Home for pregnant adolescents, and the Gary Community School Adolescent Health Center.

In 1992 we observed Black History Month by distributing packets on famous African Americans to the public and giving eight elementary schools Black History booklets for their school library. In 1993, Gamma Psi Omega purchased a chapter banner and hosted the Area Retreat at the Radisson

Hotel. Over 70 sorors were in attendance to explore the theme, "Building Our Roots."

1994 was a big year for Gamma Psi Omega. Along with Cluster VIII, we hosted the 60th Central Regional Conference, "Soaring to New Heights." To kick off the wonderful weekend, a reception for honorary Soror Jan Spivey-Gilchrist, artist and illustrator, was held at the Gary Public Library. "The Ivy Notes" singing group was formed the previous year to provide music expressly for this conference. The initial group consisted of sorors from Gamma Psi Omega, Sigma Phi Omega, and Eta Kappa Omega Chapters. Since that time, the Ivy Notes have continued to provide entertainment and ceremonial music for chapter, regional, and other Alpha Kappa Alpha activities as well as for various functions within the community.

During the fall of 1994 the chapter also celebrated its 50th Birthday at Marquette-on-the-Lagoon. The Keynote speaker was Soror Eva Lois Evans, Supreme Basileus. It was a memorable event!

As the 90's progressed, so did the chapter. Many successful program activities continued to be implemented. Worshipping together at various churches and rededicating ourselves during Founders' Day activities always started the year off right.

In 1997, Gamma Psi Omega introduced activities centered on the international theme: "The Alpha Kappa Alpha Strategy: Making the Net Work." We networked with various venues within the community by spearheading the donation of books authored by African Americans. This celebration of Black History Month culminated with a community-wide Women's History Celebration held at Indiana University Northwest. Sponsoring youth participation in the "Competitive Edge" summer program fulfilled the program target "Partnership in Math and Science." Through this program, skills for middle school girls in Math and Science were fostered and developed.

That same year, we participated in a letter-writing campaign to Congress to support the appointment of Dr. Henry Foster as the United States Surgeon General. Books and school supplies were sent to storm-damaged Jamaica. What a jump-start into 1998, when we embraced the Health Target by participating in various community health activities for the first time. In the "Walk for Aids," we won first place for money collected by an organization.

Sorors also participated in "Call a Friend Tuesday" for Breast Cancer and "Coat Day." Coats were donated and distributed to the Rainbow Shelter and The Ark. Our focus was again turned to developing math and science skills in middle school girls and they participated in competition at Valparaiso University and Chicago State University during the 1998 Boule.

1999 was a time of focusing within. In addition to completing program targets, service projects and community outreach, Sorors of Gamma Psi Omega took time for themselves, fostering "Togetherness." There were Christmas Luncheons and End-of-the-Year Socials. Also, the chapter participated in an All-Greek Picnic at Lake Etta and sponsored the All-Greek Dance at Marquette Park. That fall, reactivation became a main focus. Cards were sent out, invitations were mailed and a party was held. What a success! Over 20 sorors were reactivated.

We're proud to say our scholarship awards totaled $64,000.00 during this decade. And, in the first four years of the new millennium, we have awarded $44,600.00. What a great way to begin!

THE NEW CENTURY

To continue the Gamma Psi Omega tradition of participating on the regional and international level, we started 2000 with a joint Founders' Day; sent a large delegation to the 66th Central Regional Conference in St. Louis and 15 sorors traveled to the Boule in Dallas. The chapter then participated in the News Election Service project where we reported the results of 80 precincts to the national media. This netted a profit of $1,000.00 and a commendation from The Associated Press for a job well done.

In 2001 and 2002, we served as ushers for the Miss USA pageant, which was held in Gary, IN and looked exquisite in black tuxedos. Our partnership with the West Side Theatre Guild was also initiated during this time as we helped with ticket sales for Bill Cosby, "Fences" and Ray Charles. Hosting book signings for Mr. Randall Robinson and Soror Carla J. Cargle were great successes. We were honored to be able to furnish a room at the local YWCA in memory of our own soror Katherine Beckman for a contribution of $4,000.00. The chapter also began advising Epsilon Rho chapter during this time.

2003 and 2004 were full of activities which showed our "SPIRIT." An outing to see The Lion King on stage at the Cadillac Palace Theatre in Chicago provided an opportunity for fellowship during dinner prior to the performance.

Sisterhood and Service were highlighted as we continued making our presence felt in Gary through our many annual service projects. We served as hostesses at programs for Indiana University Northwest and for the African American and Hispanic Legislators Prayer Breakfast.

Scholarship was highlighted as we judged 57 entries in the Young Authors Program, supported the publications of our own members, sorors J. Moffett-Walker and Dharathula Millender and successfully implemented The Ivy Reading AKAdemy.

Partnership was the focus as we volunteered with Ispat Inland, Inc. during Martin L. King Day and involved family members and friends, as well. Joining hands with Junior Achievement allowed sorors to focus on financial literacy with ages from Kindergarten through High School.

Involvement and Innovation are definitely important as we explore other ways to create wealth. Supporting the local basketball team was a fun partnership that netted profits. The Tea Rose Rental Committee was established after we made chair covers for our Spring Social. Renting the chair covers to other organizations will garner additional revenue. We continue to move forward with Technological advances by using automated calling services and developing our website.

We celebrated our 60th year with an elegant affair on October 23, 2004 with the support of our surrounding Alpha Kappa Alpha Sorority, Inc. chapters, other Greek organizations and business and community leaders. It was fulfilling to see the "Respect" we've gained. Sixty years of service rendered — many years of service ahead to continue in the SPIRIT of Alpha Kappa Alpha Sorority, Inc.

The years 2005 — 2007 had many notable highlights. We partnered with West Side Theatre Guild to welcome Soror Coretta Scott King to Gary, IN. Supreme Basileus Linda M. White sent a gorgeous floral arrangement to honor Soror King, as well and several sorors were granted a private audience with her after the program to present our chapter gift. We were on hand to welcome Jasmine Guy as a part of the Library's Black History Month celebration.

The devastating effects of Hurricanes Katrina and Rita moved sorors to action as we donated gift cards and phone cards to aid families in their recovery efforts. We also donated coats and continuous support to the 35 evacuees temporarily relocated to the Marion Home in Gary, IN. We continued our participation in the various health walks to raise funds and awareness for Breast Cancer, Sickle Cell Anemia, MS and for personal fitness during our annual Power Walks through the mall.

Socially, we enjoyed the live performances of The Lion King and The Color Purple. But these plays paled in comparison to our own original production of "History in a Flash" presented at our Joint Founders' Day celebration in 2006. Sorors portrayed our sorority's founding as told by a mother and grandmother to a young, aspiring "skeewee wannabee." Soror Dolena Mack was the musical director. Soror Joyce Price wrote the script and Soror Kellauna Mack-Jackson choreographed the dance interludes. Luckily, Soror Karen Nolan videotaped our ever-so-talented chapter members and other Sorors perform this innovative production.

Another successful partnership which began in this century and has lasted until now is the Tax Freedom Day initiative spearheaded by Soror Ida Gillis. This activity provides free tax preparation for low-income and senior citizens each year. Soror Gillis also forged our partnership with Money $mart week held each October since 2006 for Northwest Indiana residents. Our Tea Rose Rentals partnership with organizations throughout the city brought in much needed funds for the chapter. But we had no idea at the time that decorating the reserved seating at our Annual Ebony Fashion Fair with our beautiful chair covers would be such a big hit. We were just making Ebony's 50th anniversary of the premier African American fashion show more special. What a beautiful affair it was!!

On the regional and international scene, our chapter began to gain additional prominence through the dedication of sorors working on regional and national committees. Our Ivy Reading AKAdemy won a regional award in 2006, thanks to Sorors Linda Daniels and Helen Turner. Soror Sharon Haney chaired the decorations for the 62nd Boule Luncheon's "Motown" theme in Detroit, MI and the Ivy Notes transformed into the Jackson Five, The Supremes and Tina Turner and delighted the audience with their unique brand of showmanship. Soror Dolena Mack served as a workshop speaker discussing "Balancing Family, Work and Sorority" and as a facilitator for the presentation of the International Program Chairman, Soror Loann J. Honesty King. Soror Ida Gillis worked diligently for EAF and actually won a 2 year lease on a Mercedes Benz during its fundraiser. Eight sorors will never forget travelling to New Orleans and working on a house for Habitat For Humanity and distributing food for Feed The Children. Our lives were enriched again by rendering service to those in need. Plus it helped us work towards our "Million Pounds" challenge under the E.S.P. theme.

E.S.P. entered our vocabulary in a new and dynamic way when Soror Barbara McKinzie became our 27th Supreme Basileus. Oh what fun we had with that acronym and creating programs to fit an Extraordinary Service Program. Our first foray into continuous mentoring of young males was a great success as we partnered with the Boy Scout Troup of St. Timothy Community Church in Gary, IN to provide First Responder training for them and our own families. Entrepreneurs graced our meeting regularly as we spotlighted women and minorities in business under the E.S.P. theme. AKAnomics, Junior Achievement, Youth Economic summit (Y.E.S.) and a focus on financial literacy kept the chapter busy finding ways to make "Money Matter" to all of our members and constituents. Basileus Lori Benford Bryant charged sorors Ida Gillis, Joyce Price, and Karen Nolan with this task and they did not disappoint. Sorors Kimberly Wooden and Tanya Burns watched over our Emotional Health while Soror Kellauna Mack-Jackson ignited our Physical Health activities each week under the Health initiatives. She also led all of the First Responder events. What a fun time transitioning to the new program.

In 2007, we had to say good bye to two of our Charter members. Sorors Ruth Battle on 4/19/07 and Soror Clemette Armstrong on 5/1/07. Our chapter owes them both so much for their dedication and leadership throughout the years. They both reached the milestone of Diamond Sorors that year. Life always gives you 'highs' for 'low' moments like this. When Soror Dolena Mack penned the official Central Region Song, both the lyrics and the music, our chapter was once again lifted to happier moments and AKAlades. The Ivy Notes were rewarded for their dedication and hard work with a personal invitation from Soror McKinzie to perform at the 63rd Boule celebration our 100th anniversary in Washington, D.C. in 2008.

The Centennial Year — 2008 — deserves a section all to itself. Eight Sorors from the chapter started the year off celebrating our Founding at the gala event held at Howard University in Washington, D.C. We then welcomed Soror Rev. Bernice King at a celebration in honor of her father's day of service at Indiana University Northwest. 4 Sorors went to AKA Day at the Capitol in Indianapolis and Tea Rose Rentals decorated a 1000 chair event for Mayor Rudolph Clay's Inaugural Ball. Sadly, Sorors Janie Pratt and our beloved chapter members Soror Alice Mack Hytche and Soror Opal Burleson passed and would not live to celebrate our Boule festivities in DC.

Notable events in our city included honoring former Black Mayors, including Mayor Richard G. Hatcher, and our own Soror Dharathula (Dolly) Millender was congratulated on preserving the historical data on the Mayors. Rev. Jesse Jackson applauded Soror Dolly's accomplishments in person. Additionally, the National Sorority of Phi Delta Kappa held its Midwestern Regional Conference in nearby Merrillville with Gamma Psi Omega Sorors playing prominent roles. Soror Lori Benford-Bryant was the Co-Host of the event and Sorors Joyce Price, Penny Cochran, Kellauna Mack-Jackson, Clari

Benford, Patricia Lovelace and Dolena Mack served as judges for their various competitions. Finally, the opening of the "Y-Jean Chambers Hall" on the campus of Purdue University Calumet to honor the life-long work of Dr. Chambers as a Professor of Communications and Theater on the campus.

A fabulous 74th Central Regional Conference in the home of Founder Soror Ethel Hedgeman Lyle was topped off with awards for our scrapbook and our stroll and the wonderful invitation for the Ivy Notes to sing at the Centennial Boule. But since work is never done, we had to come down out of the clouds and serve as hostesses at the IMEC Entrepreneur Supplier Diversity Conference in nearby East Chicago, host a Pink Ribbon Breast Cancer Awareness Family Survival Fair, conduct a Black Male Community Forum, and the Ivy Notes filmed their singing to be included in the National Centennial Historical documentary aired at the Boule in July. Nu Lambda chapter taught senior citizens how to use their cell phones more effectively — including our chapter members and we joined hands with Sigma Phi Omega and Eta Kappa Omega chapters and inactive Sorors and friends in the "ESP 1908 Global Centennial Walk" at Gleason Park.

On the Civic front, we registered 600 voters, and assisted citizens in getting to the polls with "Take 5 to the Polls." Our efforts were spearheaded by Soror Barbara Mack and they were multiplied with assistance from the Urban League, Indiana University Northwest, and the Gary Literacy Coalition. The Gary Community School Corporation sponsored a "Reading Chairs on Parade" event for children in grades K-3 and our chairs were beautifully painted to resemble 2 children's books — "101 Dalmatians" and "Dora the Explorer."

In July alone, we received a proclamation from Gary Mayor Rudy Clay proclaiming July 11 – 18 as "Alpha Kappa Alpha Centennial Celebration Week."Large "100th Birthday" car magnets were ordered and displayed proudly on Sorors' cars. Other organizations celebrating their centennial within the city were presented with a commemorative AKA history collage and $100 each (Gary Public Library, First Baptist Church and Emerson School of Visual and Performing Arts). Pink and green pencils were presented to the community during the 4th of July parade and 200 books were collected to give to the new children's library at Howard University. Soror Dolena Mack penned "Celebrating 100 Years" and "For 100 More" for use at the Boule. The Ivy Notes were featured in the *Gary Post Tribune* newspaper July 15th on their upcoming performance and 60 Sorors attended the Boule.

Our many annual service projects mentioned throughout this chapter's history were held in 2008, as well as a very full, productive and wonderful Centennial Celebration for our chapter. But of course, the year was made even more special as our chapter celebrated the election of the first African America President of the United States of America — Mr. Barack Obama. That is the only thing that could outshine Soror Jackie Garlin being named Soror of the Year for 2008.

2009 – SUMMER 2012

The final years of this historical accounting will only highlight new or special initiatives by our chapter. Soror Shemia Jackson of Nu Lambda chapter was the General Conference Co-Chairman for the Diamond Jubilee 75th Central Regional Conference. Sorors Dolena Mack and Kellauna Mack-Jackson continued their legacy of attending every Boule and Leadership conference since Kellauna's initiation by being the only Sorors to brave the wilds of Anchorage, Alaska. And, Soror Mack-Jackson chaired the Area Retreat at the Radisson Hotel, in Merrillville, IN in September of 2009. Sorors Quanda Davis and Jerri Floyd chaired our 65th Anniversary Celebration luncheon and brought Soror Peggy Lewis LeCompte, 19th and 24th Central Regional Director as our guest speaker who delivered a powerful and inspirational message. This wonderful event was held in 2 phases on 10/24/09 and 10/25/09 which was the kick-off to our now annual Wine Tasting event and the aforementioned luncheon activity. The highlight of the weekend event was a commemorative DVD produced for the occasion featuring Charter Member Joyce Tatum Morgan and other former Basilei and Sorors. It described the history of our chapter in a manner made more special since Soror Morgan passed away later in 2009.

Since our partnership with Ebony Fashion Fair ended after 49 years, we supplemented our fund raising efforts by partnering with the West Side Theatre Guild to host "Lyrics: A tribute to Michael Jackson." In honor of the singers' untimely death, Sorors donned MJ-like hats, silver gloves and socks, and specially-made shirts with Michael's Smooth Criminal pose in silver. Soror Charius Haney was responsible for reactivating this new avenue of revenue generation.

We went green with the new term of Soror Ida Gillis as Basileus. We eliminated all paper reports except for those senior Sorors who do not have emails, and used technology to display reports on a large screen at our meetings. The chapter participated in the 1st Annual Boys and Girls Club's Keystone Leadership Group Reality Store. Sorors Angela Boone and Rosalyn Whitfield hosted our first webinar entitled "Entrepreneurial Success Plan: How to make it Happen" where panelists discussed the critical steps to establishing a business and how to turn passions into profits.

We partnered with Indiana University to present two Black history programs during this time. We hosted and the Ivy Notes performed along with members of Delta Sigma Theta Sorority, Inc. as BET's Jeff Johnson, Hezekiah Griggs, the youngest millionaire in the world spoke in 2010. We repeated our participation as the university brought living Freedom Riders to the campus and debuted the documentary of their story in 2012.

We enjoyed the play "Wicked" in Chicago as a sisterly relations event and began to almost embrace wearing red for "Pink Goes Red for a Day" under the "Global Leadership Through Timeless Service" program designed by new Supreme Basileus Carolyn House Stewart. Our "Emerging Young Leaders" program has blossomed to over 20 girls over the last 2 years and they have learned valuable life lessons, made several craft projects to reinforce what they learned and participated in several service projects to enhance their awareness of giving back to the community. This signature program for Soror Carolyn House Stewart is a delight to the chairman Soror Quanda Davis and her Co-Chairmen, Sorors Karen Barber-Walker, Kellauna Mack-Jackson, Ayronn Newman, Tracey Hamilton, and Soror Karen Nolan and their willing committee members.

Soror Sharon Haney coordinates a "Spa Day" and "Barber Shop Day" each year with the Gary Literacy Coalition to provide free haircuts by licensed barbers at the Bernard C. Watson Academy for Boys and free manicures, pedicures, facials and shoulder massages by licensed beauty and health technicians for girls at the Frankie Woods McCullough School for Girls.

We've taken the health initiatives to new heights by participating in a Zumba exercise activity hosted by Sorors Veronica Collins and Nikki Dates and a "Diabetes Alert Day" forum consisting of keynote speakers Dr. Michael McGee of Methodist Hospital Northlake Campus and Kristina Green, a Diabetic Educator from Methodist Hospital Midlake Campus who provided information on diet and exercise. Our own Soror Nurses Karen Nolan and Tyra Morgan were on hand to provide insight, as well. All of this while continuing our many health-inspired 'walk-a-thons' and fun walks and adding a new one for The Lupus Foundation in honor of Soror Charius Haney who has been stricken with the disease.

To end this section, we highlight three events. First, the 4th Annual Wine Tasting was held at the newly renovated Aquatorium off of Marquette Beach with both an inside and outside venue decorated beautifully to beckon our patrons to enjoy the festivities for a good cause. Sorors Quanda Davis, Jerri Floyd, Sharon Haney and the other repeating committee members have continued to elevate the expectations of our guests and have not disappointed. Their bedazzled 'Got Wine" T-Shirts were outshined only by their smiles of welcome hospitality and the over-sized lighted A.K.A. sign perched high on the balcony for all to see.

Second, the wonderful job done by the 2012 Boule Luncheon Committee where we took the Sorors of Central Region on a "Fantastic Voyage" in San Francisco, CA. Chairman Kellauna Mack-Jackson is still getting AKAlades from Central Regional Director Gisélé Casanova on the job well done by her committee. The work to pull off 3 separate special events plus refreshments in the hospitality suite twice by hosting region-wide conference calls and assigning tasks to sub-chairmen was a textbook case of how to make a committee work well together.

And third at the request of Soror Casanova, the soon-to-be produced recording of the most popular renditions of "Ivy Note" selections that have been sung over the recent years at various Central Regional conferences and Boules will document and highlight the joy and hard work this band of 10 Gamma Psi Omega Sorors have had using their God-given talents for their sisterhood. Soror Dolena Mack's original music along with "AKAcised" popular tunes where the lyrics reflect Alpha Kappa Alpha themes will tickle the fancy of Sorors for years to come.

In summary, Gamma Psi Omega has continued to find innovative ways to meet the challenges of each new program of our Supreme Basilei. Our chapter is yet proud to be productive, supportive and making a difference in Gary and the Northwest Indiana communities. We thank Sorors Penny Cochran, Dolena Mack and Joyce Price for their consistent efforts to document, preserve and report our history for the last decade or more.

Gamma Psi Omega Advises Nu Lambda Chapter and Advised Epsilon Rho Chapter From 2002 — 2004 and Zeta Phi Chapter Until Its Dissolution In 1980.

GAMMA PSI OMEGA CHAPTER BASILEI

Frances Renfoe	1944 – 1945
Ruth Battle	1946 – 1946
Jane Schell	1947 – 1947
Joyce T. Morgan	1948 – 1948
Clareon Hinkson	1949 – 1949
Gladys Johnson	1950 – 1951
Jean Washington	1952 – 1953
Hattie Leonard	1954 – 1955
Alberta Newsome	1956 – 1957
Freda Coney	1958 – 1959
Yjean Chambers	1960 – 1963
Clytee Gibbs	1964 – 1965
Coleen Williams	1966 – 1967
Bloomie Kirkland	1968 – 1969
Emogene McMurtrey	1970 – 1971
Ferne Browne	1972 – 1973
Ollie Mackey	1974 – 1975
Clemette Armstrong	1976 – 1977
Ollie G. Minor	1978 – 1979
Ruth G. Hoyle	1980 – 1981
Diane Ross Boswell	1982 – 1983
Opal Burleson	1984 – 1985
Alyverne Coopwood	1986 – 1989
Willie Mae Taylor	1990 – 1991
Janis E. Culver	1992 – 1994
Rise Ross Ratney	1995 – 1997
Nina Graham	1998 – 2000
Lori Benford-Bryant	2000 – 2005
Dolena M. Mack	2006 – 2009
Ida L. Gillis	2010 – 2013
Kellauna Mack-Jackson	2014 –

Delta Delta Omega Chapter

EAST ST. LOUIS, ILLINOIS
MAY 25, 1946

Left to Right: Ruth Brinkley Brown, Iona F. Reed, Eartha P. Williams, Beatrice Miller, Kathryn M. Fagen, Thelma Blackwell, Johnetta Haley and Anita Wallace

CHARTER MEMBERS

THELMA BARNES BLACKWELL
RUTH BRINKLEY BROWN
KATHERINE FLOYD FAGEN
JOHNETTA R. HALEY

BEATRICE BURSON MILLER
EVELYN MOORE
IONA FIDLER REED
ANITA MAE WALLACE

1946 – 1956

Delta Delta Omega Chapter was chartered May 25, 1946 when a small group of graduate members, having experienced and enjoyed sisterhood as undergraduates at their respective colleges, sought to establish a graduate chapter in East St. Louis, Illinois. Because of the proximity of the city to St. Louis, Missouri, they encountered some difficulties. But, the sorors persevered and the Directorate gave its approval and granted the charter.

The eight charter members who served as chapter officers were: Basileus, Beatrice Burson Miller; Anti-Basileus, Ruth Brinkley Brown; Grammateus, Thelma Barnes Blackwell; Epistoleus, Anita Mae Wallace; Tamiouchos, Evelyn Moore; Parliamentarian, Katherine Floyd Fagen; Reporters, Iona Fidler Reed and Johnetta Randolph Haley.

Soror Eartha Perryman became an associate member the same year. In addition to Soror Beatrice Miller, who was the first chapter Basileus, four of the charter members (Ruth Brinkley Brown, Iona Fidler Reed, Evelyn Moore, and Thelma Blackwell) were chapter Basilei. When Soror Iona Fidler (1948-1949) was Basileus, she served as the chairman of the chapter's annual Easter Monday Fashionetta®, held to provide funds for scholarship awards to a deserving high school graduates.

Soror Evelyn Moore (1950-1951) succeeded Soror Reed as Basileus and outlined a program which included the play "Angel Street," directed by Soror Beatrice Miller. Under the leadership of Basileus Thelma B. Blackwell (1952-1953), Delta Delta Omega was well established by now and recognized in the community. All of the sorors became involved in the 33rd Annual Boule' held in St. Louis December 26 through December 30, 1953, where Soror Evelyn Moore served as a co-chairman of the Boule Steering Committee.

During the years 1954-1955, the chapter had a successful, well-rounded program with Soror Katie Barbee Walker as Basileus. Program activities were a Vespertine Hour, a Career Day, and Fashionetta. The Vespertine Hour was given in honor of our Founders' at Pilgrim C.M.E. Church with a reception given later in the afternoon at the Annette Center. Present at the reception were Parliamentarian Soror Gladys C. Gordon and Supreme Grammateus Soror Evelyn H. Roberts. In cooperation with the Future Teachers and Nurses Clubs of Lincoln High, a Career Day was conducted as a guidance program. Fashionetta® presented a skit, A Land of Dreams, written by Soror Evelyn Murrell, at the Lincoln High School Auditorium.

In 1956, Soror Bessie Hairston West served as Basileus. The chapter had a Fashionetta® Dance with the theme of A Night in Mexico where Soror Sarah King was crowned "Miss Mexico." The chapter co-hosted with Gamma Omega and Beta Delta the Central Regional Conference in St. Louis. And the Health Committee, chaired by Soror Evelyn Moore, furnished "PolyVisol" to indigent families of all races through the East Side Health District for rickets and scurvy.

1957-1967

Anti-Basileus Soror Willa Irene Green served as Basileus when Soror Bessie West became ill. Subsequently, Soror Green was elected Basileus in 1957 and served two years. Her administration continued the chapter's many worthwhile service, health, and community programs. One of her special memories was the 1958 Boule' held in Washington, D.C. It was the Fiftieth Anniversary of Alpha Kappa Alpha Sorority, Inc. In 1959-1960, Soror Eartha Perryman Williams succeeded Soror Willa Irene Green and Soror Susie Mann was Soror Green's successor in 1961.

Another dynamic leader was Soror Patricia Kelley, Basileus (1962-1964). Because of a change in the sorority's program structure, Soror Kelley served for two and a half years. Officers were now elected to serve based on a calendar year of January to December. As the chapter continued its many diverse activities, the sorors remained personally committed to provide service to mankind. This was evident by the scholarships given to deserving youth and financial support to such agencies as the NAACP and Sickle Cell Anemia. Fashionetta® became a debutante cotillion in 1963 to present outstanding young ladies to society. It offered enriched experiences for the participants, their families, and friends. A Fashionetta® pin, conceived by Sorors Helen Jones and Leola Johnson, and designed by Soror Yvonne Campbell, is given as a memento to each debutante. Proceeds from this cotillion continue to be used for scholarships and community programs.

At the Central Regional Conference held April 10-11, 1964, Delta Delta Omega was one of three hostess chapters and Soror Patricia Kelley chaired the Undergraduate Workshop and Graduate Panel Discussion on Chapter Programs. Soror Marcella Donald was Basileus from January 1965 through December 1966. During these two years the membership increased from approximately 27 to 48 active sorors. One of the prime goals set by Soror Donald was the establishment of an undergraduate chapter at the East St. Louis Resident Center of Southern Illinois University. With the advice and assistance she received from Soror Ordie Roberts and Regional Director Soror LeAnna Shelburne, the chapter requested and was granted a mixed chapter status at the 1966 Boule. This opened the door for undergraduates to join Alpha Kappa Alpha. (See Epsilon Iota). Soror Donald also collected the data and wrote the chapter's first historical manuscript covering the period of 1946-1980.

1968-1978

Soror Mary Wren served as Basileus during 1967 through December 1968. The chapter awarded funds to send mentally and physically challenged children to camp. Contributions were made to local charities and other programs, such as the United Fund, Emily Willis Day Care Center, Mary Martin Center, March of Dimes, Veterans Hospital, and Cancer Society. A donation of $1,000 was given to an East St. Louis Community Center.

The chapter moved with greater aspirations with Soror Lena Weathers as Basileus (1969-1970). Then, Delta Delta Omega Chapter began its twenty-fifth year with Soror Peggy LeCompte as its Basileus (1971-1972). Negro Heritage Week was observed February 7-13, 1971, with a Negro Heritage Forum at State Community College and a youth panel discussion "Rapping with Black Youth" at Lincoln High School. Negro Heritage brochures published by the sorority were distributed to the public library, schools, and community. Public forums were sponsored for local city and school board candidates.

The twenty-fifth anniversary of Delta Delta Omega, celebrated May 21-23, 1971, included a dinner dance and special Founders' Day Worship Services especially for charter members Eartha P. Williams and Anita Wallace who had become Ivies Beyond the Wall.

There was a rededication to work diligently in specific program areas of Alpha Kappa Alpha, when Soror Dianna Logan was elected Basileus (1973-1974). The financial system was revised and funds were increased. The first Night At the Races, chaired by Soror Beatrice Crawford, was held as a fundraiser.

January 1975 began Soror Vivian Brightharp Green's tenure as Basileus, which ended December 1976. The highlights of local programs included a public outcry for dismissal of Judges Billy Jones and Ora Polk; support of NAACP, by purchasing a Golden Heritage Membership for $1,000 and UNCF by sponsoring a local banquet, which resulted in a donation of $4,000. The chapter was rewarded for its effort by having two National Committee members selected with Soror Peggy LeCompte — NAACP followed by Soror Green — UNCF.

Soror Sheryl Howard Clayton served as Basileus from 1977 to 1978. Her theme was Boost Your Sorors. There were many accomplishments during her term of office. The first Central Regional Director from our chapter, Soror Peggy Lewis LeCompte, was elected. A Supreme Basileus, Soror Bernice Sumlin, visited the chapter and observed a summer reading program at the East St. Louis Public Library. Vignettes of various sorors were written by Soror Doris Epps and printed in the weekly newspaper. A yearbook with a profile of each soror was printed. Soror Leureatha Griffin served on the Boule' Luncheon Committee and created the Hats idea to represent each chapter at the luncheon. Buford Norris, a Straight An electronics student became our first male scholarship recipient.

1979-1989

Like all other organizations, Delta Delta Omega was beginning to feel the crunch of inflation and the chapter began January 1979 with 78 active sorors. Soror Lora Jones became the Basileus of the chapter (1979-1980). The highlights of chapter programs were the sponsorship of the first roadblock for UNCF; contributing to Community Hospital Pediatric Ward; distributing AKA History books to the public library, public schools and colleges; continuance of Miss Fashionetta" cotillion; a Negro Heritage Program; project youth to include sponsoring a Khoury League Girls Softball Team; revitalization of a reading program based on the National Life-Long Learning Project; and scholarship awards to youth. Delta Delta Omega was designated prime hostess to the 45th Central Regional Conference held at the Breckenridge Inn in Frontenac, Missouri. At the end of this decade, one of our charter members, Soror Iona Fidler Reed joined other charter members as an Ivy Beyond The Wall.

The threshold of the new decade began with expanding programs and a stabilizing membership. The Basilei included Soror Marjorie Preston (1981-1982) when the chapter co-sponsored a reception to introduce the National Directorate to the St. Louis Metropolitan area and collaborated with

Anheuser-Busch for the unveiling of their Great Kings of Africa Art Series.

The term of office for Soror Katrina C. Thomas (1983-1984), involved supporting the following: State Representative Wyvetter Younge in fundraising events; voter registration drives; Soror Rosetta Wheadon (a community college president), who was named Illinois State University Alumni of the Year; Reading is Fundamental, where students had an opportunity to select books of their choice from 1,000 books purchased. For Founders' Day Soror Loraine Green, 2nd Supreme Basileus was the speaker at the public meeting. Members from all Black Greek organizations were among the 400 guests in attendance. The next year Soror Thomas initiated the first joint Founders' Day celebration with graduate and undergraduate chapters of the St. Louis Metropolitan area.

With Soror Cathryn Mason's (1985-1986) emergence the chapter participated in one of the largest fundraisers for UNCF in the Metro East area. A total of $32,592.97 was raised during a two-month period. Soror Maya Angelou was given a reception at SIU-Edwardsville and Soror Sheryl Clayton campaigned for a School District 189 Board seat.

Basileus, Soror Louella Hawkins (1987-1988), instituted creative writing and Soror Burena Howard added computer literacy to the chapter's Assault on Illiteracy. The program chaired by Soror Howard won 1st place awards for Assault on Illiteracy at the Central Regional Conferences.

From 1989-1990 Soror Luereatha Griffin was Basileus. During her leadership, AKA poems written by Soror Griffin were published; Soror Susie Mann endowed the Desiree Haire Scholarship in honor of her mother for an outstanding student attending an HBCU; Dr. Henry Ponder became the first male speaker for Founders' Day, chaired by Soror Judith Higgins; and, to reactivate inactive sorors, the first Pink and Green Extravaganza...With Pizzazz, chaired by Soror Katrina Thomas was given.

1990 – 2000

For the nineties, the chapter realigned its programs consistent with the international theme: Creative Strategies for Action-Addressing the Crises of the 1990's, and six target areas of Back to the Basics in Education, Health Concerns, the Arts, Economic Empowerment, the Black Family, and the World Community. Soror Luvenia Long, Basileus (1991–1992), implemented the IVY AKAdemy with a ribbon-cutting ceremony in January 1992.

The torch was passed to the Basileus, Soror Burena Howard, (1993–1994) for the AKAdemy's anniversary celebration. The chapter continued the successful computer literacy classes of the Assault of Illiteracy target within the Ivy Akademy. Within the Arts the chapter held the first Kalendar Kids Pageant. The chapter also implemented the first and largest Black Exposition Business and Health Fair in East St. Louis; participated in the City-Wide Baby Shower donating items needed by expectant mothers and newborns, and adopted the Rukavena Senior Citizens Apartment and delivered food baskets during key holidays.

Soror Gail McClellan's administration (1995 – 1996) saw the celebration of fifty years of service for Delta Delta Omega Chapter. Celebration activities included: a Reception/Cruise on the Casino Queen; Sister-to-Sister activity at the Holiday Inn and a luncheon at the Marriott Pavilion Hotel, both in Downtown, St. Louis Mo; Public meeting at the East St. Louis City Hall Rotunda which included the unveiling of Former Basilei Portraits and the Parade of Pan Hellenic Flags.

Soror Helen Jones, administration (1997 – 1998) saw the inception of a Black Salute to Volunteers Program that included a Tribute to Trail Blazer, Thelma Wair, a member of the Little Rock Nine. In addition, American Red Cross disaster unit kits were made and donated, and a Foster Care Parent luncheon was sponsored. The Chapter held its first Gospel Explosion. It also participated in the Shriner's Parade network Cancer Society roadblock, donated teddy bears to the East St. Louis Public Library, sent books to Africa, and initiated the P.I.M. Math and Science Program. The chapter also made and designed the Pan Hellenic Flags for Regional Conference.

Soror Juanita Brown (1999 – 2000) led the chapter in the Cancer Walk for the Cure and raised more money than any other participating organization. Gospel Fest was initiated during this administration and the chapter won a Regional Conference Award for sponsoring a play and reception event at the Black Repertory Theater. Chapter efforts resulted in the creation of an Alpha Kappa Alpha room at the Call for Help women's' transition and homeless shelter. A reception was held to celebrate at the completion of the project. The sorors of Delta Delta Omega helped to make the Central Region Quilt. Soror Juanita then won the quilt in a raffle. The Guidance Program was expanded and the P.I.M.S. Celebration (Math and Science Program was held. The chapter was the first local Greek organization to purchase bricks for the building of the Jackie Joyner Kersee Community Center.

2001 – 2010 (The Millennium)

The sisterhood activity, Run for the Roses, was initiated during Soror Alice Aldridge's reign (2001 – 2002). This activity involved sorors acknowledging the kind acts or giving encouragement to another soror. It was an instant hit. Soror Alice also realigned the programs of the local chapter to match national programs without conflict. Delta Delta Omega partnered with the East St. Louis Public Library and donated audiovisual equipment for the facility. The chapter also partnered with Call for Help, women's transition and homeless shelter. It was under this administration that the Delta Delta Omega website was launched. A local scholarship for high standards and moral character was presented to Miss Fashionetta®. Debutantes and Escorts (in addition to Miss Congeniality) were created. A reception for Soror Thelma Wair, one of the Little Rock Nine, was held.

Relay for Life, a fundraiser for the American Cancer Society, saw Alpha Kappa Alpha collect the largest amount of money of all participating organizations under the administration of Soror Donna Bender (2003-2004). During this administration, the chapter also maintained one hundred percent membership in the Educational Advancement Foundation and received regional certificates for the largest percentage of chapter members in attendance and reactivation of sorors at the 2004 Regional Conference in Milwaukee, WI.

Soror Lola Key's tenure ran from January 2005 to December 2006. To-date, the chapter sponsored the first Dr. Martin Luther King, Jr. Program/Reception and decorations for a service organization; sponsored the Save the Library Reception, and refurbished the Call for Help AKA room and sponsored a reception to celebrate. Delta Delta Omega also celebrated its 60th Anniversary under Soror Lola's leadership, which included a reception honoring all of our golden sorors, and a grand hat luncheon.

Basileus Kathy Walker Steele was the guiding force as Delta Delta Omega reached its largest membership of 110 sorors. The chapter also received the Five Heartbeat Award for its efforts in reclaiming sorors, and retained sorors through exciting membership activities like the very successful Sisterhood Summit and a trip to Kansas City, MO. As Alpha Kappa Alpha Sorority, Inc. celebrated her 100th Anniversary, the chapter responded overwhelmingly to the ESP Program. Platform I — The Non-Traditional Entrepreneur — inspired the members to learn more about opportunities for entrepreneurship. Platform II — The Economic Keys to Success initiative — was instituted at chapter meeting training sessions where topics were discussed which pertained to financial development and security. Platform III — The Black Family — was the catalyst for the adoption of an East St. Louis Family. Platform V — Health Resource Management and Economics — was the motivation needed as sorors answered the call to become healthy by group exercise and mall walking. This was a time of high energy and excitement as Delta Delta Omega sorors exuded Efficiency, Service and Pride in the name of sisterhood and service!

During her reign, Soror Doris Stewart Morgan (2009-2010) instituted Adopt-A-Family through East Side Heart and Home Catholic Organization by providing appliances and helping to finish their new home. A Passport to Success Workshop was conducted which emphasized the Economic Growth of the Black Family and was presented to teens in the local area. The Pearls, Pumps and Polo's Dance fundraiser was started as a means to raise funds for Relay for Life. The chapter partnered with TLOD in the Diabetes Walk and Workshop. Finally, Delta Delta Omega served as host, with other chapters, for the 2010 Boule. Soror Kathy Walker-Steele served as General Chairman.

2011 – Present

Touching Hearts to Change Minds was the theme of Soror Gwendolyn Childs' (2011-2012) administration. This included igniting the "Key to My Heart" activity, which allowed sorors to recognize a Soror who had touched her heart by giving them a green key that could be inserted into a pin heart which could be worn on the lapel. It was under Soror Gwen's leadership that the GLTTS national initiatives were launched. Along with programs targeting Health, Internal Leadership, Global Poverty and Economic Security, Delta Delta Omega instituted the Emerging Young Leaders (EYL) and Social Justice and Human Rights initiatives. The chapter partnered with Opal's House, a safe house for abused women, and the Center for Domestic Violence where we conducted a candlelight vigil to bring light to issues surrounding domestic violence. Other programs that were initiated during Soror Gwen's tenure were a City-Wide Easter Egg Hunt, a College Trunk Giveaway, and a program to help Veteran women get a better understanding of local and regional program offerings. An All-White Soiree' fundraiser was also started to help support chapter service programs.

The first order of business for our 36th Basileus, Soror Courtney Vales Robinson (2013-2014), was to launch and introduce the chapter's new website, www.akaddo.com. The website is one of several key steps Delta Delta Omega has taken to promote and support environmental stewardship and sustainability. We also partnered with the U. S. Attorney's Office of the Southern District of Illinois, U.S. Attorney's Office of the Eastern District of Missouri, and Southwestern Illinois Law Enforcement Commission to co-sponsor a Human Trafficking workshop. Again, we worked with the Violence Prevention Center of Southwestern Illinois to serve as co-chairman of the Second Annual Domestic Violence Awareness Ceremony and Candlelight Vigil. Other than the joint Founders' Day Observance, the 2013 Susan G. Komen Race for the Cure, Martin Luther King, Jr. Day of Service, and the formation of an Alpha Kappa Alpha Step Team marked the first of many future joint activities among the five St. Louis Metropolitan Chapters.

Delta Delta Omega Advises Epsilon Iota Chapter, SIU—Edwardsville.

Chapter Members Who Have Held International/National Office or Been Elected to the International/National Nominating Committee

Peggy Lewis LeCompte	Central Regional Director	1978 – 1982
	Supreme Grammateus	1982 – 1986
	Central Regional Director	1997 – 1998

Delta Delta Omega Chapter Basilei

Beatrice Miller *	1946
Ruth Brinkley Brown *	1947
Iona Fidler Reed *	1948 – 1949
Evelyn Moore *	1950 – 1951
Thelma Blackwell *	1952 – 1953
Katie Barbee Walker *	1954 – 1955
Bessie Hairston West *	1956 – 1957
Willa Irene Green *	1957 – 1958

Eartha Perryman *	1959 – 1960
Susie Mann	1961 – 1962
Patricia Kelley	1962 – 1964
Marcella Donald	1965 – 1966
Mary Wren	1967 – 1968
Lena Weathers	1969 – 1970
Peggy LeCompte	1971 – 1972
Dianna Logan	1973 – 1974
Vivian Green	1975 – 1976
Sheryl Clayton	1977 – 1978
Lora Jones	1979 – 1980
Marjorie Preston	1981 – 1982
Katrina Thomas	1983 – 1984
Cathryn Mason	1985 – 1986
Louella Hawkins	1987 – 1988
Luereatha Griffin	1989 – 1990
Luvenia Long	1991 – 1992
Burena Howard	1993 – 1994
Gail McClellan*	1995 – 1996
Helen Jones	1997 – 1998
Juanita Brown	1999 – 2000
Alice Aldridge	2001 – 2002
Donna Bender	2003 – 2004
Lola Key	2005 – 2006
Kathy Walker-Steele	2007 – 2008
Doris Morgan	2009 – 2010
Gwendolyn Childs	2011 – 2012
Courtney Vales Robinson	2013 –

Ivy Beyond the Wall

Lucille B. Wilkins
11TH CENTRAL REGIONAL DIRECTOR
AUGUST 1946 – DECEMBER 1950

Lucille Robinson Wilkins was initiated in Beta Chapter in 1920 and transferred to Theta Omega Chapter upon receiving her B.A. Degree from the University of Chicago in 1922.

Soror Wilkins served as Basileus of Theta Omega in 1933 when the chapter was busily preparing for the 16th Boule and Alpha Kappa Alpha's silver anniversary in Chicago, IL. She also served the sorority as First Supreme Anti-Basileus.

Soror Wilkins received the M.A. Degree from the University of Chicago in 1940. She taught at Willard Elementary School and served as Adjustment Teacher at Phillips Elementary School for a number of years. She was teaching at Wendell Phillips High School at the time of her retirement in 1954. Soror Wilkins became an Ivy Beyond the Wall in 1964.

Soror Wilkins brought to her administration a commitment to the National Programs of the Sorority. The Central Regional Conferences emphasized the National Non-Partisan Council on Public Affairs, the American Council on Human Rights, the sorority's Endowment Fund, health, and Gamma House.

Five graduate chapters were chartered during her administration, Delta Phi Omega, Delta Chi Omega, Epsilon Epsilon Omega, Epsilon Kappa Omega, and Epsilon Lambda Omega.

Delta Phi Omega Chapter

TWIN CITIES — MINNEAPOLIS/ST. PAUL, MINNESOTA
APRIL 17, 1948

Left to Right, Back Row: Jean Riffe, Juanita Schuck Harris, Francis Hughes, Beatrice Reed, Frances Brown, Rachel James and Edna Smoot Griffin. Front Rrow: Mary Jane Cyrus Hewitt, Margaret Young, Lillian Howland, Lucille Wilkins (Regional Director) Ethel Maxwell Williams and Hazel Warricks Mann

CHARTER MEMBERS

ALLIE BALLENGER
FRANCES SMITH BROWN
MARY JANE CYRUS (HEWITT)
EDNA GRIFFIN
JUANITA SCHUCK HARRIS
SHIRLEE HARRIS THOMASON
LILLIAN HOWLAND
FRANCES HUGHES
RACHEL JAMES
HAZEL WARRICKS MANN
BEATRICE REED
JEAN RIFFE
BELLA SHELTON
ETHEL MAXWELL WILLIAMS
MARGARET YOUNG

MAJOR CHAPTER EVENTS OR PROJECTS:

FASHIONETTA®: In 1986, the chapter initiated the Miss Fashionetta® Program and Pageant. The program provided special contact between girls aged 12 to 15 and the professional women of our chapter. During the Fashionetta® season, various topics were addressed in a variety of ways: leadership development, self-awareness, cultural and career awareness.

Also, a scholarship/financial plan, as a base for an education fund, was started for each participant who received up to 50 percent of all monies raised in her name. This program provided funds for the yearly scholarships offered by the chapter. The last year it was held was in 2005.

TURNING POINT: Turning Point began as a chapter program in 1990. The program provided ongoing support to mothers and children affected by the use of crack cocaine. The committee worked closely with a representative of the staff of Turning Point (AA place where you can change your mind.") to design and implement monthly programs for chapter involvement, which has included such activities as tutoring for mothers and children, donations of blankets, toys, books, clothing, accessories for mothers and children; child care — story time for children; rides for mothers; providing Thanksgiving food baskets; sponsoring a holiday party with gifts for children and adults; Just Us Girls talk sessions; sponsoring a series of speakers for cultural awareness programs; and parenting skill building programs. The chapter also provided dinner and talks on occasion.

AFRICAN AMERICAN ACADEMIC ACHIEVEMENT AWARDS: This program is an annual event, started in 1990. Graduating seniors, who have achieved at least a grade point average of 3.0, are honored at a special convocation ceremony. Each student receives a bronze medallion and a certificate as they are introduced to the community by the chapter. Other sororities, fraternities and groups who award scholarships, such as The Links, are also invited to present their awards at this occasion. A keynote speaker provides words of inspiration. A reception follows the event.

A unique aspect of this program is the effort of African American individuals and businesses to sponsor this event as an example of African Americans recognizing the accomplishments of African American students in their community.

FOOD SHELF CONTRIBUTIONS: Beginning in 1990, Delta Phi Omega sorors had contributed food and money to the Emergency Food Shelves at St. Phillips Episcopal Church in St. Paul. Members of our chapter, some of whom are members of the church, delivered the food and money and also helped with distribution at selected times.

Ivy House: The chapter began a partnership with St. Joseph's Home for Children in the mid-1990s. St. Joseph's is a residential facility for children who have been physically or emotionally abused or neglected. A majority of the children are African American. Once a month, sorors spent two hours with the children. Time was spent, reading, playing games, braiding hair or just giving attention to individual children.

Scholarships: Since it's chartering, Delta Phi Omega has emphasized supporting students through scholarship awards. Fundraising efforts to provide scholarship funds included AKADazzle, a Neiman Marcus Fashion Show and an all soror Telethon. AKADazzle was the annual scholarship dance held at the Minneapolis Women's Club each January. Despite the weather, this was a popular Twin Cities social event. Delta Phi Omega partnered with Neiman Marcus to present a breakfast fashion show followed by make-overs and shopping. During the telethon, sorors used a bank of telephones to call active and inactive sorors in the Twin Cities to obtain pledges for the scholarship fund. Delta Phi Omega also hosted the Ebony Fashion Fair for 3 years. In 2011, Delta Phi Omega hosted the Pink Carpet Affair, a formal event, honoring a local community leader. A silent auction was held as well.

The Ivy Foundation, Inc.: The Ivy Foundation was established in 2000 as the philanthropic arm of Delta Phi Omega. All financial sorors of Delta Phi Omega are members of the foundation. The foundation sponsors and co-sponsors with the chapter many fundraising and community service activities.

American Red Cross: In 2001 Delta Phi Omega entered a partnership with the American Red Cross. Annual blood drives are held at a local church. The chapter recruits donors and works on the day of the drive. The Red Cross handles all of the medical aspects of the drive. The Red Cross has commended Delta Phi Omega for the success of the blood drives. In addition, the chapter recruits for other Red Cross blood drives in the community.

Regional Conferences: Delta Phi Omega hosted Central Regional conferences in 1951, 1981 and 1999. In 2011, Delta Phi Omega as part of Cluster II was a host chapter for the 79th Central Regional Conference held in Madison, WI.

Cluster: Delta Phi Omega is the primary hostess chapter for the 2013 Fall Cluster. Clusters I, II, and VIII sorors attending.

Family Picnic: A highlight of the year is the annual family picnic. Sorors, families and friends gather at a local park for an afternoon of good food and fellowship.

Twin Cities Men Who Cook: The inaugural event was held in October 2012 and is a fundraiser with proceeds benefiting the programs of Delta Phi Omega Chapter. Local men are invited to participate as a chef and show their culinary skills. There are 3 female judges, who are well known community leaders.

Delta Phi Omega Advises Mu Rho Chapter and Advised Eta Chapter Until Its Dissolution.

Chapter Members Who Have Held International/National Office or Been Elected to the International/National Nominating Committee

C. Elizabeth Johnson	Supreme Grammateus	1939 – 1941
	Editor-in-Chief, *Ivy Leaf*	1937 – 1939
Delta Irby	Undergraduate Member of Large	1978 – 1982
Mabel Evans Carson	Central Regional Director	1982 – 1986

Delta Phi Omega Chapter Basilei

Margaret B. Young	1947
Mary Taylor Pyburn	1956
Wilma Allison	1958
Mable Evans Cason	1976
Irece Winans	1977
Beatrice Bailey	1978
Shirley Jumelle -Y- Picokens	1979
Linda Garrett	1980 – 1981
Rosa Smith	1982 – 1983
Phyllis Norris Sanders	1984
Beverly Johnson	1985 – 1986
Virginia Sims	1987
Gloria Marks	1988 – 1989
Shirley Gordon	1990 – 1991
Cynthia S. Tyson	1992 – 1993
Teressa White-Cooper	1994 – 1997
Andrea Hayden	1997 – 1999
Peggye Mezile	2000 – 2003
Gloria Marks	2004
Rubye Walker	2004 – 2006
Valerie Perkins	2006 – 2007
Lorraine Griffin Johnson	2007 – 2009
Lori Jackson	2010
Leshia Lee Dixon	2011
Lisa Tittle	2012 –

Delta Chi Omega Chapter

EVANSTON, ILLINOIS
JUNE 25, 1948

Standing, left to right: Jacquelyn Baskin, Carrie Arleta Gatlin, Dr. Elizabeth Hill, S. Ruth Haith, Leonia Burton, Ophelia Otey, Annie Johnson, Fredrica Smith, Wilhelmina Burroughs, Audrey Fountain and Lastinia Warren; Seated, left to right: Sorors Vivian Garry, Doris Cunningham, Irma Clark (Supreme Tamiouchos), Lucille Wilkins (Regional Director), Lucile Roberts (Basileus), Elaine Woodson Levy and Christine Evans; Not pictured: Sorors Margaret Allen, Gloria Hilliard and Anna Watson.

CHARTER MEMBERS

MARGARET ALLEN	S. RUTH HAITH
JACQUELYN BASKIN	ELIZABETH HILL
WILHELMINA BURROUGHS	GLORIA HILLIARD
LEONIA BURTON	ANNIE JOHNSON
DORIS CUNNINGHAM	ELAINE WOODSON-LEVY
CHRISTINE EVANS	OPHELIA OTEY
AUDREY FOUNTAIN	LUCILE ROBERTS
VIVIAN GARRY	FREDRICA SMITH
CARRIE GATLIN	ANNA WATSON
	LASTINIA WARREN

From February 20, 1944 to June 25, 1948, a group of Evanston-area women had a dream, a dream of forming an Evanston chapter of Alpha Kappa Alpha Sorority. They saw the need for work to be done in a community that was expanding and building. There was the need to encourage and give guidance to the youth at the Evanston Township High School. Post-war problems with racial overtones were beginning to arise as social service agencies were making pleas for help.

In April 1948, a volunteer group of determined AKA's compiled a list of 25 persons in Evanston identified as sorors. All were invited to a meeting. The wheels were set in motion to activate this Evanston, Illinois chapter and make a dream a reality. A charter had been granted in 1944, paid for by Fredrica Smith of Waukegan, Illinois. It was learned from the Regional Director, Lucille Wilkins, that the charter was still valid and only 10 members were needed to start an official chapter. Nineteen women were willing to be charter members. Their names were submitted and approved by the Regional Director. On June 25, 1948, during Soror Edna O. Campbell's term as Supreme Basileus, Soror Wilkins, Irma Clark, Supreme Tamiouchos and Arlene Washington, a former Regional Director, traveled to Evanston and established Delta Chi Omega Chapter. Soror Lucile Roberts was selected as the first Basileus.

Sorors marked the occasion with a dinner celebration at the home of Soror Roberts, which also was the site of the installation ceremony. Afterwards, Delta Chi Omega entertained Greeks and other guests at a reception held at the Evanston YMCA.

During the first 20 years of the chapter, Delta Chi Omega established one precedent after another, being responsible for innumerable innovations and contributions to the life, progress, and culture of the North Shore. Delta Chi Omega focused its concerns on the academic achievement and social, personal, and educational development of our African American youth of high school age. A vocational guidance committee was established to cooperate with homeroom teachers, counselors, parents and students in an effort to improve standards in every area of high school life.

Delta Chi Omega was one of the first African American community groups to use private facilities (the Swedish Hall and the North Shore Hotel) in Evanston for chapter activities. One of the first fundraising activities undertaken by the chapter was a Queen Mother Contest. For several years, a group of selected women in the community vied for the title of Queen Mother of Delta Chi Omega. Lest this activity continue too long and become stagnant, a Fashion-Cocktail Hour was conceived. Delta Chi Omega was the first in the community to host this type of affair. The first fashion show was the most lavish. The facility chosen could not contain the crowd. The next year, the event was moved to the North Shore Hotel, where it was standing room only.

Scholarships have always been a thrust for Delta Chi Omega throughout its existence. Initially, two small scholarships were granted to a graduating senior of the North Shore community. One of these awards was for a college bound student and the other was directed toward a student pursuing a trade. Through the years, the scholarship focus has evolved into five to ten annual awards directed toward college-bound students and students continuing their pursuit of a degree.

Members of Delta Chi Omega have made outstanding contributions locally and nationally. Special recognition must be given to the late Soror Helen Cromer Cooper, who was honored as a recipient of numerous community and statewide awards. She dedicated herself to Alpha Kappa Alpha Sorority on the national level. Soror Helen served as Financial Director 1962-1966, Supreme Tamiouchos 1966-1970, Supreme Parliamentarian 1970-1972, and Chairman of the Personnel Committee 1972-1974. She honored Delta Chi Omega with her membership, and served Alpha Kappa Alpha for more than six decades.

Delta Chi Omega Chapter has a long tradition of leadership in the Evanston-North Shore community, covering all areas of endeavor, including education, health, law, religion, public service and social justice. Among the chapter's charter members in 1948 was Dr. Elizabeth Hill, part of a pioneering team of physicians attending to the healthcare needs of Evanston's African American community at a time when the city's hospitals were segregated. Determined to replace the ill-equipped converted houses that served as medical centers for our community, Dr. Hill mounted a fundraising effort that, in 1952, resulted in the opening of a new Community Hospital, with 54-beds, two delivery rooms, a nursery and two operating rooms. Along the way, Dr. Hill made history as the first African American woman in Illinois to hold the title of hospital chief-of-staff. Community Hospital closed in 1980 and now houses people with disabilities. These Hill Arboretum Apartments are named in memory of Dr. Hill.

Soror Mayme Spencer became the first African American woman to serve as an Evanston alderman in 1963. She was known for her community activism, providing pro bono legal services and advocating fair housing. Soror Spencer remained a practicing lawyer until her death in 2011. Her legacy continues through the free legal services provided by the Mayme F. Spencer Memorial Street

Law Center.

In 1993, Soror Lorraine H. Morton became Evanston's first African American mayor and, when she retired in 2009, she again made history as Evanston's longest-serving mayor. The Evanston Civic Center has been renamed in her honor.

In 2008, Mayor Morton joined the Supreme Basileus of Alpha Kappa Alpha Sorority, Incorporated, and all of Delta Chi Omega in celebrating both the sorority's centennial year and the chapter's 60th anniversary by becoming the first Black Greek-letter Organization to serve as grand marshal of Evanston's annual Fourth of July parade.

This type of groundbreaking activity is not new to Delta Chi Omega: when the newly chartered chapter celebrated its first Founders Day at the North Shore Hotel in 1950, it became the first African American organization of any kind to hold an event in one of Evanston's previously segregated hotels.

In 2009, when Soror Patricia A. Vance became chapter basileus, she distinguished Delta Chi Omega as the only chapter with a sitting basileus who is also Cook County's only African American female elected to the office of Township Supervisor.

Today, Delta Chi Omega Chapter continues to boast a bevy of accomplished community leaders and inspired volunteers. Additionally the chapter is known for its collaborative work with other community groups. Examples of successful collaborations include: the partnership with Dress for success, which provides career clothing for women seeking or returning to work; the Unity Reception, which brings nearly 30 college-scholarship-granting organizations together to celebrate their award winners and recognize high school honor roll students; the Evanston-North Shore Community Consortium, which involves sororities, fraternities, and churches in hosting candidates forums to help educate voters; the Women's History Project, in partnership with the Evanston Historical Society, and the Dreams Delivered prom boutique, held in conjunction with the Evanston Women's Club.

From the beginning, Delta Chi Omega has consistently executed the sorority's program initiatives. As part of the 2004-2006 Young Authors initiative, the chapter successfully engaged local youth in a series of writing workshops that included recognition awards for the best prose and poetry submissions and the publication of their work in a book. Additionally, the chapter's after-school money seminars and online investment game activities won Financial Literacy program recognition at the Central Regional Conference in 2009. In 2012, the chapter's Martin Luther King Day of Service activity honored women veterans at the Lovell Federal Health Care Center with a specially catered lunch, musical entertainment and gifts.

Through the years, Delta Chi Omega has dreamed. Many of these dreams have become reality. Delta Chi Omega has studied and solved many problems peculiar to the American way of life. Delta Chi Omega has made scholarship and educational excellence a reality. Additionally, improving the image and socioeconomic status of the African American race continues for Delta Chi Omega. There is still much to be done and much that Delta Chi Omega must do. Delta Chi Omega will be ever pressing forward in its goal of service to all mankind.

SCHOLARSHIP

Delta Chi Omega established the non-profit Ivy Pearl Foundation in 1999 as its philanthropic fundraising and grant-making arm, focused primarily on awarding scholarships. Since that time, more than $120,000 in scholarship funds has been awarded, including a special $10,000 scholarship allocation in honor of the sorority's 2008 centennial year. We are proud to have an opportunity to assist deserving students in furthering their education. Our scholarship program reaches high school and undergraduate students.

Delta Chi Omega Advises Gamma Chi Chapter and Advised Xi Epsilon Chapter Until Its Dissolution in July 2000.

CHAPTER MEMBERS WHO HAVE HELD INTERNATIONAL/NATIONAL OFFICE OR BEEN ELECTED TO THE INTERNATIONAL/NATIONAL NOMINATING COMMITTEE

Helen Cromer Cooper	Financial Director	1962 – 1966
	Supreme Tamiouchos	1966 – 1970
	Supreme Parliamentarian	1972 – 1974

DELTA CHI OMEGA CHAPTER BASILEI

Lucile Roberts	1949 – 1949
Elaine Woodson Levy	1950 – 1951
Margaret T. Allen	1952 – 1953
Jacqueline Baskin	1953 – 1954
Anna E. Watson	1955 – 1956
S. Ruth Haith	1956 – 1959
Helen Cromer Cooper	1959 – 1961
Vivian Garry	1962 – 1963
S. Ruth Haith	1964 – 1964
Rosamond Sanders	1965 – 1966
Dorothy Magett	1967 – 1968
C. Louise Brown	1969 – 1970
Earlene Fleetwood	1971 – 1972
Blanche Smith	1973 – 1974
Ellen Reynolds	1975 – 1976
Janice Jones	1977 – 1978
Gwen Holmes	1979 – 1982
Barbara Travis	1983 – 1984
Jamilla Pitts	1985 – 1988
Charese Jordan	1989 – 1991
Yendis Gibson-King	1992 – 1996
Donna Richardson	1997 – 1998
Elreta Dickinson	1999 – 2002
Vickie Brown	2003 – 2004
Michele McClure Lacy	2005 – 2008
Patricia A. Vance	2009 – 2012
Deldri R. Dugger	2013 – Present

PART II: THE SECOND QUARTER OF THE CENTURY

Epsilon Epsilon Omega Chapter

CHAMPAIGN, ILLINOIS
APRIL 9, 1949

*Left to Right-Seated: Bernice Brightwell, Lucille Wilkens, Regional Director, Louise William Brown.
Left to Right-Standing: Carrie Alice Pope, Marie Mack-Rivera, Mary Grace Thomas, Annette Parmer Chavis, Marion Davis, Clara Smith, Marion Davis, Not Pictured: Mary Varnado-Waldon*

CHARTER MEMBERS

HELEN HITE	MARGUERITE CHISM JOHNSON
ERMA BRIDGEWATER	ANNETTA PARMER CHAVIS
BERNICE BRIGHTWELL	CARRIE ALICE POPE
LOUISE BROWN	MARIE MACK RIVERS
MARION DAVIS	CLARA SMITH
HELEN HITE	MARY GRACE THOMAS
LIZZIE JOHNSON	MARY VARNADO WALDEN

1949 was a vintage year—for it not only gave Champaign-Urbana the Epsilon Epsilon Omega Chapter, but it gave the community thirteen dynamic women. On April 9, 1949, Gamma—the mixed chapter—became Gamma, the undergraduate chapter, and Epsilon Epsilon Omega, the graduate chapter. Currently, Epsilon Epsilon Omega advises Gamma Chapter. The thirteen charter members were determined to perpetuate the idea of Alpha Kappa Alpha Sorority, "Supreme in Service to All Mankind." Since that eventful day, Epsilon Epsilon Omega continued to grow. In 2000, its membership reached thirty sorors. The continuous turnover of graduate students at the University helps to decide the size of the chapter. The last membership intake process was in May 2008. Nine women were initiated during that intake. Due to graduations and transfers, the Chapter remains a small chapter of fewer than twenty-five members.

The Chapter has maintained its effectiveness due to the belief that programs should be geared to meet the needs of the community, while at the same time, compatible with the sorority's international program. In the early days of Epsilon Epsilon Omega's inception, sorors met in each other's home and at Gamma House to conduct the business of the sorority and to plan activities that would accomplish the chapter programs. In more recent times, sorors have conducted Executive Committee and Chapter meetings at the Douglass Library, University of Illinois, Don Moyers' Boys and Girls Club, and the Danville Public Library. Other committee meetings are still held in sorors' homes.

Through the years, the Epsilon Epsilon Omega Chapter has tried to maintain her presence in the community, sponsoring some activities and supporting others. Currently, her reach extends also to Danville, IL, where Epsilon Epsilon Omega Chapter has welcomed sorors to the chapter from Danville, as well as implemented programs in the Danville community. The chapter has historically participated in community service and fund raising activities. Listed below is an overview of some of Epsilon Epsilon Omega Chapter's programs and activities through the years.

THE SALAD BOWL: The Salad Bowl began in 1966. It was one of the Chapter's smaller fundraisers. It was designed to be an annual summer community-social activity. For fifteen years, on a Sunday afternoon in July, it was held on the front lawn of Soror Maudie Edward's home. The center table had a large AKA umbrella over it. All other tables were covered with pink tablecloths. The event was a dressy affair. Many people in the community attended and for several years, many sorors attending summer school at the U of I were guests.

For this event, the chapter members made the salads. One summer, a salad cookbook was sold. In the early eighties, the Salad Bowl was moved to Douglass Center. The event expanded to include a fashion show. Local stores donated clothes to be modeled.

The funds raised were given back to the community. The activity funded the following: items for seniors at the Douglass Center, fruit baskets for seniors, the Girls Club, NAACP and helped with the senior picnic. The Salad Bowl was discontinued in the late eighties.

SCHOLARSHIP DINNER DANCE: This major fundraiser, used to promote scholarships to area graduating African American juniors and seniors, was first held in the early sixties. In the past the Chapter made a commitment to give scholarships to at least four graduating high school young ladies each year. In more recent years, the Chapter has made a commitment to give out as many scholarships as possible.

PINK PANACHE: In the year 2000, the Chapter adopted the theme, "Pink Panache." This would become the major fundraising event each year. Pink Panache has taken many forms: dance, art auction, silent auction and a book reading/signing. This event has allowed the Epsilon Epsilon Omega Chapter to give more substantially through a larger number of scholarships.

HALLOWEEN FRUIT BASKETS FOR SENIORS: Baskets were initially decorated and filled with fruit to be given to seniors in the community during the Halloween celebration. The Chapter has since incorporated this event into the sorority's National Volunteer Day. In recent years, baskets have been filled and given to a local church during the Thanksgiving holiday.

READING IS FUNDAMENTAL (RIF): Epsilon Epsilon Omega Chapter receives a grant each year to help fund the RIF program. Children's books have been distributed at the Girls' and Boys' Club, Douglass Branch Library and the Douglass Center. More recent RIF distributions have been made at Mount Olive Baptist Church and during C-U Day in the Douglas Park. Through this program, thousands of books have been distributed to area children and youth.

FAACES: In the year 2001, Epsilon Epsilon Omega Chapter adopted a community program called FAACES. It is a mentoring program for area high school female students. Since its inception, many African American teenage females have gone through the program and thought it was a worthwhile experience.

OTHER ACTIVITIES THROUGH THE YEARS

Community Service	Fund Raising
Salvation Army	Scholarship Dinner
Voter Registration	Fashionetta®
Donations to Canaan Academy	King & Queen Contest
Visits to Nursing Homes	Shopping & Theater in Chicago
Holiday Fruit Baskets for Senior Citizens	Garage Sales /Bake Sales
Gifts to Senior Citizen Club	Candy and Cookie Sale
NAACP Life Membership	Hat Making Fashion Show
Tutoring	Circle City Classic
Food Baskets to the Needy	Jazz & Jest

March of Dimes
Boys & Girls' Club Volunteers
Donations to the Woman's Place
Best Interest of Children
Donations to Canaan Academy
MLK Day of Service
Presidential Debate Watch Party

Art Auction
Pink Panache
Diabetes Awareness Walk
Breast Cancer Awareness Walk
Pink and Black Ball

Epsilon Epsilon Omega has hosted two Central Regional Conferences in Champaign, Illinois—one in 1951 and again in 1985. The officers and sorors working on the 51st Central Regional Conference under the direction of Central Regional Director, Mabel Evans Cason in 1985 were: Basileus Arnetta Rodgers, Conference Chairman Patricia Lewis, and Registration Chair Maudie Edwards. In addition, Epsilon Epsilon Omega co-hosted the 2001 and 2007 Central Regional Conferences in Springfield, IL.

Epsilon Epsilon Omega Advises Gamma Chapter.

EPSILON EPSILON OMEGA CHAPTER BASILEI

Louise Brown	1949 – 1950
Mary Grace Taylor	1950 – 1951
Margarete Johnson	1951 – 1952
Helen Mite	1952 – 1953
Hester Suggs	1954 – 1957
Bernice Pope	1958 – 1959
Michelle Grant	1960 – 1961
Judy Zackrey	1962 – 1963
Jessie Donaldson	1964 – 1965
Maudie Edwards	1965 – 1966
Helen Hite	1967 – 1968
Pernice Pope	1968 – 1969
Juanita Van Dorn	1970 – 1971
Hester Suggs	1972 – 1973
Ethel Mencie	1973 – 1974
Maudie Edwards	1975 – 1977
Karen Bagley	1978 – 1979
Patricia Lewis	1980 – 1981
Renee Renfro	1982 – 1983
Arnetta Rodgers	1983 – 1984
Hester Suggs	1985 – 1986
Rose Adkisson	1986 – 1987
Teretha M. Johnson	1988 – 1989
Nell Taylor	1990 – 1991
Hettie Collins	1992 – 1993
Hester Nelson Suggs	1994 – 1997
Frances Graham	1998
Terrilyne Cole	1998
Camille Chang-Gilmore	1998 – 1999
Deanie Brown	1999 – 2001
Murial Bondurant	2002 – 2003
Courtney Tucker	2004
Rychetta Watkins	2004 – 2005
Deloris Henry	2005 – 2007
Tanya Chillis	2007
Rhonda Williams	2008 – 2010
Alice Payne	2010 – 2011
Murial Bondurant	2012 –

Epsilon Kappa Omega Chapter

MILWAUKEE, WISCONSIN
MAY 11, 1949

Charter Members Honored at Founders' Day Banquet and Dance
Left to Right: Pauline Redmond Coggs, Mabel Raimey, Cassandra Kelley and Edwina Thomas
Not Pictured: Dorothea Carter, Phyllis Curry, Alden Freeman, Clarice Harris and Norma Humphrey

CHARTER MEMBERS

DOROTHEA CARTER	NORMA HUMPHREY
PAULINE REDMOND COGGS	CASSANDRA KELLEY
PHYLLIS CURRY	MABEL RAIMEY
ALDEN FREEMAN	EDWINA THOMAS
CLARICE HARRIS	

Epsilon Kappa Omega has grown from eight sorors to one hundred and seventy. The chapter's efforts to promote higher education and scholastic achievement have been broad. Tutorial programs for elementary, high school and college students, scholarship awards recognition, career guidance conferences for high school juniors and seniors, and seminars for college-bound freshmen have been successfully implemented. Through its Arts Alert program, the chapter has sponsored programs in fine arts for both private and public school students, with special emphasis given to students in schools wherein limited cultural exposure is provided.

The Thrust Committee's umbrella program enables Epsilon Kappa Omega to join with other chapters in implementing the Sorority's programs. From 1949 to the present time the following major chapter events have occurred:

DEBUTANTE COTILLION: Established in 1974, this annual project's purpose is to expose outstanding young ladies to the principles of Alpha Kappa Alpha—service, scholarship and high ethical standards. This dream of youth recognition, in conjunction with scholarship fundraising was conceived and initiated by Soror Jacqulyn Shropshire.

In 2013 the Debutante Cotillion which is currently sponsored by the Pauline Redmond Coggs Foundation established by the chapter in 1999 will celebrate its 40th anniversary. During the years over 900 young ladies have been presented as debutantes to the Milwaukee community in which about $900,000 has been generated for scholarships and awards. Hundreds of community service agencies have also benefitted from the debutantes service efforts. Over 90 percent of all debutantes presented go on to college and many are many are respected professionals in their chosen careers.

BRADLEY CENTER CONCESSION STAND: Established in 1990, this annual project raised funds for chapter programs and increased awareness of Alpha Kappa Alpha within the Milwaukee Community. Sorors operated a concession stand at the Bradley Center sports arena approximately twenty times per year. Not-for-profit groups such as AKA were responsible for managing a food stand and all the logistics involved in serving patrons throughout the event. Sorors handled canned and food items, prepared food, dispensed soda and beer, and accounted for cash and inventory at the end of each event.

The chapter realized $13,000 over a two-year period from this project. Over 65 percent of the chapter was involved and over 10,000 patrons were served. This project also fostered greater teamwork and cooperation among chapter members because of the nature of the work involved. In 1996, the chapter ended the project.

YOUNG, BLACK AND TALENTED SHOWCASE: Established in 1987, this annual event showcases talented young African American Milwaukee Area elementary, junior high, and high school students who are excelling in the fine arts. This program was initiated by the Arts Alert Committee as a project, yet, has grown to become one of the chapter's premiere annual events. Young people from across the city have been featured on this program during the past seventeen years and many of them are now enrolled at some of the most prestigious colleges and universities pursuing fine arts studies. Hundreds of young artists and groups have been featured since the inception of this program.

OTHER SIGNIFICANT ACTIVITIES: Countless memories include implementing the Mississippi Health Project in 1951; Annually producing the Greenwich Village theatrical fund-raiser for scholarships; canvassing the community to obtain and distribute tuberculosis information in 1952.; sponsoring a ball to benefit the Sickle Cell center of Deaconess Hospital in 1972; In 1974 the annual lawn sip was established by then Basileus M. Kathleen Coleman. hosting the Central Regional Conference in 1959, 1966 and 1987; co-hosting the central regional conference held in Madison, Wisconsin in 1990 and the Central Regional Conference held in Milwaukee, Wisconsin in 2004; celebrating the 30th Annual Debutante Cotillion in 2003, which continues to generate funds for scholarships; recognizing the 50th Anniversary of this chapter with a grand gala in 1999; unveiling a unique exhibit depicting 50 years of sorority service within the community that was displayed at the Milwaukee County Historical Society in 2000; forming the Retired Alpha Kappa Alpha Sorors (RAKAS) group in order to utilize the memorable experiences, including videotaping the reflections of Golden Sorors in 1997; introducing the annual "Day at the Capitol" where sorors meet with state legislatures and the Governor to discuss actions which impact our community; establishing the Pauline Redmond Coggs Foundation to secure additional scholarship funds and contributing $10,000 to the Pauline Redmond Coggs Endowment Fund to foster greater revenues for scholarships and generously contributing to the Milwaukee Art Museum in order to purchase Black Art for their collection. In 2009 Epsilon Kappa Omega celebrated its 60th anniversary and produced short video and community program to commemorate this event. Membership continues to grow in the chapter with a precedent set in 2005 when 39 members were initiated. The chapter most recently welcomed its newest members in 2012 with the initiation of 13 outstanding women. In 2012 the chapter was instrumental in helping to host the 2012 regional conference held in Madison, WI in which over 1300 sorors participated. Soror Teresa Brown was named as cluster coordinator.

GLOBAL INVOLVEMENT: Epsilon Kappa Omega chapter adopted an African Village in 1987. Since then our sorors have provided continuous support in the form of shoe boxes of school supplies and purchasing hand made wares from Nairobi. The chapter co-sponsored a BIAFRA benefit for the World Community Project in 1969. The Visions and Voices Against Apartheid Project was co-sponsored in 1988. Much assistance was provided to charter a chapter in Freeport, Bahamas. An annual scholarship is bestowed in the name of Soror Mildred Parrish in remembrance. Contributions have been given to Haitian relief, for Sudanese relief and the water wells in Ghana in 2004.

CHAPTER HONORS AND AWARDS: In recognition of exemplary service the chapter was presented with $10,000 from the S C Johnson Company for the 50th Anniversary celebration in 1999; $10,000 from the Bader Foundation for the On-Track Program in 2002; $1,000 EAF Grant for the Connection Committee in 2002; $5,000 contribution for the Marcia Cromwell Scholarship fund; $6,000 for the Bader Foundation for the Ivy Reading AKAdemy in 2003 and in 2004. These monetary sums enabled Epsilon Kappa Omega Chapter to fully implement the chapter's community service projects.

Other memorable accomplishments include: winning the Regional Achievement Award in 1969; Soror Edith Finlayson receiving the Eleanor Roosevelt Medallion at the Boston Boule in 1992; Soror Edith Finlayson being inducted as an Honorary Soror at the Washington DC Boule in 1994; chapter receiving the UNCF Traveling Trophy for Community Service in 1987; Soror Frances Brock Starms recipient of the International Founders Graduate Service Award at the New Orleans Boule in 1992 and was also the first and only living individual to have a Milwaukee Public School named in her honor (Frances Brock Starms Early Childhood Center and Starms Elementary School).; chapter was selected as one of 20 chosen from over 200 chapters to be recognized internationally for Excellence in Programming featured in the *Ivy Leaf* in 1998.

Chapter Undergraduates which we supported received these honors: Frances Wilkerson—1988 Foreign Travel Winner; Hasannah Fair—1988 Leadership Fellow; Sheri Crosby — 1997 Leadership Fellow; Denise Perry 1998 — Leadership Fellow; Erica Horton - recipient of $1,000 EAF Scholarship in 2002; Kimberly Troutman — highest GPA in Central Region receiving a trip to Spain with the Directorate; Erica Horton — 2003 Leadership Fellow and appointed to the National Nominating Committee; also, Erica Horton elected as the International Undergraduate Member-at-Large at the Nashville Boule in 2004.

Epsilon Kappa Omega Chapter is proud of its accomplishments and is committed to continuing to provide exemplary service to the greater Milwaukee community.

Epsilon Kappa Omega Advises Mu Beta, Lambda Xi, Iota Delta, Omicron Xi, Uw-Oshkosh-General Members And Advised Epsilon Delta Chapter.

CHAPTER MEMBERS WHO HAVE HELD INTERNATIONAL/NATIONAL OFFICE OR BEEN ELECTED TO THE INTERNATIONAL/ NATIONAL NOMINATING COMMITTEE

M. Kathleen Coleman	Nominating Committee	1980 – 1982

EPSILON KAPPA OMEGA CHAPTER BASILEI

Pauline Redmond Coggs	1949
Edwina Thomas	1951
Clarice Green	1953
Anna Mae Fisher	1955
Jodora Middleton	1957
Mildred Pollard	1959
Lorraine P. Carter	1960
Juliana Rhoten	1962
Delores Casey	1964

Frances Brock Starms	1965
Frances Jefferson	1967
Mary K. Ball	1969
Melbia Rhodes	1971
M. Kathleen Coleman	1973
Geraldine Goens	1975
Elvira Dicks	1977
Mildred Parrish	1979
Jacqulyn Shropshire	1981
Irajean Haynes	1983
Ernestine Hansbrough	1985
Ethel Walker	1987
Annie J. Carlisle	1989
Dorothy W. Buckhanan	1991
Deidra Y. A. Edwards	1993
Carol Brown	1995
Jenelle Elder-Green	1997
Joyce King-McIver	1999
Margaret A. Rogers	2001
Joyce A. Peoples	2003
Catherine E. Miles	2005
Michelle Crockett	2007
Teresa Brown	2009
Sandra Hubbard	2011
Khyana Pumphrey	2013

Epsilon Lambda Omega Chapter

CAIRO, ILLINOIS
MAY 28, 1950

Four Charter Members Pictured — Left to Right: Carita Caldwell Trotter, June Moss Anderson, Mattie Williams and Agnes Holt Williams

CHARTER MEMBERS

JUNE MOSS ANDERSON	C. NELLE RUSSELL HARRIS
MARY D. WILSON BASS	CARITA CALDWELL TROTTER
DOROTHY SAVADA MURRAY DENNIS	AGNES HOLT WILLIAMS
GLADYS ENGLAND	MATTIE WILLIAMS
ADDLENE HOLLOWAY LIGHTFOOT	LOUISE LEWIS YOUNG

Soror C. Nelle Russell Harris spearheaded the push to establish a graduate chapter in Cairo, Illinois. She worked diligently over a four month period to find ten (the number required for chartering a chapter at that time) sorority members who were interested in chartering a chapter.

Soror Russell pulled off a small coupe by convincing a couple of sorors from the Carbondale area and one from the Paducah area to transfer to Boule membership.

These sorors along with those already in the city met the number required for chartering.

On May 28, 1950 this happy group of sorors assembled at the home of Soror June Moss Anderson at 2:30 p.m. for the chartering. The chartering ceremony was conducted by Soror Ida Scott for Central Regional Director, Lucille B. Wilkins. Sorors Cox and Storey of Paducah came to witness the joy of the new chapter members and to offer encouragement.

Through the years, Epsilon Lambda Omega Chapter has maintained a high profile in the community and received recognition for the many projects that have benefited the area. Scholarships have been given annually on a rotating basis to the three area high schools. The initial scholarship in 1951 was $25.00. Today that amount has increased to $1,000.00. In addition, in the 1960's, one of the schools had no lunch program and Epsilon Lambda Omega provided milk and snacks to three first grade classes.

During the 1970's the chapter contributed pajamas, a television, and sponsored fundraisers for the pediatric ward of St. Mary's Hospital (later renamed P.A.D.C.O.). Another project that received recognition was Epsilon Lambda Omega's help for the School for the Deaf in Marion, Illinois. Fundraisers and activities were sponsored to publicize the needs and to make contributions of the school.

Epsilon Lambda Omega programs also include a literacy program and the Chapter's signature program: The annual Sickle Cell Walkathon. For the last three years the Chapter has raised approximately $1,000 annually for the foundation.

The chapter's program of service continues with its adoption of the local women's shelter. A food drive for the shelter is organized annually, and unwrapped gifts for teen girls and women and toys for the children are donated for Christmas. The chapter is also one of the sponsors of the Valentine's Day party and St. Patrick's Day party at the local nursing home.

Epsilon Lambda Omega Advised Nu Sigma Chapter, Cape Girardeau, Missouri, From 1981 Until its Dissolution in 2002 and Advised Delta Beta Chapter, Carbondale, Illinois, Until 1961.

EPSILON LAMBDA OMEGA CHAPTER BASILEI

June Moss Anderson	1950 – 1952
Agnes Williams	1952 – 1954
Mattie Williams	1954 – 1956
Flora Chambliss	1956 – 1974
Laverna Thomas	1974 – 1976
Flora Chambliss	1976 – 1978
Merle Wilson	1978 – 1979
Laverna Thomas	1979 – 1980
Linda Woods Robertson	1980 – 1982
Laverna Thomas	1982 – 1984
Karla Seavers Patton	1984 – 1986
Naomi Lewis Mcpherson	1986 – 1988
Glenda Winters Jones	1988 – 1990
Debra Newell Houston	1990 – 1992
Laverna Thomas	1992 – 1993
Karla Seavers Patton	1993 – 1995
Charolette Mallory	1996 – 1997
Faye Howard	1998 – 1999
Karla Muriel Patton	2000 – 2002
Constance Williams	2002 – 2004
Janice Quarles Couch	2004 – 2006
Lela Humble	2006 – 2008
Karla Seavers Patton	2008 – 2010
Constance Williams	2010 – 2012

Part III

The Third Quarter of the Century

1951 – 1975

The Third Quarter of the Century

America was forced to make many adjustments during the post-war years. Among them was the press for full equality by Negro organizations. We can, to some extent, credit President Truman's Fair Deal policy with setting the climate for some gains made by the Negro in the late forties and early fifties. In 1948, a federal order was issued requiring fair employment in the federal services and by 1956 sixteen states and thirty-six cities had committees working toward the elimination of discrimination in employment.

On the sorority's front, the 1948 Boule would vote to establish a national headquarters under the supervision of an administrative secretary. A major economic self-sufficiency move, the doors opened to the first office on October 8, 1949. The office was located in a suite of rooms on the fourth floor of the Washington Park Bank Building at 63rd and Cottage Grove in Chicago, IL. Carey B. Maddox (Preston), Administrative Secretary was at the helm. The sorority never looked back from these humble beginnings. Approval by the Boule for the purchase of the building at 5211 South Greenwood in Chicago came in 1951. In October 1952, Alpha Kappa Alpha Sorority, Inc. became the first Black Greek letter organization to own a permanent headquarters building. In 1984 Alpha Kappa Alpha Sorority, Incorporated would open the doors to its debt free multimillion dollar Corporate Office at 5656 South Stony Island Avenue, Chicago. IL.

The location of the Corporate Office in Chicago, Illinois and Central Region has directly impacted the prestige of the organization in the community and the region. Each of the ten Executive Directors contributed to this prestige in their own distinct way. But, there is one that stands as a legend in both the sorority and in Chicago, Carey B. Maddox Preston.

Soror Preston (pictured at left) was initiated in Beta Delta Omega Chapter, Jackson Mississippi and transferred to Xi Omega, Washington, D.C. in 1944. She attended Tougaloo College and received the Master of Arts degree from Atlanta University of Social Work. She returned to Jackson after graduation to serve as Director of Social Work at the Wm. Johnson Community Center. She went on from Jackson to serve as Assistant Superintendent of the Krauss School in Wilmington, Delaware and Director of the National Training School for Girls in Washington, D.C., while doing further study at the Pennsylvania School of Social Work and Western Reserve University.

In 1948, Carey B, Maddox Preston was chosen from a large group of well-qualified applicants as Alpha Kappa Alpha's first employed officer, Executive Secretary. For more than twenty-five years, she interpreted the rules for graduate and undergraduate members and chapters; oversaw management of the sorority's property and finances and arranged its Boules.

Her unique influence helped move the sorority from a traditional focus on self-development toward a broadened service role. This included funding research on the causes and treatment of sickle cell anemia, and the operation of a Job Corps Center in Cleveland, Ohio. During her watch, the sorority also expanded its member reach and inducted Eleanor Roosevelt, Marian Anderson, and India's Mme. V.I. Pandit, into its ranks as honorary members. She also arranged for Dr. Martin Luther King, Jr. to address one of AKA's largest Boule audiences drawing thousands of middle class women closer to the protest phase of the civil rights movement.

Carey B. Maddox Preston made a strong contribution to civic affairs serving as a Director and later President of the Board of Directors of the Chicago Urban League. She served as a member of

District 158 Junior College Board; followed by an appointment by Mayor Richard Daley to the Chicago Board of Education where she served for seven years, including a term as Vice President. Other positions held by her included membership on the Women's Board of the University of Chicago, Board of Directors of Hyde Park Federal Savings Bank, Board of Good Shepard Church and President of the Chicago Pan Hellenic Council of Greek letter college sororities and fraternities.

After her retirement as Executive Director in 1974, following 26 years of service, she soon was called upon to help Baird and Warner Company lease up the Dearborn Park Development that began the revival of Chicago's South Loop. In addition, she returned twice to the Corporate Office: once to supervise construction of the third floor to the National Headquarters, in 1984 and again for several months in 1998 to serve as Interim Executive Director. She graciously served Alpha Kappa Alpha in its times of greatest need. Carey B. Maddox Preston became an Ivy Beyond the Wall in December 2000, feisty and commanding to the end.

By 1950, the Supreme Court and the Interstate Commerce Commission were protecting the rights of Negroes to travel without restrictions that had been imposed upon them by state segregation laws. The discrimination and segregation practices of hotels, public institutions, and restaurants were eased and frequently eliminated. Negroes had been 30 percent integrated in the armed services by 1951. In addition, Blacks were registering to vote in record numbers, while simultaneously striking down discriminatory state voting policies. However, these gains met stern resistance, hostility and even violence. In 1956, the Montgomery bus boycott ignited the largest civil rights movement in history.

Throughout these events, Alpha Kappa Alpha Sorority was there leading the way and cooperating with other organizations such as the American Council on Human Rights (ACHR) to guarantee that the gains made would not be lost.

During the third quarter of the century the sorority became the first organization to receive a federal contract to operate a job corps for women (Cleveland Job Corps Center); turn its attention to preservation and legacy with the commission of the sorority's first history, issued the African American Women Heritage Series and purchase of the home of the birthplace of Dr. Martin Luther King, Jr.

The National Health Program was revamped and several institutions received "Grants-In-Aid" for research in diseases directly affecting Negroes, i.e., sickle cell anemia. Internally, the sorority initiated its first long-range strategic plan: "To Capture A Vision Fair" and in June, 1953 secured the trademarks on Fashionetta® and the sorority's crest and pin. Several initiatives in support of Undergraduate Members were implemented including Leadership School, Foreign Travel Tour and the Ethel Hedgeman Lyle Endowment Fund.

As the sorority positioned itself to move into the final quarter of the century Central Region chapters continued to vigorously embrace the sorority's programs.

Evelyn Roberts
12TH CENTRAL REGIONAL DIRECTOR
DECEMBER 1950 – DECEMBER 1954

Soror Roberts attended Stowe Teachers College from the fall of 1936 to June 1940 and was invited to join the Ivy Leaf Club during her sophomore year. During her third year at Stowe, she was initiated into Beta Delta Chapter and was elected to serve as Anti-Basileus and later as Basileus.

A few years following her graduation from Stowe Teachers College, where she earned her B.A. degree, she joined Gamma Omega Chapter in St. Louis and went on to earn a M.A. and Ed.D. degree.

Beta Iota Chapter

Evansville College
Evansville, Indiana
June 2, 1951 – July 1962

Evansville, Indiana — A Dream Realized — Charter Members.

Charter Members

MARY E. COLEMAN
WYLENE ECHOLS
EDNA FORD
ALLENE LAMBERT
GERALDINE SHELTON

LAURA WATT
JOYCE WATSON
JACQUELINE WILEY
AGNES H. MANN
HENRIETTA SEALS

The first Beta Iota Chapter was established in Portsmouth, Ohio, in 1934 and dissolved in 1937. In 1951, the chapter was reestablished at Evansville College in Evansville, Indiana. Beta Iota Chapter existed on the campus of Evansville College, Evansville Indiana until its dissolution in July 1962 due to lack of membership. The Directorate assigned the name to the chapter at Northern Michigan University in Marquette, Michigan, in 1969.

Delta Beta Chapter

SOUTHERN ILLINOIS UNIVERSITY
CARBONDALE, ILLINOIS
APRIL 19, 1952

CHARTER MEMBERS

MALINDA BALINGER
IANTTHA BROWN
EVELYN COLEMAN
LAVERNA CORNELIUS
GWENDOLYN HALLIDAY

LOVENGER HAMILTON
JANETTA HICKMAN
DORIS JAMES
CHRISTINE MCKINNEY
JOYCE TABORN

Sorors Lucille Walker and Jenolar Hillsman McBride of Gamma Kappa Omega Chapter organized Delta Beta Chapter on the campus of Southern Illinois University at Carbondale. These two sorors convinced Central Regional Director Evelyn Roberts that an SIU chapter could be viable and maintain a presence on campus.

Prior to the chapter's chartering, women matriculating at SIU who wanted to become a member of the sorority participated in an interest group called the "Alpha Kappa's." Upon receiving their Bachelor's degrees and graduating, the interest group members were initiated into the sorority.

The charter group was deemed "goddesses." Each of the women had to select the name of a goddess and write about her attributes. No physical hazing took place; however, each pledge had to carry a basket of Ivy containing an egg. The women wrote and recited original poetry and had mandatory study sessions. After completing all assigned tasks, Delta Beta Chapter was chartered on the campus of Southern Illinois University at Carbondale on April 19, 1952.

Initially, Delta Beta held its chapter meetings at the home of Soror Lucille Walker (Gamma Kappa Omega Chapter) or at one of the private homes on the Northeast side where Delta Beta sorors resided. During that time, Blacks were not allowed to live in university housing. Eventually, the chapter was able to procure a sorority house. Delta Beta's first house was located at 108 East Park Street, at the site of the Brush Towers residence halls.

In the late 1950s, SIU built a Greek Row, officially known as Small Group Housing. Delta Beta was supervised and sponsored by Epsilon Lambda Omega Chapter in Cairo when it moved onto "the row." The chapter was one of the original tenants and, initially, the only Black sorority. The house, at 109 SGH, was located between the Alpha Phi Alpha and Kappa Alpha Psi houses. Later, the chapter maintained private housing on both Park Street (prior to the building of the Brush Towers residence halls) and Chautauqua Street.

THE KABACHIO: Delta Beta's signature event was "The Kabachio," a sweetheart ball. The idea was first suggested by charter member Ianttha Brown. No one knew or could explain the origin of the term Kabachio. Rumor was that it meant "stud" in Greek (or possibly Italian, depending on who you talked to). The winner, or Delta Beta's sweetheart, would be crowned "Mr. Kabachio." Runners-up were Mr. 20 Pearls (1st runner-up), Mr. Delta Beta (2nd runner-up) and Mr. Pink & Green (3rd runner-up). Several of the first Kabachios were held at the Carbondale City Hall and emceed by the then up-and-coming comic, SIU alumnus Dick Gregory. The Kabachio was always held in February as close to Valentine's Day as possible and was always well-attended by SIU students. After a long hiatus, The Kabachio was reborn in 1995.

During the 1960s, Delta Beta hosted Autumn Haze, a presentation honoring new women students. The 1970's saw the advent of SIU's All-Sorority Rush held each year in the fall with the other three Black sororities (Delta Sigma Theta, Zeta Phi Beta and Sigma Gamma Rho). This annual event gave new students an opportunity to obtain information about all of the Black sororities at one place and time in an expo-type setting. Each organization set up a booth with informational materials, paraphernalia, and other items. The rush included each chapter president giving an organization overview (history, purpose, philanthropy, etc.) and each chapter's Dean of Pledges outlining the membership process including qualifications and the application process. The event ended with a performance (step show) by each sorority.

Throughout the years, Delta Beta was an integral part of SIU Greek life. The chapter and its members participated in events such as the Tau Kappa Epsilon Olympics, Theta Xi Variety Show, Kappa Alpha Psi Scroller Talent Show, Sigma Pi Volleyball Tournament, and Inter-Greek Council Welcome fest and Fashion Show.

In 1964, 1967 and 1968, Delta Beta won or placed in the TKE Olympics. The chapter won the Sigma Pi Volleyball Tournament in 1968 — the first Black Greek-letter organization to do so — and was treated to a steak dinner by the Jewish fraternity members.

The early 1970s marked tremendous growth in Delta Beta. In January 1971, Pamela Bates, 27th Central Regional Director, was initiated with 16 other sorors. In May of that same year, 30 young women were initiated constituting the largest line in Delta Beta history to date. During this period, Delta Beta organized a signature event, AKA Olympics, a track and field competition involving members of other Greek-letter organizations on campus. In addition, members remained active in the breakfast program for low-income youth on the northeast side of Carbondale and the Black Student Union. In 1973, Marsha Callahan (spring '71) was inducted into the Sphinx Club, becoming one of the first African American undergraduates to be honored. In the mid-1970s, Sheila Colvin and Chrislyn Cross (both fall '75) were a part of a well-known singing group called Saks 5th Avenue. Terri-Ann Stinnette, Rose M. Taylor and Para L. Jones (all fall '78) made up the sensational singing group, Brown Sugar. Both groups captured several talent show awards, and regularly performed at campus and community events.

At the Central Regional Conference in 1964, the chapter won first place undergraduate chapter award and second place in the overall exhibit category. At the 33rd Central Regional Conference, Delta Beta took home the Arnetta G. Wallace award for scholastic achievement. The chapter received the highest undergraduate chapter GPA award at the 1994 Regional Conference.

Delta Beta sorors have always been a part of SIU campus royalty. Delta Beta sorors who were Kappa Alpha Psi sweetheart included Pearlie Little (winter '61), Sherry Brame (Spring '68), Cheryl Randolph (Winter '71) and Cynthia Williams (Spring '71). The 1966 Kappa (Alpha Psi) Karnival Queen was Gayle Purnell (Winter '66).

Alpha Phi Alpha had various names for their royalty and sorors picked up many of their crowns, including Norma Morris (Winter '60), Alpha Sweetheart; Rosalyn Smith (Winter '66), Alpha Playmate; Paulette Berry (Winter '68), Sweetheart; Enid Redden (Winter '73), Sweetheart; Laura White (Spring '74), Miss Eboness; Sandra Martin (Fall '75), Mack's Mate; and Keeyana Riley (Spring '00), Miss Black & Gold.

Paulette Berry (Winter '68) also reigned as the Phi Beta Sigma Sweetheart and Charsetta Reed (Spring '83) was the Sigma's "Ms. Touch of Blue." Other sorors who served as fraternity sweethearts include: Connie King (Winter '61), Lun Ye Crim (Fall '61), Cecile Williams (Spring '62), Carol Rancifer (Winter '63), Cheryl Cole (Winter '68), Carol Sanders (Spring '68), Jackie Howard (Spring '71), Pamela Akins (Winter '73), Vikki Davis (Spring '74), Gail Drish (Fall '75), Karen Harris (Fall '75), Patricia Waller (Fall '75) Lawanda Young (Spring '00), and Norma Brown (?). SIU AKA Homecoming Queens include: 1981 Denise Wells (Spring '77); 2007 Shannon Page (Fall '06); 2011 Autumn Anthony (Fall '10); and 2012 Whitney Clark (Fall '10). Susan Smith (Fall '75) and Leah Hemphill (Fall '01) were Homecoming Court finalists.

The chapter and its members also fully participated in campus life. Several sorors worked as dormitory resident assistants and in various divisions within Student Affairs. With the implementation of a Black Studies Department at SIU in 1969, 20 undergraduate student leaders — known as Learning Group (or L-Group) Leaders — were chosen to work as teaching assistants. Crystal Campbell (Spring '67) was a part of the initial L-Group. Charsetta Reed (Spring '83) was elected a Student Senator as were Keeyana Riley and Charisma White (both Spring '00). Brittany Greathouse (Spring '13) served as President of the Undergraduate Student Government (USG) during the 2012-13 school year. Teresa Hudson-Handy (Spring '93) served as president of both the National Society of Black Engineers and Blacks in Engineering & Allied Technologies, and Julia Anderson (Spring '93) was named one of SIU's 25 Most Distinguished Graduating Seniors. SIU recognized Delta Beta in 1994 for both outstanding service and academics. Also in 1994, Delta Beta planted and dedicated an "Alpha Kappa Alpha" tree near the Student Center. Kaliah Liggons (Fall '10) was presented the Outstanding Senior of the Year and Living Your Values awards by the Inter Greek Council in Spring 2013.

Mauri Thomas (Spring '71) and Harriet Wilson (Spring '71) represented Delta Beta on the organizing group to establish the National Pan-Hellenic Council (NPHC) on the SIU campus under the guidance of then graduate assistant and member of Kappa Alpha Psi, Lou Hines. In the 1980s, Charsetta Reed (Spring '83) served SIU in many capacities including National Pan-Hellenic Council President and Treasurer as well as NPHC's rep to SIU's Inter-Greek Council (comprised of the NPHC, Inter-Fraternity Council and PanHellenic Council). Denise Wells (Spring '77), Laura Becerra (Spring '09), and Vanessa Mosley (Fall '09) held the office of NPHC President. Susan Smith (Fall '75) was NPHC Vice President, and NPHC Secretaries included Julia Anderson (Spring '93), Keeyana Riley (Spring '00), Vernessa Streater (Spring '01), and Porche Noble (Spring '09).

Delta Beta commemorated the 30th anniversary of its chartering in 1982 with a weekend-long reunion in Carbondale. A new tradition, AKApollo was started in 2002 and modeled after the shows at the Harlem's Apollo Theater. It is now an annual affair. The 50th chapter anniversary was celebrated with a brunch in Chicago following the 68th Central Regional Conference in 2002. Delta Beta celebrated its 60th chapter anniversary in conjunction with the SIU Black Alumni Group Reunion in Carbondale and hosted a breakfast for sorors.

WELL-KNOWN DB ALUMNAE INCLUDE:
- Pamela Bates (Porch), Spring 1971 — 27th Central Regional Director
- Minniejean Brown, Fall '61 — Member, Little Rock 9Crystal Campbell (Kuykendall), Spring '67 — Motivational Speaker — Attorney — Minister — Educator — Human Resources Expert — Founder, KIRK (Kreative & Innovative Resources for Kids)
- Cheryl Cole (Young), Winter '68 — First Black female sales representative, Santa Fe Railway, featured in both Essence and Ebony for this accomplishment.
- Sheila Colvin (Fuller), Fall '75 — Vocalist — well-known jingles such as Osco Drug (At Osco you can count on people who care) and WNUA-FM/Smooth Jazz 95.5 (call letter vocalist: W-N-U-A 95.5), was one of the Budweiser Spudettes (Spuds Mackenzie).
- Jacqueline Heath (Parker), Winter '61 — Past National President, Top Ladies of Distinction
- Tracy Holliway-Wiggins, Spring '85 — Actress/Singer (Soul of the Game) — Company Manager, St. Louis Black Repertory Company
- Teresa Hudson-Handy (Williams), Spring '93 — Corporate Diversity Manager, Toyota Motor North America
- Norma Morris (Ewing), Winter '60 — Associate Dean, College of Education — Southern Illinois University at Carbondale
- Thelma Mothershed (Wair), Winter '61 — Member, Little Rock 9
- Lonnae O'Neal (Parker), Spring '85 — Reporter, Washington Post — Freelance Writer (Essence) — Author of White Girl? Cousin Kim is Passing, an infamous piece on racial identity in the US; originally published in the Post in 2000 and featured on ABC's Nightline.

- Barbara Rudd, Winter '69 — Vice President, Advertising — Johnson Publishing Company
- Cheryl M. Toles, Spring '77 — Artist
- Challis Waller (Lowe), Winter '65 — Executive Vice President of Human Resources, Public Affairs & Corporate Communications — Ryder System, Inc. — Chairman, Board of Directors, Florida A & M University
- Harriet Wilson (Barlow), Spring '71 — Assistant Vice President of Diversity Initiatives, University of Nevada-Las Vegas

DELTA BETA CHAPTER BASILEI

Beverly Smith	1961
Linda Alexander	1967 – 1968
Paulette Berry	1968 – 1969
Winona Clayton	1971
Peggy White (Yaseem Brown)	1971 – 1972
Cheryl Randolph	1972 – 1973
Lynn Cain	1973 – 1974
Pamela Akins	1974 – 1975
Sharen Watson	1975 – 1976
Gail L. Drish	1976
Susan M. Smith	1977
Pamela D. Hatchett	1978
Gena S. Gunn	1979
Debra A. Kimbrough	1980
Terri-Ann Stinnette	1981 – 1982
Audrey Wilson	1982
Erica F. Ginwright	1984
Lonnae O'Neal	1985
Tatia Jones	1986
Leah Denise Drue	1993
Sharon Thomas	1994
Teresa Hudson-Handy	1995
Rochelle Wilson	1997 – 1998
Christina Smith	1998 – 1999
Helena Paschall	2000
Shanna Harris	2001
Melynnda Demery	2001
Nancy Hanks	2001 – 2002
Shavell Pelote	2002 – 2004
Antoinette Arnold	2004 – 2005
Adrienne Head	2005 – 2007
Denell Scott	2007 – 2008
Staci Hurt	2008
Canita Martinez	2009
Carla Yerger	2010
Dontevia Hall	2010 – 2011
Autumn Anthony	2011 – 2012
Kaliah Liggons	2012 – 2013
Brittany Greathouse	2013 – 2014

Zeta Zeta Omega Chapter

EVANSVILLE, INDIANA
MARCH 13, 1954

First Row: Ada Chester, Agnes Mann, Alberta Stevenson, Willie Effie Thomas, Evelyn Hoberts, Allene Lamoert, Madaglene George, Jacqueline Neal. Second Row: Allouise Story, Lillian Bell, Ruth Slaughter, Rosalind Hunter of St. Louis, Mo., Mandleen George; and: Third Row: Thelma Lovelace, E. Carolyn Wilson, E. Joy Mays, Claudine Cabell, Bertha D. Hodges, Mary E. Coleman and Joyce Watson.

CHARTER MEMBERS

LILLIAN BELL	WYLENE MORSE*
CLAUDINE CABELL	JACQUELINE NEAL*
ADA CHESTER	MARGORIE PERRY
ELFRIEDA CHURCHILL	MARY ROBINSON
MADELINE GEORGE	ALBERTA STEVENSON
ALLENE LAMBERT	ALLOUISE STORY
THELMA LOVELACE	WILLIE EFFIE THOMAS
AGNES MANN	JOYCE WATSON
JOY MAYS	CAROLYN WILSON

*Surviving Members

Willie Effie Thomas, a native of Tyler, Texas and an Elementary School Teacher was inspired by the distinguished reputation of Alpha Kappa Alpha Sorority and became an Alpha Kappa Alpha woman. Upon arriving in Evansville, she dreamed of establishing a local chapter. She gathered some of her friends, fellow teachers and other AKA's in the tri-state area including graduated members of Beta Iota Chapter from the campus of Evansville College to discuss the possibilities. After much planning and many meetings, Zeta Zeta Omega Chapter was chartered on March 13, 1954 under the leadership of Regional Director, Evelyn Roberts and Supreme Basileus, Arnetta G. Wallace. The Charter Members were Lillian Bell, Claudine Cabell, Ada Chester, Elfrieda Churchill, Madeline George, Allene Lambert, Thelma Lovelace, Agnes Mann, Joy Mays, Wylene Morse, Jacqueline Neal, Marjorie Perry, Mary Robinson, Alberta Stevenson, Allouise Story, Willie Effie Thomas, Joy Watson and Carolyn Wilson. The chapter chartering was held at the McCurdy Hotel.

In the early years of the chapter many of the women of Zeta Zeta Omega were active in the NAACP and were pioneers in the local civil rights movement, organizing stand-ins and sit-ins in Evansville theatres, hotels and restaurants. They worked to give equal access to Mesker Park, lodging for women of color at the YWCA and to secure jobs from local companies that did not hire people of color. Zeta Zeta Omega women were in the forefront of the struggle for fair housing and education in the Evansville Community. As NAACP Youth Advisors, they also mentored young people to work for equality and justice locally and through travels to other cities.

These dedicated women fought to break down barriers to opportunities for school teachers of color who, while educated with advanced degrees and certifications, were often overlooked for administrative assignments and principal positions. Their efforts were rewarded when Jacqueline Neal was named the first Black Female principal in the Evansville Vanderburgh School Corporation. On the shoulders of this AKA woman, other AKA women ascended. Mattie Miller became assistant principal of Plaza Park Elementary then principal of Harper Elementary. Joan Finch was named the first Female Principal of an EVSC High School when she was assigned to Central High School. Cateena Johnson became principal at Delaware Elementary. Martharee Mays became principal at Stringtown Elementary. Tijuanna Tolliver was named principal of Stockwell Elementary. In addition to educators, Zeta Zeta Omega women have excelled in various careers and disciplines, positively impacting the Evansville Community. These careers include Social Workers, Nurse Practitioners, Counselors, Corporate Managers, University Administrators, Accounting and Finance Directors, Attorneys and Entrepreneurs.

More than a networking vehicle for outstanding educators and professionals, Zeta Zeta Omega was also a catalyst for cultural enlightenment and community service. During the late 1950's and the early 1960's, Zeta Zeta Omega held Debutante Balls in the Rose Room of the McCurdy Hotel annually. These elegant galas educated young ladies in the social graces and trained young men in gentlemanly behavior. Ada Chester and Mattie Miller gained acclaim for their "charm school" expertise. Parents financially sacrificed to enable their daughters to participate in this coveted social event.

In the early years of its existence, Zeta Zeta Omega advised Beta Iota undergraduate chapter on the campus of University of Evansville until Beta Iota's dissolution in July 1982.

Since the chapter's inception in 1954, several projects and activities have been sponsored by the chapter to foster the ideals of Alpha Kappa Alpha Sorority. Zeta Zeta Omega has supported the international programs and targets of each international administration of the sorority. These programs included the Charles Drew Blood Drive, "Reading is Fundamental" book giveaways to under-privileged elementary school children, a Young Author's program to encourage the development of writing skills, the adoption in 2005 of Caze Elementary School to participate in the Ivy Reading AKAdemy, Voter Registration and Get Out the Vote, Family Day in the Park, Pink goes Red for women's heart disease awareness, participation in the YWCA Chalk It Up domestic violence awareness campaign and the Emerging Young Leaders mentoring program targeting middle school girls.

One of the chapter's main focuses for the past 20+ years has been "Breakfast with Santa" which began in 1985. Through this event, Zeta Zeta Omega provides a holiday memory for over 150 inner-city African American children each year and provides information to parents for their economic empowerment.

Starting in 1987 and continuing through 1991, Zeta Zeta Omega Chapter held its "Atlantic City on the Ohio," a casino night fundraiser. In the spirit of friendly gaming patrons vied for AKA dollars that were used to bid on prizes donated by local businesses.

Zeta Zeta Omega continues various fundraiser events such as Balls, Bowl-a-thons for Scholarships, plays and dances. Over the years, Zeta Zeta Omega has raised over $120,000 to provide scholarships for college bound students and to provide other services and projects that benefit the Evansville Community.

Zeta Zeta Omega Chapter has always fostered a can-do attitude. In 1992, with less than 45 active members, Zeta Zeta Omega was the prime host chapter of the Central Regional Conference.

Throughout its existence, Zeta Zeta Omega has supported the international program goals and targets of each administration. In addition to the above, projects have included blood drives, "Reading is Fundamental" book give-a-ways to underprivileged elementary school children, Black Dollar Day, and the Young Authors program. In February 2005, Zeta Zeta Omega adopted Caze Elementary School to participate in the Ivy Reading AKAdemy. Second grade was the grade selected to prepare students for ISTEP testing in reading comprehension. Sorors of Zeta Zeta Omega willingly volunteer their free time to support this program and to prepare our young leaders of the future.

In subsequent years, Zeta Zeta Omega actively participated in the "2008 Centennial Walk" celebrating Alpha Kappa Alpha's 100 year anniversary, "Pink Goes Red" for Heart Disease awareness, Asthma Awareness initiatives, Tree Plantings on Arbor Day, participation in the YWCA's "Chalk It Up" Domestic Violence Awareness campaign and Emerging Young Leaders activities.

Today, Zeta Zeta Omega is again advising an undergraduate chapter, Tau Rho, chartered on April 21, 2013 and located on the campus of the University of Southern Indiana.

Reflecting the values of the women who founded Alpha kappa Alpha Sorority on the campus of Howard University in 1908, Zeta Zeta Omega women continue striving to provide "Service to All Mankind" thru advocacy, awareness and action. Our illustrious history is still being written.

Zeta Zeta Omega Advised Beta Iota Chapter Until the Chapter's Dissolution in July 1982. And Currently Advises Tau Rho Since its Chartering on the Campus of the University of Southern Indiana in April 2013.

Zeta Zeta Omega Chapter Advises Tau Rho Chapter.

ZETA ZETA OMEGA CHAPTER BASILEI

Willie Effie Thomas	1954 – 1955
Alberta Stevenson	1956 – 1957
Lillian Bell	1958 – 1959
Ada Chester	1960 – 1961
Carolyn Wilson	1962 – 1962
Mattie Miller	1963 – 1968
Marjorie Perry	1969 – 1970
Allouise Story	1971 – 1972
Jacqueline Neal	1973 – 1974
Irene Saucer	1975 – 1976
Cateena Johnson	1977 – 1978
Joyce Washington	1979 – 1980
Jennifer Miller	1981 – 1982
Cora Hall	1983 – 1984
Frankye Calloway	1985 – 1986
Frances Johnson	1987 – 1987
Jennifer Miller Douglas	1988 – 1989
Earsie Kelley	1989 – 1990
Vicki White	1991 – 1992
Edmonia Pringle	1993 – 1994
Cateena Johnson	1995 – 1996
Avril Miller	1997 – 1998
Carla Rice	1999 – 2000
Kimberly Redding	2001 – 2004
Deborah Raspberry	2005 – 2008
Pamela Hopson	2009 – 2013

Maude Lillian Mann

13TH CENTRAL REGIONAL DIRECTOR
DECEMBER 1954 – AUGUST 1958

Soror Mann was initiated into Beta Chapter in 1940 and transferred to Theta Omega in 1942. She received the B.A. degree from Lewis Institute and the M.A. degree from Northwestern University. She taught at the Mendel Elementary School.

During her administration as Basileus of Theta Omega Chapter a program was initiated to encourage sorors to get to know each other. At each Chapter meeting five sorors were introduced and a brief resume was given to the body on each.

A mental health program for adolescents was held and the chapter funded physical examinations for each student entering the Coleman School in Chicago at a cost of one dollar per student. Immediately following her tenure as Basileus of Theta Omega Chapter (1951 – 1953), Soror Mann was elected Central Regional Director. Her interest in youth and health were carried into her administration as Central Regional Director. She presided over the 22nd, 23rd and 24th Central Regional Conferences. During her tenure as Central Regional Director there were no chapters chartered in the region and the state of Kentucky joined the ranks of Central Region.

Soror Maude Lillian Mann served admirably as Central Regional Director from December 1954 – August 1958. Four months after the end of her tenure as Central Regional Director, Soror Mann became an Ivy Beyond The Wall in December 1958.

Annetta Moten Lawson

14TH CENTRAL REGIONAL DIRECTOR
AUGUST 1958 – DECEMBER 1962

Soror Annetta Moten Lawson was elected Central Regional Director at the Washington, D.C. Fiftieth Boule of Alpha Kappa Alpha Sorority, Inc. Her administration was guided by the National Program theme "Assessing the Strength of Alpha Kappa Alpha For Future Investment For Service."

Soror Lawson was initiated into Alpha Chapter at Howard University and received her undergraduate degree from Howard University. She received a Master's degree from Boston College and Butler University and later affiliated with Alpha Mu Omega Chapter, Indianapolis, Indiana.

She was a teacher in the Indianapolis Public School System, having taught at School #17 and Crispus Attucks High School. She retired from Crispus Attucks in 1973 after many years of service. She had previously been employed by the YWCA in Philadelphia in supervision and administration.

She was a member of the American Federation of Teachers, Indiana Retired Teachers Association, Indianapolis Links, Inc., the Patrician, Les Finesseurs and Les Femmes bridge clubs, Fortnightly Literary Club, and the senior guild of Alpha Home.

With her warm smile and pleasant personality she presided over the 25th, 26th, 27th and 28th Central Regional Conferences. Also during her term of office she chartered Delta Omicron, Northern Illinois University in DeKalb; Eta Kappa Omega, East Chicago, Indiana; and Eta Mu Omega, South Bend, Indiana. Soror Lawson became an Ivy Beyond The Wall on December 8, 1986.

Delta Omicron Chapter

NORTHERN ILLINOIS UNIVERSITY
DEKALB, ILLINOIS
MAY 22, 1960

Top Row — Left to Right: Betty Byrd and Lynn Campbell; Second Row: Gwen Davis, Loretta Dunn, Norma Gant; Third Row: Betty Gunn, Barbara Hinton, Eurise Joseph; Fourth Row: Donna Lucas and Ethel Richards.

CHARTER MEMBERS

GWENDOLYN BRAXTON	BETTY GUNN
BETTY BYRD	BARBARA HINTON
LYNN CAMPBELL	EURISE JOSEPH
GWENDOLYN DAVIS	EDNA KELLEY
LORETTA DUNN	DONNA LUCAS
NORMA GANT	ETHEL RICHARDS
	WANDA SMITH

In 1958, twelve young women: Ethel Richards, Ladonna Watson, Norma Gant, Martha Collier, Elizabeth Gunn, Barbra Hinton, Eurice Joseph, Eleanor Key, Donna Lucas, Loretta Dunn, Ethlynn Campbell and Judy Ashby met and decided that there was a need for an organization that would unite the African American Women at Northern Illinois University. They had a vision of being a part of an organization that accepted and respected them, as well as one that would allow them to play an active role socially, charitably and intellectually.

In 1958, such an organization did not exist at Northern Illinois University. There were many white sororities on campus; however they did not accept Black members. Also, in order to use campus facilities for any activity, students had to belong to a university organization.

Determined to pursue a way to become a viable part of the university and tired of having to travel to Sycamore, IL, which had a small African American settlement, for any social outlet these young ladies pursued their dream. The dream to form their own organization with the hope that one day they would become a national organization.

The first stumbling block was the university's policy that stated that any student organization needed a faculty sponsor. Since there were no Black female faculty members at the Northern Illinois

University at that time, Dr. Elizabeth Lang, a Jewish Physical Education Professor, agreed to sponsor the group and Tau Delta Sigma was born. Tau Delta Sigma existed as an organization for a year and a half and sponsored programs such as: Homecoming and Father's Day Teas and Banquets, all-school mixers, making scrap books and tote bags for children's hospitals and baskets for needy families, to name a few.

After careful deliberation, it was decided by the group that the goals of Alpha Kappa Alpha Sorority Inc., were most congruent to those of Tau Delta Sigma. Thus on May 22, 1960, Delta Omicron was chartered as the 107th chapter of Alpha Kappa Alpha Sorority Inc. The Charter Members are: Gwendolyn Braxton, Betty Byrd, Ethlynn Campbell, Gwendolyn Davis, Loretta Dunn, Norma Gant, Wanda Smith, Betty Gunn, Barbara Hinton, Eurice Joseph, Edna Kelley, Donna Lucas and Ethel Richards.

Since 1960, Delta Omicron has had the distinction of having many "first" on the campus of Northern Illinois University:

- Dorothy Jackson (1968) was the first Black Homecoming Queen in 1969 sponsored by the Black Student Union;
- Sharon Stevens was the first editor of the first black newspaper published in 1969-1970;
- Phyllis McIntosh was the first Black NIU cheerleader in 1970;
- Joan Dameron received one of the highest scores (980), ever achieved by a student at NIU on the GRE exam in 1972;
- Tiffany Abrahams was Miss Black Illinois, 1992-1993, while a student at NIU;
- Carol Briggs (1974) was the first Black Homecoming Queen sponsored by NIU in 1975;
- Tiffany Abrahams was Miss Black Illinois, 1992-1993, while a student at NIU

In 1982, Xi Nu Omega became the graduate chapter for Delta Omicron and in 1988, the chapter initiated "The Pink and Green Extravaganza" which is the chapter's major fund raising activity.

Delta Omicron is involved in many community service projects. Sorors have participated with the Illinois Department of Transportation raising awareness of wearing seatbelts and not drinking while driving. Seminars have been conducted to raise awareness of SIDS (Sudden Infant Death Syndrome) and women's health issues. In economics the chapter has sponsored seminars on financial planning and economics in the African American community.

Delta Omicron is a 100 percent EAF chapter and has a proud history of supporting the International Program and is committed to Sisterhood, Scholarship and Service as evidenced by the numerous awards received at Regional Conferences.

Delta Omicron celebrated 50 years of service on May 22, 2010 on NIU's campus. Sorors representing every year were in attendance at the celebration. The DO history continues with the recent initiation of 17 young college women on November 20, 2011.

Delta Omicron Chapter Basilei

Eleanor Key	1960
Ethel Richards	1962
Gwen Davis	1963
Elaine Thigpen	1964
Alma Roberts	1965
Janice Bell	1966
Marilyn Jennings	1967
Linda Mills/Cynthia Draper	1968
Ella Gray	1969

Phyllis Moore	1970
Jewel Willis/Joan Dameron	1971
Patricia Hill	1972
Vanora Grover/Floradine Bell	1973
Polly Bridges	1974
Robin Reed	1975
Carol Briggs	1976
Delores Cooper	1978
Evelyn Smith	1981
Dalphine Anthony	1982
Robin Wilson	1983
Romona Davis	1984
Renee Harris/Carolyn Franklin	1985
Joy Terrell/Linda Perry	1986
Linda Perry	1987
Rosalind Agee	1988
Carmencita Johnson	1989
Michelle Smith	1990
Kimberly Burt	1991
Kai Love	1992
Monique Davis	1993
Hope Towns	1994
Neelege Terrell	1995
Terronni Johnson	1995
Terronni Johnson	1996
Rubye Wilson/Stephanie Avery	1997
Kelli T. Bentley/Tiffany Gordon	1998
Tiffany Gordon	1999
Andrienne Bond	2000
Courtney Jackson	2000
Sarah Kilgore	2001 – 2002
Kimberly Williamson	2002
Gina Marie Jones	2003 – 2004
Jasmine Wideman	2006 – 2007
Tiffany Smith	2008
Tiffany Via	2009
Lonnette Miller	2010
Jasmyne Portee	2011-2012
Jessica Gray	2012-2013

Eta Kappa Omega Chapter

East Chicago, Indiana
February 20, 1960

Charter Members

LUCY BROOKS	AMELIA JACKSON
JOHNNIE UPSHAW BROOKS	HATTIE LEONARD
CLARA BROWNING	PATRICIA MCKINNIE LOWE
WARRIES DANIELS BUGGS	BARBARA MOORE
MARY CHAVIS	THELMA COMER MORRIS
ERNESTINE COFIELD	ELIZABETH PARRISH
MAXINE WINBUSH COLE	MADONNA PERKINS
LAURETTA FACTORY	ANNA MARIE PORTER
MYRTLE LEWIS FIKES	EMMA RANSOM
OCIE FLYNN	MOZELLE WILSON RIVERS
RUTH HARDAWAY GROSS	LETHA COFIELD SNEAD
JORITHA WALKER HARPER	SEDALIA TURK
HELEN HARPER	BARBARA HARRIS WEBB
DOROTHY HENDERSON	JESSIE GOODE WHITE
	ANN HARRELL WILSON

Eta Kappa Omega Chapter began as an idea of two sorors, Hattie Leonard and Dorothy Henderson (who were active in a nearby chapter) in 1958. The two accessed the situation and determined there were enough graduate Alpha Kappa Alpha Sorors in the cities of East Chicago and Hammond to begin a new chapter. The new chartered chapter would service those cities. The chapter colonized under the name "FRIENDS." Sorors began an association with Gamma Psi Omega Chapter from whom there was much support and in turn were supportive of Gamma Psi Omega Chapter's activities — namely "Fashionetta®" and Ebony Fashion Fair. The association continues with the mutual support of these two chapters.

After two years of organizing, Eta Kappa Omega Chapter was chartered in February of 1960. The focus of the chapter was on the local and national programs of Alpha Kappa Alpha Sorority, Inc. There were many endeavors to benefit youth and the communities. They included the following:

- Free Dental Screening for children in the West Calumet neighborhood of East Chicago with services donated by Dr. Jerry Henderson, husband of Soror Dorothy Henderson.
- Children's Benefit Annual Toy Dance around the Christmas holiday with a donated toy(s) as admittance to the formal event.
- Sponsored Cultural Enrichment activities for the two communities, including concerts and off-Broadway plays.
- Health Forums with emphasis on Black health issues.
- First sponsors of the local Cotillion and Beautillion held in 1967. Many of the debutants participating in the event went on to become Alpha Kappa Alpha sorors.
- The Shoe Box Give-a-Way provided school supplies to needy youth.
- AKATeens was a mentoring program for adolescents and teens offering guidance and support in various areas.
- "Take a Senior to Breakfast" was a real treat for senior citizens. Each soror treated one to three senior citizens to breakfast at one of the areas restaurants.

Many of the programs have been altered to meet the needs of youth and the community today but our commitment to service continues strong. Some additional programs include these:

- Annual Fall Scholarship Dance offering food and entertainment while benefiting our scholarship fund.
- "Men of Valor" held annually in June recognizing African American men in particular professions servicing the two communities. This formal event benefits our scholarship fund as well.
- The Lauretta Factory/MaryAnn Jimerson Scholarships are available for graduating high school seniors needing financial assistance who have a 2.5 GPA or higher. The scholarship is named for two dedicated sorors who are Ivies Beyond the Wall. We also offer the matching Presidential Scholarships to local high school students.
- "A Day On, Not a Day Off" in commemoration of Dr. Martin Luther King, Jr. is supported in a variety of ways — attending prayer breakfasts, ecumenical services and a candle light walk. We incorporate this activity with a Voter's Registration effort. Chapter sorors participate in one or more of the events.
- The annual Easter Egg Hunt is co-sponsored with two other local organizations offering an egg hunt, baskets, toys, and bikes given as prizes, along with a visit from a "chocolate Easter Bunny." As part of our literacy thrust, the chapter uses this opportunity to offer free books to the children attendees.
- AKA Coat Day is held in October donating coats and business attire to a local homeless shelter, churches and a battered women's shelter.
- Family Volunteer Day includes food basket donations to at-risk families and elderly residents. Sorors spend time with the recipients as they share the donations.
- The chapter participates in the East Chicago Health Department's American Cancer Society's Breast Cancer Walk-a-Thon. Sorors walk in the event, host an information booth, representing a group, and makes a yearly monetary donation to the worthy cause. Eta Kappa Omega Chapter has received trophies for largest number of participants.
- AKA Mix is the Sisterly Relations activity held prior to each meeting with games, food and fun. Volunteers alternate monthly which is a welcome treat giving sorors the opportunity to show their creative talents in their own way.
- Reactivation efforts continue inviting inactive sorors to our monthly chapter meetings. The chapter gained gained regional recognition at the Tea Rose Level; as reported in The *Ivy Leaf*, for reclaiming sorors.

50 Years of Service to All Mankind — On Saturday, February 20, 2010 at the Ameristar Casino and Hotel, Eta Kappa Omega celebrated its 50th Anniversary "Golden Gala." Sorors past and present circulated throughout the room reminiscing and viewing the chapter scrapbooks and other chapter memorabilia. Seven Charter members: Soror Warries Daniels Buggs, Soror Maxine Winbush Cole, Soror Ocie Flynn, Soror Ruth Hardaway Gross, Soror Dorothy Henderson, Soror Mozell Wilson Rivers and Soror Ann Harrell Wilson were present. These sorors were honored for their trailblazing efforts and also treated sorors with tales of their day as "Friends" and how they ultimately became Eta Kappa Omega. A chapter photo was taken to commemorate this golden moment. The event was uplifting, inspiring and filled with excitement. Sorors left with their AKA spirits re-energized, bonds of sisterhood were strengthened and their passion to serve was reignited. We invited inactive members to join us as we continue to serve the communities of East Chicago and Hammond and as we embark on our next 50 years of service. Each year since, the chapter celebrates its Anniversary with a themed event.

50 Years of Service and Beyond — While continuing legacy programs that still benefit the community, new programs and fundraisers have been implemented in an effort to increase the visibility of the chapter and its initiatives, to support community efforts and create awareness of key issues impacting our community.

Martin Luther King Day — The chapter continues yearly support for MLK Day "A Day On, Not A Day Off." Over the years MLK Day has been expanded to include support of Veterans, recognition of outstanding Alpha Phi Alpha Men in the community and the Annual NAACP Breakfast where we serve as hostesses. The chapter has been recognized by the East Chicago Public Library for its continued support of MLK Day.

Mobile Food Pantry — The chapter developed a partnership with the Northwest Indiana Food Depository to help feed residents of the community. After unloading and separating food items (bread, canned goods, dried vegetables, boxed goods and soups) sorors pack bags for individuals in need. The chapter donated eco-friendly bags to ensure each person has a sizeable bag to fit all their items. Sorors also participate in the "Back Pack Program" filling weekend lunch bags with food for students who are in need of food over the weekend. The chapter has been recognized by the Northwest Indiana Food Depository for outstanding service to the community.

Child Abuse Prevention — The chapter participates in a walk-a-thon with other community organizations to promote child abuse prevention and awareness.

Health — Each year, the chapter organizes and participates in a number of service projects designed to bring awareness to various health issues impacting the African American community; Diabetes Awareness (focus on juvenile diabetes), AKA Goes Red (American Heart Association), Breast Cancer Awareness Walks, Bowling for a Cause (Breast Cancer Awareness) and Stroke Prevention.

Ivy to Pearls Workshop Series — Young ladies 6th through 12th grade are invited to have lunch with chapter members. Prior to the luncheon, two workshops are held. Workshop I discusses self-image and mental health. Workshop II focuses on college and career choices. (Subjects Vary) Open dialogue is had on topics of education, self-esteem, relationships and sorority life. This program was eventually transitioned into our EYL program.

Boys to Men Workshop Series — Under our ESP Program, young men ages 11 to 18 were invited to participate in an informational forum with the theme of Educate…Support…Prepare. Men from local organizations, East Chicago Police Department and College Admission Officers educated young men who wanted to excel in their future on conflict management, career choices and money management.

Local Church Partnerships

- Breast Cancer Awareness — In the month of October 3 breast cancer awareness events are held simultaneously at local churches to promote breast cancer awareness. Pink ribbons and informational pamphlets are provided to all members of the congregation.
- Meet the Candidates Forum — Chapter sorors organized a meet and greet with local candidates for the upcoming election. The community had the opportunity to meet with the mayoral, city treasurer and council-men at large candidates prior to the election to hear directly from the candidates about their platforms. The meet and greet was held at Zion Missionary Baptist Church.
- Diabetes Alert Day — Sorors encouraged families, friends and colleagues to take the Diabetes Risk Test to find out if they are at risk of developing type 2 diabetes. The chapter collaborated with local churches and schools to administer the test.
- Spirit Day Promotion — The chapter participates annually in Spirit Day at Zion Missionary Baptist Church. All members of the Divine 9 are represented to promote higher education and awareness of sorority/fraternity mission, goals and initiatives.
- Launch and Implementation of EYL — In 2010 under the leadership of Supreme Basileus, Soror Carolyn House-Stewart and Eta Kappa Omega Basileus, Soror Schundra Hubbard Eta Kappa Omega launched the Emerging Young Leaders Initiative. Girls 6th through 8th grade and their parents/guardians were invited to an information session to learn about the EYL program and participation requirements. Four young ladies were part of the original selection of girls, Kayla Broady, Chelsea Jackson, Antoinette Phillips and Nuri Muhammad.
- Since the program began, the chapter has provided mentorship for the young ladies, supervised them during service projects, organized fun activities (bowling and pizza party), recognized them for their academic achievements and oversaw their participation in the Chicagoland EYL Summit. As participants of the EYL Summit since its inception, they attended workshops focused on health, self-image, effective use of social media, traits of a healthy relationship, public speaking, conflict management, body image and fashion etiquette.

Fundraisers

- Breast Cancer Breakfast — Honored breast cancer survivors in the East Chicago and Hammond, IN communities. In addition, the breakfast raised awareness of breast cancer and its impact in the African American community. The importance of mammograms and how it aids in early detection was shared. An aggressive form of breast cancer, triple negative breast cancer, was highlighted. The Laini Fluellen Charities was acknowledged for their work in the community and awarded a financial contribution toward their efforts to fight breast cancer.
- Annual Holiday Bazaar — Local entrepreneurs and small business owners have an opportunity to gain visibility, showcase and sell their goods and services. Vendors sell a variety of products including greek paraphernalia, women and men's clothing, jewelry, Christmas decorations, art, purses and bed linen and cooking products. Other local businesses donate items for the silent auction. All proceeds benefit recipients of our Loretta Factory Scholarship Award, Mary Ann Jimerson Scholarship Award and Service Award.

Eta Kappa Omega continues to move forward in service and sisterhood. Chapter members will continue to implement programs that support our national initiatives and benefit the community we serve and dedicate ourselves to the ideals and beliefs of Alpha Kappa Alpha Sorority, Inc.

Notable Mention:

As Basileus of Eta Kappa Omega, Soror Schundra Hubbard was the first Northwest Indiana Chapter Basileus invited to join the Chicagoland Basilei Council since the Council's inception. In 2011 Soror Schundra Served as Anti-Basileus of the Council where she served as Chairman of the Emerging Young Leaders Youth Summit, a collaborative partnership among the 16 participating chapters of the council. In 2012, Soror Schundra served as Basileus of the Chicagoland Basilei Council.

Eta Kappa Omega Advised Epsilon Rho Chapter Until 1980.

Eta Kappa Omega Chapter Basilei

Hattie Leonard	1960 – 1961
Rosemary Mitchell	1962 – 1963
Dorothy Henderson	1964 – 1965
Ocie Flynn	1966 – 1967
Hattie Leonard	1968 – 1969
Dorothy Henderson	1970 – 1971
Clara Browning	1972 – 1973
Ernestine Cofield	1974 – 1975
Ann Holland	1976 – 1978
Kathryn Brantley	1979 – 1980
Maryann Jimerson	1981 – 1982
Cynthia Warner	1983 – 1986
Tracey Williams	1987 – 1988
Gwendolyn Hatcher	1989 – 1990
Thelma Morris	1991 – 1992
Wilsetta Mitchell	1993 – 1994
Ann Holland	1995 – 2996
Loris Bradford	1997 – 1998
Judith Bridgeman	1999 – 2002
Paulina Johnson	2003 – 2004
Michelle Rushing	2005 – 2008
Schundra Hubbard	2009 – 2012

Eta Mu Omega Chapter

South Bend, Indiana
March 26, 1960

Left to Right Standing: Bessie Woolridge, Josephine Curtis, Ruth Bell, Effie Myrtle Roe, Bernice Ware, Mayme H. Ross, Mattie Carey, Marguerite Pinkard, Kathrynn Jeffries and Inez Johnson. Seated: Mary Mullins, Joan Ballard, Maenell Hamilin Newsome, Past Central Regioonal Director, Annetta Moten Lawson, Central Regional Director, Ruby Jarrett-Joyce and Ada Yates Parr, Not Pictured: Y. Ernestine Grayson and Elizabeth Fletcher Allen.

Charter Members

ELIZABETH FLETCHER ALLEN	ALLEN INEZ JOHNSON
JOAN BALLARD	MARY MULLINS
RUTH BELL	ADA YATES PARR
MATTIE CAREY	MARGUERITE PINKARD
JOSEPHINE CURTIS	EFFIE MYRTLE ROE
Y. ERNESTINE GRAYSON	MAYME H. ROSS
KATHRYNN JEFFRIES	BERNICE WARE
RUBY JARRETT-JOYCE	BESSIE WOOLRIDGE

Eta Mu Omega began as the dream of a young college woman who had been active in Alpha Kappa Alpha Sorority, Inc. She had experienced all the benefits of sisterhood and service to the community inherent in being in an undergraduate chapter and did not relish the thought of leaving them behind. After graduating from college in 1950, Soror Ruby Jarrett attended Boule that year in Kansas City, Missouri. She returned to South Bend, Indiana, inspired and determined to start a chapter.

After ten years of perseverance, Soror Jarrett received a commitment from fifteen other Sorors who were college graduates and interested in starting a chapter. On March 26, 1960, Eta Mu Omega was chartered into Alpha Kappa Alpha Sorority, Inc. The ceremony was held at the Morris Inn on the campus of the University of Notre Dame with Central Regional Director, Soror Annetta Moten Lawson presiding. The first chapter meeting was held on April 10, 1960 at the home of Soror Bessie Woolridge. At this time, the officers were installed.

Eight of the chapter's charter members are still active - professionally and in the sorority — in South Bend and various cities across the country. Soror Joan Ballard is a retired teacher residing in Colorado; Soror Mattie Carey is a retired social worker who lives in Washington, D.C.; Soror Y. Ernestine Grayson is retired from the South Bend (Indiana) Community School Corporation (SBCSC); Soror Kathrynn Jeffries is a retired teacher, residing in Michigan; Soror Ruby Jarrett Joyce is retired and residing in Herndon, Virginia (and is a member of Lambda Kappa Omega of Fairfax, Virginia); Soror Mary Mullins is on the faculty at Tuskegee University; Soror Marguerite Pinkard is a retired teacher, residing in Nashville, Tennessee; Soror Mayme H. Ross is a retired teacher in Los Angeles, California. Sorors Allen, Bell, Curtis, Johnson, Parr, Roe, Ware and Woolridge have joined the Ivies Beyond the Wall. Soror Effie Myrtle Roe was a charter member of Theta Rho Omega Chapter. Soror Y. Ernestine Grayson is the only charter member still residing in the South Bend community. Since our last historical update only two charter members are living, Sorors Y. Ernestine Grayson and Ruby Jarrett Joyce.

Eta Mu Omega's first major service project, which spanned a number of years, was an outreach to women who lived in the apartments that belonged to the South Bend Housing Authority. With the support and guidance of Soror Josephine Curtis, who was director of the Housing Authority at the time, the chapter provided programs and services that helped these women take pride in their homes and encouraged them to project a positive attitude within their families.

Over the years, Eta Mu Omega's annual programs have incorporated the targets and goals of the international organization, touching the lives of the South Bend community while enhancing the bonds of sisterhood within the chapter. A partial list of programs includes: work with the Babies-at-Risk Program and the Memorial Hospital Healthy Babies Program; implementation of a comprehensive, weekly reading program and an annual, month-long summer reading, writing and self-esteem program for elementary school children; involvement in a weekly mentoring program with disadvantaged teenage girls; sponsoring of dance troupes, theatrical groups and cultural, educational and career forums and seminars in the community; donations of Thanksgiving and Christmas baskets to needy families; volunteer work for the Northern Indiana Historical Society; support of the Women's Shelter, St. Margaret's House and other programs that help the disadvantage women; participation in various projects with the American Lung Association, Christmas Seals and the American Cancer Society; visiting, caroling and assisting at several nursing homes in the city; presenting an annual Senior Citizens' and Women's Health Forum that provides health and care information for the women of the community; donations to the United Negro College Fund, the National Council of Negro Women, the Urban League, and life membership in the NAACP.

The chapter has always used local and national program projects to strengthen the bonds of sisterhood. Black Dollar Month provides an opportunity for Sorors and their families to shop and fellowship together. The chapter sets aside one Sunday each year for Sorors to worship together. The dinner/dance and Christmas Mixed Social are an important part of our program, as is the summer family picnic. Other Greek-letter organizations are invited to join in our Survival Walk. The Eta Mu Omega Singers sing at chapter and chapter-sponsored community functions.

We are continuing our commitment to community through the Global Leadership and Timeless Service Initiatives.

Social Justice and Human Rights Initiative:

Through this initiative we are able to continue our collaboration with St. Margaret's House with the following programs:

- Winter Walk
- Ice Cream Social
- Fashion Show
- Workshops

- Voter Registration
- Toiletry Donations

Also under this initiative we participated with the YWCA in the following activities:

- Penny Harvest
- Christmas Gift Wrapping Project
- **Health Initiative:**

Under the Health Initiative Eta Mu Omega has participated in several health fairs with African American Women In Touch, a local grass roots breast cancer organization.

- **Leadership Initiative:**

Eta Mu Omega concentrated not only in cultivating the leaders in our sorority but also recognized the leadership in our Michiana community.

Debutante Cotillion History:

The chapter held its first Debutante Scholarship Cotillion Ball in 1962, with Sorors providing most of the finances for pre-ball activities and scholarships. The goal has been to repeat this function every two or three years. At the March 25, 1995, Ball, seventeen young ladies were awarded more than $8,100 in scholarships. The debutantes raised most of these funds.

The Cotillion continues to grow; in 2013 we will introduce 36 young ladies and their escorts to the Michiana community. We expect to award over $20,000 in scholarships to the Debutantes.

Fashion Show:

The chapter presents an annual Fashion Show Luncheon, using members of local women's organizations as models. Originally begun as a scholarship fundraiser, this event has become a social function that the community expects to occur each year. It is now presented as a service, with the funds raised being an added benefit. The fashion show has been replaced with a new fundraiser "Jazz In Pink."

Beginning in 2005, Eta Mu Omega became a member of the South Bend Chapter of the National Pan-Hellenic Council. The group has sponsored several fundraising social events, donating the proceeds to local high schools. As part of the Pan-Hellenic Council and in conjunction with other local African American Churches and organizations, we held a successful citywide voter registration drive. In 2006 we partnered with Delta Sigma Theta with their girls conference. We assisted with the financial, career and health workshops. To end 2012 the Divine 9 of South Bend participated in the Civil Rights Heritage Center's Christmas tree competition. The purpose of this competition was in celebration of the 150th year anniversary of the Emancipation Proclamation signed by President Abraham Lincoln. The pink and green tree was absolutely beautiful.

Eta Mu Omega's name and commitment to community service are further immortalized by its purchase of a history brick, bearing the chapter's name and chartering date, which is part of the walkway on the grounds of the Northern Indiana Center for History. In 2010 Eta Mu Omega celebrated 50 years of tireless service to the Michiana community. A luncheon was held honoring our Charter Members and Golden Sorors. Eta Mu Omega, which began as the dream of one Soror, continues to build the future through service to all mankind, while fostering the bonds of true sisterhood.

Chapter Members Who Have Held International/National Office or Been Elected to the International/National Nominating Committee

Gloria E. Bond	Central Regional Director	1978-1982

Eta Mu Omega Chapter Basilei

Ruby Jarrett-Joyce	1960 – 1961
Y. Ernestine Grayson	1961 – 1962
Joanne Ballard	1963 – 1964
Kathrynn Jeffries	1965 – 1965
Ruth Bell	1966 – 1966
Ruby Jarrett-Joyce	1967 – 1969
Phyllis Bowerman (resigned because of illness)	1970 – 1970
Gloria Bond	1970 – 1971
Inez Johnson	1972 – 1973
Elizabeth Wolf	1974 – 1974
Alma Powell	1975 – 1976
Iris Outlaw	1977 – 1978
Carolyn Threatt	1979 – 1980
Maureen Roberts	1981 – 1982
Ellen Sayles	1983 – 1984
Felice Dudley-Collins	1985 – 1986
Linda McDougal	1987 – 1988
Wilma Gary	1989 – 1990
Virginia Calvin	1991 – 1992
Linda Murphy	1993 – 1994
Velma Harris	1995 – 1996
Carolyn Threatt	1997 – 1998
Felice Dudley-Collins	1999 – 2000
LaTanya Reese	2001 – 2001
Terrilyn C. Walton	2001 – 2002
Irene Eskridge	2002 – 2002
Giovanna Edwards	2003 – 2006
Iris Outlaw	2007 – 2008
Loretha Buchanon	2009 – 2010
Carolyn Threatt	2011 – 2014

Lee Anna W. Shelburne

15TH CENTRAL REGIONAL DIRECTOR
DECEMBER 1962 – AUGUST 1966

Lee Anna W. Shelburne was nominated at the 1962 Central Regional Conference in Evansville, Indiana, and elected Central Regional Director at the December 1962 Boule in Detroit, Michigan. Soror Shelburne's served for a three-and-a-half year term.

The three-and-a-half year term was a unique situation. At the 1962 Boule the Alpha Kappa Alpha's Study Commission, presented a recommendation to the Boule that would change the Boules schedule of every eighteen months to every two years, in the summer months. The recommendation passed, and those officers elected at this Boule would serve an additional year-and-a-half, or until the next Boule scheduled for August 1964 (three-and-a-half years later).

Soror Shelburne was initiated into Beta Epsilon Chapter, Louisville, Kentucky, on November 2, 1936, and later transferred her membership to Eta Omega where she served as Basileus, Anti-Basileus, Tamiouchos, Parliamentarian and Graduate Advisor. Her professional career included serving as an elementary school teacher and a school librarian.

As Central Regional Director, Soror Shelburne initiated the monthly newsletter of the Regional Director, the Regional Nominating Committee and the celebrating of Joint Chapter Founders Day. She presided over the 29th, 30th, 31st and 32nd Central Regional Conferences. Soror Shelburne did not charter any chapters but she laid the groundwork for the chartering of two chapters in the region.

The 64th Central Regional Conference adopted a resolution presented by Central Regional Director, Peggy Lewis LeCompte in memoriam to Soror Lee Anna Shelbune for her love, time, and service to Alpha Kappa Alpha Sorority. Soror Shelburne became an Ivy Beyond the Wall in 1998.

Ordie Amelia Roberts

16TH CENTRAL REGIONAL DIRECTOR
AUGUST 1966 – AUGUST 1970

Initiated into Gamma Chapter in 1934, Soror Ordie Roberts received a B.S. in Physical Education from the University of Illinois in 1936. She joined the faculty at A & T College in Greensboro, North Carolina, where she headed the Women's Department of Physical Education.

In the early forties, Soror Roberts returned to her birth place, Chicago, and began her teaching career at DuSable High School. Following several years as a physical education instructor at DuSable she transferred to Doolittle Elementary School where she remained until her retirement.

Soror Roberts joined Theta Omega Chapter in 1943 where she held several offices including Basileus. In Soror Roberts own words "I had the good fortune of being Basileus of Theta Omega during Alpha Kappa Alpha's 50th Anniversary."

Soror Roberts was elected Central Regional Director in 1966. During her administration, the idea of a chapter "Round-Up" as a reactivation method was introduced. She presided over the 33rd, 34th, 35th, and 36th, Central Regional Conferences, and chartered eight chapters of Alpha Kappa Alpha: Beta Phi, Gamma Chi, Epsilon Delta, Epsilon Zeta, Epsilon Eta, Epsilon Iota, Epsilon Xi and Theta Rho Omega. She holds the distinction of having chartered all of the undergraduate chapters starting with the Greek letter Epsilon in Central Region.

Soror Roberts had a down-to-earth, no-nonsense approach to solving the problems of the region. But, more importantly, Soror Ordie will always be remembered for her unstinting support of Gamma Chapter. She served on the National Housing and Advisory Committee and established the Gamma House Association. Before her incapacitation, sorors could always count on seeing Soror Ordie at Regional Conferences and Boules selling Alpha Kappa Alpha paraphernalia to support the Gamma House Association. Our Golden Soror Ordie became an Ivy Beyond the Wall on July 15, 1995.

Epsilon Delta Chapter

University Of Wisconsin-Madison
Madison, Wisconsin
May 18, 1968

Charter Members

MARGARET BALSLEY	SARA JACKSON
CAROL BRUNSON DAY	DEBORAH MCCORMICK
KAREN DIXON	GWYNETTE MCDONALD
PRISCILLA FLORENCE	RENEE THOMAS
JUDITH GORDON	CHERYL TURNER
LACHARION GRIFFIN	CARMA WHITFIELD

The Epsilon Delta Chapter of Alpha Kappa Alpha Sorority, Inc. was on chartered Saturday, May 18, 1968 at the University of Wisconsin-Madison, Madison, WI. Charter members were: Margaret Balsley, Carol Brunson Day, Karen Dixon, Priscilla Florence, Judith Gordon, LaCharion Griffin, Sara Jackson, Deborah McCormick, Gwynette McDonald, Renee Thomas, Cheryl Turner and Carma Whitfield.   The chartering of the Epsilon Delta Chapter made Alpha Kappa Alpha Sorority, Inc. the first black sorority on University of Wisconsin-Madison's campus, as well as the first undergraduate chapter of Alpha Kappa Alpha in the state of Wisconsin.

At the time of Epsilon Delta's chartering, Dr. Larzette G. Hale was the 17th International President of Alpha Kappa Alpha Sorority, Inc, having served from 1966-1970. Soror Ordia Amelia Roberts was the Central Regional Director, and during her time as regional director, she also chartered seven other chapters—all the undergraduate chapters starting with the Greek letter Epsilon in the Central Regional. These women, with the help of Epsilon Kappa Omega Graduate Chapter in Milwaukee, WI, provided the Epsilon Delta Charter Members with the support and guidance needed in order to make their vision a reality.

As the Charter Members described to the Chairman of Fraternal Societies and Social Life at the University of Wisconsin-Madison on February 6, 1968, the vision of Epsilon Delta's Charter Members was to organize a chapter with the purpose of promoting the scholastic, cultural, ethical, and social development of its members, and implementing the program of the National Organization. Special program plans for the chapter included new student orientation and counseling, career guidance, developing potential for leadership, social action in terms of controversial issues, encouraging scholastic achievement, extending travel grants, aid to women's job corps, research on African American heritage, and participating in Pan-Hellenic and campus functions.

Even though the University of Wisconsin-Madison had over 31,000 enrolled students in 1968, there are only about 450 black students, and according to Epsilon Delta Charter Members, they are not well organized like black students on some other campuses. This lack of organization motivated the women to individually work "to promote black unity and black heritage" on campus, while as a group they worked to get the Epsilon Delta Chapter well known on campus.[1]

In addition to promoting African American heritage on campus, the women who chartered Epsilon Delta focused on distinguishing themselves separately from the majority white sororities on campus by focusing on community service over social activities. Because of their service emphasis, they did not fully consider Alpha Kappa Alpha Sorority, Inc. part of the Greek system at the University of Wisconsin-Madison—they felt that their community service focus would help them grow, while the more socially oriented Greek organizations may dwindle.[1]

[1] Quoted From: Julie Kennedy, "Black Sorority Stresses Service and Unity; Repudiates Typical Greek Social Stereotype," *The Daily Cardinal*, October 8, 1968.

Theta Rho Omega Chapter

MARKHAM, ILLINOIS
NOVEMBER 17, 1968

Left to Right Seated: Joyce Marvel, Rebecca Ross, Dororthy Bradford, Josephine Franklin, Emma Bakeman, Amerike Warren, Marie Smith. Left to Right Standing: Winta Massey, Lita Holmes, Linda Johnson, Renee Green, Effie Roe, Laruth Colbert, Nellie Scott, Helane Davis, Christine Ponquinette, Barbara Geaither.

THETA RHO OMEGA CHARTER MEMBERS

EMMA BAKEMAN	JOYCE MARVEL
DOROTHY BRADFORD	WINTA MASSEY
LARUTH COLBERT	CHRISTINE PONQUINETTE
HELANE DAVIS	EFFIE ROE
JOSEPHINE FRANKLIN	REBECCA ROSS
BARBARA GEAITHER	NELLIE SCOTT
RENEE GREEN	AMERIKE WARREN
LITA HOLMES	MARIE SMITH
LINDA JOHNSON	

The mustard seed is the smallest of all seeds, less than one millimeter in length or diameter. When planted, like other seeds, it gathers nourishment from its surroundings, sprouts roots and stems, and after a time pokes its head above the soil. If once the seedling is above ground and it does not successfully weather the elements, the mustard plant will die or grow gnarled and misshapen. On the other hand, if the plant holds firm to its purpose and endures, then it flourishes and becomes a bountiful member of God's good earth.

So it is with an idea, a tiny flicker of thought, and a glimmer of what could be a sketch on the drawing board of someone's mind. Once conceived, an idea must be nourished and nurtured. During this period of development, the idea must maintain a true course of growth, not deviating for improvement's sake or for lack of interest on another's part. If it does, then the original idea is lost and something entirely different results; or it dies, never reaching its greatest potential. As Thomas Edison so aptly put it, "Genius is 1 percent inspiration and 99 percent perspiration." There is a struggle involved in bringing an idea to fruition.

In 1968, change and movement in housing patterns were the rule in the area outside Chicago. As the southern suburbs expanded, so did the number of Alpha Kappa Alpha women with their families. Two of those women, Soror Emma Bakeman and Soror Josephine Franklin, found commuting to the city so intrusive into their family's lives that they joined forces to establish a chapter in their community.

They enlisted the aid of Sorors Effie Roe, who had moved from South Bend, Indiana, to the area, and Soror Winta Massey Mallory, a classmate of Soror Bakeman's. Soror Roe was a special addition because while a resident of South Bend, Indiana, she worked with the sorors there, helping to charter Eta Mu Omega Chapter. She would be an "old hand" for the Markham chapter's establishment. Together the four sorors scoured the surrounding communities in search of interested sisters. Soror Ordie Roberts, Central Regional Director, was contacted, and the process began.

The chartering date was set to occur before 1968 ended. With sorors helping sorors, the ad hoc group grew to eighteen. The sorors petitioned the Boule for a charter and elected temporary officers. Soror Franklin was chosen to serve as interim chairperson. Soror Barbara Geaither served as chairperson for the community project.

Soror Geaither wrote and directed a pageant entitled "Born Free." The extravaganza was a tribute to the culture of Black people everywhere. It also created a place of renown for the sorors in the hearts and minds of the local youth. In addition to the community project, the sorors performed two fundraising projects, a Kiddie Party at a local movie theater for the children in the community and a cards and games party. The work was started during the winter months of 1968 and was completed during the fall of the same year.

That day, when Soror Bakeman walked over to Soror Franklin's house with the idea of forming a new chapter, neither knew what to expect. So they nurtured the idea, gaining momentum from the work and the love of other sorors, eventually bringing Theta Rho Omega Chapter to her place among the other chapters of our illustrious sisterhood on Sunday, November 17, 1968. Soror Ordie Roberts was joined by Soror Lauretta Naylor Thompson, Supreme Grammateus; Soror Beatrice Murphy, Basileus of Theta Omega, Chicago; as well as Sorors from Chicago and South Bend, Indiana, in chartering the chapter. Once chartered, Theta Rho Omega held its first election. The first officers elected were: Soror Josephine Franklin, Basileus; Soror Dorothy Bradford, Anti-Basileus and program Chairman; Soror Amerike Warren, Grammateus; Soror Emma Bakeman, Anti-Grammateus; Soror Joyce Marvel, Epistoleus; Soror Rebecca Ross, Tamiouchos; Soror Marie Smith, *Ivy Leaf* Reporter; and Soror Barbara Geaither, Historian. THETA RHO OMEGA WAS ON HER WAY.

During Theta Rho Omega's initial years, two projects were developed which have become permanent fixtures in Theta Rho Omega Chapter's program: The annual scholarship awards and the public program. Other projects initiated during this period were a tutoring service for young people, a Sickle Cell Anemia Drive, a Meet the Candidates" night and a skating party for youth. Proceeds from the skating party were used to support the NAACP and the Cleveland Job Corps. Membership was also a concern during the first four years. Recognizing the need for new members, in 1970, the chapter initiated their first new members.

Theta Rho Omega Chapter members were involved in several noteworthy events and programs during the mid to the late seventies. The chapter hosted the 1973 and 1978 Central Regional Conferences, saluted fine arts and Black heritage through theater parties, dances, and public programs and printed the first chapter yearbook in 1974. In addition, the chapter initiated its Community Action Program. The program involved rendering service at an area nursing home, senior citizen's residence or children's hospital. A very successful project, the Community Action Program (CAP) became an integral part of the chapter's program and would be expanded to include fundraising and other community service projects.

The beginning years of the 1980's, "blossomed like a rose." The chapter initiated six new members and reactivated eight sorors. Chapter interest and participation was high. The chapter named its first "Honey-Do" of the year, held a workshop luncheon on consumerism and money management, initiated Secret Pal activities and sponsored a reception honoring renowned educator, Marva Collins.

During this period, Theta Rho Omega Chapter became involved in the sorority's connection focus.

The chapter joined the South Suburban Chamber of Commerce and distributed information, to chapter members, on community action activities. A focus on health program at the Harvey Library consisted of presentations on Toxic Shock Syndrome, Nutrition and Women, Blood Pressure and Weight, and Women and Cancer. Several first-time activities were also initiated by the chapter, among these activities were, a Trans African forum, a teen's work shop and a "Little Miss AKA" Pageant. Several of the chapter's projects have endured the span of time and deserve special recognition. These projects are:

SCHOLARSHIP PRESENTATIONS: Scholarships were publicly presented in 1969 at the fundraising event and the annual presentation has continued today. The high school seniors in the community look forward to applying for the opportunity to seek scholarship assistance.

ANNUAL SKATING PARTY FUNDRAISER: In 1975, a skating party was started as a fundraiser to meet the public service responsibilities of the chapter. It was continued until 1990. Soror Dorothy Bradford, third Basileus, was chairman of the event during the entire time.

LITTLE MISS AKA: The "Little Miss AKA" Pageant was first presented in 1985 as a part of the "Spring Affair," the chapter's one big push for scholarship funds. The combination of the two events resulted in the most profitable event ever sponsored by the chapter. This event continued for several years.

CHICAGOLAND METROPOLITAN FOUNDERS' DAY: In 1991 the Chicagoland Metropolitan Founders' Day Observance was formed and in 1992 Theta Rho Omega chapter became one of the five chapters to participate at the time. The guest speaker that year was soror Yvonne Perkins, 22nd Central Regional Director. Since 1992, Theta Rho Omega has participated in the annual observance, chairing the committee of now 19 participating chapters (13 Graduate and 6 Undergraduate) in 2001and 2012. The annual observance is attended by over 300 sorors and follows the tradition of wearing all white, the attire worn for induction into the sorority.

SILVER ANNIVERSARY: In 1993, the chapter celebrated its silver anniversary. Theta Rho Omega has survived more than two decades of success through the creative, imaginative leadership of capable Alpha Kappa Alpha women as presidents and stellar members. Year after year at the regional conferences, it has garnered its share of honors and awards. The chapter is most proud that its name is engraved on the roll of honor for corporate giving (CIP), which hangs in the International Headquarters, Chicago, Illinois.

THE THIRTY-FIFTH ANNIVERSARY: On Saturday, November 22, 2003 at the Flossmoor Country Club the chapter celebrated its 35th Anniversary "Pink and Green Persuasion." Soror Faye Terrell-Perkins served as chairman for this elegant affair which was attended by many community and civic leaders from the Chicago land area including Soror Linda M. White, Supreme Basileus and Soror Barbara A. McKinzie, First Supreme Anti-Basileus. Theta Rho Omega Chapter looks forward to celebrating the chapter's accomplishment and future anniversaries as it continues its service to the communities in the South Suburbs.

THE FORTIETH ANNIVERSARY: On Saturday, November 15, 2008, Theta Rho Omega celebrated its 40th anniversary at the Olympia Fields Country Club. Soror Marie Smith, chapter charter member, served as chair. On displayed during the celebration was forty years of achievements and awards from Regional Conferences, community activities and the 3ft-high scholarship plaque displaying every scholarship recipient's name and year of recognition since the first scholarship awarded. Also in recognition of forty years of service and sisterhood, the chapter's first history book was compiled and given to each charter member and active chapter member of that year.

THE FORTY-FIFTH ANNIVERSARY: On Saturday, November 16, 2013, Theta Rho Omega will celebrate its 45th anniversary: Pearls of Service — 45 Years, at Flossmoor Country Club. The formal event will feature a Theta Rho Omega "Oscar Night" awards ceremony and celebration of forty-five years of accomplishments and community service in south suburban Chicago.

Josephine Elizabeth Seaton Franklin Foundation: In 1995 the chapter established and incorporated a 501(C) (3) nonprofit and philanthropic entity: The Josephine Elizabeth Seaton Franklin Foundation named to honor the chapter's first Basileus and charter member.

THE TRADITION CONTINUES: Theta Rho Omega Chapter continues its presence in service to the south suburbs. Beginning in 1999, funds for the chapter's scholarship program and national programs were generated by the "Vision Quest Awards." This was an annual fund raising luncheon that recognized outstanding community leaders who have excelled in service. The event also resulted in the chapter awarding an average of $12,000 in scholarship funds each year. In October, 2004, the luncheon format for this fund raising event was replaced by a Vision Quest Black Tie Masquerade Ball and in October, 2005, the 7th Annual Vision Quest Awards fund raising event was another elegant evening affair at the Tinley Park Holiday Inn. The Vision Quest Awards fund raising tradition will continue with the 14th Annual fund raising event taking place in 2013 at the Matteson Holiday Inn.

Other chapter programs have included: E.S.S.E.N.C.E., Buckle Up, On Track, the Arts, Robbins Fest, AKA Connection, health forums, Black Dollar Day, Black family activities, a senior program, coat drives, Holiday Marketplace, Black Women's Health Study, Washington D.C. presence, African American art fairs, ACT-SO support, business round tables, UNCF Walkathon, investment club, mathematics, science and literacy program, March of Dimes Walk America, blood and organ donor drives, mobile mammograms, Habitat for Humanity, tutoring, the Ivy AKAdemy, Financial literacy workshops, including the male focused Real Men Are Financially Astute, voter registration at local churches and colleges, community outreach with PADs residents and their children, several years of Angel Tree participation, EYL mentoring and guidance, back to school supply donations, Relay for Life, and Pink Goes Red for a Day.

Programs to foster sisterly relations inside the chapter are annual Sistah Fests, monthly chapter hostesses, leadership training, theater, movie and opera outings, dining out and chapter retreats. Membership in Theta Rho Omega has increased through reactivations, transfers and MIP's in 1996, 2003 and 2011.

In 2011 Theta Rho Omega went high tech by establishing its first website, troaka.org, providing the community it serves an insight into the chapter's long history of programs and service projects in the south suburbs. The chapter has also begun to video the chapter history through interviews and service of the chapter's charter members, golden sorors and former Basileus. The videos are archived to the chapter's website.

Theta Rho Omega continues to be represented and support Central Regional Conferences, cluster retreats, Leadership Conferences and Boule. During 1998, Theta Rho Omega was one of the hostess chapters for the Boule held in Chicago and the chapter was also a joint hostess for the 68th Central Regional Conference in 2002. In 2009 the chapter was once again a joint hostess for the 75th Central Regional Conference held in Schaumburg, Illinois. In 2012 the chapter hosted Clusters 1, 2 and 8 retreats held in Orland Park, Illinois.

THETA RHO OMEGA CHAPTER BASILEI

Josephine Franklin	1968 – 1972
Muriel Brown Walker	1973 – 1974
Dorothy Bradford	1975 – 1976*
Helane Elizabeth Daves	1977 – 1978
Emma Jean Bakeman	1979 – 1980
Genrose Harwell	1981 – 1982*
Dorothy Bryant	1983 – 1984
Andrea Harris	1985 – 1986
Jacquelyn Heath Parker	1987 – 1988
Anita Harmon	1989 – 1990
Jacqueline Lewis	1991 – 1992
Alfreda Keith Keller	1993 – 1994

Dorothy Bryant	1995 – 1996
Faye Terrell-Perkins	1997 – 1998
Mary Palmore	1999 – 2000
Brenda Montgomery	2001 – 2002
Patricia Jones-Banks	2003 – 2004
Loester M. Lewis	2005 – 2006
Vanessa M. Vavasseur	2007 – 2008
Andrea Sanders	2009 – 2010
Doncella Pamon	2011 – 2012
June Cole Boulware	2013 – 2014

Ivy Beyond the Wall

Epsilon Zeta Chapter

WESTERN KENTUCKY UNIVERSITY
BOWLING GREEN, KENTUCKY
NOVEMBER 22, 1968

Charter members pictures (from left) are Sorors Carolyn Seay, Linda Dickson, Benita Lynch, Rose Robinson, JoAnne Sandifer, Frances Sandifer, Carolyn Witherspoon, Brenda Lee, Patricia Garrison, Carrie Jpnes, Sherrie Buttler, Susie Jackson, Alice Adams, Carolyn Victor (center), Christola Clark and Veronica Cross.

CHARTER MEMBERS

PATRICIA GARRISON (CORBIN)
CARRIE JONES (DAVIS)
FRANCES SANDIFER (COTTON)
SHERRIE BUTLER (LYONS)
CAROLYN VICTOR (LAMBERT)
BENITA LYNCH
CHRISTOLA CLARK (DAVIDSON)
LINDA DICKSON
CAROLYN WITHERSPOON (HAYES)

BRENDA LEE
VERONICA CROSS (MCGILL)
ALICE ADAMS (MORRIS)
LINDA THOMPSON (PEARSON)
ROSEMARY ROBINSON (RAMSEUR)
SUSIE JACKSON (RILEY)
CAROLYN SCOTT (SEAY)
JOANNE SANDIFER (SHELTON)

The Epsilon Zeta chapter of Alpha Kappa Alpha Sorority Incorporated was chartered on the campus of Western Kentucky University by seventeen profound young women led by the late Soror Patricia Garrison-Corbin. Originally an Alpha Kappa Alpha study group was formed in the fall of 1967 with twenty young ladies Beta Rho Omega graduate chapter served as their sponsor and advised the young ladies that they would need to prove their ability to work together.

On February 25th 1968, Soror Odie Roberts, Central Regional Director at the time, visited Western Kentucky University to explain the qualifications of being a member of Alpha Kappa Alpha Sorority, Inc. Later in the spring of 1968, these interested young women sponsored a "Spring Fashion Show" as a way to raise funds for a community project that provided assistance to young elementary school girls living in low income housing.

On September 30th 1968, seventeen girls who qualified were pledged by the Beta Rho Omega Graduate Chapter and on November 22, 1968 these prestigious young women were inducted into Alpha Kappa Alpha Sorority as charter members of the Epsilon Zeta chapter at Western Kentucky University. Mrs. A.G. Gaston spoke at the Installation Banquet on the topic of "Effective Service to Humanity." The officers, installation and Rush Tea was the conclusion of the chartering of the Epsilon Zeta chapter on November 24th 1968.

Epsilon Zeta has accomplished many endeavors throughout the forty-three, almost forty-four years of its existence and several of its charter members have been recognized for their accomplishments.

- Soror Garrison-Corbin held the position of president of the chapter until she graduated in May of 1969. Not only that, but she was inducted and recognized as a member of The Hall of Distinguished Alumni on October 25th 1969.
- Soror Frances Sandifer Cotton held the position of Tamiouchos as member of Epsilon Zeta. She held the positions of Basileus, Philacter, and *Ivy Leaf* Reporter. Also, she was chairman of the Education, and Scholarship committees of the Eta Omega chapter in Louisville, Kentucky. F or Central Regional Conferences, she was the chairman of Logistic and Kit Committees. Not only that, but Soror Sandifer-Cotton is a Silver Star, a Life Member, and has received the Soror Through the Years award.
- Soror Carolyn Witherspoon-Hayes is a former principal and was featured in the National Association of Elementary School Principals' Principal magazine. She was recognized as the 2000 National Distinguished Principal of Kentucky and a 2001 YMCA Adult Black Achiever.
- Soror Veronica Cross-McGill was elected as Western Kentucky University's first Black cheerleader in 1969.
- Soror Linda Thompson Pearson was the first African American woman at Western to be elected to the Homecoming Court in fall of 1968.

Throughout the years Epsilon Zeta has continued a deep legacy of upholding the purpose of Alpha Kappa Alpha while being great citizens and role models in the community. We will continue to press on and strive for higher endeavors in everything that we do.

Epsilon Zeta Chapter Basileus

Melody Samuels	1990
Nicole Orr	1991 – 1992
Uykia Smith	1993
Nikita Stewart	1994
Christa Bell	1995
Melissa Bush	1996
Brenda Dawson	1997
Adrian Lane	1998
Sanee Smith	1999
Rana Barnes	2000
Aisha Alexander	2001
Felicia Williams	2002
April White	2003
Konika Malone	2004
Dedra McDowell	2005
Camira Warfield	2006
Jocelyn Fernandez	2007
Jessica Sutherland	2008
Jessica Sutherland	2009
Sabra Wilson (Sept.-Dec.)	2009
Josclynn Brandon	2010
Adenikkei Adeniran	2011
Jessica Nichols	2012

Gamma Chi Chapter

NORTHWESTERN UNIVERSITY
EVANSTON, ILLINOIS
MARCH 1, 1969

Charter Picture Identification: Front row, left to right: Jinx (Smith) Kenan; Sandra (Small) Hill; Debra (Avant) Hill, PhD; Loester (Lewis) Lewis, and Janice (Sims) Powells, MD. Second row: Adrianne (Thomas) Hayward; Regina (Rice) Luster; Nona M. Burney, PhD; Barbara (North) Lightning, Esq., and Dorothy J. Harrell, Esq.
Not pictured: Lillian (Jordan) Daley, Josephine Bronaugh, Saundra Malone.

CHARTER MEMBERS

DEBRA JEAN AVANT
JOSEPHINE BRONAUGH
NONA MICHELLE BURNEY
DOROTHY JEAN HARRELL
LILLIAN CECILE JORDAN
LOESTER MAE LEWIS
SAUNDRA MALONE

BARBARA CLARK NORTH
REGINA ROSALYN RICE
JANICE RUTH SIMS
SANDRA DENISE SMALL
JINX COURNEY SMITH
ADRIANNE AURELIA THOMAS

Author's Note: The chapter name is out of sequence for a new undergraduate chapters in Central Region because the Boule initially assigned the chapter name to an undergraduate chapter in Dayton Ohio in 1950. That undergraduate chapter was dissolved and the name was reassigned to Central's undergraduate chapter at Northwestern University.

Gamma Chi Chapter began as a TIAKA Club (Those Interested in Alpha Kappa Alpha) which was formed in March of 1968 by a group of twenty-one coeds. These young women had attended a rush party given by the Beta Chapter of Alpha Kappa Alpha earlier that year. Under the guidance of two members of the Sorority, Josephine Bronaugh and Saundra Malone, the TIAKA group set the goal of obtaining a chapter on the campus of Northwestern University.

After many organizational meetings, petitioning and the drawing of a constitution, the TIAKA group obtained the approval of the Student Senate. Thus, on March 28th, 1968, the TIAKA group became an official colony on the campus. On October 6, 1968, these women were inducted into the

Ivy Leaf Pledge Club of Alpha Kappa Alpha. These 11 young women became the charter members of Gamma Chi Chapter on March 1, 1969.

With the chapter's beginnings amidst the Black studies movement occurring on Northwestern's campus, many chapter members were a part of major political activism that would shape the University's history during the post-Civil Rights era. After the 1968 takeover of the Bursar's office at Northwestern, many sorors of the Gamma Chi Chapter along with other African American students, who would later form the Black Student Union (For Members Only), were responsible for the creation of an African American Studies department, as well as a mandatory 10% enrollment of Black students at the University. Dr. Debra Avant Hill, Dr. Nona M. Burney, Sandra Hill, and Adrianne Thomas Hayward were featured in the 2012 Boule museum exhibit "Unsung Heroes of the Civil Rights Movement."

Through over 40 years of service, Gamma Chi chapter has held true to the values of activism, service and sisterhood under which it was established. Each passionate and dedicated woman has done her part to ensure that the campus as well as the community of Evanston are served through relevant, socially conscious programming that have followed the platforms of every International President since the chapter's inception. Though remaining a smaller chapter amongst other undergraduate chapters, the members have expanded their vision toward making a bigger impact on the world's stage. The chapter continues to broaden its scope to incorporate global programming initiatives that will empower women and girls all across the Black diaspora.

As the Beta site of the (2006-2010) National program, The Heart of E.S.P. An Extraordinary Service Program, Gamma Chi chapter took part in Alpha Kappa Alpha's Extra Special Project of developing strong leaders and ensuring economic advancement for all mankind. Under the leadership of International President Carolyn House Stewart (2010-2014), Gamma Chi chapter was selected as an EPA ambassador in the fall of 2012. With the United States Environmental Protection Agency, Gamma Chi chapter helps to promote educational programming around health risks associated with bio-hazards, and to serve as an advocate to the nation's most under-resourced and most vulnerable populations.

In 2012, Monique L. Brown, a member of Gamma Chi chapter, was also appointed to the International Undergraduate Activities Committee where she serves as the Central Region representative until 2014.

Epsilon Eta Chapter

BRADLEY UNIVERSITY
PEORIA, ILLINOIS
DECEMBER 14, 1968.

CHARTER MEMBERS

BEVERLY LOUISE ALSTON (BETTS)
JOYCE ANNE BOX (BROWN)
CANDACE LENORE BURCH
LONA CAROL COOLEY (BIBBS)
SHARMON MARIE DAVIS (JAMINSON)
CECELIA ANN DUNCAN
KARLA RENEE KINARD (GREEN)
ROMAINE FRANCES LEE
JUNE ODELL LEWIS (TAYLOR)
CASSANDRA MING (DOCKINS)
MICHELLE MINOR
GERALDINE PARSONS
CHERIS DIANE SIDDALL
CHERYL MARIE TURNER (STALLINGS)
ROSALIND YVETTE ZANDERS (LOWRY)

In the early and mid-1960s, a small group of young women enrolled at Bradley University sought to establish an undergraduate chapter of Alpha Kappa Alpha Sorority, Incorporated. The name of this interest group was the Ivettes. Many graduated before seeing their dream become a reality. They were aided in their bid for a charter by local graduate sorors Kathryn Kendall, Josie Russell, Barbara Penelton, Jeanne St. Julian and Alice Taylor.

In the fall of 1968, Soror Sylvia Stafford, a former Ivette, who was initiated at the University of Illinois, returned to Bradley to serve as Dean of Pledges for the first group of Ivies. With the support of the Central Regional Director, Ordie Roberts' fifteen charter members were initiated on December 14, 1968. This new chapter became Epsilon Eta.

With the chartering of Epsilon Eta Chapter, Alpha Kappa Alpha became the first black Greek sorority at Bradley University. Since then there have been 46 membership intake groups for a total of 216 sorors initiated into Eta Chapter, Alpha Kappa Alpha Sorority, Inc.

Upholding the vision of our founders to be of service to all mankind has always been the legacy of Epsilon Eta Chapter. From the very beginning of its chartering, the first group of women wasted no time in providing meaningful contributions to the Peoria area and Bradley community.

Epsilon Iota Chapter

SOUTHERN ILLINOIS UNIVERSITY
EDWARDSVILLE, INDIANA
MAY 30, 1969

Epsilon Iota Chapter — Seven sorors graduate from Southern Illinois University. From left Sorors Lolita Shelby, Bernice Faulkner, Gloria Jones Dickerson, Susan Falls, Karen Gill and Yvonne Jordan. Not pictured is Soror Maxine Jackson.

CHARTER MEMBERS

GLORIA JONES DICKERSON	ETHEL JOSHWAY
SUSAN FALLS	CHERYL KILLIN
BERNICE FAULKNER	ELLA MICHELS
MAXINE JACKSON	LOLITA SHELBY
KAREN JENKINS	NOLA JONES WILLIAMS
YVONNE JORDAN	RUTH BRUCE WILSON

With the establishment of the East St. Louis Residence Center of Southern Illinois University in 1959, Delta Delta Omega became interested in the chartering of an undergraduate chapter. In several instances, a group of interested girls banded together and formed an interest group in preparation to become a chapter. But the chapter was unable to secure the necessary information and guidance to organize an undergraduate chapter.

The establishment of an undergraduate chapter became one of the prime goals set by Soror Marcella Donald who was Basileus (1965-1966). While attending the regional conference in Milwaukee, Soror Donald discussed the situation with Soror Ordie Roberts, a candidate for Regional Director.

With the advice and assistance from Soror Ordie Roberts and the Regional Director, Soror Le Anna Shelburne, mixed chapter status was requested and granted at the 1966 Boule. Seven undergraduate young ladies became members of the Ivy Leaf Club of Delta Delta Omega on January 15, 1967. The first young ladies inducted into the Ivy Leaf Club were: Dorothy Smith, Victoria Goode, Pearl Washington, Phyllis Haynes, Karen Gill, Mary Granger, and Maxine Jackson. Gloria Jones, formerly a student at the Carbondale Campus of Southern Illinois University, transferred her membership to the East St. Louis Ivy Leaf Club. With the continuous interest and growth of the undergraduate sorors, Delta Delta Omega applied for and was given an Undergraduate City Chapter at the 1968 Boule. The undergraduate chapter, Epsilon Iota, has been under the chapter's guidance since it was chartered in 1969.

Alpha Kappa Alpha Sorority, Epsilon Iota Chapter, held its first annual Racism Seminar on February 1, 1990. The seminar is usually in observance of Black History Month and generally features various speakers on a panel. The first seminar featured our very own soror and the director of the SIU-East St. Louis Center, Johnetta Haley; John Farley, a professor in the Sociology Department and Benjamin Quillian, vice president for Administration; Sheila Ruth, a professor in the Department of Philosophical Studies; and Rudolph Wilson, associate professor in the Department of Curriculum and Instruction. The seminar is free and open to the public and welcomes college students to come and discuss racism on campus and figure out ways to improve race relations on campus. This event has continued. The speakers have included John Farley, Patricia Brauley, vice president of the racial harmony organization and civil rights activist, Marcus Garvey Jr.

For more than 44 years, Epsilon Iota has served SIUE and mankind through the following annual and award-winning programs:

- AKA Coat Day
- Buckle-Up For Safety
- Breast and Testicular Cancer Awareness
- Circle of Friends
- Mr. MiAKA Scholarship Pageant
- SIDS and Sickle Cell Anemia Awareness
- Welcome Back Chat

And a host of other educational seminars and social enrichment events!

Epsilon Iota Chapter Basilei

Ruth Wilson	1969 – 1970
Joyce Williams	1978 – 1979
Wrenetha Glover	1979 – 1980
LaTonda Dillworth	1980 – 1981
Sharon Shepherd	1981 – 1982
Francella Jackson	1982 – 1983
Angelita Triplett	1983 – 1984
Somulra Ball	1984 – 1985
Cristeen Oneal	1985 – 1986
Kimberly Hopkins	1986 – 1987
Cristeen Gavin	1987 – 1988
Leslie Young	1988 – 1989
Traci Johnson	1988 – 1989
Demetria Russell	1989 – 1990
Renita Perry	1990 – 1991
Pam Williams	1991 – 1992
Deborah Hartwell	1992 – 1993
Marian L. Bunting	1993 – 1994
Rosalyn Smith	1995

Beta Phi Chapter

BALL STATE UNIVERSITY
MUNICIE, INDIANA
NOVEMBER 14, 1969

Beta Phi Charter Members and Pledges — This photo was recovered from a fire at Thornburg Studios in Muncie, Indiana years ago. The new owners decided to keep the old photos in storage in the event that someone would inquire.

CHARTER MEMBERS

PAMELA BARNES
DEBORAH BARNETT
CONNIE BENTLEY
SHARON BURCH
EQUILLA COLEMAN
JUNE COLLINS
PAMELA DABNER
BRENDA GIRTON
CHERYL HUNT
HERMETTA JENNINGS

CARNICE LAMBERT
BEVERLEY MATTHEWS
DELORES MOORE
JANET THOMAS
BARBARA SIMMONS
CARMEN MARKS
BETTY WATTS
PATRICIA WILSON
SANDRA YOUNG
NETTIE KELLEY SENTER

Author's Note: Once again, a Central Region Undergraduate Chapter would be named out of sequence. In 1938 the Boule initially assigned the chapter name Eta Phi to an undergraduate chapter at Xavier University, New Orleans, Louisiana. The name was reassigned with the establishement of Beta Phi at Ball State University.

Creating Sisterhood — Living For More Than A Moment
Striving A Lifetime To Achieve
Giving What We Have To Offer, In A Creative Way,
Forms, Molds and Strengthens The Sisterhood of AKA.

Beta Phi Chapter of Alpha Kappa Alpha Sorority began as a special interest group. This interest group organized as a social club in January 1961. The club consisted of eight members called the "Coettes." As the Coettes grew in membership and status, they sought local affiliation on campus and the name was changed to Kappa Tau Sigma Social Club.

In May 1964, the group achieved local campus standing under the name of Alpha Omega Chapter of Kappa Tau Sigma Sorority with about twenty-five members. Local standing for the interest group had to be maintained for at least two years. In doing so, the goal of achieving national status could be reached.

Becoming a recognized chapter of Alpha Kappa Alpha Sorority, Inc. was always the goal of the women of Kappa Tau Sigma Sorority on the campus of Ball State Teachers' College, which became Ball State University in 1965. Under the astute leadership of Cassandra Bailey and Susan Settles, AKA was brought to fruition. These ladies with their incredible insight, kind nature and focused guidance provided the direction to move the agenda for affiliation with Alpha Kappa Alpha Sorority, Inc. As well as sharing information to the group on the history of AKA, with its founding chapter at Howard University in 1908; the sorority's focus on "Service to all Mankind;" and AKA as the first sorority to operate the Federal Cleveland Job Corps Center.

In its effort to achieve recognition, Kappa Tau Sigma participated in numerous community projects, including a freedom project with NAACP to improve integration, while supporting the culture of scholarship and friendship. These ladies had the acumen to see that such an affiliation was crucial to the professional and personal growth of women.

Martin Luther King was assassinated in April of 1968 leaving a major leadership void in the African American community and a frustrating period of despair across the nation. The non-violent movement faced many challenges. Sorority and fraternity members participated in numerous meetings and events on campus, keeping our campus a safe place for dialogue and interaction on race relations.

In June of 1968, sorors were among thousands of BSU students in the stadium who rallied support for Senator Robert Kennedy in his run for the President of the United States of America. He spoke to an overflow crowd of enthusiastic student supporters. Who later left the stadium euphoric, truly believing that they too could 'make a positive difference' in the world, only to wake up the next morning to the devastating news of Kennedy's assassination in Los Angeles.

James Brown's single, "I'm Black and I'm Proud," lifted the hopes of African American sororities and fraternities. The Kappa Tau Sigma sorority sisters, who could, sported Afro hairstyles, which were immediately noticed on campus as a statement of pride. The women of Kappa Tau Sigma continued the diligent work for AKA affiliation with the help of members of AKA. The chapter had begun procedures to become a chapter of the sorority a year prior to its induction and was granted permission during the Boule. Committee and financial reports, social services, and pledge activities were sent to the Chicago national office for the process.

Sunday, November 9, 1968, with a banquet in Cardinal Hall, Hazel Moore, Dean of Pledges for the Alpha Mu Omega Graduate Chapter of AKA delivered the speech, "Your Day Has Come." This theme was selected based on "Ruby & the Romantics," a popular song of that time, "Our Day Will Come." Also in attendance from the university were: Martha Wicham, Dean of Women; Pat Ryan, Assistant Director of Student Programs, Victor Lawhead, Dean of Undergraduate Studies, and Doris Lawhead, Faculty Sponsor for the sorority once it became recognized as a part of AKA as the Beta Phi chapter.

On November 14, 1969, twenty members of the former Kappa Tau Sigma Social Sorority became charter members of the Beta Phi Chapter of Alpha Kappa Alpha Sorority, Inc. Following the charter ceremony, an Open House was held in the suite for all friends and supporters. AKA was the first African American sorority to have a suite in Tichenor Hall of Ball State's campus. Charles Sappenfield, Dean of the Architectural College, designed the suite.

The first Beta Phi Pledge Class included the following: Gwendolyn Byrd, Tommy Campbell, Chrisandra Douglas, Wanda Henderson, Barbara Hampton, Patricia Holbert, Sandra McCants, Beverly Muldrow, Rosemary Rogers, Marilyn Rogers, Marilyn Trevis, Toni Trice, Jeanette Elliott, Levenia Fountain, and Maurine Harper.

In 1969, Betty Watts was elected Basileus of the Beta Phi chapter for the new school year starting in September and the Beta Phi lineage of notable members continued.

When accepting the pledge to be of service to all mankind, the Beta Phi Chapter made sure to uphold it in all gravity. Programs were created and carried on to leave an impact on the Ball State campus such as conducting a 3.0 Grade Point Average Reception to honor minority students with a grade point average of a 3.0 or higher and awarding two scholarships per year.

Beta Phi chapter held eight initiations between 1998 and 2008 resulting in 64 new, talented sorors into our illustrious sisterhood. Like many of those who paved the way for us, the Beautiful Beta Phi chapter set out to maintain the legacy of sisterhood, service and scholastic achievement.

Programs Conducted On The Ball State Campus

- Jump-A-Thon for American Red Cross- where the members would jump rope for hours at the Ball State Scramble light to raise money that was donated to the American Red Cross.
- An annual health fair
- Adopt a family where the chapter provided for them during the Thanksgiving and Christmas holidays. Some years the chapter was able to provide a complete dinner and gifts in the campus suite for the family during the Christmas holiday.
- Weekly tutoring at the Madison Center and Motivate our Minds which yielded over 1,000 hours of service each school year.
- The AKAdemy Awards which is an after-five event still continued on the campus presently; which focuses on the performing arts and recognizes students for their campus accomplishments.
- And we even re-introduced a Beta Phi tradition with the Mock Playboy Scholarship Week.

Some notable accomplishments were:

- April 5, 1994 Public Service Award : Beta Phi was named an Honoree Indiana Conference of Higher Education in Indianapolis
- AKA Regional Conference 1993: Three awards — Step Show, Scrapbook and a program award.
- AKA Regional Conference 1994: Awarded for Scrapbook.
- April 1993 Phi Beta Sigma Statewide Step Show: Beta Phi — 1st place
- BSU Awards: Beta Phi received the end of the year (in spring) service awards for community service in 1993 & 1994 from the Multicultural Center.
- Regional conference 1998- Beta Phi received awards for highest percentage of sorors in attendance as well as highest GPA.
- From 1997-1999: The Beta Phi Sorors maintained the highest GPA award for all NPHC chapters and outstanding service and philanthropic awards amongst the campus Greeks.
- Regional conference 2003-Beta Phi won the step show award, highest GPA, and several 1st place awards for programs.

Over this time period, Sorors held leadership positions as President or Vice President of the Student Government Association, Black Student Association, Student chapter of National Association of Black Journalists and National Pan Hellenic Council and on the Ball State Board of Trustees.

2010-Present

Since the return of Beta Phi in the fall of 2010, the chapter has held many events as well as earned some of the highest recognitions on campus. In the spring of 2011, The Pristine 17 held their first week of events titled "The Epitome of Pretty Girls." During the week the chapter members completed two community service projects as well as held their first AKAdemy Awards event. That same year in the fall, the chapter held another week of events titled "AKAlades to the Decades." With music themed events, the chapter put on community service projects, financial and political seminars as well as held a volleyball tournament benefiting Muncie's youth.

The fall of 2012 was a very eventful and exciting semester for the Beta Phi chapter. The chapter held its third week of events and inducted new members into our organization. The third week of events was titled "TAKAstand" which included events such as AKArobics, an Election Day watch party and a masquerade ball. Within weeks following 13 new members, S.U.B.L1M3, were initiated on November 18, 2012.

With a chapter size well over twenty, members made strides to serve not only the Ball State campus but the Muncie community as well in ways that they haven't in the past. Beginning February 2013 with the "AKA's for Cans" event, the chapter collected over 300 pounds of non-perishable items to donate to Muncie's Second Harvest Food Bank. In March, the chapter had a successful Arbor Day event at the Muncie Boys and Girls club where flowers were planted with the youth. Finishing out the school year, members held their annual AKAdemy Awards event and "Taste Test for the Heart" honoring the American Heart Association.

In the fall of 2013, the remaining seven members of the chapter held a week of events titled "AKAdemics First: Skoolin' life." This week of events contained a Zumba class encouraging AKArobics, a financial simulation game, a seminar on confidence for ladies, community service at Motivate Our Minds, a pool party as well as an event titled "Karnival." With each event mimicking a class subject, the ultimate "class project" was to send a girl to school. During this event students were able to play minute to win it games to raise money to help send a girl in a third world country to school. The chapter raised over $300 and was able to send two girls to school.

Throughout the chapter's history, Beta Phi Chapter members have achieved recognitions such as earning the highest NPHC GPA on campus and winning many student organization awards for service and philanthropy. Members have been Deans List recipients, editor of two campus magazines, Black Alumni Constituent Society Scholarship recipients, Black Student Association president, the first African American Miss Greek at Ball State University, crowned Miss Black and Gold, Miss Ball State and Ms. Unity.

Through the years, Beta Phi Chapter has strived to render service through participation in the Sorority's International/National programs; involvement in community and campus activates; and sisterly relations. Some of the key activities which have been a part of Beta Phi's programming history were: exposition weekend founders' appreciation and Vanna Lounge Playboy Club (later adopted as Mock Playboy). Services include: drives for the United Negro College Fund, Sickle Cell Anemia, the National Urban League and continued service to the Muncie community. We take pride in our history and past as we do in our present and future as being ladies of Alpha Kappa Alpha Sorority, Inc., Beta Phi Chapter.

Our Light Along The Way As We Strive Toward Our Goals; Lamenting The Burdens We Bear, We Should Always Remember Alpha Kappa Alpha Is Always There!

Beta Phi Chapter Basilei

Aidrenne Wells-Hart — 1992 to 1993
Ithream Blackman-Atwell — 1993 to 1995
Tina Hunter-Milhouse — 1995 to 1996
Ebony Rutherford — 1996 to 1997
Kyna Willis — 1997 to 1998
Erica Hogan-Hewlin — 1998 to 1999
Kristen Quarles-Bostic — 1999 to 2002
Mia Fields-Lamar — 2002 to 2003
Erica Long-Roberson — 2003 to 2005
Shermelle White — 2010 to 2011
Kelli Bennett — 2011 to 2012
Brandilyn Muir — 2012 to 2013
Stephanie Woolley — 2013 to 2014

Epsilon Xi Chapter

Indiana State University
Terre Haute, Indiana
December 6, 1969

Charter Members

W. DIANE ADKISSON
VALARIE A. BAILEY
DORIS J. BRYANT
SHARON E. BURGE
CORLISS J. BURTON
DIANE DEBOWLES

VICKI E. HARRIS
BARBARA L. HATCHER
JENNIFER JONES
ADRIENNA LENOIR
CAROLYN D. ROSS
LINDA G. SMITH

For many years prior to the chartering of Epsilon Xi, young college women at Indiana State University (ISU), located in Terre Haute, Indiana, were interested in becoming members of Alpha Kappa Alpha Sorority, Inc. History shows that in the 1940s, Soror Maenelle Newsome, 10th Central Regional Director visited Indiana State University at the request of the Dean of Women to discuss the possibilities of establishing an undergraduate chapter. Fortunately, young women had the opportunity to pledge Alpha Kappa Alpha Sorority, Inc., through Alpha Eta Omega Chapter, the Graduate Chapter located in Terre Haute, prior to Epsilon Xi's fruition.

Late in the 1960's, an interest group known as the TI-AKAS (Those Interested in AKA), moved forward with the desire to obtain an undergraduate chapter of Alpha Kappa Alpha Sorority, Inc. on campus. Towards the end of April 1969, the undergraduate sorors applied for a national charter. On Saturday, December 6, 1969, Epsilon Xi Chapter of Alpha Kappa Alpha Sorority, Incorporated was chartered on the campus of Indiana State University in Terre Haute, Indiana in Erickson Hall. Soror Ordie Roberts, 16th Regional Director, was present to charter the chapter and participate in the weekend of events.

The dream of having our illustrious organization recognized on the campus of Indiana State University came to fruition beginning at 1 p.m. and continuing until 8 p.m. The twelve charter members of Epsilon Xi are all still alive today. They are:

- Soror Diane Adkisson Cargile, the first Basileus of Epsilon Xi and a life member of Alpha Kappa Alpha. She retired from Vigo County Schools in 2011 as the President of the National Association of Elementary School Principals.
- Soror Diane Debowles, the first Anti- Basileus of Epsilon Xi, is married and resides in Evansville, Indiana.
- Soror Jennifer Jones Richie, the first Grammateus of Epsilon Xi, resides in Bakersfield, California and has a career as a speech and hearing pathologist.
- Soror Sharon Burge Byrd, the first Tamiouchos of Epsilon Xi, is married and now resides in Detroit Michigan.
- Soror Adrienne LeNoir, the first Dean of Pledges of Epsilon Xi, is still an active member of Alpha Kappa Alpha Sorority, and resides in Gary, Indiana.
- Soror Linda Gail Smith, the first Hodegos of Epsilon Xi, was originally from Florida.
- Soror Doris Bryant who is an administrator for the county government in Oakland, California;
- Soror Valerie Gail Bailey, a social worker, is an active member of Alpha Eta Omega chapter;
- Soror Carolyn Ross Love, an active member of Alpha Kappa Alpha, is married and resides in Denver, Colorado
- Soror Barbara Hatcher, an active member of Alpha Mu Omega Chapter of Alpha Kappa Alpha, is retired from Eli Lilly and Company, and today resides in Indianapolis, Indiana
- Soror Corliss Burton, a retired Atlanta, Georgia educator, resides in Indianapolis, Indiana
- Soror Vicki Harris Tomlin, is a psychologist who retired from Denver Public Schools. She currently works part-time in research and evaluation. Soror Vicki resides in Denver, CO and is an active member of the Epsilon Nu Omega chapter.

Since the chartering of Epsilon Xi Chapter, we have continued to reach out to the campus of Indiana State University and the surrounding community. Epsilon Xi was a charter member of the National Pan-Hellenic Council chapter at Indiana State University; is a member of the ISU Black Student Union, and was the first African American organization to participate in Donaghy Day, an ISU day of service implemented for the beautification of the campus. Epsilon Xi has the distinction of being the only African American Greek Letter Organization to win the Overall All Greek Competition sponsored by the ISU Office of Greek Affairs. Several members of Epsilon Xi have been crowned the winner of the ISU "Miss Ebony" Pageant that showcases the talents of African American women on campus. Epsilon Xi is currently advised by Alpha Eta Omega chapter. In the past, Alpha Mu Omega chapter in Indianapolis, Indiana has also advised the chapter. There have been 46 lines of exquisiteness to pass through Epsilon Xi.

A pleasant memory for Epsilon Xi is the frequent visits of Soror Mabel Evans Cason, 20th Central Regional Director. The chapter had the pleasure of hosting Soror Mabel, a Terre Haute Native and

Indiana State University Alumnus, as she received the Distinguished Alumni Award presented by the President of ISU. The entire chapter of the time greeted and serenaded Soror Mabel as she arrived at the Terre Haute Regional Aiport. Soror Mabel stayed in contact with the chapter and was instrumental in the growth and leadership development of the chapter.

Through the years, Epsilon Xi has won several awards at various Central Regional Conferences including: Overall Chapter Achievement, Chapter Scrapbook, Black Family, Health, the Arts, Economic Empowerment, Education, Chapter with Most in Attendance, and various individual soror awards. The chapter has had the pleasure of hosting an Area Retreat on several occasions, and has contributed donations to the Educational Advancement Foundation (EAF).

Community service and programming have been the heart of Epsilon Xi from its inception. Some of our programs through the years include:

Trick O' Treat For Unicef

For over 30 years, Epsilon Xi has raised money for Unicef. Sorors dress up in costumes during the day and give candy to those students, staff, and faculty who donate to this important charity. It is a popular event that the ISU campus looks forward to every year.

Little Miss AKA

In 1992, Epsilon Xi initiated the Little Miss AKA Pageant on the campus of Indiana State University. Young ladies who reside in the Wabash Valley are presented to the community. Two categories are presented: 8-10 year olds and 10-13 year olds. The young ladies prepare for the event by spending time with the sorors of Epsilon Xi learning choreographed dances for the pageant, receiving tutoring, and completing community service projects in the community. During the pageant, the young ladies are judged on the categories of talent, question/answer, and presentation. A savings bond of $500 is presented to winners in both categories and all participants receive wonderful prizes. Some of our former winners are now members of Alpha Kappa Alpha.

Black Male Appreciation Dinner

Black Male Appreciation is an annual event that recognizes the African American men on the campus of Indiana State University. Dinner is served to all men who attend and awards and prizes are presented to let the men know that they should continue to strive for excellence and success.

Many sorors initiated in Epsilon Xi have gone on to serve Alpha Kappa Alpha Sorority, Inc. and Central Rgion in leasership roles:

Diane A. Cargile	National Constitution Committee	1984
Nadine C. Bonds	National Honorary Members Committee	1990-1994
Nadine C. Bonds	Central Regional Director	1998-2002
Nadine C. Bonds	International Regional Director	2002-2006
Nadine C. Bonds	International Finance Committee	2002-2006
Nadine C. Bonds	International Rituals Committee	2002-2006
Sheila R. Bonds	International Protocol Committee	2002-2006
Tonya Branch	International Technology Committee	2010-2014

Epsilon Xi Chapter Basilei

W. Diane Adkisson	1969 – 1970
Diane DeBowles	1970 – 1971
Pamela Fentress	1971 – 1972
Deborah Long	1972 – 1973

Denise Cummins	1973 – 1974
Jacqueline Jones	1974 – 1975
Lisa Cheatham	1975 – 1976
Vendetta Green	1976 – 1977
Joyce Washington	1977 – 1979
Sabrina King	1980 – 1981
Stephanie King	1981 – 1982
Natalie Brunson	1982 – 1983
Anitra Parrish	1983 – 1984
Gina Foster	1984 – 1985
Syvaline Miller	1985 – 1986
Saundra Lee	1986 – 1987
Toyka Cunningham	1987 – 1988
Lana Hannah	1988 – 1989
Meca Theadford	1989 – 1990
Sheila Rowland Bonds	1990 – 1991
Pamela Cox Starks	1991 – 1992
Wynona Davis	1992 – 1993
Felicia R. Short-Gates	1993 – 1994
Mariatu A. Abdullah Swayne	1994 – 1995
Felicia R. Short-Gates	1995 – 1996
Miranda Thompson	1996 – 1997
Toree Edge	1997 – 1998
Rukiya Bey Campbell	1998 – 1999
Aaryn Miles	1999 – 2000
Paryis Housley	2000 – 2001
Yamelia Williams	2001 – 2002
Afton Simpson	2002 – 2003
Crystal Williams	2003 – 2004
Crystal Williams	2004 – 2005
Bonita Wiggins	2005 – 2006
LaShaunda Starks	2006 – 2009
Adrienne Fields	2009 – 2010

Epsilon Rho Chapter

PURDUE UNIVERSITY
WEST LAFAYETTE, INDIANA
DECEMBER 13, 1969

Charter Members

LADYS L. BARLOW
MARSHENELL M. CONLEY
VICKI L. EPPS
PAMELA J. FORD
JANE L. HART
CHERYL P. JACKSON
PHYLLIS A. JOHNSON
BETTY L. POINDEXTER
CAROLYN P. ROSS
HARRIETTE M. SCOTT
CATHERINE C. TOMPKINS
CARMILLA WARE

As the turbulent 60's drew to a close in our country, Black students at Purdue University in West Lafayette, Indiana found ways to unite to make their collective voices heard. The assignations of President Kennedy, and then his brother, Robert, followed by the deaths of Black leaders Malcolm X and Reverend Dr. Martin Luther King, Jr. led to violent rioting in cities with significant Black populations. The peaceful, non-violent messages of Dr. King seemed impossible for many Black people in the face of his tragic murder. Amongst the cornfields of Central Indiana were approximately seventy Black Purdue University students, most of them on academic or athletic scholarships, on a campus of thirty thousand.

Taking the lead of Dr. King's non-violent protests, these Black students began peaceful protests at the administration building. They walked the campus carrying bricks to signify their discontent with University policies and began to speak about their dissatisfaction with the lack of social opportunities that the university provided for them. Upon this backdrop of discontent, a group of six Black women began to explore the possibility of establishing a second Black sorority on Purdue's campus. Their vision was to provide a choice for the Black women at Purdue. Alpha Kappa Alpha had been very impressive and could offer that choice so they sought the establishment of a chapter at Purdue.

That first group of young women was encouraged by Central Regional Director, Soror Ordie Roberts, and members of Alpha Mu Omega Chapter in Indianapolis, Indiana to begin the process of Alpha Kappa Alpha membership. These visionary undergraduates began to meet together and traveled monthly to Indianapolis to network with and to study Alpha Kappa Alpha's history with undergraduates from Butler University, John Herron Art Institute, and Indiana Central College, who were also seeking membership through Kappa Chapter. The ladies from Purdue were embraced, encouraged, and trained for their important leadership role on Purdue's campus.

On May 6, 1968, these six became the first women from Purdue's campus to be initiated into Alpha Kappa Alpha. These six new sorors then had three major obstacles to establish a chapter at Purdue: the number of women needed to charter an official chapter on the campus was twelve, three of these ladies were preparing to graduate, and Purdue administration didn't think the small Black population could sustain two Black sororities. The small but determined group of sorors responded by continuing the work to fulfill their vision to provide a choice and give Black women of Purdue the freedom to choose.

By December of 1969, nine women, representing three pledge lines, had followed to become AKAs. The third of these pledge lines, "Jive Five," was the first Ivy Leaf Pledge Club allowed to pledge entirely on Purdue's campus, and with their initiation, Epsilon Rho Chapter was chartered on December 13, 1969. Soror Clara Marie Browning, a dietician on Purdue's campus who had been an advocate for the chapter's chartering, was appointed to serve as Epsilon Rho's first Graduate Advisor.

Major Chapter Events and Historical Programs

MOCK PLAYBOY SCHOLARSHIP WEEKEND — From the 1950s and through the 1980s, the "Playboy Club" was the epitome of swank and posh entertainment that Showcased American beauty without respect to race or color. Originally set as a replication of the very chic and trendy "Playboy Clubs" of the day, the "Mock Playboy Club" was established at Purdue by Epsilon Rho Charter Members in 1970 to showcase the beauty and talent of the sorors of this new Chapter.

Through the years, the "Mock Playboy Club" has evolved into a weekend of purposeful and enjoyable activities for the Greater Lafayette community, family and friends as well as an annual reunion for Charter Members and Chapter Alumnae.

The program's original objective, to emphasize the importance of high academic standards by issuing monetary awards recognizing academic achievement, continues to be realized after more than 35 years. Since the program's inception, a scholarship has been awarded to a worthy Purdue University student; an additional scholarship award has been issued to a local Lafayette-area high school student since 1972. Monetary awards and formal recognitions are presented to the chosen scholars at the "Mock Playboy" Scholarship Luncheon/Formal Banquet — a staple and a focal point of the weekend.

"Mock Playboy" Weekend has become Epsilon Rho's major fundraising endeavor through a variety of activities. The central fundraising venture is the sale of ad space in the annual program ad book supported by local businesses, campus organizations, faculty members, Chapter Alumnae, family and friends.

Other programs, such as "LaughFest" and "AKApollo" (highlighted below), also provide considerable contributions to the fundraising efforts. The highlight of the weekend is the "Bunny Line Show" where Chapter members perform a welcome back routine for visiting sorors as well as other entertaining "step" performances in a traditional costume of "Tuxedo Tails" and "Bunny Ears." The "Bunny Line Show" is always a rousing success — thus contributing significantly to the overall fundraising campaign.

It was the vision of Epsilon Rho's Charter Members to create a program in "Mock Playboy" that would establish a tradition that would exist at Purdue long after their time on campus had past. This annual activity, one of the longest-running continuous programs at Purdue University and within Alpha Kappa Alpha Sorority, continues to capture their vision more than 35 years later.

SIX BILLION DOLLAR MAN / PURDUE'S MOST WANTED MAN CONTEST — The "Six Billion Dollar Man" Contest, a very popular male pageant launched at Purdue in the late 1970s, was revamped and renamed "Purdue's Most Wanted Man" in 2001. In these pageants, the contestants are judged in various fashion categories including swimwear and after-five attire. The contestants are judged in various fashion categories such as swimsuit and after-five attire. They are also given the opportunity to display their intelligence and quick wit in a question and answer segment. The proceeds from the event are donated to the United Negro College Fund and other charitable organizations and causes.

AKAPOLLO — This program has been held continually since 1990. It is a talent competition with a format similar to the television show, "It's Show Time at the Apollo." The money generated from the event is donated to various local aand national charities.

LAUGHFEST — Capitalizing on the immense popularity of Black Comedy of the 1990s, "LaughFest" was established to bring nationally and regionally recognized comic talent to Purdue's campus. Proceeds generated from this program are donated to various charitable organizations.

OPERATION SOAP — This project is a campus-wide toiletry drive. Items such as soap, toothpaste, deodorant, and the like are collected and donated to area shelters.

Chapter Members Who Have Held International/National Office or Been Elected to the International/National Nominating Committee

Dayna Johnson   National Nominating Committee   2002 – 2004

Epsilon Rho Chapter Basilei

Jane Hart	1969
Catherine Tompkins	1970
Julia Boone	1971 – 1972
Angela Buie	1973 – 1974
Gloria Booth	1975 – 1976
Linda Holland	1977
Jeretha Fields	1978 – 1979
Carmen Dent	1980
Shirley Satterfield	1981
Karen Burnett	1982
Stephanie Tatum	1983
Stacy Lawrence	1984
Sandra Sherard	1985
Beverly Peaches	1986
Stephanie Jordan	1987
Daphne Williams	1988
Kristy Dotson	1989
Tracey Nelson	1990
Kellie Rouse	1991
Jody Banks	1991
Jenean Palmer	1992
Jonta French	1993
Tiffany Roberts	1994
LaDonna Williams	1995
Charlene Lovings	1996
Monica Crain	1997
Charius Haney	1998
JessicaKimbrough	1999
Dana Boyd	1999
Brittney Carelock	2000
Terri Smith	2001
Salana Oliver	2002
Shalisa Sanderlin	2003–2004
Brandi Hogan	2005
Kara Williams	2006
Jasmin Pettigrew	2007
Juliette Smith	2008
Celeste Taylor	2009
Taneisha Springfield-Jones	2010
Marissa Lyles	2012-2013

Johnetta Randolph Haley

17TH CENTRAL REGIONAL DIRECTOR
AUGUST 1970 – AUGUST 1974

Johnetta Randolph Haley was elected the 17th Central Regional Director at the Kansas City Boule in 1970. This event culminated twenty-five years of constant activity in Alpha Kappa Alpha since being initiated into the Alpha Iota Chapter at Lincoln University, Missouri in 1945, where she also served as president of the Ivy Leaf Pledge Club.

She is a charter member of Delta Delta Omega and Omicron Theta Omega, and Former Basileus of Gamma Omega Chapter all located in St. Louis, MO.

A civil rights activist, Soror Haley brought to the region a greater awareness of black concerns in their communities, and encouraged the strict adherence to Alpha Kappa Alpha's policies and procedures.

Her first Regional Conference was held in Chicago, where for the first time chapter representatives were asked to come on Thursday to attend an evening workshop on chapter operations. Because this had never been done, many members were apprehensive. However, the workshop room was packed to capacity and the sorors were lavish in their praise for the idea and planning. The National Program theme was "PIN" (Personal Involvement Now), and Soror Laura N. Banks, the Far Western Regional Director set the tone of the conference with her stirring speech.

At each Regional Conference Soror Haley began something innovative and new for the Region. Her Second Conference was held in Evansville, Indiana, and there she began the Sunday morning rededication breakfast, which she patterned after the Mid-Atlantic Regional Conference.

The Third Conference held after her reelection in 1972 was at the Holiday Inn in Gary, Indiana. It was the last conference held at the "failing" hotel and the then Mayor Richard Hatcher was so grateful to Alpha Kappa Alpha for this gesture that he stated so in his address at their Public Meeting.

Sorors had become acclimated to the Sunday morning rededication breakfast and turned out in full force to hear Soror Etta Moten Barnett as the keynote speaker and to donate, by individuals and chapters, $10,000 to the Cleveland Job Corps Center. It was at this conference that the "Undergraduate Dress Out" that Soror Haley had initiated gained numerous participants, and her "All Night Party" for undergraduates became an overwhelming success.

Soror Haley was an ardent advocate for undergraduates, visiting each chapter in the region, and appointing an undergraduate soror as co-chairman of every Regional Committee, as well as appointing one undergraduate as assistant to the Regional Director. Undergraduate members almost equaled the attendance of graduate members at the Regional Conferences.

On the first Saturday in December of each year, Soror Haley held a "Basileus — Graduate Advisor's Work-Day" at cities within the region, such as Minneapolis, Paducah, and Indianapolis. These sessions were for program planning, chapter procedures, awareness and fellowship.

At Soror Haley's last conference, which was held in her home city of St. Louis in 1974, over 800 sorors were in attendance. Congressman William L. Clay, a friend, brought Congressman Louis Stokes with him to greet and address the sorors at their public meeting. Also in attendance was Supreme Basileus Mattelia B. Grays and outgoing Executive Director Carey B. Preston. Soror Preston was given a retirement gift from the region.

It was Soror Haley who suggested designating the month of March as Job Corps Month. In addition, while serving as Central Regional Director, she organized a visit by the chapters of Central Region and accompanied them to the Cleveland Job Corps Center (no other Region has done this). Soror Haley chartered nine undergraduate chapters and two graduate chapters during her administration. Following her tenure as Central Regional Director, she continued to serve Alpha Kappa Alpha as the National Chairman of the Job Corp Committee; Standards Committee, Constitution and Bylaws Committee and the Honorary Members and Awards Committee. From 1990 – 1994 she served as Supreme Parliamentarian.

Soror Haley is a retired Professor Emeritus of Music and University Administrator at Southern Illinois University at Edwardsville and has the distinction of having the Minority Academic Program at Southern Illinois University at Edwardsville named the Johnetta Haley Scholar's Academy. Her other recognitions include: inducted in 1988 into the Greater St. Louis — Women of Achievement Society; 2010 — Legacy Award-St. Louis, "Women in Leadership Award," entered into the congressional record; and the "Olive Branch Award" in 2013 for professional excellence as an educator, mentor and community leader.

Soror Haley remains active in her church: St. Phillips Evangelical Lutheran Church Council, Former President and serves as the pianist for the church choir. She is a National Alumna, Platinum Member Affairs Committee, the Links, Inc., a member of the Money Bee Investment Club and Hollywood Poker Club.

Soror Haley is the proud mother of two children, Karen and Michael (deceased) and one grandchild (Jonathan). She has two nieces Sharon and Jazzmine a cousin, Pari and her daughter Karen who are all Alpha Kappa Alpha women.

Her leadership in education, higher education, administration and community service has earned her numerous awards and honors. She received Alpha Kappa Alpha's Founders Graduate Service Award at the Boule in Orlando, Florida in 2002.

Zeta Zeta Chapter

Murray State University
Murray, Kentucky
January 9, 1971

Charter Members

ROSETTA BACON
SHARON ANNE BRONAUGH
MARETHA BURGESS
DEBORAH DAVIS
JANICE DIGGS
BRENDA LOUISE HAYES
SUR CAROL LAUDERDALE
CHERYL ANN LONON

LUCRETIA MARIE MCCLENNEY
TERRY LISA MCGRUDER
ANITA MUNFORD
GALE M. NOAH
GLORIA OWEN
DONNA ELAINE PARRIS
DOROTHY RAY
VIVIEN ANGELENE WALLS
LAURA WILFORD

Zeta Zeta Chapter has participated in the Murray State University Minority Students College Preparation Program since 1980. The sorors serve as mentors to middle school students from the Jackson Purchase area. The program lasts for one academic year. In addition, the chapter assists Needline in Murray, Kentucky, a family resource center that provides clothing, food, and other items to local families. Financial support is possible through fundraising efforts such as Water Day. Water Day is held on the campus with students purchasing spring and flavored waters from the sorority.

Chapter Basilei

Vivien Walls	1971 – 1972
Lacy Mae Hardison	1972 – 1973
Yvette D. Henley	1973 – 1974
Beverly A. Garrad	1974 – 1975
Martha McHenry	1975 – 1976
Cheryl Parker	1976 – 1977
Pamela Stocks	1977 – 1978
Theresa Mathis	1979 – 1980
Angela Cox	1980 – 1981
Beverly Hutcherson	1981 – 1983
Linda Faye Anderson	1983 – 1984
Daveeda E. Roper	1984 – 1986
Rhonda Kaye Sullivan	1986 – 1987
Theresa Ann Cathey	1987 – 1988
Faye Laverne Williams	1988 – 1989
Dianne Woodside	1989 – 1989
Naretha Timberlake	1989 – 1991
Raco Halloway	1991 – 1991
Allene Houston	1991 – 1994
Michelle Lane	1994 – 1995
Rosita Gillespie	1995
Renita Avery	2001-2002
Eryn Murray January	2005 – May 2006
Kristye Russel June	2006 – May 2008
Tiffany Beauregard June	2008 – May 2009
Tiffany Gartley June	2009 – June 2010
Angela Glore June	2010 – May 2010
Brittany Toney	2012
Charzetta Pittman	2013

Zeta Iota Chapter

Western Illinois University
Macomb, Illinois
February 20, 1971

Charter Members

YVONNE ALFORD	CYNTHIA SHERMAN
YVONNE EILAND	CLAUDIA SIDNEY
CELESTINA ESISO	BEVERLY WARREN
LUEVESTER LEWIS	CHERYL WASHINGTON
SHIRLEY ODOM	LINDA WILLIAMS
RUBY ROBERSON	RENE WILLIAMS
	LINDA YOUNG

No history submitted.

PLEDGED TO REMEMBER: THE HISTORY OF CENTRAL REGION

Zeta Nu Chapter

EASTERN KENTUCKY UNIVERSITY
RICHMOND, KENTUCKY
APRIL 25, 1971

CHARTER MEMBERS

LENISE ROSE BELL
DONNA FAYE BLACK
TONI JO CHAMBERS
NATALIE COOK
SHARON FERMAN
PATRICIA ANN HILL
JULIA ELAINE HUGUELY

MARSHA HELEN HUGULEY
GAIL L. LYTTLE,
LINDA BEA MARSH
RUTH ANN MEADOWS
LASANDRA ELIZABETH RIDLEY
TERESA ANN SEARCY
JOYCE WANNOIA WILSON

Alpha Kappa, the early seed of what was later to become Zeta Nu Chapter, Alpha Kappa Alpha Sorority, Inc. was established on Eastern Kentucky University's campus in April 1970. This was a procedure required by the university in order to pursue the chartering a national sorority. The moving force in the establishment of this local sorority consisted of twenty-six socially conscious dedicated young women who, like our founders, were determined to make their college experience as positive and as meaningful as possible. The officers of Alpha Kappa were: Donna Black — President, LaSandra Ridley — Vice President, Toni Chambers — Treasurer and Gail Lyttle — Recording Secretary.

180 ALPHA KAPPA ALPHA SORORITY, INCORPORATED®

After months of hard work, relentless preparation and the undying support from the first appointed Graduate Advisor, Soror Dr. Joyce Berry of Beta Gamma Omega Chapter in Lexington, Kentucky, Zeta Nu Chapter of Alpha Kappa Alpha received its National Charter on April 25, 1971.

The fourteen charter members, in keeping with Alpha Kappa Alpha's ideal of academic excellence, proudly received the Scholastic Cup in the spring of 1971. This award was presented by the faculty of Eastern Kentucky University to the Greek organization obtaining the highest grade point average per semester.

Remaining true to a "Legacy of Excellence" initiated by the fourteen charter members, over the years that follow, the chapter has and continues to be a driving force for social change. Over 175 young women have become a part of the phenomenal sisterhood of Zeta Nu and the chapter's presence continues to make an enormous impact on both the campus of Eastern Kentucky University and in the community of Richmond, Kentucky as a whole.

Supporting our National motto of "Service to All Mankind," Zeta Nu has sponsored numerous cultural, social and academic initiatives. One of the chapter's first and most successful projects was the establishment of the annual Miss Black EKU Pageant. Zeta Nu also supported a local senior facility, The Pine Street Old Folks Home and provided an annual tuition for one black child attending the K-12 Model Laboratory School located on the campus.

In 2007, the Chapter purchased a "Kiddy Car" for Safety City in Lexington, Kentucky to aid in teaching good vehicular safety practices to young children. The chapter maintained its commitment to the Richmond community during the holidays through the funding of Thanksgiving Baskets for underprivileged families; Toy Drives; sponsoring a local family for Christmas; and a campus wide activity making Veteran Thanksgiving cards of "Thanks" to the brave women and men who have fought unselfishly for our country.

Zeta Nu's signature programs for 2012-2013 targeted empowering young women on campus, Health & Fitness Programs, Texting & Driving Awareness Seminars, American Cancer Association Wig Drives, and various other fundraising activities to support international organizations to target global poverty.

Zeta Nu's commitment to service continued to receive recognition on campus when the chapter was presented with the African-African American Studies 2012 Best Educational Program Award for Mission AKAcomplished (Domestic Violence Awareness Program) and 2013 Best Sorority Award.

In 2012 and 2013, Zeta Nu received the Community Service Award for Freshman Move-In Day, Eastern Kentucky University's Relay for Life, October Domestic Violence Awareness Day, and "Rock the Vote" voter's registration event. They were honored with the Triple Star Standard Award in 2011 for Leadership and Involvement, Membership Intake, Chapter Management, and Risk Management by EKU Greek Life.

Just as we thank God for the dream, drive and determination of our sixteen founding sorors, we will also forever be thankful to God for the vision, initiative, and, fortitude, of Zeta Nu's fourteen prodigious charter members.

The spirit of Alpha Kappa Alpha will endure through "Zealous" Zeta Nu's merit and culture.

Zeta Phi Chapter

INDIANA UNIVERSITY-NORTHWEST CAMPUS
GARY, INDIANA
DECEMBER 12, 1971 – FEBRUARY 26, 1980

Front, from left: Denise Harris, Karen Nixon. Second row: Gloria Love, Jeanete Shivers, Dollye Coleman, Barbara Barbara Steverson, Johnetta Holly, Central Regional Director; Millicent Ross, Emogene McMurtrey, Basileus, Gamma Psi Omega. Standing: Patricia Toppin, Mary Ann Alexander, Joquella Berry, Jackie Thompson, Lois Ann Outlaw, transfer from Alpha Rho, Veronica Rollins, Stacy Johnson, Brenda Gould, Jackie Mulligan.

CHARTER MEMBERS

MARY ANN ALEXANDER	KAREN NIXON
JOQUELLA BERRY	LOIS HICKS OUTLAW
BRENDA LOUISE GOULD	VERONICA ROLLINS
DENISE HARRIS	BARBARA STEVERSON
STACY JOHNSON	JACKIE THOMPSON
JACKIE MULLIGAN	PATRICIA TOPPIN

Thanks to Gamma Psi Omega Sorors Gloria Love, Dollye Coleman and Jeanette Shivers, the interest group TIAKA's was organized in order to get an undergraduate chapter chartered. Zeta Phi, a chapter consisting of only Sorors attending Indiana University was chartered on December 12, 1971 in Gary, Indiana at the home of Soror Juanita Grant. Gamma Psi Omega served as its advising chapter.

Six Sorors of Zeta Phi attended their first Central Regional Conference in Evansville, Indiana on April 13 – 16, 1972. With no time to rest, they joined Gamma Psi Omega and six other chapters and immediately began planning for the 39th Regional Conference to be held in downtown Gary the next year.

Zeta Phi Sorors attended the joint regional Founder's Day celebration in 1973. They worshipped with Sorors from Epsilon Rho of Purdue University, West Lafayette, IN, Gamma Psi Omega, and Eta Kappa Omega of East Chicago, IN on February 25, 1973. After service at St. Augustine's Episcopal Church, they rededicated themselves at the home of Soror Juanita Grant. Then in April, they watched their hard work and plans pay off at the very successful Regional Conference.

They continued serving mankind and increasing in number. In October of 1978, they hosted the Area Retreat under the guidance of Soror Clytee Gibbs. The theme for this event was "Serving Mankind with Knowledge and Responsibility."

In 1979, they again observed Founders Day with the immediate past and current Regional Directors in attendance. Sorors Gloria Bond and Peggy L. LeCompte made an impression on them to stay active and take advantage of learning opportunities often. So of course they followed their advice and made sure they were represented at the next retreat by sending their Basileus Ada Crosby to Fort Wayne, IN on December 8, 1979.

Zeta Phi was dissolved in 1980 as a new city chapter was formed. On Sunday, February 24, 1980 six women were pledged at Valparaiso University as a beginning step towards developing the city chapter. This city chapter, Nu Lambda, consisted of Sorors attending Indiana University Northwest, Purdue University Calumet, Valparaiso University and Calumet College. It was chartered on May 4, 1980. The following sorors served as Basilei during the period of the chapter's existence: Brenda Gould 1972; Brenda Winters 1973; Iris Faulkner 1976; Anita L. Thornton 1979 — spring; Ada Crosby 1979 — fall.

Eta Alpha Chapter

ILLINOIS STATE UNIVERSITY
NORMAL, ILLINOIS
MARCH 4, 1972 – JULY 2002

CHARTER MEMBERS

ALVA BAILEY	VEATRICE LEATHERWOOD
ALBERTA BELL	BEVERLY LYNCH
LOIS BRIDGES	LEONA MCPHERSON
CAROL COOLEY	SHERRY PARROTT
HELENA GILL	JOANNE PERRY
PATRICIA GREEN	PAMELA RICE
PAULA JACKO	DIXIE SMITH
LOIS KELLY	GAIL WALLACE

In April 1971, sixteen young ladies interested in becoming members of Alpha Kappa Alpha Sorority organized under the name of the TIAKA Club. After working diligently with several service projects, they were inducted into the Ivy Leaf Pledge Club on November 4, 1971. The merging of sixteen distinct personalities was tantamount to rocky mountain climbing, but was a challenge well worthwhile. The successful journey was celebrated at their initiation night on March 4, 1972.

Three hundred-sixty four days after the chartering, Eta Alpha's first line was initiated March 3, 1973. More than 200 sorors shared the thirty year history of sisterhood and service in Eta Alpha Chapter. Following suspension for violations of Alpha Kappa Alpha Sorority, Inc.'s membership process Eta Alpha Chapter was dissolved in July 2002 at the 60th Boule in Orlando, Florida.

Eta Gamma Chapter

Eastern Illinois University
Charleston, Illinois
October 28, 1972 – July 2000

Charter Members

PAULA LOUISE ALLEN,
CORA LEE BERRY
VALERIE LOUISE DREW
LAURA FLOYD
DEBORAH GRANT
STEPHANIE LOIS HOWARD

PHYLLIS KNOX
GWENDOLYN MILLER
LINDA COLLETTE O'CONNOR
MARTHA REED
DORIS MAXINE STEWART
BARBARA J. THORNTON
STEPHANIE J. WRIGHT

Due to inadequate members for a period in excess of three consecutive years Eta Gamma was dissolved in July 2000 at the 59th Boule in Dallas, Texas.

Eta Rho Chapter

MOREHEAD STATE UNIVERSITY
MOREHEAD, KENTUCKY
APRIL 29, 1973

CHARTER MEMBERS

BEVERLY G. BUCKNER	LINDA JOHNSON
KAREN DAVIS	MARITA L. KINNIARD
MARY L. DAWSON	ROSE LIVINGSTON
NETTIE FERGUSON	ANITA PALMER
ANITA FORD	ELLA RICE
LEONA E. JOHNSON	SANDRA TURNER

The moving spirit of Eta Rho was Linda Johnson. She surveyed and interviewed those women who were not affiliated with the existing sororities on campus. Many responded claiming their interest in Alpha Kappa Alpha, which resulted in the formation of TIAKA (Those Interested in AKA). Six members formed the Alpha Kappa Alpha interest group on the campus of Morehead State University in February of 1971. Those six members were Linda Johnson, Leona Johnson, Marita Kinnaird, Beverly Green (Buckner), Jo Ann Davis, and Bonita Flynn. These six strong Black women, led by Linda Johnson (president), determined to bring sophistication and distinction to the campus of Morehead State University, were the moving forces to the chartering of Eta Rho. After almost two years of anxious waiting, Miss Johnson's dream...our dream, came true.

Four women of Eta Rho's prospective elements held general membership in the sorority prior to chartering. They were made Alpha Kappa Alpha women on February 3, 1973 by Beta Upsilon Chapter in Louisville, KY. These four members were Marita Kinnaird, Linda Johnson, Mary Dawson, and Leona Johnson. The remaining charter members were initiated into the Ivy Pledge Club and then into the sorority on April 28, 1973. Mrs. Johnetta R. Haley, Central Regional Director, presided at the initiation ceremonies.

Eta Rho Chapter of Alpha Kappa Alpha Sorority, Incorporated was chartered and officers installed on April 29, 1973, in the Alumni Cafeteria at Morehead State University, Morehead, KY. Presiding at the chartering and instillation of officers was Mrs. Johnetta R. Haley.

Eta Rho's first officers were Basileus Beverly Buckner, Anti-Basileus Ella Rice, Grammateus Marita Kinnaird, Epistoleus Sandra Turner, Tamiochous Leona Johnson, and Dean of Pledges, Rose Livingston.

Eta Rho Chapter has a tradition of excellence. Jerica Kelso was a Summer 2012 Leadership Fellow; Eta Rho was awarded the chapter with the highest GPA for Central Region at the 2012 Regional Conference; and "Love at First Date — Date Auction" benefited Global Poverty and Domestic Violence was held February 2013.

ETA RHO CHAPTER BASILEI

Beverly Buckner	Spring 1973
Rose Livingston	Spring 1975
Cynthia Bush	Fall 1975 – 1977
Debra Spotts	Spring 1977
De'Ondrea Bowman	Fall 1977

Karen Ross	Spring 1978
Rhonda Barnes	Spring 1980
Rudene Nelson	Spring 1981
Donna Parham	Spring 1982 – 1983
LaDonna Soles	Spring 1984
Renee Warfield	Spring 1985 – 1986
Y. Dionne Coate	Spring 1991
Natasha Woods	Spring 1992
Cynthia Eddings	Fall 1992
Stacie Reed	Spring 1993
Tyree Gaines	Spring 1999
Yolanda E. Stone	Spring 2000
LaTasha Smith	Fall 2001- 2002
Camilla Tillman	Spring 2003
Vontrese Warren	Fall 2003 – 2004
Kimberly Williams	Spring 2005
Jerica Kelso	2011 – 2013
Zhanna McDole	2013 – 2014

Iota Chi Omega Chapter

FORT WAYNE, INDIANA
DECEMBER 15, 1973

Left to Right: Ella M. Green, Wilhelmina L. Ricks, E. Sharon Banks and Johnetta Randolph Haley, Central Regional Director

CHARTER MEMBERS

SANDRA BAKER
ESTELLE SHARON BANKS
PATRICIA CASEY
JUANITA ELDRIDGE
ELLA GREEN
CHARLEY HARDY
BERNICE HENDERSON
H. DELORES MOORE
SHARRON NORMAN
SHERBY OLIVER
WILHELMINA RICKS
MAMIE SMITH
BRENDA TILLER
JACQUELYN WILLIAMS
GLORIA WILSON

In 1971, a few women armed with a little knowledge of how to but with a strong desire to affiliate with Alpha Kappa Alpha Sorority, Inc., led Sorors E. Sharon Banks, Juanita Eldridge, Ella Green, Charley Hardy, H. Delores Moore, Sharron Norman, Wilhelmina Ricks, Beverleigh Starke, and Gloria Wilson to form a committee.

The first course of action was to contact the Central Regional Director, Soror Johnetta Randolph Haley, to determine the procedure for establishing a chapter in Fort Wayne, Indiana. She willingly shared her expertise in organizing what became known as an Alpha Kappa Alpha Colony. As the Colony continued the search for fifteen members, officers were elected, monthly meetings were held, and several service projects were implemented.

On December 15, 1973, Fort Wayne Indiana's Alpha Kappa Alpha Colony received its charter and became known as Iota Chi Omega Chapter.

In order to strengthen its chapter, Iota Chi Omega Chapter initiated a class on March 8, 1974. This class exemplified determination, fortitude, stamina, and a true love for Alpha Kappa Alpha Sorority. The members of the first class were Ethel Jean Adams, Anita Dortch, Gussie Green, Verdia Greene, Joy Johnson, Mossie Phillips, Caherine Ridley Middleton and Hana Stith.

Having gained the strength of additional members, Iota Chi Omega Chapter set out on the journey of promoting the goals and ideals of the sorority. The sorors attended Regional Conferences, Area Retreats and Boules, in order to fully implement the national programs.

The chapter worked diligently to enhance Alpha Kappa Alpha's presence in the local community. Following are some of Iota Chi Omega's activities in the community:

- Presenting the Harlem Boys Choir to the Fort Wayne Community
- Presenting a "Fashionetta®"
- Hosting an annual Scholarship Dinner/Dance/Fashion Show
- Awarding an annual scholarship at a Sorority Tea
- Participating in the local Black Expo, where the chapter's "Barbeque Turkey Legs" were a hit
- Providing an annual "Breakfast With Santa" for underprivileged children
- Sponsoring a comprehensive Health Fair
- Serving Thanksgiving meals in conjunction with Kappa Alpha Psi Fraternity to the needy community
- Providing school supplies and book bags for Chapter I schools
- Donating African American books to a local community center
- Participating in the local "Breast Cancer Walks"
- Donating monies to the Fort Wayne Children Zoo's African Veldt
- Contributing to the Dr. Martin Luther King, Jr. Annual Essay Contest
- Participating in the organizing of the community based "Stop the Madness" program
- Participating in the African American Read-A-Thon
- Knitting afghans for a local nursing home
- Hosting several Area Retreats and a Regional Conference
- Supporting local sororities and fraternities in their community endeavors

One of Iota Chi Omega Chapter's greatest accomplishments was hosting the 55th Central Regional Conference which was held on April 6-9, 1989, in Fort Wayne Indiana. The Regional Conference was conducted under the superb leadership of Soror Loann J. Honesty King, Central Regional Director. The chapter not only hosted a dynamic conference for approximately 900 sorors but was able to return all seed monies contributed by the host chapters. This was a first in the Central Region. Sorors in the Central Region still remember the conference and frequently compliment the chapter on a job well done.

The history of Iota Chi Omega Chapter is about "hellos" as we embrace and welcome new sorors who relocate to Ft. Wayne and those graduating from college. Iota Chi Omega Chapter opens its heart and graciously accepts sorors who affiliate with the chapter and offer full participation as in the spirit of our chartering members.

Our history is also about "goodbyes" to our beloved sorors who have joined the Ivies Beyond the Wall: Sorors Juanita Bedenbaugh, Verdia Greene, Mossie Phillips and Wilhelmina Ricks.

Iota Chi Omega's journey has been a relatively short one. However, the journey has been filled with sharing, laughter, handwork, pride, determination, courage, a few tears, loss and most of all love and respect for each other and for our beloved sorority, Alpha Kappa Alpha.

Theta Omicron Chapter

Eureka College
Eureka, Illinois
January 20, 1974 – July 1992

Charter Members

PATRICIA BROOKS
WENDOLYN CARLEY
CALVITA JO FREDERICK
ELIZABETH J. HAULCY
DEIRDRE L. JAMES

PAULINE C. JACKSON
EDLOIS MITCHELL
KATHYE P. SELLERS
LAJOIE M. THOMPSON
SHELLIE E. THURMAN
LINETTE WALKER

Following several years of struggling to sustain chapter membership; the chapter was dissolved in July 1992 at the 55th Boule in New Orleans, Louisiana.

Kappa Epsilon Omega Chapter

Anderson, Indiana
May 25, 1974 – July 2010

Charter Members

BARBARA BROOKS
BESSIE CAMPBELL
BARBARA DUERS
KAREN FIGURES
CARNICE GORIN
JEANETTE GORIN
DEBORAH GOVERNOR
JUNE GREGORY

THELMA HUGGINS
LAVERIA HUTCHISON
CASSANDRA JACKSON
CAROLYN JOHNSON
SYLVIA MCMURRAY
MARILYN RHINEHART
WYNELLE SCHEERER
JORETHA THORNS

There was a great desire by sorors in Anderson, Indiana to begin an alumni chapter of Alpha Kappa Alpha Sorority. Because of this desire, Sorors Karen Figures (Johnson), Carolyn Johnson, June Gregory, Barbara Dures, and Deborah Henson Governor met on August 12, 1973 formed a committee, and began the search for more sorors of Alpha Kappa Alpha Sorority.

It was decided on August 19, 1973 that the Regional Director, Soror Johnetta Haley, would be informed of the existence of these interested sorors in Anderson, Indiana. Sorors from Both Madison and Delaware counties were located and contacted. These sorors were Bessie Campbell, Joretha Thorns, Wynell Scheerer, Barbara Brooks, Jeanette Gorin, Cassandra Jackson, Carnice Gorin, Lavera Hutchinson, Thelma Huggins, and Sylvia McMurray.

On September 30, 1973, a colony was formed — a major step in becoming a chartered chapter of Alpha Kappa Alpha Sorority. The colony began its preparation for chartering with monthly meetings concerning talks of how the chapter would function and goals that would be achieved. Members attended workshops at Indiana University and in Fort Wayne. The colony distributed the Heritage Series in the Anderson community schools as a service project.

Chartering took place on May 25, 1974, and Kappa Epsilon Omega chapter of Madison and Delaware counties became the 461st chapter of Alpha Kappa Alpha Sorority Inc.

In 1974, the first chapter event held was in the local churches. This project was to become an annual affair—blood pressure screening to educate the African American community about the dangers of high blood pressure. It is with the assistance of our chapter pharmacist and the local nurses of each church in the community, that this project continues each May. Also, due to the efforts of the sorority by the distribution of educational literature to the African American community about high blood pressure preventive health measures, there has been an increase in health care by the overall community. The chapter joined the Anderson Panhellenic in 1975. This organization consisted of seventeen sororities. Kappa Epsilon Omega Chapter of Alpha Kappa Alpha, as the only African American sorority of the group and the community, was reintroduced to the Black and white community. Representatives from each of the national college-or university-affiliated social sororities joined to increase the awareness and enlighten young ladies about the benefits of sisterhood. From the proceeds of the sorority fundraiser, the sorority was able to purchase playground equipment for a local pediatrics unit of the community.

The chapter sponsored a perceptual motor skills program through the sorority's Adopt-a-School project in 1976 with Anderson community schools. A toaster oven was presented to the Madison County head start program. The sorority presented $1,000 to an outstanding graduating senior.

The Madison County Urban League, in 1977, benefited from the services of the sorority through many hours donated toward its membership telethon with a pledge of $200 from Kappa Epsilon Omega Chapter of Alpha Kappa Alpha Sorority. A scholarship of $1,000 was awarded from the chapter as a result of a successful fashion show presented by the J. Stanley Crowe Revue.

Ceramics classes were offered by the chapter in 1978 to Shadeland Elementary School as a community service project. A scholarship of $500 was awarded to a graduating senior. The community was given an "appreciation affair" for supporting the local chapter of Alpha Kappa Alpha Sorority.

Kappa Epsilon Omega triumphed in 1979 with first place honors in the Madison County head start basketball extravaganza. A $1,000 scholarship was awarded to a local high school senior.

The chapter designed and compiled, a Community Pamphlet listing various services available to senior citizens in 1980. A play was sponsored by the chapter during Black History Month at Anderson University. Nabisco posters of African- American writers were presented to the community in 1981 as a commemorative to the African American children killed in Atlanta, Georgia. Other chapter projects were continued through the year including a Professional Career Expo to present African- American professional women role models working in various careers to high school, junior, and senior female students. This exposure resulted in several of these young ladies going on to college and becoming professionals in their chosen fields.

Anderson's first African American pioneers in 1982 were recognized in a tribute with plaques and certificates. The chapter began a nightly tutorial program at a local church with assistance from African American professionals of the community.

The chapter continued in 1983 its support of the Adopt-a-School Project. A Black History art exhibition was set up by the chapter for culture enrichment. A

$1,000 scholarship was given to a local high school senior. The chapter participated in the Lou Rawls United Negro College Telethon.

Members of the sorority in 1984 worked diligently with the East Central Madison County Chapter of the March of Dimes as hostesses for its annual gourmet fundraising affair. The chapter served as hostesses for the NAACP ladies auxiliary Thanksgiving dinner aiding senior citizens.

A clothing drive with donations given by each soror was sponsored by the sorority in 1985, free to the community. The chapter sponsored a local youth to attend a YWCA camp program. Proceeds from the chapter's costume ball fundraiser funded other community and national projects. The chapter received its first life membership plaque from the local NAACP.

A minority business listing in 1986 was organized and distributed by the chapter to the community. The sorority assisted a local church in opening a free clothing bank. The chapter sponsored in 1986 and 1987 a trip to the Indiana Black College Fair held in Indianapolis each year in September. The purpose is to enhance the awareness of the historical Black colleges. Graduating seniors were presented with an annual scholarship of $500 each.

In 1988 and 1989 the chapter sponsored many activities for the benefit of senior citizens in the community. A bake-a-rama sponsored by the sorority to feed the hungry of the community benefited many. The chapter supported the NAACP ladies auxiliary program in feeding the hungry. Graduating seniors were presented with the annual scholarship of $500 each.

From 1990-1991, the chapter's yearly activities included participation in the annual blood pressure drive, senior citizens Thanksgiving dinner drive, and the Black Expo parade. The fundraiser enabled the chapter to sponsor a student scholarship of $500. In 1992, the chapter sponsored a gospel extravaganza as the scholarship fundraiser and awarded a $500 scholarship. A food drive benefited needy families and the local food bank. In 1993, the chapter participated in workshops with the local university students to educate them on the surroundings of the community. The chapter distributed applications for the Domestic Travel Tour and a local high school senior was chosen to attend. The chapter served as hostesses for a local nursing home and the local Urban League Annual Dinner.

Due to a membership of less than eight and inactivity for more than three years the Chapter was recommended for dissolution and approved by the Boule in 2010.

Kappa Epsilon Omega Advised Beta Phi.

KAPPA EPSILON OMEGA CHAPTER BASILEI

Karen Johnson Figures	1974 – 1975
Deborah Henson Governor	1976 – 1976
June Gregory	1977 – 1977
Henson Governor	1978 – 1979
Mildred Powell	1980 – 1980
Delia Stuart Williams	1981 – 1982
Melanye Floyd	1983 – 1985
Faye Barber	1986 – 1987
Carolyn Johnson	1987 – 1987
Fredonia Yvonne Harris	1988 – 1989
Helen Wilkins	1990 – 1992
Normine Allen Brown	1993 – 1994
Colletta Cooper	1994

Iota Delta Chapter

University Of Wisconsin
Milwaukee, Wisconsin
July 21, 1974

Charter Members

CLEMMEL ANTHONY	KATE GRAY
KATHY BARNES	JOLYNN GUNN
FRANCES BROWN	WENDI HARPER
RENEE BURKETT	LENA JONES
LORENA CHICOTE	WANDA JONES
PATRICIA GIBSON	LESLIE RAY

Iota Delta Chapter of Alpha Kappa Alpha Sorority, Inc. was chartered on July 21, 1974 at the University of Wisconsin-Milwaukee. It was the 2nd undergraduate chapter chartered in the state of Wisconsin. The first Basileus of Iota Delta was Wendy Harper, an Education major.

Iota Delta's debut event on the campus of University of Wisconsin-Milwaukee was a benefit dance to support a foster child named Benet in Africa. On May 6, 1975, Iota Delta initiated 5 new members, Diane Beckley, Faith Hughes, Wanda McReynolds, Susan Stephen and Marcella Williams. The 2nd Basileus was Kathy Barnes.

The early chapter programs included co-sponsoring a performance by University of Minnesota gospel choir, hostess for the Cluster Retreat, various fund raisers for the United Negro College Fund and annual donations at Thanksgiving to needy families. Iota Delta became the 1st sorority from the NHPC to attain office space in the University of Wisconsin-Milwaukee Union. Soror Genise Perry was the only undergraduate from Central Region honored as a Leadership Fellow 1998. In 2002 Iota Delta was the first chapter in the region to assist the Regional Director with implementing "Tax Freedom Day." The chapter held its 30th anniversary celebration in 2004 where many members returned to help celebrate the legacy of the chapter.

To the present date, Iota Delta has initiated many Alpha Kappa Alpha women. Iota Delta alumni are active professionals in Education, local politics, Physicians, college academic advisors and Nursing. The chapter is excited to celebrate its 40th anniversary in 2014.

Part IV

The Final Quarter of the Century

1976 – 1999

The Final Quarter of the Century

As the 20th Century neared the finish line, equality, justice and empowerment were the rallying calls that echoed across the globe. The nation and the world grabbed the baton passed by the civil rights movement, yet the struggles for democracy and freedom persisted.

Full participation in the democratic process was still being denied to African American's through prohibitive voter registration processes in the Southern states and affirmative action gains in education and employment were being challenged in the courts.

Determined to make a difference, Alpha Kappa Alpha Sorority, Inc., with brilliance and "Facets of Dynamic POWER," entered the Diamond Years of her existence.

From 1975 to 1999, Central Region would grow from twenty-seven undergraduate chapters and twenty-four graduate chapters to thirty-four undergraduate chapters and forty-seven graduate chapters. Active membership went from 1,300 to over 3,000.

Throughout this final quarter of the century, Central Region chapters and sorors would continue to carry out their tradition of service and were among the movers and doers as the sorority took giant steps during this period.

Soror Gloria E. Bond established the Graduate Advisor's Council in 1975. The sorority mandated at the 46th Boule that every graduate chapter have a Graduate Advisor's Council. The officers of the first Central Region Graduate Advisor's Council were: President, C. Louise Brown, Delta Chi Omega, Evanston, IL; Vice President, Essie Blaylock, Theta Omega, Chicago, Illinois and Helen Comer Cooper, Secretary, Delta Chi Omega, Evanston, IL.

In 1976, the sorority held the first reading experience workshop in Chicago, with Theta Omega Chapter as host. Constance Kinard Holland, Kappa Tau Omega, drafted the articles of incorporation for the Educational Advancement Foundation and Loann J. Honesty King, Theta Omega, was the first treasurer and an incorporator of the foundation. Doris Parker, Alpha Mu Omega, was appointed the EAF's first Executive Secretary.

The sorority's first Economic Development Conference in Washington, D.C., was chaired by Soror Loann J. Honesty King, Chairman of the Economic Development Program Sub Committee. The sorority's multimillion dollar International Headquarters "The Ivy Center," stands on Loraine Richardson Green Drive in Chicago, because of the efforts of Soror Doris Powell, a member of Theta Omega Chapter, at that time, and approval by the Directorate.

During the Final Quarter of the Century, six Central Region sorors were elected to national offices besides those elected as Central Regional Director. Four of these sorors were elected Supreme Tamiouchos: Loann J. Honesty King, Yvonne Perkins (twice), Martha Levingston Perine and Barbara A. McKinzie; two were elected Supreme Grammateus: Peggy Lewis LeCompte and Linda Marie White. Also, Sorors Johnetta Randolph Haley and Constance Kinard Holland served as Supreme Parliamentarian.

Central Region was the host to four Leadership Conferences: 1981 in Indianapolis, and 1983, 1985, and 1991 in Chicago; Indianapolis, Indiana and was the host for the 56th Boule in July 1994.

The first Leadership Fellows program was held in Spencer, Indiana (near Bloomington) at the McCormick Creek State Park. The 17th and 18th Leadership Fellows program was held in Minneapolis, Minnesota in 1997 and 1998 respectively at the Sheraton Minneapolis Metrodome in partnership with Pillsbury.

Since the first Boule of the 20th Century held outside of Howard University, the second in 1919, was convened in Chicago. It was only befitting that the sorority would return to Chicago in 1998 for the 58th Boule to close out the 20th Century. With the election of Soror Linda Marie White, Theta Omega Chapter as First Supreme Anti-Basileus and Soror Barbara A. McKinzie, Theta Omega Chapter as Supreme Tamiouchos, at the 58th Boule, Central Region was poised to enter the next millennium with "Greater Laurels to win and Greater Tasks to Begin."

Gloria Elouise Smith Bond

18th Central Regional Director
August 1974 – July 1978

Soror Gloria Elouise Smith Bond, a member of Eta Mu Omega Chapter in South Bend, Indiana was initiated in Alpha Psi Chapter, Tennessee State University. Soror Bond earned her Master of Science degree in Business Administration and Education from Indiana State University. Her professional career which included a period in Chicago, IL where she affiliated with Theta Omega Chapter mirrors her sorority involvement with many firsts and outstanding achievements.

While working for the Veterans Administration the agency cited her performance as a pioneer in automated data processing and programming and editing. As a member of Delta Kappa Gamma Society International, she was the first minority to hold an Indiana State elected office. Governors, mayors and community organizations have recognized Soror Bond's volunteer service. The National Program Theme: "A Salute to Women: Past, Present, and Future," personified her tenure as Central Regional Director. Soror Bond:

- published the first Who's Who in Central Region;
- chartered the FIRST Alpha Kappa Alpha Sorority Chapter on a Military Installation;
- along with Soror Anne Mitchem Davis (Executive Director) and on the recommendation of Soror Leola Travis, wrote and incorporated into the regional conference the First Protocol Guidelines in 1976;
- conducted the most area retreats on college campuses with undergraduate chapters as host, to help these sorors learn how to prepare for group meetings;
- gathered historical data from all past Directorate members in Central Region and formed a Past Regional Directors Council that functioned as a committee;
- honored Past Directorate members at Regional Conferences and extended the first gratuitous registration for these sorors;
- established the Graduate Advisors Council;
- was first to include the cost of awards in the conference budget and name awards in honor of former Regional Directors;
- incorporated the new procedures for analyzing Chapter Reports for Regional Awards after chairing a committee to set standards and design the evaluation form under Central Regional Director Johnetta R. Haley;
- established two Regional Awards, one for highest percentage of undergraduates transferring to a graduate chapter upon graduation and another for highest percentage of membership reactivation in a graduate chapter, to increase membership.

Soror Bond holds the record and distinction of being the Regional Director who chartered the most chapters in the region during her term of office. She chartered fourteen chapters (six undergraduate and eight graduate chapters). As Central Regional Director she presided effectively and efficiently over four Central Regional Conferences.

During her tenure as Central Regional Director she was elected twice, by her peers, to serve as National Chairperson of the Regional Directors Council. This position entailed representing all Regional Directors at Directorate meetings, visiting each of the other eight regional conferences, analyzing and preparing a report for the Directorate on all General Membership applications, and assisting other Regional Directors when requested to do so.

On of Soror Bond's fondest memories in her own words was: "A great highlight of my tenure was to have the honor of presenting the first 50-year Gold Medallions to Central Region's Golden Sorors at the 1976 Boule in New York at the Waldorf-Astoria Hotel."

Soror Bond always greeted her sorors and others with a smile. Following her tenure as Central Regional Director Soror Bond continued to serve the sorority on the national and regional level including chairman of the national Personnel Committee. One could expect her presence at Central and other Regional Conferences, Boules and other sorority functions.

In 1994, she became a Golden Soror and remained a vital part of the organization until for health reasons she moved to Marietta, Georgia to live with her son. She later relocated to the Sugarland care facility in Houston, TX, a few miles from her daughter, Tony. She remained active in heart with a room filled with AKA paraphernalia Soror Bond became an Ivy Beyond the Wall on September 22, 2013.

Iota Epsilon Chapter

National College Of Education
Evanston, Illinois
September 28, 1974 – July 1982

Charter Members

WILLA ADAMS	AUDREY MORRIS
MELTRAS W. AMMONS	WANDA H. NEWELL
SINIE E. HICKS	ELAINE RAY
LEE OLA HOOSMAN	MARCIA ROEBUCK
GAIL MAYES	ARNITA R. ROWE
BEVERLY MILTON	KYMBERLY C. SCOTT
	RENEE D. WILLIAMS

Following several years of low membership, Iota Epsilon Chapter was dissolved in July 1982 by the 50th Boule in Boston, Massachusetts.

Iota Sigma Chapter

University Of Kentucky
Lexington, Kentucky
May 5, 1975

Charter Members

ANGELA CHAMBERS	ROSALYN MACK
TONI DAVIS	ANTOINETTE MORROW
JUDITH DOWNS	VICKIE WHITE
TERESA GORE	VANESSA NEWMAN
KIM HATCH	TERESA ORR
SENORA HIGGINS	MARTA PEARSON
CHARLENE HINES	RITA HAWKINS PHILLIP
ALANA JACKSON	JANICE RIPLEY

The following sorors served as Basilei of Iota Sigma Chapter from 1999-2005: Keyon Moss Massey, 1999; Lisa Gaines, 2000; Miranda Martin, 2001; Keisha Carter, 2002; Maquiba Ballentine, 2003; Ahlishia Shipley, Fall 2003; April Eaves, 2004, and Brittany Johnson, Spring — 2005.

Kappa Mu Omega Chapter

JOLIET, ILLINOIS
APRIL 5, 1975

Left to Right, Seated: Ruth Griffin, Beverly Reed, Linda King, Central Regional Director, Gloria Boind, Janetta Hickman, Marilyn Regulus, Christine Ponquinette. Left to Right, Standing: Jennifer Johnson, Pearl Bush, Vivian Pennymon, Maxine Gillespie, Lita Holmes, Mary Gibson, Alberta Richie, Thelma Rush Kirkland.

CHARTER MEMBERS

PEARL BUSH	LINDA G. KING
MARY L. GIBSON	THELMA KIRKLAND
MAXINE G. GILLESPIE	GLENDA MONTGOMERY
RUTH GRIFFIN	ANNETTA B. OBRYANT
JANETTA HICKMAN	VIVIAN PENNYMON
LITA HOLMES	CHRISTINE A. PONQUISETTE
INGRID JACKSON	BEVERLY REED
JENNIFER JOHNSON	MARILYN REGULUS
	ALBERTA RICHIE

In November of 1973 Soror Lita Holmes invited all known Alpha Kappa Alpha women in Joliet to a get-acquainted meeting at her home. The purpose of the meeting was to garner support for a newly formed interest group at Lewis University in Romeoville, Illinois, where Soror Holmes was employed.

The nine sorors attending the meeting reminisced, discussed ideas, and shared and exchanged information. The meeting provided impetus for months of hard work, perseverance, and a firm renewal of the spirit of our sisterhood and the goal of establishing a graduate chapter in Joliet.

As the sorors continued to seek out and involve other sorors, meetings were held bi-monthly at each soror's home. The result of this beginning was the formation of a working group of seventeen committed sorors.

In preparation for the task at hand, the sorors began an intensive program of fundraising, which ran throughout the year. Activities included; garage sales, casino parties, and the selling of tickets for the annual Spring Scholarship Ball.

Kappa Mu Omega Chapter was chartered on April 5, 1975 by the Regional Director, Soror Gloria Bond. The ceremony was conducted at the Joliet Holiday Inn followed by a workshop and a dinner for sorors and guests.

Following their chartering, the chapter immediately established a Coretta Scott King Scholarship, which was financed by its annual Scholarship Ball and moved quickly to incorporate all of the National Programs. Also, in an effort to serve area residents at a grass roots level, Kappa Mu Omega committed to monetarily support the Joliet Community Action Agency's Emergency Relief Fund and initiated an intense Consumer Education Program.

The sorors of Kappa Mu Omega never forgot the reason that they were originally called together and with their support Lambda Psi chapter was established on the campus of Lewis University in Romeoville, IL in 1978.

In the years since chartering Kappa Mu Omega has kept pace with all of the international programs as well as tailoring them to meet the needs of our local community. The Miss Fantasia Contest and Cotillion has become a family and community tradition. This biennial cotillion is the chapter's major fund raiser, which financially supports our scholarships and public service programs.

Over the years, Kappa Mu Omega's education program activities have evolved as the chapter's strongest initiative. These programs encompass a full range of activities for grade school students including teaching, tutoring, and mentoring under the umbrella of the Ivy AKAdemy.

A program for high school students consisting of teaching, mentoring, college preparation, college selection, scholarship award and support in locating, and obtaining other scholarships is provided on a continuum beginning with Fantasia and usually continuing through their completion of college.

In the years since chartering Kappa Mu Omega has maintained its active presence in the Joliet community. Today it is the only historically Black Greek letter sorority functioning as a unit in the city.

A major change took place in 2007 when the Tealight foundation was established as the fundraising arm of the chapter. This has increased and expanded our scholarship capability. Scholarship grants were received from the Silver Cross foundation and awarded with existing scholarships. Partnerships with other community groups and agencies increased as well as participation with Silver Cross Hospital, St Joseph Hospital, The Joliet Public Schools, Catholic Charities., Back to school Fair, Take-Back-the-Night, (Anti-Domestic violence event), several Walkathons, and health fairs.

Overall, Kappa Mu Omega Chapter has remained active, viable and productive in the Joliet Community. The Miss Fantasia Contest and Cotillion continues as the chapter's major fund raiser and most known sorority event. The Chapter is now in its thirty-seventh year of existence and remains committed to rendering service to the Joliet community. The sorors of Kappa Mu Omega look back with pride, humility, and thanks for the difference we have made and the lives we impacted.

Kappa Mu Omega Chapter Has Advised Lambda Psi Chapter Since Its Chartering In 1978.

KAPPA MU OMEGA CHAPTER BASILEI

Christine Ponquinette	1975 – 1976
Jennifer Johnson	1976 – 1977
Lita Holmes	1977 – 1978
Elsie McLemore	1978 – 1979
Jennifer Johnson	1979 – 1981
Billie Terrell	1981 – 1983
Faye Downey	1984
Ernestine Boston	1984 – 1987
Cornelia Malone	1988 – 1990

Jeanette Hamilton	1990 – 1992
Jennifer Johnson	1992 – 1994
Veryl Boykin	1994 – 1996
Lita Holmes	1996 – 1998
Martha Johnson	1998 – 2000
Allison Shade	2000 – 2002
Thelma Kirkland	2002 – 2004
Delois Standfield	2004 – 2006
Bobbie Bates	2006 – 2008
Martha Johnson	2008 – 2010
Patricia Meade	2010 – 2012
Jennifer Johnson	2012 – 2014

Kappa Tau Omega Chapter

BLOOMINGTON, INDIANA
APRIL 10, 1976

CHARTER MEMBERS

IRIS COOPER
SHIRLEY A. FLUELLEN
LINDA GROOMS
WANDA F. HARRIS
EPSEY Y. HENDRICKS
CONSTANCE KINARD HOLLAND
LINDA LELAND

L. L. MICHELLE LIGON
ANNA KATHELEEN MOORE
PATRICIA ANN SHIPP
LA VERTA LORENE TERRY
CAROLYN ANN THOMAS
EDITH PEETE THOMAS
DELORIS WALKER (BIRCH)
ARTEE F. YOUNG

On Sunday, September 28, 1975, twelve members of Alpha Kappa Alpha Sorority, Inc. convened at the home of Soror Constance Kinard Holland. One of the issues discussed during this first meeting was whether there was the opportunity for potential growth as an established chapter in the area. It was determined that there were other members of the sorority among the ranks of graduate students who were interested in forming a graduate chapter. Based on this information, the sorors who were present made some immediate decisions.

It was decided that the sorors would call themselves the Sisters of Ivy; those members who were currently not financial would become general members; the current Regional Director, Soror Gloria Bond, would be contacted and invited to come to Bloomington to meet with the group; that the chapter would hold monthly organizational meetings; that they would identify community service needs that the group could respond to, and they would begin to identify potential women in the community who would make membership growth possible.

The Bloomington Community was ideal for the development and growth of an Alpha Kappa Alpha chapter in 1975-1976. Tau Chapter had existed in the community without local sponsorship for more than fifty years; there were no Greek organizations among blacks at the graduate level; there was a cadre of faculty and staff wives with college degrees who were not affiliated with any Greek letter organization; and there was a definite need in the local community to demonstrate the black presence both socially and through service projects. The Sisters of Ivy immediately began to fill the gap.

Soror Gloria Bond came to Bloomington in late October or early November of the year. She met with the Sisters of Ivy and declared them a functioning group. The Sisters of Ivy initiated a Saturday tutorial project; took lessons on storytelling so that they could engage the minds of young children in the community; held bake and garage sales to raise funds; and made plans for the chapter chartering date proposed for April 1976.

The chartering ceremony was held on Saturday, April 10, 1976, in the Bryan Room. National officers in attendance included Central Regional Director, Soror Gloria E. Bond; First Supreme Anti-Basileus, Barbara K. Phillips; Supreme Parliamentarian, Elizabeth Randolph; and Executive Director, Anne Mitchem Davis. A representative number of sorors from Alpha Mu Omega Chapter in Indianapolis and Tau Chapter in Bloomington joined the Sisters of Ivy in the Bryan Room. More than three hundred Bloomington residents joined the chapter for the charter luncheon.

The mayor of Bloomington brought greetings and offered a challenge to the new chapter to make a difference within the community. Soror Barbara K. Phillips delivered a well-received message entitled "There Is a Balm in Gilead." The community talked about the speech and the luncheon, held in the Indiana University Tudor Room, and the program for months. Bloomington has not witnessed anything like this classy charter luncheon before or since. Soror Anne Mitchem Davis delivered the charter officially naming the Sisters of Ivy, Kappa Tau Omega Chapter, and Soror Gloria Bond presented the chapter with the president's gavel.

Bloomington has not witnessed anything like this classy charter luncheon before or since. The chapter has been on the move since that glorious day in April, and the community truly felt their presence.

The chapter purchased three life memberships in the NAACP within the first two years of their existence. The chapter has also for many years been the only organization holding a Golden Life membership in the NAACP. Within eighteen years, chapter contributions to Cleveland Job Corps and to the United Negro College Fund have exceeded $3,500. Nine women were initiated into Kappa Tau Omega Chapter in December 1976.

Locally, the chapter contributes to the Boys and Girls Clubs; they support AIDS, Breast Cancer and Diabetes Awareness, and they provide a local scholarship and an incentive award, and they annually contribute to the Bloomington Hospital Foundation.

Kappa Tau Omega continues to hold book drives related to the African Diaspora to both primary and secondary schools, and they hold Economic Empowerment Summits to teach the community about financial planning, consolidation, and reviewing credit reports.

Kappa Tau Omega also provides a local scholarship: Constance Kinard Holland and an incentive award. The Constance Kinard Holland Scholarship is given out annually to an African American high school senior who not only exemplifies leadership and community service but, academic excellence. The scholarship is in honor of one of the charter members, Soror Constance Kinard Holland, who has exemplified the true meaning of serving mankind through educational philanthropy by dedicating her professional and personal time in the Bloomington community.

Kappa Tau Omega sorors make an annual contribution to the Educational Advancement Foundation, and have historically maintained a 100 percent membership in the foundation. In addition, the chapter has contributed scholarships and grants to local community agencies.

In the twenty-first century, Kappa Tau Omega Chapter has been blazing new trails by implementing more local programs for both the Indiana University campus and Bloomington community. The chapter has hosted three Cluster Retreats; two in Bloomington, Indiana and one in Columbus, Indiana. The 2002 Cluster Retreat was one of the most well attended clusters in Alpha Kappa Alpha history. In 2001, the chapter hosted its twenty-fifth anniversary celebration at the Oliver Winery which was well attended by people in both the Columbus and Bloomington communities.

In 2003 Kappa Tau Omega sorors started a teen etiquette workshop called "Cultured Pearls." The Cultured Pearls workshop prepares high school ladies for the world through career building, professional etiquette, and leadership training with various workshops that target these areas of concern for today's young women. The chapter has also been a part of the Adopt a Family program for the Thanksgiving and Christmas holidays.

Kappa Tau Omega is steady in its operations, although its membership is transient. The chapter's membership has been as high as twenty-six sorors and as low as seven sorors. This is due primarily to the members' connections with Indiana University (professors come and go).

In its thirty-seven year history the chapter has had two of its sorors win a distinguished national award—the "Founders Graduate Service Award." Sorors from the chapter have chaired and served the sorority on national committees and eight of its members have been certified as Graduate Advisors.

Kappa Tau Omega Has Advised Tau Chapter.

Chapter Members Who Have Held International/National Office or Been Elected to the International/National Nominating Committee

| Constance K. Holland | Nominating Committee | 1986 – 1988 |
| | Supreme Parliamentarian | 1994 – 2000 |

Kappa Tau Omega Chapter Basilei

Constance Kinard Holland	1976 – 1977
Prudence Bridgwaters	1978 – 1979
Adele Dendy	1980
Audrey McCluskey	1981 – 1982
Caramel Russell	1983
Constance Kinard Holland	1984
Joanne Washington	1985
Adele Dendy	1986
Margaret McDay	1987
Thurman Gordan	1988 – 1989
Denise Hayes	1990 – 1991
Tammey Ramey	1991
Constance Holland	1992 – 1994
Richelynn C. Douglas	1995
Constance K. Holland	1996 – 1998
Denise Hayes	1999 – 2000
Y. Grace Raby	2001 – 2002
Aisha Goens	2003 – 2004
Jesulon Gibbs	2005

Pledged to Remember: The History of Central Region

Kappa Psi Omega Chapter

Madison, Wisconsin
May 15, 1976

*Seated Left to Right: Alicia Allen, Cynthia Knox, Barbara Archia, Velma Richardson, Rebecca Graves.
Standing Left to Right: Diane Hendrix, Mary Wilburn, I. Lorraine Davis, Darlene Hancock, Ethel Swonigan, Betty Reneau Rowe, Mariann Keller, Laura Turner, Bobbie Curtis, Frances Huntley-Cooper. Not pictured: Marie Best, Lucia Sernorma Mitchell, Lessie Fort, Bettie Peevy, Linn Hairston*

Charter Members

ALICIA V. ALLEN	DIANE P. HENDRIX
BARBARA P. ARCHIA*	MIRIAM E. KELLER
MARIA L. BEST	CYNTHIA H. KNOX
FRANCES HUNTLEY-COOPER	LUCIA MITCHELL
BOBBIE J. CURTIS	BETTIE E. PEEVY
I. LORRAINE DAVIS	VELMA J. RITCHERSON
LESSIE C. FORT	BETTY J. RENEAU-ROWE*
REBECCA V. GRAVES	ETHEL M. SWONIGAN
LINN HAIRSTON	LAURA TURNER
DARLENE HANCOCK*	MARY N. WILBURN

*Ivy Beyond the Wall

Twenty Madison, Wisconsin sorors chartered Kappa Psi Omega graduate chapter in May 1976. The spring chartering ceremony, led by then Central Regional Director, Gloria E. Bond marked a first for Madison. Soror Barbara Archia, the chartering Basileus made contact with and brought together nearly thirty sorors from Madison's community and the University of Wisconsin's graduate student ranks. Pushed untiringly by Soror Archia, the sorors formed an interest group intent on planning a comprehensive program of service with four goals: 1) Providing guidance and assistance to the minority community, particularly in the areas of education; 2) Personal involvement and professional skills devoted to youth and children; 3) Support and sisterhood to the graduate members at the University of Wisconsin-Madison and; 4) Leadership and sisterhood to the undergraduate women on the University of Wisconsin campus, Epsilon Delta Chapter.

Following Kappa Psi Omega's chartering other Alpha Kappa Alpha women joined the chapter, and they included: Gloria Dickerson, Deborah B. Cureton, Valerie Leon, Maxine Thompson and Gwen Highsmith. At that time, Soror Deborah Cureton served as the Chancellor, University of Wisconsin-Richland Center campus.

THE FIRST TEN YEARS: 1976 to 1986 the chapter promoted its goals by: sponsoring fashion shows; Career Days for high school seniors; joint Founders Day with Epsilon Delta; organized a health fair at East Towne Mall; partnered with the NAACP's voter registration drives; donated AKA Heritage series of books on Black women to a local neighborhood center; hosted a Golden Years Luncheon for senior citizens; mentored middle school students; and held a joint Founders Day with Pi Gamma Omega Chapter, Rockford, Illinois. Soror T. Ella Strother, third Basileus introduced the first annual spring dance for raising scholarship funds.

1987 TO 1997 — the years of growth and new leaders emerging. During these years, the chapter was recognized as a community leader for sponsoring such projects as: canned food drives for African American churches and the homeless shelter; hosting a health information booth at Juneteenth Day both in Madison and Beloit, Wisconsin; awarding savings bonds to middle school students; and awarding tuition funds to African American Ethnic Academy, summer school enrichment program.

In 1991, Kappa Psi Omega Chapter was the prime hosting chapter for the 57th Central Regional Conference. Under the leadership of Soror T. Ella Strother, Men Who Cook was launched in 1994 as the primary scholarship fundraiser. "Men Who Cook" has become a staple in the Madison community. The sorority invites male cooks from a variety of organizations such as, elected officials, public and private sector workers, retirees, members of the media, students and many others –to cook a specialty dish that community members sample. A panel of working chefs judge to determine the chef's awards while the community participate in a ballot which determines the "people's choice" awards. In recent years Kappa Psi Omega has combined the "Men Who Cook" event with aspects of the Alpha Kappa Alpha Sorority, Inc. International Programs in order to bring attention to issues like womens' health, obesity, heart health, breast health, and domestic violence abuse. Each year, this events provides the bulk of the resources for the chapter's scholarship proceeds

BUILDING A BRIDGE TO THE NEW MILLENNIUM THROUGH PROGRAMS OF SERVICE, 1997 TO 2012: Due to the high number of interracial families living in Madison, Wisconsin Soror Eleanor Higgins' administration held classes and workshops for biracial families on hair care, hair care products and skin care. In 1998, Kappa Psi Omega co-sponsored Epsilon Delta's 20th Anniversary Rededication Breakfast.

The Ivy Academy for sixth graders was implemented in year 2000. The academy was held at Wright Middle School and organized by Soror Lilada Gee, Nehemiah Corporation, a community social services agency. The chapter celebrated its tenth year scholarship fundraiser Men Who Cook, February 2004. Kappa Psi Omega Chapter also became a charter member of the Pan-Hellenic Council at the University of Wisconsin.

In 2005, Kappa Psi Omega's Basileus, Soror Marcia Lovett was elected President, Pan-Hellenic Council. Four women were initiated as new members: Sorors Enid Glenn, Tanya Smith, Camille Townsend and Kim Williams.

In commemoration of Alpha Kappa Alpha's centennial year, 2008, Kappa Psi Omega initiated the "Walk it Out" Health Fair. This free community activity, now held annually, includes a two mile walk, a set of health and fitness workshops, massage and relaxation services, and a healthy foods cooking demonstration. Our community partners for this event include GHC Health, 100 Black Men of Madison Wisconsin, UW Credit Union and Susan G. Komen for the Cure of South Central Wisconsin.

At the end of each summer Kappa Psi Omega joins with 100 Black Men of Madison and other service organizations to stuff and distribute backpacks full of school supplies for needy students. These efforts have earned the chapter special recognition by 100 Black Men of Madison for being a strong community supporter.

Each fall, Kappa Psi Omega teams with other African American Greek organizations to participate in the "Divine 9 Food Drive" The drive is a friendly competition to collect the most non-perishable foods to donate to a local food pantry. Not surprisingly, Kappa Psi Omega often wins this contest.

Located in Madison, Wisconsin, the state capital, Kappa Psi Omega frequently plays a prominent role in the state's "AKA Day at the Capital" activities. Being in the capital city has given members excellent access to lawmakers and policy setters enabling Kappa Psi Omega to advocate for issues that directly impact women, and the African American community.

In 2011 Kappa Psi Omega hosted the first annual Wisconsin statewide Founders' Day. More than 100 sorors from chapters in Milwaukee, WI and Rockford, IL joined us to remember and rededicate ourselves to the purposes and ideals of our beloved founders.

In April 2012 Kappa Psi Omega hosted the 78th Central Regional Conference at Madison's beautiful Monona Terrace. More than 1400 Central Regional sorors attended the conference where they had the opportunity to provide service at the Second Harvest Food Pantry and host a youth summit for more than 100 area youth

Kappa Psi Omega is home to some of the Madison community's most distinguished citizens. Among the chapter's members are the state of Wisconsin's first and only African American elected mayor (Frances Huntley-Cooper, former Fitchburg Mayor), a diamond soror (Fannie Frazier Hicklin) who was the first African American professor at the University of Wisconsin-Whitewater, the first African American Nurse to both serve as President of the American Nurses Association and head a Wisconsin state agency (Barbara Nichols), and the first African American women to earn tenure in the University of Wisconsin-Madison School of Education (Gloria Ladson-Billings)

Currently, Kappa Psi Omega is implementing the Alpha Kappa Alpha Sorority, Inc., International Program: Emerging Young Leaders (EYL) with middle school girls in the Madison metropolitan area. With a core of more than 20 girls, chapter members are engaging in leadership development and mentoring activities to ensure that our community will have a ready supply of talented and willing leaders for decades to come

Kappa Psi Omega Has Advised Epsilon Delta Since 1977.

Kappa Psi Omega Chapter Basilei

Barbara P. Archia*	1976 – 1978
Theresa Sanders	1980 – 1982
T. Ella Strother	1983 – 1986
Michelle Bledsoe	1987 – 1988
Linda Gordon	1991 – 1992
Theresa Sanders	1993 – 1996
Alfie Breland	1997 (Limited term)
Eleanor Higgins	1997 – 2000
T. Ella Strother	2001 – 2004
Marcia Lovett	2005 – 2006
Theresa Sanders	2007 – 2008
Frances Huntley-Cooper	2009 – 2012
Gloria Ladsen-Billings	2013-present

**Ivy Beyond the Wall*

Lambda Alpha Omega Chapter

WESTERN SUBURBS
CHICAGO, ILLINOIS
MAY 29, 1976

Row 1-Left to Right: Arthalia Jackson, Carol L. Benson, Wylmarie Reid, Joyce Moore, Arlene Dantzler, Jacqueline Mitchell, Frances Maxine Planer, Alexanne Williams, Rose J. Thompson, Goldie Brown, Lynne McGraw, Connie Williams, Joyce D. Luckett, Vivian Sturgis, Ethel L. Gary. Row 2-Left to Right: Janice B. Lewis, Edna W. Randolph, Patricia Bauldrick, Janice McNair, Lue Ellen McGee, Nola Williams, A. Lorene Hunt, Beverlynn Ivory, Ruth Lawson.

CHARTER MEMBERS

PATRICIA BAULDRICK	LYNNE MCGRAW
CAROL L. BENSON	JANICE MCNAIR
GOLDIE BROWN	JACQUELINE MITCHELL
ARLENE DANTZLER	JOYCE MOORE
ETHEL L. GARY	FRANCES MAXINE PLANER
A. LORENE HUNT	EDNA RANDOLPH
BEVERLYNN A. IVORY	WYLMARIE REID
ARTHALIA JACKSON	VIVIAN STURGIS
RUTH LAWSON	ROSE THOMPSON
JANICE LEWIS	ALEXANNE WILLIAMS
JOYCE LUCKETT	CONNIE WILLIAMS
LUE ELLEN MAGEE	NOLA WILLIAMS

As a result of the turbulent civil rights movement of the 60s and early 70s, an onslaught of young, African American professionals initiated another major migration of African Americans to all parts of this country. The Chicago western suburbs were a great recipient of this group; doors opened to job opportunities never imagined. The beginnings of what would be known as Lambda Alpha Omega originated at a tea in the home of Soror Ethel I. Gary of Wheaton, Ill. Ten sorors were in attendance: Goldie V. Brown, Carla Edwards, Beverlynn A. Ivory, Arthalia E. Jackson, Ruth Lawson, Joyce Luckett, Lue Ellen (Magee) Moore, Edna Randolph, Vivian J. Sturgis and Rose M. Thompson; Patricia A. Bauldrick joined the group at the second meeting. Four officers were named as organized efforts continued: Soror Rose M. Thompson — Chairman, Soror Ethel I. Gary — Co-Chairman, Soror Joyce M. Luckett — Secretary and Soror Lue Ellen Moore — Treasurer. The group met monthly and by February they had chosen a name, West Suburban Associates of Alpha Kappa Alpha Sorority.

While continuing to organize, the size increased and the first fundraiser was held. A social outing/dance at Northlake Hotel in Northlake, Ill. was held in February 1976. The theme for the first fundraiser was "Leaping into '76 with AKA." Proceeds from this activity were donated to the United Negro College Fund (UNCF) and the National Association for the Advancement of Colored People (NAACP).

On May 29, 1976, the group received its charter at the Hyatt Oak Brook Hotel (currently the Doubletree) where the beautiful ceremony was led by 18th Central Regional Director Soror Gloria E. Bond of South Bend, IN. Following the installation of the first officers of Lambda Alpha Omega, the charter members joined their families, friends and visiting sorors for a luncheon, where the chapter's donations of $500 to the UNCF and the NAACP were formerly presented. The Second Supreme Basileus of Alpha Kappa Alpha Sorority, Incorporated, Loraine R. Green of Chicago, IL, Theta Omega Chapter, was the luncheon speaker.

Other contributions and projects for 1976 included distributing baskets to five needy families in Wheaton and Maywood; forming a young girl's enrichment group; volunteering time for the DuPage County Cancer Society; supporting the sorority's National Program, which included the Cleveland Job Corps Center; Leadership Training; the Boule in New York; the Regional Conference in Chicago; and contributing to the sorority's half million dollar commitment to the UNCF by 1978. Ms. Ella Jenkins was presented in concert, a Disco Night was sponsored in Bolingbrook, a family picnic and family Christmas party were held, and a life membership plaque was received at the NAACP Scholarship Banquet in November 1976.

Throughout the seventies and eighties, Lambda Alpha Omega continued its support of sorority programs and local community organizations. The chapter supported several organizations: the Peace Corps Partnership Project (San Rafael de Bordon Community Center in Costa Rica), the Urban League, Operation Push, DuSable Museum of African American History, National Council of Negro Women, Sickle Cell Anemia, local churches, and the Y.W.C.A. The chapter participated in World Food Day and aid to the victims of Hurricane Hugo.

Also, the chapter sponsored reading and tutorial services, career guidance through Black College Forums and Miss Fashionetta®. The chapter donated to the Educational Advancement Foundation, Historically Black Colleges and Universities, the Oak Park Council on International Affairs, and the Assault on Illiteracy program.

One of the most exciting experiences for Lambda Alpha Omega was being prime hostess for the 56th Central Regional Conference on April 19-24, 1990. The conference was held under the dynamic guidance of Loann J. Honesty King, Central Regional Director at the Hyatt Hotel in Oakbrook, IL. Basileus Rose Thompson, and Chairman Patricia Bauldrick provided chapter leadership for the occasion.

On May 25-27, 2001, under the leadership of Vera Wilcox, Basileus and Brenda Ladipo, Chairman, Lambda Alpha Omega had a "Sterling Celebration" marking 25 years of "Service to All Mankind" in our local communities. Charter members: Patricia Bauldrick, A. Lorene Hunt, Lue Ellen Moore-Magee, Joyce Moore, F. Maxine Planer, Edna Randolph, Rose Thompson, Goldie Brown, Ethel Gary, and other chapter members, including Barbara Wade and Sharece Spivey, performed a skit, "The Way it Was," written by Beverlynn A. Ivory. Special guests included First Supreme Anti-Basileus, Linda White, Central Regional Director, Nadine Bonds, Former Central Regional Director and Former Supreme Grammateus, Peggy LeCompte, National Building and Properties Committee member, Mae Carr and Pamela Porch from Xi Nu Omega.

By the year 2004, Lambda Alpha Omega's chapter membership included two Golden Sorors: Beverlynn Ivory and Dolores Register, 18 Silver Stars and 12 Life Members. From 2003-2004, the chapter retained 95% of its members and had 5% reactivation. Although the majority of the members lived in west suburban Chicago, several members—newly initiated and transferees—came from Chicago's south and west sides and south suburban Chicago. As a result, some programs extended to Chicago. Examples are the Miss Fashionetta® activities, scholarship recipients and partnerships with the Chicago Public Schools and Chicago Defender Education Department.

Lambda Alpha Omega Chapter was delighted and proud when two of our chapter members were appointed to national committees. In 1994, Supreme Basileus Eva Evans appointed Emily Dilworth Jones to the National Membership Committee and in 2004, Supreme Basileus Linda White appointed Mae Helen Smith to the National Honorary Members Committee.

The 2004 Cluster I Area Retreat was held in Itasca, IL, September 17-18, 2004. Central Regional Director, Dorothy Buckhanan provided enthusiastic and purposeful leadership. Chairman Christa Wyatt-Small, Basileus Barbara Wade, Melinda Riddick, Mae Smith and Josephine McClellan contributed to the success of the retreat.

Graduate Advisor Sharece Spivey and Assistant Graduate Advisor Marquita Curry provide leadership and counsel to Omicron Alpha Chapter, which is composed of undergraduate sorors from Aurora University, Aurora, IL, and Dominican University, River Forest.

Some of the chapter's continuing and new activities, based on the international program initiatives, are: AKA-Lade (named by Soror Patricia Bauldrick) featuring Miss Fashionetta®; AKA-Dettes, a young women's enrichment group; Pre-Kwanzaa Bazaar, and the Ivy Reading AKAdemy.

AKA-Lade/Miss Fashionetta® has generated more than $800,000 for scholarships and book grants to college bound students through the Arthalia E. Jackson and Janice B. Lewis Scholarship Funds.

Debutantes, escorts, "extras" and parents who participate in this event also participate in seven months of activities including: a series of workshops such as financial literacy, cultural field trips and social graces in preparation for the gala cotillion and dinner-dance.

Other scholarships awarded to community youth included the Educational Advancement Foundation (EAF) in 2001 and the Presidential Freedom Scholarship in 2003 and 2004.

The Pre-Kwanzaa Bazaar has afforded unparalleled community involvement. The bazaar is a marketplace in which Black vendors and others from the surrounding communities present and sell all manner of unique quality merchandise in a family oriented setting. The vendors share the day with educational forums, health venues and performances of the arts.

More than 50 vendors and companies participated in the 2004 Pre-Kwanzaa Bazaar held at the College of DuPage in Glen Ellyn, IL. Partnerships include the College of DuPage, DuPage County NAACP, Jack and Jill, Urban League, Top Ladies of Distinction, Benedictine University and River Forest Community Center. Chairmen for the event have been Dolores Register, Nola Williams, Anna Simeon and Valarie Watkins.

The Ivy Reading AKAdemy began in 2003 under the directorship of Mae Helen Smith and continues today. Working closely with Mae Helen Smith were Basileus Barbara Wade, Anti-Basileus Osie Davenport and A. Lorene Hunt.

The Ivy Reading AKAdemy program has led to significant partnerships with professors and students at Concordia University, River Forest. The university provided twenty-seven students in 2004 to tutor at the AKAdemy.

Honorary member Jan Gilchrist, author and illustrator, was a presenter at the 2003-2004 Ivy Reading AKAdemy culminating event held at Emerson School in Maywood, IL.

Forum-Senior Issues: Health, Safety and Quality of Life was presented to approximately 80 community residents in 2004. The forum was led by Anti-Basileus Osie Davenport, Co-Chairmen Beverlynn A. Ivory and A. Lorene Hunt, Health Committee Chairman Kimberly Brown, and Edna Randolph. Partners involved were the Church and Society Committee and the Health Committee of Neighborhood United Methodist Church, and the National Organizations of Black Law Enforcement Executives (NOBLE). Special speakers were Dr. Dorothy Lucas, Medical Director of Cook County Department of Public Health and Mr. Williams Simmons, Criminal Division Chief Investigator, DuPage County State's Attorney Office.

In 2004, Lambda Alpha Omega program activities earned the chapter many accolades at the 70th Central Regional Conference in Milwaukee, WI: First Place Overall Achievement for Chapter Programs, Gold for Chapter Operations/Standards Reporting and First Place for Achievement in Economic Development.

Lambda Alpha Omega has and continues to eagerly implement programmatic thrusts as mandated by the administration of each Supreme Basileus. It is our focus to deliver "Service to All Mankind." Since

2005 several of the aforemention programs have expanded and the following programs have been added:
- Reading Is Fundamental Distributions
- ET Tutorial Programs
- Carter G. Woodson Essay Contest
- AKA-DETTES (a young girls' enrichment group)
- African American Family Forum
- Collaboration Luncheon for Black Organizations in the Western Suburbs
- Teen Pregnancy Prevention Program
- Health Awareness Workshops for Senior Citizens
- Children's Halloween Parties
- Hayrides with Square Dancing
- Children's Christmas Parties
- Pre-Kwanzaa Bazaar
- African Village
- Golf Outings

Lambda Alpha Omega has grown to approximately 100 members and continues its legacy of service. The Chapter and its members continue to address community needs as recommended by the sorority's international leadership.

Lambda Alpha Omega Has Advised Omicron Alpha Since 1986.

Lambda Alpha Omega Chapter Basilei

Rose Thompson	1976 – 1978
Beverlynn A. Ivory	1979 – 1980
Patricia Bauldrick	1981 – 1982
Emily Jones	1983 – 1984
Ruby Campbell	1985 – 1986
Nell Santos	1987 – 1988
Rose Thompson	1989 – 1990
Rebecca Smith-Andoh	1991 – 1992
Flora Green	1993 – 1994
Frances Planer	1995 – 1996
Mae Helen Smith	1997 – 1998
Brenda Ladipo	1999 – 2000
Vera Wilcox	2001 – 2002
Barbara Wade	2003 – 2004
Osie Davenport	2005 – 2006
Anna Banks Simeon	2007 – 2008
Kimberly Brown	2009 – 2010
Sharion E. Wade	2011 – 2012
Jacquelyn Pipkin	2013 – 2014

Lambda Mu Omega Chapter

CHICAGO, ILLINOIS
MARCH 5, 1977

First Row—from left: Former National Officer Irma Clark, Special Guest Carolyn Thomas, Former Supreme Basileus (2nd) Loraine Richardson Green, Supreme Basileus Bernice I. Sumlin, Juanita Van Dorn, Executive Director Ann Mitchem Davis, Connie Shields and Mary Shears. Second Row—left to right: Jessie M. Shaw, Florence Robinson, Valeria Parks, Genevieve Walker, Lois Ward, Arlene Pierce, Carmen Fair, Binarozelle Ferguson, Vera Materre. Third Row—left to right: Melba Wilson, Amaralize Dejoie, Ellouise Cantrell, Dorothy Lamar, Maryann Shanklin, Arwilda Burton, Evelyn Daniels, Gloria Collins. Fourth row—Brenda Williams, Belinda Williamson, Claudette McFarland, Geraldine Jackson, Earnestine King, Geraldine Jones, Florice Green, Carol Smoot, Slettie Vera Bondurant, Lillie Wyatt and June McClanahan.

LAMBDA MU OMEGA CHARTER MEMBERS

CARMELITA ANSON	JUNE MCCLANAHAN
DOROTHEA AVANT	CLAUDETTE MCFARLAND
SLETTIE VERA BONDURANT	VALERIA PARKS
ARWILDA BURTON	ARLENE PIERCE
ELOUISE CANTRELL	JUNE RHINEHART
EMMERINE CLARKSTON	FLORENCE ROBINSON
GLORIA COLLINS	MARYANN SHANKLIN
EVELYN DANIELS	JESSIE M. SHAW
AMARALIZE DEJOIE	MARY SHEARS
CARMEN ERCELL FOWLER FAIR	CONNIE SHIELDS
BINAROZELLE FERGUSON	CAROL SMOOT
MOLLY FREEMAN	ZENOBIA STRODE
FLORICE GREEN	JUANITA A. VAN DORN
GERALDINE JACKSON	GENEVIEVE WALKER
GERALDINE D. JONES	LOIS WARD
EARNESTINE KING	BRENDA WILLIAMS
DOROTHY LAMAR	BELINDA WILLIAMSON
GLADYS BEAVERS LEWIS	MELBA WILSON
VERA MATERRE	LILLIE WYATT

In April 1976, Soror Jessie M. Shaw, a former Basileus of Theta Omega Chapter, expressed her desire to form a second, small chapter in Chicago. This chapter would meet during the day. After several sessions with interested sorors, the women decided that this chapter would emphasize service.

A few months later, Sorors Jessie M. Shaw and Claudette McFarland Winstead formed an interest group called the Satellite Associates of Alpha Kappa Alpha Sorority, Inc. The name was the brainchild of Soror Winstead. Officers were: President, Claudette McFarland Winstead; Secretary, Carmen E. Fair; Treasurer, Florice Green; and Historian, Genevieve Walker.

The Satellites met and demonstrated their ability to carry out Alpha Kappa Alpha programs. Taking the leadership role, Soror Winstead formulated and guided most of the program activities. A highlight was a public tea featuring classical music at the DuSable Museum of African American History. Through Soror Winstead and her family, the Satellites were able to present a piano to the museum.

On March 5, 1977, the Satellite Associates was chartered and named Lambda Mu Omega Chapter. The beautiful chartering ceremony, conducted by Supreme Basileus Soror Bernice Sumlin, was held at the Harris YWCA of Chicago.

Lambda Mu Omega became the second alumnae chapter in the city of Chicago. They met during the day, and demonstrated their ability to carry out Alpha Kappa Alpha programs throughout the years. Lambda Mu Omega Chapter has contributed through individual sorors,\ and collectively as a chapter. Some of the outstanding program activities are:

- More than 27 years of financial and in-kind service to the Harris YWCA. Health Fairs and consultations were given
- More than 27 years of support for the Boy Scouts of America, Troop 717 and Pack 3717, resulting in a member of the chapter earning the Silver Beaver Award for service
- More than 27 years of visitations (with monthly parties) to the Dawson Nursing Home
- Participation in Tag Days, chapter meetings, letter campaigns (and of course, life membership) of the NAACP. Several chapter members have personal life memberships.
- Participation in canned goods campaigns, referrals to the colleges, financial donations and annual telethon, local and national Alumni Council of UNCF.
- Tutoring sessions and enhancement sessions in reading, young authors, and other studies in service to Chicago youth and teens in the Ivy AKAdemy I and II programs (Coleman and Ross Schools and Geer Home).
- Participation in meetings, influencing city leaders through Citizens Alert. One of the chapter members is the president.
- Presented concerts to assist aspiring young artists and to help develop community appreciation.
- Domestic Travel Tour, Cleveland Job Corps and other Alpha Kappa Alpha programs were uppermost in the activity schedule.
- Volunteering as receptionists, helping with registrations, doing community education for Cancer Society, Diabetes Association, Planned Parenthood, Heart Fund, Cook County Hospital, etc.
- Providing scholarship grants and Presidential Freedom Scholar grants for needy students at predominantly Black institutions of higher learning.
- Tutoring, sponsorship of the 4th Ward Health Fairs, AKA coat drive and donations of clothing and supplies for a shelter for women and children.
- Sponsoring educational college fairs, Black Dollar Month, Buckle Up, Martin Luther King, Jr. Service Day and voter registration drives.
- Sponsoring support for an African Village through CARE and the Oak Park council on International Affairs. This on-going project features a different village each year. In addition, the chapter sends boxes of supplies and coordinates letter exchanges between African American and African students.
- Established "The Gala Foundation" to provide scholarships for college students and donations for selected local and national charitable organizations.

- Annie R. Pope was selected in 2011 by Supreme Basileus Carolyn House Stewart as Central Region Archives Representative to the International Archives Committee.
- Lambda Mu Omega is an original founder of Chicago Joint Founders' Day celebration as a united effort.
- Joy E. Pilcher was the second president of the Chicagoland Area Basileus Counci, an opportunity to unite chapters in sisterhood and as service partners.

In our "SERVICE TO MANKIND," sisterliness, cooperation, loving support, caring and sharing with one another, gives Lambda Mu Omega Chapter members the roots and stamina to spread this same love to others.

Lambda Mu Omega Has Advised Xi Kappa Undergraduate Chapter Since 1982.

LAMBDA MU OMEGA CHAPTER BASILEI

Juanita A. Van Dorn	March 1977 – December 1977
Carmen E. F. Fair	1978 – 1979
Glady B. Lewis	1980 – 1981
Brenda Williams	1982 – 1985
Patricia Mosley	1986 – 1987
Phyllis Wilson	1988 – 1989
Marguerite Barlow	1990 – 1991
Comella Smith	1992 – 1993
Cristal L. Clay	1994 – 1995
Lois E. Robinson	1996 – 1997
Valerie Jones-Bland	1998 – 1999
Joy E. Pilcher	2000 – 2001
Simona M. Haqq	2002 – 2003
Crystal J. Washington	2004 – 2005
Nancy B. Coleman	2006 – 2007
Michelle (Lee) Murrah	2008 – 2009
Leona Paytes	2010 – 2011
Annie R. Pope	2012 – 2013

Lambda Xi Chapter

UNIVERSITY OF WISCONSIN
WHITE WATER WISCONSIN
MAY 14, 1977

Picture of 2003 Initiates: First Row — Left to Right: Taketa Causey, Ramycia Cooper, Myia Donley; Top Row: Brittany Clark and Marquita McCoy.

CHARTER MEMBERS

VYNESSA ALEXANDER	TONI HOPKINS
TONI BANKS	PATRICIA JAMISON
JACKIE BATTISTE	CHRISTINE JOHNSON
JOYCE BLAND	ZENA LOVE
DEBRA BROWN	MARY METCALFE
WAVERLY HENDERSON	LAVERN POPE

Since the early days of Lambda XI, the chapter has worked diligently to uphold the purpose of Alpha Kappa Alpha Sorority on the campus. The members have always involved themselves in several service projects to benefit both the campus and community.

IN THE BEGINNING

The chartering of Lambda XI chapter was no easy feat, several young women worked for four years to bring Alpha Kappa Alpha Sorority to the campus of the University of Wisconsin at Whitewater.

It all began in the fall semester of 1974, when seven young women began expressing their interest in Alpha Kappa Alpha. These seven women began to meet with two young women who were members of Alpha Kappa Alpha Sorority, Liddie Collins and Elaine Stephene. After several meetings, it was decided to form a club of interested women and chose the name TIAKA (Those Interested in Alpha Kappa Alpha) Club.

As the TIAKA club, this group of women began to organize themselves. They elected officers and sponsored a variety of campus activities and service projects while promoting the good name and goals of Alpha Kappa Alpha. Those efforts were all centered toward their goal of becoming women of Alpha Kappa Alpha and officially bringing the sorority to the campus.

A year later, in the fall semester of 1975, the graduate chapter from Milwaukee, Epsilon Kappa Omega became aware of the TIAKA club and offered their assistance in helping them to either pledge or charter a chapter. They sent a representative to campus to discuss these possibilities with the young women. She discussed with the young ladies several options, which included the requirements for chartering, and the option of pledging general membership in the sorority. The TIAKAS were still interested in chartering a chapter but at this time their membership was only 7 strong and they needed 12 in order to charter a chapter. With this in mind, five of the TIAKAS decided to pledge general membership under Epsilon Kappa Omega and then later continue working on chartering a chapter.

In November of 1975, five young women from the University of Wisconsin-Whitewater began the process for general membership. They were: Debra Brown, Paulette Blake, Joyce Bland, Christine Johnson and Florida Norman. Three other young ladies from around the state joined them. These young women became members of Alpha Kappa Alpha Sorority, Inc on February 14, 1976.

After becoming general members and still keeping their original goal in mind of chartering a chapter, they began to reorganize the TIAKA club. They held a rush, which had an overwhelming turnout of more than 25 girls in which 9 young women joined the TIAKA club. They were Vynessa Alexander, Jackie Battiste, Jill Cavanaugh, Toni Hopkins, Debra Stephens, Eileen Critz, Susan Young, Zena Love, and Dorothy Williams.

The TIAKA club and the four women of Alpha Kappa Alpha began holding meetings, sponsoring activities and planning for beginning the chartering process. After one semester of hard work, in January the chartering process was ready to begin. At this time the TIAKA club was reorganized with just the interested young women on the campus who met the chartering requirements.

Once the chartering process began the group started to formulate a chapter by developing a constitution, devising chapter goals for programming, completing several services projects, and learning the history and operations of Alpha Kappa Alpha.

During this process Regional Director Gloria A. Bond and various representatives of Epsilon Kappa Omega visited the campus to assist this group of young women. After four long months of work and dedication Regional Director Gloria Bond chartered Lambda Xi on Saturday, May 14, 1977 in the reception room of the Center of the Arts. After the ceremony a reception was held for family and friends of the new chapter. Several campus administrators were there to offer their congratulations on bringing such a fine organization as Alpha Kappa Alpha Sorority, Inc to the campus of UW-W.

As a young chapter, the Sorors of Lambda XI continually strived to be of service to the Whitewater Community and the campus. The chapter sponsored annual benefits such as the Misletoe Dance, Halloween Costume Ball and a Cabaret/Casino Weekend for the UNICEF/UNCF, Walworth County Social Services and the Cleveland Job Corp.

During Black History month the chapter would set up a display about the achievements of black people. Also they distributed copies of various heritage series to the students, and Nabisco black history posters.

Reactivation and Revitalization

Since the reactivation of the chapter on December 9, 1989, the Lovely Ladies of Lambda Xi Chapter have continued its legacy to be of Supreme in Service to All Mankind through the following:

BLACK FAMILY: The Black Family is a target in which Lambda Xi focuses on the improvement of the "status quo" of the Black community. Each year the chapter holds a Beautillion that honors black males for outstanding achievements on and off campus. The purpose of this event is to show the chapter's gratitude for the positive Black man and to step away from the negative stereotypes given to Black males. The importance of the Black male to the family as a community role model and the Black woman is also expressed in this event. Attendance at this event is always great

Other programs in which the chapter has been involved are the food and clothing drive, free facials and bake sales in which all proceeds went to Hurricane Katrina relief efforts. The annual food and clothing drive runs during the holiday season in which non-perishable food items and clothing are distributed to local churches and the Salvation Army. During the winter months, Lambda Xi attended the hunger task force and assisted with the assortment of non-perishable food items, toiletries and more.

ECONOMICS: The economic target area is supported each year by patronizing Black-owned businesses. Chapter members frequently dine at Granny's Nook, a soul food restaurant in the inner city of Milwaukee, owned by the parents of former Lambda Xi Soror JaDawn Muhammad. In Whitewater, the ladies often dine at Big Jim's Soul Food Restaurant on Main Street and in Milwaukee at Mr. Perkins Restaurant. Each year during Skee-Week Lambda Xi purchases items from Lena's Grocery store, a Black family owned business.

The support of Black businesses helps promote the empowerment of the Black community. The service of these businesses is conducted with pride. Seeing the employers and employees taking such pride in the businesses that they have established enhances our overall pride in ourselves and our culture. Patronizing these businesses is one way for the members to engage and uplift the Black community and support the economic target.

HEALTH: A Health Week is held to address the health target area. During this week, chapter members set a table in the University Center building of our campus. The table has a variety of literature and pamphlets dealing with various issues in health and its relevance to our fellow college peers such as breast cancer awareness, SIDS (Sudden Infant Death Syndrome) awareness and STD (Sexually Transmitted Disease) awareness.

The first Health Seminar emphasized natural health. The seminar educated students about the effect of fast foods, processed foods and soda.

Other health activities have included: basketball, volleyball, aerobics, blood pressure checks, and a seminar on AIDS awareness. The Health Week is a service to the student body to help them to develop healthy relationships and to be more aware of their health. Also these health events help to keep the participants and chapter members in shape and a lot is learned each year.

ARTS: In the Arts, Lambda Xi chapter holds an annual Apollo night, which allows students to showcase their talents through dance, poetry and music. A newly implemented event that Lambda Xi has targeted is the "Mr. Pink and Green" Pageant. The Mr. Pink and Green scholarship pageant gives male students at UW-Whitewater an opportunity to interact with members of the chapter through community service.

The Heritage Arts Show was a prelude to the annual Apollo night. This event displayed art work by elementary school children; highlighted the talent of upcoming generations and celebrated visual art as part of our culture.

EDUCATION: A mentor/mentee program was initiated during the '92-'93 academic school term. Through this program each soror became a mentor to a freshman young lady. The program was later extended to female upperclassmen. Sorors assist and get acquainted with these young women academically and personally. The program helps students adjust to college life. The sorors become friends with some of the young ladies and, in one way or another, role models to all of them.

Lambda Xi has participated in university sponsored programs such as Adopt-a-School and America Reads. Weekly study nights have also been available for students to improve scholastic achievements

OTHER PROJECTS: Also in 1992-1993, the chapter initiated a world community program. This project was the Somalia penny drive to help alleviate famine in Somalia. The chapter's contribution to world causes promoted better relations and gave the sorors a greater understanding that as a part of the world everyone is affected by what happens in other places.

The chapter does many other service projects of equal significance including: Participating in various walk-a-thons, visiting mental care homes in the local Whitewater community and volunteering their services at different city festivals in the summer and entertainment events throughout the year. The sorors of Lambda Xi Chapter are committed to the fulfillment of our purpose as sorority sisters of Alpha Kappa Alpha Sorority, Inc. rendering service to mankind.

LAMBDA XI CHAPTER BASILEI

Debra Brown	1977
Vynessa Alexander	1978 – 1980
Not Recorded	1981 – 1983
Brenda Hodges	1984 – 1984
Sonia Davis	1985 – 1986
Michelle Buchanan	1987 – 1987
Racquel Cobbler	1989 – 1991
Janie Pope	1992 – 1993
Khyana Pumphrey	1993 – 1994
Michelle Kahl	1994 – 1995
Hope Jones	1995 – 1996
Nichole Bronson	1996 – 1997
Shelly Conner	1997 – 1998
Quanisha McAllister	1998 – 1999
Tanika Listenbee	1999 – 2000
Chavette Chatman	2000 – 2001
Not Recorded	2001 – 2003
Narasha Nabors	2003 – 2004
Brittany Clark	2004 – 2006

Lambda Nu Omega Chapter
LAKE COUNTY, ILLINOIS
MAY 27, 1977

From left-to-right, first row: Helen Watkins,* Gwen Jones,* Delores Crews, Edna Warren,* Mary Alston, Minnie Baldwin,* Eloise Williams, Robbie Lightfoot* and Thelma Luther. Second Row: Helena Johnson, Faye Warren, Arminta James,* Cleo Turk, Rosie Madison, Isabelle Buckner, Past Supreme Basileus (2nd) Lorraine R. Green,* Central Regional Director Gloria Bond,* Cynthia Hardin, Brenda Head, Johynne Tate,* Joyce Epperson, Past Central Regional Director Ordie Roberts*

*IVY BEYOND THE WALL

CHARTER MEMBERS

MARY ALSTON	THELMA LUTHER
ISABELLE BUCKNER	ROSIE MADISON
MINNIE BALDWIN	BRENDA READ
DELORES CREWS	JOHYNNE TATE
JOYCE EPPERSON	CLEO TURK
CYNTHIA HARDIN	EDNA WARREN
ARMINTA JAMES	FAYE WARREN
GWEN JONES	HELEN WATKINS
HELENA JOHNSON	ELOISE WILLIAMS
ROBBIE LIGHTFOOT	

Lambda Nu Omega Chapter was formed through the interest of a few sorors in the Lake County area, spearheaded by Soror Isabelle Buckner. An Alpha Kappa Alpha Roundup was held in her home on Sunday, February 8, 1976. Efforts were put into action, which eventually led to the chartering of Lambda Nu Omega Chapter of Lake County, IL. This chartering has the distinction of being the first Black sorority in Lake County.

Lambda Nu Omega was chartered May 27, 1977, at the Waukegan Public Library in Waukegan, Illinois. Soror Bernice I. Sumlin was the Supreme Basileus and the Central Regional Director, Soror Gloria Bond of South Bend, IN, performed the chartering ritual. Also present for this event were Soror Ordie Roberts, Past Central Regional Director and Soror Loraine R. Green, 2nd Supreme Basileus. Two sorors, Angela Alexander and Karen Wright were unable to be a part of the chartering ceremony but are considered charter members.

After the ceremony a chartering reception was held at the home of Soror Edna Warren and chaired by Soror Arminta James. Saturday morning festivities continued with a chartering luncheon chaired by Soror Brenda Head and held at the Deerpath Inn, Lake Forrest, IL. Sorors reviewed Alpha Kappa Alpha's past, present and future via films, slides, songs, books and speakers.

Lambda Nu Omega chapter is committed to carrying out the programs of Alpha Kappa Alpha Sorority, and has sponsored several major projects prescribed by its leadership:

EBONY FASHION SHOW — The Ebony Fashion Show was the chapter's largest fundraiser and was held in the month of May around Mothers' Day every year. The chapter has held this event since 1977 when Soror Isabelle Buckner served as Basileus. Four scholarships were awarded to the Lake County community at the show. The fashion show continued to be the chapter's most anticipated event until 2009.

FALL DANCE — An annual fall fundraiser of the chapter was held at Great Lakes Naval Base at Port-O-Call. The Fall Dance was held from 1977-1990.

MARTIN LUTHER KING, JR. DAY — The first Martin Luther King, Jr. Day celebration was actualized during the tenure of Soror Isabelle Buckner. A commemorative service was planned in the community to remember the work of Dr. King. This tradition has continued through the years. The service, though initiated by Lambda Nu Omega Chapter, is now planned by the ministerial alliance. But the chapter participates as a member of the Pan-Hellenic council which sponsors the social hour before the service begins. This year Lambda Nu Omega partnered with Alpha Phi Alpha, Kappa Alpha Psi and the Family First Center to provide pre-teens and teenagers with a venue to share their thoughts, ideas and opinions about the state of the nation in the aftermath of the Civil Rights Movement. The program consisted of video clips from the "Little Rock Nine" and "Whatever it Takes," which focus on education in America. There was discussion with the youth about their thoughts on racism in the 1960s through today and the progress that has been made. Parents and mentors who helped facilitate the discussion attended this event. After the presentations, everyone shared a meal of sandwiches, chips, and juice, followed by a cake to celebrate Dr. King's birthday.

SENIOR CITIZENS NIGHT OUT — About 80 seniors are entertained through song, dance and stories by chapter members. The sorors and seniors play Bingo. The senior citizens can win door prizes and refreshments are served afterwards. This function is held in an area nursing home in Lake County during the month of November. This project was initiated in October 1977 but was no longer implemented after 1992.

AKA BOWL — For more than 10 years, LNO has hosted a bowling event open to the chapter and their family and friends for an evening of glow in the dark 'cosmic bowling' experience. Each year more than 80 guests participate, and all proceeds go to the scholarship fund. The event has been held annually since 2000.

ADOPT-A-HIGHWAY — This beautification event began on June 12, 2003 when LNO accepted an agreement between Lake County, IL, to adopt Section 38A of O'Plaine Road between IL Route 137 and Celano Drive. Sorors, honey — dos and don'ts, and guests met at 8:30am to clean up the highway, and then congregated afterward for breakfast and fellowship. This practice occurs annually.

EMERGING YOUNG LEADERS — As the signature program of Soror Carolyn House Stewart, this mentoring and coaching workshop activity occurs monthly on the second Saturday directly following chapter meetings. Girls ages 11-14 attend workshops on self-esteem, hygiene, fashion, and other related coming of age topics facilitated by chapter members. EYL was initiated in 2011 and will continue throughout this administration. There are currently 7 girls enrolled in the program.

GREEK DAY AT THE CAPITAL — This event occurs every March. The LNO chapter has joined other AKA chapters and members of the Pan Hellenic for a visit to Springfield, IL to talk to state legislators about their legislative agenda. More than 300 individuals were in attendance in 2012.

Lambda Nu Omega chapter is also notable in the Lake County community by their service projects and well-known events.

STOMPFEST STEPSHOW — Lambda Nu Omega along with Kappa Alpha Psi launched its newest fundraising activities in February of 2012. Undergraduate chapters from the surrounding region were invited to participate in a step show showcase held at the College of Lake County in Grayslake,

IL. This fundraiser is scheduled to repeat the February of 2013, and will be an annual event with proceeds going toward the scholarship fund.

In 2000 Lambda Nu Omega spearheaded the formation and chartering of Sigma Gamma Chapter at Lake Forest College, in Lake County IL Thirteen young collegiate were initiated at the Lilly Reid Holt Chapel on April 11. Alpha Kappa Alpha was the first African American Sorority or Fraternity to be established at Lake Forest College. Soror Linda Baskin-Wilson was the Graduate Advisor.

Lambda Nu Omega Chapter is proud of its contributions to the community and the longevity of its members in the sorority. Our Golden Sorors include: Isabelle Buckner, Robbie Lightfoot,* Joyce Epperson, Edna Warren,* Naomi Peters and Helen Watkins. Our Silver Star members are: Brenda Baskin-Pearson, Cynthia Hardin, Gloria Greer, Sharon C. Allen, Cynthia Alexander, Denise Simon, Lynn Garrett, and Linda Baskin-Wilson.

Lambda Nu Omega Advises Sigma Gamma Chapter

LAMBDA NU OMEGA CHAPTER BASILEI:

Isabelle Buckner	1977 – 1978
Arminta James	1979 – 1980
Gwen Brown	1981 – 1982
Naomi Peters	1983 – 1984
Earnestine White	1985 – 1986
Joyce Green	1987 – 1988
Sarah Haggerty	1989 – 1991
Linda Baskin — Wilson	1992 – 1993
Karen D. Haggerty	1994 – 1996
Sharon C. Allen	1997 – 1998
Traci Hines	1999 – 2000
Jeanne Lucas	2001 – 2002
Pamela Foster-Stith	2003 – 2006
Cynthia Alexander	2007 – 2011
Sharon C. Allen	2011 – 2012
Jacqueline Jones	2013 –

Lambda Psi Chapter

Lewis University
Romeoville, Illinois
February 19, 1978

Charter Members

MAGGIE ADAMS	EMMA LIGGONS
KAREN ALEXANDER	CORNELIA PATTERSON
LETITIA BATES	JANIS SANDERS
PATRICIA CORBIN	JOHNNIE SIMS
VALERIE DAVIS	RHONDA TRAMEL
FAYE FLYNN	CYNTHIA J. WALLACE
SHELIA LEWIS	MATTIE WILLIAMS

Lambda Psi chapter was conceived in the minds of two Sorors who were employed at Lewis University (Sorors Lita Holmes and Kathleen Bolden). When Soror Holmes was elected Basileus in 1977, she enlisted the assistance of Soror Christine Ponquinette, who accepted the position of Graduate Advisor. Both of these Sorors moved to fulfill their commitment to charter a chapter at Lewis University-Romeovillle

During the time between 1973 and 1977, there had been some students initiated as general members, but by 1977 they had all graduated or were at least close to leaving campus leaving no official Alpha Kappa Alpha presence on campus. As a result, 14 young women were recruited to become members of the Ivy Leaf Club and the chapter to be established.

Under the watchful guidance of Soror Ponquinette, the group organized and coalesced as they created the Alpha Kappa Alpha presence and image on the Lewis University campus. Chosen to lead as president of the Ivy Leaf Club was Patricia Corbin, a mature student quickly moving toward completion of her requirements for graduation. The club's activities included many campus fundraisers such as dances and product sales. They also established a formal representation of Alpha Kappa Alpha in campus life.

The Peter Claver Center in Joliet became their community service project and many hours were spent with the children they served. Culminating the Ivy Leaf Club activities was the decision to purchase a $500 life membership from the Joliet Branch NAACP.

Lambda Psi Chapter was chartered February 19, 1978, in Joliet, IL at the Sheraton Joliet Motor Inn. The ceremony was conducted by Central Regional Director Soror Gloria E. Bond. Soror Corbin was elected Basileus and would serve until September of 1978 when her status would change and the new school term would begin. In September of 1978 Soror Karen Alexander was elected Basileus. The newly formed chapter carried the torch and set the bar high for Alpha Kappa Alpha's Attitude, Action, Behavior, Image and Spirit.

Lambda Psi chapter continues to be a dynamic force on the campus of Lewis University and obtaining many awards and recognitions. In 2008–2009 they were awarded the Mission Star Award — Organization of the Year. This award is given to the Student Organization that exemplifies the value of Knowledge, Fidelity, Wisdom, Justice and Association among its membership and throughout any of the events they host throughout the year.

In 2010 -2011 Lambda Psi was awarded two Spirit Awards. Spirit Awards are in recognition of specific events. They received the Spirit of Diversity and Unity Award for their 4 Shades of Pearls event. The Spirit of Diversity and Unity Award is given to the organization that hosts an event that celebrates what it means to celebrate unification among diversity. They also received the Spirit of Education Award for their Breast Cancer Seminar. The spirit of Education Award is awarded to the organization that hosts an event that provides the Lewis University community with an enriching educational experience.

Now in Lambda Psi's 36th year we pledge a renewal of commitment and continue to be "Supreme in Service to All Mankind." We do so in loving memory of the chapter's second Basileus, Ivy Beyond the Wall, Soror Karen Alexander-Gousman who led with love.

Lambda Psi Chapter Basilei

Patricia Corbin	1978
Karen Alexander	1978 – 1979
Linda Johnson	1979 – 1982
Celeste Trammel	1982 – 1984
Monica Johnson	1984 – 1985
Sonia Horn	1985 – 1987
Marla Heflin	1987 – 1990
Tessn McKinzie	1990 – 1991
Karen Calloway	1991 – 1992
Julie Houston	1992 – 1993
Latice Baker	1993 – 1993
Ayanna Fisher	1993 – 1994
Tiffany Seay	1994 – 1995
Natasha Sawyer	1995 – 1996
Regine Nazaire	1996 – 1997
Niquitta Berry	1997 – 1998
Concitta Cavin	1998 – 1999
Samantha Powell	2000 – 2001
Symara Michelle Hearon	2001 – 2002
Shaundra Heavens	2002 – 2003
Devon Ellis	2003 – 2004
Ashuanta McCormick	2004 – 2005
Ashley Caridine	2005 – 2005
Marie A. Clarke	2005 – 2006
Miriam Muhammad	2006 – 2008
Kellie E. Griffin	2008 – 2009
Kasmir Quinn	2010 – 2010
Victoria Jorden	2010 – 2012
Danielle Blocker	2012 –

PART IV: THE FINAL QUARTER OF THE CENTURY

Lambda Tau Omega Chapter

FAR SOUTH SUBURBAN CHICAGO
FEBRUARY 26, 1978

Seated from left: Audrey Carter, Bessie M. Flint, Lauretta Naylor-Thompson, Regional Director Gloria Bond, Willene Buffett, Gertrude Tandy, Tamyra Johnson and Janie Cooper. Standing, from left: Lois Merritt, Ethel T. Brown, Carolyn Hutton, Beverly Roseborough, Carolyn Washington, Constance Shorter, Maxine Morgan, Ruby Campbell, Anita Walker, Yvonne West, Jacqualine F. Scott and Jeanette W. Rogers.

CHARTER MEMBERS

ETHEL T. BROWN	MAXINE MORGAN
WILLENE BUFFETT	JEANETTE W. ROGERS
RUBY CAMPBELL	BEVERLY ROSEBOROUGH
AUDREY CARTER	JACQUELINE SCOTT
JANIE COOPER	CONSTANCE SHORTER
BESSIE FLINT	GERTRUDE TANDY
CAROLYN HUTTON	ANITA WALKER
TAMYRA JOHNSON	CAROLYN WASHINGTON
LOIS MERRITT	YVONNE WEST

THE EXPLOSIONS OF LAMBDA TAU OMEGA

The year 1976 not only commemorated the 200th birthday of America, but it also marked the beginning of what was to become Lambda Tau Omega Chapter of Alpha Kappa Alpha Sorority, Inc. The nucleus group was comprised of six Alpha Kappa Alpha women who resided in the far south suburban communities of Chicago.

The first meeting was organized by Anita Walker and Beverly Roseborough and attended by Ruby Campbell, Tamyra Johnson, Janie Cooper and Yvonne West. The main intent of the interest group was to continue locating sorority sisters who shared the enthusiasm of perpetuating the ideals of the sorority through community involvement. As Far South Suburban Associates of Alpha Kappa Alpha grew in numbers, it grew in confidence and determination in realizing its goal of becoming a chartered alumnae chapter. Through many months of planning and arduous work the number of sorors increased to 18.

On February 26, 1978, the aspirations of these 18 members became a reality. Regional Director Soror Gloria Bond conducted the chartering ceremony at the Left Bank Restaurant and the Far South Suburban Associates of Alpha Kappa Alpha became Lambda Sigma Omega Chapter. Imagine the surprise of the charter members when it was discovered that they had been chartered with the name of an existing chapter. Actually, before most members were aware of the mistake, new certificates were in the mail bearing the name: Lambda Tau Omega.

LAMBDA TAU OMEGA CHAPTER INITIATIVES

Since traditionally Alpha Kappa Alpha Sorority, Inc. has stressed scholastic achievement and service, it seemed fitting that Lambda Tau Omega Chapter continue to make significant contributions to facilitate academic excellence and service to the community. The following programs illustrate those efforts:

ADOPTION OF SOCIAL SERVICE AGENCIES

In 1978, Lambda Tau Omega selected to support Respond Now, an agency which is located in Chicago Heights, IL, and provides for the social welfare needs of residents in the Southern Suburbs. The services provided include health care, housing, food and/or clothing assistance. Lambda Tau Omega continues its canned food drive and annual monetary donations to Respond Now.

Since 1978, the chapter branched out to include support to a number of other local and international social service agencies/initiatives and Southland schools. Among these agencies/initiatives were: The Cleveland Job Corps, Crisis Center of South Suburbia, Rebuilding Together, Soles 4 Souls, World Water Day, American Cancer Society, Relay for Life, and Lupus Foundation.

CHARM AND CAREER CLINICS 1979-81

Lambda Tau Omega held Charm and Career Clinics at Freedom Hall in Park Forest, IL, sponsored by John H. Johnson Company of Chicago, IL. The clinics were for young ladies in grades 9-12. The purpose was to provide information on grooming, etiquette, health care, self-esteem, manners and career paths for the future.

LIFELONG LEARNING—READING EXPERIENCES 1982-1985

The purpose of this program was to identify problems relating to reading difficulties among minority students. The chapter provided tutoring and enriching experiences, which focused on reading, writing and study skills. Thus Lambda Tau Omega held Creative Writing Workshops/Contests for students in the South Suburbs. Savings Bonds were presented to the winners.

AFRICAN VILLAGE PROJECT

Initially the chapter adopted the village of Keur-Galle in 1985 where the main focus was the Waterwell Project. The chapter continued to enhance the global perspective through its support of and care for African villages. In subsequent years the chapter donated shoeboxes filled with school supplies for the children.

THE BLACK FAMILY

In the mid-1980's it became very obvious that many problems interfering with the success of our youth and adults could not be solely addressed within the family structure. Members of Lambda Tau Omega contacted resources to provide services to families in the South Suburban communities. Utilizing information gained from family interviews, the chapter was able to develop plans to meet the needs of various families with the "Adopt a Black Family Program."

BLACK COLLEGE FAIR

In 1984, Lambda Tau Omega felt that there was a need to inform their South Suburban youth of the opportunities that Historically Black Colleges offered and how they could be accessed. For several years, the Chapter chartered buses and took students to college fairs in Chicago, IL. Students received pertinent information and attended workshops on college life and financial aid from representatives from these colleges.

VOLUNTEER ENRICHMENT PROGRAM (VEP)

The Volunteer Enrichment Program (VEP) began January 4, 1986, at Charles E. Gavin School in Chicago Heights, IL, following a year of extensive planning. The intent was to provide an academic enrichment program for students in the areas of math, science, reading, writing, Black History, creative dramatics, and arts and crafts. It was a collaborative effort of four organizations: Lambda Tau Omega; South Suburban Links, Inc; Dr. Charles E. Gavin Women's Auxiliary; and Jack-and-Jill of America.

MISS PROMINENT PEARL COTILLION

The goals of Miss Prominent Pearl Cotillion were to enhance the debutantes in the areas of culture, college preparation, the arts, etiquette, ethics, community involvement, character building and social dancing. The cotillion allowed family and friends to share in the debutantes' joys of accomplishment and completion and offered the debutantes lifelong memories and bonds of friendships as they prepared for lives of higher achievement.

This event served as a major fundraiser 1989-2002. In 2010 Miss Prominent Pearl Cotillion was resurrected and continues to be an elegant and successful affair. It is now an initiative under the Twenty Pearls Foundation, Inc.

RISING STARS

In 1990, an all-male mentor program was developed for teenage boys. It was very successful and the only male group that had been organized by a sorority in any South Suburban community. One of its most outstanding programs was its "First Responder Disaster Training Program," in 2006. The program's success resulted from the Chapter's collaboration with the local fire departments and Christ Hospital. In addition to learning to prepare for a disaster, the young men learned to develop Disaster Preparedness Plans and Kits. The kits were distributed to residents in the local communities.

ACT TEST PREPARATION

In 1991 Lambda Tau Omega established a program to provide assistance to local minority students who wish to prepare for the American College Test (ACT). Specific areas of the ACT test such as math, science, English and reading were targeted each week. The results of the program were overwhelmingly positive and the students were quite appreciative of Lambda Tau Omega for taking time to enrich and enhance their test-taking skills.

EDUCATION/HISTORICALLY BLACK COLLEGE TOURS 1993-1999

Since Alpha Kappa Alpha Sorority, Inc. stressed the importance of high scholastic achievement, Lambda Tau Omega planned Historically Black College Tours for students in grades 11 and 12 during the mid-'90s. Students were able to visit numerous campuses in the South, talk with college personnel, visit the dormitories, cafeterias and classes… thus helping our students to make informed, intelligent decisions regarding their college choices.

ON TRACK

In 1998, this initiative embraced the Black Family. The Chapter provided educational services for at risk youth, which included tutoring in mathematics, science and reading. The program was monitored for a three year period at Chateau School in Hazel Crest, IL.

BUCKLE-UP/CHILD SAFETY SEAT INITIATIVE

This collaboration with State Farm Insurance in Palos Heights, IL was begun during the SPIRIT administration in 2006 and continued until 2010. Through this initiative families were provided with infant/child seats for their autos and were instructed on the correct procedure for placing the seats in the cars and for securing the infants in the seats.

AKA EXPO

The AKA Expo began in 2001 to provide a community program that highlighted many of the sorority's targets, which at that time included Health, Education, Arts, Black Family and Economics. During the AKA Expo, more than 50 African American vendors and social service/health providers were spotlighted; authors held book signings and health screenings were available. Voters were registered and instructed on the use of the new touch screen voting process.

The event was hosted over the years at the following venues: Prairie State College in Chicago Heights, IL, New Covenant Baptist Church in Phoenix, IL, Lincoln Mall in Matteson, IL and River Oaks Mall in Calumet City, IL. Currently, we have transitioned to the Markham Illinois Sixth Municipal District courthouse, in Markham, IL, "Going to School is Cool, Back to School Rally." Its sponsors are the Adult Probation Department, Twenty Pearls Foundation, Inc. and Kappa Alpha Psi Fraternity, Inc.

FOOD DRIVES

Hunger became an important concern in many areas and Lambda Tau Omega used Family Volunteer Day in 2004, 2005 and 2006 to culminate its annual food drives. Chapter members, family and friends joined together to sort hundreds of donated items for distribution to the Rich Township Pantry in Richton Park, IL. In 2012, Lambda Tau Omega is still supporting the Pantry.

MENTORING PROGRAMS

In 2004, Lambda Tau Omega established the Strands of Pearls, a mentoring program for girls ages 9 through 13. The program focused on education, creative writing, etiquette, inter-relationships, financial literacy, grooming and self-esteem. The Precious Pearls program for girls 14-18 was established in 2007 and those graduating have been rewarded with computers to assist with their college work. In 2009, the Emerging Pearls program was developed for girls 4-8 years old. These three mentoring programs are still operational and highly effective today.

EMERGING YOUNG LEADERS (EYL)

Lambda Tau Omega's Emerging Young Leaders (EYL) mentoring program was created in 2010 to address and align with the tenets of the Global Leadership Through Timeless Service Program initiative. Girls in grades six to eight are program participants.

TWENTY PEARLS FOUNDATION, INCORPORATED INITIATIVES

The Twenty Pearls Foundation, Inc. is the charitable arm of Lambda Tau Omega Chapter of Alpha Kappa Alpha Sorority, Inc. The Foundation established in March 2001 was designed to generate funds needed to develop philanthropic programs to serve many of the unmet needs of citizens of the Chicago Southland Community. Our chapter uses funds raised through the Foundation to support its programs.

The Foundation has written and received several grants. Among these were grants to address HIV/AIDS awareness, other health related issues, support for scholarship and educational issues and other community concerns. The following programs have been supported by Twenty Pearls Foundation, Inc.:

SCHOLARSHIPS

The Foundation awards the following scholarships on an annual basis: Shirley J. Phillips Scholarship, HBCU Scholarships; Betty George Scholarship, Stella Hardin Scholarship, Mae Solomon Financial Need Scholarship and Marva Campbell Academic Scholarship.

SPIRIT AND ESP INITIATIVES (2006-2009)

The chapter won five program awards at Central Region Conference in 2007 for its outstanding program implementation.

LTO GOES GREEN

LTO developed a website in 2006 and "went green" with all reporting in 2010.

TAX SEMINARS

From 2006-2009, annual tax seminars were sponsored by the Program Committees and held at Mayo Church in Matteson. These seminars were used to guide residents through the tax filing process.

REBUILDING TOGETHER

Twenty Pearls Foundation, Inc. collaborated with the national non-profit group "Rebuilding Together" in 2007-2009 on the last Saturday in April in each of the years listed here to renovate a home in an impoverished area for a low-income family who could not afford to do home repairs. Both organizations donated money and labor to the project.

EYEGLASS INITIATIVE

Lambda Tau Omega Collaborated with Lens Crafters and Luxottica Foundation, Inc. to provide vision testing and free eye glasses to more than 500 students in Southland schools in 2006 and 2007. The students were referred by vision screeners and school nurses.

MILLION POUND CHALLENGE

Lambda Tau Omega members formed teams and walked enthusiastically to shed pounds. Sorors signed up at the 50 Million Pound Challenge web-site and recorded all pounds shed by June 2010. Chapters with the greatest loss were awarded prizes at Boule 2010. LTO did not win a prize for shedding the most pounds at Boule but did win first place in its category for Platform V.

HEALTH RESOURCE MANAGEMENT AND ECONOMICS EMOTIONAL EMPOWERMENT SOCIAL SUPPORT PUBLIC AWARENESS

Members of the Foundation supported this initiative at the Central Region Conference in 2010.

SENIOR HEALTH OUTREACH INITIATIVES

The Senior Outreach Committee planned and implemented a variety of activities during 2005-2011 to entertain residents of Glenwood Healthcare and Rehabilitation Center in Glenwood, IL, and at Victory Centre Assistive Living Facility in Park Forest. Events were planned in conjunction with the following holidays: Martin Luther King Day, Valentine's Day, Memorial Day, Veteran's Day and Christmas. Activities consisted of senior survival and health related workshops, music, games, movies, food, gift giving and conversation.

GLOBAL LEADERSHIP THROUGH TIMELESS SERVICE INITIATIVES

The following activities were held during 2011-2012 to support and address the objectives of the Global Leadership through Timeless Service program initiatives:

EMERGING YOUNG LEADERS (EYL)

- Chicago Basilei Symposium
- Golf and tennis clinic
- Run the World: Girls Symposium
- Black Family Day Symposium
- Tour of Illinois State Capitol where EYLs served as Pages to State Senators and Representatives
- Gabrielle "Gabby" Douglas "Pink Pearls and Pretty Dresses: Empowerment Brunch
- "Pink Goes Chic" (3 part series) — Hair, Skin and Make-up

HEALTH

- Sorors participate in the Gift of Hope organ donation program at Ingalls Hospital
- Sorors Participated in Walk for Lupus and Walk for Hope programs in Chicago Southland.

GLOBAL POVERTY

Sorors worked with students at Algonquin School, Meadowview School and Lincoln School to raise money to donate to the Heifer Foundation in order to purchase heifers to send to Africa to help families farm and to supply them with food.

Sorors and mentor groups collected, cleaned and donated shoes to " Share Your Soles" Foundation to send to families in Third World countries.

Sorors and mentor groups collected and donated canned goods to needy families at Mayo Church and Praise Alive Church for their "Feed the Hungry" Programs.

Sorors and the mentoring groups partnered with Respond Now and the Village of Sauk Village to develop community gardens.

ECONOMIC SECURITY

Sorors collaborated with two other Southland organizations to sponsor a Back to School Rally at Cook County Municipal Court House in Markham, IL. Several hundred children were given school supplies for the year.

Sorors hosted community workshops to teach residents how to maintain their homes during this sluggish economy and how to write wills. The following were the themes for the three workshops: Keep Your Home, Thy "Living Will" Be Done and Conscious Consumption

"Women Wine Down" was an entrepreuneur chat session to help African American women start their own businesses.

SOCIAL JUSTICE AND HUMAN RIGHTS

Workshops were held at various locations in the south suburban communities to address the following topics:
- Teen Dating Violence
- Get Hands On for Hands Off Domestic Violence (in partnership with a local Crisis Center)
- Youth aging out of foster care
- Angel Tree Foundation to provide gifts to children of incarcerated parents.

These workshops were well attended by teenagers with their parents, community members and sorors.

INTERNAL LEADERSHIP FOR EXTERNAL SERVICES

A Speak Up Toasters Workshop and Leadership Conference were hosted by Lambda Tau Omega Chapter to help members enhance their communication skills. The premise: "Strong speaking skills enhance leadership capacity."

ACCOLADES

The explosion of Lambda Tau Omega continues to echo in the Central Region and in Alpha Kappa Alpha Sorority, Inc. The chapter has been the recipient of many regional, international and community awards. In 2010, Lambda Tau Omega chapter won three program awards at the Regional level and the individual soror awards:
- Outstanding Silver Soror
- Outstanding Golden Soror
- Soror Through The Years
- Runner-Up for Outstanding Soror in Communications/Journalism

In 2012, the chapter won at the Central Regional Level, the Outstanding Basileus of the Year and five program awards listed below:
- Emerging Young Leaders (EYL)
- Health
- Global Poverty
- Economic Security
- Social Justice and Human Rights

Lambda Tau Omega Chapter through its Foundation received special recognition for its contribution of $5,000 to Africare and is a four star contributor to the Educational Advancement Foundation.

In 2012 and beyond, we will face new challenges that will require us to mount with renewed fervor and tenacity. We must keep open minds and a willingness to do tasks differently to achieve maximum success. Our theme for 2012-2013 is: "The Dream Is Easy… The Journey Is Not."

35TH ANNIVERSARY CELEBRATION

January 2013 ushered in the year that we finalized plans for celebrating the Chapter's iconic chapter's 35th Anniversary, how it started, its past accomplishments and future undertakings. The centerpiece of the celebration was the 35th Anniversary Luncheon held Sunday, February 24, 2013 at Dream Palace in Lynwood, IL. Joining us in this celebration were our esteemed charter members, former chapter Basilei and the 28th Central Region Director Soror Giselé M. Casanova.

The Journey Continues!

LAMBDA TAU OMEGA CHAPTER BASILEI

Willene Buffett	1978 – 1979
Janie Cooper	1980 – 1981
Jeanette W. Rogers	1982 – 1985
Ceola Barnes	1986 – 1989
Shirley J. Phillips	1990 – 1991
Emily Turner	1992 – 1993
Anntionette L. Austin-Austin	1994 – 1995
Beckie A. Harris	1996 – 1997
Bertha H. Pugh	1998 – 1999
Sonya L. Bowen	2000 – 2001
Toya T. Harvey	2002 – 2003
Linda T. Varnado	2004 – 2005
Lynda Tarver	2006 – 2007
Jacqueline Toler	2008 – 2009
Rose Butler-Hayes	2010 – 2011
Joyce L. Nelson	2012

Mu Beta Chapter

MARQUETTE UNIVERSITY
MILWAUKEE, WISCONSIN
MARCH 4, 1978

CHARTER MEMBERS

MIRIAM ADAMSON	AIDA ORTIZ
FRANCES AGNEW	JENETTE PERKINS
MARY BELL	TRINETTE PITTS
GERILYN FLOWLER	MONICA RAY
DARLENE HAYES	JUDY ROGERS
JOANN HENRY	SHEREE ROBERTSON
THERA MARTIN	

The development of Mu Beta Chapter started with the tiaka Club (Those Interested in Alpha Kappa Alpha) in October of 1975, at O'Donnell Hall. There were 21 ladies in the club working toward the goal of establishing a chapter of Alpha Kappa Alpha on Marquette's campus.

The ladies worked diligently for nearly a year with appointed officers, goals and programs proposed and implemented. E. Kathleen Coleman, a member of Epsilon Kappa Omega Chapter was appointed to serve as liaison between the interest group and Epsilon Kappa Omega Chapter. One project stood out as they continued to give community service for another year. It was a monthly newspaper drive that gave the TIAKA Club an opportunity to meet and fellowship with all of Milwaukee AKA's.

This dream finally came true on Marh 4, 1978 when thirteen young ladies know as the "The Midnight Specials" became Mu Beta Chapter. The chapter was established under the direction of the Milwaukee Graduate Chapter Epsilon Kappa Omega with E. Kathleen Coleman the leader and organizer, and later the Graduate Advisor, and Central Regional Director Gloria E. Bond.

Mu Beta Chapter located at Marquette University was the second Alpha Kappa Alpha Undergraduate Chapter formed in the city of Milwaukee and the fourth in the state of Wisconsin and was the first chapter chartered at a private university in the state.

The first line for Mu Beta consisted of five ladies who referred to themselves as "The First Addition." The hope of becoming women of Alpha Kappa Alpha became a reality for Connie Cobb, Barbara Henry, Donna Oldham, Carla Wethers and Windy Williamson on December 10, 1978.

At this time at Marquette the African American population was less than one percent and there was a question on whether a chapter could be maintained. A line was made every semester through the mid-'90s with lines averaging four to six people. They included the Tres Chic, Jewels of the Nile, etc.

Monica Ray was the first Basileus, Joann Henry second, Donna Oldham third and Connie Cobb fourth. The graduate advisor was E. Kathleen Coleman for four years. Connie Cobb and Donna Oldham would later become graudate advisors of Mu Beta.

Mu Beta has won numerous awards through the years: for scrapbooks, in 1979 won highest GPA of Central Region and in 2005 won the Greek chapter of the year at Marquette University.

Mu Beta hosted the fall 1980 area retreat at Marquette under the direction of Central Regional Director Peggy Lewis Lecompte. Mu Beta lead the university's Pan-Hellenic Council 1978 through 1981 because because they were the largest Greek organization on campus.

Various community and national programs that the chapter participated in were: national smoke-out day for the American Cancer Society — "Kiss Me, I Don't Smoke," Pink Ribbon Week for breast cancer, prostate cancer screening, Food For Families, Campus Kitchen, Muscular Dystrophy Dance Marathon, Take Back the Night Walk, United Negro College Fund, Cleveland Job Corps and many other local service projects.

Sorors of Mu Beta Chapter have gone on to contribute professionally to society as attorneys, teachers, dentists, morticians, police lieutenants, social workers, engineers and various other careers. Many remain active in graduate chapters in the cities that they live, upholding the sorority's motto of "Service to All Mankind."

MEMORIES: Mu beta was a hit at the 1979 Regional Conference in St. Louis. They wore matching tee-shirts and visors, something that was not done at that time.

"We had unity then. There was a pride.
It was somehting to see AKA's walk into a party together with at least 12 deep
and we walked!
It wasn't a party until the AKA's came.
We made a statement and made people want to be an AKA.
We were so polished.
When I was a freshman I saw 12 women walk across the campus in Pink & Green and I said wow!
We helped each other become young women!
Sorors would pull you aside to tell you about yourself which was meant to help."

Mu Beta Chapter 2005 continues its service under the leadership of Basileus Cheri Howard, Graduate Advisor Liddie Collins, Assistant Graduate Advisors, Brenda Roshell and Christly Stanley.

MU BETA CHAPTER BASILEI

Monica Ray
Joann Henry
Donna Oldham
Connie Cobb
Cheri Howard

Mu Delta Omega Chapter

FORT KNOX, KENTUCKY
JUNE 3, 1978

CHARTER MEMBERS

RHONDA BIVENS
PAULA BROOKS
FAYE BROWN
MILDRED BROWN
BETTYE ESKRIDGE
ROSIE HAGLETT
KAREN JACKSON

SANDRA LINEN
GLORIA MCFADDIN
THELMA OWENS
PAT RAINEY
LOTTIE ROBINSON
KATHREEN SMITH
ESTHER WHITTLESEY
GWENDOLYN YARBROUGH

In 1977, members of Alpha Kappa Alpha Sorority, Inc., decided to form a post chapter on Fort Knox, Kentucky Military Installation. Through the tireless efforts, hard work and determination of these Alpha Kappa Alpha women Mu Delta Omega Chapter was chartered on June 3, 1978.

Mu Delta Omega Chapter has the distinction of being the first chapter of Alpha Kappa Alpha Sorority, Inc. established on a military installation and the first National Pan-Hellenic Council, Greek-lettered organization established at Fort Knox. The members of Mu Delta Omega Chapter were instrumental in assisting other fraternities and sororities with chartering their chapters on Fort Knox Military Installation.

Mu Delta Omega Chapter provided a plethora of service and community based activities within the Fort Knox area, staying true to the Sorority's main purpose and goal of "Providing Service to All Mankind." Some of the events and service projects since chartering in June 1978 included:

- Fashion show that featured "Lloyd Morton Designs
- Summer Reading Enrichment Programs (which were geared toward Fort Knox students' kindergarten through third grade at Barr Memorial Library).
- Service Project — volunteered annually with the "Golden Days" Special Olympics
- Service Project –volunteered at Debutante Cotillion(s)

Mu Delta Omega Chapter was placed on inactive status due to low membership for several years, however the interest of reestablishing the chapter at the Fort Knox Army Installation never waivered. A group of interested women formed an interest group, The Exquisite Pearls of Service.

The Exquisite Pearls of Service made initial contact with Dr. Giselé Cassanova, Central Regional

Director of Alpha Kappa Alpha Sorority, Inc., on June 20, 2011 to express their desire to become an official Interest Group on Fort Knox Military Installation in Kentucky. The group was guided under the tireless direction and leadership of Sorors Naomi Johnson, Renee Wingate and Geri Deshautelle-Renaud.

The Exquisite Pearls of Service participated in many events on Ft.Knox and the surrounding areas including:
- March of Dimes for Babies — Elizabethtown, KY — Top Ten Donating Team
- Red Cross Run for the Red — Fort Knox, KY
- 9-11 Torch Run, Radcliff, KY
- Wounded Warriors Run — Greek Organization NPHC's
- New Hope Mentoring Program, Radcliff, KY
- Radcliff Community Breakfast, Radcliff, KY
- Hospice Tea, Elizabethtown, KY
- Founder's Day Celebration & Brunch
- Fundraisers: Raffles for Gift Baskets, (2) Yard Sales
- Kappa Kruze — Louisville, KY
- Men Can Cook — Louisville, KY
- Women's Shelter — Donations for Transition living
- Yard Sale
- Voters Registration Drive
- Fort Knox Greek Picnic
- Attendees at 2011 Leadership Conference in Atlanta and the 2011 Regional Conference & Cluster K

On Saturday, June 2, 2012, Mu Delta Omega was chartered on Fort Knox Army Installation at the Knox Hills Community Center, Fort Knox, KY. The Central Regional Director of Alpha Kappa Alpha Sorority, Inc., Dr. Giselé Cassanova led 22 Alpha Kappa Alpha members through the chartering ceremony. They were: Sorors Terry Carr, Geraldine Deshautelle-Renaud, Cortney Evans, Veronica Heno-Henderson, Naomi Johnson, Nakesha Millsap, Veronica Murry, Janice Nickie-Green, Zepel Otey-Robertson, Terry G. Owens, Deshana Pandy, Lynell Peace-Trent, Charlee Renaud, Minnie Robinson, Chastic Steele, Melanie Sullivan, Ellen Thompson, Talisha Thompson, Angela Veney, Cathy Walter, Arthella Wingate and Lucretia Starnes-Young.

Following the chartering ceremony, Sorors were tasked with electing officers. Soror Terry G. Owens was elected Basileus; Soror Veronica Murry was elected Anti-Basileus, Soror Nakesha Millsap was elected Grammateus, Soror Ellen Thompson was elected Anti-Grammateus, Soror Deshana Pandy was elected Tamiouchos and Soror Geri Deshautelle-Renaud was elected Pecunious Grammateus. Soror Veronica Heno-Henderson was elected Hodegos, Soror Melanie Sullivan was elected Epistoleus and Soror Talisha Thompson was elected *Ivy Leaf* Reporter. Soror Lucretia Starnes-Young was elected Historian and Soror Charlee Renaud was elected Parliamentarian. Soror Sheree Brown was elected Chaplain and Soror Lynell Peace was elected Philacter.

Immediately following the ceremony a luncheon was held at the General George Patton Museum. Guests viewed a slide show presentation as they were entertained with live music and a dramatic dance performance. Mu Delta Omega's very own Soror Chastic Steele blessed everyone with a heartfelt solo. Dr. Gail Phoenix, the keynote speaker, gave an inspiring message to the charter members and guests challenging each person to demonstrate leadership and get involved in the community.

Those in attendance at the celebratory luncheon included visiting Sorors, members of the Divine Nine Greek Organizations, dignitaries, senior military officials, various civic leaders, family members and friends.

Since the reemergence of Mu Delta Omega on the Fort Knox Army Installation the chapter has been involved in several new program initiatives such as:

(1) The Clean Water Project via TheWaterProject.org. MDO will venture into a long term

commitment and be connected to proven partners who are drilling fresh water wells, providing sanitation and hygiene training and constructing other sustainable water projects around the world. This project will support the international global poverty initiative.

(2) The Thanks4Giving Program via Soles4Souls "Thanks4Giving" (T4G) is a campaign to raise 250,000 pairs of shoes for S4S to distribute where they will be needed most. We are encouraged to donate new or gently worn shoes in the spirit of the holidays (NOV-DEC). The point of T4G is to be thankful for the gifts in our lives and give recyclable shoes in that gratitude. This project will support the international global poverty initiative.

(3) "Feeding America" Kentucky's Heartland volunteers.

MDO will help pack food items such as cereal, canned fruits, juice, cheese, shelf-stable milk or evaporated milk, rice, pasta, peanut butter and more for distribution to coordinating agencies to assist school age children and seniors. This event will take place on Saturday, November (10 or 17, it's still being worked out by the Army Volunteer Corps Program Coordinator) at the Feeding America Volunteer Center located at 300 Peterson Drive, Elizabethtown, KY from 9 a.m. to noon. Feeding America's mission is to serve those in need by acquiring and distributing donated food, grocery items and government commodities through member network of charitable agencies in 42 Kentucky counties. This project will support the international global poverty initiative.

(4) "Hearts of Hope Homeless Shelter" Building Project.

MDO will assist with building of the Homeless Shelter located at 6869 North Dixie Highway, Elizabethtown, KY, on Saturday, October 27, from 8 a.m. to 2 p.m. The shelter will provide transitional housing and appropriate support services to people who are homeless or who are close to homelessness. The transition is to help them be more self sufficient to move toward independent living on their own.

(5) MDO participated in the 2012 Run for Fun 5K at Freeman Lake Park in Elizabethtown on Saturday, November 10, at 9 a.m. The event is co-sponsored by Hardin Memorial Hospital. All proceeds from the race go to Project Fit America which is a national agency that works at the grassroots level with school and front line educators to create new opportunities for kids to be active, fit and healthy. They work with communities to bring in funding, equipment, teacher training, curriculum and the resources schools need to actually get kids fit and foster a love of movement. This event will support the international health initiative for personal fitness and living healthy lifestyles.

(6) Annual Women's Empowerment Conference, Saturday, January 12, 2013 at the Colvin's Community Center located at 233 Freedman Way, Radcliff, KY from 10:30 a.m. to 3:30 p.m. Guest speakers are: Brigadier General Margarett Barnes (and DST), Deputy Commanding General, U.S. Army Human Resources Command, Honorable Denise Clayton, Judge Jefferson Circuit Court and first African American woman appointed to a circuit judgeship in Kentucky; Dr. Mari Mujica Diversity Consultant, LLC and our charter luncheon speaker, Dr. Gail Phoenix, Lindsey Wilson College — Adjunct Professor. MDO sorors attending this event should lend us credit for the Social Justice and Human Rights initiative.

Chapter Basilei

Gwen Yarbrough	1978
Gloria McFadden	1980
Thelma Owens	1983
Kathreen Smith	1985
Angela Weathers	1986-87
Eloise F. Denson	1987-91
Jacqueline Hodge	1991-1994
Naomi Johnson	2011 June 2012)
Soror Terry G. Owens	2012

Peggy J. Lewis LeCompte

19TH CENTRAL REGIONAL DIRECTOR
JULY 1978 – JULY 1982

ACTING CENTRAL REGIONAL DIRECTOR
1985 – 1986

24TH CENTRAL REGIONAL DIRECTOR
JULY 1997 – JULY 1998

Soror Peggy Lewis LeCompte was initiated at Lincoln University, Alpha Iota Chapter in 1958 and served as Basileus of both Alpha Iota and her current chapter, Delta Delta Omega in East St. Louis, IL, from 1972-1974. Soror LeCompte is an educator, television host, newspaper columnist and is the president and CEO of LeCompte Unlimited, a PR and Marketing Company and Marketing Consultant for *Coverings Magazine*. She received her B.S. Degree from Lincoln University and her M.A. from Southern Illinois University. Soror LeCompte's administration as the 19th Central Regional Director was highlighted by several innovations and firsts. She initiated and introduced: the Soror of the Year Award for both graduate and undergraduate Sorors, the first chapter to pay per capita awards, Rapping with the Regional Director for Undergraduates and an Evening with the Regional Director.

Soror LeCompte recognized the importance of developing leadership skills among undergraduates. She initiated the Undergraduate Round-up, utilized undergraduate Sorors as Regional Conference Parliamentarians, committee chairmen and workshop leaders; appointed undergraduate chapters as hostesses for Area Retreats, wrote and disseminated a Central Regional Handbook for Undergraduates and reinstituted the Undergraduate Step Show at Regional Conferences and initiated the first Undergraduate Luncheon, which was held at the 1979 Central Region Conference in Minneapolis, MN with Mu Rho Chapter as the first host chapter.

She also expanded the duties of the Graduate Advisors Council, introduced potpourri sessions at area retreats, re-instituted the Central Regional Conference Public Meeting, published two editions of Who's Who in Central Region, published the first Central Region history which was authorized and compiled by Dr. Sheryl Howard Clayton and revised the Regional Chapter Awards Booklet. She edited and published the first Protocol Handbook in collaboration with former Executive Director Anne Mitchem Davis.

Nine chapters were chartered during her tenure: Mu Rho, University of Minnesota; Nu Lambda, City Chapter of Gary, IN, Nu Omicron Omega, Springfield, IL; Nu Pi Omega, Peoria, IL; Nu Sigma, Southeast Missouri State University; Xi Epsilon, National-Kendall Colleges; Xi Zeta, Illinois Wesleyan University; Xi Eta Omega, Moline, IL; Xi Nu Omega, Chicago Heights, IL and Xi Kappa, Chicago State University.

In addition, Soror LeCompte wrote and disseminated monthly issues of the Central Region newsletter, *THE LOVE LINE,* and visited every chapter in Central Region. During her term of office Anita McCollum was elected to the position of Undergraduate Member-At-Large, and chapters in Central Region overwhelmingly participated in CIP to build the national headquarters and to help establish the Educational Advancement Foundation.

Soror LeCompte effectively and efficiently managed four successful regional conferences. One grew to expect a profusion of Directorate members, distinguished and very special guest from her first Central Regional Conference at the Frontenac Hilton Hotel in Frontenac, MO, with State Comptroller Roland Burris as speaker for the Public Meeting to her last at the Sheraton West in Indianapolis, IN with Dr. Lenora Cole Alexander as the public meeting speaker.

Soror Peggy Lewis LeCompte was elected Supreme Grammateus in 1982 and reelected for a second term in 1984. During the last year of her second term (1985-1986) as Supreme Grammateus she was appointed Acting Central Regional Director due to the illness of Soror Mabel Cason. During this period, she planned and presided at the 1986 Conference and organized and chartered Omicron Alpha Chapter in Aurora, IL.

Prior to her election as Central Regional Director, Soror LeCompte served the sorority as a member of the National NAACP committee, 1974-1978. During her term as Central Regional Director, she served as a member of the National Building and Properties Committee from 1978-1982.

As Supreme Grammateus she served as secretary for the National Constitution and Bylaws Committee and as the first Recording Secretary of the Educational Advancement Foundation Board of Directors and Chairman of the National Ad-Hoc Policy Committee.

In 1994, Soror LeCompte was appointed chairman of the International Membership Committee, a position which she held until 1997 when she was once again called on to serve as the 24th Central Regional Director to complete the unexpired second term of the 23rd Central Regional Director, Soror Martha Perine who due to career advancement was relocated to Memphis, TN. She was installed as the 24th Central Regional Director by Soror Eva Lois Evans, Supreme Basileus.

Soror LeCompte graciously and effectively accepted the torch and her incomparable leadership was demonstrated as she planned and executed the 64th Central Regional Conference in Indianapolis, IN; reactivated Beta Zeta—Kentucky State University; Gamma Chi-Northwestern University, Delta Beta—SIU, Carbondale; Zeta Iota-Western Illinois University; Beta—City of Chicago; Lambda Xi—University of Wisconsin, Omicron Xi—City Chapter of Milwaukee; and Alpha Eta Omega-Terre Haute, IN; chartered Upsilon Phi Omega Chapter in Edwardsville, IL (the first Greek letter organization to be chartered in Madison, County, IL); held an Undergraduate Leadership Seminar with 162 Sorors in attendance in Collinsville, IL, conducted eight record attendance area retreats and led Central Region to receive the 1998 EAF Overall Achievement Award.

Soror LeCompte served as an Honorary Chairman of the 2010 Boule held in St. Louis, MO. Among her many awards is the Alpha Kappa Alpha "Graduate Founders' Award."

Soror LeCompte's outstanding leadership is not limited to the sorority. She has served National President of TOP LADIES OF DISTINCTION, INC., as president of the East St. Louis Federation of Teachers, Local 1220; as vice-president of the Illinois Federation of Teachers; as president of the Southwest Area Council of Teachers; as president of the Board of Directors of the Boy's Club of East St. Louis; Chairman, president of the GEMM Board of Directors; president of the St. Clair County

Comprehensive Mental Health Center Board of Directors; secretary of the NAACP Board of Directors; Board of Directors of the Metro East Council of Churches; Area Council Chairman of the South Central Area Council of Boy's Clubs; Chairman of Christian Unity and Interreligious Concerns Board of Directors; East St. Louis Civic Guild president; Executive Committee, Board of Global Ministries; Urban League of Metropolitan St. Louis, and three time chairman of the Salvation Army Tree of Lights.

She is currently President of the Trinity Unity Methodist Women, member of the Illinois Great Rivers Conference Board of Directors of UMW; Board of Directors of the Franchell Boswell Foundation Board of Directors; Board of Directors of the Illinois United Way, Board of Directors of the Dred Scott Foundation; and member of the Domestic Violence Coalition.

Soror LeCompte has one son, Larry Jr., and two Alpha Kappa Alpha siblings: Sorors Money Dent Guiden and Louella Hawkins.

Mu Rho Chapter

Twin City Chapter
Minneapolis/St. Paul, Minnesota
March 25, 1979

Charter Member

LAURIE BAINES	MATZARENE HUGGA
SHIRLEY BUCKANON	CAROL JENKINS
DEBRA BUCKNER	CAROL JOHNSON
MRYNA CAMPBELL	DEMETRIA JONES
CREMELLA CAMPBELL	TONYA LA GRONE
GLORUSHIA DAVIS	LINDA LARKINS
DAWN DOGAN	PAM MATHIS
ROBBIE GARDNER	ANNA PEEBLES
BETTYE GRIFFIN	DEBRA SCOTT
JOANN HOLLIES	DEBRA SHAW
HERIETTA HOLLY	MICHELLE THOMAS
	KIM TRUMBO

The first undergraduate chapter chartered at the University of Minnesota in St. Paul, MN was Eta Chapter in 1922. The chapter functioned in the area until the mid-'50s. The chapter was unable to sustain a membership and as a result was dissolved in 1969. The chapter name Eta was assigned to the undergraduate chapter at Bowie State College in Bowie, MD.

It would not be until 1979 when an undergraduate chapter would once again be established at the University of Minnesota. Soror Peggy L. Le Compte, Central Regional Director at the time, chartered Mu Rho Chapter as a City Chapter that included the University of Minnesota, Saint Catherine University and Macalester College on March 25, 1979.

Twenty-four outstanding ladies became charter members of Mu Rho Chapter. Mu Rho continues to be the only undergraduate chapter of Alpha Kappa Alpha Sorority, Inc., in Minnesota.

The chapter flourished from 1975 until 2005. Mu Rho Chapter was awarded the runner-up for the Carolyn Blanton Cup Undergraduate Achievement Award in 1983.

In 2005, the chapter became inactive due to lack of membership but a call to action occurred in 2010. Mu Rho was reactivated November 20, 2011, with 10 new Sorors during the tenure of Central Regional Director Giselé M. Casanova. Those Sorors were: Lekie Dwanyen, Alana Eason, Charissa

Jones, Jael Kuehl, Mercedes McKay, Foluso Ogundepo, Titilayo Ogunrinde, Nekey Oliver, Mary Taylor, and Kelsey VanCleve.

Mu Rho has continued its legacy of holding campus and community service events. In 2011, the chapter began a major annual event titled "Race in the Media: A CritAKAl Analysis." The event was recognized by local publications such as the *Minnesota Daily*. In addition, Mu Rho received campus-wide recognition for raising awareness of AIDS and HIV in a special gala reception that was attended by more than 100 people.

CHAPTER BASILEI

Anna Maria Peebles, 1979
Michelle Thomas, 1980
Michelle Thomas, 1981
Dawn Dogan, 1982
Lady Cecil Sutphen, 1983
Kim Calvin, 1984
Michelle Herron, 1985
Lisa Estes, 1986
Unknown 1987-1988
Given Brown 1989
Given Brown, 1990
Heidi Farmer, 1991
Nikki Thompson, 1992
Latika Russell, 1993
Josephine Howell, 1994
Rhonda Chakolis, 1995
Santanya Caufield, 1996
Marcia Wade, 1997
Angelita Brown, 1998
Janelle Peralez, 1999
Unknown — 2000-2005
Inactive — 2005 – 2010
Lekie Dwanyen, 2011-2012
Mercedes McKay, 2013

Nu Lambda Chapter

CITY CHAPTER
GARY, INDIANA
MAY 4, 1980

CHARTER MEMBERS

DEBORAH BARTON
BARBARA BLADE
CORNELIA BROWN
ADA CROSBY
JENI GRIFFIN
DARGEELING LEONARD

FELICIA I. PRINGLE
BENITA JO RICHARDSON
ANDREA SCOTT
GLORIA SMITH
JENNIFER D. SMITH
VENESSA WILSON

Nu Lambda Chapter's charter encompasses Indiana University Northwest, Purdue University Calumet, Valparaiso University and St. Joseph's Calumet College. On Sunday, February 24, 1980 six women were pledged at Valparaiso University as a beginning step toward developing a city chapter.

Six additional young ladies from the area colleges joined the initial group and Nu Lambda Chapter was chartered on May 4, 1980. The ceremony took place at the home of Soror YJean Chambers in Gary, IN. Gamma Psi Omega served as the advising chapter.

The new chapter members participated in tutorial programs for underprivileged youths and helped Gamma Psi Omega with their annual Ebony Fashion Fair scholarship fundraiser in November 1980. This began a tradition of serving refreshments and providing a coat check for the show's guests. They also hosted their first undergraduate "Dress Out Extravaganza." Soror Gloria G. Smith served as Basileus.

Soror Janis Culver assumed the Graduate Advisor duties and mentored them as they assisted with Founders Day. They met Soror Loraine R. Green, Second Supreme Basileus when she served as the luncheon speaker. Winning the award for highest GPA and having Basileus Smith win the second highest GPA in the region was a true highlight of the year. Singing and stepping at Gamma Psi Omega's "Smarty Party" ended the spring semester in style. They continued their winning ways by receiving the attendance award at the Regional Conference in 1982. Soror Janis Culver won for Annetta M. Lawson Best Graduate Advisor as well.

In the early 1990s, Nu Lambda continued being very active in Central Regional Conference activities. Soror Tracey Hamilton served on the Undergraduate Activities at the 56th conference in 1990 and Soror Karen Saunders was a Philacter at the 58th Central Regional Conference in 1992.

The late '90s saw Soror Akesha McClain being appointed to the Regional Constitution and Bylaws committee by Soror Yvonne Perkins, Central Regional Director. Nu Lambda produced a beautiful calendar commemorating Black History Month with notable African Americans on the cover of each month. They also began the tradition of bowling with Gamma Psi Omega in honor of Undergraduate Activities Week and participated in the News Election Service with their graduate chapter, as well.

They partnered with the other Greek organizations on the Indiana University Northwest (IUN) Campus and hosted a Spring Dance. Of course, Nu Lambda sold the most tickets of all the participating Greek organizations and showed them why we were and remain first in service.

BLACK HISTORY MONTH — Beginning in February 1992, the annual chapter activity for Black History Month consisted of an annual essay contest, with the topic relating to different aspects of African American History. Prizes are awarded to entrants for first and second place.

CARNATION DAY — In 1993, for Valentine's Day, "We Appreciate Our Black Men" Carnation day was added. The chapter purchases pink carnations and pins them on African American males attending the universities. This gesture is to let them know that although they might not know it, they are appreciated.

TUTORING — The chapter also participates in tutoring and volunteering at the area local John Will Anderson Boys and Girls Club. The chapter members tutor children from ages 7-18, participate in numerous activities and provides positive leadership and role models for the club members to encourage them to do positive things with their lives. This project was implemented in March 1993.

SOUP KITCHEN PROJECT — In March 1993, the chapter began participating in a soup kitchen project. The sorors volunteer Saturday mornings twice a month and serve food to the homeless and less fortunate. The chapter also donates money and clothes to the sponsoring church. Both of these projects are annual events.

BAKE SALE — The bake sale is an annual event that began in April 1992. It is held at Indiana University Northwest and proceeds are donated to a worthy cause. Proceeds from the 1992 sale were used to purchase school uniforms and pay the book rental fee for an elementary school student whose family was less fortunate.

HALLOWEEN PARTY — In October 1991, the chapter began sponsoring its annual Halloween costume party. Prizes are awarded to the best costume and canned goods are accepted for admission and then later used for a food basket to be donated to a needy family or charity.

THANKSGIVING PARTY — The chapter holds an annual Thanksgiving party. This event was started in November 1991. Canned goods are collected for admission and are used for food baskets donated to a needy family or charitable organization. Also during November, since the early 1980s the chapter works a concession stand and sells refreshments at our graduate chapter, Gamma Psi Omega's, annual Ebony Fashion Fair. Proceeds from the concession stand are donated to the United Negro College Fund or UNICEF.

MARION HOME PROJECT — In March 1992, the chapter decided to design the Marion Home Project. This event is held twice a month. Sorors from the chapter go to the Marion Home for Adolescent and Unwed Mothers and provide a big sister atmosphere. Our goal for the project is to give the residents of the Marion Home positive role models. Sorors offer advice and suggestions on dealing with different aspects of female life. It is a learning experience for the sorors as well as the young female residents.

THE NEW MILLENNIUM — The new millennium brought many new ideas. The Chapter held Back-to-School activities on the campuses of both Indiana University Northwest and Purdue University Calumet. Hosting outings to the Gary Railcats baseball team for Sorors and friends proved to be a homerun event. They visited Clark Nursing home, gave donations of food and/or money to The Marion House and ARC centers for women and children and provided assistance for the Gary Neighborhood Services Center's "Tall Project: A Midnight Retreat." Thanksgiving and Christmas baskets were routine in their annual program schedule. Additionally, they held successful Ivy AKAdemy projects at Ernie Pyle and Washington Elementary schools, distributing brochures on Sickle Cell Anemia, attending events at Emerson School of Visual and Performing Arts and West Side Theatre Guild.

Assisting Gamma Psi Omega with their annual Smarty Party, hosting bake sales, "08 minute dating," AKAcise and study nights, sisterly relations activities and participating in Marktin Luther King Day of Service kept the sorors busy for sure. But they still had time to participate with the Tax Freedom program, AKA Coat drives, decorate the campus display cases to introduce themselves and sell coupons for the Carson Pirie Scott Sales as a fundraiser. Their dances with stepping brought in additional funds. Some of these funds went for two scholarships awarded at the Smarty Party.

But of course, learning about Alpha Kappa Alpha never ceases. Soror Dakita Jones proved this as she served as the 68th Central Regional Conference Co-Chairman and the chapter assisted with the Undergraduate Luncheon. Learning about a birth defect which impacted all of the males in one African American family was another highlight for Nu Lambda as they hosted a book signing for Creola A. Colon's "Born With a Broken Heart." As the years progress, Nu Lambda proves to be a chapter with good ideas, great energy and tenacity.

Throughout the years Nu Lambda Chapter has consistently excelled by winning numerous chapter awards at Regional Conferences. In 2009, Nu Lambda served on the steering committee that hosted Central Region's 75th Diamond Conference. The chapter's Basileus served as Conference Co-Chairperson with the chapter hosting the Undergraduate Luncheon and the Community Service Event where they encouraged all sorors to GO Green.

Nu Lambda has continued their services to the community with visits to nursing homes, assisting at area shelters, offering scholarships to High School students, hosting study nights, adopting families during the holiday season, helping low income families prepare their taxes, conducting Ivy Reading AKAdemies, helping individuals become more technologically savvy, creating awareness by participating in local health walks, encouraging individuals to "Know their Status" by getting tested for HIV and empowering and mentoring 6th – 8th grade girls through the Emerging Young Leaders (EYL) Program.

Nu Lambda Chapter Basilei

Gloria Smith	1980 – 1982
Deborah Barton	1982 – 1983
Barbara Moore	1983 – 1984
Yvette Gibson	1985
Diana Hollingsworth	1986
Delarese McFadden	1987 – 1988
Rhonda Gary	1988 – 1989
Millina Hicks	1989 – 1990
Karen Saunders	1990 – 1991
Katrina Winfred	1992
Stephanie Brown	1993
Akesha K. McClain	1993 – 1994
Nichole Whitehead	1995 – 1996
Sharon Lyles	1997
Tomeka Brown	1997 – 1998
Kerre' Berry	1998 – 2000
Tanya Pierce-Burns	2000 – 2002
Charlinda Jones	
Dakita Jones	2002 – 2003
Kimberly Veal	2003 –
Jennifer Petty	
Elizabeth Harris	2010 – 2011
Shavon Smith	2011 – 2012
Ge'Tina Williams	2013 – present

Nu Omicron Omega Chapter

SPRINGFIELD, BLOOMINGTON, DECATUR, ILLINOIS
DECEMBER 13, 1980

From left, front row: Shirley J. Gordon, Georgia Rountree, Peggy L. LeCompte, Central Regional Director, Pamela Hammond-McDavid, Helyn Clem Perry; Back Row: Sue Satisfield, Jeane Morris, Janice Roundtree (Thompson), Abbey Perry Adenje, Jacqueline Jones, Lolita Spinks (Hickman), Donnita Barton-Dulania (Davenport), Glenda Montgomery, Nedra H. Joyner (Triplett), Alma Taylor Jones, Doretta Donald Ellis, Leona Demons, Doris C. Parker, Terry R. Irby

CHARTER MEMBERS

LEONA MARIE DEMONS	PAMELA HAMMOND-MCDAVID
DORETTA JEANNE DONALD (ELLIS)	JEANNE MORRIS
DONNITA BARTON OWANIA	DORIS COFFEE PARKER
SHIRLEY J. GORDON	BERTHA A. PERRY
TERRY R. IRBY HELYN	CLEM PERRY
ALMA TAYLOR JONES	GEORGIA ROUNTREE
JACQUELINE D. JONES	JANICE ROUNTREE (THOMPSON)
NEDRA H. JOYNER (TRIPLETT)	SUE SATISFIELD
GLENDA MONTGOMERY	LOLITA L. SPINKS

MAJOR CHAPTER PROJECTS:

HEALTH PROJECT — From 1982 to 1984, Nu Omicron Omega Chapter, with the help of interns from SIU School of Medicine, conducted blood pressure screenings in local churches on Sunday evenings. This project helped to make the Black community aware of the importance of watching their blood pressure as well as provided the community as a whole with information on how to monitor their diet to maintain the proper blood pressure. Sorors participated by helping people fill out the information cards, interpreting blood pressures and providing informational literature.

AFRICAN-AMERICAN HISTORY EXHIBITS — In 1986 and 1987, Nu Omicron Omega Chapter brought to Springfield, from the Smithsonian Institutes Traveling Exhibits Collection, exhibits on the contributions of Blacks in the legislature and Black women. The CILCO utility company graciously provided their lobby for display of the exhibits. Sorors hung the exhibit, provided tours and passed out informational literature on the exhibit. These exhibits exposed the community to the positive contributions made by blacks in the development of this country and raised the awareness level of everyone who passed through the lobby of the utility company.

Nu Omicron Omega has continually assessed the needs of the community providing quality services and programs. Over the years, through diversification of our Chapter's membership, Nu Omicron Omega's outreach efforts have expanded to include a significant portion of West Central and Central Illinois. The Chapter through creative collaborations has been able to reach out and provide services to areas such as Macomb, Danville and Decatur, Illinois. These efforts have significantly enhanced the quality of life for the citizens of these communities.

The Chapter has been very diligent in developing programming initiatives which address our sorority's international programming target areas. Through these efforts, the Chapter has established a number of long standing partnerships with organizations such as Western Illinois University, Gwendolyn Brooks Cultural Center and P.R.I.M.E. Youth Group in Macomb, IL. In Springfield, these collaborative partnerships have grown to include: The Boys and Girls Club, the American Business Club, Mini O'Brien Crisis Center, Pleasant Grove Baptist, Springfield Terrace Senior Facility and a number of the schools throughout Springfield. Other chapter projects:

FASHIONETTA® DEBUTANT COTILLION: The Chapter began hosting a Fashionetta® Debutant Cotillion in 1999. Over the years we have worked with over a hundred young ladies presenting workshops such as career exploration, academic enhancement, financial management, cultural exploration, etiquette and service learning projects. Everyone involved in this activity has expressed their appreciation of our commitment to helping with the development of our most precious asset, our youth. We are no embarking upon our 16th Fashionetta® in the Springfield community.

THE SAMARITAN WELL: Several times a year Nu Omicron Omega donates toiletries to this facility which serves abused and single women with children.

A CELBRATION OF AFRICAN-AMERICAN MALE ACHIEVEMENTS: This program recognizes the contributions of male leaders in the communities served.

HIV AND AIDS AWARENESS OUTREACH: In 2004 the Chapter received a $15,000 grant from the State of Illinois to provide educational opportunities and workshops to all age groups regarding the significance of HIV and AIDS and its impact upon the African American community.

SCHOLARSHIP ACTIVITIES: Nu Omicron Omega has developed a variety of programs that support scholarship initiatives. Through its outreach efforts, the Chapter has awarded over $100,000 in financial scholarships. In 2004 the Chapter established the following scholarships in honor of two of our charter members: The Georgia Pillow Roundtree Scholarship and The Alma Taylor Jones Scholarship. These two scholarships are awarded to students attending a Black college or university and a student majoring in education respectively. We also have a new scholarship which is awarded to a student in graduate school. Plans are to name the scholarship after Soror Pam McDavid who is a chartering member and has a Ph.D. We want to encourage continued learning.

CONNECTIONS/POLITICAL ACTION: The Chapter has continually sought to provide empowerment activities such as voter education and registration projects. These activities have been successfully transformed into an established Get out the Vote Campaign targeting all levels of government.

Additionally, the Chapter continues to provide support to organizations such as the United Negro College Fund, Springfield Chapter of the NAACP, Urban League and the American Red Cross.

In 1999, Nu Omicron Omega under the leadership of Central Regional Director, Nadine C. Bonds served as the primary host chapter for the Central Regional Conference.

The members of Nu Omicron Omega Chapter are indeed a viable entity providing quality service to all mankind in the Springfield and Macomb communities. On December 3, 2005, the chapter celebrated twenty-five years of service to these communities at an elegant dinner-dance held at the Northfield Inn Suites and Conference Center in Springfield, Illinois. The rich diversity among our chapter members and their willingness to serve are shining examples of our great sisterhood!

Nu Omicron Omega also supports the HEIFER Foundation by making annual donations to the Corporate Office. The Chapter has also made donations in the amount of $500.00 each for Hurricane Katrina, Sandy and Cairo victims.

Nu Omicron Omega Chapter began encompassing the Springfield, Bloomington and Decatur communities. Bloomington and Decatur have now chartered their own chapter. However, Nu Omicron Omega continues to serve the Springfield Community and celebrated the 31st Chapter Anniversary with a community wide celebration to thank the entire Springfield community for their support of our efforts in the community.

The chapter anticipates providing a Graduate Advisor for an undergraduate chapter on the campus of University of Springfield, IL. The University recently voted to have Greek life.

Nu Omicron Omega Advised Eta Gamma and Zeta Iota Through the Early 1990's.

Nu Omicron Omega Chapter Basilei

Georgia Roundtree	1981 – 1982
Pamela Hammond-McDavid	1983 – 1984
Nedra Joyner-Triplett	1985 – 1986
Kim White	1987 – 1988
Paula Stadeker	1989 – 1992
Barbara Streeter-Montgomery	1993 – 1994
Edna Shanklin	1995 – 1996
Belinda Carr	1997 – 1998
Marian Goza	1999 – 2000
Paula Stadeker	2001 – 2002
Pauline Betts	2003 – 2004
Pat Carpenter	2005 – 2006
Kisha Hortman	2006 – 2007
Nicole Staple	2008 – 2010
Pat Carpenter	2011 – 2012

Nu Pi Omega Chapter

Peoria, Illinois
December 14, 1980

Central Regional Director Peggy LeCompte (front row, 4th from left) with sorors of Nu Pi Omega Chapter.

Charter Members

JOYCE K. BANKS	THEA MOSES
JOYCE BROWN	BRENDA MOTEN
DIANE EDMONDS	BARBARA PENELTON
FLORENCE EDMONDS	MARY REED
JACQUELYN GREER BUCHANAN	JOSIE RUSSELL
RUTHIE T. HAMER	MARLENE SPOTTS
ROSE HULUM	JEAN ST. JULIAN
SUSAN HUBBARD	MARILYN RAGIER
BEVERLY JOHNSON THOMAS	MAXINE WORTHAM
DARICE LINDSEY	LINDA BINGHAMYOUNG

In January of 1980, several Alpha Kappa Alpha women were eager to make new acquaintances for the purpose of better serving the Peoria community. Beverly Johnson Thomas, Jackie Greer Buchanan, and Marlene Spotts began to identify other Alpha Kappa Alpha women within the Peoria area. National officers were contacted and names of local Alpha Kappa Alpha women were submitted with the intent to establish a graduate chapter.

Over the next several months the procedures for chartering a new graduate chapter were followed and on December 14, 1980, Nu Pi Omega Chapter was chartered with twenty charter members. Because of her outstanding leadership in the chartering process, Beverly Johnson Thomas was elected the first president of Nu Pi Omega Chapter.

One of the first endeavors the chapter took on was becoming the sponsor of the Peoria Black Arts Festival in August 1981. First organized in 1974, the festival offered a cultural experience through artistic expression for the Peoria community. Nu Pi Omega charter member Soror Joyce Banks, who was also a co-founder of the festival, served as the Chairman and Talent Coordinator.

Under the sponsorship of Nu Pi Omega, the festival grew to include a Miss Black Arts Festival Pageant, a scholarship fund, booth exhibits, and souvenir publications. The chapter turned over sponsorship to the African American Hall of Fame Museum in the summer of 1989.

In addition to sponsoring the Black Arts Festival, Nu Pi Omega Chapter has been very active in promoting the arts and culture. In the early 1990s, at a time when Peoria did not sponsor entertainment that catered to the African American demographic, Nu Pi Omega was instrumental in working with the Peoria Civic Center to bring big name musical acts and theatrical productions. In particular, the chapter sponsored two Patti LaBelle concerts which were financially successful, thus proving that these types of events were profitable. This opened the door for more major R&B, gospel, and hip-hop acts to be booked at the Peoria Civic Center in the 1990s including Luther Vandross, MC Hammer, Stephanie Mills, Boyz to Men, BeBe and CeCe Winans, just to name a few.

In the mid-1990s, the chapter was again at the forefront of providing cultural events to the Peoria community when it produced its first Juneteenth Gala. This event brought the community together to celebrate the Emancipation of slavery, while raising thousands of dollars for the chapter's scholarship funds. The gala would remain a signature event of the chapter for more than 10 years. Other cultural events have included art shows, poetry readings and praise dance celebrations.

Another major contribution of the chapter is its support of youth through programs such as Peoria Reads, tutoring middle school students in the Tri-County Peoria Urban League's Tomorrow Scientists, Technicians and Managers, and presenting workshops for Upward Bound. In addition, the chapter donated black dolls each Christmas to children with incarcerated parents and outerwear to Irving Primary School. The coat, hat and glove drive initially began to support chapter member Alice Taylor, who was a principal at the school. When she became an Ivy Beyond the Wall, the chapter continued the annual drive, as a way to honor her memory, until the school closed in 2011.

With a desire to impact the lives of adolescent girls, the chapter created the annual Little Miss Pink and Green program and pageant in 2003. The goal of the program is to provide mentorship and guidance to fifth through eighth grade girls in the areas of social graces, etiquette, self-esteem, community involvement and personal development. It also allows participants an opportunity to raise money toward their future financial goals.

Scholarships have been a central theme in the programs that have been undertaken. Through the years, more than $50,000 has been awarded to local high school seniors who were enrolling into a four-year university or college. With a desire to financially assist local students who were pursuing an associate's degree, the chapter established an endowed scholarship in 2006 at Illinois Central College. The chapter has also been very supportive of the Dr. Barbara Penelton Endowment Scholarship at Bradley University, which is named after one of the chapter's charter members.

Over the past 33 years, Nu Pi Omega Chapter has inducted many outstanding women. Its first membership intake was in March 1982, less than two years of chartering in Peoria. Since that time the chapter has had nine additional membership intake groups. The chapter has also welcomed many more who have moved to the Peoria area, having been initiated in undergraduate and graduate chapters throughout the country.

Despite its small size, with the largest number of active members peaking at 30, Nu Pi Omega Chapter played a part in the Central Region hosting several area and cluster retreats. It was also the host chapter for the 59th Central Regional Conference, April 22-25, 1993.

The chapter has been fortunate to have been led by dedicated and talented members who came from all walks of life. The chapter has also had several members who have received various awards and honors, including induction into Peoria's African American Hall of Fame Museum. They include:

1993 Alice Taylor — Education
1994 Dr. Barbara Penelton — Education
2000 Jeanne St. Julian — Education
2004 Beverly Johnson Thomas — Community Service
2004 Thea M Robinson — Business
2006 Rosalind Zanders Lowry — Community Activism

Nu Pi Omega Advises Epsilon Eta Chapter.

Nu Pi Omega Chapter Basilei

Beverly Johnson Thomas	1980 – 1982
Joyce Banks	1983 – 1984
Irene Eskridge Bohannon	1985 – 1986
Joyce Brown	1987
Barbara Penelton	1988
Rose Hulum	1989 – 1990
Ann Watkins	1991
Wanda Higgins	1991 – 1993
Peggy Heath	1994 – 1995
Davina Sharee Frazier	1996 – 1997
Jocelyn Hazlewood	1997
Rose Hulum	1998 – 1999
Diedra McQuitery	2000 – 2001
Wanda Higgins	2002 – 2003
Shann Tunks	2004 – 2005
Rosalind Zanders Lowry	2006 – 2007
Joyce Banks	2008 – 2009
Tracy Gathers	2010
Angela Anderson	2011 – 2012
Davina Sharee Frazier	2013

PART IV: THE FINAL QUARTER OF THE CENTURY

Nu Sigma Chapter

SOUTHEASTERN MISSOURI STATE UNIVERSITY
CAPE GIRARDEAU, MISSOURI
MARCH 22, 1981 – JULY 2002

Shown are sorors of Nu Sigma Chapter with Regional Director Peggy LeCompte, and Graduate Advisor Flora Chambliss after the chatering at Southeastern Missouri State University, Cape Girardeau, Missouri.

CHARTER MEMBERS

MARTHA ANN CASSELL
NEECHELLE DEAN
MICHELLE MARIE DEBAUN
MONICA LOUISE HOUSTON
KATHLEEN RUTH HUDSON
LINDA JEAN JACKSON

MARILYN MARIE JACKSON
BEVERLY SUE SLAUGHTER
GWENDOLYN EVETTE SQUIRES
DELESA CLAUDETTE SUGGS
DONNA MARIE TAYLOR
SHIRLEY DENISE WALTON

The chapter was suspended in 1996 and had no members from that time to the chapter's dissolution in 2002 at the 60th Boule in Orlando, FL

Xi Epsilon Chapter

National-Kendall College
Evanston, Illinois
December 12, 1981 – July 2000

Charter Members

GEREATHA C. AKINES	KEITHEIA JOHNSON
BERNETTA COLEMAN	CHERYL L. MCCLURE
DORORTHY C. FRANKLIN	MICHELLE MCCLURE
WENDY GLINTON	IRMA L. MITCHELL
CONSTANCE HANSBROUGH	CHERYL Y. TOWNSEND
DEVORA M. JOHNSON	DEBORAH L. VOLTZ

Due to inadequate members for a period in excess of three consecutive years Xi Epsilon Chapter was dissolved in July 2000 at the 59th Boule in Dallas, Texas.

Xi Zeta Chapter

Illinois Wesleyan University
Bloomington, Illinois
April 1, 1982 – July 1992

Xi Zeta Charter members pictured with former Central Regional Director, Peggy Lewis LeCompte, fourth from left.

Charter Members

CHERI ARMSTEAD
DIANNE BENNETT
GISELÉ M. CASANOVA
LAURA FLEMING
SHEREE FLOYD
TOMMICA FOSTER
ROSALIND GLANTON

JANET GLENN
DIANA JORDAN
LYN MORRIS
MICHELLE NORWOOD
SHEILA SIMS
VICKIE THOMAS
DEBRA WILLIAMS

The idea of chartering a chapter of Alpha Kappa Alpha Sorority, Inc., on Illinois Wesleyan University's predominantly white campus was the dream of several charter members. They saw Alpha Kappa Alpha as a vehicle through which African American women with common interests and goals could become part of a sisterhood that provided service to the community.

Eight of the Charter members, Sorors Cheri Armstead, Dianne Bennett, Giselé M. Casanova, Laura Fleming, Rosalind Glanton, Janet Glenn, Lyn Morris, and Sheila Sims were initiated, as general members, into Alpha Kappa Alpha on December 10, 1981. These sorors worked along with Soror Peggy L. LeCompte to lay the foundation for the chartering of Xi Zeta Chapter. The remaining six charter members were initiated on April 1, 1982, and following their initiation, at the 48th Central Regional Conference, Xi Zeta Chapter was chartered, becoming the first chapter to be chartered at a Central Regional Conference. Sorors Laura Fleming, Giselé M. Casanova and Tommica Foster served as Basilei. Charter member Giselé M. Casanova went on to be elected to the National Nominating Committee and served as Chairman, 2006 — 2010 and the 28th Central Regional Director, 2010 – 2014.

Xi Zeta Chapter was very active in providing service to the Bloomington-Normal, Illinois community. However, maintaining an active membership of eight or more was a continual struggle for the chapter due to Wesleyan University's extremely small enrollment of minority students. After several years of struggling with low membership, the chapter was dissolved in 1992 at the 55th Boule in New Orleans, Louisiana.

Xi Eta Omega Chapter

MOLINE, ILLINOIS
MAY 15, 1982

Standing Left to Right: Esther Caudle, Betty Oney, Grace Holmes, Sherry Davis, Dorothy Wilson, Marcia Wilson, Anna Martin, Visiting Soror, Loyce Lambert, Jolinda Glenn, Visiting Soror, Ann Mathis. Seated Left to Right: Lillian Glass, Viann Davis, Donna Harbor, Patricia Pegues, Bobbie Lastrapes, Central Regional Director Peggy Lewis LeCompte, Barbara Edwards, Deloris Henry, Gloria Covington, Cynthia Alexander, Terry Moore

CHARTER MEMBERS

CYNTHIA ALEXANDER	LOYCE LAMBERT
ESTHER CAUDLE	BOBBIE JEAN LASTRAPES
GLORIA COVINGTON	ANNA MARTIN
SHERRY DAVIS	ANN MATHIS*
VIANN DAVIS	TERRY MOORE
BARBARA EDWARDS*	BETTY ONEY*
JOLINDA GLENN	PATRICIA PEGUES
DONNA HARBOR	DIANNE WILDER
DELORIS PALMER HENRY	DOROTHY WILSON
GRACE HOLMES*	MARCIA WILSON
GWEN JONES*	DEBRA WILLIAMS

Ivy Beyond the Wall

The small but mighty Xi Eta Omega Chapter was born in 1982 in Moline, Illinois, on the curve of the similarly mighty Mississippi River. The chapter is based in Moline, but the welcoming arms of Xi Eta Omega Chapter have always reached out to the surrounding communities, even across state lines. As one of the "Quad Cities," Moline shares a metropolitan area with Rock Island, Illinois, and Davenport and Bettendorf, Iowa. Together, this metropolitan area has a population of over 250,000. Guided by the ideals of our illustrious founders, the women of Xi Eta Omega Chapter have successfully incorporated the spirit of the Alpha Kappa Alpha Sorority, Incorporated, in all their undertakings for over 30 years.

THE CHARTERING OF XI ETA OMEGA CHAPTER

The Quad Cities is a small but vibrant community, with proximity to a number of excellent collegiate institutions: such as Augustana College, St. Ambrose University and the Quad Cities campus of Western Illinois University. However, as of the late 1970s, the Quad Cities had not been home to an undergraduate chapter of Alpha Kappa Alpha Sorority, Incorporated. In fact, although a number of African American professionals were living in the area by the late 1970s, the area was not home to any official chapters of the National Pan-Hellenic Council Incorporated organizations. There were certainly sorors in the area; they just didn't have a local "center." Naturally, an enterprising group of sorors set out to create one — by chartering a new chapter. However first, they had to learn how to do it.

These enterprising women called themselves the "Quad Cities AKA's." In this age before personal computing and mobile phones, the Quad Cities AKA's armed themselves with unwavering commitment, pink passion, and inquiring minds, and then set out to find and contact all of the sorors in the Quad Cities and surrounding towns who might become chartering members.

Chartering Soror, Bobbie Lastrapes, explained that the chartering process was not easy, and was not quick. The process began in late 1978 and culminated in May 1982, under the guidance of the Central Regional Director, Soror Peggy LeCompte. However, the process was frustrated by the transitional nature of the community. The list of potential charter members would grow — and then it would shrink, as potential charter members moved to the area, and then moved away. Major employers in the Quad Cities area such as Alcoa, John Deere, and the Rock Island Arsenal always attracted talented and educated African American families for various employment opportunities. Consequently, the same employers who brought new families to the area were also responsible for transferring potential charter members to other areas of the country for further employment opportunities.

Fortunately, the Quad Cities AKA's never gave up. They kept looking, and they stayed organized. They held fundraisers to get ready. They educated themselves on the process. When they had a solid and steady group, they were ready. Soror Peggy LeCompte performed the chartering ceremony on May 15, 1982 and installed the officers at the historic Deere-Wiman House in Moline, Illinois. Xi Eta Omega Chapter was born.

Xi Eta Omega Chapter's First Officers were: Bobbie Lastrapes, Basileus; Deloris Henry, Anti Basileus; Dorothy Wilson, Grammateus; Barbara Edwards, Corresponding Secretary; Patricia Pegues, Tamiouchos; Gloria Covington, *Ivy Leaf* Reporter; Gwen Jones, Parliamentarian; Jolinda Glenn, Membership Chairperson; Terry Moore, Graduate Advisor; and Sherry Davis, Hodegos.

By the time Xi Eta Omega Chapter celebrated its 10 year anniversary in May 1992, Soror Betty Oney, one of the chartering member was a Golden Soror. She also was the guest speaker for the occasion. Several chartering sorors returned for the festive occasion.

Xi Eta Omega chapter also never forgot the importance of enriching its members with SISTERHOOD ACTIVITIES. The chapter has at least one annual sisterly relations activity. Countless sorors have opened their homes to the chapter in the name of "sisterly relations." Other activities included weekend retreats, recreational activities, celebration of sorors' birthdays, card showers and other fun filled fellowship. Xi Eta Omega always extends welcoming arms to visiting sorors and new sorors in the area.

XI ETA OMEGA CHAPTER THROUGH THE YEARS

Xi Eta Omega Chapter's programs consistently focused on community service, health, education, mentorship, scholarship and sisterly relations, while also mirroring the Sorority's international programs and agenda.

Xi Eta Omega Chapter began hosting the Little Miss Fashionetta® in 1985. There were 14 participants in that inaugural program, and Ms. Eneetria Livings was crowned the first Little Miss Fashionetta®. By the early 1990s, Xi Eta Omega Chapter aimed to present the program biennially, generally in the month of May.

The success of the program grew along with the reputation of Xi Eta Omega Chapter. For example, the chapter's second Little Miss Fashionetta® program in April 1991 netted over $13,000.00 to support community service projects.

Nearly a half dozen accomplished and charming young girls have been crowned "Little Miss Fashionetta®" over the years: 1991, April Farley; 1993, Janelle Hester; 1997, Alexis Lowe; 1999, Rosemary Twyner-Mayberry; 2001, Janea Jacobs; 2003, Kiah Earl; 2005, Rolanda Crawford; 2007, Jasmine Thomas; 2009, Breyanna Clark; 2011, Charla Swift; and 2013, Deliah Harris.

Over the years, this enrichment program included workshops and activities providing a format for the young girls to meet and interact with other African American girls in the community; workshops on self esteem and self awareness; lessons on etiquette and social skills; and substantive interactions with positive role models. Funds raised during this program were used to support future Little Miss Fashionetta® programs, along with other community programs, projects and scholarship awards.

Xi Eta Omega Chapter programs in the 1990s included an annual Black Family Conference and Teen Conference both held at Blackhawk College. One of the fundraisers during that time was "AKA Night at the Races," held at the Quad City Downs racetrack in East Moline, Illinois, which raised thousands of dollars for the United Negro College Fund and local scholarships.

Xi Eta Omega Chapter also worked diligently through the years to support local young women with its SCHOLARSHIP PROGRAM. Annually, since the chartering of the chapter, a number of scholarships have been presented to deserving young ladies chosen from a pool of qualified applicants. For example, in 2005, Xi Eta Omega Chapter presented four scholarships; in 2011 presented eight scholarships, in 2013 we presented ten scholarships, all to young women from the Quad Cities area high schools to assist with college costs. Over the years Xi Eta Omega has awarded $250,000.00 in scholarship funds to deserving individuals and community service organizations in the Quad City community.

The sorors of Xi Eta Omega Chapter have been responsible for initiating one of the signature Greek events of the year for African Americans — the Xi Eta Omega Chapter ANNUAL HOLIDAY EVENT. Beginning in 1989, the chapter sponsored a holiday sharing event in the form of a New Year's Eve Party. Initially, the parties were held in the Davenport, Iowa, and Rock Island, Illinois facilities. By the 2000's the holiday event morphed into the Annual Holiday Luncheon and Fashion Show, held on the first Saturday in December. The first iterations of the Luncheon and Fashion Show were held in Rock Island, Illinois, at the Holiday Inn. The event grew in scope and popularity, and in the years 2009, 2010, 2011, and 2012, the Fashion Show attracted over 200 attendees to a packed ballroom at the Radisson Hotel in Davenport, Iowa and showcased the personal style of over a dozen community members and the fashions of several local businesses.

XI ETA OMEGA CHAPTER'S REGIONAL CONTRIBUTIONS

Xi Eta Omega Chapter has been active on a regional level from the very beginning. Less than a year after it was chartered, Xi Eta Omega Chapter was one of the hostess chapters for the 49th Annual Regional Conference in South Bend, Indiana (April 1983). Over the years, Xi Eta Omega Chapter remained active on a regional level. The chapter served as one of the hostess Chapters for the 57th Central Regional Conference in Madison, Wisconsin (April 1991) and the 65th Central Regional Conference in Minneapolis, Minnesota (April 1999). At the 70th Central Regional Conference in Milwaukee, Wisconsin (April 2004), Xi Eta Omega Chapter supported the Central Region by presenting the "Tribute to Leaders" Dinner. The chapter again served as a hostess chapter at the 78th Annual Regional Conference in Milwaukee, Wisconsin (April 2012). Through the years, regional conferences committees chaired or assisted by Xi Eta Omega Chapter included Standards, Timekeepers, Tellers, Evaluation, Vendors and the Tribute to Leaders Breakfast Committees.

In 1993 Xi Eta Omega hosted a Cluster Retreat in Rock Island, IL at the Sheraton Hotel. The two day event welcomed one hundred plus sorors.

XI ETA OMEGA CHAPTER'S INTERNATIONAL LEVEL CONTRIBUTIONS

January 2011, Xi Eta Omega Chapter contributed to the success of the International Founders Day. The observance was held in Little Rock, Arkansas, the location for one of the most famous battles for equal education. AKA conducted nine service projects to pay homage to the Little Rock Nine for the historic role the group played in Civil Rights. Under the Social Justice and Human Rights Initiative we worked with other chapters to assemble emergency personal hygiene kits. These kits were presented to Better Community Developers, Little Rock, AR, for distribution to low income, underserved, disadvantaged families.

XI ETA OMEGA CHAPTER LINEAGE

Dynamic programming and an unrelenting presence in the community helped Xi Eta Omega Chapter grow its reputation in the community. Xi Eta Omega Chapter also grew internally, through the initiation of some of the most outstanding women in the Quad Cities area.

- 1984 — "Magnificent Ladies" — Carolyn Bibbs, Diedra Carter, Marie Christian, Joan Jackson, Mary Jones and Mary Alice Walker
- 1986 — "Fabulous Five" — Gail Porter Davis, Berlinda Tyler Jamison, Claranne Perkins, Edna Scott Kee and Kathy Williams
- 1987 — "Three Musketeers" — Raye E. Hawthorne, Patricia Dunbar and Diane Simmons
- 1988 — "Sensational Ladies" — Louise W. Davis, Sandra Easter, Sandra Gillispie, Loretta McClemore and Hope Williams
- 1989 — "Unique Line of '89" — Juanita Bates, Lisa Foust, Vanessa Newkirk, Frances Viers and Kimberly Washington
- 1993 — "Five Elegant Ladies" — Denise Clark, Christine Hester, Gwenda G. Edgeworth, Kialyn Walker and Angela Mikel
- 2000 — "Supreme Three" — Trina Clark-Johnson, Bettina J. McWilliams and Lisa D. Peer
- 2002 — "Trio Divine" — Karen Boyd, Denise Robinson and Krystin Simmons
- 2011 — Torri H. Smith and Michelle Yates

Given the absence of an undergraduate chapter in the Quad Cities, in November 1991, Xi Eta Omega Chapter hoped to pursue development and establishment of an undergraduate chapter at Augustana College. Although an undergraduate chapter was not chartered, in April 1992, Xi Eta Omega initiated two general members, "Diamond and Pearl," Marian Dozier and Chandra Guinn.

To perpetuate the sorority locally and nationally two legacies have come: Kristen Simmons and Kialyn Walker. Additionally, to date we have eighteen Silver Sorors and two Golden Sorors.

XI ETA OMEGA CHAPTER 30 YEARS LATER

May 2008, Xi Eta Omega Chapter celebrated its 25th birthday. There were activities at Deere Wiman House and reception at Johnnies Steakhouse, both located in Moline, IL. Invitations were sent to our community supporters, Greek brothers and sisters, government dignitaries and other community service organizations. We all gathered and celebrated the birthday in style. Several people came out to help in the celebration, to applaud the Chapter's success and encourage Xi Eta Omega to continue to be a positive and vital presence in the Quad Cities Community.

Xi Eta Omega Chapter turned 30 in 2012. Still a small but busy chapter, it boasts of a membership composed of various professions. Soror Bobbie Lastrapes, one of the charter members and the first Xi Eta Omega Chapter Basileus, is still an active member of the chapter. Xi Eta Omega Chapter's activities in 2012 included its annual Holiday Luncheon and Fashion Show, Emerging Young Leaders program, participation in the Greek Unity winter coat drive, "Pink Goes Red," participation in Komen Quad Cities Race for the Cure, Making Strides, Relay for Life, Diabetes Awareness Alert Day, and the 78th Central Regional Hostess Chapter.

XI ETA OMEGA CHAPTER RECOGNITIONS AND AWARDS

Xi Eta Omega chapter have received various awards throughout their 30+ plus years existence including the following:

- 1988 — 54th Central Regional Conference Loann J. Honesty King Connection Award
- 1998 — 64th Central Regional Conference in Indianapolis, Indiana, the Mabel E. Cason Overall Chapter Program Award.
- 2000 — Operation Buckle-Up and AKA Coat Day Recognition
- 2004 — Retention Reactivation Initiative Certificate of Recognition
- 2011 — 77th Central Regional Conference in Louisville, Kentucky, ESP Platform II Economic Keys to Success, Chapter Program Award.
- Multiple EAF recognition Certificates
- Multiple local recognition program awards

Xi Eta Omega Chapter has been led by women of extraordinary vision and commitment over the last 30+ years. The Chapter will continue for years to come to provide "Service to All Mankind" through our local and national programs both here in the Quad Cities and Internationally. Accolades received shows Xi Eta Omega, that we are needed and appreciated in the community we serve. Therefore, we will continue to be "Supreme in Service to All Mankind."

XI ETA OMEGA CHAPTER BASILEI

1982 – 1983 — Bobbie J. Lastrapes
1984 — Barbara Edwards
1985 — Esther Caudle
1986 — Betty Oney
1987 – 1988 — Berlinda Tyler Jamison
1989 — Claranne Perkins
1990 – 1995 — Hope D. Williams
1996 – 1999 — Brenda J. Hanes
2000 – 2004 — Mattelyn Pritchett-Joplin
2005 – 2006 — Soinnya Kelly
2007 – 2008 — Bettina J.C. McWilliams
2009 – 2010 — Brenda J. Hanes
2011 – 2012 — Yolanda K. Grandberry
2013 – 2014 — Diane Simmons

Xi Nu Omega Chapter

CHICAGO HEIGHTS, ILLINOIS
JULY 9, 1982

Front Row Seated — Left to Right: Kathy L. Spencer, Carmelita Rivera, Patricia Berry, Claudia Brooks Russell, Diana Hamilton James, Peggy L. LeCompte-Central Regional Director, Patricia Hill, Doris Powell Kyle, Carolyn D. Schanette, Kevena Turner Williams. Middle Row — Left to Right: Belinda Brown Williamson, Valencia McCord Watkins, Audrey R. Sanders, Vanora Grover, Joan DamersonCrisler, Carol Briggs, Phyllis McIntosh McCune, Valerie M. Everett. Top Row — Left to Right: Adrienne Patricia Lofton, Carolyn Dean, Brenda Mills Morgan, Willa Young-Jennings, Gail Street-Coe, Kathy G. Simms, Loyce Mason Epps.

CHARTER MEMBERS

PATRICIA BERRY
CAROL J. BRIGGS
JOAN DAMERON CRISLER
CAROLYN DEAN
LOYCE MASON EPPS
VALERIE MICHELE EVERETT
VANORA YVETTE GROVER
PATRICIA ANN HILL
BRENDA LYNN MILLS MORGAN
DIANA HAMILTON JAMES
WILLA YOUNG JENNINGS
DORIS POWELL KYLE

ADRIENNE PATRICIA LOFTON
PHYLLIS MCINTOSH MCCUNE
CARMELITA RIVERA
CLAUDIA BROOKS RUSSELL
AUDREY RENAE SANDERS
CAROLYN DAISE SCHANETTE
CATHY G. SIMMS
KATHY L. SPENCER
GAIL STREET-COE
VELENCIA L. MCCORD WATKINS
KEVENA TURNER WILLIAMS
BELINDA BROWN WILLIAMSON

While attending a Founders' Day Celebration in February 1980, five graduate sorors initiated in Delta Omicron Chapter began discussing the forthcoming 20th anniversary of their undergraduate chapter's founding in DeKalb, Illinois. From this discussion evolved the Delta Omicron 20th Anniversary Celebration Committee. These sorors became diligent in their efforts to bring all sorors initiated into Delta Omicron together again. As plans were being formulated to herald this event, it became apparent that Delta Omicron was no longer a functioning chapter and was in jeopardy of losing its charter.

Rededication to Alpha Kappa Alpha and to Delta Omicron proved to be a powerful and emotional experience. In July 1980 several concerned Delta Omicron alumnae met to discuss the plight of their former chapter. From this meeting, the Delta Omicron Reactivation Committee was formed. More than a dozen alumnae of the chapter were reclaimed as financial members.

Upon receiving the enthusiastic approval and support of Soror Peggy LeCompte, Central Regional Director, a series of informational meetings were held in DeKalb and Chicago with young women who were interested in joining the sisterhood of Alpha Kappa Alpha Sorority, Inc. Sixteen of these young women were inducted into the Ivy Leaf Pledge Club on February 23, 1981. On March 28, 1981, in a ceremony conducted by the Central Regional Director, the fifteen members of the Ivy Leaf Pledge Club became women of Alpha Kappa Alpha Sorority, Inc., Delta Omicron Chapter.

With the reactivation of Delta Omicron completed, the Reactivation Committee turned its attention toward the fulfillment of another goal. The unity and sisterhood regained in its efforts of reactivation proved to be the nucleus of the desire to charter a new graduate chapter of Alpha Kappa Alpha Sorority, Inc. In a short time the chartering committee met its tasks and assignments. The reward was the sanction from the Directorate of Alpha Kappa Alpha Sorority to be presented with a charter. On July 9, 1982, Xi Nu Omega was chartered. Soror Peggy LeCompte, Central Regional Director, conducted the chartering ceremony and sorors from all over the metropolitan Chicago area were in attendance.

Eager to be about the work of Alpha Kappa Alpha Sorority, Inc., Xi Nu Omega, unable to afford the luxury of a summer hiatus, worked diligently through the summer. Just five months after the chapter's chartering, Xi Nu Omega awarded a small scholarship, affiliated with the Pan-Hellenic Community Action Council (a politically active official subordinate of the National Pan-Hellenic Council, Inc.), made donations to several charitable civic and social organizations, and began what would become a tradition—giving Christmas gift stockings to the children confined to Provident Medical Center and St. James Hospital.

In 1983, Xi Nu Omega started its first full year of operation as a chapter with renewed spirits and an abundance of energy. Chapter members attended the Central Regional Conference in South Bend, Indiana, making the chapter's presence felt by recommending that the region adopt as a resolution a boycott of the Nestle Corporation and its subsidiaries because of their racist policies regarding mothers and infants in Third World countries. That year, chapter sorors also participated in the March of Dimes Walk America, the Midwest Association for Sickle Cell Anemia Bike-A-Thon, a candy sale and a flea market.

Fall 1983 was busy as the chapter made plans to sponsor its first major fundraiser. Conceived by several sorors during a brainstorming session at the regional conference, responsibility for the fundraiser was taken on by an ad hoc committee. Christened "The Monarch Awards," the first awards dinner dance was dubbed "A Tribute to Black Men." Twelve Black men who had made outstanding contributions to the community through their professions were honored. The first Monarch Awards was held on November 11th at the Holiday Inn City Center with more than 200 guests in attendance. The year 1983 ended on an extremely high note. In addition to continuing the Thanksgiving and Christmas holiday tradition of giving baskets and Christmas stockings, Xi Nu Omega participated in the United Negro College Fund's "Parade of Stars." A check was presented during this event in the amount of $500 from proceeds raised from the Monarch Awards. Other donations were also presented to various organizations that year.

At the beginning of 1984 the highly successful ACT/SAT preparation seminars were instituted. Under the auspices of the Program Committee, the seminars and workshops assisted high school juniors and seniors with test-taking skills needed for the college entrance examinations. Held at the DuSable Museum of African American History, the seminars attracted more than seventy-five students from Chicago and suburban high schools.

Later that same year, chapter members enthusiastically served as hostesses for the 50th Central Regional Conference. Two thousand sorors descended upon Chicago for "Chicago Gold." Chapter members served as chairmen of the Gifts and Souvenir Journal Committees and as members of the

Regional Conference Steering Committee. All chapter members were involved in registration, manning the hospitality suites and showing visiting sorors around the Windy City.

The chapter decided late in 1983 to sponsor candidates for membership into the sorority, and on May 12, 1984, the first candidates of Xi Nu Omega Chapter were initiated. Fifteen women joined the membership ranks of the chapter during a beautiful ceremony held in Dearborn Park.

The second annual Monarch Awards dinner was held on October 27, 1984 at the Holiday Inn Center. More than 300 guests attended the 1984 gala affair where Supreme Grammateus, Soror Peggy LeCompte, an inspiration behind the chartering of Xi Nu Omega, delivered the keynote address. In addition to hosting the annual Monarch Awards, sorors gleaned for UNICEF, donated Thanksgiving baskets and Christmas stockings and participated in the UNCF "Parade of Stars."

The year 1985 found Xi Nu Omega's calendar of activities full. Sorors held the second ACT/SAT preparation workshop, sponsored a dance, walked in the March of Dimes Walk America, held the annual Monarch Awards Affair (attendance by this time doubling to more than 400), and donated Thanksgiving and Christmas baskets and Christmas stockings. In addition, sorors attended the 51st Central Regional Conference and the sorority's Leadership Conference and participated in the traditional chapter activities: Founders' Day, chapter retreat, membership activities and a chapter anniversary and Christmas celebrations.

Xi Nu Omega's calendar of events continued to grow. In addition to the chapter's traditional programs and activities, the first Teenage Pregnancy Prevention Workshop was held in early April 1986. Later that month at the 52nd Central Regional Conference, held in Lexington, Kentucky, a Xi Nu Omega soror vied for a seat on the National Nominating Committee. The month of May found many sorors reminiscing about their own exciting induction day experiences as they welcomed thirteen new sorors into Alpha Kappa Alpha Sorority, Inc., on June 1, 1986.

In 1987, Xi Nu Omega continued to touch the lives of their members, the sorority and the community through a planned program of activities. That year the chapter sponsored a party at a local African American health club and a late night boat ride on Lake Michigan. Attendance at the annual Monarch Awards event also continued to grow. Xi Nu Omega's major program activities continued to address the concerns of the teenage population. In March of that year the chapter held the annual ACT/SAT Test Preparation Seminar and in the following month sponsored the annual Teen Awareness Program. In addition to the above, the chapter placed a renewed emphasis on reviewing chapter procedures and retaining sorors through an innovative series of membership activities.

The success of the chapter's major fundraiser, "The Monarch Awards: A Tribute to Black Men," helped to make the event synonymous with Xi Nu Omega throughout Chicago land. With the growth and popularity of the "The Monarch Awards," sorors felt that the time had come to identify alternative means to solicit funds for the event. Consequently, in 1987, planning began to incorporate the Monarch Awards into a 501 (c) (3) foundation. In 1988, the Monarch Awards Foundation was established to expand the scope of services upon which Alpha Kappa Alpha Sorority, Inc. was founded and in 1989, tax-exempt status was granted. Xi Nu Omega Chapter sponsors programs, raises funds, awards scholarships, and makes charitable contributions through its Monarch Awards Foundation.

The 1990's found Xi Nu Omega poised and ready to meet the challenges presented during the last decade of the 20th century. In 1991, Xi Nu Omega established its Ivy AKAdemy at the Harriet Harris YWCA, located on the south side of Chicago, and launched the first "Music Arts Explosion." This free community event is held annually to celebrate African American cultural heritage by showcasing Chicago artists and musicians. One of the highlights of the event is the "African Market" which allows local entrepreneurs to display and sell their products. The African Market also gives Xi Nu Omega Chapter and the Monarch Awards Foundation the opportunity to promote economic support of African American businesses.

The Monarch Awards Foundation's major fundraiser, A Tribute to Black Men, had come to be known as an elegant, formal, black-tie affair where patrons were treated to dinner, dancing, and a variety of entertainment. Consequently, the fundraiser became known as the "Monarch Awards Gala: A Tribute to Black Men" during the early 1990's. The categories were expanded to include an "Outstanding Youth" award and the scholarship committee introduced the "Community Colleges" scholarship, of which the recipient would receive monies from the proceeds of the Gala.

In April of 1991, Xi Nu Omega initiated thirty-seven new sorors. During the same year, two young ladies who were undergraduate students at Northeastern Illinois University, located in Chicago, expressed their desire to become a part of Alpha Kappa Alpha's sisterhood. Their request was brought to the attention of Xi Nu Omega and the young ladies were initiated in April 1991 as General Members along with the chapter's thirty-seven candidates. The two undergraduate General Members desired to charter a chapter of Alpha Kappa Alpha on their campus and began the process with the assistance of Xi Nu Omega. Their dream became a reality with the chartering of Pi Nu Chapter on Northeastern Illinois University's campus in 1992. Consequently, Pi Nu Chapter became the second undergraduate chapter under Xi Nu Omega's sponsorship.

In 1993, Xi Nu Omega launched its Ivy AKAdemy's "Reading is Essential" program at the Harriet Harris YWCA. This program provided weekly reading groups for young children. In an effort to provide service to our senior citizens, sorors volunteered monthly at the Harris YWCA's Adult Day Care program. The Music Arts Explosion continued to be presented to the community with the introduction of a performance by a professional singer in 1993.

Xi Nu Omega's support of the Educational Advancement Foundation (EAF), earned the chapter "Four Star" status in 1993 and 1994. Regional recognition included Xi Nu Omega being the highest donor of COIP contributors in the region in 1993, being ranked fifth highest in the region with respect to monetary contributions to program activities in 1994 and ranked as the third highest chapter in the region with respect to scholarship donations in 1994. The chapter membership continued to increase with the initiation of fifty-two new sorors in April 1994.

In 1995, Xi Nu Omega partnered with Doolittle West Elementary School in an effort to promote Alpha Kappa Alpha's program target "Partnership in Math and Science (PIMS) Literacy. Sorors served as judges for Doolittle's Science Fair and awarded certificates of participation to each student and trophies to the winners. Xi Nu Omega sorors also provided math tutoring at the Pullman Library for 3rd and 7th graders in preparation for taking the Iowa Test of Basic Skills. The chapter collaborated with the American Red Cross to train sorors to become certified HIV/AIDS instructors. As a result, sorors presented HIV/Aids workshops and Xi Nu Omega co-sponsored an informational booth along with the Red Cross at Chicago's Black Expo. Through the chapter's Ivy AKAdemy, sorors served as mentors to young mothers in the "Parents Too Soon" program at the Harris YWCA and the annual Music Arts Explosion featured a "Back to School Jam." The Monarch Awards Foundation supported the Jackie Robinson West Little League through a monetary donation and participation in the Season Opening Parade.

Regional recognition in 1995 included achieving "4 Rockets to Venus" status for the chapter's contribution to the EAF, receiving a certificate of recognition for outstanding support of the Alpha Kappa Alpha international program, and receiving the award for the most sorors in attendance for chapters with 75-126 members. Additionally, the chapter's first step team was organized to perform at the conference and Xi Nu Omega won first place at the Step Show.

Xi Nu Omega Chapter continued its "Partnership in Math and Science" in 1996 with Doolittle West Elementary School. Additional programs included serving as volunteers with girls who were wards of the state, residing at Sadie Waterford Manor, sponsoring a foster care and adoption workshop, participating in the Sickle Cell Walk-Bike-Jog-A-Thon, and volunteering at Youth Empire Services and at a senior residence building. The Monarch Awards Foundation continued its support of the Jackie Robinson Little League.

The chapter received "4 Rockets to Venus" status again in 1996. At the 62nd Central Regional Conference, Xi Nu Omega won 1st place for its chapter program exhibit, 1st place for most sorors in

PART IV: THE FINAL QUARTER OF THE CENTURY

attendance, and was 1st runner-up for overall achievement for an alumnae chapter. Computer technology helped to change the look and production of the chapter newsletter — the "Xi News" and the first Xi Nu Omega Chapter and Monarch Awards Foundation websites were launched by the basileus in 1996.

Xi Nu Omega's PIMS affiliation with Doolittle West Elementary School continued during 1997 and 1998. Through a partnership with the Harriet Harris YWCA, a grant was secured to help establish a Teen Reach (Teen — Responsibility, Education, Achievement, Caring, and Hope) program for girls ages 10-17. Sorors served as mentors to the Teen Reach participants providing academic enrichment, recreational activities, and life skills training. Additional programs that Xi Nu Omega continued to support included Jackie Robinson West Little League and the American Red Cross. The 7th annual Music Arts Explosion featured "Groovin' at the Music Arts Café" while the theme of the 8th Music Arts Explosion was "Akarnival."

A new program introduced in 1997 was "Take Flight." The program was sponsored through a partnership with the Tuskegee Airmen and gave youth the opportunity to learn about the field of aviation as well as the history of African Americans in aviation. The "Pearls of Wealth" investment club was formed to offer sorors the opportunity to learn about and participate in the financial investment process. The Monarch Awards Foundation sponsored its first "Graduate Greek Step Show" fundraiser in 1997. The event was the first of its kind in the Chicago area and was held at Malcolm X College.

The year 1999 was significant in that it marked the end of the 20th century and set the stage for Xi Nu Omega Chapter to "Blaze New Trails" of service into the new millennium. The chapter continued its partnership with the Harriet Harris YWCA as its Ivy AKAdemy by providing mentoring services to the "Girls World" program and continuing its work with the senior citizens. Xi Nu Omega received an EAF grant for the Music Arts Explosion and earned the highest level of achievement for its EAF contributions. A time capsule was created that contains historical information about the chapter. This capsule will be opened at the chapter anniversary celebration in 2012. Once again, Xi Nu Omega saw a large increase in membership after the initiation of fifty-nine new sorors in April 1999.

During the year 2000, Xi Nu Omega's regional recognition for its programs of service continued to grow. The chapter took first place for the following program targets: Education, Health, Economics, and the Black Family. Additionally, Xi Nu Omega received the chapter achievement award, the award for the greatest percentage of sorors in attendance, and tied as the winner for the chapter scrapbook award. The chapter was the runner-up for the following awards: membership reactivation, chapter heritage, chapter exhibit, and overall chapter achievement.

The year 2000 was also notable for the Monarch Awards Foundation of Xi Nu Omega Chapter in that the 18th annual Monarch Awards Gala raised a record amount of funds. Consequently, the Foundation was able to award six of the largest scholarships to college students to date.

The Monarch Awards Foundation established an EAF Endowment Fund in 2001. During 2001 and 2002, Xi Nu Omega continued many of the chapter's traditional programs of service such as the Music Arts Explosion. A new program addition in 2001 was "Teen Esteem." This program provides leadership development for high school aged young women. It promotes and facilitates organized community service activities amongst the teens. In 2002, at the 68th Central Regional Conference, a Xi Nu Omega soror ran for the office of Central Regional Director.

As the year 2003 approached, Xi Nu Omega was ready to launch its "Spirit" programs that included the Dr. Martin Luther King (MLK) Day of Service that featured a Teen Summit. The theme of the summit was conflict resolution and a panel of experts facilitated the discussion with the audience. Additional programs included: identification of participants for the "Young Authors" program, participating in the National Family Volunteer Day by assisting at the Chicago Food Depository, awarding Presidential Freedom Scholarships, attending the SIDS Summit in Detroit, MI, providing free income tax preparation for low-income individuals and families, and participating in Denim Day at the October chapter meeting for Breast Cancer Awareness month. The Teen Esteem "Trunk Party" was implemented to assist those participants who were graduating seniors, preparing to go to college. Sorors donated basic essentials that a college freshman would need, such as toiletries, laundry items, school supplies, and linen. The size and scope of the Music Arts Explosion continued to grow as guests were treated to "Everything Under the Sun" in 2003 and experienced "The Heart of Arts" in 2004.

In recognition of the chapter's excellent programs of service, the Chicago National Pan Hellenic Council awarded Xi Nu Omega several chapter program awards. A partnership between Malcolm X College and the Monarch Awards Foundation was developed as the Foundation served as a sponsor for the college's "Series of Symposium" for Women's History month in 2003 and as a sponsor of the college's 10th annual Kwanzaa celebration in 2004. The Foundation's "Community Colleges" scholarship category was changed to the "Chicago Metropolitan Area Colleges/ University" scholarship to expand the type of eligible institutions and their location. In December of 2003, Xi Nu Omega initiated eighty new sorors and for the first time in the chapter's history, membership consisted of more than two hundred and forty sorors.

At the 70th Central Regional Conference, in 2004, history was made for Xi Nu Omega. The chapter received first place awards in each of the five program target areas for chapters with one hundred twenty-six members or more. Xi Nu Omega also received first place awards for chapter program exhibit, most members in attendance, and AKA Connection. Additionally, at the 70th Central Regional Conference, a Xi Nu Omega soror was elected to the position of Central Region Representative to the International Nominating Committee — making her the first soror in the chapter to win an elected regional position.

Another historical event occurred in 2005. For the first time in the history of the chapter, the Basileus was a soror who was initiated in Xi Nu Omega. The chapter continued to provide its spirited programs of service to the community including the MLK Day of Service, free tax preparation for low-income families and individuals, the Young Author's program, National Family Volunteer Day, the Teen Esteem program and the Music Arts Explosion. Xi Nu Omega Chapter's first "official" list serve was created and new and improved websites for both Xi Nu Omega Chapter and the Monarch Awards Foundation were developed. Xi Nu Omega continues to host a variety of creative and fun sisterly relations activities to help foster the spirit of sisterhood within the chapter and to present enjoyable fundraisers of a smaller scale than the annual Gala.

In 2006, Xi Nu Omega experienced another historic event at the 72nd Central Regional Conference when Soror Pamela Bates Porch was elected as the 27th Central Regional Director. Her legacy in the Region would continue the Region's service and impact on advancing local communities and strengthening sisterhood among chapters. She would pass on her torch of service to a former Xi Nu Omega Chapter President who would become the 28th Central Regional Director.

In 2007, Xi Nu Omega Chapter celebrated the 25th anniversary of her chartering. Sorors had the opportunity to reflect on the growth and development of the chapter, from its genesis with a nucleus of twenty-four charter members to its current status of over two hundred forty professional women. The Monarch Awards Gala: "A Tribute to Black Men" has become a well-known annual social event in Chicago with over 1300 guests in attendance. Through its Monarch Awards Foundation, over half a million dollars has been awarded in the form of scholarships, donations to charitable organizations, and to provide programs to the Chicago area community. Through the years, the chapter's commitments to service, guidance by its leadership, and the devotion of its members have made Xi Nu Omega Chapter a premier chapter in Central Region.

In 2008-2011, Xi Nu Omega would strengthen it's signature programs that would incorporate an Annual Community Expo featuring it's Annual Music and Arts Explosion engaging as many as 700 local community residents encouraging students "back to school" with offerings of free book bags with school supplies, health examinations, economic empowerment workshops, fitness demonstrations, entrepreneur's marketplace, fashions show and talent showcase with local community talent. Through it's foundation, the chapter continued to host it's Annual Martin Luther King Teen Summit to promote education and service among tweens and teens in the community. The event ranged from 150 participants to well over 400 students through these years. The Annual Community Feeding Program, in partnership with Beautiful Zion Baptist Church Food Pantry of the Englewood Food Pantry Network, serviced over 600 families by providing a meal for the day and a bag of groceries including a turkey or cornish hen for the Thanksgiving holiday for local residents. Finally, the Emerging Young Leaders program was instituted with fifteen six grade through eight grade girls in partnership with the Academy of St. Benedict the African school in Chicago, IL.

In 2012, Xi Nu Omega celebrated her 30th anniversary of her charting and its monumental year of service, leadership and sisterhood. Over three hundred chapter members, family and friends joined Xi Nu Omega at its annual chapter anniversary celebration held at the Marriott Midway in Chicago. Soror Peggy Lewis LeCompte, the chapter's chartering Regional Director, served as the keynote speaker. It was a homecoming of the Chapter's charter members, former presidents,currect leadership, former and current members, and sorors around the region. The Chapter recapped its accomplishments of 30 years of service, leadership and sisterhood remembering its most current accomplishments at the 78th Central Regional conference where the chapter would once again receive first place in all program initiative awards (accept one where she received runner-up) including membership reactivation and would represent the Region at the 2012 Boule in San Francisco, CA as an award nominee for the signature program initiative Emerging Young Leaders.

Xi Nu Omega chapter is posed to continue to extend her global legacy of sisterhood, service and leadership that will forever remain a timeless contribution to her community as evidenced by the National Pan Hellenic Council of Chicago (NPHCC). NPHCC named Xi Nu Omega Chapter its 2012 Large Sorority Chapter of the Year for her stellar service to the Chicago land community. Further, as its next level of leadership marks change in the chapter, the chapter remains real, strong and together in service, sisterhood and leadership.

Xi Nu Omega Chapter Advises Delta Omicron and Pi Nu Chapters.

Chapter Members Who Have Held International/National Office or Been Elected to the International/National Nominating Committee

Giselé M. Casanova	Nominating Committee	2006 – 2008
Pamela Bates Porch	Central Regional Director	2006 – 2010

Xi Nu Omega Chapter Basilei

Patricia Hill	1983 – 1983
Susan Smith	1984
Joan Dameron Crisler	1985 – 1986
Zerrie Campbel	1987 – 1988
Shelly Thompson	1989 – 1990
Cynthia Armster	1991 – 1992
Phyllis McCune	1993 – 1994
Giselé M. Casanova	1995 – 1996
Pamela Bates Porch	1997 – 1998
Carolyn Franklin	1999 – 2000
Janeen Turner	2001 – 2002
Nancy Banks	2003 – 2004
Eugenia Reese	2005 – 2006
Adrienne Upchurch	2007 – 2008
Michelle R. Willis	2009 – 2010
Latrice E. Eggleston	2011 – 2012
Alenda V. Young	2013

Xi Kappa Chapter

Chicago State University
Chicago, Illinois
July 10, 1982

Charter Members

CRISTAL L. CLAY	JACQUELYN G. WILLIAMS
VENUE COLE	PAMELA D. COTTON-ROBERTS
SERITA EVANS-ARNOLD	CAROLYN HANKINS
JUDY HODGES	YVETTE M. HOUSE
DENITA M. HUNTER	CHERRI D. HURSEY-RAY
KIM J. JOHNSON	LARITA JONES-WRIGHT
SANDRA R. JONES-GONZALEZ	CECELIA MOORE
PATRICIA L. MOORE	TONIA SADLER
VALENCIA SMITH-CARSON	DENISE STOWER
LESLIE A. STUBBLEFIELD (DECEASED)	CHARON THOMAS
CERELOUS A. DOUGLAS-MARBERRY	GAIL TURNER

Xi Kappa undergraduate chapter of Alpha Kappa Alpha Sorority Inc. was chartered July 10, 1982, at Chicago State University in Chicago, Illinois. Lambda Mu Omega Chapter is the sponsoring graduate chapter. The Supreme Basileus at the time was Barbara K. Phillips, the Regional Director was Peggy LeCompte, and the graduate advisor was Harriet Brown Hughes.

Several Xi Kappa members have served on international committees including: Crystal J. Evans-Washington, Membership Committee, 1989-90; Kaweemah Bashir, Central Region's representative to the Undergraduate Activities Committee, 1985-88; and Chantel Hays, Central Region's representative to the Undergraduate Activities Committee, 1992-94.

Several chapter members of Xi Kappa have won the Highest GPA award for Central Region: Chantel Hays (1992-first place), Donica Glass (1991-first place), Crystal Washington (1986-first place), Kaweemah Bashir (1986-second place), Bethsheba Bullock (1984-first place) and Cherri Hursey-Ray (1984 second place).

Xi Kappa has had a legacy of hard working graduate advisors with regional acclaim from Lambda Mu Omega Chapter. Soror Comella Smith was Central Region's Graduate Advisor of the Year in 1988.

Soror Valerie Jones-Bland received the Central Region's Graduate Advisor of the year award in 1993, and was first runner-up in 1992.

Most important are Xi Kappa's contributions and service to the community. Historically, the chapter has adopted an African student annually; conducted a voter's registration drive; volunteered at the Dawson Nursing Home; participated in the UNCF Telethon, blood drives, Anti-Drug/Anti-Gang Rallies, NAACP Tag Day, UNCF Walk-a-thons, and Jump Rope for Hearts, Sickle Cell Anemia Walks; and supported Black Greeks for Harold Washington. The chapter also sponsored an Ivy Academy Center at Chicago State University and participated in the university's Senior Citizens Pre-Thanksgiving dinner, Alumni Telethon, Senior Citizen Fitness/Wellness Fair, and Popular Issue Forums/Workshops with topics that included AIDS, grooming, racism, women, Black Greeks, relationships, and family. The chapter financially supports many organizations including the Cleveland Job Corps, Urban League, UNCF, CSU Book Scholarships, South Central Community Center, Food Pantry, Chicago State University, National Council of Negro Women, NAACP, and EAF.

As Xi Kappa approached and entered the new century several new programs were added to the chapter's list of service to the community: Making Strives to Breast Cancer Awareness Walk; Sickle Cell Disease Walk/Run/Bike-A-Thon; Mr. Pink & Green Scholarship Pageant and Freshman Orientation & Freshman move in day.

In addition to the chapter's outstanding record of service, Xi Kappa Chapter continues its tradition of academic achievement:

- In 2002 and 2004, Xi Kappa Chapter received the First Place Award for highest Central Region City Chapter G.P.A.
- In 2002, Soror Kelley Debbs received the Second Place Award for the highest Central Region individual G.P.A.
- In 2004, Soror Alexia Gist received the Foreign Travel Grant Award for having the highest individual G.P.A. in Central Region. She was sponsored to attend the post Boule Tour in Europe with Supreme Basileus, Soror Linda White and other highest GPA sorors from the other regions.

The legacy of hard working graduate advisors from Lambda Mu Omega Chapter also continued with Soror Cynthia Mitchell-Dunbar's second place recognition as Graduate Advisor of the Year in 2004.

Truly, Xi Kappa Chapter exhibits all the qualities that bring to Alpha Kappa Alpha Sorority Inc. the pride and dignity she deserves. This chapter will continue in its role of making excellent educated women a positive impact on society.

XI KAPPA CHAPTER BASILEI

Crystal Clay
Cerelous A. Douglas-Marberry
Bethsheba Bulluck
LaTanya DeRamus
Alice Durham
Crystal J. Washington
Carla Hill
Daphne Robinson
Felicia Cobb
Paulette Conway
Donica Glass
Chantel Hays
Angela Chambers

Tamara Lumas	1994
Simona Haqq	1995
Dewana Taylor	1996
Lisa Abston	1996
Equilla Green	1997
Felicia Coleman	1997
Antandra Bailey	1998
Quandra Wilcoxen	1999
Nikita Mitchell	1999
Konawetish Fields	2000
Danielle Wallington	2001
Regina Wilborn	2002
Tamlyn Wright	2003
Valeaka Hooks-Brown	2004
Dena High	2005

Mable Evans Cason
20TH CENTRAL REGIONAL DIRECTOR
JULY 1982 – JULY 1986

Soror Mabel Evans Cason, a native of Terre Haute, Indiana, was initiated into Alpha Kappa Alpha Sorority through Beta Xi Omega Chapter, Tuskegee, Alabama. She received her bachelor's degree from Indiana State University in Home Economics, with a minor in Physical Education and French. She received her master's degree from the University of Wisconsin in Nutrition and Biochemistry.

Soror Cason began her career as a Food and Nutrition Instructor at Tennessee State University. She taught at Taylor High School in Jeffersonville, Indiana, and was head of Foods and Nutrition at Tuskegee Institute. Later she moved to New York and was the Food Editor of Our World Magazine. She was also a Field Nutritionist with Wheat Flour Institute and the American Institute of Baking. Her final career move was to Minneapolis/St. Paul, as Assistant Director of Personnel for the St. Paul Public School system. She held this position until her retirement.

Soror Cason was a dedicated and committed member of Delta Phi Omega Chapter as well as an active participant in many civic, professional and educational organizations. Her involvement in the National Heart and Lung Advisory Council, Minnesota State Advisory Council for Vocational Education, National Human Nutrition and Research Advisory Board of the U.S. Department of Agriculture, National Sickle Cell Disease Program, and the American Association of Retired Persons, has earned her many notable achievement awards and special recognitions.

A promise of power in collaboration, sisterliness and mutual support between sorors and between chapters, was the motto by which Soror Cason led Central Region. To quote her, "we are a sharing, we are a caring, and we are a loving sisterhood." Soror Cason emphasized the importance and necessity for closer relationships and open communication between undergraduate and graduate chapters.

All of the Central Regional Conferences during her tenure drove home the meaning of the national Program theme "Facets of Dynamic Power" with the "P" for political action at the forefront. The public meetings spotlighted history-making guest speakers such as the Honorable Roland Burris and the late Harold Washington, Mayor of Chicago, at the 50th Anniversary Conference. Other highlights of her conferences included: the adoption of the Gamma Omega Choir as her official performing group, the open forum with the Regional Director, and the V.I.P. breakfast. The community workshops and the open session's presenters epitomized the word connection.

Soror Cason stated in one of her reports: "My strength, if I have any, I think is not on the building of new chapters that is in saying let's start another chapter, but in reclaiming members." Apparently, her strength was in both. She chartered six graduate chapters and one undergraduate chapter during her administration.

Due to illness, Soror Cason was unable to preside over her final conference. Soror Peggy Lewis LeCompte the 19th Central Regional Director accepted the responsibility of finalizing the plans for the 52nd Central Regional Conference and presided in her stead. In lieu of a report by the Regional Director, a letter from Soror Cason was read. Following are excerpts from that letter.

"To all my beautiful and loving sorors of Central Region, you must understand how difficult it is for me to be absent from my last conference as your Regional Director. I have attempted to find some way to join you for a part of the conference, but my doctors said, "No,"

. . . There is no doubt in my mind that the conference will be an exemplary one and you will leave knowing that you had a part or role to plan in its success. My spirit will be with you throughout each hour and day.

. . . Special thanks to all participants on the program and best wishes to those who seek office. Have a joyous, enlightening experience! Thanks again, Sorors Peggy, Johnetta and members of the steering committee, for your assistance and loads of love to Sorors Teresa, Leola and Ida Nell that I worried with many calls. I love each of you and miss being in your midst."

In later years, Soror Cason attended Regional Conferences and other organizational meetings, even with the assistance of a wheel chair, when her health permitted. She continued to serve as a community activist, an advocate for the rights of children and to enjoy her family and friends.

Her graciousness and caring spirit was once again demonstrated when she hosted a "Thank You" party for her friends for their many years of support on the occasion of her 80th birthday. Soror Mabel Evans Cason became an Ivy Beyond the Wall on June 28, 2004.

Omicron Delta Omega Chapter

BLOOMINGTON-NORMAL, ILLINOIS
MARCH 24, 1984

CHARTER MEMBERS

WANDA BRADFORD	JEANNE B. MORRIS
SOPHRONIA BREEDLOVE	MARY ANN ROSEMOND
ANGELA DANIELS	SUE ADAMS SATISFIELD
GLORIA JEANNE DAVIS	PAMELA HENDERSON SAUNDERS
ALINDA GHOLAR HALL	FARRIS AVERY SMITH
ROBIN JACKSON	JAMESEVA WEBB
JACQUELINE D. JONES	LINDA FAYE WHITE
VENESSA M. LOTT	SHARON ELAINE WHITTAKER
ETHEL B. MINCEY	

The Bloomington-Normal community has historically been a transient community. Prior to Omicron Delta Omega's chartering, sorors traveled to Springfield, Illinois to be affiliated with a chapter. Omicron Delta Omega and Nu Omicron Omega chapters have three charter members in common. Several Omicron Delta Omega members were initiated into the sorority by Nu Omicron Omega.

As the numbers improved, Sorors Shirley Gordon and Sue Satisfield became the moving force in forming the Bloomington-Normal interest group which resulted in the new chapter's chartering. Soror Mabel Cason, Central Regional Director conducted the chartering ceremony. Soror Gordon was transferred out of the area before the chapter was officially chartered and Soror Sue Satisfield became the first Basileus.

Since it's chartering, Omicron Delta Omega has participated with other Cluster IV chapters as a host for several Central Regional Conferences held in Springfield and Peoria, Illinois. The chapter has hosted several Cluster Area Retreats and joint Founders' Day Celebrations in Bloomington-Normal. Omicron Delta Omega has a legacy of hard working sorors and has been the recipient of Regional Conference program awards.

Activities sponsored by the chapter support the goals of the international organization. Over the years, provided countless volunteer hours and financial support for activities focused on children's learning and mentoring, senior citizen's needs, critical care facilities, academic, economic and health education events.

The chapter awards multiple annual scholarships to high-school seniors entering an accredited college or university. Other notable programs and public service events include:

Breakfast With Santa — A program developed by the chapter so that the African American children in the community could have breakfast with a soulful Santa. This event is not a fundraiser; it is an opportunity to provide the community with African American images that they can relate to. Breakfast consists of pancakes and other activities include caroling, storytelling and a snapshot with Santa. This has become an annual event to which the community looks forward. This event was the brainstorm of Soror Eartha Nicholson.

Walk For Mankind — Is a community event that the chapter lends its woman power to on an annual basis. We help register the participants and make sure that their pledge sheets are complete. The organizers and the community view the members of Alpha Kappa Alpha as hard-working volunteers that can be counted on to help with this event.

Chefs' At Play — Is an annual fundraiser that has been held in the summer since 1989. Soror Gloria-Jeanne Davis borrowed this idea from her mother's church. The chefs are males who donate their favorite dish for the participants to sample. After everyone has sampled the tantalizing delicacies they participate in board games. The proceeds of this event go to the scholarship fund. This event was also coordinated in previous years to occur the day that the men of Omega Psi Phi have their golf tournament.

- Renovation of a Women's Lounge at a local shelter.
- Participation in American Heart Association's Heart Walk, Rally and Race for the Cure (Susan G. Komen).
- Annual Holiday Food Baskets give-a-ways.
- Women's Forum & Luncheon
- Voter Registration Drives
- Special Olympics
- Make-A-Difference Day
- Black Dollar Days
- Easter Seals Telethon
- Precious Gems Pageant,
- AKATR (All Kids Achieve Through Reading) storytelling

The chapter also contributes to other charitable organizations and causes.

Omicron Delta Omega Advised Eta Alpha And Xi Zeta Prior to Their Dissolution.

Omicron Delta Omega Chapter Basilei

Sue Satisfield	1984 – 1985
Mary Ann Rosemond	1986 – 1987
Eartha Shelby Nicholson	1988 – 1989
Rosalyn Lang Wilson	1990 – 1991
Edna Shelby-Lewis	1992 – 1993
Sharon Francis	1994 – 1995
Nichele Taylor	1996
Natalie Brunson-Wheeler	1996 – 1997
Brigitte Byrd Spencer	1998
Marietta Wicks	1998 – 1999
Ayanna Price Vinson	2000 – 2001
Marcia Thompkins	2002 – 2003
Tracye Rollins	2004 – 2005
Edna Shelby-Lewis	2006 – 2007
Carolyn LaVere	2008 – 2009
Ayanna (Price) Vinson	2010 – 2011
Jennifer Palmer	2012 – 2013

Omicron Eta Omega Chapter

UNIVERSITY CITY- ST. LOUIS, MISSOURI
MAY 26, 1984

CHARTER MEMBERS

RACHEL B. ADKISSON BURSE	SHARON IRBY MOORE
MELANIE S. CHAMBERS	SHEREYL HOSKIN O'NEAL
MICHELLE CHAMBERS	CHERYL MILTON ROBERTS
CHARLENE GARY	CAROLYN KIDD ROYAL
ANGELA HAYWOOD GASKIN	JACQUELINE SLAUGHTER
ESTHER HAYWOOD	RHONDA BUCKNER TAYLOR
WANDA DIANE JACKSON	MARCELLA CURRY WATKINS*
EULA KEEN	CASSANDRA YOUNG PINKSTON

Ivy Beyond the Wall

On May 26, 1984, after operating for a year as an interest group, the Mystical Pearls became an official chapter of Alpha Kappa Alpha Sorority, Incorporated. Our 20th Central Regional Director, Soror Mabel Evans Cason, chartered Omicron Eta Omega.

Behind the leadership of Soror Angela Haywood Gaskin and fifteen charter members, Omicron Eta Omega instituted programs of service that were designed to empower the communities surrounding the city of St. Louis. These programs developed a model that has sustained the chapter's existence for nearly thirty years. Voter registration drives, scholarship fundraisers, tax preparation assistance programs, job skills training and resume writing are among the many programs implemented along with an international initiative of funding a water purification plant in the African country of Rwanda.

The chapter has had representation at every Boule, Leadership Conference, Central Regional Conference, and Area Retreat since 1984 ... California, the Bahamas, Washington D.C., Jamaica, Las Vegas, Alaska, Atlanta, New Orleans ... Omicron Eta Omega chapter was present. Our chapter Basileus, Soror Wanda D. Jackson attended the First International Regional Conference held July 1989 in Freeport, Bahamas. Representation at these conferences has allowed Omicron Eta Omega to develop and implement chapter programs that parallel the current national programs ensuring that Omicron Eta Omega continues to render service to the St. Louis metropolitan community. The administrative focus has always centered on the needs of the chapter:

SMILE (Strengthening Membership through Involvement, Leadership and Empowerment) — This innovative program, implemented in 1994 under the leadership of Soror Melanie Chambers, was designed to enhance sisterly relations and to build and maintain membership. Some highlights of this program were soror of the month recognition awards, monthly workshops following every meeting designed to empower the membership, and a secret soror program designed to enhance relationships among the membership. Soror Chardial Samuel and Soror Cecily Curry carried program SMILE through their administrations.

BUILDING A MORE COHESIVE SISTERHOOD WITH GROWTH AND QUALITY — Initiated by Soror Seletha Curtis in 1999, this program initiative was developed to efficiently utilize the skill base within the membership. It also offered an opportunity for Omicron Eta Omega chapter to collaborate with other organizations affiliated with our chapter members. Sorors Angela Lampkin, Colette Cummings and Cheryl White continued this programmatic theme through their administrations.

STRIVING TO CAPTURE A VISION FAIR — Initiated in 2007 under the second term of Soror Wanda Jackson and continuing through with Soror Rachel Burse, sorors were encouraged to show their AKA pride through service. Preparing for the sorority's 100 year celebration, this initiative focused on the concept created by our founders that our membership is comprised of ladies that are beautiful in spirit, generous in sharing good deeds, passionate in their dedication to serve others and always striving to "capture a vision fair."

CHANNELING THE SPIRIT OF OUR FOUNDERS — Soror Yolanda Lockhart initiated this 2011 focus to ensure that Omicron Eta Omega is "Supreme in Service to All Mankind." This initiative utilized a spirit of inclusion and a spirit of sisterhood to ensure that all were instrumental in the success of our mission of serving and servicing the St. Louis community. The diversity within the chapter was used to help define our commitment to the community.

Chapter Pearls

REGIONAL POSITIONS & RECOGNITIONS

- 2007-2014 — Soror Carolyn Kidd Royal, Central Region Technology Committee
- 2008 Central Regional Conference, Primary Hostess chapter, Omicron Eta Omega chapter; first to implement online registration for Central Region conference attendees.
- 2008 Central Regional Conference Chairman, Soror Melanie Chambers; Conference Co-chairmen, Soror Veronica D. Stacker and Soror Wanda D. Jackson
- 2009-2010 — Central Region Connections Coordinator, State of Missouri, Soror Wanda D. Jackson
- 2011-2014 — Soror Pamela Westbrooks-Hodge, Central Region Technology Committee
- 2011-2014 — Soror Wanda D. Jackson, Central Region Standards Committee
- 2011-2014 — Soror Rachel A. Burse, Central Region Constitution & Bylaws Committee

INTERNATIONAL POSITIONS & RECOGNITIONS

- 2007 — 2010 — Heritage Committee Member, Soror Wanda D. Jackson
- 2008 — Boule Luncheon Committee Member, Soror Taina Charleston
- 2010 — Boule Luncheon Committee Co-chairman, Soror Taina Charleston

LOCAL RECOGNITIONS

- 1992 — Soror Pamela Coaxum, first executive director of the greater East St. Louis community fund under the US District Courts of Southern Illinois
- Greater St. Louis UNCF Walkathon Co-chairman, Soror Crystal Momon-Reed with husband Thomas Reed
- 1999 — Soror Pamela Coaxum, St. Louis American "Yes I Can" Awardee for Non Profit Leadership at the YWCA
- 2008-2012 — Soror Pamela Coaxum, Co-founder of the St. Charles Human Rights Commission, and currently serves as the commission President
- 2009 — Soror Pamela Coaxum, awarded the Bronze Hammer for the Habitat for Humanity "St. Charles County"
- 2000-2010 — Soror Esther Haywood served in the Missouri House of Representative, District 71
- 2009 — Soror Melanie Chambers received the Unsung Heroine Award in recognition of outstanding community service presented by the Top Ladies of Distinction, Inc. St. Louis Chapter
- 2010 — Soror Wanda D. Jackson received the Unsung Heroine Award in recognition of outstanding community service presented by the Top Ladies of Distinction, Inc. St. Louis Chapter
- 2012 — Soror Yolanda Lockhart received the Unsung Heroine Award in recognition of outstanding community service presented by the Top Ladies of Distinction, Inc. St. Louis Chapter
- 2011 & 2012 — Soror Delores Clayton received a President Barak Obama National Service Award for AARP Volunteerism, 10 year Service Award for working with Tax Aide Program

- 2011 & 2012 — Soror Delores Clayton received a President Barack Obama National Service Award, for Volunteering 296 hours & 497 hours, respectively, with Missouri Claims, State Health Insurance Program(SHIP) Office
- 2012 — Soror Rachel A. Burse, Minority Business Development Manager for Save-A-Lot was featured in the June 2012 issue of the Black Enterprise as a Hero for Hire
- June 2012 — Soror Angela Haywood Gaskin, teacher at Ladue Horton Watkins High school, was recipient of the Benjamin Lawson Hooks Exceptional Educator of the year award winner by the St. Louis County Branch of the NAACP
- June 2012 — Soror Rachel A. Burse, Minority Business Development Manager for Save-A-Lot, was recipient of the 2012 NAACP Most Inspiring St. Louisans Award presented by the St. Louis County Branch NAACP
- June 2012 — Soror Cheryl Milton Roberts, Manager, Organization Development and Training, Energizer North America; was recipient of the 2012 NAACP Most Inspiring St. Louisans Award presented by the St. Louis County Branch NAACP
- July 2012 — Pamela Westbrooks-Hodge, co-founder of the Scholarship Solution, was featured and interviewed on KPLR-TV 11 News for providing an organized and efficient approach to obtaining college scholarships
- 2013 — Soror Seletha R. Curtis, received the Unsung Heroine Award in recognition of outstanding community service presented by the Top Ladies of Distinction, Inc. St. Louis Chapter

Chapter Legacies
- Mother-Daughter: Soror Esther Haywood (1971), and Soror Angela Haywood Gaskin (1978),
- Sister Sorors: Soror Melanie Chambers (1977), Soror Michelle Chambers (1979), and Soror Chandra Chambers Henley (1988)
- Mother-Daughter: Soror Wanda D. Jackson, 1974 and Soror LaKeisha McKeown(2003)
- Mother-Daughter: Soror Rachel A. Burse and Soror Crystal Adkisson, (2004)
- Mother-Daughter: Soror Shereyl O'Neal (1976) and Soror Ashley O'Neal (2005) both in Delta Tau
- Mother-Daughter: Soror Dorothea King-James (1985) and Soror Trinita James-Hobbs, 2012
- Sister Sorors: Soror Davina Hughes and Soror Sunnie Hughes
- Sister Sorors: Soror Marcella Curry Watkins (1979) and Soror Allieze Ruby Curry

To enhance our membership and strengthen procedures, the following have been instituted in our chapter's structure:

SOROR ASSIST FUND — created in the early 1990's, the main function of this fund is to assist chapter sorors who have experienced a financial crisis. It was created to assist active chapter sorors with their per capita and chapter dues. Assistance can be in the form of a grant or loan and the request for assistance can be made by a current chapter soror on behalf of the soror in need, or by the soror herself. All fines collected from chapter sorors are included in the Soror Assist Fund Account.

OMICRON ETA OMEGA FUND, INC. — This organization, established in 1998, under the leadership of Soror Cecily Curry, Basileus and Soror Wanda D. Jackson, Incorporator, functions as the philanthropic organization for Omicron Eta Omega chapter, providing financial assistance to the community. It was organized exclusively for the purposes within the meaning of Section 501(c) 3 of the Internal Revenue Code. In 2011, the nonprofit corporation was renamed IVY FOUNDATION OF ST. LOUIS.

POLICIES AND PROCEDURES MANUAL — initiated in 1994, this chapter document compiled expectations for chapter officers. The concept was presented to the chapter under the leadership of Soror Melanie Chambers, Basileus and Soror Wanda Jackson, Standards Chairman. In 2004, under the leadership of Soror Colette Cummings, the current format was established to include all chapter practices and to insure that our chapter practices would be documented and standardized.

It compiles all of Omicron Eta Omega chapter's policies, procedures and protocol under one binder so they could be readily accessible to all chapter sorors. It is used in conjunction with Omicron Eta Omega Bylaws, Ivy Foundation of St. Louis Bylaws, Fiscal Fitness Guide to Chapter Financial Procedures, and the Bylaws and Constitution of Alpha Kappa Alpha Sorority, Incorporated.

OMICRON ETA OMEGA CHAPTER SIGNATURE PROGRAMS INCLUDE:

SALUTE TO BLACK MEN AWARDS — The purpose of this project is to honor Black men from the St. Louis Metropolitan area who have positively impacted the St. Louis community, and who have distinguished themselves professionally. Since 1986, our chapter has honored over one hundred men who continually serve our community. The proceeds from this event have been used to present scholarships and book stipends to deserving college students. This program concept was first presented to the chapter by Soror Melanie Chambers, who was also the first chairman for the event.

LITTLE MISS FASHIONETTA — Since 1991, this program has been offered annually for young African American girls. The total experience, which lasts about five months, includes a series of life skill enhancement activities, community service and a formal luncheon. The culminating event is a spring pageant where the girls receive awards, showcase a talent and are presented to the community in cotillion attire. Many of our participants have participated in Fashionetta® activities for high school seniors and several have also become members of Alpha Kappa Alpha Sorority, Incorporated. This activity was presented to the chapter and first chaired by Soror Sonya Wilson and Soror Seletha Curtis.

SCHOLARSHIP RESEARCH WORKSHOP — partnering with "The Scholarship Solution", the workshop is dedicated to providing college bound students and parents with the knowledge and tools needed to conduct a successful scholarship search. The first workshop was held in 2006 with Soror Pamela Westbrooks as the chairman. Scholarship Solution is the brainchild of Soror Pam who used her scholarship research experience of obtaining funding for her Morehouse college bound nephew. Her nephew, Brandon, has since graduated from Morehouse, completed medical school at SLU, and is now in his residency program.

BLACK COLLEGE ROAD SHOW — Since 2007, our chapter has arranged travel to and a tour of colleges and historical sites. The bus trip is offered to students in grades 8-12 to visit Historically Black Colleges and Universities such as Grambling State, Southern, Alabama A&M, Lincoln, Fisk, Tennessee State, Spelman, and Morehouse. A chaperoned bus load of students journey over a three or four day period, visiting college campuses and planting the seed of higher education … helping these young students envision their lives as college students on these campuses. This activity was first presented to the chapter by Soror Andrea Boyd and first chaired by Soror Sharita Shelby.

IVY LEAGUE AKADEMY — A mentoring program to build leadership and character in young girls at the Hanranhan Elementary School, Ferguson-Florissant school district. Funding for the project was obtained through a grant from the AKA Educational Advancement Foundation for the 2010-2011 school years. This activity was presented to the chapter by Soror Rachel Burse and first chaired by Soror Sharita Shelby.

Philanthropic contributions have been given to countless organizations to help further their causes. The United Negro College Fund, AKA Educational Advancement Foundation, Lupus Foundation, NAACP, American Cancer Society, American Red Cross, United Way and the YWCA are among Omicron Eta Omega chapter's many recipients. Community outreach activities, in addition to financial contributions, have allowed Omicron Eta Omega chapter to fulfill our sorority's purpose as established by our Founders… "Service to All Mankind."

Chapter projects and activities throughout the service life of Omicron Eta Omega include:

Joint Founder's Day Celebrations; Africare Assistance Program; "Save the Children" Sponsor; Letter Writing Campaign; Education Awareness Workshops; Shoeboxes for Africa; South African Struggle Campaign; Health Fair & Health Awareness Workshops; Mother's Day Banquet for Teenage

Mothers; Buckle Up America; Book Donations for Nurseries and Libraries; Black Dollar Day Sponsor; American Red Cross Blood Drives; Distributed Fire Detectors to Needy; Masquerade Ball Costume; Masquerade Ball Formal; "Meet the Candidates" Forum; Adopt A Family Program; AKA Coat Drive for the Needy; Komen Race for the Cure; UNCF Walk A Thon; Energy Assistance Program; Census 2000 & 2010 Partner; Career Fair & Job Skills Workshop; Fundraising at Busch Stadium; "Charles Drew Blood Drive" Sponsor; "St. Louis Gateway Classic" Support; "St. Louis Black Repertory Theatre" Support; "Greenley Community Center" Support and Assistance; "West End Academy Community Center" Support and Assistance; Collaborative Programs with city of St. Louis Fire Department; Collaborative Voter Registration Drive with RAMS Football Team and League of Women Voters; Centenary Bridge Program; Salvation Army Harbor Lights Homeless Shelter Program

Serving the St. Louis Community and Retaining a Loyal Sisterhood, Omicron Eta Omega chapter remains in The Spirit of Alpha Kappa Alpha.

OMICRON ETA OMEGA CHAPTER BASILEI

Angela Haywood Gaskin	1984 – 1985
Melanie Chambers	1986 – 1987
Mary Stoddard	1988 – 1988
Wanda D. Jackson	1988 – 1990
Carolyn Kidd Royal	1991 – 1992
Melanie Chambers	1993 – 1994
Chardial A. Samuel	1995 – 1996
Cecily Curry	1997 – 1998
Seletha R. Curtis	1999 – 2000
Angela Lampkin	2001 – 2002
Colette Cummings	2003 – 2004
Cheryl L. White	2005 – 2006
Wanda D. Jackson	2007 – 2008
Rachel A. Burse	2009 – 2010
Yolanda Lockhart	2011 – 2012
Pamela Westbrooks-Hodge	2013 – 2014

Omicron Theta Omega Chapter

St. Louis, Missouri
May 27, 1984

Left to Right, First Row: Barbara Epps, Hazel Mallory, Doris Jones, Dorothy Solomon, Virginia Gilbert, Doris Roberts, Mary Louise Franklin, Thelma Osborne, Shirley Armstrong. Second Row: Sally Holland, Elveeta Macon, Betty Lee, Mildred Simmons, Velma Martin, Armatha Jackson. Third Row: Rosetta Moore, Faye Johnson, Pamela Johnson, Arlene Antognoli, Jamesanna Jones. Fourth Row: Alice Windom, Helen Downs, Inez Griffin, Pearlie Evans Fifth Row: Johnetta Haley, Mary Brewster, Mary Robinson, Erma Shelton. Sixth Row: Vertrella Lewis, Karen Haley Douglas, Margaret Bush Wilson, Gloria Dismukes. Not Pictured: Madeline Franklin

Charter Members

ARLENE ANTOGNOLI*
SHIRLEY ARMSTRONG
MARY BREWSTER
GLORIA DISMUKES
HELEN DOWNS
KAREN HALEY DOUGLAS
BARBARA EPPS
PEARLIE EVANS
MADELINE FRANKLIN
MARY LOUISE FRANKLIN
VIRGINIA M. GILBERT*
INEZ GRIFFIN
JOHNETTA HALEY
SALLY HOLLAND
ARMATHA JACKSON*
FAYE JOHNSON
PAMELA JOHNSON
DORIS JOHNSON
JAMESANNA JONES*
BETTY J. LEE*
VERTRELLA LEWIS
ELVEETA MACON
HAZEL MALLORY
VELMA MARTIN
ROSETTA T. MOORE
THELMA OSBORNE
DORIS ROBERTS
MARY ROBINSON*
ERMA SHELTON
MILDRED SIMMONS
DOROTHY SOLAMON
MARGARET BUSH WILSON*
ALICE WINDOM

*Ivy Beyond the Wall

Omicron Theta Omega Chapter's history speaks of work, and the realization that all work is eased when there is love and commitment and so it is with Omicron Theta Omega. Our work record over the past years is our history. It began on May 27, 1984, when thirty-three sorors became charter members and formed the third Alpha Kappa Alpha Sorority Graduate Chapter on the Missouri side of the Mississippi River. At the time of the chartering of Omicron Theta Omega, the Regional Director was Soror Mabel Cason.

Many of the sorors, having gained active experiences in other chapters, were ready to take on new activities and build on others, and Alpha Kappa Alpha could thus spread its services to meet an ever-increasing need.

EDUCATIONAL EQUITY: Since 1984, Omicron Theta Omega Chapter has addressed quality education as a programmatic activity. Our first community forum on education, "Education Reform: Equity For Black Children was presented to inform the community, to assess the problems, to collaborate on solutions, and to devise a course of action to guarantee quality education for black children in St. Louis. The concerns and issues presented were drafted into a resolution and forwarded to appropriate officials as a document of educational reform.

Moving from facilitation of issue to presentation, membership and chapter participation in school bond issues and tax campaigns became a prime activity for supporting quality education. Omicron Theta Omega has been involved in every tax proposition for the schools since the chapter was established.

In 1987, the city-wide election for four new members of the Board of Education became a critical issue for the community when four of the ten candidates came from a white-rights group. Chapter members voted to endorse an alternative slate of candidates for Quality Education. An incumbent Black member was re-elected and one of the white-right coalition candidates lost.

A similar scenario developed in 1991, when four seats on the board were up for election. A slate of reform candidates ran against a white rights group. One of the reform candidates was a chapter member and Omicron Theta Omega solidified a support campaign for all the candidates that helped in a landslide victory for the Four Candidates for Kids.

Believing that the future lies in today's youth, Omicron Theta Omega has sponsored memberships for the Mathews-Dickey Boys' Club and was involved in a program presentation for the initiation of girls' activities. In 1987, a drug and alcohol abuse program for middle school students was sponsored by the chapter. Later, the top ranking St. Louis Public School seniors were recognized at a reception featuring Huel Perkins, TV anchorman, and special guest speaker. Soror Stephanie Brown chaired this project.

A previous youth thrust involved the participation of Omicron Theta Omega Chapter with three other Alpha Kappa Alpha chapters in a collaboration workshop designed to address the problems of teen pregnancy. Our chapter was able to bring experiences to the workshop based on a Teen Pregnancy Project initiated prior to our becoming a chapter. In this project, led by Soror Shirley Armstrong, our members worked with middle school girls, helping them in the development of positive goals, self-esteem, and new, caring experiences.

GLOBAL CONCERNS: In developing a concept for involvement in Global Concerns, the chapter launched plans for the establishment of a South Africa Resource Center. Soror Alice Windom, who has lived and traveled extensively in Africa, chaired the committee to plan activities for program implementation. The goal of the center was to increase awareness in the St. Louis community and to focus attention on the continuing struggle of front-line states. The concept was introduced to the community in 1984 and based on public response the center was fully developed in 1985.

With the awareness of South Africa increased through printed materials, films, books, and other resources coordinated through the center, it was decided that a long-range project should involve collaboration with other groups and individuals. Omicron Theta Omega organized a panel and film presentation that stimulated the interests of others and became a participant in the founding of the St. Louis Coalition Against Apartheid.

Continuing with organizational impact and collaboration, the chapter joined the Committee for a Free South Africa and the United Mine Workers in picketing a local Shell Station to protest the company's presence in South Africa; picketed the Martin Coin Shop in Clayton, Missouri, seller of the South African Krugerrands; cooperated with the women's group of a Presbyterian Church on presenting Elizabeth Sibeko, Women's Wing coordinator, Pan Africanist Congress of Azania; supported the development of divestiture action for city pension fund; and presented a forum on African Development featuring Melvin Foote, with participation by Gamma Omega and Delta Sigma Theta.

As a way of enhancing knowledge and acquiring information about people all over the world, Soror Alice Windom coordinated chapter membership in the African American Cultural & Arts Network (AACAN). AACAN is a travel organization with a black focus on cultural trips and, through organizational affiliation. Omicron Theta Omega received revenue from recruitment of individual travel. Income was directed to the Africare Project. This has become an annual travel opportunity.

CONNECTION/POLITICAL ACTION: Under the leadership of Soror Jamesanna Jones, State Connection Coordinator, a series of activities was implemented in 1984 for chapter involvement in voter education and registration. Sorors were encouraged to participate in state caucus meetings. A list was developed outlining each soror's ward and precinct as a guide for meeting attendance. Soror Jones represented the chapter at a Town Hall meeting in which the restrictive policies of the St. Louis Board of Election Commissioners were discussed. Support was given to the Women's Vote Project to assist with voter registration. The chapter received a $6,000 grant, facilitated by Soror Pearlie Evans, Central Region's Connection Representative, for voter education and registration projects.

Political empowerment was the thrust of the Social Action Committee's coordination of participation in key political campaigns. Omicron Theta Omega's earlier involvement in voter education was transitioned into a Get out the Vote action project to sustain a base of black political power in the city of St. Louis. The committee chairperson, Soror Mary Franklin, outlined ways that sorors could give individual support and Soror Margaret Bush Wilson addressed the chapter on the St. Louis political scene and the importance of the Black vote. The Black incumbent office-holders were re-elected.

The involvement of the chapter has expanded to overseeing public housing tenant management elections, including the supervision of the Cochran Gardens Tenant Management Board elections; presenting community issue forums; and actively participating in the area of reproductive rights and the African American woman.

Other activities since the chapter's inception include the contribution of more than $4,000 to the United Negro College Fund, and the renovation and furnishing of a room at the Phyllis Wheatley YWCA.

The resources and talents of members of Omicron Theta Omega have enabled the chapter to achieve a status of recognition in the community. We have distinguished ourselves among the many fraternal, community, and civic organizations in the St. Louis Metropolitan area. We were honored for our service on behalf of Alpha Kappa Alpha with a LEADING THE WAY Award from the Coalition of 100 Black Women. The community involvement and public service contribution of our members continues to enhance the chapter, the traditions of our great sorority, and the quality of life in the St. Louis community.

ETHEL HEDGEMAN LYLE ACADEMY: In 1998, Omicron Theta Omega chapter members wanted to identify a multi-year program that would be significant in scope and varied enough to appeal to the interests of all sorors. Soror Paula Smith, who had just completed her term as a member of the St. Louis Board of Education, suggested that the chapter apply for a charter to operate a school.

The Omicron Theta Omega Chapter had always been a very strong and visible supporter of public education and many of its programs were conducted through the city's public schools. Additionally, several of its members opposed the charter school legislation because of the anticipated negative impact it would have on the St. Louis Public School System. However, when the charter school legislation did pass and became law, there was a desire by many chapter members to ensure continued African

American involvement in the decisions made for educating Black youth. The charter school initiative was seen as a way to address the chapter's need for a significant long-term program and a way to have a "seat at the table" during public education policy making.

Soror Ruby Bonner suggested naming the charter school for the sorority's first member and St. Louisan, Ethel Hedgeman Lyle. Implementation of the strategies necessary for acquiring the charter fell to chapter Basileus, Soror Joan Hubbard. Members of the first committee were: Andrea' Allen, Nancy Anderson-Tayborn, Ruby Bonner, Sharilyn Franklin, Laura Elaine Flipping, Sheilah Glaze, Johnetta Haley, Joan Hubbard, Hazel Mallory, Romona Miller, Paula Smith, Charlotte Ijei, Laura Mabry, Loretta Striplin, Hattie Stunson, and Barbara Wilkins.

The charter was written, and an educational management company was employed. Based on the contacts of Soror Pearlie Evans and in accordance with State Statute, application for sponsorship was made to Harris Stowe State College. Harris Stowe State College accepted our application on February 23, 2000, thereby making Ethel Hedgeman Lyle Academy the first charter school to receive sponsorship in the City of St. Louis.

Due to the lack of available adequate facilities, the Academy was forced to open its doors in September, 2000, in a building that was shared with another charter school, Thurgood Marshall Academy. This was a building leased from the Federal Government located at 4300 Goodfellow Boulevard.

The Academy opened with 208 youngsters in grades pre-kindergarten through 2. The first principal was Delores Guyton, a soror who had held principalships in St. Louis suburban school districts. Soror Guyton guided the Academy to its growth to grade 4 and to its reputation as a school of excellence.

In 2003, the chapter's charter school committee (Academy's Board of Directors) located space on the 7th and 8th floors of a stellar downtown office building at 1509 Washington Avenue. This space was renovated to accommodate classrooms and in September, 2003 became the current home of the Academy. Also during the summer of 2003, Soror Guyton resigned her position and Mrs. D'Anne Tombs-Shelton was appointed as the Academy's principal. Additionally, due to state budget cuts, the pre-kindergarten program was eliminated.

The Academy grew. At the start of the 2004-2005 school years, there were 356 students enrolled in grades kindergarten through six, housed on four floors of 48,000 sq. ft of space at 1509 Washington Avenue.

The Image Schools, Inc. our management company expanded EHLA to a Middle/HS in 2006 at 706 N Jefferson, STL, Mo after much debate and resistance by the charter holders and founders. Each year, gradually, a grade level was added. By 2007 this facility housed grades six thru eleven, W. Harrison and later S. Pittman served as principals.

In 2007, chapter members approved separation from Imagine Schools, Inc., Arlington, Va., due to unacceptable academic performance per state standards and overall lack of transparency of school operations. This became delayed for one year. Subsequently, the termination of the agreement became final, with an effective date of July 1, 2008.

Under the leadership of Basileus Karen Haley Douglas and appointed Board President Margaret Ann Berry, steps were initiated to address the ongoing challenges of providing a quality education for our students. Access Management Co., Clayton, MO., under CEO Charles Farris, was hired to take the helm of EHL Academy, replacing Imagine Schools, Inc. EHLA opened doors at a new middle/high school site at 1881 Pine Street, St. Louis, MO. a 90,000 sq. ft.; 4 story office building and the rent expense was reduced by 40% from prior site.

January 2009, Ivy Leaf Foundation, Inc. was created for the chapter by Basileus, MA Berry. A new and separate tax ID number assigned to EH Lyle Academy with assistance from legal counsel of Danna McKitrick Law firm. Its purpose was to address the ongoing concern and need to separate EH

Lyle Academy from Omicron Theta Omega Chapter in every aspect of its operations. This became a very important action in later years for the chapter members. In February, 2009, the Ivy Leaf Foundation, Incorporated, became official and is the property of Omicron Theta Omega Chapter.

February 2009, at AKA Day at the Capital; Basileus MA Berry requested needed legislation regarding Charter school governance and oversight. Approximately two months later, notice was received by the chapter and EHLA- AKA Board of the intent to discontinue sponsorship by MBU (Missouri Baptist University) St. Louis, MO. The issue stated was the request for a more diverse and Independent Board with residents from City of St. Louis. Chapter members voted to comply, turning over total operations to MBU and their designees, effective June 2009.

January 2010, Correspondence from the State of Mo. reflected an ongoing concern for operating the following school year; a nationwide recession was looming large. Funding for education was being dramatically affected as well for many school districts; St. Louis was not an exception. April 2010, Mo. Dept. of Education ordered a transition of EHLA students to the St. Louis Public School system, effective May 1, 2012. May 1: EHLA is transitioned to St. Louis Public Schools System, as mandated by the Mo. Dept. of Education.

At its peak, EHL Academy boasted an attendance of some 1400 students, and an annual budget of $15 million. Two stellar locations; 1509 Washington Avenue served grades K thru 5 and 1881 Pine Street for grades 6-12. Its first graduating class saw 18 students receive their long awaited diplomas and a hope for a better life. The dream continues...

We were pleased to have had the distinct opportunity to be the trailblazers for the Charter School movement in St. Louis, Missouri from 2000 thru 2010. We chose to dream that we could "make a difference" in the life of a child. That dream persists today. May the dream live forever in the hearts and minds of one and all. Three sorors stand out as true soldiers in this vein. They are: Board Members: Sharon Burroughs, Dr. Dorothy Fiddmont, and Margaret Ann Berry, Past Board President and two term Basileus.

Additionally, individual chapter members donated their time as tutors and/or mentors. Members of the charter school committee functioned as the State required Board of Directors. These sorors served as policymakers for the Academy, oversaw a budget of $3M for compliance with State law, for excellence in educational strategies, and for acceptable business practices. They also served as advocates for the Academy in the community and within the sorority. Following are the names of sorors who have served a on this committee: Allen, Andrea, 02-24-00 – 03-31-01; Bennett, Christina, 07-01-01; Berry, Margaret, 07-01-01; Bonner, Ruby, 02-24-00 – 12-31-01; Douglas, Karen, 07-01-03; Ellington-Twitty, Norma, 07-01-02 – 06-30-04; Epps, Beatryx, 07-01-03 – 12-31-03; Fiddmont. Dorothy, 07-01-02 – 06-30-03; Flipping, Elaine, 02-24-00 – 06-30-03; Franklin, Sharilyn, 02-24-00 – 12-31-01; Glaze, Sheilah, 02-24-00 – 12-31-01; Haley, Johnetta, 02-24-00; Hall, Jasmine, 07-01-03; Harper, Rhonda, 07-01-04; Hubbard, Joan, 02-24-00; Ijei, Charlotte, 02-24-00 – 06-30-02; Mabry, Laura, 02-24-00 – 12-31-01; Mallory, Hazel, 02-24-00 – 12-31-01; Miller, Romona, 02-24-00; Striplin, Loretta, 02-24-00; Stunson, Hattie, 02-24-00; Terrell, Dorothy, 07-01-01 – 06-30-03; Wilkins, Barbara, 02-24-00 – 12-31-01. Soror Marquita Wiley, Delta Delta Omega Chapter and Missouri State Senator Soror Rita Days also worked with the Academy as advisory board members.

OTHER CHAPTER PROGRAMS:

The chapter's program committees routinely conducts the following social service projects:
- Education — Ivy Reading Academy; Young Authors' Program; book donations.
- Black Family — Family to Family (a donation of food and clothing in collaboration with the Academy's PTA); Young Ladies' Day (etiquette training for both Academy girls and daughters of sorors); Mom's and Dad's Day essay contests.
- Economic Empowerment — Youth Financial Literacy Program (teaching youngsters the ABC's of managing money).

- Arts — Exhibit of student artwork at local mall.
- Connections — Get out the vote project in collaboration with Academy PTA.
- Angel Tree Project — Donate holiday gifts to children whose parents are incarcerated
- Change for Change — Support the Heifer International programming efforts.
- Global Poverty — Operation Food Bank-Donated can goods to help stock and restock the food pantries.
- Sky Is the Limit — Academic Scholarships in Partnership with Mathews Dickey Boys and Girls Club
- CWHA — Community Women Against Hardship- conducted life skill workshops

Pink Pizzazz-Annual Jazz Brunch Scholarships & Program Fundraiser
- AKApe — outreach to sorors who are sick and/or shut in, this includes a visit and showering them with pink and green love

REGIONAL POSITIONS & RECOGNITIONS
- 1970 – 1974, Johnetta Randolph Haley, Central Regional Director
- 1972 – 1974, Pearlie Evans, Connections Committee Chairman
- 2008 – 2009, Margaret Ann Berry, Standards Committee Member
- 2009 – 2010, Margaret Ann Berry, Awards Committee Member

INTERNATIONAL POSITIONS & RECOGNITIONS
- 1990 – 1994 — Johnetta Randolph Haley, Supreme Parliamentarian
- 1972 – 1974 — Pearlie Evans, Connections Committee Member
- 2010 – Margaret Ann Berry, St. Louis Boule Workshop Facilitator
- 2010 — Nina Patterson Caldwell, St. Louis Boule Transportation Co-Chair
- 2012 — Margaret Ann Berry, San Francisco Boule: Unsung Heroes of the Civil Rights Era
- 2012 — Pearlie Evans-San Francisco: UnSung Heroes of the Civil Rights Era
- 2012 — Margaret Bush Wilson-San Francisco, UnSung Heroes of the Civil Rights Era

LOCAL POSITIONS & RECOGNITION
- 2004 — Elveeta Macon, Initiated Spanish Lake Business Association
- 2010 — Nina Patterson Caldwell, Mathews Dickey Boys & Girls Club Service Award
- 2011 — Elveeta Macon, President of Trinity High School Executive Board
- 2011 — Margaret Ann Berry, Mathew Dickey Boys & Girls Club Service Award
- 2012 — Pamela Wall-Dover, Corporate Executive of the Year- St. Louis American
- 2012 — Elveeta Macon, Spanish Lake Youth Association- Youth Program Award
- 2012 — Nina Patterson Caldwell, Who's Who In Black St. Louis
- 2013 — Margaret Ann Berry, Emerald Award: Pioneer Woman in business (Int'l Trade & Finance)
- Iota Phi Lambda Sorority, Inc. (Alpha Zeta Chapter)
- 2013 — Nina Patterson Caldwell, Outstanding Dean of Student Award-NASPA Region IV

CHAPTER LEGACIES
- Mother-Daughter: Soror Velma Martin and Soror Deborah Ratliff
- Mother-Daughter: Soror Johnetta Haley and Soror Karen Haley
- Mother-Daughter: Soror Robin Britt and Soror Portia Britt
- Mother-Daughter: Soror Henrietta Mackey and Soror Morgan Mackey
- Sisters: Soror Michaela Thomas and Soror Christina Thomas

Chapter Members Who Have Held International/National Office or Been Elected to the International/National Nominating Committee

1970–1974, Johnetta Randolph Haley, Central Regional Director *
1990–1994 — Johnetta Randolph Haley, Supreme Parliamentarian

Member of Gamma Omega Chapter at time of election.

Omicron Theta Omega Chapter Basilei

Virginia Gilbert	1984 – 1985
Jamesanna Jones	1986 – 1989
Hazel Mallory	1990 – 1991
Velma Martin	1992 – 1993
Margaret Ann Berry	1994 – 1995
Madeline Franklin	1996 – 1997
Joan Hubbard	1998 – 2002
Elaine Flipping	2002
Ramona Hawkins Miller	2003 – 2005
Karen Haley Douglas	2006 – 2008
Margaret Ann Berry	2009 – 2010
Nina Patterson Caldwell	2011 – 2014

(Terms begin January 1 – December 31 for each year)

Omicron Sigma Omega Chapter

BOWLING GREEN, KENTUCKY
MARCH 31, 1985

Left to Right — Seated: Theresa Cowheard, Kelley Campbell, Shirley Malone, Bettie Esters, Mabel Cason-Central Regional Director, Shirley Sisney, Marilyn Mitchell, Ersa Austin, Patricia Cooke. Standing: Shirley Rainey, Emma Kendrick, Wanda Snead, Dorothy Shanklin, Greta Fishback, Sarah Sweatt, Sylvia Payne, Vivian Glass, Brenda Bell, Anna Senter, Amanda Barlow.

CHARTER MEMBERS

ERSA AUSTIN	EMMA KENDRICK
AMANDA BARLOW	SHIRLEY MALONE
BRENDA BELL	MARILYN MITCHELL
KELLY CAMPBELL	SYLVIA PAYNE
PATRICIA COOKE	SHIRLEY RAINEY
THERESA COWHERD	ANNA SENTER
BETTIE ESTERS	DOROTHY SHANKLIN
GRETA FISHBACK	SHIRLEY SISNEY
VIVIAN GLASS	WANDA SNEAD
	SARAH SWEATT

The closest chapter of Alpha Kappa Alpha Sorority, Incorporated to Bowling Green, KY was Beta Rho Omega Chapter, chartered in 1937 and located in Hopkinsville, Kentucky. It was composed of members from Clarksville, Tennessee, and five other cities in Kentucky—Auburn, Bowling Green, Franklin, Hopkinsville, and Russellville. Women interested in joining the chapter, reactivating, participating in chapter meetings, sorority functions or sisterly relations activities traveled 128 miles to and from Hopkinsville, when not hosting at home during monthly rotations.

As years passed, the number of sorors increased in the Auburn, Bowling Green, Franklin, and Russellville areas. Gasoline prices were also on the rise. With a growing desire to decrease travel time and the vision to implement more effective programs in Bowling Green and the surrounding areas, sorors began to discuss the possibility of establishing a chapter of Alpha Kappa Alpha in Bowling Green, KY.

Sorors Shirley Malone and Shirley Sisney spearheaded the effort to make the new chapter a reality. As a result of growth and increasing need in the communities, action to establish a chapter in Bowling

Green began. An interest group met on October 20, 1984 at the Dero Downing University Center on the campus of Western Kentucky University. At this meeting the following officers were elected: President, Shirley Sisney; Vice President, Bettie Esters; Recording Secretary, Marilyn Mitchell; Corresponding Secretary, Patricia Cooke; Treasurer, Ersa Austin; Parliamentarian, Shirley Malone; and Publicity Chairman, Kelly Campbell. Other sorors who expressed an interest in establishing a chapter were: Amanda Barlow, Brenda Bell, Theresa Cowherd, Greta Fishback, Vivian Glass, Emma Forte Kendrick, Sylvia Payne, Shirley Rainey, Anna Senter, Dorothy Shanklin, Wanda Snead, and Sarah Sweatt.

On October 24, 1984, the interest group met at the home of Soror Shirley Sisney, constructed the Constitution and Bylaws and selected the name Alpha-Ettes. Three days later at 5:00 p.m. the Regional Director, Soror Mable Evans Cason, met with the sorors on Western Kentucky University's campus to explain the procedures for chartering a chapter of Alpha Kappa Alpha Sorority, Inc. Each soror was assessed $100 to help charter the chapter. The first regular meeting was held on November 10, 1984 at the George Washington Carver Center in Bowling Green. The charter requirements were finalized on November 13, 1984 at the home of Soror Greta Fishback, thus enabling the Alpha-Ettes to fulfill the obligations and requirements to become chartered members of Alpha Kappa Alpha Sorority, Incorporated.

At 3:00 p.m. on March 31, 1985, the chartering ceremony was held at State Street Baptist Church, the oldest African American church in Bowling Green, Kentucky. The program began with a prelude by Soror Wanda Snead. Next the Reverend O. A. Moses, Interim Pastor at State Street Baptist Church, provided the invocation. Then Soror Marilyn Mitchell presented the occasion. The Honorable Charles Hardcastle, Mayor of Bowling Green, gave greetings along with the following: Soror Marsha Holloway, Beta Rho Omega Chapter, Alpha Kappa Alpha Sorority, Hopkinsville, Kentucky; Mr. Jimmy Stewart, Western Kentucky Regional Director, Alpha Phi Alpha Fraternity; Soror Louvenia Peavie, Nu Kappa Omega Chapter, Alpha Kappa Alpha Sorority, Clarksville, Tennessee; Mr. Gregory McKinney, Kappa Alpha Psi Fraternity; Miss Marilyn White, Delta Sigma Theta Sorority; Mr. Herbert A. Oldham, Omega Psi Phi Fraternity; Mrs. Collen Wilhite, Zeta Phi Beta Sorority; Mr. Michael W. Coleman, Phi Beta Sigma Fraternity; Mrs. Gwendolyn Downs, National Association for the Advancement of Colored People (NAACP); Mr. Herbert Oldham, Ancient Landmark #93, and Mrs. Wanda Johnson, AWARE (Association With Aspirations For Real Equality).

After the greetings, Soror Shirley Rainey sang an uplifting solo. Soror Shirley Sisney introduced the speaker who was the Regional Director, Soror Mable Evans Cason. Soror Shirley Malone made a presentation to Soror Mable Evans Cason, followed by remarks from Soror Sisney. To conclude the ceremony, the sorors sang the National Hymn and the Reverend O. A. Moses delivered the benediction. Under the leadership of Supreme Basileus, Faye B. Bryant, the Alpha-Ettes accomplished their mission of becoming the newly chartered Omicron Sigma Omega Chapter of Alpha Kappa Alpha Sorority, Incorporated.

Major Chapter Events And Service Projects

THE DEBUTANTE COTILLION

The Debutante Club/Cotillion became the signature event for Omicron Sigma Omega Chapter in 1986. The Debutante Club has positively impacted young women in their junior and senior years of high school as well as their escorts. The debutantes participated in a series of workshops and community service projects designed to strengthen cultural and civic involvement, to encourage academic and professional growth, and to promote superior achievement. Workshops and community service projects include:
- Etiquette for business luncheons or social events
- (LEAP) Litter Education and Abatement Program
- Bowling Green Christmas Parade

- Scholarship application strategies
- Study skills and test preparation
- Talent showcase

An average of $5000 has been awarded in scholarships to debutantes and other students in the surrounding communities as a result of this fundraiser. The community enthusiastically looks forward to seeing the young ladies along with their parents, and escorts as they are presented to society, receive awards, and dance the Minuet.

OTHER FUNDRAISERS

Fashion shows have been integral to fundraising for the chapter with sorors, children, debutantes, and community members serving as models. The Male Fashion Shows have strengthened intergenerational bonds ranging from toddlers to grandfathers. The men not only commanded the runway in style, but furthermore prepared their special dishes for the receptions following the shows. Ever mindful of delicious food, participating in "The Taste of AKA" has continually offered sorors opportunities to showcase their favorite prepared dishes, going from appetizers to desserts. During the "Taste of AKA," local talent provides entertainment while entrepreneurs sell their products which include: cosmetics, books, holiday crafts, jewelry, and other items. As a continued effort to raise monies, the chapter has also partnered with Kappa Alpha Psi Fraternity in sponsoring Masquerade Balls.

HEALTH FAIRS

Through health fares, Omicron Sigma Omega has taken action in response to the negative statistics of minorities disproportionately suffering from heart disease, breast cancer, obesity, diabetes, prostate cancer, and asthma. These fairs operated at the Bowling Green Housing Authority, Parker Bennett Elementary School, and Shake Rag Festivals. Sorors have also disseminated pamphlets and brochures about nutrition, wellness, and the importance of exercise with said materials being provided at the Juneteenth Festival, Unity in the Community, International Festivals, in churches, and through other venues.

Use of a mobile screening unit from Western Kentucky University Health Services has given free health screenings that have saved lives and increased awareness of healthy and unhealthy levels of cholesterol, blood sugar, and blood pressure. Other topics covered were seat belt safety, self-defense, stress reduction, and beauty tips. Omicron Sigma Omega sorors have frequently participated in Relay for Life and the Komen Race for a Cure by walking and raising funds to support treatment and research. In partnership with the Community Health Department and Community Action of Southern Kentucky Head Start, the chapter sponsored an Asthma Awareness workshop.

EDUCATION AND THE ARTS

Through its activities spanning over six years, the Ivy Akademy stressed the value of a good education for success in life. Students from grades K-2 and 3-6 received tutoring in reading, math, writing, and science; saw cultural events (such as The Boys Choir of Harlem, Peter Pan, Jungle Book, Beauty and the Beast, African Drummers and Dancers of Nashville); and participated in other social or learning experiences. The Little Mr. and Miss AKA Pageant provided a chance for youth to showcase their artistic creations or talents for their parents and attendees. Several Kentucky State University Choir Concerts and Gospel Extravaganzas have enriched the community with diverse music—classical, opera, jazz, spiritual, and contemporary—while raising funds for chapter programs. Omicron Sigma Omega donated money for students attending the Historically Black Colleges and Universities Tour and students going to Beijing, China. The chapter also continues to annually honor many students for excellence in scholarship, athletics, the arts, and community service.

COLLABORATION WITH OTHER ORGANIZATIONS

In helping the needy, Omicron Sigma Omega has collected food, coats, and clothing in addition to distributing Thanksgiving baskets to families in Auburn, Bowling Green, Franklin, Glasgow, and

Russellville, Kentucky. Realizing the necessity of broadening the impact of Alpha Kappa Alpha Sorority's programs, the chapter has also combined efforts with other organizations to improve the community. Some or the collaborators have included: the NAACP, Greek fraternities and sororities, the Housing Authority of Bowling Green, various Western Kentucky University departments, local churches, the George Washington Carver Center, the Bowling Green Human Rights Commission, Masonic organizations, the Association of Black Social Workers (ABSW) of South Central Kentucky, Girl Scouts of the USA, area schools, and various other civic organizations. In fact, some of these same groups have worked with the sorority to help with Habitat for Humanity building projects. Broadening its outreach even more, Omicron Sigma Omega members participated in the Dr. Martin Luther King, Jr. (MLK) Day events—including the symbolic annual march—along with debutantes, Emerging Young Leaders (EYL), and other organizations and people from across the community. Afterwards, they attended more events at State Street Baptist Church. A month later in February at AKA Day at the Capitol, sorors, other Greeks, and supporters from across Kentucky met with legislators in Frankfort to advocate for justice, equal rights, and needed changes to current laws. Further emphasizing civic endeavors, the chapter has also worked in partnership with additional likeminded organizations to build political empowerment through voter education, voter registration drives, candidate forums, and get out the vote campaigns.

OSO—THE NEXT CENTURY

In 2008, Omicron Sigma Omega Chapter sorors symbolically marched towards Washington, D.C. into the next century, doing so simultaneously with sorors throughout the world, other sororities, fraternities, friends, family, and members of the community. Continuing its forward movement in celebrating Cluster Seven's Centennial Founders' Day, Soror Dorothy Buckhanan, 26th Central Regional Director and current Supreme Anti-Basileus, spoke to both sorors and the community attendees. Her topic was "Extending Service as We Progress into the Next Century." The collection of canned goods, coats, and cell phones gathered at the event went to the State Street Baptist Church food pantry, the Salvation Army, a women's domestic abuse shelter, and to families of deployed soldiers.

Emerging Young Leaders (EYL) was launched on January 16, 2011. It is a mentoring program for middle school girls in grades 6-8. EYL activities have included: visiting a monthly Bowling Green City Commissioners' meeting to observe leadership practices, including use of parliamentary procedures; attending the formal "Mom Prom" for breast cancer awareness; supporting First Lady Michelle Obama's "Get Moving" initiative; participating in weaving plastic bags into mats for the homeless at the Juneteenth Festival; and collecting donations for the Heifer project. In "Going Green," the girls each received a tree sapling while attending a local park's Arbor Day event, obtained bicycle safety certificates after successfully riding a road course and passing a written test, and participated in the Litter Education and Abatement Program (LEAP), picking up trash to clean a local road.

Throughout the years, many Omicron Sigma Omega sorors have been honored as: Kentucky Colonels by the governor, Trailblazers by the Trailblazer committee representing several community churches, Women of Achievement by the Bowling Green Human Rights Commission, and as Outstanding African American Community Leaders by the MLK Committee. In 2011 as another honor, the chapter was recognized as a Historical Community Advocacy Organization. Its history, along with a group photo, was included in the 2011 Legacy MLK calendar which was sold as a fundraiser. In 2012, Omicron Sigma Omega received President Obama's Service Award from the WKU Alive Center, a volunteer outreach agency. The chapter was also recognized at the 2012 Central Regional Conference and was chosen to be featured in the Spring 2012 issue of the *Ivy Leaf* for its MLK Day of Service "Sunday Supper." This event was to spotlight active and inactive duty service members, veterans, and their families. A Military Star Salute memorialized deceased veterans and honored living service members. Those present had the opportunity to post a star on a tree which was followed by a military panel sharing its experiences of service to the country.

IVIES BEYOND THE WALL

Three dynamic Omicron Sigma Omega sorors inspired others and actively served until they joined the Ivies Beyond the Wall. Soror Amanda Barlow, the eldest member, opened her home and gave guidance along the journey. Soror Wilsonya Watts, as a past Basileus, left her mark as an example of strong leadership. Soror Dorothy Shanklin mentored debutantes, escorts, and youth she met along the way. Chapter sorors hold dear the bonds of sisterhood greatly enriched from knowing them.

Omicron Sigma Omega Has Advised Epsilon Zeta Since 1985.

CHAPTER MEMBERS WHO HAVE HELD INTERNATIONAL/NATIONAL OFFICE OR BEEN ELECTED TO THE INTERNATIONAL/NATIONAL NOMINATING COMMITTEE

Brandi M. Smith   International Nominating Committee   2008-2010

OMICRON SIGMA OMEGA CHAPTER BASILEI

Shirley Sisney	1985 – 1986
Emma Forte Kendrick	1987 – 1988
Vivian Glass	1989 – 1990
Wilsonya Watts	1991 – 1992
Emma Forte Kendrick	1993 – 1994
Wanda Snead	1995
Thelma Jackson	1996
Cassandra Little	1997
Wanda Snead	1998 – 1999
Cassandra Little	2000
Cheryl Lewis Smith	2001
Joan Sanders	2002
Cheryl Lewis Smith	2003 – 2005
Vivian Glass	2006
Cheryl Lewis-Smith	2007 – 2008
Emma Forte Kendrick	2009 – 2010
Barbara Pollock	2011 – 2012
Cheryl Lewis-Smith	2013 –

Omicron Phi Omega Chapter

KOKOMO, INDIANA
MAY 18, 1985

Front Row, Left to Right: Jeannetta Burbridge, Alice Marshall, Loraine Richardson Green, 2nd Supreme Basileus, JoAnn Obie and Gerry Stroman. Second Row, Left to Right: France Gibbons, Mary Ann Nolcox, Delores Davis, Narvie Scott, Kimberly Queen, Kathy Donald, Tyjuanna LaBennett, Jacquelin Cole, Mattie Daniels, Cherresa Johnson, Sharon Grier. Not Pictured: Tova Ellison.

CHARTER MEMBERS

JEANNETTA BURBRIDGE	TYJUANNA R. STRICKLAND LABENNETT
JACQUELIN BELLAMY COLE	ALICE RUTH BURNS MARSHALL
MATTIE LOUISE MCGILL DANIELS	MARY ANN LIGGIN NOLCOX *
ETHEL DELORES GRIFFIN DAVIS	JOANN WARD OBIE
KATHRYN KUYKENDOLPH DONALD	KIMBERLY ANN QUEEN
TOVA JASELLE ELLISON	NARVIE LEE KENNEDY SCOTT
SHARON LEE CREWS GRIER	GERRY FRANCES GUNNINGS STROMAN
CHERRESA VERNEA JOHNSON	FRANCES R. FOSTER GIBBONS SWEATT

*Ivy Beyond the Wall

The Pearls of Kokomo was officially established on September 23, 1984, after three months of recruitment by Soror JoAnn Obie. Soror Obie successfully recruited Delores Davis, Sharon Grier, Gerry Stroman, Tyjuanna LaBennett and Mattie Daniels.

By October, 1994 the Pearls of Kokomo had grown to sixteen, including members from nearby Marion, Indiana. With hopes of a spring chartering, the Pearls of Kokomo met with Soror Mable Cason, Central Regional Director.

Seven months later, the Pearls of Kokomo had earned the right, privilege, and responsibility of becoming a graduate chapter of the nation's oldest and most esteemed Black sorority—Alpha Kappa Alpha. In the afternnoon on May 18, 1985 Soror Loraine Richardson Green, 2nd Supreme Basileus conducted the chartering ceremony held at the Ramada Inn in Kokomo. Omicron Phi Omega was the first Black sorority established in Kokomo.

The chartering of Omicron Phi Omega was the start of a stream of notable women, in the area, becoming members of Alpha Kappa Alpha Sorority, Inc. On May 24, 1986, the first group of candidates was initiated. They were Theresa Lang, Patricia Alsup,* Gwendolyn Williams, Juanita Martin and Darlene Poulard.

A second group of candidates was initiated on June 27, 1988. Included among them were Virginia Anglin, Celia Reed and Celestine Johnson. On September 21, 1991, Mary Lou Johnson, Jean Burnett, Leesa Wilson, Lois Motley Harris, Terrye Garrett, Lynne Rieser and Muriel Haywood were initiated into Omicron Phi Omega. Other sorors have joined the chapter through the years from undergraduate chapters. They were Michelle Lee, Reashonda White, Anita Bellamy and Charlene McCarter.*

Charter member, Mary Ann Nolcox became an Ivy Beyond the Wall on August 12, 1989. She was much beloved by her fellow sorors. A scholarship was established in her memory. In 1994, Inez Patricia Alsup and her husband Johnny, on their retirement from teaching, funded a scholarship with the chapter.

Charter member and former chapter Basileus, Delores Davis became an Ivy Beyond the Wall on December 8, 1996. On November 9, 1997 four new sorors joined the chapter. They were Kimberly R. Sinclair, Debra E. Williams, Anita L. Upchurch and Joanne Onkes. This was an inspiring event for all of the sorors involved.

October 10, 1999 saw yet another increase in the chapter's membership with the initiation of Sorors Dondra Ewing, Camille Johnson, Kelee Mitchell, Alessia Harrell, Lisa Taylor and Bobbie Owensby.

January 15, 2000 marked a memorable occasion. Soror Mary Lou Johnson chaired the 15th Annual Dr. Martin Luther King, Jr. Celebration. The celebration was underwritten by Soror Johnson's cousin, Robert Knowling, Jr., who sponsored the Reverend Jesse Jackson's coming to Kokomo and presented the chapter with a check for $100,000 for Omicron Phi Omega Chapter's scholarship fund.

Also, during January 2000 Sorors Alice Marshall and Jean Burnett reactivated with the chapter. In the summer of 2001, Soror Thomanisa Noble-Ash transferred to Omicron Phi Omega from Gamma Psi Omega in Gary, IN.

In January 2002, Qianna Kimbrough joined the chapter upon graduation. And on March 24, 2002 the sixth group of candidates was initiated. They were: Angekla Jones, Mallorie Marshall, Heather Smith, Lisa Washington, Donnika Trice and Latisha Poulard.

MIP for the seventh group of new sorors was the weekend of March 17-19th, 2006. The new sorors were: Jade Jackson, Jacquelyn Thomas-Miller and Brooke Weatherspoon. Soror Reashonda White Breckenridge reactivated with the chapter in January 2007.

On October 19, 2009, Omicron Phi Omega hosted a Cluster Retreat with Central Regional Director Pamela Porch. Soror Robin Scott also joined the chapter during the year from Alpha Mu Omega. Soror Patricia Alsup became an Ivy Beyond the Wall in 2010 and Soror Charlene McCarter became an Ivy Beyond the Wall on July 21, 2012.

Soror Brooke Weatherspoon reactivated with the chapter in 2012 and Soror Debbie Williams reactivated with the chapter in 2013.

SERVICE PROGRAMS:

During the weekend of January 18-19, 1986, Omicron Phi Omega Chapter sponsored its first community collaboration in celebration of Dr. Martin Luther King, Jr.'s first national holiday. This celebration continues to receive overwhelming support from the community. In 1987 an award from Mayor Stephen Daily for the chapter's Dr. Martin Luther King, Jr. Celebration was presented to the Basileus, JoAnn Obie.

MLK CELEBRATION TIME LINE:

1986 — Theresa Anglin

1987 — Brunch with Mayor Daily and Kokomo's Kids — Teen Express Gospel Choir (Grissom)

1988 — High school students (vocal, instrumental, creative speaking, and dancing)

1989 — Musical Program by area churches

1990 — Co-sponsored with the Affirmative Action Committee, IUK, Dr. Herbert Miller, and Emerson School

1992 — Cherresa Lawson (soloist)

1993 — Angela Brown (soprano)

1994 — Songfest

1995 — Indiana University Afro-American Choral Concert

1996 — The Master's Touch Production presented "Sacred Movement"

1997 — Kimberly Vaughn (vocalist-pianist)

1998 — Catherine Carson (vocalist)

1999 — Established Omicron Phi Omega Chapter Emita B. Hill Indiana University-Kokomo Scholarship

2000 — The Rev. Jesse L. Jackson was the guest speaker and the special celebration was underwritten by one of Kokomo's own, Robert Knowling, Jr. President, and CEO of COVAD Industries. The culmination of the event was the presentation by Robert Knowling, Jr. of a check to the chapter for $100,000 for the scholarship fund!

2001 — Karen Freeman-Wilson (Attorney General, State of Indiana)

2002 — Charles Moore

2003 — Chris Washington

2004 — Pastors Michael Carson, Lonnie Anderson, and Robert A. Lee

2005 — Pastor Clarence Moore

2006 — Dr. Eugene G. White (Superintendent Indianapolis Schools)

2007 — Dr. Rev. Robin Scott (Wayman A.M.E. Chapel)

2008 — Dr. Terri Jett (Butler University)

2009 — Dr. Kenneth Williams (Williams Medical Clinic and Alliance Healthcare Systems)

2010 — Patricia Payne (Indianapolis Public Schools Crispus Attucks Center)

2011 — McKenzie Scott Lewis (Founder, President and Chief Executive Office of the MSL Group, LLC)

2012 — Robert Knowling, Jr. (Author and Chairman of Eagles Landing Partners)

2013- Dr. Harold Smith, DDS

OTHER PROGRAMS OF THE CHAPTER

- Scholarship Program
- Dinner/Dance Scholarship Cruises
- Annual Scholarship Golf Tournament- est.1991
- Relay for Life
- NAACP — support
- EYL — est. 2012
- Kokomo Rescue Mission
- Carver Community Center
- HESP
- Tutoring/ Mentoring Programs
- Nursing Home Activities

- Health Program — workshops and health fairs
- Debutante Ball — support
- College Tours
- Heifer Campaign
- African American Reading Chain

Omicron Phi Omega has been a 100 percent supporter of the Educational Advancement Foundation since its beginning and annually gives an Alpha Kappa Alpha, Martin Luther King, Jr. and Indiana University-Kokomo, scholarship. Through the years, the community has supported our efforts and without their support, we would not have been able to support the children of the area with scholarships.

Omicron Phi Omega Chapter Basilei

Jo Ann Obie — 1985 – 1986
Sharon Grier — 1987 – 1988
Darlene Poulard — 1989 – 1990
Delores Davis — 1991 – 1992*
Gerry Stroman — 1993 – 1994
Gwendolyn Williams — 1995 – 1997
Sharon Grier — 1998 – 2001
Alessia Harrell — 2002 – 2003
Sharon Grier — 2004 – 2005
Virginia Anglin — 2006 – 2007
Leesa Gold — 2008
Juanita Martin-Davis — 2009-2011
Jackie Thomas — Miller – 2012
Virginia Anglin — 2013 –

Ivy Beyond the Wall

Pi Gamma Omega Chapter

ROCKFORD, ILLINOIS
JANUARY 25, 1986

Charter members are shown with Central Regional Director Mabel E. Cason.

CHARTER MEMBERS

KIMBERLY CARMEN
CAUJUANA FAYE DUCKSWORTH
GAYLE DURHAM
GAIL HARPER
PAMELA HENNING
MARGO JOHNSON
ADORN LATRICE LEWIS
PEACHERA RHODEN MCCLENDON
CARLA ORTIQUE
LYNDA SIMMONS
VICKIE SCACLING
MARY BROUGHS STALLWORTH
KAREN GLADNEY STEWART
PAMELA G. THOMAS
ADRIAN J. WRIGHT

Fifteen women came together to form the interest group that was to be Pi Gamma Omega Chapter, Rockford Illinois. Following several months of hard work and involvement in community projects this group of women realized their dream and on January 25, 1986, the chapter was chartered at Fisher Chapel on the campus of Rockford College.

Eight months had passed since the chartering of Pi Gamma Omega Chapter by Central Regional Director, Mable E. Cason. All seemed well but was it really? Word had begun to spread in the Rockford community that a chapter had been chartered in the area. Many Alpha Kappa Alpha women residing in Rockford became concerned because they knew nothing of the events that had led to the chapter's chartering nor had they been contacted regarding affiliation.

In July 1987, the newly elected Central Regional Director, Soror Loann J. Honesty King was contacted to investigate the concerns of these sorors. The investigation revealed that the majority of the charter members did not reside in Rockford, Illinois, but in Chicago. In addition, the majority of the chapter's meetings and functions were being held in Chicago (approximately 95 miles from Rockford).

The then Supreme Basileus, Soror Janet Jones Ballard and Regional Director Soror King met with the chapter members to discuss the issues. Following a review of the issues and facts, the chapter was informed by the Supreme Basileus that the charter clearly stated that the chapter was established in Rockford, Illinois, and therefore the chapter would have to function in the Rockford area. The result was a reorganization of the chapter and the affiliation of several sorors residing in Rockford.

Even with somewhat of a stormy beginning, the chapter persevered and is involved in several major chapter events and projects. The chapter awards annual scholarships to outstanding female seniors who will attend a historically Black college or university. Monies for these scholarships are raised through annual fundraising trips. Chapter members participate in an annual Black Dollar Day and attend Black churches to establish an AKA presence in the Black community.

Pi Gamma Omega Chapter continues to make strides forward. The chapter's membership continues to have a stable count of between 33 and 40 sorors. Over the years we have seen many sorors relocate to other areas or become inactive because of family needs. Working to reactivate sorors has a high priority as well as sponsoring a membership intake as often as possible.

The chapter's fundraising efforts have stepped up a notch with the advent of the annual Fashionetta® event. The first Fashionetta® in Rockford, Illinois took place in the spring of 1994. Monies raised have allowed the chapter to continue the scholarship program, and fund community initiatives including the Ivy Reading AKAdemy for grade school students.

In 2004 Chrysler Corporation presented a one-thousand dollar grant in support of the Ivy Reading AKAdemy and its goals. An annual bus trip mini-fundraiser has also been successful and augments the Fashionetta® income.

In 2003, Soror Annie Blackwell established a scholarship Endowment Fund, and sponsors an annual $1,000 scholarship for the winner of Miss Fashionetta®. Other sorors who have sponsored scholarships are Jacci Mannery, and Caryl Brown. Pi Gamma Omega no longer restricts scholarship awards to high school graduates attending historical Black colleges and universities.

The chapter has also forged a partnership with the Community Foundation of Northern Illinois. Pi Gamma Omega has set up a scholarship Endowment Fund under the Foundation's umbrella of charitable accounts. This allows the chapter to operate as a 501C(3) tax exempt fundraising entity when using the Foundation account. More importantly, this partnership establishes a lasting Pi Gamma Omega legacy that will yield scholarships into perpetuity.

Pi Gamma Omega hosted one of the Central Region Clusters in 2000. It received many accolades for the organization and implementation. This was especially forthcoming for the luncheon place settings and decorations.

Basileus Estelle Black was the Awards Chair for Central Regional Conferences in 2003 and 2004. Soror Carol Craig chaired the evaluations committee for Central Regional Conferences 2003 and 2004 and Soror Anetral Buckles chaired the Reception Committee for the 2004 Regional Conference.

Soror Coleen Williams has written poems (especially for chapter functions) that are part of our history also. The titles are: "Silhouette (Ancestors)"; "Silhouette (Mirror)"; "Silhouette (Shadow Twin)"; "If Pearls Could Choose"; "Pearls for the World"; "Myself"; and "Rhapsody in Pink."

Soror Marcella Harris (Ivy Beyond the Wall) established a CD for Pi Gamma Omega in 1998. The purpose of the C.D. is to provide operational funds for the chapter should it ever face an operational budget crisis. The chapter consistently looks for new ways to raise funds, achieve national and local goals and be of service to all mankind.

PI GAMMA OMEGA: SAVORING THE MEMORIES
(AN EXPANSION AND UPDATE OF PI GAMMA OMEGA HISTORY) WRITTEN IN 2012 BY SOROR COLEEN MARTIN WILLIAMS
[SELECTED INFORMATION EXTRACTED]

It has been 28 years since ten sorors worked with Loann J. Honesty King (Central Regional Director, 1986 -1990) to clarify that Pi Gamma Omega was a Rockford Chapter and could not have an operational base in Chicago. Because of the dedicated persistence of Soror King and nine Rockford sorors, Pi Gamma Omega has become a respected community resource in the Rockford community. These ten sorors were Coleen Martin Williams (1st Chapter Basileus from Rockford), Jacqueline

Mannery, Mary Hawks, Nora Wilson, Oda Bell Campbell*; *Emma Stubblefield, Constance Lane,* Marcella Harris,* Barbara Pickett,* and Harriet Treadwell.*

When Soror Williams became Basileus, the chapter had thirteen Rockford members. The original ten were joined by Faye Cox, Jeanette Franklin, and Judy Smoots.* Every member had to handle multiple tasks in order to meet local goals and national expectations.

Pi Gamma Omega's first local service initiative was the establishment of a Scholarship program. To raise funds, Pi Gamma Omega sponsored a 'February Sweetheart Dance'. This event was held two years in a row. One of the Sweetheart Dance highlights was a raffle. The most popular item was a 'Money Hat' worn by different sorors during the course of the evening. The hat had 100 one-dollar bills placed around the hat band. Soror Coleen Williams was Basileus, and when her husband, Loranzie, won the Money Hat, he graciously gave it back for another raffle number to be called. Another early scholarship fundraiser was organizing garage sales. Sorors Mary Hawks and Emma Stubblefield* allowed the chapter to use their garages. The best customers were the sorors themselves! Soror Stubblefield,* who was Anti-Basileus during Soror Williams' term, proposed another fundraiser in the early days: Compiling and selling a PGO cookbook. Recipes from sorors and their friends went into the book which sold well. Another early fundraiser was hosting chartered bus trips. Bus trips included shopping excursions and one venture to the dog races. After Sweetheart Dances, garage sales, cook books, and bus trips, the main scholarship fundraiser became Fashionetta®.

Soror Joy Chase presented the idea of Fashionetta® for a Pi Gamma Omega fundraiser. The chapter held its first Fashionetta® in 1994. Girls were selected from grades seven through nine. Soror Joy Chase was the first Fashionetta® Chairman, and Sorors Joyce Price and Caryl Brown* were the first Fashionetta® Co-Chairs. The first Pi Gamma Omega Miss Fashionetta® was Katia Brown, daughter of Soror Vera Brown. In its sixth year, Fashoinetta® became a cotillion for girls who were high school juniors or seniors. Mentoring activities and educational workshops were an integral part of every Fashionetta® Pi Gamma Omega sponsored. Through Fashionetta®, thousands of dollars were raised for the Pi Gamma Omega Scholarship Program and generated monetary awards for each girl. In 2010, the chapter discontinued Fashionetta® because community attendance had declined.

To augment scholarship monies generated by Fashionetta®, a chapter Fundraising Committee was established. Soror Coleen Martin Williams was the first Fundraising Chairman. Her committee chose to plan a chartered bus trip to the Chicago DuSable Museum and the Woodfield Mall. It was an event that sold out the capacity of the two Van Galder chartered buses. Pi Gamma Omega provided snacks for the guests. Soror Annie Blackwell* followed Soror Williams as Fundraising Chairman. Soror Blackwell* was a special soror. Though she was legally blind, she did not let that deter her from living life to the fullest. This included accepting the Fundraising Chairman's responsibilities. She also knew that her Pi Gamma Omega sorors were there for her. Soror Blackwell* chaired two bus trip events that included shopping and casino trips in Illinois and Wisconsin. The bus trips were discontinued when Pi Gamma Omega accepted a proposal from Soror Kimberly Buchanan to sponsor an event called "Hair Expo and White Party." It was a two-day event. The Hair Expo was held on Friday, the White Party was held on Saturday. Separate tickets were sold for each event. Soror Buchanan was the first chairman, Soror Karen Marks the second. One of the "Hair Expo and White Party" events has the distinction of raising the most money (after expenses) of any single Pi Gamma Omega fundraiser held before 2013 ($27,000). This event was produced three times before it was discontinued in 2010 due to the declining interest of event participants and declining ticket sales. The next chapter fundraiser is scheduled to take place in the spring of 2013. It will be an event that honors those who complete the Pi Gamma Omega Emerging Young Leaders (EYL) Program.

PI GAMMA OMEGA SERVICE AND VOLUNTEERISM

Pi Gamma Omega is well known for the service it provides in the Rockford area. The chapter has provided nearly $100,000 in annual scholarships to African American female scholars graduating from Rockford area high schools. Pi Gamma Omega expands its service by collaborating with and supporting schools and other organizations. Pi Gamma Omega gives service in various ways including monetary donations, sponsoring educational programs, donating holiday food baskets, distributing gifts of clothes, personal items, and furnishings. The following examples give testimony.

Coats for Kids — Each fall, Pi Gamma Omega sorors donate coats to the Salvation Army annual Coats for Kids drive. The chapter has participated in their food drives and has made cash donations for meals they serve at no cost to those who come.

Rockford Rescue Mission — Sorors sign up several times a year as servers for meals that are free to men, women and children who come to the Mission meal center. Pi Gamma Omega has also furnished the Barean Room for Women with chairs, tables, and wall decorations.

Workshop in the Bahamas — In 2005, out of admiration for the leadership of Basileus Estelle Black, and in recognition of three excellent examples of written chapter communications, Soror Linda Putney and Soror Jacqueline Torry authored a workshop presentation on effective written communications for chapters. It was sent as a proposal to planners of the 2005 Alpha Kappa Alpha Leadership Conference in the Bahamas. The proposal was chosen for presentation. Because all workshop presenters were volunteers, Sorors Putney and Torry flew to the Bahamas at their own expense. The centerpiece of the Effective Written Communications Workshop incorporated the written communications of three PGO sorors: (1) Pi Gamma Omega Finances written by Soror Rebecca Cook Kendall, Tamiouchos; (2) Pi Gamma Omega Newsletters designed, edited, and printed by *Ivy Leaf* Reporter, Soror Linda Putney; and (3) Fashionetta® Plans and Time Lines prepared by Fashionetta Chairman, Soror Coleen Martin Williams. Sorors Putney and Torry reported that the workshop was well received and appreciated by workshop participants.

soles4souls, inc. — This organization is based in Old Hickory, TN and has collection sites throughout the United States. In 2009, anti-basileus Karen Marks proposed a collaborative effort with soles4souls that the chapter approved. Sorors donated gently worn shoes and placed collection boxes in churches. 500 pairs of shoes were sorted, boxed, and shipped. Pilgrim Baptist Church and Providence Baptist Church gave monetary donations to cover shipping costs. Most of the shoes went to Honduras. A small number was given to Rockford's Patriots' Gateway for local distribution.

Donations for Lewis Lemon School — In 2010, in celebration of Pi Gamma Omega's twenty-fifth year, winter clothing items were donated by chapter members and taken to Lewis Lemon School. This was followed by a chapter commitment to collect items at each chapter meeting. Donated items were broadened to include toiletries, baby items and personal supplies. This program initiative places emphasis on helping homeless children and families.

Captain Murphy's Box — In 2011, Soror Karen Marks brought the Captain Murphy's Box initiative to Pi Gamma Omega's attention. Kennedy Middle School was collecting items to be sent to Captain Murphy who was on duty in Afghanistan. Pi Gamma Omega sorors donated non-perishable food and personal items. The chapter invited the captain's family to Montague Public Library where the items were presented to Captain Murphy's wife, young daughter, and the school principal. The chapter learned that Captain Murphy received a number of boxes and enough items he generously shared with his company comrades.

Emergency Preparedness for Survival — On Saturday, September 28, 2012 Sorors Jacqueline Mannery, Basileus Rebecca Cook, Helen Gibbons, Joyce Higgins, and Coleen Martin Williams represented Pi Gamma Omega Chapter at the Public Library event called Emergency Preparedness for Disaster. Soror Faye Muhammad, the library Assistant Director, coordinated the services of the sorors who passed out emergency survival kits. Soror Terry Wilkerson gave her service, though inactive at the time of this event. Utitilizing the services of inactive sorors is one of the ways Pi Gamma Omega encourages reactivation.

Emerging Young Leaders (EYL) — After months of planning, in the fall of 2012, Pi Gamma Omega launched their pilot program for Emerging Young Leaders at Kennedy Middle School. This program is an International Program initiative of Alpha Kappa Alpha Sorority, Incorporated. The girls who have been selected to participate will be guided through genealogical self-awareness by Soror Joyce Higgins who has written a book on the subject. Other sessions will focus on exploration of self, civic engagement, getting to know community leaders, and writing narratives from interviews participants conduct with local leaders. The program culminates with a fundraiser that will give recognition to the EYL participants. The program is a collaboration with the school district and the Kennedy School principal and staff. Soror Lamata Mitchell, chairman, and Soror Ayesha Horton, co-chairman worked closely with Basileus Rebecca Cook Kendall, Anti-Basileus Fayrene Muhammad, and Soror Joyce Higgins, to launch this pilot initiative.

Scholarship Workshop — In 2010, Pi Gamma Omega initiated an annual scholarship workshop that is held annually at the Montague Branch of the Rockford Public Library. Library computers are used by participants during the workshop. The purpose of the workshop is (1) to make the participants aware of scholarship opportunities and (2) to familiarize participants with the application process. Parents and guardians are encouraged to accompany their children to these informative sessions. Chapter Basileus Linda Putney and sorors Tiana Cooper and Anqunette Parham designed, planned, and launched this annual workshop that utilized the expertise of the Community Foundation of Northern Illinois (CFNIL).

Ethnic Heritage Museum — Sorors Fayrene Muhammad (Board Member) and Joyce Higgins worked on two new fundraisers for the Ethnic Heritage Museum African American wing. One fundraiser was a dinner held at Rockford College and billed as The Divine Nine. At the request of Soror Muhammad, Soror Coleen Martin Williams participated in the program by presenting an original poem called The Divine Nine Chronicles. The other museum fundraiser was the 2012 Jazz and Blues Festival held at the Sullivan Center. Pi Gamma Omega provided refreshments for the performers. Sorors Anqunette Parham, Karen Marks, Monique McClurge, Kelli Jackson, and Terry Wilkerson (a volunteer inactive soror), and Basileus Rebecca Cook Kendall, were food hostesses and ushers. Soror Coleen Martin Williams was among the featured performers. She gave a spoken work presentation of her poems that incorporated musical interpretations of those poems. All performers were volunteers for this fundraiser.

Taus Total Woman Expo and Conference — In 2012, Pi Gamma Omega was a $1,000 sponsor for this Taus event. With that sponsorship came 10 conference/dinner tickets. Ten sorors volunteered to buy the $75 tickets, which meant the actual cost of the PGO sponsorship, from its treasury, was $250. BMO Bank of Rockford sponsored two tables for the 14 participants in the chapter's EYL program. The conference dinner featured speaker, Soror Donna Brazile. Soror Brazile is a frequent political analyst/commentator on major T.V. and cable stations. Many sorors were in attendance, including former Central Regional Director, Pamela Porch who gave the dinner invocation. After Soror Brazile spoke, Chapter Basileus, Rebecca Cook Kendall, presented Soror Brazile with the chapter's gift of a Kosta Boda® figurine. After the Friday dinner, there were Saturday workshops and a vendors room. Soror Porch was a workshop presenter. Sorors Estelle Black, Joyce Higgins, and Coleen Martin Williams were at vendor booths. Soror Higgins was promoting her magazine, *Chromelight II,* and Soror Williams was in the author's section where she sold copies of her book, *Stems With Flowers.*

Support for Other Community Activities — (1) At the annual National Council of Negro Women (NCNW) Black Family Reunion and annual Tommy-Meeks-organized Juneteenth, Pi Gamma Omega arranges to have a booth. This gives the chapter a grand opportunity to interface with the community. Sorors distribute Pi Gamma Omega program information, health pamplets, free books and school supplies. The chapter has also served flavored ice cones and provided a giant 'bounce toy' for children. (2) In 2010 Pi Gamma Omega began an annual partnership involving a Kantorei Concert performance at Pilgrim Baptist Church. Sorors usher and help serve refreshments at the fellowship that follows. This concert benefits the Kantorei Boy Choirs of Rockford, Illinois. (3) At the annual Booker (Community Center) Fest, Pi Gamma Omega volunteers serve in the ticket booth and give assistance as needed.

Many members of Pi Gamma Omega have distinguished themselves through their service on local boards, in their professions, and in community service. The chapter has made its mark on the community of Rockford and educated its populace regarding the programs of Alpha Kappa Alpha Sorority, Inc.

PI GAMMA OMEGA CHAPTER BASILEI

Adrian Wright	1986 – 1987
Coleen Williams	1987 – 1989
Emma Stubblefield	1990 – 1991
Constance V. Lane	1992 – 1993
Marcella E. Harris	1994 – 1995
Vera Brown	1996 – 1997
Joyce Price	1998 – 1999
Barbara Pickett	2000 – 2001
Carol Craig	2002 – 2003
Estelle M. Black	2004 – 2005
Aloura Hudson	2006 – 2007
Linda (Patterson) Putney	2008 – 2009
Linda (Patterson) Putney	2010 – 2011
Rebecca Kendall	2012 – 2013

Omicron Alpha Chapter

College Consortium
Northwest Suburban Illinois
April 20, 1986

Charter Members

FELICIA ARJONN DUNNING	MONIQUE P. MADLOCK
JOSIE FAULKNER	OLIVIA METGOZA
LOVIE ANDRE FOXWORTH	ELESA R. PATTON
JO LISA JOHNSON	KAREN POLK
CICELY MONIQUE KILLINGSWORTH	BRENDA K. STRONG
VICKI L. KINDRED	TERESA MICHELLE SPEARS
TANYA BONITA LANTON	VICKIE VEARNEAL WELLS
YOLANDA MICHELLE LEWIS	TANYA WHITEHEAD

Omicron Alpha Chapter's existence began with the graduate chapter Lambda Alpha Omega recognizing a need to promote unity and friendship among college women enrolled in the colleges of the Western Suburbs.

Due to the graduate chapter's assistance in organizing the interest group, Omicron Alpha Chapter was chartered in Aurora, a western suburb in Illinois, on April 20, 1986. The chapter was a College Consortium of Aurora University in Aurora, Elmhurst College, Elmhurst, George Williams College, Illinois Benedictine (Benedictine University), Lisle, Rosary College (currently Dominican University) and Concordia University both of River Forest, and Wheaton College, Wheaton, all of Illinois. The chartering Central Regional Director was Mabel Evans Cason and Faye B. Bryant was Supreme Basileus. Sorors Joyce Moore and Margaret Crawford Jordan were the chartering Graduate Advisors.

Through the years, University dynamics and needs of students have changed but Omicron Alpha Chapter continues to provide service in the Western Suburbs.

Omicron Alpha Chapter Basileus

Felicia Dunning	1986
Jennifer Powe	2006
Jetta Walker	2007
Crystal Sherrill	2008
Vanessa Underwood	
Bonnie Hampton	2009
Alia Parker	2010
Kaydene DeSilva	2011 – 2012
Jennie Bell	2012 –

PART IV: THE FINAL QUARTER OF THE CENTURY

Pi Lambda Omega Chapter

EASTERN JEFFERSON COUNTY, KENTUCKY
JUNE 28, 1986

First Row (L-R): Dorothy Ray, Margaret Williams; Second Row (L-R): Stephanie Mudd, Marcia Smith, Margery Duvall, Margaret Dunbar, Third Row (L-R): Carla Fulton, Valerie Jackson, Gloria Irvin, Cassandra Hall, Beverly Johnson, Back Row (L-R): Janis Brown, Beverly Gaines, Janice Hodge, Heri Etta Gray, Portia Wade, Mable Cason, Central Regional Director, and Danna Jones

CHARTER MEMBERS

JANIS BROWN	GLORIA IRVIN
MARGARET DUNBAR	VALERIE JACKSON
MARGERY DUVALL	BEVERLY JOHNSON
CARLA FULTON	DANNA JONES
BEVERLY GAINES	STEPHANIE MUDD
HENRI ETTA GRAY	DOROTHY RAY
CASSANDRA HALL	MARCIA SMITH
JANICE HODGE	PORTIA WADE
	MARGARET WILLIAMS

A new beginning was the cry echoed by the Alpha Kappa Alpha women gathered at the home of Soror Stephanie Mudd, on an evening in January 1986. The vision of the sorors gathered was the creation of a chapter in Eastern Jefferson County to extend toward Shelbyville, Kentucky.

The five sorors: Janis Brown, Gloria Irvin, Danna Jones, Stephanie Mudd and Margaret Williams, were full of enthusiasm and excitement about the possibilities of founding a chapter of Alpha Kappa Alpha Sorority, Inc. Each soror possessed her own individual expertise and abilities after having served in the sorority and the community.

After the initial meeting, these sorors began the process invigorated and they moved zealously forward. The Regional Director at the time was Soror Mabel Cason. She was immediately contacted by Soror Jan Brown for advice and guidance on forming a new chapter. Soror Cason shared information, directed them to the national office for the appropriate forms, and soon planning was underway.

Sorors who had similar concerns about a new chapter were contacted and asked to meet at Masterson's Restaurant for brunch on January 25, 1986. At that meeting, designated sorors were slated to explain various qualifications and individual responsibilities necessary for the formation of a chapter. The response was overwhelmingly positive and sorors attending began to share their own ideas, hopes and dreams for a chapter in Eastern Jefferson County. Through this meeting and other contacts, twelve other sorors decided to join the group. Plans for the future continued.

In the meetings to follow, sorors labored to fulfill all the requirements to make their dreams become a reality. It was thought that the group needed a sorority-related name, as they had been approved as an interest group bearing all rights and privileges of such a group. Thus they became the "Alpha Jewels."

Meetings were held at the Louisville Free Public Library and at sorors' homes in planning and preparation for the new chapter. All sorors were willing to assume leadership roles. Soror Dana Jones, a soror new to Louisville for one year, was elected as president symbolizing a fresh start or a new beginning for the local sorors.

The Alpha Jewels worked diligently on service projects, such as (1) volunteering at the Kentucky School for the Blind, (2) donating to the Home for the Innocents, (3) giving birthday parties for the residents of Mount Lebanon Nursing Home, and (4) presenting a series of seminars on major concerns of our community at the First Baptist Church of Jeffersontown. Fundraisers included raffle tickets for a University of Louisville basketball print, and a Derby Gala held at On Broadway Restaurant and Lounge.

A growth plan for the group was one requirement for chartering. This was addressed along with concerns about the proximity to another Alpha Kappa Alpha chapter through a plan written by the President, Soror Dana Jones. The plan was submitted and accepted by the Directorate of Alpha Kappa Alpha Sorority, Inc.

Correspondence with the national office and frequent communication with the Regional Director assured the Alpha Jewels that they were on target in preparation to be chartered. Finally, qualifications were met and the charter date was set.

Invitations to sorors of the surrounding chapters, families and friends of sorors were sent asking them to be our guests at the special occasion of the chartering and dinner/dance. The sight for the evening's festivities was the newly completed Hilton East Hotel in Jeffersontown, Kentucky. The response was warm and supportive. Soror Janis Brown was program chairperson.

The Alpha Jewels were chartered on June 28, 1986, at a beautiful, inspiring ceremony conducted by the Regional Director, Mabel Cason. At that moment, the vision of the five sorors who dared to dream and that of the other charter members wanting an opportunity to serve became a reality. Pi Lambda Omega Chapter of Alpha Kappa Alpha Sorority, Inc. was formed.

Immediately after the chartering, sorors prepared to meet and greet their guests. The program participants applauded their efforts and wished them well. The evening's activities crystallized the vision of the seventeen charter members of Pi Lambda Omega Chapter.

Pi Lambda Omega Chapter has continued the journey to make Alpha Kappa Alpha Sorority, Inc., supreme in "Service to All Mankind." The chapter continues to be actively involved in the numerous community programs aimed at further enhancing the quality of life for the citizens of the Jeffersontown/Louisville community. Since the chapter was chartered, the major service program has been the Leadership Program.

THE LEADERSHIP PROGRAM — The Leadership Program began in September 1986. The program was designed to encourage and motivate the total student to achieve, and by that, develop well-rounded individuals. Students were reached through schools and churches. The members of Pi Lambda Omega who were teachers were helpful in informing students at their respective schools about the Leadership Program. Word of mouth became the most effective way of gaining students for the program.

Chapter sorors were given responsibilities for each meeting. A car pool was planned to provide rides for the students. Professionals throughout the community were invited to the meetings, held bimonthly, to inspire and motivate the students by sharing their personal goals and aspirations and elaborate on their career choices. Soror Brown-Thompson wrote a motto and creed for the program. They are recited at the beginning of each meeting, to instill in the students the purpose of the program and to reach beyond the regular classroom activities.

CREED: We, the members of the Leadership Program, are encouraged each day, to seek knowledge and experience, to set higher, lofty goals, and to work to attain those goals, to seek God and to love ourselves, and to always strive to do the very best that we can. MOTTO: I am responsible for my own success.

The chapter sponsored a Black History Quiz Bowl, coordinated by Soror Danna Jones-Wilson, to address self-esteem and Black heritage with the students. Also a calendar contest was recommended as a fundraiser for the students but this proved to be too expensive. Instead, Soror Brown-Thompson presented the idea of holding a Fashionetta®, a trademark of Alpha Kappa Alpha Sorority, Inc. This became a reality the second year of the program.

Another goal of the Leadership Program was to expose the students to the HBCUs. The first college tour occurred in 1987. It was a one-day trip visiting Fisk, Tennessee State, Meharry and Vanderbilt.

The need for the Leadership Program was apparent as the student numbers grew with the growth of the chapter. It is used to encourage self-realization, human relationships, economic efficiency and civic responsibility to the full potential of the individual student. It is an effective means to prepare students to meet the challenge of the future. Any student, grades nine through twelve, showing interest and enthusiasm toward achieving and exhibiting leadership ability may be a member of the Leadership Program.

Under Supreme Basileus Eva Evans' national program, the name was changed to the Ivy AKAademy as the program goals were the same. The Ivy AKAdemy continues to nurture and encourage the academic, social, and spiritual growth with an emphasis on the program thrust of math and science. The Ivy AKAdemy students were pleased to be regional winners of the Math and Science Quiz competition and to have competed in the national competition at the Baltimore, Maryland Boule.

The Ivy AKAdemy includes students from the elementary through high school years. Special reading programs have been developed and implemented by sorors of Pi Lambda Omega for the Ivy AKAdemy for students in the Jefferson County Public and Parochial Schools. The students share experiences with role models from the local community and State. Workshops or seminars on youth concerns are addressed through speakers, tours, parent-student forums and group discussions. During the month of February the chapter has hosted a city wide Black History Quiz Bowl. Schools, churches and other organizations were invited to participate in this educational and fun-filled event. Certificates and trophies were given to the winners and runners up.

Supreme Basileus Linda White administration's signature program was the Ivy Reading AKAdemy. The chapter participates in the Jefferson County Public School Literacy Initiative Program, Everyone Reads, in conjunction with the Ivy Reading AKAdemy. Chapter sorors have completed training and tutor students at various Jefferson County Public Schools and at churches throughout the community.

Pi Lambda Omega Chapter also sponsors a Day of Service, as one of the programs designed to celebrate the works and birthday of Dr. Martin Luther King, Jr. During the day, a program is presented which allows students to be engaged in crafts, discussions, dramatizations, poems, and song presentations.

Black Heritage tours were designed for high school students to tour different Historical Black Colleges and Universities as well as local universities. The African American Heritage tour was established to involve Ivy AKAdemy and other community students. Students visit historical communities, churches, and businesses in the greater Louisville and Jefferson County with African American historical significance.

Pi Lambda Omega was proud to present the Torchbearers and Trail Blazers program, initiated by Soror Danna Jones Wilson, giving recognition to individuals throughout the state of Kentucky for their contribution and dedication in their career fields. These fields included service in education, community involvement, arts and business. Each recipient received a trophy especially designed by the Torch Bearers and Trail Blazers program committee.

In May 1987, Pi Lambda Omega Chapter held the first Derby City Men Who Cook. This program idea was presented to the chapter by Soror Janis Brown-Thompson whose friend had attended a similar function in New York City. The chapter was excited about the idea and decided to make it the chapter's annual fundraiser. Derby City Men Who Cook a gala affair is now in its 25th year and continues to be a successful event that grows each year. The community looks forward to this event each year as it attracts many distinguished and high profile men in the community.

Our Manual of Policies and Procedure was developed in 1999. The purpose of the manual was to document the agreed upon policies and procedures for the chapter to follow in an effort to ensure efficiency and consistency in chapter operation. This manual is now in its 3rd revision.

Under the outstanding leadership of the 25th Central Regional Director, Soror Dorothy W. Buckhanan, the 69th Central Regional Conference, with over 1,200 sorors in attendance was held in the "Derby City" (Louisville). Pi Lambda Omega Chapter had the distinct honor of being the prime host chapter. Although small in number (31) we were blessed. Soror Antoinette S. Davis-Jones our Basileus and also the conference chairperson showed us through prayer and diligent work all things are possible. Soror Janis Brown-Thompson served as conference co-chairperson and public meeting chair. Other chapter members also shared and had leadership roles in all committees including: Grammatues, Wanda Borden; Tamiouchos, Janice Hodge; Registration Sonia Suggs; Workshops, Yolanda Allen; Kits, Valerie Collins-Moore; Courtesy, Henri Etta Gray; Public Meeting Reception, Denise Franklin-Williams; Protocol, Margaret Williams; Logistics and Security, Celestia Brown; Corporate Underwriters, Gladys Barclay; Printing, Danna Jones Wilson; Welcome, Hope Johnson; Exhibits/ Awards, Susan Ray; Social Activities, Gloria Irvin; Grand Gala and Publicity, all members of Pi Lambda Omega Chapter. This will be remembered by all sorors of Pi Lambda Omega Chapter as a labor of love.

In 2003 the Kentucky Historical Society Museum, Frankfort, Kentucky, displayed Soror Mary Clarke's uniform and honored her as a Black female officer. She was commissioned as a Lieutenant which was very rare in the sixties. Soror Clark retired from the Air Force as a Lieutenant Colonel.

During the 2004 Boule, the chapter celebrated its first Golden Soror, Margaret Williams. In recognition of this accomplishment, one of the scholarships given annually has been named in her honor. Soror Eliza Young, Soror Margaret's sister, was also crowned Golden in 2008 at the 100th year celebration in Washington DC.

2006 was a long heartfelt year. In June of 2006 the Articles of Incorporation (nonprofit Corporation in Kentucky) papers were filed for the Derby City Tea Rose Foundation. By November our foundation was incorporated. The organization is for charitable purposes to promote the involvement of our members in civic and charitable endeavors and to provide services and programs to the communityi. The chapter's community service initiatives are largely funded by grants from the Derby City Tea Rose Foundation.

Our first Ivy Beyond the Wall, Soror Wanda Borden passed away in July 2006. With this Pi Lambda Omega performed its first Ivy Beyond the Wall ceremony. Before this we had participated in several ceremonies but had not been the lead chapter. Three years later, Soror Muriel Meriweather became our second Ivy Beyond the Wall.

In December of that year, the sorors of PLOC celebrated the chapter's 20th Anniversary with a

Formal Birthday Bash. The chapter recognized its many accomplish- ments over the years and gave special thanks to its charter members.

The chapter is pleased to have several Life members: Wanda Borden (deceased), Janis Brown-Thompson, Mary Clark, Henri Etta Gray, Janice Hodge, Gloria Irvin, Margaret Williams and Danna Jones Wilson. The chapter's Silver Sorors are: Wanda Borden (deceased), Janis Brown-Thompson, Mary Clark, Henri Etta Gray, Janice Hodge, Gloria Irvin, Sybil Ramsey, and Danna Jones Wilson.

The official chapter website www.pilambdaomega.com was launched in 2006 to provide the public with information about our chapter's history, members, programs and upcoming events. This website has been created in accordance to the Alpha Kappa Alpha Sorority website guidelines. Chapter members have access to electronic chapter reports and documents through the Member Login section of the website. The official chapter Face book account is aka-pilambdaomega. This account is utilized to post announcements of chapter activities to the chapter's Face book fans. Only sorors designated by the Basileus and Technology Committee are able to post information to this account.

Over the years, there've been numerous states that have successfully secured Alpha Kappa Alpha License Plates for motorists to buy at their local DMV. When Soror Richelle A. McCoy and her family moved to Kentucky, she knew that the Sorors of The Bluegrass State would also be able to accomplish this historic task! The quest to have the Kentucky AKA License Plate began in September of 2010 with the members of Pi Lambda Omega Chapter formally being approved by the Kentucky Transportation Cabinet to begin receiving the 900 required applications. Soror Janice Hodge created the beautiful design that was praised by members of the KTC. A picture of the plate and an application can be found of the PLOC website – www.pilambdaomega.com. The Committee continues to work on a monthly basis to reach Sorors in each of the graduate and undergraduate chapters. In-active Sorors can also purchase the plate if they have proof of membership and an active Soror vouches for them on an affidavit form. To fulfill the pledge of "being of service to all mankind," $5.00 from every plate purchased will go to benefit programs at The Kentucky Center for African American Heritage in Louisville.

Twenty-one Pi Lambda Omega Sorors were present in Lexington, KY for the 77th Central Regional Conference in the spring of 2010. Our chapter sorors played an integral role in the success of this conference. Sorors Richelle McCoy and Jan Brown-Thompson planned a beautiful Tribute to Leaders Breakfast. Soror Giselé Casanova, CRD, recognized and honored the Chapter Basilei of Central Region. Sorors Toni Davis-Jones and Celestia Brown organized the Rededication Breakfast on Sunday morning.

Under the guidance of Basileus Kellye Singletary and the Executive Committee PLOC Went Green in February of 2011! What did this mean? It meant that paper reports will no longer be distributed at chapter meetings. All reports will be projected on the screen in the meeting room. Officer and Committee reports will be posted on the Member Login section of the website prior to each chapter meetings. Each Soror is able to print copies of reports from our Members Only section of the website prior to the monthly meeting.

The PLO 2011-2015 Strategic Plan was developed with great anticipation, excitement and expectation. It was initiated in 2010 by the Standards Committee, under the direction of Soror Yolanda Allen. The Strategic Planning Team, a subset of the Standards Committee, developed the plan utilizing soror input through surveying, retreat workshops and chapter committee response. This 5 year plan details the chapter's mission, vision and long term goals. It will provide direction for the chapter as we progress forward toward our desired outcome.

Our chapter hosted the 2011 Cluster Founders' Day brunch and Rededication Ceremony on January 11, 2010. Pi Lambda Omega Chapter and over 100 Sorors of Clusters 6 and 7 celebrated our Precious 20 Pearls. We also honored our chapters' Soror of the Year and Soror educators across the state. Our Regional Director, Soror Giselé Casanova, served as guest speaker. Soror Giselé reminded us all of the "secrets to preserving our pearls". She pointed out that we must "adapt and prosper to stay relevant and time-less."

2011 marked 25 years of service to all mankind for our chapter. Throughout this 25th Anniversary Year, the Ivy Vine Connection, the Basileus monthly newsletter, saluted our charter members that continue to dedicate themselves to the growth and evolution of our Chapter.

The 25th Anniversary committee recommended having our 25th Anniversary "Pink Ice: A Night of Decadent Indulgence" event on December 3, 2011. This was an event to celebrate the 25 years of service that Pi Lambda Omega has contributed to Alpha Kappa Alpha Sorority Inc. and it was time for us to celebrate ourselves at the 25th Anniversary Celebration—Pink Ice! The committee recommended that gifts be purchased for active charter members. Presenting these gifts to the charter members was the chapter's way of saying "Thank You" for their hard work over the years. We have dedicated 25 years to outstanding community service programs, supporting higher education through scholarships and displaying sisterly love.

PLOC Sorors hosted the Cluster 6&7 Retreat October 5-6, 2012. Our chapter hosted a fun-filled and educational weekend, led by our Central Regional Director, Soror Giselé M. Casanova. Over 100 sorors from clusters 6&7 attended. The retreat included updates on program initiatives, financial practices and recognitions around the region. We also had workshops on basic parliamentary procedures, conflict resolution and the use of prayer in our everyday chapter activities. What an awesome weekend and Tea Roses go out to Sorors Marie Walker and Latrice Shannon for their leadership as well as all sorors that were involved in the planning and success of the weekend

This year (2012) we are very proud to announce that Soror Celestia Brown, a member of our first pledge line will become a Silver Star. She has been a dedicated and active member of our chapter for 25 years and counting. Congratulations Soror Celestia.

PLOC embraced our Supreme Basileus Carolyn House Stewart's "Global Leadership through Timeless Service," 2010-2014, signature program initiatives. Throughout the past two years we have been very involved in all aspects of each of the six initiatives; however, our two pearls were Emerging Young Leaders and the Health Initiatives.

Our Emerging Young Leaders Program was named Pearls of Perfection AKAdemy. Soror Brandye Moore was the winner of the contest to name the program. The program was designed to cultivate and encourage high scholastic achievement through Leadership Development, Educational Enrichment, Civil Engagement, and Character Building. On January 25, 2011, the Emerging Youth Leaders Signature Program (EYL), Pearls of Perfection Akademy opened for business with a parent/student orientation at Meyzeek Middle School. Enrollment at Meyzeek approaches 1075 students across grades six through eight, and represents the full diversity the city offers. The Math, Science, and Technology magnet program attracts students from the immediate neighborhood and the northern third of Jefferson County. Meyzeek's unique mix of students made it the location we were looking for to launch our Program. We were welcomed with open arms. The program meets every other Tuesday from 6:00 to 7: 30pm. We begin and end each session with our PEARLS pledge: I am a Pearl, I am Elegant, I am Abstract, I am Regal, I am Loved, I am Somebody. Topics of discussion include: Who Do They Say I Am, Setting Goals / Self Esteem, Intro to Branding Yourself, Does the World Influence Our Behavior, Martin Luther King, Jr. Community Project, Lifestyle Choices, Your Body is Your Temple (Zumba & Healthy Eating), Black History Quiz Bowl, Reality Fair – Can You Count, Internet Etiquette, Community Service Projects, and Field Trips to- the Performing Arts, UofL Girls' Basketball Game Outing, and Cinderella (the opera).

Because the Presidential and local elections are this November, in October we focused on: what it means to be a citizen, why it is important to vote, leadership skills and a brief over view of how our government works. To help our EYL participants learn more about the inner workings of our local Government, Soror Valerie Moore, our program chairman, accepted an invitation from Councilman Tandy, a member of our Louisville Metro Council, to attend an open session of the council. Soror Valerie along with Sorors Jan Brown-Thompson, Janice Hodge, Brandye Moore and 15 EYL participants attended their first Metro Council session.

Soror Valerie gave a well prepared explanation of our program before the council. The girls were very impressed seeing how new laws were introduced and passed. Votes are placed electronically, so we could actually see how each councilman voted. After the session we met with Councilman Tandy for a photo session.

During our first year at Mezeek our program was recognized by the Jefferson County Public School System as an outstanding program for young girls. It has been our pleasure to work with each young lady as they have progressed towards becoming our next generation of leaders. The Sorors of Pi Lambda Omega hosted a summer lock-in for the young ladies of the Emerging Young Leaders—Pearls of Perfection program. The girls were treated to a workshop on healthy hair and skin by the daughter of Soror Jackie Baker and gave each other manicures. They also ate pizza, watched a movie and had girl talk into the early hours of the morning. The young ladies have also had the opportunity to attend local government council meetings and be recognized on the council floor for their accomplishments.

Our Through the Health initiative The Women's Health Symposium was created.

PLOC hosted its first Women's Health Symposium, Reclaiming Our Health: Putting Your Health Mask on First, October 29, 2011. This was a day of education, enrichment and empowerment for all women who attended. Applause goes out to Soror Sonia Suggs and her committee for an outstanding Health Symposium. High praises were expressed throughout the event by attendees. The Health Symposium targeted many of our initiatives by providing reading material and handouts and vendors with expertise in wealth building, health related illnesses and prevention, and empowerment tools for women. Excess lunch boxes from the symposium were donated to Salvation Army, Center of Hope rounding off the Global Poverty Initiative. The Health Symposium was truly an event that sorors and participates learned and shared together.

The 2012 Women's Health Symposium "I'm Worth It"; was held on October 27 at the Kentucky Center for African American Heritage. The symposium format included a continental breakfast, The Doctor's in the House panel discussion with local African American female doctors, and various workshops on eating healthy on a budget, wealth building, weight loss, putting the best you forward, healthy relationships, healthy hair and AARP classes – Retirement Planning (Partnership with The Links). There were also health screenings/mobiles – Cervical cancer, Skin cancer, Mammography sign ups, Hypertension, Glucose, HIV, Diabetes, Chiropractor, Dental, Bone Density, and Body Mass Index.

We have contributed much to the community both individually and as a chapter including: awarding numerous academic scholarships to students throughout the community; a NAACP Life Membership; contributor to the United Negro College Fund (annually), Urban League (annually), American Cancer Society, NCNW Girl's Day Out Program, Kentucky African Americans Against Cancer, African American Women's Literacy Series and the Ambassador to Ambassador Program empowering youth in the community. The chapter also participates in the activities of the Urban League, AKA Day at the State Capital, Cloth-A-Child program at Christmas, NCNW Girl's Day Out Program, African American Women's Literacy Series, the National Council of Negro Women (membership), Habitat for Humanity, Salvation Army Center of Hope, and Family Scholar House. Programs that the chapter has sponsored include joining with the Kentucky African Americans Against Cancer to present a Breast Cancer Awareness Seminar, an annual Student/Parent Forum and aWellness Fair focusing on Heart Disease. The Chapter has also supported the Fern Creek Traditional High School Science Club; a Christmas Party and life skills workshops for the Save America's Youth Program; sending a student to attend a Red Cross Leadership Camp; and tours for youth to the Kentucky Center for the Arts and the Speed Museum.

In addition the chapter awards a scholarship to the YMCA Black Achiever's Scholarship Program; encourages sorors and the greater community to support Black businesses during Black Dollar Day; serves as mentors for the Minority Teacher Recruitment the chapter continues to be a pioneer in educating, providing resources, establishing partnerships with organizations that impact the well-being of minorities in the community. As a chapter we have volunteered, assist other agencies with administrative duties, raised funds to assist in the cause, and actively participated in numerous walks signifying our commitment to a healthy lifestyle Program, and chaperones youth presentations at the Kentucky Center for the Arts.

Starting out as a vision of a few, PLOC has grown to live up to our unofficial motto of being "small but mighty." We are all proud of our accomplishments as a chapter and may we continue to grow in a positive light and continue to shine throughout our community. As time continues to march on, the sorors of Pi Lambda Omega Chapter will continue to carry out the goals and commitments of Alpha Kappa Alpha Sorority, Inc. with determination, dedication and love.

Pi Lambda Omega Chapter Basilei

Danna Jones-Wilson	1986 – 1988
Janis Brown	1989 – 1990
Regenia Moore-Lee	1991 – 1992
Martha Dorsey	1993 – 1994
Antoinette Davis-Jones	1995 – 1996
Annette L. Toler	1997 – 1998
Janis Brown-Thompson	1999 – 2000
Antoinette Davis-Jones	2001 – 2002
Margaret Williams	2003 – 2004
Denise Franklin-Williams	2005 – 2006
Yolanda Allen	2007 – 2008
Sybil Ramsey	2009 – 2010
Kellye Singletary	2011 – 2012
Richelle McCoy	2013 – 2014

PART IV: THE FINAL QUARTER OF THE CENTURY

Loann Julia Honesty King
21ST CENTRAL REGIONAL DIRECTOR
JULY 1986 — JULY 1990

November 21, 1959, was the beginning of a career of service to Alpha Kappa Alpha Sorority, Inc. This was the date of initiation of Loann Julia Honesty into Beta Chapter in Chicago while attending Chicago Teachers College (Chicago State University).

She earned her Master's Degree from Northeastern Illinois University in Inner City Studies and completed additional post-graduate studies at DePaul and Roosevelt Universities.

Soror King has been an active financial member since the day of her initiation and a member of Theta Omega Chapter for more than fifty years where she currently serves on the Basilei Council, Graduate Advisors Council and the Theta Omega Chapter and AKArama Foundation, Inc. Executive Committees

Her record of service has included almost every aspect of membership participation. She has served as a consultant to the Corporate Office; Basileus of both Beta and Theta Omega Chapters; elected, as an undergraduate, to the National Nominating Committee; elected Supreme Tamiouchos in 1976 and served two terms; an Incorporator and the first Treasurer of the Educational Advancement Foundation; member of the National Program Committee; Chairperson of the National Economic Development Sub-Committee and chaired the sorority's first Economic Development Conference, held in Washington, D.C; and the International Program Committee Chairperson 2006 — 2010.

On her election as the 21st Central Regional Director, she pledged to execute the responsibilities and duties of the office with tenacity, loyalty, dedication and sisterly love. Soror Loann fulfilled her pledge and brought a rejuvenated vision, a deeper understanding of the sorority's organizational structure, and an exciting, innovative, and creative style to the Region. Soror King promoted equity, fairness and sisterly cooperation by using the skills, talents and expertise of the membership.

She introduced the Chapter Roll Call and titled the Regional Director's Report as the "State of the Region Report." Chapters were kept informed via thirty issues of the Central Times and instructed in correct chapter operations and procedures at twenty area retreats. Central Region received special recognition at the 1990 Boule for having contributed the highest amount, of any region, to the Educational Advancement Foundation, and the Loraine Richardson Green Endowment Fund was established.

Central Region also experienced an audio/visual explosion—from the dynamic multimedia awards presentation at her first conference banquet to the inspiring video presentation, "Soror to Soror, a Conversation with Soror Loraine Richardson Green."

In addition, Central Regional Conference attendance soared, setting several records. The Reverend Jesse Lewis Jackson was among the many dignitaries who were special guests at the conferences. The traditional public meeting became a showcase for exhibiting the talents of young people throughout the region and the undergraduate step show was revitalized.

Omicron Xi Chapter in Milwaukee, Wisconsin and Pi Nu Omega Chapter in Gary, Indiana were chartered during her administration. In addition, she laid the ground work for the establishment of an undergraduate chapter at DePauw University.

Following her tenure as Central Regional Director, she was appointed to the newly created International Business Round Table Committee by Supreme Basileus, Eva Evans. She continues to serve the sorority as a guest speaker at sorority functions, workshop presenter and as a resource person at the local, regional and national level.

Soror King has written three editions of "The History of Central Region Pledged to Remember" and was appointed Central Region Historian in 2011by the 28th Central Regional Director, Giselé M. Casanova. She also Co-Chaired Beta Chapter's 100th Anniversary weekend Celebration in October 2013.

Soror Loann is a life member, charter member of the Heritage Club, a member of the Capital Improvement Project (COIP) Loraine Green Club, and a charter life contributor to the Educational Advancement Foundation.

Her volunteer and community service is not limited to the sorority. She is an Alumna member of the Links, Inc. She has served as President of the Parkway Community House Board of Directors, and served on the boards of Jane Adams Hull House and HRDI (Human Resources Development Institute). Currently she serves on the African American Legacy Board of the Chicago Community Trust and the Advisory Board of Urban Prep Academies.   In 2001, she with her husband, Paul J. King, Jr. established the Loann and Paul King Philanthropic Fund with the Chicago Community Trust, becoming the Trust's first family donor advised fund established by African Americans. They have two adult sons, Paul J. King III and Timothy Jay King.

Soror King was the recipient of the Sorority's highest honor presented to a member: The Founders Graduate Service Award, in 2008. In addition to her sorority awards and recognition, Soror King has been the recipient of numerous professional and community service awards including :Special Commendation, U.S. Department of Education; Meritorious Service Award, Chicago State University; Speaking of People, Ebony Magazine 1982; 2002 Outstanding First-Year Student Advocate Award from the National Resource Center for the First-Year Experience and Students in Transition, University of South Carolina, and Houghton Mifflin Company; 2002, inductee to the Englewood High School Alumni Hall of Fame; 2000 and 2003 recipient of the Outstanding Woman Award, American Association of Women in Community Colleges (Harold Washington College Chapter), and Outstanding Service Award City Colleges of Chicago, 2003.

Omicron Xi Chapter

City Chapter
Milwaukee, Wisconsin
December 3, 1988

Charter Members

WENDY BARRIERE
LISA BELL
MICHELE CARTER
DARSELLE GILMORE
URSULA HARDY
STARLET HAYES
NICOLE JAZZETTE JOHNSON

CONNIE RENEE LEA
KATHI LEWIS
VIVIAN MAYS
SHERRI MARISSA METTS
CHERYL COX-NEWSON
SHEILA PAYNE
LOLITA L. THOMAS

Omicron Xi City Chapter was conceived by Epsilon Kappa Omega of Milwaukee, Wisconsin. The rationale: EKΩ was the sponsor of three undergraduate chapters, but there were several other top rating colleges and universities who attracted minority students, here in the city of Milwaukee.

M. Kathleen Coleman, a member of EKΩ, accepted the challenge in 1986 to spearhead a committee and perform all the necessary requirements to establish a city chapter consisting of Alverno College, Cardinal Stritch University, Concordia University, and Mount Mary College.

With Soror Ethel Walker as the Basileus, and eight other members of EKΩ, the committee attracted 14 energetic, vivacious, and talented ladies. They served diligently, rendering "Service to All Mankind" for over a year, awaiting and preparing for chapter formation. At such time the group was known as the AKA-C4 or 4-Cs, which represented Cooperation, Commitment, Competency, and Community Pride.

These fourteen young ladies became the charter members of Omicron Xi Chapter on the 3rd of December 1988. The chartering ceremony was conducted by Central Regional Director, Soror Loann J. Honesty King at the D & R Building on North Avenue. The first Basileus was Soror Lisa Bell; the Graduate Advisor was Soror M. Kathleen Coleman and the Assistant Graduate Advisor was Soror Rosalind Bordain.

Cooperation, Commitment, Competency, and Community Pride has guided the programs of Omicron Xi since its chartering. Annual programs include the:

BREAST CANCER BAKE SALE — For the month of October the chapter conducts a bake sale at one of the four colleges and distributes breast cancer awareness information. Proceeds from the event are donated to the Susan G. Komen foundation.

SOUL FOOD DINNER — In an effort to celebrate Black History month, the chapter hosts a soul food dinner event at Alverno College. Dinners are sold for $5.00 and the proceeds are either donated to a charity or used for other fundraising events.

CHRISTMAS APPRECIATION DINNER — During the Christmas holidays the chapter sponsors an appreciation dinner for all the people who have helped the chapter through the year.

PROM — Chapter members volunteer to help students at CYD alternative school prepare for their prom by donating gently used prom dresses, helping with hair, nails and makeup and attending the prom as chaperones.

Other Chapter Activities:

- National Black HIV/AIDS Day, spring 2003: During this event Omicron Xi distributed information and encouraged African Americans to go out and get tested.
- Tax Freedom Day, spring 2003: Chapter members went to a local library and provided tax services to over 100 community residents. The chapter received a $2,000 grant for this project.
- AKAerobics, fall 2004: To celebrate Skee Week, the chapter hosted a night of aerobics. A trained instructor came and taught a few basic exercise routines and offered healthy living tips to sorors and other participants.
- Essence of a Successful Woman, fall 2005 — Omicron Xi hosted a roundtable discussion where young women had the opportunity to speak to professional women in various career areas on issued that concerned them. This was a first for the chapter and Omicron Xi looks forward to a successful discussion next year.
- Adopt a Highway, spring 2005: During the cleaning season, chapter members adopted a stretch of the highway and designated days to clean it up.
- Pretty in Pink BBQ, spring 2005: The ladies of Omicron Xi and Iota Delta held this 1st annual event which was a collaborative effort that provided food, fun and games for the community.
- Anti-Hazing Forum, 2009: This activity addressed the anti-hazing policy and procedures and strategies of Alpha Kappa Alpha Sorority, Incorporated. To implement our zero-tolerance policy and to establish a better understanding of hazing as well as the seriousness and consequences of participation.
- Dr. Martin Luther King Day of Service, 2009 — (Repairers of the Breach): A day of serving food to the homeless in collaboration with Epsilon Kappa Omega. Donations of toiletries and clothing items were distributed.
- 2010 — Platform 1 — The Non-Traditional Entrepreneur (Entrepreneur Round Table): This activity incorporates platforms 1 & 3. Three business owners spoke of how they got started, the pitfalls and successes of their operation. One included a young man under the age of 30 who owns more than three companies/partnerships.
- 2010 — Platform 2 — The Economic Keys to Success (Financially Green): A dedicated event to the financial success of college students. Loan Officers from local banks spoke to students about various financial options.
- 2010 — Platform 3 — The Economic Growth of the Black Family (Purposefully PINK and Generously GREEN Pillow Talk): Promoting unity and friendship amongst college women. Discuss issues currently plaguing the black family and community. Interact with attendees by painting nails to show our appreciation.
- 2010 — Platform 4 — The Undergraduate Signature Program: Economic Educational Advancement through Technology (Technology 101/FemininiTea and Informational): To help others grasp the importance, dangers and meaning of various technologies. To know how they can be helpful and harmful to every age group.
- 2010 — Platform 5 — Health Resource Management and Economics (AKAerobics– Let's Get PhysAKAl w/Zumba): The purpose of this event is to reach that stratosphere of satisfaction where one is physically and mentally fit and poised to embrace all of life's rewards and challenges. This will require a balance of emotional intelligence, optimal psychology and spirituality. It can be accomplished in one full hour of ZUMBA.

Omicron Xi Chapter has been the recipient of many regional awards for community service and scholarship. In 2002, Soror Kimberly Trottmen received the Loraine R. Green award for the undergraduate in the region with the highest cumulative average and was the Foreign Travel Grant winner.

In 2003 and 2004, the chapter was the winner of the overall chapter achievement award and the Chapter Achievement Award in the target areas of Art, Black Family, Economics, and Health and was the runner-up in 2005. Omicron Xi also was the winner of the connection award for 2003, 2004, and 2005.

Soror Erica S. Horton was the runner-up for the Outstanding Basileus award in 2003 and 2004; Soror of the Year award in 2003, and the Service Leadership Award in 2002 and 2003.

With Cooperation, Commitment, Competency, and Community Pride, the chapter and its members continued to render service to Alpha Kappa Alpha and the community. The chapter also initiated seven new members during the 2006 – 2007 school year; four new members in 2007 – 2008; one new member in 2008 – 2009; and five new members in May 2009.

Regrettably, in the spring 2011 members of the chapter were suspended for hazing. These members remain suspended until the last member graduates.

Chapter Members Who Have Held International/National Office or Been Elected to the International/National Nominating Committee

Erica S. Horton	Undergraduate Member-at-Large	2004 — 2006

Omicron Xi Chapter Basilei

Lisa Bell	1988 – 1989
Erin Koehler	1999
Jennifer Coleman	2000
Tracee Cooper	2001
Michelle Hill	2002
Erica Horton	2003 – 2004
Janell Robinson	2005 – 2006
Tiffany Foster	2006 – 2007
	2007 – 2008
Marquita Taylor	2008 – 2009
Jasmine Aleem	2009 – 2011

Sigma Phi Omega Chapter

Gary, Indiana
June 21, 1990

Charter Members

DIONNE BALLARD
JACQUELINE EVANS BLUE
VALENCIA CARSON
MARIAN WILSON COMER
SHARMA CROOM
CHERYL CYLAR
DENISE COMER DILLARD
JANET DOUGLAS
LINDA DRAKE
PAMELA EDGINGTON
ANN ELDRIDGE
MONETTIA FISHER
CECILIA JOHNSON
GWENDOLYN BYRD LEE
JOAN WOOD MOORE
MALLINE MORRIS
DEBRA SMITH MOSLEY
CYNTHIA PARKER
FAY PRICE
DORETHA ROUSE
TONIA SADLER
LEZLIE J. WILSON THOMPSON
LARCENIA TURNER
GLENDA MILES WILLIAMS
CONSTANCE WINFREY

The motivation to charter a new chapter of our great sisterhood can come in a number of ways. Sigma Phi Omega Chapter of Alpha Kappa Alpha Sorority traces its genesis to the actions of Soror Marian Wilson Comer who was inspired by a series of conversations between several Alpha Kappa Alpha women. These sorors joined together to form a third chapter of Alpha Kappa Alpha in the Northwest Indiana area. Other friends and interested inactive sorors were invited and plans to start an interest group were formulated.

The Central Regional Director, Soror Loann J. Honesty King, was invited to explain the necessary steps to achieve chapter status. Membership expanded to twenty-five sorors and the Dimensions Interest Group became an active service organization.

Dimensions Interest Group selected dynamic leadership in the person of Soror Lezlie Thompson. To promote sisterly relations among members of Dimensions, activities were held to mold the group into a cohesive unit. The group assembled to participate in a Founders' Day Ceremony and immediately thereafter started conducting activities to enhance the lives of local groups and individuals. Dimensions actively participated in a number community service projects. These projects not only served to form a cohesive working unit, but also introduced members to the many diverse needs of the community. The group participated in the following:

HOME FOR BATTERED PERSONS: Located in Gary, Indiana, the home provides temporary residence for abused persons. Dimensions made corsages for the residents of the home for Mother's Day.

BROTHER'S KEEPER: This is a shelter for homeless men. Dimensions collected newspapers in support of the shelter's drive to raise funds. Sorors have continuously saved newspapers to periodically deliver them to help support the shelter.

EAST CHICAGO PUBLIC LIBRARY: During Black History Month, Sorors sponsored a reading program for children featuring black authors. Sorors took turns reading favorite works of Black novelists to many young listeners.

NORTHWEST INDIANA FOUNDATION FOR SICKLE CELL ANEMIA: This disease affects many African Americans. Dimensions supported their annual fundraising activities in the form of a dribble thon. The group continues to donate funds to the organization.

NATURE WALKS: In an effort to provide our Black youth with as many positive experiences as possible, Sorors have provided guided tours through the Indiana Dunes National Lakeshore for teenagers involved in the Summer Work Program.

THANKSGIVING BASKETS: Sorors gathered to prepare and deliver Thanksgiving food baskets to needy families selected by the Welfare Department.

DISADVANTAGED SINGLE MOTHERS: Dimensions sponsored an "outing" for the children of disadvantaged single mothers who were busy attempting to better their lives through training programs.

EASTER BASKETS: Dimensions made and presented Easter baskets to patients in nursing homes.

The industrious women of Dimensions proved to be cohesive, concerned and resourceful and they were ready to become chartered as the newest chapter of Alpha Kappa Alpha Sorority. The commitment of Dimensions was recognized by the Corporate Office of Alpha Kappa Alpha and a date was set for chartering. The beautiful Chartering Ceremony conducted by the Central Regional Director, Soror Loann J. Honesty King, converted Dimensions Interest Group into the Sigma Phi Omega Chapter of Alpha Kappa Alpha Sorority, Inc. The ceremony took place on June 21, 1990, and was witnessed by many well-wishing sorors from various chapters in Central Region.

Sigma Phi Omega was chartered as the eightieth chapter in the Central Region. Twenty-five Alpha Kappa women were charter members. The women of Sigma Phi Omega are of one mind in their dedication to be of service to all mankind. In other ways they are diverse: Thirteen of these women had not been active since graduating from college. With the exception of one, none of the women had been affiliated with a chapter the previous year. Four women had been financial with the Boule at the time Dimensions was started. The youngest Soror was twenty-two years old, the oldest was fifty-one, and the average age was thirty-three years. In terms of careers they are employed in the private and public sectors and are involved in a number of different professions.

The first public activity of Sigma Phi Omega was an Economic Development Forum featuring Judy O'Bannon, wife of the Lieutenant Governor of the State of Indiana. During this forum the Sigma Phi Omega's 1990-1991 Program was presented. The chapter also had a Christmas Party and decorated the Miller Town Hall and evergreens at the corner of Miller and Grand Avenues with pink and green lights for the Holiday Season.

Sigma Phi Omega sorors remain proud of the accomplishments of its first full year of operation and activities that were supported by the reactivation of several energetic sorors: Sorors Renetha Rumph, Sharon Emery, Toyka Cunningham, and Kimberly Turner. Joining the ivy vine, they instantly strengthened the ranks of experienced sorors. They infused ideas, energy and affection into the new organization.

One of the most exciting ventures undertaken during the year was the processing of a group of nine dynamic new sorors. Lovingly, Soror Denise Dillard chaired the committee responsible for counseling and indoctrinating the women who were carefully selected to have the honor of being among the first group to be initiated into Sigma Phi Omega. Each of these women brought her individual vitality and spirit.

Embracing the Alpha Kappa Alpha ideals, they joined the ivy vine and widened our circle. On March 24, 1991, Soror Patricia Bolden, Soror Pamela Creed, Soror Elaine Gordon, Soror Marika Gray, Soror Bridgett Hoye, Soror Sandra Mosley, Soror Vanessa Nichols, Soror Dana Phillips, and Soror Jannie Pratt were welcomed as neophytes. During 1991 Sigma Phi Omega Chapter promoted community relations through the following:

TENNIS CLINIC: A tennis clinic was conducted with the Boys and Girls Club of Northwest Indiana. The program was well received and the students were eager in their participation.

LIBRARY SERVICES: Students from the Boys and Girls Club were given an overview of the services of the public library. These students were given library cards and encouraged to participate in the ongoing activities for teens.

NATURE WALK: A nature walk was provided for some of the summer jobs students by the Douglas Environmental Center and Sigma Phi Omega.

BROTHER'S KEEPER: Sigma Phi Omega supported Brother's Keeper by providing newspaper for their ongoing fundraising activities. In addition, Sigma Phi Omega also provided food during the holiday season for the men.

SICKLE CELL: Sigma Phi Omega supported the Sickle Cell Foundation by donating funds for their fundraising "Dribble-A-Thon" and by purchasing tickets to their annual fundraising dinner.

MEET THE CANDIDATES: Sigma Phi Omega held a successful "Meet the Candidates" program to provide a forum for the public to hear candidates' views.

BUY IN GARY DAY: The "Buy in Gary Day" campaign to promote economic development in the city was appreciated by the local businesses.

CHRISTMAS BASKETS: Sorors provided financial support and donated canned goods to provide baskets for needy families at Christmas.

The first year of activities was financed mainly by volunteer contributions by the sorors. This state of affairs could not continue if the chapter were to make a significant impact upon the community, a fundraiser was planned. To provide "seed" money to prepare for a major fundraiser, raffle tickets were sold. The first major fundraiser was a formal brunch—the first annual "Special Gifts" brunch. A new singing group, The Too Totally Toughs, or T3 performed. We look forward to seeing more of them.

Sigma Phi Omega received recognition at the Central Regional Conference for having the largest number of sorors present and Soror Lezlie Thompson was honored as "Soror of the Year." Several Sigma Phi Omega sorors participated as hostesses in the "World Conference of Mayors" meeting that was held in Gary. The Basileus, Lezlie Thompson, represented the chapter as a guest when Miss Black America, a native of Gary, was greeted by the city.

Sisterly relations were promoted through joining with Gamma Phi Omega to celebrate Founders' Day, working together to accomplish goals, holding a Christmas party for sorors, and participation in a very successful first anniversary party.

The chapter's ranks have grown and the sorors can look back on an initial year that established our presence in the community, produced the following high quality programs, and set a standard for our future development.

SCHOLARSHIP — The Scholarship Committee selects recipients of tuition wavers and text book awards. These awards are presented at the annual "Special Gifts" brunch and dance. In addition, this committee selects a student to go on a bus tour of the Black Colleges by the Young Women's Christian Association. Sigma Phi Omega provides the funds to make this activity possible.

SISTERLY RELATIONS — The committee selects a host of activities to involve the chapter membership. Activities have included a beach party, workshops on sisterly relations, a card party, and

"Hen Sessions." A suggestion of Soror Renetha Rumph was to select secret sorors to remember during the year. This activity has become a tradition for Sigma Phi Omega Chapter.

TEEN ASSISTANCE — A new thrust was instituted in 1991. The chapter conducted a series of workshops designed to encourage students to seek higher education, help them find money to attend college, instruct them on how to study, manage time, and select a school. In addition to the library, workshop sessions took place at the Boys and Girls Club of Northwest Indiana.

THANKSGIVING BASKETS — were prepared by the sorors of Sigma Phi Omega Chapter. The baskets were distributed to families deemed needy by the Public Welfare Department.

SUMMER SIZZLE II — In 1991 the sorors decided to conduct a new fundraising activity. Summer Sizzle II, summer dance with a Caribbean theme, provided an energy outlet for sorors and their guests.

SPECIAL GIFTS II — A spectacular extravaganza. Sorors were attired in pink satin trimmed in pink and green brocade. The band played music that inspired everyone to stay on the floor. The evening was a great success.

The year's activities are traditionally ended with a Soror Christmas party and the decoration of Miller Town Hall, our meeting place.

In 1995 Soror Denise Dillard became our second Basileus. Under her leadership, the chapter focused on developing partnerships, and working with the youth in our community. Our commitment to high quality programs and service continued with:

HEALTH AWARENESS: Information on health issues, prevention methods, and organizations providing assistance were disseminated to the community. Topics included water safety, nutrition, healthy living, organ donation, and AIDS awareness and prevention. Various agencies including, The Aliveness Project of Northwest Indiana, the Gary Health Department, the Methodist Hospitals, MOTTEP, Healthy Start, The American Red Cross and the American Heart Association assisted with presentations, or provided supplies and materials.

GOVERNMENT AFFAIRS: Members of Sigma Phi Omega Chapter actively took on the fight against legislation when proposed changes (local or national) could dramatically impact our communities.

NAACP: We began payment on a Life Membership for our chapter and continued to participate actively with the local branch.

BLACK DOLLAR DAY: An economic empowerment endeavor in which we exercised our "green power" by spending only with black-owned businesses.

STEPS TOWARD SUCCESS: This was a one-day workshop designed to help prepare high school students for college and introduce them to the working world. Students were taught the basics of developing a resume, job interviewing techniques, and dressing for success. Sorors and representatives from Workforce Development served as presenters.

SENIOR APPRECIATION LUNCHEON: We hosted our third annual Senior Appreciation Luncheon. The event was designed for us to honor the senior citizen women of our community. The seniors used the luncheon as an opportunity to meet new friends. The event had grown to be so popular that a larger venue was needed to accommodate more guests.

BOYS AND GIRLS CLUB: Sorors served as tutors, storytellers and activity chaperones for events throughout the year.

SISTERLY RELATIONS: Sigma Phi Omega also maintained her commitment to sisterhood. We hosted our first Joint Founders' Day celebration. We welcomed sorors from Cluster VIII as well as inactive sorors to an elegant event at the Center for Visual and Performing Arts in Munster, IN. Soror Sharon Emery served as chairman for the occasion and presented each attending soror with a lovely original poem about sisterhood. We also hosted our first Area Retreat in October of 1996 at the beautiful Indian Oaks Resort in Chesterton, Indiana.

Soror Patricia Bolden commenced her tenure as Basileus of Sigma Phi Omega in 1999 as we hosted our second Joint Founders' Day celebration with the focus on retention and reactivation. Ever on the move, Sigma Phi Omega sorors served on the Steering Committee for the regional AIDS Walk, volunteering many hours as well as collecting pledges and contributions in the amount of $2,000.00 over the two-year period. Soror Lezlie Thompson trained and completed the Chicago Marathon in the name of Sigma Phi Omega Chapter with pledges going to the Leukemia Foundation. As we approached the new millennium, the chapter continued to expand its horizons and grow in leadership. For the second time, Sigma Phi Omega Chapter hosted the Area Retreat at Indiana University Northwest in October of 1999.

Additionally, the chapter accepted the charge to become the Graduate Advisors for Epsilon Rho Chapter at Purdue University — West Lafayette, Indiana; Soror Barbara Bolling led us in this responsibility.

Locally, Sigma Phi Omega completed payment for Life Membership in the NAACP through our own Soror Barbara Bolling, who was serving as president of the Gary branch. Led by Soror Denise Dillard, we also became involved with the NAACP ACT-SO program, which recognizes black youth in The Arts, Science and Technology. In addition, sorors helped organize and participate in the Annual Pan-Hellenic Picnic with other local Black Greek organizations.

The year 2000 saw Sigma Phi Omega Chapter's continued growth and increased involvement. At the 66th Central Regional Conference in St. Louis, MO, the Time and Place Area Retreat Committee was chaired by Sigma Phi Chapter's Basileus, Soror Patricia Bolden. Through its Connections Committee, sorors solicited support in a letter-writing and email campaign for a Congressional Gold Medal for Rosa Parks.

Sigma Phi Omega celebrated it 10th Anniversary in June of 2000. Sigma Phi Omega's former Basilei and many of the charter members recognized the chapter's accomplishments over the short span of 10 years. Although Sigma Phi Omega remained a small chapter during this period, its goal continued to be reactivation and retention. Ending her tenure as Basileus, Soror Bolden accepted the Norma Solomon White Reactivation Award at the Dallas Boule in the name of Sigma Phi Omega Chapter.

Under the leadership of Basileus Malline Morris Sigma Phi Omega Chapter continued to build on the programs initiated under previous administrations while initiating several new ones. Successful programs under her administration include:

EDUCATION: Ivy Reading AKAdemy — Sigma Phi Omega partnered with the H.O.P.E. program in Michigan City, IN tutoring at-risk students in reading after school. Sorors volunteered one day a week to read to 25 youths grades K-3. Additionally, Sigma Phi Omega partnered with the men of Omega Psi Phi Fraternity at their annual Back-To-School Jamboree. The chapter purchased 500 notebooks and helped stuff goody bags.

Scholarships: Sigma Phi Omega continues to offer academic scholarships to deserving female high school seniors and college young women. Additionally, the chapter participated in the Presidential Freedom Scholarship Program which awards matching funds; thus far, four young ladies have received an additional $500.00 each from that program.

HEALTH: Breast Cancer Awareness — Sorors distributed posters and flyers on Breast Cancer and urged women to have annual mammograms. "Bowl for the Cure"- Since 2003, sorors have raised monies to benefit the Susan G. Komen Breast Cancer Foundation. Additionally, Sorors visited the Marion Home for pregnant teens where sorors discussed the risks involved in unprotected sex, diabetes, SIDS, Heart Disease, and other health issues.

THE BLACK FAMILY: Mothers Day Baskets & Cards — Baskets were created and delivered to the mothers at the Rainbow Shelter (for battered women). Sorors donated health and beauty items for each basket in the theme of "Beautiful Healthy Moms." Additionally, Mothers' Day cards were designed by a soror in the chapter and mailed to area mothers.

Senior Appreciation: In 2004 we were honored to have our first centurion guest. Mrs. Percy Anderson Barber, age 107, who participated in marches with Dr. Martin Luther King, Jr.

Outreach Funds: Sigma Phi Omega continues to support area churches and agencies with monetary donations for their food pantries and emergency/homeless ministries. We also donated Christmas gifts to seniors at the Linden House in Gary, IN.

AKA COAT DAY: Over the years we have collected in excess of 250 coats which, in turn, have been donated to organizations throughout Northwest Indiana. THE ARTS: Our annual fundraiser, 'Melodies from Heaven' is a concert featuring gospel choirs, praise dancers, and soloists who perform songs of praise and inspiration to celebrate the holiday season.

LEADERSHIP DEVELOPMENT: In 2005, Sigma Phi Omega received a $5,000.00 grant to augment the monies generated from our fundraisers. The grant will afford the chapter the opportunity to provide additional workshops, scholarships and programs.

VOTER'S REGISTRATION: While celebrating Dr. Martin Luther King's birthday, sorors partnered with the local branch of the NAACP to register new voters and distribute literature.

Sigma Phi Omega Chapter is continuing to grow and is definitely making a difference in the community. On Friday, June 24, 2005, Sigma Phi Omega Chapter celebrated the chapter's 15th Anniversary during "A Pink Karpet Affair" at the Dynasty Banquests in Hammond, Indiana.

LEADERSHIP — 2006 — Parts of these same funds were used to help send five (5) high school seniors to Washington, D.C. to study the working government of our country. Lezlie, I can't remember the name of this venture, perhaps you can, as your daughter was a part of this group.

VOTERS' REGISTRATION — Under the leadership of Soror Janet Douglas, several teachers from Lew Wallace High School in Gary, IN successfully registered over 65 new voters (all students). Once registration was completed and students received their Voters' Registration Card, they were escorted and transported by bus to the Lake County Government Complex to vote in the 2006 Presidential Primary. The actions of Soror Douglas was applauded by the Gary Community School Board.

Soror Keisha L. White, the chapter's 5th Basileus, had the honor and distinction of serving as the Centennial Basileus of Sigma Phi Omega Chapter. Twenty-four chapter members registered and participated in the Centennial Boule. Soror White moved the chapter toward the direction of Every Soror Participates (ESP), with our Supreme Basileus Barbara A. McKinzie. Our focus was accountability, auditing, and standards. The chapter began to embrace this vision with new policies and procedures.

EDUCATIONAL ADVANCEMENT FOUNDATION (EAF) — Beginning in 2008 — Under the direction of Basileus Keisha White and Soror Sondra Craig, Sigma Phi Omega became 100% compliant with supporting our EAF initiative. Soror Craig, as the chapter's representative to EAF, made sure that we each understood and embraced the purpose of EAF. This year the chapter's By Laws were changed to include that EAF was part of our dues, thus ensuring that the chapter was 100% compliant each year. Additionally, Sorors made contributions to the Endowment Funds of Alpha Kappa Alpha Directorate Members.

REACTIVATION — To celebrate our Centennial 2008 our chapter soared with record number reactivation. The number of Sigma Phi Omega Sorors reached 58 financially active members.

EXTRAORDINARY SERVICE PROGRAM — (ESP) — Our national platform focused on raising awareness within our own chapters. For four years we focused on ESP as acronyms to exemplify AKA service to all mankind.

FREEDOM FRIDAY FUNDRAISER — Every Friday during the month of July 2008 we held Friday mixers to support our scholarship / programs. Meeting at a local restaurant, we were able to help increase the restaurant's business while we raised the community's awareness of our activities thereby increasing our program coffers.

REAL MEN WEAR PINK — Combining the sorority's ESP platforms II & IV, members presented the first annual fashion showcase and dinner entitled "Real Men Wear Pink." The idea was formed with neophyte, Soror Karla Brackett Wiley, to raise money for our Annual Scholarships and programs. Over 450 guests attended this premiere event. The showcase featured an all-male modeling troupe of 23 men; including fraternity members, firemen, policemen, educators, entrepreneurs, fitness trainers, steelworkers and public officials, including the Mayor of Gary. Models wore pink attire. Partnerships were formed with Bacharach and K & G clothing stores, who donated some of the clothing modeled. The event helped to raise awareness of both male and female Breast Cancer. Two local men were honored with plaques for the care they provided their loved ones who suffered from Breast Cancer. Twenty BC survivors in attendance were pinned with ribbons and presented with a cancer survivor medallion provided courtesy of the American Cancer Society. Charitable donations were presented to the Princess Nikky Foundation of Africa and the Gary Community Health Center. The event's proceeds were raised for Sigma Phi Omega's innovative programs and unique second semester scholarships.

NEW YEARS EVE COLLABORATION with Omega Psi Phi Fraternity fundraiser — 2008 — We celebrated New Year's Eve at Marquette Park Pavilion with the Que's bringing in the New Year. All proceeds benefited our chapter programs and scholarships.

POLITICAL AWARENESS — SPO members banded together to register citizens to vote.

NAACP — Sigma Phi Omega chapter members gathered to attend the attend Frontiers Drum Major program at the Genesis Center in Gary, IN. Yearly we purchase table to help honor the works of MLK and honor those who best walk in his footsteps. The not only supports the community event it has also become a sisterly relations activity for chapter members.

BREAST CANCER WALK — Beginning in 2009 and in conjunction with Real Men Wear Pink, we started our increased our efforts for fight against breast cancer awareness to cover our Health initiative platform. We participated in the Breast Cancer Walk to support the American Cancer Society. As chapter we raised over $1500.00 in effort to fight this horrific disease.

CENTRAL REGIONAL CONFERENCE — In 2009 our chapter assisted with hosting, planning, implementing Central Regional conference held in Schaumburg, IL. This conference was under the leadership of Soror Pamela Bates Porch. Our chapter signified the event by chairing the decorations committee.

CHAPTER ANNIVERSARY — June 2010 we celebrated 20 years of AKA service to our local, central region as well as on a national level. This celebration involved other sororities and fraternities within our local area who joined us in the festivities. During this celebration we asked former charter members, basilei, and members to attend this momentous occasion. All in attendance celebrated with lunch that included guest speaker Soror Loann Honesty King, our Chartering Regional Director.

SIGMA PHI OMEGA SCHOLARSHIPS: During our 20th year, we honored members who became Ivies Beyond the Wall by naming scholarships in their memory. The book scholarships are named for Sorors Bridgette Hoye and Edith Blanchard, both of whom were initiated in to Alpha Kappa Alpha during our first and second membership intake processes. The Freshman Scholarship is named for Soror Cecilia Johnson, a Charter Member of Sigma Phi Omega. Both Soror Johnson and Soror Blanchard lost their battle with Breast Cancer. We will remember them always.

IVY'S CLOSET: Each year Sorors both accepted donations and cleared their closets of unused or gently or seldom worn clothing items such a blouses shirts, skirts, and pants. Sorors also collected toiletries, for local homeless shelters.

CENTRAL REGION CONFERENCE — E.S. P. Community Service Event: Sorors joined in the effort by giving back to women and foster children in need of a new start. Members provided new, sealed cosmetics and hosiery that will be distributed to agencies working with abused women. And Sorors provided laundry bags for agencies working with foster children.

PROVIDING FOR HOMELESS — Sigma Phi Omega members continually support projects for the homeless. Initially by collecting newspapers for My Brother's Keeper, which aided them in their fund raising efforts to raise funds, and by supplying needed items to various organizations supporting the homeless. The effort continues as Sigma Phi Omega joined others in Central Region to collect wigs as an on-site community service project "Wig Drop for ACS" This project l supports the Lexington branch of the American Cancer Society's Patient Service Room whose mission is to restore hope to cancer patients battling the effects of chemotherapy.

Soror Janet Brackett Douglas became our 6th Basileus in 2011. Under Soror Douglass' leadership, Sigma Phi Omega continued her service to all mankind.

AKA GOES PINK FEBRUARY 4, 2011: Members joined in this endeavor by wearing red to raise awareness of how heart disease affects women especially African American women.

SISTERLY RELATIONS: During chapter meetings, time is set aside to recognize members for a variety of reasons. Under the leadership of Soror Douglass, Soror Jacki Walker Sims provided a variety of activities so that we each get to learn a bit more about each member. Additionally, at the end of each meeting, we gather to have lunch at a local restaurant. The outings are endearing as we learn more about each other.

POLITICAL FORUM: Sigma Phi Omega along with the Urban League of Northwest Indiana Young Professionals sponsored a Mayoral Forum. The forumn featured 9 candidages for the office of Mayor in the City of Gary, Indiana. With 100 guests in attendance, Basileus Janet Douglas prvided the welcome and Honey-Do Ben Sims, husband of Soror Jacki Walker Sims, served as moderator. Candidates gave a brief introduction shared their politiacal ideopology and vision for the city. Chapter members and along with the Young Professionals selected questions from the audience for the candidates. Karen Freeman-Wilson, a member of Delta Sigma Delta, be came the first female mayor of Gary, Indiana defeating Republican Charles Smith in the November General election.

Sigma Phi Omega Sorors, along with the Sorors of Gamma Psi Omega and Eta Kappa Omega joined together as members of the new Mayor's Inaugural committee participating in a weeklong celebration for Gary's new mayor.

EMERGING YOUNG LEADERS (EYL) began during 2011. Seven young ladies were given tidbits of life lessons throughout the academic year. The topics ranged from looking your best, table manners, etiquette, getting along with each other, fellow students and the adult leaders. The young ladies acted as served as hostesses at our annual fundraiser. The young ladies also provided service food banks, homeless projects and churches.

FRIENDSHIP AWARD Soror Lezlie Thompson, Sigma Phi Omega's first Basileus, was honored by Delta Sigma Theta Gary Alumnae Chapter, at their first annual High Tea. Soror Thompson was the recipient of the Delta's first Friendship Award. Soror Thompson exemplifies the true meaning of friendship regardless of affiliation.

REAL MEN WEAR PINK continues as the chapter's primary fundraiser. In 2011, the chapter honored Soror Benita Nicks as the first female who supported her husband as he battled Breast Cancer during the preceding year. We were able to find a pink Eiffel Tower to help carry out our Parisian theme. 2012 marked our 5th year of Real Men Wear Pink. There were several surprises that occurred at this event. First, we honored two of the show's participants as Real Men. The first was one of our models was a caretaker for his mother, a breast cancer surveyor. Secondly, one of the band members who also cared for his mother who lost a ten year battle with breast cancer. Next, we honored the male models who have participated in the fashion showcase for the event for five years. The final surprise came as we noticed that a number of Real Men in the audience who wore pink — either shirts, ties, or a combination of both, suit jackets and other accessories with the color pink.

FEEDING THE HOMELESS — Under the direction of our Basileus, Soror Jan Douglass, chapter members meet each week to serve meals to the homeless at St. Monica Luke's Catholic Church.

CHAPTER ANNIVERSARY: The celebration in 2012 was twofold. First, Sorors met at the Habitat for Humanity to assist with preparation for the new store. Sorors helped place items, and signs on shelves as well as assisted with unpacking new items. Sorors continued the anniversary celebration at a luncheon reminiscing chapter activities and accomplishments throughout the years. Chapter members look forward to even greater achievements in the years to come.

Sigma Phi Omega Advised Epsilon Rho Chapter From 1999-2001

Sigma Phi Omega Chapter Basilei

Lezlie J. Thompson	1990 – 1994
Denise C. Dillard	1995 – 1998
Patricia A. Bolden	1999 – 2000
Malline Morris	2001 – 2007
Keisha White	2008 – 2010
Janet Douglas	2011 –

PART IV: THE FINAL QUARTER OF THE CENTURY

Yvonne Perkins

22ND CENTRAL REGIONAL DIRECTOR
JULY 1990 – JULY 1994

Soror Yvonne Perkins was initiated into Kappa Chapter, Butler University in 1970 and served as Basileus of the chapter from 1970-1971. She received her MBA from Indiana Wesleyan University.

On her transfer to Alpha Mu Omega Chapter, her service continued as Alpha Mu Omega Chapter Basileus (1973 – 1975), Tamiouchos, Parliamentarian and Chairman of numerous committees. She has served as a member on the Ivy Endowment Board since 2008.

Alpha Mu Omega Chapter has recognized this outstanding soror by selecting her Soror of the Year in 1976 and Soror through the Years in 1983.

Soror Perkins' organizational skills and leadership abilities beyond the chapter level were first exhibited as the General Chairperson for the 1982 Central Regional Conference. From there it was AKA Connection Coordinator for the State of Indiana from 1982-1986, to Supreme Tamiouchos, from 1986-1990, to Central Regional Director, from 1990-1994, to Supreme Tamiouchos, from 1994 to 1998. As Supreme Tamiouchos, Soror Perkins served as chairperson of the International Finance Committee, Treasurer of the Educational Advancement Foundation, and Treasurer of the Housing Foundation. She also revised the Guide to Chapter Financial Operations and co - authored A Handbook for Regional Directors in 1998.

Since serving as Supreme Tamiouchos, Soror Perkins has been National Standards Committee Chairman, 1998 – 2000; National Protocol Team Chairman, 2002 – 2006; Centennial Traveling Exhibit Committee member, 2005 – 2006; Financial Advisor to Supreme Basileus Linda M. White, 2002 – 2006; and International Regional Accounting System Task Force member, 2006.

Beyond giving of her time and energies, Soror Perkins has financially supported the programs of the sorority. She is a member of the CIP, Loraine Green Club, Educational Advancement Foundation Charter Life Contributor, 1988 and has joined the Ivy Tree of Honor. Following are several notable highlights of her administration as Central Regional Director.

- published twenty-four Central Region Newsletters
- published an annual Central Region Directory
- conducted thirty-two area retreats
- established the Regional Basileus of the Year Award for each Undergraduate and Graduate chapter
- established a regional fund to provide matching funds for undergraduate chapters as they submitted the chapter Corporate Office Improvement Project (COIP) Assessment

Soror Yvonne Perkins was at Central Region's helm for both the 1991 Leadership Seminar in Chicago, and the 1994 Boule in Indianapolis. Also, the Educational Advancement Foundation (EAF) Loraine Richardson Green's Endowment Fund was capitalized during Soror Perkin's administration;

Central Region received the Educational Advancement Foundation's Overall Achievement Award in 1994; and Central Region reached the Corporate Office Improvement Project (COIP) regional goal. In recognition of Soror Perkin's service, Central Region established the Educational Advancement Foundation (EAF) Yvonne Perkins' Endowment Fund which was fully endowed in 1994.

During her administration, Soror Perkins effectively presided over the 57th (1991), 58th (1992), 59th (1993) and 60th (1994) Central Regional Conferences. Three chapters were chartered during her term in office Pi Lambda (DePauw University, Greencastle, Indiana), Pi Nu (Northeastern Illinois University, Chicago, Illinois) and Tau Gamma Omega (Oak Park, Illinois). . In addition, approval was given to Former Central Regional Director, Soror King to write the history of Central Region.

Professionally, Soror Perkins has been a professional in the utility industry for more than 35 years. As Vice President, Community Relations at Citizens Gas & Coke Utility, her major areas of responsibility included corporate communications, media relations, community redevelopment, community investment, brand management and diversity strategist.

She is an advocate for issues impacting children and women, and has participated with the governing boards of local, regional and national non-profit organizations for more than 25 years. In addition to being well versed in board governance and strategic planning, Yvonne's expertise as a Certified Public Accountant often brings the much need financial acumen to non-profit boards. Her current involvements include leadership with the National Board of Girl Scouts of the USA, King Park Area Development Corporation, Coburn Place, Planned Parenthood of Greater Indiana, Madame Walker Center, Circle City Chapter of The Links and Indianapolis Public Schools Education Foundation.

Her family includes a daughter, Soror Kimberly Black, grandson, Davyd Hall, and an enduring love, Art Carter, Sr. She is a Steward and Financial Secretary of Allen Chapel African Methodist Episcopal Church.

Pi Lambda Chapter
DePauw University
Greencastle, Indiana
March 23, 1991

Left to right, Back Row: Angela Smith, Tonya Walker, Erika Boykins, Nadine Bonds (Graduate Advisor), Yvonne Perkins (Central Regional Director), Kara Endsley, Jill English, Dana Ransom, Robin Batties, Anita Lawrence Front row: Joy Armstead, Ingrid Wilder, Johari Miller, Alicia Hite, Charnita West, Buffy Bryant.

Charter Members

JOY ARMSTEAD	ANITA LAWRENCE
ROBIN BATTIES	JOHARI MILLER
ERIKA BOYKINS	DANA RANSOM
BUFFY BRYANT	ANGELA SMITH
KARA ENDSLEY	TONYA WALKER
JILL ENGLISH	CHARNITA WEST
ALICIA HITE	INGRID WILDER

In the spring of 1986, three DePauw University women, encouraged by Gina Ross, expressed interest in affiliating with Alpha Kappa Alpha Sorority, Inc. Initial contact was made with Epsilon XI Chapter (Indiana State University, Terre Haute, Indiana), however, since Epsilon XI is chartered as a campus chapter, the young women from DePauw could not be invited into the sisterhood. Determined to become members, Gina spearheaded the quest throughout the summer of 1986.

Gina then contacted Maenell Newsome, Past Central Regional Director and a member of Alpha Mu Omega (Indianapolis, Indiana) for assistance. After discussions with Central Regional Director Mabel Evans Cason (Delta Phi Omega, St. Paul, Minnesota) Soror Newsome was referred to the newly elected Regional Director Loann J. Honesty King (Theta Omega, Chicago, Illinois) and Nadine C. Bonds, Basileus of Alpha Mu Omega.

Throughout the fall of 1986 and the first half of 1987, regular conversations and correspondence flowed between Regional Director King; Alpha Eta Omega (Terra Haute, Indiana) Basileus Ivonne Jones; Alpha Mu Omega Basileus Bonds and Kappa Tau Omega (Bloomington, Indiana) Basileus Margaret McDay to determine which of the three graduate chapters would sponsor the young women.

Because of small memberships in Alpha Eta Omega and Kappa Tau Omega, it was determined that Alpha Mu Omega would guide the young women through the membership process.

In the early fall of 1987, the Alpha Mu Omega Executive Committee received chapter approval to begin the general membership process. Soror Bonds met with DePauw University officials to obtain permission to distribute materials regarding Alpha Kappa Alpha membership to interested students. With university approval, Soror Bonds provided DePauw students Ronda Henry and Natasha Dotson with necessary instructions and forms.

At the January 30, 1988, Directorate meeting, Central Regional director, Soror Loann J. Honesty King presented the names of six young women for approval as general members. They were: Joy Armstead, Robin Batties, Ronda Henry, Gina Ross, Angela Smith and Ingrid Wilder. The four young women were initiated into Alpha Kappa Alpha Sorority, Inc. on May 1, 1988, at St. Peter Claver Center in Indianapolis. The chapter incubation period had officially begun.

Early spring 1989 brought together eight young women for general membership: Erika Boykins, Buffy Bryant, Kara Endsley, Jill English, Anita Lawrence, LaShauna Lawton, Angela Smith (president) and Ingrid Wilder. They were initiated April 15, 1989 in Indianapolis. The Pearls of DePauw were formed and Robin Batties served as president. The spring of 1990 (March 9) yielded three additional general members: Dana Ransome, Tonya Walker and Charnita West. They were initiated March 23, 1990, in Indianapolis, Indiana.

In 1990, DePauw University, a small private Midwestern college located in Greencastle, Indiana, had an enrollment of approximately 2,700 students—and the minority population was just under 100. Even with a small prospective membership pool, the Pearls of DePauw moved forward to the next step in becoming a chapter. In the fall of 1990, Sorors Robin Batties and Ingrid Wilder made a presentation to the DePauw University Board of Fraternal Affairs seeking official recognition as a university organization.

Central Regional Director Soror Yvonne Perkins received the required paperwork from the Pearls of DePauw and recommended at the January 26, 1991

Directorate meeting that approval is given to initiate two additional general members and to charter a chapter on the campus of DePauw University.

Alicia Hite and Johari Miller, initiated March 23, 1991, became the first sorors to be initiated on the DePauw campus. Following the general member initiation, Soror Perkins performed the ceremony to charter Pi Lambda Chapter. Pi Lambda was the first chapter chartered under the regional leadership of Soror Perkins. Soror Nadine Bonds served as the Graduate Advisor.

In April 1991, Pi Lambda Chapter received its first public accolade: The Chaplin's Award was presented by DePauw University in recognition of 100 percent chapter participation in campus sponsored service projects. Pi Lambda went on to win the Chaplain's Award in 1992 and 1993.

Soror Ingrid Wilder was appointed in the Summer of 1991 by Supreme Basileus Mary Shy Scott to serve as Central Region representative on the International Constitution Committee.

October 13, 1991 produced the first initiates of Pi Lambda Chapter. They were Michele Adams, Velyndea Clark, Lisa Henderson, Vonda Mitchell, Keri Paniagua, Lisa Ross, Keysha Webb, twins Stella and Wilma (Priscilla) Williams and Veneese Williams.

At the 1992 Central Regional Conference held in Evansville, Indiana, Central Region was proud to recognize its baby chapter as first place winner in various program award categories, including Outstanding Undergraduate Basileus (Jill English) and Outstanding Graduate Advisor (Nadine Bonds). Pi Lambda was also recognized by the Educational Advancement Foundation as a 4-Star EAF chapter. Also in 1992, Soror Vonda Mitchell was honored as a Leadership Fellow.

The 55th Boule in New Orleans, Louisiana again saw recognition for Pi Lambda Chapter when Soror Johari Miller was presented as a candidate for the office of Second Supreme Anti Basileus.

On October 18, 1992, Pi Lambda Chapter initiated eight sorors. They were Alison Chaney,

Shatrese Flowers, Darrianne Howard, Karen Henry, Ericka Jeter, Glenita Ruffin, Deborah Russell and Anne Thomas.

In 1993, Soror Karen Henry attended the first Job Corps Summit held in March at the Cleveland Job Corps Center. The 59th Central Regional Conference held in April in Peoria, Illinois, again saw Pi Lambda Chapter recognized as a first place winner in numerous program categories including Undergraduate Chapter with the Highest Percentage of Sorors in Attendance (19 of 20 members were present).

The chapter was privileged to entertain Soror Berna Rhodes, Second Supreme Anti-Basileus during Think Pink week program activities held April 12 – 18, 1992.

Throughout the years Pi Lambda continued to build a positive image on the DePauw campus. From the March 23, 1991 chapter chartering through the spring of 2005, Pi Lambda initiated seventy-three sorors who were dedicated to enriching the DePauw Campus, the Central Region, and Alpha Kappa Alpha as a whole.

In 2000, Pi Lambda assisted in developing a chapter of the National Pan Hellenic Council at DePauw in order to provide a recognized governing body for the growing historically Black Greek-letter organizations represented on campus. Pi Lambda was also named DePauw's "Sorority of the Year" for 2000.

Pi Lambda celebrated its 10th anniversary in March of 2001 and hosted Dr. Mae C. Jemison to commemorate the occasion. Pi Lambda consistently served as a model chapter to undergraduates through their accomplishments at regional conferences, boules, and participation in the Leadership Fellows. At the 69th Central Regional Conference (Louisville, Kentucky), Pi Lambda received accolades in almost every award category. The chapter received runner-up recognition for Communication/Journalism (Leslie Williams) and Outstanding Neophyte (Moneaka Bonham). Pi Lambda won awards for Outstanding Basileus (Devonne Inman); Undergraduate Soror of the Year (Deonna Craig); and Chapter Achievement in Education, Health, the Black Family, Economics, and the Arts.

The 2003/2004 school year came as a rebuilding period for Pi Lambda as only two sorors remained on campus following the moratorium. Pi Lambda was one of the first undergraduate chapters in the Central Region to initiate new members in the fall of 2003. Those sorors were Chanelle Henderson, Joy Conway, Erin Scott, Miriam Grays, and Alysia Sargent. In the spring of 2004, Pi Lambda continued rebuilding and initiated Jessica Daniel, Jennifer Hinton, Devonii Reid, and Osemuede Osemwota.

In 2005, the 71st Central Regional Conference was held in Indianapolis, Indiana. Pi Lambda was named one of the host chapters and was responsible for all Undergraduate Activities. The Undergraduate Event Chairmen were Alysia Sargent (General Conference Co-Chairman and Undergraduate Activities Chairman), Miriam Grays (Undergraduate Luncheon Chairman) and Joy Conway (Step Show Chairman).

ANNUAL CHAPTER EVENTS

1. **Think Pink Week** — During the fall semester of each year, the chapter designates a week to focus on the programming targets. Various Think Pink Week events have included investment workshops, literary displays, health awareness tabling, and educational discussion forums.
2. **Skee-Week** — The events held during Skee-Week also focus on national programming. Skee-Week features the "Tea Rose Scholarship Ball" where Pi Lambda's PIMS Scholarship is awarded to one student for their response to a scientifically based essay question. The week also includes the crowning of Mr. MiAKA who is chosen based on his dedication to encouraging African American men to become involved in community service.
3. **AKAessence Awards** — The first AKAessence Award Ceremony was spearheaded by Erin Scott during the fall of 2004. Students are given the opportunity to nominate peers and faculty who have

contributed to DePauw's African American community. During the ceremony, the nomination entries are read and two students and one faculty member are chosen to receive the awards.

The chartering of Pi Lambda Chapter at DePauw University was a historic event. Pi Lambda was the first Greek letter organization organized at DePauw since 1945 and to this date remains the only historically Black Greek-Letter organization to be charted on the campus.

Pi Lambda Chapter Basilei

Robin Batties	1989 – 1990
Jill English	1991
Dana Ranson	1992
Johari Miller	1993
Alison M. Chaney	1994
Aisha Geaither	1995
Nataki Landrum	1996
LaShon Fincher	1996 – 1998
Carvana Hicks	1999
Greta Smith	2000
Ashley Barnett	2001
Devonne Inman	2002
Deonna Craig	2003
Alysia Sargent	2004
Miriam Grays	2005

Tau Gamma Omega Chapter

Oak Park, Illinois
November 2, 1991

Charter Members

EUNEVA ACKER	JODICE R. LEE
VALERIE LEON BROWN	BERTHA J. KYLES
THERESA CALDWELL	CYNTHIA M. LOGUE
RUBY M. CHAPMAN	GLAMORA JORDAN MAEWEATHER
WANDAMARIE B. CRAWFORD	CAROL J. MARLEY
TINKI D. DELANEY	JOYCE MCCLAIN
CAROL K. DORSEY	WILMA Y. MCCLENDON
PATRICIA B. EASLEY	MAYE J. MORRISON
PAMELA F. THOMAS-HALL	BARBARA ROBERTSON
CYNTHIA A. HARDEN	KAREN SCOTT
STELLA W. HARDEN	MARJORIE JUDITH VINCENT
ALBERTA S. HOLLISTER	ROSEMARY YORK
ELOISE KELLY	

The Sorors of Tau Gamma Omega Chapter of Alpha Kappa Alpha Sorority, Inc., are a group of graduate members of the international sorority who have organized to expand the presence of the sorority, to reclaim members who have not been active with the sorority, to pass on the torch of Alpha Kappa Alpha, and to provide service to all mankind in an atmosphere of sisterhood and love.

In the summer of 1990, four sorors met to discuss the possibility of forming a chapter to serve West Cook County, including the west side of Chicago and the near west suburbs. Those sorors were Flora Green, Jodice Lee, Wilma McClendon, and Luellen Moore.

In January 1991, two sorors, Jodice Lee and Wilma McClendon met with three other sorors, Sandra Bempah, Alberta Hollister and Sonya Parker to formulate a plan for a new chapter. By March, the group had grown to sufficient size to request permission from the international organization to become an official chapter of Alpha Kappa Alpha Sorority, Inc.

The interest group was known as the West Cook County Associates of Alpha Kappa Alpha Sorority, Inc. The first officers were Jodice Lee, President; Patricia B. Easley, Vice-President; Alberta Hollister, Treasurer; Valerie Leon Brown, Secretary; and Wilma McClendon, Membership Coordinator. As the group gained momentum, other members took on the responsibilities of committee chairmen and began to work in earnest toward receiving a charter from the international organization.

With the goal in mind of becoming a chapter in Central Region and the Sorority, the group began to function as an interest group of the sorority, and in May 1991, the West Cook County Associates of Alpha Kappa Alpha, Inc., performed its first community service program. The interest group sponsored a luncheon and health awareness program for Sarah's Inn, a shelter for abused women and children on the west side of Chicago.

In July 1991, the group launched its first fundraiser, a theater outing and reception at the ETA Theater. The fundraiser was a very successful venture and also served to introduce the group to other charitable organizations, sororities, and fraternities in Chicago.

Keeping in mind the need for additional knowledge and organization; the group had its first workshop on August 10, 1991. Soror Barbara McKenzie, immediate past executive director of Alpha Kappa Alpha Sorority, Inc., conducted the workshop on chapter operations and parliamentary procedure.

On November 2, 1991, the members of the West Cook County Associates of Alpha Kappa Alpha Sorority, Inc., received their official charter as the 82nd graduate chapter of Central Region. The presiding Regional Director, Soror Yvonne Perkins, chartered the group at the Ramada Inn-O'Hare. Soror Loraine Richardson Green, Second Supreme Basileus was also in attendance.

Since its charter, Tau Gamma Omega Chapter has conducted seven initiations. The first initiation of eight new members ("First Edition") was held in May 1993. Subsequent initiations: three members ("Total Recall") in March 1994, seven members ("Quiet Storm") in December 1996; nineteen members ("SS BAM") in March 1998; nineteen members ("SS Edge") in March 2000; twenty-three members ("Destined Endeavor 23") in March 2004,and four members ("4Titude ") in September 2012 added to the membership of Tau Gamma Omega Chapter.

Tau Gamma Omega Chapter has sponsored several fundraising events including theater outings, Celebration of Youth, luncheons, calendar kids, bachelor/bachelorette bids, White Linen Party, The Roses and Ivy Ball, and after work socials. The Roses and Ivy Ball became the chapter's signature event in 1996 presenting entertainers such as the Gentlemen of Leisure, Jazz Trio, comedian Damon Williams, among other very talented individuals.

TEA ROSE EDUCATIONAL FOUNDATION: In November, 2000, the chapter established the Tea Rose Educational foundation to improve the quality of life for underserved communities by promoting and supporting educational and social activities. The chapter has also done an outstanding job in implementing the national program since the chapter's chartering.

PROJECT P.O.I.S.E. Spearheaded by the chapter's first initiates, "First Edition," the chapter conducted Project P.O.I .S.E. mentoring program for teen girls ages 11-17. The acronym P.O.I.S.E stands for Positive Ongoing Intellectual and Social Experiences. It provides positive role models and social seminars on social graces, proper etiquette, and finances. The girls are encouraged to give back to the community.

AKAZAAR: AKAzaar, a village bazaar, was developed in 2000 to serve as an umbrella for the national programs. It allowed the members to present effective programs for the community and the chapter's service areas.   Tau Gamma Omega Chapter has partnered with the Chicago Public Schools, The Chicago Park District, The Homan Square Foundation, Family Focus, The Chicago Westside Branch of the NAACP, John H. Stroger Hospital, and elected city and suburban officials in carrying out these programs.

ON TRACK: One of Tau Gamma Omega's award winning programs, which was awarded a $25,000.00 grant from Ameritech. This program partnered with a school on the west side of Chicago to provide tutoring. On Track also won an award for its excellence at the 2002 Central Regional Conference.

IVY READING ACADEMY: This program partnered with two schools on the west side of Chicago. The reading program addressed the needs of the students. Tutoring provided by the sorors contributed to the improvement of many of the student's standardized test scores. The student's self-esteem also improved as a direct result of their academic improvement and interaction with the sorors.

SCHOLARSHIPS: Scholarships were awarded to deserving young men and women. A nursing scholarship named in honor of Soror Glamora Jordan Maeweather. Soror Maeweather, a charter member, was the chapter's first Ivy Beyond the Wall. This nursing scholarship is given annually. To date, the chapter has awarded approximately $50,000 in scholarships.

CHAPTER AWARDS: Tau Gamma Omega Chapter has won a number of awards at regional conferences. These awards include:
- 3rd place Step Show
- 2nd place Step Show
- Black Family, Economics, Attendance, 2nd place Step Show, and 2nd Place "Soror Through the Years"

- Journalism, Arts, Black Family, Economics and Health
- "On Track," Arts and Attendance
- Basileus of the year and Trail Blazer Award
- Soror Through the Years
- Neophyte of the Year, Soror of the Year, Soror Through the years, Standards Blue Ribbon Award (runner-up), and Attendance
- Health, Global Poverty, Emerging Young Leaders (EYL), and Human Rights first place awards as part of the platforms for Soror Caroline House Stewart's administration

Sorors of Tau Gamma Omega chapter remain dedicated to providing service to all mankind with a special emphasis on the chapter's target area—the west side of Chicago and the near west suburbs.

It is the sincere desire of the sorors of this chapter to be of assistance to those in need, to be friends to other community organizations, to give service to all mankind with and through the guidance of Alpha Kappa Alpha Sorority, Inc. May the chapter continue to grow in love and sisterhood.

Tau Gamma Omega Chapter Basilei

Jodice R. Lee	1991-1993
Stella Ward Harden	1994-1995
Johnna Anderson	01/1996-04/1997
Wanda Marie Crawford	05/1997-10/1997
Cynthia Harden	11/1997-12/1997
Vera G. Davis	1998-2000
Carol K. Dorsey	2001-2002
Shari A. Johnson	2003-2004
Annie Marie Ford	2005-2006
Lisa Jackson	01/2007-03/2007
Annie Marie Ford	04/2007-12/2008
Bertha J. Kyles	2009-2010
Annie Marie Ford	2011-2012
Kimberly R. Morton	2013

Pi Nu Chapter

NORTHEASTERN ILLINOIS UNIVERSITY
CHICAGO, ILLINOIS
MARCH 21, 1992

Seated Left to Right: JoMarie Brown, Danielle Porch, Carmen Hampton, Murneka Harris and Giselé Casanova (Graduate Advisor). Standing Left to Right: Kyna Simpson, Dorsey Evans, Rukaiyah Goodwin, Alisa Campbell, Leisha Kimbrough, Cindy Larry, Sylvia Woods and Keisha Williams

CHARTER MEMBERS

JOMARIE BROWN	LEISHA KIMBROUGH
ALISA CAMPBELL	CINDY LARRY
DORSEY EVANS	DANIELLE PORCH
RUKAIYAH GOODWIN	KYNA SIMPSON
CARMEN HAMPTON	KEISHA WILLIAMS
MURNEKA HARRIS	SYLVIA WOODS

During the fall semester of 1989, the idea of starting a chapter of Alpha Kappa Alpha Sorority, Inc., on the campus of Northeastern Illinois University came to life. Danielle Lorraine Porch and Carmen Nicole Hampton decided that Northeastern needed something to attract the African American women on campus to band together. They both knew what the campus needed, Alpha Kappa Alpha.

The sorority stood for everything in which they believed. Danielle and Carmen decided to get all the information that they needed to start on what proved to be a long journey in search of their goal. On April 28, 1991, the first general members were initiated by Xi Nu Omega Chapter. During that same year Xi Nu Omega agreed to sponsor the Northeastern Illinois interest group, thus paving the way for the establishment of an undergraduate chapter on the campus of Northeastern Illinois University.

Determined to go further and establish an undergraduate chapter, at Northeastern, and with the help from Soror Yvonne Perkins and dedicated graduate sorors, more women joined the quest. On December 22, 1991, four more dedicated women matriculating at Northeastern Illinois were initiated into the sorority. Other interested and capable women, seeing our numbers grow on campus joined the interest group.

Then on March 21, 1991, the quest to capture a vision fair became a reality. The chartering of Pi Nu Chapter at Northeastern Illinois University was a historic event. Not only for the women who had struggled with making their dream a reality but, it also was a historic moment for Northeastern Illinois University. Alpha Kappa Alpha is the first Black Greek-letter organization on campus. "For this was a day Alpha Kappa Alpha had made, let us rejoice and be glad in it."

CHAPTER PROJECTS:

ACT/SAT WORKSHOP — This workshop is held in September for high school students. The high school counselor who conducts the workshop also provides the students with college and scholarship information. This project was initiated in 1992 and it is a continuing project. The purpose of this project is to provide students with ACT/SAT testing strategies and college information that they might not regularly get.

READING IS ESSENTIAL PROGRAM — The purpose of this project is to get children more interested in reading. This project was initiated in 1993 and it is a continuing project. Sorors take an hour out of their day to read to children every second Saturday of the month. Other achievements of Pi Nu Chapter and its members have included: Recognition as the chapter with the second highest grade point average at the 1993 Central Regional Conference, and Danielle Porch, recipient of Xi Nu Omega's Monarch Award Scholarship.

ADDITIONAL PROJECTS AND ACHIEVEMENTS — The later 1990's would continue the spirit of chapter achievements at the regional and national levels for Pi Nu. In "addressing the crisis of the 1990's," Pi Nu began a series of family discussions entitled "The African American Family Series" to promote communication and "creative strategies" for families of African descent to address the crisis of the black family by offering possible solutions to resolve the prevalent issues within the black family structure.

With many achievements recognized at the chapter and regional level, Pi Nu Chapter and its leadership would participate in more activities beyond the chapter level. Chartering basileus, Danielle Porch, would run for 2nd Supreme Anti-Basileus at the 56th Boule in Indianapolis, Indiana. Pi Nu Chapter members Nanette Casanova and Laura Crenshaw and June Earley would represent Central Region and Pi Nu Chapter as Leadership Fellows in 1994 and 1997, respectively.

Following 1997, stability in chapter leadership yielded higher expectations in chapter program standards and more participation on programs beyond the chapter level as well as regional recognition. Soror June Earley was honored as the "Outstanding Basileus" and "Outstanding Soror of the Year" at the 1997 Central Regional Conference and Soror June along with Soror Laura Crenshaw would grace the cover of the 1998 Boule Edition of the *Ivy Leaf*. Pi Nu would continue to display their leadership beyond the chapter level as subcommittee chairman on the Chicagoland Joint Founders' Day Committees, Area/Cluster Retreats and represent the chapter at the Undergraduate Luncheon at the Central Regional Conference in the late 1990's.

The mid-1990's marked another turn in chapter programming for Pi Nu. In 1995, Pi Nu chapter would establish the Martha L. Perine Mathematics Award as chapter members worked to continue to excel in program development and implementation with its P.I.M.S. Scholarship Ball to honor high school students excelling in math and science. Other chapter programs included "Sista Speak" a forum for African American female students to address the pressing issues of self-esteem, self-respect, health, and sisterly relations. Additional programs also included a mentoring program for young girls age 11-14 years at the Harris YWCA in Chicago, Illinois, volunteering at local women's' shelters, annual Breast Cancer Awareness seminars, annual AIDS Awareness seminars with the American Red Cross, coat drives, book drives, blood drives and reading/tutorial programs to combat illiteracy. Chapter programs have also included making monetary donations to the Cleveland Job Corps, American Red Cross, DuSable Museum of African American History, Midwest Association for Sickle Cell Anemia, March of Dimes, United Negro College Fund and Oprah Winfrey's Angel Network.

The 20th century would mark a new beginning for the growth and development of chapter programming. In 2004, Pi Nu would move in the "Spirit of AKA" in programming and visibility of service on the local and regional levels. The key to chapter programming success would be collaborations made with campus departments and units at Northeastern Illinois University, various student organizations including neighboring NPHC members and their sponsoring graduate chapter, Xi Nu Omega to broaden the reach and scale of service to the university community.

Led by chapter Basileus, Sarator Whitehead, Pi Nu would establish its Ivy Reading AKAdemy at Faraday Elementary School located on the westside of Chicago, Illinois in collaboration with the College of Education at Northeastern Illinois University, the Student Muslim Association organization and the Alpha Mu Chapter of Alpha Phi Alpha Fraternity, Incorporated at Northwestern University located less than 20 miles from Northeastern campus. Pi Nu Chapter members also continued to collaborate with their sponsoring graduate chapter sorors for MLK Day of Service in the Chicago Public Schools through Chicago Cares by joining them in painting classrooms and school hallways and by providing entertainment at the Monarch Awards Foundation 14th Annual Music Arts Explosion "The Heart of Arts." An additional program honoring the life and legacy of Dr. Martin Luther King would also be held in conjunction with the NEIU President and various NEIU campus departments.

A number of "first" were also made in chapter programming activity during the 2004 and 2005 year. In collaboration with Alpha Mu Chapter of Alpha Phi Alpha Fraternity, Pi Nu Chapter co-hosted the largest Midwest Greek Step Show, K.A.O.S. (Kappas, Alphas, Omegas, Sigmas) with a little D.A.Z.S. (Deltas, AKAs, Zetas, and SGRhos), planned by undergraduates where over 1500 guests were in attendance at the physical education building at Northeastern Illinois University in 2004 and 2005. In promoting the arts, Pi Nu Chapter also instituted annual "Poetry Jams" in 2004 to allow students, faculty and staff the ability to display their artistic talents in performance and creative writing. In 2005, Pi Nu Chapter would also be the first undergraduate chapter to participate in AKA Day at the State Capital held in Springfield, Illinois.

In its quest for perpetuity, Pi Nu has held membership intakes each semester since it's chartering (minus a brief period during a national moratorium in 2002 and chapter inactivity in 2003). Historically, the chapter has initiated less than five members at a time. As preparation to increase chapter membership began in 2004, who could predict what the future would hold for chapter membership in Pi Nu? In the spring of 2005, Pi Nu made chapter history by initiating 9 members, thus making it the largest group of women initiated in its chapter history while still maintaining a chapter grade point average of 3.5 (on a 4.0 scale).

The future of Pi Nu continues to look bright as standards in program development and implementation increase in its level of excellence, as scholarship and service soar, and as greater heights of sisterhood are reached.

PI NU CHAPTER BASILEI

Danielle Lorraine Porch	1992-1993
Jo Marie Brown	1994
Alisa Campbell	1995
Karen Bundy	1995
Natasha Turner	1996
June A. Earley	1997 – 1998
Jerelyn D. Porch	1998 – 1999
Ursula Hoskins	1999 – 2001
Natashee Noble	2002
Sarator Whitehead	2002
Toyya Proctor	2003
Sarator Whitehead	2004 – 2005
Rhonda Cobbin	2005

Martha Levingston Perine Beard

23RD CENTRAL REGIONAL DIRECTOR
JULY 1994 – JULY 1997

Martha Levingston Perine Beard, the 23rd Central Regional Director, graduated Summa Cum Laude from Clark Atlanta University in 1969, with a bachelor degree in Business Administration. In the summers of 1967 and 1968 she studied at Harvard University and Yale University respectively, and in 1971 she earned a master's degree in Economics from Washington University.

Job responsibilities transferred her to Memphis, Tennessee in 1997 where she is Senior Branch Executive for the Memphis Region of the Federal Reserve Bank of St. Louis. In this role, she is responsible for the Federal Reserve's operation in western Tennessee, eastern Arkansas and northern Mississippi. As Central Regional Director, she was a vice president at the Federal Reserve Bank in St. Louis.

Soror Martha married Savoyd Beard in February 1998. Soror Beard has continued her active community service in Memphis. She serves on the boards of Memphis. She serves on the boards of Memphis Tomorrow (an organization comprised of Memphis chief executive officers), St. Jude Children's Research Hospital (Board Vice Chairman), Memphis Regional Chamber, United Way of the Mid-South (Board Chairman), Better Business Bureau of the Mid-South (Board Chairman), Women's Foundation for a Greater Memphis, Mid-South Minority Business Council and the New Memphis Institute (Board Chairman). She is a graduate of the 1987 Class of Leadership St. Louis and the 1998 Class of Leadership Memphis.

In St. Louis she received various honors from Top Ladies of Distinction (Community Service Award), Clark Atlanta University Alumni Association (Alumnus of the Year), and the United Negro College Fund (Volunteer of the Year). In Memphis, she has been honored by Leadership Memphis (Alumnus of the Year), the University of Memphis (Economic Educator of the Year), the Federal Bureau of Investigation (Corporate Citizenship Award) and Grace Magazine (Corporate Excellence Award). She has also been profiled in the Commercial Appeal (Memphis' daily newspaper), the Memphis Business Journal, Crossroads Magazine, Southern Woman Magazine, Memphis Woman Magazine, and RSVP Magazine.

In 2013, she was selected as a member of the inaugural class of Leadership Tennessee, a leadership program sponsored by the Governor of Tennessee; membership in the class was limited to 30 persons statewide. In 2013, she was also named as one of the Outstanding Female Corporate Executives in the City of Memphis by the Memphis Business Journal.

Within Alpha Kappa Alpha, she has been recognized as Gamma Omega Chapter's Soror of the Year and the chapter's 75th anniversary recipient for business leadership. In the Southeastern Region, she has received awards from Beta Epsilon Omega Chapter (Humanitarian of the Year), Epsilon Epsilon

Chapter at the University of Memphis (Empowerment Award for Business Leadership) and was the region's 2002 Membership Chair of the Year.

Soror Perine's personal and professional accomplishments are mirrored by her service to Alpha Kappa Alpha Sorority, Inc. In addition to her service as Central Regional Director, she served as Central Region's Parliamentarian during the administration of Soror Loann J. Honesty King. Immediately before her election as Central Regional Director, Soror Martha served as Supreme Tamiouchos, 1990 – 1994. National Committee involvement includes Chairman of the Human Resources Committee for two administrations, Chairman of the Finance Committee, and membership on the Building and Property Committee and the Economic Development Subcommittee. She has also served as Treasurer of the Educational Advancement Foundation and Treasurer of the Alpha Kappa Alpha Housing Foundation. She also chaired the committee responsible for developing the sorority's regional accounting procedures. At the local level, she served as Basileus, Anti-Basileus, Pecunious Grammateus and Grammateus of Gamma Omega Chapter. She has served as Parliamentarian for Beta Epsilon Omega Chapter.

Soror Martha's first Central Regional Conference was convened in her hometown, St. Louis, Missouri in April 1995. Also, during that same month she chartered Rho Lambda Chapter, Indiana Institute of Technology. In 1997 she chartered Upsilon Mu Omega Chapter, Milwaukee, WI.

Throughout Soror Perine's tenure her commitment to ensure that Central Region was "second to none" as the region carried out the national program theme: Building the Future: Making the Net Work was evident as she fulfilled her duties and responsibilities. Soror Perine kept communications open, disseminated information to the region through her newsletter, chapter visits and 22 area retreats. In addition, her leadership brought to the region a renewed sisterliness. One of her hallmarks was her gracious recognition of former and present leadership.

Each of her three regional conferences: 61st in St. Louis, MO, 62nd in Louisville, KY and the 63rd in Chicago, IL were informative, entertaining, and allowed for engagement in sisterly fellowship. Sorority leadership from across the regions was always present at Central's Regional Conferences including a first with three Central Regional sorors as National Officers: Supreme Parliamentarian, Constance Kinnard Holland, Supreme Grammateus, Linda Marie White, and Supreme Tamiouchos, Soror Yvonne Perkins.

Soror Martha is the proud mother of three children — David A. Perine, Jr, Soror Alissa Lynette Perine and Soror Alison Lynette Perine Olson. She is also the proud grandmother of Hannah Perine, Alexander Perine and Michael Olson.

PART IV: THE FINAL QUARTER OF THE CENTURY

Rho Lambda Chapter
INDIANA INSTITUTE OF TECHNOLOGY
FORT WAYNE, INDIANA
APRIL 30, 1995 – JULY 2010

Rho Lambda Chapter charter members with Soror Martha Perine, Central Regional Director.

CHARTER MEMBERS

TONISHA P. BELCHER
NIKKI BLAINE
NICOLE BRYANT
LATASHA BOYD-JONES
SAUNA J. KELSAW
KEYLA L. MORTON

SHAWNA PEMBERTON
LA'KIA R. RADCLIFF
SHUNTAI ROBINSON
TYLIA CASHE SMITH
KELSIE L. SMOOT
MALINDA ANN TINSLEY

PLEDGED TO REMEMBER: THE HISTORY OF CENTRAL REGION

Upsilon Mu Omega Chapter

MILWAUKEE, WISCONSIN
MARCH 29, 1997

UPSILON MU OMEGA CHARTER MEMBERS

WILLETTE BOWIE
SHAVONN M. BROWN
DOROTHY WILSON BUCKHANAN
MICHELLE BUCKINGHAM
ANNIE J. CARLISLE
RACQUEL COBBLER
HELEN COLLINS
KATRICE COTTON
KEELY L. CRAWFORD
DELDRI DUGGER
DEIDRA Y.A. EDWARDS
SARAH MARTIN ELAM
SUSAN FIELDS
DAWN E. GILLESPIE
BEVERLY HARRELL
MICHELLE HATCHER
IRAJEAN HAYNES
JOANN HENRY
VALARIE HILL
STEPHANIE L. HOUSTON
MIRTLEAN JENKINS
GWENDOLYN D. JOHNSON
DARSELL JOHNS
FRAN ASHLEY JORDAN
SANDRA JORDAN

MONICA KELSEY-BROWN
DONNA KEY
MABEL LAMB
STEFANIE LAMON-REID
LARISSA LAMPKINS
RUTH LAMPKINS
SUZANN LANDINGHAM
JULIE LANDRY
THERESA LAURA
MELANIE LAWRENCE
DEBORAH D. LEDBETTER
KIMBERLY LEE
DEBORAH LEWIS
GWENDOLYN F. LEWIS
ALEXIS LIGGINS
DAPHEN D. LITTLE
SANDRA A. LOCKETT MELCHER
CRYSTAL M. LOCKRIDGE
LINDA F. LUCAS
LA'SONJA LUCKETT
MARLA LUMPKINS
CHERYL MAYES
BERTHENA MAYS
VIVIAN MAYS
LOIS A. MCKISSICK

MICHELE MCKNIGHT
LAUREL NOBLES
TONI M. PACE
JANIE M. POPE
VICTORIA PRYOR
JACQUELYN A. RICE
MICHELLE SAPP
KRISTINA SHANNON
MARY SHAW
PATRICIA B. SHIRLEY
TAMERA SIMPSON
TARI L. SLEDGE
DOMINIQUE SMITH
PAULI TAYLORBOYD
LENA C. TAYLOR
MARQUITA M. TEASLEY
IRIS BOWIE THOMAS
JENNIFER A. TILLMAN
JULIE A. TOWNS
CAROL BROWN TURNER
DEBORAH WALLACE
LISA S. WANZO
MARLENA WARD
NICOLE WATKINS
MICHELLE E. WATTS

Upsilon Mu Omega Chapter was chartered March 29, 1997, in Milwaukee, Wisconsin by seventy-six dynamic women. Inspired by our tenet of "Service to all Mankind," the charter members were committed to the belief that there was an opportunity for the establishment and growth of a second chapter of Alpha Kappa Alpha Sorority, Incorporated in the greater Milwaukee area. A "new" incubator for leadership and empowerment of women of "high scholastic and ethical standards" was the vision and driving force behind the chartering of Upsilon Mu Omega. This effort was led by our organizers: Dorothy Buckhanan Wilson, Irajean Henry, Deidra Edwards, and Carol Brown Turner.

Since 1997 the members of Upsilon Mu Omega have proudly continued the traditions of our noble sisterhood. During this time, there have been many unique international program platforms addressing the pressing needs of men, women and children all over the world. To affirm our commitment to service and bring to life the vision of each Supreme Basileus, Upsilon Mu Omega has sponsored programs and partnered with other organizations to promote the health and welfare of the community-at-large. As a result, we are confident that the global community has been fulfilled through the exemplary programs listed below.

HEALTH AND WELLNESS PROGRAMS
- Family Fun Day — health and wellness festival
- Sponsored blood/bone marrow donation drives in the African American community
- Collecting toiletries, clothing and other items for survivors of domestic violence
- Education programs
- $25,000 in educational scholarships
- Emerging Pearls Enrichment Program
- Emerging Young Leaders program

ECONOMIC PROGRAMS
- AKA Money Camp for Kids
- Black Dollar Days
- Featuring female entrepreneurs at chapter events

CONNECTIONS PROGRAMS
- Hosting Dr. Martin Luther King Day of Service activities to support veterans
- Serving as Poll workers for the City of Milwaukee (Adpot-A-Poll)
- AKA Day at the Capital
- Arts and Cultural programs
- Hosting Kwanzaa celebrations
- Supporting the African American Children's Theater
- Supporting young musical and dance organizations

COMMUNITY PARTNERSHIPS
- UNCF Walk/Run
- Susan G. Komen Walk
- Alzheimer's Association Memory Walk
- American Heart Association Pink Goes Red celebration
- Sister's Network awareness campaign
- African World Festival
- NAACP
- Boys and Girls Club
- Girl Scouts of Greater Milwaukee
- Milwaukee Public Library

To financially support our pursuits of excellence in service, Upsilon Mu Omega members established the Diamond Jubilee Pearls Foundation in 2003. The mission of the Foundation, a 501(c)(3) organization, is to raise and distribute funds to support educational scholarships and impactful community service programs. Over the years, the Diamond Jubilee Pearls Foundation fundraisers have included: Miss Fashionetta®/Mr. Esquire, A Tribute to Women Leaders, and Mother-Daughter Brunch. Some of the nationally recognized guest speakers for the fundraisers have been the late Ms. Bebe Moore Campbell (best-selling author), Ms. Glinda Bridgforth (President And CEO of Bridgforth Financial & Associates), Ms. Kim Coles (Actress, Author and host of BET show "My Black is Beautiful"), and Ms. Susan L. Taylor (Editor Emerita of Essence Magazine).

Through our pursuits of excellence in service and unity in the fellowship of sisterhood, we dedicate ourselves to the ideals and tenets of Alpha Kappa Alpha. May we continue to grow in wisdom, service and exemplify the values to which we hold dear.

Chapter Members Who Have Held International/National Office or Been Elected to the International/National Nominating Committee

Dorothy Buckhanan Wilson	Central Regional Director	2002 – 2006
Dorothy Buckhanan Wilson	Supreme Grammeteus	2006 – 2010
Dorothy Buckhanan Wilson	First Supreme Anti-Basileus	2010 – 2014

Upsilon Mu Omega Chapter Basilei

Dorothy Buckhanan Wilson	1997 – 2000
Valarie A. Hill	2001 – 2002
Sandra A. Melcher	2003 – 2004
Jacquelyn B. Rice	2005 – 2006
Latisha Gray	2007 – 2008
Tammi Summers	2009 – 2010
Laurel Nobles	2011
Felicia M. Miller	2012 – 2014

Upsilon Phi Omega Chapter

EDWARDSVILLE, ILLINOIS
JANUARY 31, 1998

CHARTER MEMBERS

NICOLE ALEXANDER
ADELE CARPENTER
ZINA CRUSE
GLORIA DICKERSON
KENYA DRIVER
VERONICA FISHER
SHEILA HAMILTON
LATONGIA HAYES

CAROLYN JASON
JENNIFER JOHNSON
NOLA JONES
YVONNE JORDAN
GAIL MOSLEY
SANDRA MOSLEY
DAVINA PULLIAM
ETHEL PICKENS
PATRICIA PENELTON

On March 15, 1997, a small group of Alpha Kappa Alpha women met to form the beginnings of an interest group to develop a chapter in the Edwardsville, Illinois community. The hostess for that meeting and those that followed, the woman whose vision and persistence led to the development of this chapter, was Soror Nola Jones. Under the presidency of Soror Davina Pulliam, these sorors named their club Sisters with Pearls. It was the genesis of the first graduate chapter of a Greek letter organization of primarily African American membership in Madison County, Illinois. On Saturday, January 31, 1998, at Mount Joy Baptist Church, Edwardsville, Illinois, Upsilon Phi Omega Chapter was chartered under the leadership of Central Regional Director Soror Peggy Lewis-LeCompte, during the tenure of our Supreme Basileus Soror Eva Evans. Following the charter ceremony the following officers were installed: Patricia Penelton, Basileus; Gail Mosley, Anti-Basileus; Adele Carpenter, Grammateus; Yvonne Jordan, Pecunious Grammateus; Sheila Hamilton, Tamiouchos; LaTongia Hayes, Epistoleus; and Davina Pulliam, *Ivy Leaf* Reporter.

At the gala that followed, the seventeen charter members greeted Madison County and the Greater St. Louis metropolitan community. History was made that day.

At the chartering program, greetings came from many dignitaries, including 17th Central Regional Director Soror Johnetta Randolph Haley, Edwardsville's mayor, our district's state representatives, the governor, the local NAACP president, and representatives of the cluster's alumnae chapters (Gamma Omega, Delta Delta Omega, Omicron Eta Omega and Omicron Theta Omega), and representatives of other Pan-Hellenic alumni chapters in the St. Louis area. The new chapter made certain its presence was known by presenting thousands of dollars of gifts to the Edwardsville NAACP, Alpha Kappa Alpha's Educational Advancement Fund, Lincoln School Alumni Association (the historically black elementary school in the city), undergraduate chapter Epsilon Iota, and a newly established fund for human service awards, named after Soror Marla Rene Dickerson, Ivy Beyond the Wall. The program was followed by an elegant reception where charter members joined family, friends and other VIPs. On this occasion, the first Basileus of Upsilon Phi Omega Chapter, Soror Patricia Penelton, launched an energetic local program to meet the national sorority's initiatives.

During the chapter's relatively short tenure, the women of Upsilon Phi Omega have made a significant impact on their community, as well as the national focuses of the sorority. To earn the monies to support that programming, the chapter holds the Annual Scholarship Dance, usually a formal affair scheduled near the Christmas holidays; annual sales of Great Boars of Fire Barbecue, eagerly awaited just before Memorial Day by our supporters; and a new enterprise, Twilight in the Vineyard, an elegant, widely successful wine tasting event. A more recent and very successful event is the chapter's annual Hattitude Luncheon, held in collaboration with one of the area's most respected and oldest community colleges, Lewis and Clark Community College, located in Godfrey, Illinois.

With these funds, the chapter has sponsored educational programs for children of different age groups. Magical Morning, an annual affair since 2002, is a springtime event for preschool and early elementary school age children, featuring performers, games, gifts and snacks. Read Across America is celebrated each year when sorors go into day care and elementary school classrooms to read to children and when the chapter makes gifts of books to schools and libraries. Summer picnics have been held for the area's black families at which the chapter gave away school supplies and gifts, and each year school supplies are donated to the local pantry for the start of the academic year. Each year since its chartering, the chapter has presented two to three scholarships to graduates of our county's high schools.

In 2002, the chapter also hosted the St. Louis Metropolitan Chapters' Joint Founders' Day Celebration in Collinsville, IL.

In the summer of 2005, a new program, Tomorrow's Pearls, was launched. For this first club of thirteen- to sixteen-year-old girls, seminars were held that focused on etiquette, their self-worth, and their educational and economic potential.

Emerging Young Leaders (EYL), a program for middle school girls, was created in the summer of 2012; the thrust of this program allows girls to experience and participate in personal development and community service activities.

Making the community aware of Alpha Kappa Alpha Sorority's legacy of civic responsibility, Upsilon Phi Omega maintains a high profile in the area. Since 2004, the chapter has made monthly visits to volunteer at an area nursing home, specifically selected because it is the longtime home of one of our sorors and past community leaders, Dr. Willie Pyke.

In October of each year, the Buckle-Up for Safety Campaign is coupled with a Food and Coat Drive, netting one of the largest collections for our local food pantry. Successful educational presentations have included two economic seminars—one on investments and financial planning and a second one entitled "Financing and Re-financing Your Home." The chapter also has sponsored Dress for Success collections, and participated in the March of Dimes Walk, Susan G. Komen Race for the Cure, Relay for Life Walk, the Lupus Foundation Walk and sponsored a Red Cross Blood Drive.

The chapter maintains an active presence in special programs that are specific to its local community: the Southern Illinois University-Edwardsville International Street Fair, the NAACP Welcome Back Program for students, and the YMCA & Edwardsville High School Building Funds, netting an Upsilon Phi Omega Chapter/ Alpha Kappa Alpha Sorority commemorative brick in the courtyards of these institutions. Each year, as part of the Southern Illinois University-Edwardsville Black History Month festivities, the chapter is invited and serves as hostesses for the art exhibit reception.

An enormously successful local program which Upsilon Phi Omega co-sponsors, along with local chapters of AAUW, is G.E.M.S., Girls Explore, Experience, and Experiment in Math and Science. Since 1998, the chapter has been part of this educational program for girls in grades six, seven, and eight. Our involvement has meant rapidly increasing access to African American participants and the inclusion of women-of-color as presenters, professionals in the focus fields.

Sorors with lifelong membership in Alpha Kappa Alpha Sorority are recognized with special recognition as Silver Stars, 25 year members and Golden Soror, 50 year members. Upsilon Phi Omega is honored to have nine Sorors who have earned the status of Silver Stars and one Golden Soror. In addition, the chapter is proud of those Sorors whose exceptional commitment to Alpha Kappa Alpha Sorority earned them special recognition from the chapter as Soror of the Year.

From its inception, Upsilon Phi Omega Chapter has continued to make history in Madison County, Illinois. As we make our presence widely known, we introduce many in our community to the long-established history of Pan-Hellenic organizations and educate them, though demonstration, about Alpha Kappa Alpha Sorority's historic record of dedication to service.

Upsilon Phi Omega Chapter Basilei

Patricia Penelton	1998
Zina Cruse	1999 – 2000
Carolyn Hart Jason	2001 – 2002
Jimmie Cooper	2003 – 2004
Shana Carpenter	2005 – 2006
Annette Stewart	2007 – 2008
Cornelia Smith	2009 – 2010
Devon Bruce	2011 – 2012
Mary Nicholson	2013 – 2014

Nadine C. Bonds
25th Central Regional Director
July 1998 — July 2002

Nadine C. Bonds is a life member of Alpha Kappa Alpha Sorority, Inc. She was initiated through Epsilon Xi Chapter, Indiana State University and transferred to Alpha Mu Omega Chapter where she served as Basileus, Anti Basileus, Graduate Advisor, Mentor and Membership Chairman. A graduate of Purdue University, Soror Bonds has business experience in the private sector with the GTE Corp. as the former Director of Public Affairs, Manager of Corporate Contributions and Executive Trainer.

In the not-for-profit arena, she is the former Executive Director of the Madame C.J. Walker Urban Life Center. Currently, she is a licensed Personal Realtor with JB Real Estate Consultants.

Soror Bonds is an active member of University United Methodist Church and Board member of the Greater Indianapolis Progress Committee, President of the National Coalition of 100 Black Women, Inc., Indianapolis Chapter. She is a Life Member of the NAACP, Indianapolis President's Round Table, Indianapolis Silhouettes and National Association of Realtors.

In addition to many community awards, Soror Bonds has been recognized as the Central Region Soror of the Year, Soror through the Years, Outstanding Graduate Advisor (twice) and has earned the sorority's highest volunteer honor, the Founders' Graduate Service Award. She is noted on the Ivy Tree of Honor and is a member of the Alpha Kappa Alpha Heritage Club.

Soror Bonds was elected the 25th Central Regional Director during the 1998 Central Regional Conference in Indianapolis, Indiana where she served as the General Conference Chairman. Her reelection, for a second term in 2000, put Soror Bonds at the helm as Central Region entered the new century.

During her tenure, Soror Bonds presided over the 65th, 66th, 67th and 68th Central Regional Conferences; visited all chapters of the Central Region; published forty-one issues of the Trailblazer newsletter and participated in all Directorate meetings/Conference Calls. The Nadine C. Bonds EAF Endowment Fund was also capitalized during her tenure.

In 1999 she chartered Phi Epsilon Omega Chapter, Harvey, IL; Phi Kappa Omega, Evergreen Park, IL, 2000; Sigma Gamma, Lake Forest College, 2001; Sigma Eta, Northern Kentucky University, 2002; Chi Alpha Omega, Schaumburg, IL, 2002.

The Bonds' Greek household includes Richard, Marcel, Rodney, all Life Members of Kappa Alpha Psi Fraternity, Inc. and all EAF Men of Money. Daughters-in-law Soror Sheila and Soror Vicki are both members of Alpha Mu Omega Chapter. Grandson Austin also a member of Kappa Alpha Psi Fraternity, Inc., remains to this day the youngest EAF Man of Money, recognized at age two at the 56th Boule in Indianapolis. Soror Bonds has four grandchildren: Coutland, Windsor, Chole and Ethan.

At the 60th Boule in Orlando, she was appointed by Supreme Basileus, Soror Linda M. White to serve as the Fourth International Regional Director. Soror Bonds also served as a member of the National Finance Committee (Secretary), Rituals Committee and, when required, served as Chairman of the Directorate Ethics Committee.

PART IV: THE FINAL QUARTER OF THE CENTURY

Phi Epsilon Omega Chapter

HARVEY, ILLINOIS
JANUARY 23, 1999

Front Row, Left to Right: Tanya Foucher-Weekley, Anjanette Johnson, Bakahia Madison, Nadine C. Bonds, Central Regionsl Director, Tina Kenebrew, Germayne Smith and Latonya Gunter. Second Row, Left to Right: Desirie Howard, Detra Reynolds, Cindy Sanders, Marsha Golliday, Nisa Ahmad, Natasha Buckner, Lisa Joe, Sharice Fox, Theresa Singleton, Tanya McCray and Daneen Edmond Not Pictured: Ebony Gallaher and U. Schanee Woods

CHARTER MEMBERS

NISA AHMAD (LISA JOHNSON)
NATASHA BUCKNER
GERMAYNE CADE
DANEEN WOODARD EDMOND
TANYA FOUCHER-WEEKLEY
SHARICE MCCANTS FOX
EBONI ZAMANI GALLAHER
MARSHA GOLLIDAY-EILAND
LATONYA GUNTER

LISA JOE
ANJANETTE IVY JOHNSON
TINA ROBERSON KENEBREW
BAKAHIA REED MADISON
TANYA MCCRAY
DESIRIE HOWARD MCKAY
DETRA MCCLARITY REYNOLDS
CINDY SANDERS
THERESA ANDREWS SINGLETON
U. SCHANEE WOODS

In November 1997, several members of Alpha Kappa Alpha Sorority, Inc met to discuss the chartering of a new graduate chapter of Alpha Kappa Alpha Sorority in the Chicago area. They wanted to use their time and talents to better serve the community and the Sorority. On November 16, 1997, this group of women named themselves "The Ultimate Women of Pink and Green." Under the leadership of Bakahia Madison, the group's membership increased to nineteen members.

The officers of the Ultimate Women of Pink and Green Interest Group were Bakahia Madison (president), Tina Roberson (vice president), Schanee Woods (recording secretary), Germayne Cade (corresponding secretary), Tanya Foucher (treasurer), Marsha Eiland (membership chair), Desirie Howard (hostess), Anjanette Ivy (fundraising chair), Cindy Sanders (historian/*Ivy Leaf* reporter),

Sharice Fox (communication chair), Theresa Andrews (bylaws chair), and LaTonya Gunter (sergeant-at-arms).

Over the next year, the interest group continued to meet and develop programs for the community in Health and Education. The Ultimate Women did many service projects including grading entrance exams for a local high school, organizing and staffing "Healthy Kids Day" at the South Side YMCA, conducting "Positive Black Women" presentation for girls from age 12-18 at the Burnham Girls Group Home, and providing a skating party for the cheerleaders and basketball team at Martin L. King elementary school in Dixmoor, IL for winning first place in district. The interest group also held a health and beauty seminar and a Black Family Market, which were both well attended and well received by the community. By mid-1998, the interest group members began taking steps to initiate the chartering process; their tremendous efforts proved fruitful.

The Ultimate Women of Pink and Green Interest Group was chartered as Phi Epsilon Omega Chapter on January 23, 1999 in Harvey, Illinois. The chartering ceremony took place at the Best Western, in Homewood, Illinois. The 25th Central Regional Director, Soror Nadine C. Bonds, conducted the ceremony. The 25th Supreme Basileus, Soror Norma S. White, and the 25th Supreme Tamiouchos, Soror Barbara A. McKinzie, also attended the chartering celebration.

The first Basileus of Phi Epsilon Omega Chapter was Bakahia Madison. The other officers were Marsha Eiland (Anti-Basileus), Anjanette Johnson (Grammateus), Germayne Cade (Epistoleus), Tanya Foucher-Weekley (Tamiouchos), Theresa Andrews-Singleton (Parliamentarian), LaTonya Gunter (Philacter), Cindy Sanders (Historian), LaTisha Robinson (Hodegos), Daneen Edmond (membership chairman), Timeka Gee (fundraising chairman), and Schanee Woods (*Ivy Leaf* Reporter).

The vision of Alpha Kappa Alpha Sorority, Inc., Phi Epsilon Omega Chapter is to foster the unbreakable bonds of sisterhood from within and to service the Harvey community through programs, mentoring, and volunteering. Thus, to foster sisterhood, the chapter hosts numerous activities each year to promote sisterly relations. Each year, sorors look forward to the soror brunch, book clubs, and Christmas party. The chapter anniversary celebration, AKA Game Night, strolling parties, summer picnics, slumber parties, "A Taste of AKA" potluck dinners, AKAerobics, and soror tea are examples of other events scheduled throughout the years to promote our sisterly relations. During the annual chapter retreat in June, various activities are held to strengthen our bonds of sisterhood.

Several sorors reactivated through the chapter soon after its chartering. They were: Charlotte Curtis, Denedra Givens-Ellis, Heather Holland, Narissa Jones, LaTacia Morgan-Greene, Angela Alford Murray, Antoinette Patton, Timeka Patton Gee, and LaTisha Robinson Bell.

This new chapter decided to expand its sisterhood even further by conducting its first membership intake process. The first initiation ceremony of the chapter was held May 7, 2000. The first initiates included: Cara Alley, Yolanda Anthony, Toya Supreme, Sabrina Butler, Cleopatra Cowley, Marie Davis, LaKeisha Grace-Stewart, Ingrid Jones, Charlesnika Evans, Shayla Maatuka, Breian Meakens, Danielle Mitchell, Tamiko Mitchell, Lisa Moore, Shivonne Nelson, Keiana Peyton Barrett, Ayanna Perkins, Terrycita Perry, Dawn Phillips, Traci Powell, LaKeisha Ross, Deana Sanders, Rachel Scott (Rowell), Erika Simmons, Celeste Smith, Toi Walker, Kimberly White, and Cynette Wilson.

The second initiation ceremony was held April 7, 2002 and included: Catrice Armstrong, Bridgett F. Earls, Valencia Jones, Nikki Laury Wilson, Kamita Terrell, Katrina Terrell, and Sukari Washington Jones. Soror Tamara McClain and Soror Tonya Weatherly transferred into Phi Epsilon Omega chapter in January 2004.

The third initiation ceremony was held February 26, 2006 and included: Sorors Margo Anderson, De'Onna Cavin, Leah Humphrey, Tiffany Majors, Patrice McCoy, Michelle Rainey, Michelle Ross, Antoinette Weston, Erika Whitehead, Ceshia Wilder, Attiyya Williams, and Kim Willis.

In 2007 Sorors Shawanda Higgins, Vanessa Johnson, and Sandra Rush were welcomed into Phi Epsilon Omega chapter along with reactivated/transfer sorors Toya Campbell and Tanya Stephens-Berry.

After Soror Hareder Jackson reactivated with the sorority in 2010, she has brought numerous inactive sorors to chapter meeting many of whom have since reactivated. Sorors Dana Stafford-Menefee, Danielle Graham-Harris, Barbara Martin, Alicia Mattocks, Ursula Burns, and Tammy Scott-Brand have returned to Alpha Kappa Alpha Sorority, Inc. via Phi Epsilon Omega chapter in the last 2 years because of her enthusiasm.

The sorors of Phi Epsilon Omega chapter have "Blazed New Trails," promoted the "SPIRIT" of Alpha Kappa Alpha, pursued "Economics, Sisterhood, and Partnerships," and supported "Global Leadership Through Timeless Service" in their efforts to provide numerous programs to the community.

The chapter has participated in the "Buckle Up" program and has donated over 1,000 coats to the Harvey/Dixmoor community over the years on "AKA Coat Day."

- Books, dictionaries, and encyclopedias were sent to Africa in Project Send in 2001.
- Young Author's contest was held at King elementary. A pizza party was given to the class of the winner.
- Annually, sorors from the chapter participate as a group in the Y-Me race for breast cancer awareness to raise funds for breast cancer research. The chapter has raised over $10,000 over the years for the Y-Me race. In October, pink lids are collected and sent along with a $100 donation for breast cancer research.
- For 2 years, sorors participated in the American Diabetes Association's Walk for Diabetes and for 3 years have volunteered with the Chicago Diabetes Expo.
- At each chapter meeting, sorors donate their pocket change to the "Change Makes a Difference" program which provides a Thanksgiving dinner to a deserving family in Harvey, IL.
- 25th Supreme Tamiouchos, Soror Barbara A. McKinzie, spoke to the chapter in 2000 regarding personal investments.
- Annually, the chapter's Back to School Rally provides motivation as the students prepare to start their school year. Food, entertainment, book bags, school supplies, and health information is provided for students and their parents. A trunk party is also given for the college bound students that have been recognized by the chapter throughout the year at the Back to School Rally.
- Phi Epsilon Omega chapter has held a number of Christmas programs since its inception: singing carols and playing bingo with seniors at the Harvey YMCA; providing gifts for students in classes at various Harvey schools, children with incarcerated parents, and "Toys for Tots" at Ingalls Hospital
- Held a Christmas dinner at Deborah's Place, a not-for-profit organization that serves homeless or formerly homeless women, where slippers, hats, or gloves were given as gifts and sorors sang carols with the women of Deborah's Place.
- Annually on the MLK Day of Service, Sorors of Phi Epsilon Omega chapter have joined forces with local community groups in Harvey and Dixmoor, Illinois to provide service to the participants of the Women's Resource Assistance Program (WRAP). Chapter members provided business etiquette information, interviewing tips and resume writing advice for women seeking to reenter the workplace. Sorors also donated business suits and provided some guidelines for acceptable make-up, jewelry and attire while interviewing and working in corporate environments. Participants of the program expressed that sorors provided helpful information and were an inspiration to those women striving to reach their professional goals.
- Girls Identifying Future Targets Successfully (GIFTS) was the chapter's mentoring program with teenage girls at Rich South from 2005-2007. Each month, there was a roundtable discussion, individual outing with their mentor from the chapter, tutoring, and a group activity (laser tag, movies, plays, etc.) with sorors.
- The On Track program as well as the Ivy Reading AKAdemy was implemented at King elementary in Dixmoor, IL.
- Emerging Young Leaders is currently being conducted at St. Elizabeth's school.

Fundraisers have included Candlelight Bowling, Fashion Shows, ETA Theater Night, P.R.O.M. Night, a Chicago Bulls' game, a midnight cruise, and Sippin' Around the World (a wine tasting event). In 2003 and 2004, the chapter sponsored the Illinois Drill Team Association's Competition. With no funds from the chapter and 12 hours of volunteer time, thousands of dollars were secured for the chapter to provide scholarships and donations.

P.R.O.M. Night Awards Gala (Promote, Reward Outstanding Milestones for Today's Youth) began in 2003 to recognize youth for their achievement in Community Service, Arts, Science, Math and students living with sickle cell anemia (2003) and diabetes (2004). Scholarships were also given to students for the Presidential Freedom Scholarship and the PEARL Scholarship (Providing Education Assistance to Reward Levels of achievement). The PROM Night Awards Gala was held at the Flossmoor Country Club where sorors, friends, family, students from Rich South High School and other guests are able to 'relive' or experience Prom night.

Starting in 2007, the chapter has sponsored the annual Shades of Pink Cotillion. Dances are choreographed by Soror Ceshia Wilder and her husband for the debutantes and escorts. Chapter sorors volunteer time to teach about etiquette, health, and other topics. The debutantes also complete community service hours and sell ads and tickets. The proceeds are all given back to the debutantes as scholarships.

Each year, the chapter selects a health target to donate part of the proceeds of fundraisers. Phi Epsilon Omega chapter has supported the foundations for Sickle Cell Disease, Sarcoidosis, Diabetes Mellitus, Childhood Obesity, Systemic Lupus Erythematosus, Multiple Sclerosis, Allergy, Asthma, and more. The remainder of the proceeds of fundraisers is given as scholarships.

Phi Epsilon Omega has advised Zeta Iota Chapter since 2001 — Zeta Iota chapter at Western Illinois University was in danger of being dissolved when Phi Epsilon Omega chapter became its supervising graduate chapter in 2001. As this chapter is 3 hours from the Chicagoland area, previous graduate advisors Sorors Timeka Gee, Cindy Sanders, Bakahia Madison, and current graduate advisor Soror Sharice Fox have spent numerous hours on the road to revitalize, guide, and supervise this chapter.

Regional Contributions And Awards

Soror Bakahia Madison was the co-chair for the 2003 Joint Founders' Day Celebration and chair for the 2004 Joint Founders' Day Celebration. She also served on the steering committee for the 68th Central Regional Conference as Workshops Chairman in 2002 (Soror Tanya Foucher-Weekley was the co-chair) and on the Central Region's Technology committee from 2006-2010. Soror Madison served as one of the General Conference Chairmen when the chapter hosted the 75th Central Regional Conference along with Phi Kappa Omega in Schaumburg, IL in 2009. Several other sorors from the chapter chaired conference committees in 2009: Sorors Daneen Edmond and Tamara McClain chaired the Logistics committee, Soror Tanya Foucher-Weekley chaired the Budget and Finance committee, Soror Toya Campbell chaired the VIP/Courtesies committee and Soror Sandra Rush was the co-chairman, Soror Cindy Sanders chaired the Step-show committee, and Soror Tonya Weatherly chaired the Welcome Reception committee.

Phi Epsilon Omega Chapter was the Philacter's committee for the 2000 Central Regional Conference and assisted Phi Kappa Omega chapter as the Philacter's committee for the 2001 Central Regional Conference. The chapter won an award for the most sorors attending Central Regional Conference for a small chapter in 2001. Due to the diligence of membership chair, Soror Charlesnika Evans, the chapter reached Pearl level for membership in 2004. In 2011, the chapter started an Endowment Fund with EAF entitled the Phi Epsilon Omega P.E.A.R.L. scholarship fund.

Three chapter members were recognized by the region as "UNSUNG SHEROES:" Bakahia Madison, 2007; Timeka Patton Gee, 2008; and Tanya Foucher Weekley, 2009. Soror Daneen Edmond was voted Outstanding Basileus for the Central Region at the Regional Conference in 2006. Soror

Edmond was also a Central Region Heritage Committee member from 2006-2010 and assisted with evaluations for chapters in the Great Lakes Region and chapter re-evaluations in the Central Region.

Soror Timeka Gee served on the Central Region's Centennial Celebration planning committee in 2008 and as the chairman for the Central Region's Evaluations committee from 2010-2014 (Sorors Daneen Edmond and Antoinette Weston were also members of the evaluations committee from 2010-2014). Soror LaTonya Gunter served on the Central Region's Technology — Chapter Website Compliance committee from 2010 — 2014.

Phi Epsilon Omega chapter is a diverse chapter with sorors in all occupations. The chapter consists of teachers, counselors, accountants, lawyers, doctors, bankers, realtors, fashion designers, and numerous other fields of employment and expertise. Due to this, Phi Epsilon Omega chapter sorors know they can succeed in implementing the programs of the sorority and look forward to serving the community and the sorority for many years to come.

Phi Epsilon Omega Advises Zeta Iota Since 2001.

PHI EPSILON OMEGA CHAPTER BASILEI

Bakahia Madison	1999 – 2000
Anjanette Ivy Johnson	2001 – 2002
Tanya C. Foucher	2003 – 2004
Daneen W. Edmond	2005 – 2006
Timeka Patton Gee	2007 – 2008
Latonya Gunter	2009 – 2010
Tamara McClain	2011 – 2012
Cindy Sanders	2013 – 2014

Part V

The New Century

2000 – 2014

The New Century

Technically, the new millennium did not begin until 2001. However, the world agreed to celebrate on January 1, 2000. The traditional countdown began at 11:59:50 p.m. on December 31, 1999. The world was poised to celebrate while simultaneously anticipating disaster from the Y2K bug and terrorist attacks. The millennium entered with no terrorist attacks or disastrous computer failure. Moreover, as fireworks washed the sky across 24 time zones for a moment the world came together with high hopes and memorable celebrations.

Alpha Kappa Alpha entered the new century with a renewed energy. The Millennium Boule (59th) held in July, 2000 reemphasized the administrations theme, "Blazing New Trails." Alpha Kappa Alpha historical documents, memorabilia of the time, messages from the Directorate, Former Supreme Basilei and others were encapsulated in the Alpha Kappa Alpha Time Capsule to be opened mid-way of the 21st century (2050). Delta Phi Omega, Minneapolis/St. Paul, MN were awarded $1,000.00 from Daimler Chrysler for the Chapter's On-Track program. The 2000 Boule would also approve the appointment of Cluster Coordinators, by the Regional Director, in every region and the first Central Region Cluster Coordinators were appointed in 2001.

The high hopes and promises of the new millennium would be shattered with the terrorist attacks on September 11, 2001. The impact of 9/11 would bring greater focus on family, patriotism and faith. The world mourned and the nation moved to rebuild.

The war on terrorism would become the United States' priority. However, inequalities in education, health, employment and housing remained major concerns for the African American community. Alpha Kappa Alpha women individually and collectively remained focused on these problems and joined with others to keep these issues on the agendas of those setting policy.

A Strategic Planning Committee was appointed in 2002 to establish long-term goals in the areas of membership, structure and finance. Soror Barbara A. McKinzie, Supreme Tamiouchos was appointed Chairman. The plan established a guide and framework for what the sorority wanted to accomplish and covered a ten year period (2002-2012).

Central Region's own Linda Marie White was installed as the 26th Supreme Basileus at the 2002 Boule (60th) in Orlando, FL. Soror White adopted "The SPIRIT of Alpha Kappa Alpha" as the International Program theme for 2002-2006.

The five targets included in the International Program were: Education, The Black Family, Health, Economics, and the Arts. Alpha Kappa Alpha received a $1.5 million dollar grant from the U.S. Department of Education in support of the Signature Program of the administration: "The Ivy Reading AKAdemy." Soror Peggy Lubin, Theta Omega, Chicago, IL was appointed to head the program. Another major educational program was the Young Authors program. The first publication of children's work was released at the 2004 Boule in Nashville, TN and the second set of publications was released at the Detroit Boule in July, 2006.

The 2004 Boule would add the Technology Committee as a Standing Committee and two Central Region sorors were appointed to the new standing committee: Soror M. Denise Thomas, Gamma Omega, St. Louis, MO and Soror Brenda Ladipo, Chi Sigma Omega, Bolingbrook. IL

The 2006 Boule would ignite the sisterhood with the rallying call of "It's a New Day" by the 27th Supreme Basileus, Soror Barbara A. McKinzie. Her vision would spark an "Extraordinary Service Program (ESP)" of Economics, Sisterhood/Service and Partnerships.

More than 28 million individuals were impacted by the ESP Platforms; chapter contributions exceeded 11 million with external contributions reaching in excess of 15 million; and the first service initiative exclusively for undergraduates was initiated. Central Region's own Soror Loann J. Honesty King, Theta Omega, served as the International Program Chairman and Soror Cheryl Cole Young,

Gamma Omega, was Central Region's representative to the Committee. Soror Dorothy Wilson Buckhanan was elected Supreme Grammateus and the Investment Committee was added as a Standing Committee. In addition, Soror Deborah Dangerfield, Theta Omega, Chicago, IL would be appointed Executive Secretary (Board approved title change to Executive Director in 2007) of the Educational Advancement Foundation. Soror Dangerfield would transition to the position of Executive Director of Alpha Kappa Alpha Sorority, Inc. in 2008. Soror Barbara Sutton, Theta Omega would pick up the mantle as Executive Director of the Educational Advancement Foundation (EAF).

Soror McKinzie was at the helm for Alpha Kappa Alpha's Centennial Year and Boule. History was made! Following a year of celebrations, one region at a time, more than 35,000 members, family and friends descended on Washington, D.C. to celebrate Alpha Kappa Alpha's 100th year of sisterhood and service. And the world was put on notice regarding the heritage, service and achievements of Alpha Kappa Alpha Sorority.

Central Region's Centennial Year Celebrations included the Centennial Traveling Exhibit hosted in Milwaukee, Wisconsin by Epsilon Kappa Omega and in St. Louis Missouri by Gamma Omega. Soror Dolena Mack, Gamma Psi Omega, Gary, IN headed the Region's centennial initiative of collecting original poems, songs, musical arrangements and regional strolls that captured the individuality, togetherness and uniqueness of the region. Soror Dolena also wrote an original Central Region song that is still being sung by members of Central Region.

From the pre-conference activities to the opening sessions, to the Centennial Gala (which was entered in the Guinness World Records as the largest silver service dinner party served in one venue, 16,206 people) Central Region Sorors were well represented at the Centennial Boule. Sorors Nicole Thorne Jenkins, Omicron Eta Omega, Florissant, MO and Melody M. McDowell, General Member and Chairman, International Communications Committee served on the Centennial Celebration Committee. Central Region's "Ivy Notes" made their Boule debut and more than 15 Central Region Sorors were recognized at the Leadership Gala for their service. The Medical Response Team's Chief Medical Officer was Soror Mary K. Palmore, Theta Rho Omega, Markham, IL and one of the Team Administrators was Alfreda "Fred" Keller also from Theta Rho Omega. The International Program Service "ESP" Awards went to Gamma Omega, St. Louis, MO for Platform I – The Non-Traditional Entrepreneur; Theta Omega, Chicago, IL for Platform II – The Economic Keys to Success; and the program award for Platform IV – The Undergraduate Signature Award went to Gamma Chi, Northwestern University. Loann J. Honesty King was the recipient of the "Founders Graduate Service Award."

Central Region Sorors also added substantially to the record breaking vendor sales especially when it came to the limited edition Centennial "Barbie Doll" by Mattel. The Graduate Advisors Certification Committee was approved as a standing committee and Soror Margo S. Baines, Theta Omega; Chicago, IL was appointed Vice-Chairman of the Committee.

On November 4, 2008 at Grant Park in his home city of Chicago, Illinois (Central Region) before an estimated crowd of 240,000 the world listened to the words of United States President-elect Barack Obama: "If there is anyone out there who still doubts that America is a place where all things are possible, who still wonders if the dream of our founders is alive in our time, who still questions the power of our democracy, tonight is your answer."

The African American community celebrated and felt a renewed sense of pride, power and possibility. Central Region sorors were there in Grant Park and reveled in the fact that they had in some small part played a role in this historic victory.

The Boule (64th) would return to Central Region in 2010. Soror Kathy Walker-Steele, Delta Delta Omega would serve as General Chairman and Former Central Regional Directors' Sorors Johnetta Haley and Peggy Lewis LeCompte would serve as Honorary Chairmen. The "Ivy Notes" returned by popular demand and the Medical Response Team again provided exceptional service. Soror Peggy Lewis LeCompte, Delta Delta Omega received the "Founders Graduate Service Award."

Central Region's Boule Leadership team and committee would put their confident, competent and classy touch on every aspect of the Boule. It was truly a Grand Affair. The icing on the cake came with the official announcement that Central Region's Dorothy Buckhanan Wilson was elected First Supreme Anti-Basileus.

It was only fitting that St. Louis, the gateway city to the west, provided the gateway for the introduction of the 28th Supreme Basileus, Carolyn House Stewart administration's program theme: Global Leadership through Timeless Service. Soror E. JaNiece Bell, Chi Sigma Omega, Bolingbrook, IL was appointed to the International Program Committee and has guided the chapters of Central Region through successful implementation of the International Program.

In support of the Educational Advancement Foundation, Central Regional Director, Giselé Casanova initiated the establishment of the Haley, King, and Beard Endowment Fund. The fund was capitalized in 2011. At the 2011 Leadership Seminar EAF Luncheon, Central Region was presented an award for the "Greatest Amount of Contributions" among medium sized regions to the Educational Advancement Foundation.

Central Region is proud of the number of the region's sorors represented in the "Unsung Sorors of the Civil Rights Movement" museum unveiled at the 2012 (65th) Boule in San Francisco. Gamma Chi Chapter, Northwestern University was represented by Dr. Debra Avant Hill, Dr. Nona M. Burney, Sandra Hill, and Adrianne Thomas Hayward. Gamma Omega sorors included Minnie Perry, Alice Parham, Margaret Ann Berry, Pearlie Evans, and Margaret Bush Wilson.

Audrey Cooper-Stanton, Chairman Leadership Fellows Committee, Theta Omega was the recipient of the "Founders Graduate Service Award." Xi Nu Omega represented the Region at the 2012 Boule as an award nominee for the signature program initiative Emerging Young Leaders. And the Giselé M. Casanova Endowment Fund was capitalized in 2012.

Central Region continues to grow in numbers. As of December 31, 2013 the region has 90 Chapters (53 Graduate and 37 Undergraduate) with the reactivation of Mu Delta Omega Chapter, Fort Knox, Kentucky and 3,887 (3,509 Graduates and 318 Undergraduates) members. Chi Omega Omega in Chicago, IL still retains the distinction of having the largest number of charter members in the history of the sorority (102).

As Central Region continues to render Timeless Service we anxiously await the installation of the 29th Supreme Basileus, Soror Dorothy Buckhanan Wilson and stand ready and prepared to continue to carry the torch of "Timeless Service to All Mankind."

PART V: THE NEW CENTURY

Phi Kappa Omega Chapter
EVERGREEN PARK, ILLINOIS
JANUARY 8, 2000

Seated — Left to Right: Odas Nicholson, Pamela Rowland, Marianne C. Stallworth, Nadine C. Bonds (25th Central Regional Director), Doris B. Powell, Helen Fleming Chatman, Lilla Lissimore-Wheeler. Standing — Left to Right: Denise Gresham-Knox, Antoinette M. (Rawls) Henley, Zenobia Owens, Octavia Coleman, Pamela D. Edwards, Melody C. Williams, Yolanda Douglas, Ayanna K. Fisher, Julie Wheeler Fisher.

CHARTER MEMBERS

HELEN FLEMING-CHATMAN
OCTAVIA COLEMAN
YOLANDA DOUGLAS
PAMELA D. EDWARDS
AYANNA K. FISHER
JULIE WHEELER-FISHER
ANTOINETTE RAWLS-HENRY

DENISE GRESHAM-KNOX
ODAS NICHOLSON
ZENOBIA OWENS
DORIS B. KYLE-POWELL
PAMELA ROWLAND
MARIANNE C. STALLWORTH
LILLA LISSIMORE-WHEELER
MELODY C. WILLIAMS

On Friday, January 15, 1999 at 6:30 p.m., a group of individuals representing the fields of education, law, administration, and aviation collaborated with a vision to charter an Alpha Kappa Alpha Sorority, Incorporated graduate chapter.

The chapter, first conceived by Doris B. Kyle-Powell and organized with the charter members, the Dynamic Ladies of Pink and Green Pearls Interest group became Phi Kappa Omega Chapter of Alpha Kappa Alpha Sorority, Incorporated on January 8, 2000, and also became the first Alpha Kappa Alpha chapter chartered in the new millennium.

Chartered in Evergreen Park, Illinois, the charter members and first officers were: Doris Powell, President; Marianne C., Stallworth, Vice-President and Program Chairman; Pamela Rowland, Secretary; and Helen Fleming-Chatman, Treasurer. In addition, Pamela Edwards served as Assistant Treasurer; Melody Williams, Assistant Secretary; Yolanda Douglas, Corresponding Secretary; Julie Fisher, Publicity Chairman; Denise Gresham-Knox, Social Secretary; Odas Nicholson (retired Judge), Parliamentarian; Lilla Wheeler, Historian; Octavia Coleman, Chaplain; Ayanna Fisher, Sergeant-At-

Arms; Zenobia Owens, Membership Chairman; and Antoinette Rawls-Henley, Attorney. Sorors Lilla Lissimore-Wheeler, Julie Fisher, and Ayanna Fisher represented a legacy family among our chartering group; and we were also proud of our two Golden Sorors — Soror Odas Nicholson (Judge, retired) and Soror Lilla Lissimore-Wheeler.

Heralding our birth throughout Central Region, news of our existence was spotlighted in the first chapter newsletter "The Ivy Gazette," penned by Basileus Doris Powell, and Phi Kappa Omega Chapter of Alpha Kappa Alpha Sorority, Incorporated grew to attract other Sorority members into its ranks since 2000. Sorors Johnna Richmond, Deborah Elliott, Eloise Cheers, Rosine Bradford-Jordan, Carmella Gordon, Adrienne Crutcher, and Kimyada Wellington joined us in 2000- 2001. Among our many achievements throughout 2000-2001 were:

JOINT FOUNDERS DAY: Phi Kappa Omega has begun collaboration with 10 graduate chapters and local undergraduate chapters in preparation for Joint Founders Day 2001. A table for our Chapter was purchased.

BLACK FAMILY THEATER NIGHT: In support of the theatrical presentation by Soror Yolanda Douglas acting in "The Ancestor" on February 18, 2000 several Sorors and their families braved the worst snowstorm in Chicagoland's year 2000 winter history to attend this enjoyable event. We were proud of the talents of Soror Yolanda.

ADOPT-A-HIGHWAY: As part of the Department of Transportation Buckle Up America/Partners to Save Lives, Phi Kappa Omega joined the Adopt-A-Highway program. As a result, we have signs were posted from Western Avenue to Kedzie Avenue in Evergreen Park, Illinois heralding ALPHA KAPPA ALPHA SORORITY, INCORPORATED. We were based out of Highways District 1 of Illinois Department of Transportation.

REGIONAL CONFERENCE: Sorors Doris Powell, Marianne C. Stallworth and Pamela Rowland were in attendance at the 66th Central Regional Conference was held in St. Louis, Missouri from April 6-9, 2000.

PROTOCOL TRAINING WORKSHOP: On May 6, 2000, Soror Janis Culver, Central Region representative on the Protocol Committee provided training to Phi Kappa Omega Sorors. Materials were distributed referencing sorority protocol and sorors asked pertinent questions to clarify issues of protocol.

CHICAGOLAND FOOD DEPOSITORY WALK-A-THON: Phi Kappa Omega members along with family and friends participated in the June 2000 Walk-A-Thon to raise money for the Sixth-Grace Presbyterian Food Depository.

BOULE: Basileus Powell represented as a delegate to the July 2000 Boule held in Dallas, Texas. Soror leaders from across the country were greeted, and plenary meetings and social events were attended.

BUD BILLIKEN PARADE: Phi Kappa Omega members and friends participated in the August 2000 parade.

FAMILY AND FRIENDS SPA WEEK: During the month of June, Soror Julie Fisher organized and coordinated a Phi Kappa Omega Friends and Family spa week.

AKA COAT AND CLOTHING DRIVE: Phi Kappa Omega Sorors collected coats and formal dresses which were donated to local shelters.

AREA RETREAT: The Cluster VIII Area Retreat was held October 7, 2000 and attended by Soror Doris Powell, Soror Marianne C. Stallworth, Soror Pamela Edwards, and Soror Deborah Elliott. Sorors Marianne, Pamela and Deborah attended Membership Intake Training; while Soror Doris presented a workshop entitled "Basic Parliamentary Procedures."

RECLAIMING THE PEARLS: Phi Kappa Omega celebrated the reactivation of six sorors at a brunch organized by the program committee and the theme "Reclaiming the Pearls" Ó was presented via the history of Phi Kappa Omega. MEMBERSHIP INTAKE PROCESS TRAINING

WORKSHOP: Organized by the Membership Committee chaired by Soror Marianne and presented November 18, 2000 by Sorors Zenobia, Deborah, Johnna, and Marianne, the chapter Sorors received training on the tenets of the Intake process. In addition, the Sisterhood Video by Soror Norma S. White was presented and discussed.

OTHER PHI KAPPA OMEGA PARTICIPATION: Basileus Doris Powell represented the chapter at the National Connection Committee's AKA Day at the Springfield, Illinois State Capitol held March 29, 2000. In addition, Soror Doris attended the pink and green day at the Congressional Black Caucus Foundation's Millennial Public Policy Conference held September 14-16, 2000.

In 2001 PKO continued participation and forward momentum with:

CHAPTER ANNIVERSARY CELEBRATION: The January 13, 2001 Chapter meeting was held at the Oak Lawn Hilton. The meeting was a dinner celebration of the first year anniversary of our Chapter chartering. We are pleased that 100% of our Chapter Sorors were in attendance.

JOINT FOUNDERS' DAY: Collaborating with ten other graduate Chapters, Phi Kappa Omega attended the joint Founders' Day 2001 held on January 20, 2001 at the Marriott Hotel. Sorors Doris Powell, Marianne C. Stallworth, Helen Chatman, Johnna Richmond, Pamela Rowland, and Rosine Jordan purchased a table.

THE BLACK FAMILY AND THE ARTS: The Sixth Annual Sixth-Grace Presbyterian Church African American History Celebration showcased the theatrical talent of our own Soror Yolanda Douglas. Soror Yolanda presented her interpretation of "A Story, A Story" which was enthusiastically received by Sorors, their families, and all in attendance.

ADOPT-A-HIGHWAY: Phi Kappa Omega engaged in clean-up activities this year as part of this initiative. Sorors and family members worked together to beautify this stretch of highway between Kedzie Avenue and Western Avenue in Evergreen Park, Illinois. We are based out of Highways District 1 of Illinois Department of Transportation.

REGIONAL CONFERENCE: The 67th Central Regional Conference was held in Springfield, Illinois from April 19-22, 2001 at the Crowne Plaza Hotel. Soror Doris Powell, Soror Marianne C. Stallworth, Soror Eloise Cheers, and Soror Johnna Richmond attended.

"OUR SILVER STARS:" It was with great pleasure that PHI KAPPA OMEGA had the first of its Chapter Sorors inducted as Silver Stars. Soror Marianne C. Stallworth and Soror Eloise Cheers were honored at the luncheon and bestowed the Silver Star Medallion and Honorary Certificate. In addition, each of these Sorors received their commemorative 25-year Letter, Certificate and Pin from the National office of Alpha Kappa Alpha Sorority, Incorporated in honor of the occasion.

WALK-JOG-BIKE-A-THON: Soror Johnna Richmond, Soror Marianne C. Stallworth and Soror Melody Williams participated in the 27th Annual Walk/ Jog/Bike A-Thon on Chicago's lakefront. Phi Kappa Omega participated in this event to benefit the Sickle Cell Disease Association of Illinois (SCDAI).

CHICAGOLAND FOOD DEPOSITORY WALK-A-THON: A collaborative team representing PHI KAPPA OMEGA participated in the Chicagoland Food Depository's Hunger Walk on June 23, 2001. Pledges were solicited and donated to support the efforts of Sixth-Grace Presbyterian Church in feeding the hungry that reside in its community.

LEADERSHIP SEMINAR: The Alpha Kappa Alpha Sorority, Incorporated Leadership Seminar was held in San Juan, Puerto Rico on July 19-23, 2001. Basileus Doris Powell and Anti-Basileus Marianne C. Stallworth represented PHI KAPPA OMEGA at this conference.

CAREY B. PRESTON AKADEMY: The educational, training and human resource development opportunities provided by Phi Kappa Omega are implemented under this umbrella.

PROJECT R.E.A.D. (Reach to Educate and Develop) was implemented through the donation of books to primary and intermediate grade children. The mentoring partnership was initiated with James R. Doolittle and Ada S. McKinley for Grade 6 students. In addition, Sorors of Phi Kappa Omega donated items of warm clothing, funds and committed to purchasing a classroom library for the students with disabilities at the James Madison Elementary School.

A.K.A.S.T.L. (Acquiring Knowledge and Skills to Lead) — CHAPTER RETREAT SESSIONS: As Program Committee Chairperson, Soror Marianne C. Stallworth along with Sorors Pamela Edwards, Odas Nicholson, Pamela Rowland, and Melody Williams instituted our first annual Leadership Development Retreat Seminar series. Implemented over a three-month period, these sessions provided information pertaining to roles and responsibilities and policy and procedures of the Sorority.

AREA RETREAT: PHI KAPPA OMEGA CHAPTER was represented on the planning committee of Area Retreat by Soror Eloise Cheers and Soror Johnna Richmond. Soror Doris Powell, Soror Marianne C. Stallworth, and Soror Zenobia Owens were also participants and attendees at the Retreat held at the Holiday Inn, Matteson, Illinois September 7-8, 2001.

RECLAIMING THE PEARLS: Inactive and transferring Sorors were invited to attend our 2nd Annual Reclaiming the Pearls Brunch held September 29, 2001 at Sixth-Grace Presbyterian Church. Eight Sorors expressed an interest and committed to reactivation with Phi Kappa Omega in 2002.

PHI KAPPA OMEGA FALL BASH: Phi Kappa Omega hosted its first annual event to raise funds for scholarship awards to deserving high school youth in 2002. Sorors, family, and friends attended this gala at the Martinique on October 28, 2001.

CARSON PIRIE SCOTT FUNDRAISER: Sorors of Phi Kappa Omega implemented a unique fundraising activity this year. Sorors and friends purchased certificate packets and the Chapter received 100% or the packet price. Purchasers could use the five certificates to save money on regular, sale, or clearance prices on merchandise. All benefited from participation.

AKA COAT DRIVE: Sorors collected fifteen coats and other clothing items for the needy. Donations were targeted for a shelter for battered women in the Evergreen Park Community.

OTHER Phi Kappa Omega Activities: Basileus Doris Powell represented Phi Kappa Omega at the following events: March 22, 2001 Book signing by Honorary Soror Mae Jemison; September 27-29, 2001 attended the 31st Congressional Black Caucus annual Legislative Conference in Washington, D. C. and AKA Day at the Capitol in Springfield, Illinois, March 2001.

ESSENCE OF IVY AND PEARLS 2002 — 2003: In 2002, Soror Marianne C. Stallworth, our 2nd Basileus, initiated the motto "plan prayerfully, prepare purposefully, proceed positively, and pursue persistently." Our theme and focus became "We strive and we do…in 2002" and the chapter newsletter was redesigned and entitled "Essence of Ivy and Pearls" to acknowledge a new strength and vitality for our chapter. It would also signify the impotence for establishing a culture and to strengthen the foundation of Phi Kappa Omega Chapter. We defined the significance of its title to capture the strength of character and deed represented by the Ivy; and the elegance and grace of each of our members as the Pearls, joined together in one bond of sisterhood to serve mankind. We have been successful in advancing these qualities in the interactions with other Sorors of Alpha Kappa Alpha Sorority, Incorporated on the local, state, and international levels.

In addition to Basileus Stallworth, Johnna Richmond was Anti-Basileus; Ayanna Fisher was our 2002 Secretary, then Pamela Rowland was reappointed Secretary 2003, Adrienne Crutcher, was Treasurer; and Kimyada Wellington was elected/appointed to hold the offices of Pecunious Grammateus; and *Ivy Leaf* Reporter. Zenobia Owens, continued her appointment as Membership Chairman; Denise Gresham-Knox was appointed Fundraiser Chairman; and Rosine Bradford-Jordan was appointed Chaplain in 2002 and was succeeded by Bettye Gardner, in 2003.

On April 7, 2002 seventeen dynamic initiates joined our PKO ranks as our first intake group. Dakiti Adams, Tonietta Boyd, Rosalind Byrd, Christine Chandler, Mary Clements, Christine Craig, Carole Crutcher, Bettye Gardner, Tina Glover, Chanel Grayson, Krista Marie Hinton, Kayla Hogan, Rebecca M. Jackson, Cerrelda M. Jones, Gayle A. Jordan, Cornelia Liggans and Cassaundra Rouse became women of PKO. Linda Gresham and Raquel Betton transferred to unite with Phi Kappa Omega Chapter in May, and Jacqueline Davis, Kimberly LeFlore, and Rita Savare "Reclaimed their Pearls" at our reactivation Brunch in September 2002.

Many of our chapter programs originated and/or grew under this administration, as well. Our Sister-to-Sister Program was initiated, participation and attendance at conferences grew; our Scholarship Program awards began, and our Carey B. Preston Reading AKAdemy was initiated. We further introduced our chapter throughout the world of Alpha Kappa Alpha by exhibiting our scrapbook at the 68th Central Regional Conference; and a chapter display at the 69th Central Regional Conference.

The strength and pride of the Phi Kappa Omega Chapter lies in the participation, energy, and commitment each of its members demonstrates in making our Chapter a success! Our membership was often reminded by Basileus Stallworth that "an organization succeeds, not because it is big, or because it is long established, but because of the depth of commitment, vision, and confidence of its members who consistently plan for its future." In 2002 PKO demonstrated the SPIRIT OF AKA in the following activities:

SISTERHOOD, SCHOLARSHIP, AND SERVICE: Celebrated the Chapter's 2nd anniversary at our January 13, 2002 Chapter meeting; and initiated Project R.E.A.D. providing mentoring, tutoring, and literary support to students of James R. Doolittle Middle School and James Madison Elementary School as part of our Carey B. Preston AKAdemy, donating 100 books to our co-collaborators.

We had the greatest number of Phi Kappa Omega Chapter Sorors, both active and inactive; participate in Joint Founders' Day 2002-eleven (11), celebrating "Legend to Legacy" held at the Hyatt Regency Chicago, January 19, 2002. Phi Kappa Omega Chapter and Basileus Stallworth were recognized by the Sixth-Grace Presbyterian Church for our Carey B. Preston AKAdemy, Project R.E.A.D. (Reach to Educate and Develop) at their African American History Program on February 3, 2002 entitled "Building Strong Communities through Education."

SISTER-TO-SISTER PROGRAM: Visited Theta Omega Chapter meeting February 15 to initiate our Sister-to-Sister Program. We bestowed upon Soror Bette Reid and the Sorors of Theta Omega our Eternal Rose and the Phi Kappa Omega Chapter dossier. Our Sister-to-Sister Program is an effort to introduce Phi Kappa Omega Chapter as we meet, greet, and support other Chicagoland AKA Chapters and Sorors.

We extended ourselves Sister-to-Sister when we: attended the Theta Omega Chapter African American History Program on February 23, 2002; participated on the Basilei Council, the council of the 12 Chicagoland Chapter Basilei; attended Lambda Tau Omega Chapter's Twenty Pearls Foundation — Miss Prominent Pear Debutante Cotillion on March 16, 2002; attended the Theta Rho Omega Chapter Vision Quest Awards 2002 honoring scholarship recipients and community leaders held on May 11, 2002; attended Tau Gamma Omega's AKAzaar on May 18, 2002 which promoted health and wellness screenings and showcased African American vendors; attended and participated with the Basilei Council at the AKA Reception for Soror Linda M. White at the Hyatt on September 6, 2002; attended and participated in the AKA Buckle-Up Day in Lansing, Illinois on September 21, 2002; attended Tau Gamma Omega Chapter's "Roses and Ivy Ball" on September 27, 2002; attended the Theta Omega Chapter's AKArama AKAmericana on October 19, 2002; attended Theta Rho Omega Chapter's Holiday Christmas Bazaar on November 16, 2002; attended a good-will fundraiser for the husband of Soror Gretchen Brumley of Tau Gamma Omega Chapter. Mr. Cedric Brumley (Phi Beta Sigma) was paralyzed in a car accident while on duty as a Chicago Police Officer. We help each other. For we know there's no other like our sisterhood Alpha Kappa Alpha!

In addition:

- Nine (9) PKO Sorors participated in the 68th Regional Conference held in Chicago in April. In addition, at least eight neophytes attended the Town meeting and/or Step Show at Regional

- Eight (8) PKO Sorors attended Boule in Orlando, Florida in July
- Initiated seventeen (17) new Phi Kappa Omega Chapter Sorors, transferred in two (2) active Sorors from another chapter, and reactivated three (3) Alpha Kappa Alpha Sorors
- Participated in the Cancer Walk, the Sickle Cell Anemia Walk-a-Thon, and their Chicagoland Food Depository Hunger Walk for the third year
- Participated in the AKA Buckle-Up activity September 21, 2002
- Attended and Basileus Stallworth presented at the Area Cluster Retreat — North on October 19, 2002. — "Are You Working? The Effective Committee" to approximately 90 Sorors of AKA
- Actively participated in the AKA Coat Drive, donating 20 coats to a Chicagoland shelter

PARTNERSHIP:

- CAREY B. PRESTON IVY AKADEMY — Collaborated with Chicago Public Schools' Office of Specialized Services "The Mentor Connection, Ada S. McKinley Educational Service Program, James Doolittle Middle School, James Madison Elementary School, and Sixth-Grace Presbyterian Church to mentor and tutor students of Doolittle, and to provide books to Madison School.
- Active participants in the Pan Hellenic Council Action Committee of Chicago along with the other divine nine Greek letter organizations

INNOVATION:

- Members committed to active participation in our Sister-to-Sister Program, to link to sisterly relations with other chapters at the local, state, and international levels. Soror Zenobia presented Gamma Chapter (University of Illinois-Champaign) with our "Eternal Rose" and PKO dossier to introduce our chapter, to greet their membership, and to commemorate the induction of her daughter, Soror Jennifer, into Alpha Kappa Alpha Sorority, Incorporated.
- The Chapter adopted and continues to promote the talents of Mr. Andrew Harris who designed an African American Flag that he hopes will become a nationally recognized treasure in the Black community.
- Developed and published our Chapter brochure, our Carey B. Preston AKAdemy brochure, and revised our chapter Certificate of Training document and purchased our chapter's credential stamp to certify Leadership Training

RESPECT:

- Celebrated Phi Kappa Omega Soror Day to uplift our chapter bond and to spend "up close and personal time" with our chapter members.
- Celebrated the work of Dr. Margaret Burroughs, founder of the DuSable African American History Museum and Honorary Soror at our Autumn Bash 2002 on October 13, 2002.

INVOLVEMENT:

- Initiated and you participated in A.K.A.S.T.L. (Acquiring Knowledge and Skills to Lead) our Leadership Develop and Training forums. Phi Kappa Omega Sorors participated in training modules which took place in April, May, and June in continued preparation for leadership in our chapter.
- All Phi Kappa Omega Chapter Sorors participate on committees. To provide more active participation and involvement, Phi Kappa Omega is proud that our neophytes all Chair and/or Co-chair Chapter committees and targets. As a result, we realized greater involvement and support of our Chapter initiatives.
- Phi Kappa Omega Sorors committed to and most participated in our PKO Fall Bash 2002. We hosted over 180 family, friends, and guest Sorors at this event.

TECHNOLOGY:

- Our emphasis on technology began with our 2002 Epistoleus, Soror Ayanna Fisher. She provided

notice to Sorors by Email, as well as by U.S. mail. An electronic Essence of Ivy and Pearls Newsletter were planned for early 2003 and our Technology Committee began designing our website.
- But we didn't stop there. In 2003 we were elated to welcome Sorors Gayle Thompson, Bernadine Mabra and Ericka Carroll-Mason into PKO membership, and we continued our elation through the election of Basileus Marianne as the 4th Presiding Basileus of the Chicagoland Basilei Council.

THE BLACK FAMILY:

- Phi Kappa Omega Chapter commemorated the life and times of Dr. Martin Luther King, Jr. for MLK Day with Mr. Norman Bowen who recited the "I Have a Dream" speech at our Chapter Anniversary Celebration.
- Thirty-seven PKO members, friends and inactive Soror joined us for the Joint Founders' Day celebration of 2003 "Serving with Supreme Elegance & Sisterhood" to commemorate our Founders with Soror Linda M. White.
- Phi Kappa Omega Chapter joined with the membership of Sixth-Grace Presbyterian Church in honoring Alpha Kappa Alpha Sorority, Inc. for "Building Strong Communities through Civic and Social Action." PKO invited Chicagoland chapters and realized representation from 9 chapters as our International President, Soror Linda M. White, 26th Supreme Basileus, accepted this prestigious award on behalf of Alpha Kappa Alpha.
- Soror Cerrelda Jones, a 2002 neophyte of Phi Kappa Omega received recognition at the Regional Conference as runner-up for Neophyte of the Year — 2002. How proud we were of her!
- A.K.A.S.T.L. (Acquiring Knowledge and Skills to Lead) Leadership Development:
- Basileus Stallworth presented "Who Moved My Cheese," accepting change—at the 69th Regional conference in Louisville, Kentucky to over 95 Sorors.
- Phi Kappa Omega Chapter held Leadership Training for our chapter, but was the proud hostess chapter for the 2003 Area Retreat-North which realized the greatest number of Sorors in attendance.
- Greeted chapters "Sister-to-Sister" as Soror Marianne C Stallworth bestowed the Eternal Rose to over 47 Basilei in attendance and also hosted a "Reclaiming the Pearls" reactivation workshop. This conference also provided the only Regional training of Graduate Advisors during that time.
- PKO was very proud to bestow scholarships upon 3 High Schools Seniors and celebrated them at our 2003 Autumn Bash Gala.
- Basileus Marianne C. Stallworth experienced one of her greatest joys as a Soror of Alpha Kappa Alpha Sorority, Inc. when she had the pleasure of initiating the membership and pinning of her daughter, Soror Maricha, into Alpha Pi Chapter on the campus of Clark Atlanta University. Needless to say her pride was showing!!! And she had the pleasure of greeting the Sorors of Gamma Omega — Sister-to-Sister.

And so, Soror Marianne "Passed on the Torch" to Soror Johnna M. Richmond in 2004 and "the Spirit of AKA" continued through ESSENCE of Ivy and Pearls 2004-2005. Soror Johnna M. Richmond began her legacy as the 3rd Basileus of Phi Kappa Omega Chapter. The 2004-2005 administration and elected officers in addition to Basileus Richmond Adrienne Crutcher, was Vice-President; Carole Crutcher, was 2004 Secretary with Soror Eloise Cheers as Secretary in 2005; Cassaundra Rouse, Treasurer; Gayle Thompson, Assistant Secretary; Raquel Betton, Assistant Treasurer; and Cornelia Liggans, Sargent-at-Arms. Bettye Gardner continued as our Chaplain, Cerrelda M. Jones is the *Ivy Leaf* Reporter and Soror Denise Gresham-Knox was the 2004 Membership Chairman, with Jacqueline E. Davis as the 2005 Membership Chairman. We continue the invitation to reactivation or to transfer membership into Phi Kappa Omega to which Sorors LaTosha Mays and Monique Nunnes answered in 2004-5, and we closely observe for those who project the potential to affirm the legacy of Alpha Kappa Alpha Sorority, Incorporated and all that she stands for.

We are proud that the legacy of Phi Kappa Omega continues as we grow in service. During the 2004 year we reached out through the following activities:

HEALTH TARGET: Phi Kappa Omega participated in walk-a-thon activities, supporting Sickle Cell Anemia, Hunger /Food Depositories, United Negro College Fund, the Paul Revere School Health Fair and the Breast Cancer Walk.

THE BLACK FAMILY: Sorors of Phi Kappa Omega collected and donated (48) coats to the Mt. Pisgah Baptist Church and to Sixth Grace Presbyterian Church through a collaborative activity with the Teens Involved in Christian Knowledge (T.I.C.K.) youth group of the church.

A.K.A.S.T.L. (Acquiring Knowledge and Skills to Lead) — LEADERSHIP DEVELOPMENT: Phi Kappa Omega attended the 70th Central Regional Conference in Milwaukee, Wisconsin, the 61st Boule in Nashville Tennessee and the Area Retreat in Itasca, Illinois. We were also hostess chapter for Joint Founders' Day in 2005. In addition to the above activities, the following Sorors received awards at the 70th Central Region Conference: Soror Johnna Richmond runner up for Soror through the Years, Soror Marianne C. Stallworth runner up for Basileus of the Year, and winner of the Silver Star was Soror Doris Powell. Soror Denise Gresham Knox was Soror of the Year. How proud we are of them!

SISTER-TO-SISTER — Local Chapter Promotions: Phi Kappa Omega Sorors participated in the Martin Luther King Day On by serving hot meals to the community, Joint Founders Day Observance, AKA Buckle UP Day, partnering with other AKA chapters, AKA Coat Day, Volunteer Day and the Chicago PanHellenic Council.

In 2005, under the leadership of Soror Johnna Richmond, 38 new initiates joined the ranks of Phi Kappa Omega Chapter. How proud we were to initiate these beautiful Sorors.

The torch was passed to Soror Raquel Betton who became the fourth Basileus of Phi Kappa Omega for the years 2006 and 2007. Soror Betton led the chapter in forging collaboration with other AKA chapters in Tax Preparation for the economically disadvantaged. Phi Kappa Omega also joined forces with the Chicago Fire Department's African American Fireman's League. This organization introduced our chapter's sisterhood to the First Responders Brotherhood of Kenwood High School. Through this partnership, Phi Kappa Omega Chapter began an annual service to the community by serving lunch to the Bud Billiken Parade participants and spectators. In addition, Phi Kappa Omega initiated the Expo and Back to School Fair with Sixth Grace Presbyterian Church in Chicago which continues today.

Phi Kappa Omega continued her fundraisers in October of 2006 by presenting "Emerald City, Dreams Do Come True" our dinner to benefit the Lupus Foundation and to raise money for our Phi Kappa Omega Scholarship Fund. The event was a resounding success and achieved our goal of awarding both the Lupus Foundation and provided scholarships to eligible recipients.

Our Phi Kappa Omega Centennial Basileus was Soror Sonji G. Barnes, Ph. D. who assumed office as her fifth President. She exalted her administration in her newsletter "The Heart of the Matter." We, as members of Phi Kappa Omega, were given the charge to "evolve," inciting us to "expand, undergo gradual change, develop, and to achieve." We were further encouraged to "open our hearts to our sisterhood and have a positive outlook, a fresh perspective and the spirit of excellence."

On January 14, 2008, Soror Sonji and Soror Marianne joined Alpha Kappa Alpha Sorority, Inc. Sorors worldwide to celebrate 100 years of service to all mankind and to celebrate our Founders on the campus of Howard University. In addition to PKO Sorors attending the 74th Central Regional Conference, Phi Kappa Omega Chapter President, Vice President, and many of her officers and members attended the 100th Centennial year celebration of Alpha Kappa Alpha Sorority, Inc. also in Washington, D.C.

Our pride was heightened in 2009 because Phi Kappa Omega Chapter was one of the prime hostess chapters of the 75th Central Regional Conference. Soror Johnna Richmond of Phi Kappa

Omega Chapter served as co-chairman with Soror Bakehia Madison of Phi Epsilon Omega. Phi Kappa Omega Chapter chaired the Registration, the Public Meeting, and Transportation Committees.

Soror Sonji then passed the torch to Soror Marianne C. Stallworth, Ph.D. It was with great pride that Soror Marianne C. Bentley-Stallworth, PhD., a charter member, became the 6th Basileus of Phi Kappa Omega Chapter. This was her second administrative term for the chapter and she was ecstatic that the 2010 — 2011 years represented the 10th year Anniversary of the chapter, the first chapter chartered in the new millennium. The year 2011 also marked her second time as the Presiding Basileus of the Chicagoland Basilei Council.

The year 2010 was called our Decade of Diligence exemplifying sisterhood and service. We celebrated first by having our History Committee, chaired by Soror Maricha Stallworth Matthews, unveil and display our historical artifacts on Saturday, January 9, 2010 through June 2010 at the Evergreen Park Library. A reception was held and included the history display and a presentation from Phi Kappa Omega to Mr. Jerry Bosch, Village Trustee and Historical Commissioner. The presentation included a proclamation to the village that PKO would continue to provide support through community service to all mankind within the Village of Evergreen Park. Chapter members were pleased that Soror Pamela Bates Porch, our 27th Regional Director joined us for the celebration and presentation.

PKO continually celebrated service and sisterhood throughout the year. Service was provided through fundraising activities that would benefit the community. PKO hosted a bowling event to raise funds for the Haitian Relief Fund effort of Alpha Kappa Alpha Sorority, Inc. Phi Kappa Omega Chapter participated in the National Day of Service by partnering with other AKA chapters, fraternities, organizations and the Nuns of Fraternite of Notre Dame to prepare and serve food for the homeless and needy in the surrounding community. Chapter members also cleaned and organized inventory for the Bottomless Closet in order to provide homeless women with career services and career clothing. Along with other AKA chapters, Phi Kappa Omega assisted low income individuals and families with income tax preparation. Phi Kappa Omega Chapter made connections, led by Soror LaRita Wright, with other Greek letter organizations to attend Black History Programs, participated in a roundtable discussion hosted by Mr. Tavis Smiley and socialized in solidarity with other Divine Nine sororities and fraternities. In addition PKO partnered with the Hispanic Law enforcement Association to assist in raising funds for scholarships.

The participation of the chapter in the Glass Slipper Project, supplying prom dresses and accessories to young women brought joy to Sorors of PKO. And our Dream Girls Workshop implemented with middle school girls at Langston Hughes Elementary School initiated the Emerging Young Leaders target of Soror Carolyn House's administration. In 2010, the young ladies participated in a self-esteem and sex education forum, an etiquette forum, and a soap box question and answer session. As Emerging Young Leaders (EYL), in addition to many meetings and workshops, Basileus Stallworth along with the Chicagoland Basilei Council initiated and EYL Summit inviting all Chicago and Metropolitan chapters of Alpha Kappa Alpha Sorority, Incorporated to participate. Thirteen chapters heard the call and brought their teen girls to the Summit August 2011 event held at Langston Hughes Elementary School. Along with all of these service activities, PKO participates annually in the Mothers' Day Cancer Walk, the Chicagoland Food Depository Hunger Walk to combat hunger, and partner with the African American Firefighters and Paramedic League of the Chicago Fire Department to serve food to the community who attend the Bud Billiken Picnic and Parade.

Enhancing the State of the People has been one of the signature programs for Phi Kappa Omega. This partnership has been an annual event to focus the community on outstanding issues important to both adults and children. Our forum in 2010 was funding college attendance for high school grades. In 2011 we focused on Bullying to raise the conscientiousness of adults and children and to brainstorm some solutions and strategies to combat this behavior.

Phi Kappa Omega Chapter hosted its signature fundraiser "AKAsino," a mask ball to raise scholarship funds. This very creative fundraiser boasted formal and after-five attire and engaged attendees in dancing, casino games, and a silent auction. This gala is a signature activity for Phi Kappa Omega and will continue every few years.

PKO's 2010 initiates planned and organized a service project that supported the Chapter's desire for service. Phi Kappa Omega Chapter partnered with the Olive Branch Mission and other volunteers to clean their kitchen in preparation for feeding the hungry and homeless.

Sisterly relations activities and chapter expansion were marked by the reactivation of Sorors and the initiation of six new members into our Alpha Kappa Alpha Sorority, Incorporated sisterhood on November 7, 2010. In 2011, the newly initiated Sorors along with all Sorors of Phi Kappa Omega celebrated our Sorority's founding by attending the Chicagoland Joint Founders' Day held at the Hyatt Regency on Wacker in Chicago.

In December, 2011, Phi kappa Omega Chapter of Alpha kappa Alpha sorority, Incorporated installed its seventh Basileus, Soror Essie Mason-Purnell, to lead the chapter during 2013 and 2014. The theme for her administration was: COMMUNICATION—COLLABORATION—ACCOUNTABILITY.

The chapter aggressively embraced the tenants of the 2010-2014 Program Initiatives of the sorority and executed the following:

EMERGING YOUNG LEADERS

Under the leadership of Soror Theresa Bates, EYL Chairman, the chapter continued its partnership with the Langston Hughes Elementary School, where Principal, Soror Anita Muse, is also a member of Phi Kappa Omega Chapter. Sorors provided mentoring opportunities and workshops on personal development for young girls in grades six through eight. The girls also participated in annual EYL summits, a collaborative effort with girls from thirteen other Graduate Chapters in the Chicagoland area. During the 2013 EYL Summit, which was chaired by Basileus Mason-Purnell, the workshops focused on Social Media, Public speaking, Conflict Management, Body Image. and Fashion Etiquette. In 2013, Phi kappa Omega also hosted a graduation luncheon for graduating eighth grade students and their mothers at the South Shore Cultural Center

ECONOMIC SECURITY

Soror LeNell Watson (2012) organized a shopping extravaganza and Soror Phylis Hammond (2013) organized and implemented a yard sale in the parking lot of Jimmy Shoul's, a small business entrepreneur, to raise money for scholarships and highlight the business' presence in the community. Sorors also attended workshops on affordable home ownership and financial literacy

GLOBAL POVERTY

Empowered to be innovative in our approach to feeding the hungry and stamping out poverty, Soror Marva Franklin, Committee Chairman, creatively embraced this initiative with emphasis on financially supporting our International partner, the Heifer Foundation. A Heifer's costume was purchased in 2012 and was worn by Basileus Mason-Purnell at the June General Chapter meeting to celebrate the achievement of the financial commitment to this organization. In 2013, in partnership with the chapter's EYL program, funds were raised by the EYL participants and the Heifer costume was worn by principal and Soror, Anita Muse, to encourage the young ladies to save funds and to help feed the hungry. The Global Poverty Committee also packed food for the Greater Chicago Food Depository and spearheaded a food drive, collecting nonperishable foods to help feed those in need.

HEALTH

The chapter initiated its signature health initiative, "Paint the Lakefront Pink" to encourage healthy hearts. Under the leadership of Committee Chairman, Soror Cutina Anderson, the popularity of this weekly walk along Lake Michigan, attired in the signature pink color of Alpha Kappa Alpha Sorority, Incorporated, quickly drew the attention of other AKA chapters, family members, friends, and other individuals who wished to join an organized, energetic group of AKAs for exercise in an effort to eradicate heart disease and build healthy bodies.

This committee reached out to support the larger community through its participation in the Evergreen Park, Illinois Mother's Day Walk for Breast Cancer survivors. Phi Kappa Omega members also participated in "pin-a-Sister" ceremonies, where Sorors pinned each other with pink ribbons as a reminder to take care of ourselves and support breast cancer survivors and walked with the Chicagoland Food Depository to raise funds for the hungry.

SOCIAL JUSTICE AND HUMAN RIGHTS

Committee Chairmen LaRita Wright, (2012) led the chapter in participating in activities that directly impacted the community:

- A.K.A. C.A.R.E.S. Voter Registration — Sorors were trained and certified as Deputy Registrars and registered constituents to vote in upcoming elections
- Fraternite De Notre Dame — In partnership with Lambda Alpha Omega, Phi Kappa Omega prepared and served lunch to community residents as part of the organization's effort to feed the community. The chapter also presented the organization with a set of knives to help with the preparation of meals
- AKA Day at the Capitol — In an effort to strengthen the ties and increase our stability in the communities we serve, Sorors visited the State Capitol in Springfield, Illinois, attended legislative sessions and networked with elected officials to influence legislature consistent with the program initiatives of Alpha kappa Alpha Sorority, Incorporated.
- Angel Tree — Phi Kappa Omega Sorors purchased gifts and hosted Christmas parties for children of incarcerated parents

COMMUNITY ACTIVITIES

In an effort to strengthen the ties and increase our stability in the community, the chapter continued to reach out through the efforts of the Connections committee, under the leadership of Soror Barbara Stewart in 2013, assisted by Soror LaRita Wright, Phi kappa Omega participated in AKA at the Capitol, Martin Luther King Day of Service, trained Sorors as Deputy Registrars and managed the annual Coat Drive and The Angel Tree initiative to provide gifts to children of an incarcerated parent.

Other significant activities during Basileus Mason-Purnell's administration included:

- Participation in a collaborative effort with the First Responders to celebrate Bud Billiken Day parade encourages children to excel in school.
- Joint Founders Day Celebration — Phi Kappa Omega Sorors participated in celebrating the Founders of Alpha Kappa Alpha Sorority, Incorporated in collaboration with other Chicago Area Graduate and Undergraduate chapters.
- Ivies Beyond the Wall — In 2012, Soror Mason- Purnell facilitated the Ivy Beyond the wall ceremony for three of the chapter's members… Sorors Bettye Ann Gardner, Judge Odas Nicholson, and Deborah Elliott.
- Leadership training for all chapter members was conducted by International Committee Chairmen; — Soror Joyce Henderson — Chapter Operations; Soror Bernice Ripley — Leadership; and Soror Gayle Scott Miles — Chapter Financial Operations. 90% of Phi Kappa Omega Sorors were certified in chapter financial management
- Sorors attended the 65th Boule held in San Francisco, California; Leadership in Montreal, Canada; Central Regional Conferences in Madison, Wisconsin and Indianapolis, Indiana and Area Retreats in Bolingbrook, Illinois and Minneapolis Minnesota
- The creation of a Manual of Standard Procedures as a simple day-to-day guide to insure consistency in Chapter operations implementation
- The first off site chapter Retreat was planned and executed flawlessly by Standards Chairman, Soror

Maricha Matthews. The highlight of the retreat was a workshop on "implementing effective programming" presented by Regional Representative to the International Programming Committee, Soror JaNiece Bell
- Launched the signature "AKA at the MOVIES" Fundraiser to fund scholarships. Phi Kappa Omega was able to award scholarships in areas of technology, scholarship, books, and community, due to the diligent effort of the fundraising committee, chaired by Sorors Maricha Matthews and Michelle McClendon
- Sisterly Relations activities were an integral part of Phi Kappa Omega's ongoing programs. Hodegos and Social Chairman, Soror LaTonya Fairley in collaboration with Membership Chairman, Soror Maricha Matthews, planned and executes programs/events to not only keep current financial Soror connected but also to reach out to inactive and non-financial Sorors. This activity included celebration of anniversaries, birthdays, and special events, messages of sympathy and support, as well as events to bring together Sorors in sisterly activities began the process to establish a Foundation. The chapter voted to establish a Foundation as a way to raise monies to fund scholarships and chapter programs.

In addition to her responsibilities as Chapter Basileus, Soror Mason-Purnell also served as Anti-Basileus/Program Chairman for the Chicagoland Basilei Council, a consortium of graduate chapter presidents with the mission to share practical and consistent policies and best practices in accordance with International policies and procedures.

As we enter into a new administration in 2014, Phi kappa Omega remains strong in its commitment to providing service to all mankind. Phi Kappa Omega continues to stand tall as we highlight our commitment to Alpha Kappa Alpha's sisterhood and provide service throughout the community.

Phi Kappa Omega Chapter Basilei

Doris B. Kyle-Powell	2000 – 2001
Marianne C. Bentley-Stallworth	2002 – 2003
Johnna M. Anderson-Richmond	2004 – 2005
Raquel Betton	2006 – 2007
Sonji G. Barnes, Ph.D.	2008 – 2009
Marianne C. Bentley-Stallworth, Ph.D.	2010 – 2011
Essie Mason Purnell, MBA	2012 – 2013

PART V: THE NEW CENTURY

Sigma Gamma Chapter

LAKE FOREST COLLEGE
LAKE FOREST, ILLINOIS
APRIL 9, 2000

Charter Members: Jennifer Beal, Brandi Brice, Amani Brown, Megan Brown, Catherine Calloway, Aiyana Cox, Jane Hamilton, Christine Lipscomb, Giang Thu Autumn Nguyen, Olusholo Olabode-Dada, Lorraine Osborne, Danielle Summerville and Kamalisha White.

CHARTER MEMBERS

AMANI BROWN
MEGAN BROWN
JENNIFER BEAL
BRANDI BRICE
CATHERINE CALLOWAY
AIYANA COX*

JANE HAMILTON
CHRISTINE LIPSCOMB
GIANG THU AUTUMN NGUYEN
OLUSHOLO OLABODE-DADA
LORRAINE OSBORNE
DANIELLE SUMMERVILLE
KAMALISHA WHITE

Ivy Beyond the Wall

Establishing a chapter of Alpha Kappa Alpha Sorority on the campus of Lake Forest College was the dream of a group of young women who organized an interest group in 1999 under the name: Women for Social Change. In 1999 these young women contacted Central Regional Director, Nadine C. Bonds and inquired about the process of chartering a chapter.

This group worked with the chartering graduate advisor, Soror Linda Baskin-Wilson to complete the chartering requirements and on April 9, 2000 the dream became a reality. Thirteen young collegians were initiated at the Lilly Reid Holt Chapel and the chapter was chartered at the 66th Central Regional Conference. Soror Norma Solomon-White was the Supreme Basileus.

Sigma Gamma Chapter is the first of the Divine Nine to be a part of campus life at the College. Lambda Nu Omega Chapter is the advising chapter for Sigma Gamma.

Sigma Gamma has been an active member of the Pan Hellenic Council at Lake Forest College. The Chapter has sponsored a:

NEIGHBORHOOD FOOD DRIVE — Annually the chapter collected food in the Lake Forest neighborhood that was boxed and donated to the Lake County Food Pantry.

DATE AUCTION — Members of Sigma Gamma raised money for service projects by participating in the date auction. This event was sponsored by the college's Pan Hellenic council.

Sigma Gamma Chapter Basilei

Danielle Summerville	2000	Olayinka Owolabi	2004 – 2005
Kamalisha White	2000 – 2001	Dalavia Edmon	2005 – 2006
Catherine Calloway	2001 – 2002	Chelsea Wade	2006 – 2007
Jennifer Beal	2002 – 2003	Briana Smith	2007 – 2008
DeAnne Duncan	2003 – 2004	Cyndia Javier	2008 – 2009

Sigma Eta Chapter

Northern Kentucky University
Highland Heights, Kentucky
April 22, 2001

Charter Members

M. MARIE BAILEY	CINDY FOLSON
EBONY BROOKS	EMEICKA GRANTHAM
ALICIA CARLISLE	JOI JOHNSON
ANGEL CHICHESTER	DENISE PENN
CHERYL CRUTCHFIELD	DANIELLE PLEASANT
AMANDA DAVIS	LISA SAMUEL-HILL

Sigma Eta Chapter was chartered at the 67th Central Regional Conference.

PLEDGED TO REMEMBER: THE HISTORY OF CENTRAL REGION

Chi Alpha Omega Chapter

SCHAUMBURG, ILLINOIS
APRIL 14, 2002

Left to Right, Seated: Sheila T. Reed, Joyce A. Sinclair, Gloria Covington, Tiffany J. Morgan, Jamel Ivory Penn, Renee McMullen. Standing: Renita M. Pettigrew, Jenise Emehel, Cheryl James, Phyllis Berry, Norma Sanders, Carolyn Wilson, Kim-Collier-Jefferson, Carolyn Fitzpatrick, Bertha Covington, Tonya Branch, Chandra Wiggs.

CHARTER MEMBERS

PHYLLIS BERRY	RENEE MCMULLEN
TONYA BRANCH	TIFFANY J. MORGAN
KIM COLLIER-JEFFERSON	JAMEL IVORY PENN
BETHEA COVINGTON	RENITA M. PETTIGREW
GLORIA COVINGTON	SHEILA T. REED
JENISE EMEHEL	NORMA L. SANDERS
CAROLYN FITZPATRICK	JOYCE A. SINCLAIR
CHERYL JAMES	CHANDRA WIGGS
	CAROLYN L. WILSON

In February 2001, Sorors Gloria Covington, Yolander Dorsey, Jamel Ivory Penn and Sheila Reed met at the home of Soror Carol Dewberry in Hoffman Estates, IL to discuss the vision for a northwest suburban chapter of Alpha Kappa Alpha Sorority, Inc. The sorors agreed that the proximity of the Evanston and west suburban chapters were not conducive to active participation for sorors in the northwest suburbs.

The sorors began to plan the strategy for moving forward with the vision and agreed to meet again in a few weeks. Following the initial meeting, they began to contact sorors they knew in the area and used the Alpha Kappa Alpha Directory to locate others in the northwest suburbs that they did not know. The next meeting was held at the Barrington Library where the sorors developed their strategy further and scheduled regular monthly meeting times. They continued to meet regularly over the spring and summer months. Slowly, the sorors began to gain additional support for their vision. They selected the Northwest AKAs as the name of the group. The following sorors were elected as officers: President, Jamel Ivory Penn, Vice President, Gloria Covington, Secretary, Sheila Reed and Treasurer, Renee M. McMullen.

Soror Jamel Ivory Penn contacted Soror Nadine C. Bonds, the Central Regional Director, to discuss the requirements for establishing a chapter and the group's progress. Soror Nadine provided a thorough explanation of the requirements and agreed to meet with the Northwest AKAs during the Fall Cluster Meeting in Tinley Park, IL. The Northwest AKAs met with Soror Nadine on Friday, September 7, 2001 and the tasks that lay ahead were clearly defined. Although Soror Nadine indicated that the group had up to 2 years to complete the process of fulfilling the requirements for chartering, they were motivated to fulfill the requirements in time for consideration prior to the 68th Central Regional Conference which was to be held in Chicago, IL.

In accordance with the requirements for chartering, the Northwest AKAs began to plan and implement community service projects to meet the target programs in Arts, Black Family, Economics, Education and Health. Soror Nadine suggested Project Shoe Box as a very worthwhile project that would benefit students in Africa. The Northwest AKAs were immediately interested and excited about helping these students. Sorors were instructed to bring a shoebox filled with school supplies and personal hygiene products to the September, 2001 meeting. Some of the products were donated. However the majority were purchased by sorors.

Following the meeting, the sorors began filling shoeboxes with all types of supplies. They completed this project sending more that a dozen stuffed shoeboxes filled with pencils, pens, erasers, rulers, notebooks, soap, hair products and other toiletries to Project Shoebox in Philadelphia, PA. The sorors were overjoyed with the success of this program and the assistance provided some very deserving students.

The Northwest AKAs supported the First Annual Community-Unity Fest in the Village of Cabrini on September 29 — 30, 2001. The Arts and Music Festival was sponsored by Cabrini Green Youth and Family Services, Chicago Housing Authority and the Mayor's Office of Special Events. Prior to the festival, a soror participated in the planning meetings and also helped coordinate media communications to publicize the fest. The fest was a catalyst to bring together old and new residents for a celebration with food, music and fun. The Northwest AKAs were hands on volunteers during the 2-day event by helping with booth set-ups and as hostesses for the children's adventure play area.

On October 20, 2001, the Northwest AKAs volunteered at the 5th Annual Susan G. Komen Breast Cancer Foundation Race for the Cure in Chicago. The mission of this organization is to eradicate breast cancer as a life-threatening disease by advancing research, education, screening and treatment. The race was well attended by members of the Northwest AKAs. Their volunteer efforts helped to ensure that race participants received registration materials and directional assistance. In addition, one of the Northwest AKAs who is a breast cancer survivor walked the course. This event included 8,500 participants, 400 breast cancer survivors and raised $400,000. These funds were earmarked for national research and local breast cancer initiatives.

In support of the Arts target, the Northwest AKAs and guests enjoyed a night out at the theater for the Saturday November 17th, 2001 performance of "The Other Cinderella." This was a long running comedy mainstay in the Chicagoland area. The "Cinderella" parody was written and produced by Ms. Jackie Taylor, an African American playwright and founder of the Black Ensemble Theater.

On December 15, 2001, the Northwest AKAs partnered with the DuPage County Humanitarian Service Project organization to help provide a joyful and more meaningful holiday experience for DuPage County needy families. Sorors donated their time to help the Humanitarian Service Project group wrap Christmas gifts and prepare boxes of food that were later distributed to about 90 needy families in the DuPage County area. The Health Committee partnered with the Black Family Committee in this initiative and donated first aid kits to the needy families to help with basic health care needs.

The Northwest AKAs decided to make a difference in the lives of the seniors at the Alden Poplar Creek Rehabilitation Health Care Center in Hoffman Estates, IL during the Christmas holiday season. Sorors volunteered at the annual holiday brunch on Sunday, December 16, 2001 by serving food, carrying trays, pushing wheelchairs and sharing warm conversations. The residents were very grateful for the kind expressions extended to them.

The Northwest AKAs co-sponsored a Financial Planning and Scholarship Workshop with the Youth Ministry of Christian Tabernacle Church on December 29, 2001. The attendees included high school juniors, seniors and college students. Sorors presented information to instruct the students in establishing and maintaining good credit, saving and investing money while in high school and college and obtaining financial aid for continuing education.

By February, 2002, the Northwest AKAs had gained sufficient numbers and completed several community service projects. They eagerly anticipated the upcoming Central Regional Conference in Chicago.

Chi Alpha Omega chapter was chartered with seventeen sorors on April 14, 2002 by Soror Nadine C. Bonds, Central Regional Director. The officers elected during the first sorority meeting were: Basileus: Jamel Ivory Penn, Anti-Basileus: Gloria Covington, Grammateus: Sheila Reed, Pecunious Grammateus: Tonya Branch, Epistoleus: Chandra Wiggs, Tamiochous: Renee McMullen, Parliamentarian: Renita Pettigrew; and *Ivy Leaf* Reporter: Jenise Emehel. In addition, the following officers were appointed by the Basileus: Hodegos: Carolyn Wilson, Philacter: Joyce Sinclair, and Historian: Kim Collier-Jefferson. Tiffany J. Morgan was appointed Membership Chair.

THE FIRST 10 YEARS

Since the chapter's chartering in 2002, Chi Alpha Omega has had a baseline of 30 members. Despite its small size, Chi Alpha Omega has consistently maintained a strong presence in the Northwest suburbs of Chicago, including Villages of Arlington Heights, Barrington, Elgin, Hoffman Estates, Palatine and Schaumburg. Chapter meetings are held on the second Saturday of each month and the meeting location has primarily been at local libraries until a decision was made to move the meeting location to support a non-traditional entrepreneur. For two years meetings were held at a soulfood restaurant in Streamwood, Illinois. The chapter was provided a private area to conduct the business meetings followed by an opportunity to fellowship and have lunch while supporting a business owned by an African American female.

COMMUNITY PROGRAMS

Since 2002, Chi Alpha Omega has been a regular participant and supporter of a day of service event honoring Martin Luther King, Jr. The Martin Luther King Day of Service, January 20, 2003, culminated a three-day King celebration in which Chi Alpha Omega partnered with Destiny Church in Hoffman Estates, IL, the village of Hoffman Estates and the Park District. The Corporation for National & Community Service provided a $7,500 grant. The day began with a community breakfast attended by 300 young people and adults including state and local public officials. Civil rights activist Dr. Barbara Sizemore, professor emeritus at DePaul University, gave the keynote address for the breakfast. Following the breakfast, sorors and hundreds of northwest suburban residents locked arms and sang songs while walking down Poplar Creek Drive in a march to commemorate Dr. King. After the breakfast and march, 60 young people including students from Palatine-Schaumburg High School District 211, boarded buses to participate in service projects. Half of the youths spent three hours at Women In Need Growing Stronger (WINGS), a resale shop in Palatine where they sorted and arranged clothing and other items. The shop benefits women and children in need. The remaining youth were bused to Destiny Church to organize its food pantry and clothing closet. Afterwards, the youth visited Friendship Village in Schaumburg where they interacted with seniors by completing puzzles and word games highlighting African American history.

On Saturday, January 19th, 250 people attended the Dr. King service. Chi Alpha Omega received recognition in the Daily Herald and received an award for community service during the King Day Service at Destiny Church.

In subsequent years, Chi Alpha Omega has continued to work with the Village of Hoffman Estates in support of the Martin Luther King, Jr Commemorative Breakfast. Sorors perform many roles , including voter registration, registering guests, serving as greeters and attending to the Village's VIPs and distinguished guests.

SCHOLARSHIP PROGRAM

Chi Alpha Omega's Scholarship Program has served as the chapter's most consistent and impactful community project. The chapter held their first annual Ivy Scholarship Gala in April 2003 which produced $5,000 in scholarships for deserving college-bound students. Since 2003, the chapter has awarded over $40,000 in scholarships to graduating high school students in the Northwest suburbs. The scholarship is primarily based on academic achievement, extra-curricular activities, and personal essay. Each year scholarships are awarded to outstanding college bound students.

NON-TRADITIONAL ENTREPRENEUR

The chapter has supported the efforts of Powerhouse Productions for many years. Lead by Non Traditional Entrepreneur (NTE) Valerie Profit, Powerhouse Productions sponsors an annual Black History Theatre event during February at the Schaumburg Prairie Arts Centre showcasing local talent, while providing a history lesson thru entertainment, such as "The Black Wall Street" and "Moments in Time." This has been a meaningful partnership for Chi Alpha Omega as the chapter has provided recurring support of Powerhouse Productions, as well as helping to showcase other emerging NTEs. In addition to promoting the event and selling tickets, the chapter hosted the event receptions, worked the ticket booth and served as hostesses and ushers for the plays. Some other NTE events sponsored by Chi Alpha Omega include:

- Hosting a book signing event for two African American authors including one book by a Chi Alpha Omega member.
- A Non-Traditional Entrepreneur Symposium (2007)
- Post meeting lunches at a local soulfood restaurant (2009 -2010)
- Fundraising event at African American owned Wine Styles in Schaumburg (2010)

YOUTH ENRICHMENT PROGRAMS

Working with area youth has been one of the cornerstones of Chi Alpha Omega chapter's community involvement. Over the years the program name has changed from AKA Teen to Ivy League, and now to Emerging Young Leaders. However, the commitment to provide youth with workshops and sessions that provide valuable life, leadership, educational and study skills has remained constant. During the chapter's first years, sorors tutored and mentored youth at the Roselle Library. The program expanded to include a variety of enrichment sessions on a monthly basis. Some of the workshops offered included:

- College Bound Workshop
- Career Exploration & Career Fair
- Teen Sexuality Workshop
- Leadership Training
- Finance & Fiscal Fitness
- Stock Market Game
- 100 Black Men College Fair
- Effective Study Skills
- Ivy League Recognition & Scholarship Dinner
- Black History Workshop
- Health & Fitness Workshop
- Suzlon Wind Energy Tour
- Effectively Dealing with Conflict
- Anti-Bullying Workshop

HEALTH PROGRAMS

Chi Alpha Omega has contributed to many health initiatives. In 2003, sorors along with family and friends participated in the Multiple Sclerosis (MS) Walk. The chapter has supported the American Cancer Society for many years by serving as registrars and participating in the Komen Race for the

Cure Cancer Walk. Sorors understand the importance of supporting these organizations especially when these diseases impact the lives of those in our chapter.

As diabetes is a serious health concern in the African American community, the chapter has partnered with the American Diabetes Association for several years at the Diabetes Expo assisting with set-up, distributing informational booklets, as well as assisting with healthy lifestyles cooking demostrations and product give-a-ways. In recognizing the importance of our families and our health, Chi Alpha Omega supported the Color of AIDS Campaign and Black HIV Awareness Day in 2010. Soror Carol Ash received an Emmy nomination for the series of special reports she produced for NBC-5. The series highlighted how African American and Latino communities are disproportionately affected by HIV/AIDS.

Chapter Highlights

2002 – 2004 — JAMEL IVORY PENN, BASILEUS

- In 2004, Gloria Covington was not only voted as Soror of the Year by the chapter but was also selected as Central Region Soror of the Year. She also received recognition by the state as Teacher of the Year for District 15.
- A Black History display was created and showcased at both the Palatine Library and Village of Hoffman Estates including black inventors, national leaders and pioneers, as well as highlighting Alpha Kappa Alpha Sorority.

2005 – 2006 — GLORIA COVINGTON, BASILEUS

- Partnered with the Diabetes Association for the Diabetes Expo. The chapter received an award for having the most soror volunteers' workng the event.
- The chapter spearheaded the Car Seat –Saves Lives program in conjunction with the Chicago Basilei Council by donating $1,400 to John H. Stroger Hospital in Chicago. These funds provided infant car seats to needy families.

2007 – 2008 — TONY BRANCH, BASILEUS

- Black Family Picnic & Health Fair featured health and traditional foods, as well as provided kits that included information on health issues that impact the African American community.
- AKAnomics Fair consisted of two sessions: A Financial Planning workshop and a discussion panel on Home-buying.

2009 – 2010 — RENITA PETTIGREW, BASILEUS

- The chapter participated in multifaceted Black History Celebration that covered several of Alpha Kappa Alpha Platforms including: 1) the screening of Freedom's Song; 2) Contributed dresses and accessories to the Perfect Prom Project.
- In 2010, past chapter Basileus, Tony Branch was selected as the recipient of Powerhouse Productions Leadership Award.

2011 – 2012 — RENEE MCMULLEN, BASILEUS

- In June 2011, with funds in excess of $20K Chi Alpha Omega Chapter became the first chapter in Central Region to achieve the fully capitalized Educational Advancement Foundation Endowment.
- Chi Alpha Omega celebrated 10 years of sisterhood and service with Taste the World Soiree in September 2012.
- In October 2013 the chapter established the Chi Alpha Omega Educational Advancement Foundation Fellowship. The purpose of this Fellowship is to grant awards to scholars and support programs that provide exceptional service within our community.

Under the current leadership of Basileus Diana Sweeny, Chi Alpha Omega is positioned to continue the legacy of "service to all mankind" as the chapter continues to implement programs to benefit the Northwest suburbs of Chicago.

CHI ALPHA OMEGA CHAPTER BASILEI

Jamel Ivory Penn	2002 – 2004
Gloria Covington	2005-2006
Tony Branch	2007 – 2008
Renita Pettigrew	2009- 2010
Renee Edwards McMullen, Ed.D.	2011- 2012
Cynthia Diana Sweeny	2013 -Present

Dorothy Wilson Buckhanan

26th Central Regional Director
July 2002 – July 2006

Soror Dorothy Wilson Buckhanan was elected 26th Central Regional Director at the 68th Central Regional Conference in Chicago, Illinois and installed at the 60th Boule in Orlando, Florida. Soror Buckhanan directed the eight-state Central Region in programming activities focused on the national theme "Spirit of Alpha Kappa Alpha." The theme of her tenure centered on Journey Through Central Region.

Soror Buckhanan was initiated into Psi Chapter at Benedict College in Columbia, South Carolina. She served as Basileus of her seventy-member undergraduate chapter and introduced innovative programming in the areas of education and economics. She was named "Soror of the Year" and the "Most Outstanding Undergraduate in the South Atlantic Region," for her efforts.

Soror Buckhanan received her undergraduate degree in Business Administration and Economics from Benedict College. She received a Masters' of Business Administration degree in Marketing from Clark Atlanta University at the age of twenty-two and went on to blaze a trail, as one of the youngest African American female executives at the Xerox Corporation and S.C. Johnson Wax.

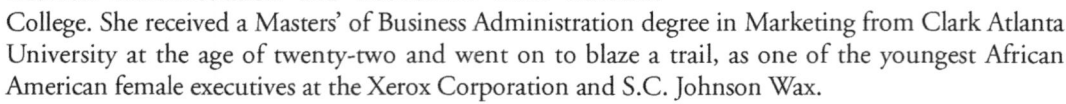

Soror Buckhanan affiliated with Epsilon Kappa Omega Chapter in Milwaukee, Wisconsin where she served in several major offices, including Basileus. She went on to serve as charter Basileus of a second award-winning Milwaukee based graduate chapter—Upsilon Mu Omega, for two terms.

Program implementation, membership retention and increased sisterly relations were the hallmarks of the Buckhanan regional administration (2002-2006). From the beginning of her tenure, Soror Buckhanan used her extensive leadership and marketing skills, to help refine the region's image as the Competent, Confident and Classy Central Region. All aspects of the region's internal and external communications, including its newsletter — the Ivy Atlas — to its website, reflected this hard working, elegant image.

Some of the most significant accomplishments during Soror Buckhanan's tenure included:

National recognition of Central Region for outstanding programs (1st and 2nd Place National Ivy Reading AKAdemy and Merrill Lynch Financial Literacy Winners) for two consecutive years.

National recognition of Central Region for its support of the Educational Advancement Foundation (EAF). Central was the first chapter in the new millennium to achieve 100% chapter participation status. The region also received recognition for raising the greatest amount of funds in the Medium Size region category. Finally, the Dorothy W. Buckhanan endowment for students in businesses established at the beginning of her tenure was fully capitalized in record time. Central region also led the way in capitalizing the Endowment Fund for Soror Linda M. White, 26th Supreme Basileus.

- National recognition as one of the two regions with all states sponsoring AKA Day at the State Capitol celebrations. Central maintained this status all four years of Soror Buckhanan's tenure.
- National recognition for registering a record number of new voters during the 2004 presidential election season.

- National recognition for collecting and donating over 10,000 books to children in grades K-3 as part of book collection drives at the Milwaukee Regional Conference and Nashville Boule.
- National recognition for donating $10,000 to the sorority's national disaster relief efforts.

Soror Buckhanan also encouraged membership growth by chartering five graduate chapters: Chi Xi Omega — Decatur, IL; Chi Sigma Omega — Bolingbrook, IL; Chi Phi Omega — Lafayette, IN; Chi Chi Omega — Indianapolis, IN; Chi Omega Omega — Chicago, IL (the largest graduate chapter chartered in sorority history with 101 members)

During her term in office, Soror Buckhanan set a new standard for productive, creative, well-attended and inclusive, regional conferences. She presided very efficiently at the 69th, 70th, 71st and 72nd meetings. A number of innovations were initiated, including the Community Outreach Project, Regional Gala, EAF Breakfast, Legacy Breakfast/Luncheon and no-lines registration. The number of workshops doubled and many other learning opportunities were added. Because of this emphasis on "Soror Centered Leadership," Central was unofficially named the "Heart of Alpha Kappa Alpha," during this period. In summary, Soror Buckhanan led Central Region with a sense of quiet competence, while moving its members forward in the Spirit of Alpha Kappa Alpha.

Following her term as the 26th Central Regional Director Soror Dorothy was elected Supreme Grammateus at the 62nd Boule in Detroit, MI and served from 2006-2010. As Supreme Grammateus she served on the International Constitution Committee and secretary for the EAF Board of Directors.

Soror Wilson's leadership skills and record of service resonated throughout the membership and propelled her to the office of First Supreme Anti-Basileus at the 64th Boule in St. Louis, MO. The Sorors of Central Region anxiously await her installation as the 29th Supreme Basileus of Alpha Kappa Alpha Sorority, Incorporated.

Chi Xi Omega Chapter

DECATUR, ILLINOIS
JANUARY 10, 2004

First Row Seated, Left toRight: Elizabeth Harden, Central Regional Director, Dorothy Buckhanan, D. Jean Reid, Frankye Morgan, and Sheryl E. Coleman. Standing, left to Right: Melverta Wilkins, Chantanell Jewett, Celestine Taylor, Kim Bond,, Naomi McPherson, Venita Edwards-Talley, Joyce Edwards, Tamara Baltimore, Beverly Norton, Eloise Warfield and Bettye Hill.

CHARTER MEMBERS

TAMARA BALTIMORE	CHANTANELL JEWITT
KIM BOND	NAOMI L. MCPHERSON
SHERYL COLEMAN	FRANKYE MORGAN
JOYCE EDWARDS	BEVERLY NORTON
VENITA EDWARDS-TALLEY	D. JEAN REID
BETTYE HILL	CELESTINE TAYLOR
ELIZABETH HARDEN	ELOISE WARFIELD
	MELVERTA WILKINS

The Decatur Elite Pearls became Chi Xi Omega Chapter during a beautiful chartering ceremony at the Marcia's Waterford Restaurant on the picturesque Lake Decatur. The chapter grew out of the forsight of Soror Edna Shanklin and the sorors of Nu Omicron Omega Chapter, Springfield, Illinois. Soror D. Jean Reid is the chapter Basileus.

Chi Xi Omega Advises Tau Rho Chapter.

PART V: THE NEW CENTURY

Chi Sigma Omega Chapter
BOLINGBROOK, ILLINOIS
DECEMBER 5, 2004

CHARTER MEMBERS

SHARON MAYS ALLEN
MARCIA MORROW BANKS
GLENDA LAWRENCE BLAKEMORE
ELIZABETH BOONE-MERRITT
JOSLYN BOWLING-JONES
VERENA BRILEY-HUDSON
TAMMIE BROOKS-LEWIS
KIM BARROW CHISM
MEGAN HALL CLARK
ADRIENNE W. COCHRANE
MELODY EASLEY COLEMAN
LISA COLEMAN-DIORO
SHEILA ABRAMS GIVENS
LINDA GRESHAM
MARCELLA HALL

TANYA D. HAUGHTON
LACHIE' M. JENNINGS
ROMELDA CROSBY JORDAN
BRENDA DORSEY LADIPO
KAREN Y. LEXING
MONICA CUNEGIN MARTIN
EMILE L. PENDARVIS-MURDEN
LYNETTE J. PHILLIPS
ANGELA A. PIETERS*
JANET L. PITTMAN
SANDRA D. PULLIAM-JOHNSON
NAQUISHA L. SMITH
REBECCA SMITH-ANDOH*
WENDOLYN SWIMS
LISA MARIE HUNTER WRIGHT

Beyond the Wall

Several Bolingbrook area graduate general members proposed to establish a new chapter of Alpha Kappa Alpha Sorority, Incorporated in the Village of Bolingbrook at the close of the Boule in July 2002. Their interest was due to the nonexistence of a graduate chapter operating close to the Village of Bolingbrook, their need to serve the exploding community where they live instead of other Chicago land locales and their need to have a chapter that addresses career women in varying family stages. The first organizational meeting took place on October 12, 2002 at the home of Verena Briley-Hudson. More graduate general members in the area who shared this interest were recruited. On September 27, 2003, this group of dedicated sorors met with Soror Dorothy W. Buckhanan, 26th Central Regional Director who made the Spirited Pearls an official interest group of Alpha Kappa Alpha Sorority, Inc.

After years of service to the southwest suburbs of Chicago, the Spirited Pearls Interest Group was chartered as Chi Sigma Omega Chapter on a glorious Sunday morning, December 5, 2004 in a beautiful ceremony at the prestigious Bolingbrook Golf Club in Bolingbrook, IL. There were 30 charter members. Among the honored guests were the First Supreme Anti-Basileus of Alpha Kappa Alpha Sorority, Inc., Soror Barbara A. McKinzie and Soror Dorothy W. Buckhanan, Central Regional Director. Both conducted the chartering ceremony. Soror Barbara A. McKinzie also conducted the chapter's installation of officers following the election. Over 200 sorors, community leaders, family and friends attended the chartering luncheon following the chartering ceremony.

The first chapter officers of Chi Sigma Omega Chapter were Sorors Emile L. Pendarvis-Murden, Basileus, Melody Easley Coleman, First Anti-Basileus, Brenda Dorsey-Ladipo, Second Anti-Basileus, Sharon Mays Allen, Grammateus, Karen Y, Lexing, Tamiouchos, Lisa Marie Hunter Wright, Anti-Tamiouchos, Marcia Morrow Banks, Pecunious Grammateus, Naquisha L. Smith, Anti-Pecunious Grammateus, Lachie' M. Jennings, Epistoleus, Romelda Crosby Jordan, Hodegos, Angela A. Pieters, Philacter, Verena Briley-Hudson, Business Manager, Megan Hall Clark, *Ivy Leaf* Reporter, Linda Hayes-Gresham, Pan Hellenic Council Representative, Glenda Lawrence Blakemore, Parliamentarian, Elizabeth Boone-Merritt, Custodian and Monica Cunegin Martin, Chaplain. Additional charter members included Sorors Joslyn Bowling-Jones, Kim Barrow Chism, Adrienne W. Cochrane, Lisa Coleman-Dioro, Sheila Abrams Givens, Marcella Hall, Tanya D. Haughton, Tammie Brooks-Lewis, Lynette J. Phillips, Janet L. Pittman, Sandra D. Pulliam-Johnson and Wendolyn A. Swims.

The goal of Chi Sigma Omega chapter is to adhere to the purpose of Alpha Kappa Alpha Sorority, Inc. and serve as a model of chapter efficiency and sisterhood. The chapter focuses on the business of the sorority and does not give lip service to "we help each other." Through our commitment to the principles of Alpha Kappa Alpha Sorority, Incorporated and our dedication to each other, using our intelligence and strength, we are effecting positive change in our community, the international organization and ourselves.

Chi Sigma Omega chapter was chartered at a time in history when information moves very fast and the methods of obtaining information changes just as rapidly. Chapter sorors are committed to using email as the preferred form of communication for chapter newsletters, committee reports, meeting minutes, directory and sister relations notifications. This method ensures timeliness of communications, minimizes postage and reproduction expenses and allows sorors to receive information when it convenient for them to do so. The chapter is activating a telephone notification system and investigating audio conferencing. The chapter's website follows the international web site guidelines.

Chi Sigma Omega chapter sorors are members that have a burning desire for friendship and unity among women, have a desire to contribute to the success of others, especially her sorors, have a willingness to mentor/coach other sorors, especially fellow chapter members, about sorority documents, procedures and programs and personal effectiveness of members. Our sorors are knowledgeable about the chapter, regional and international policies and procedures of Alpha Kappa Alpha Sorority, Incorporated through the study and implementation of its standard operating procedures outlined in the Constitution and By-laws, the Manual of Standard Procedure, Roberts Rules of Order, Sorority published guides such as So Now You Are Elected and Moving Gracefully and the Leadership Development training provided at chapter, regional and international retreats and conferences.

Conference attendance and participation had always been a priority even as interest group members. However, Chi Sigma Omega sorors were even more excited about attending the 71st Central Regional Conference in Indianapolis, Indiana in March 2005. Over 63% of the chapter registered and attended. The chapter also served as the conference Philacters. Serving as Philacters at the conference was both an honor and a privilege and they were ecstatic that our regional director asked them to do so.

Chi Sigma Omega implemented her fundraising plans immediately following chartering. Hosting two fundraisers in a three-month period, the chapter is on her way to making an indelible mark in the Bolingbrook area. Thanks to the overwhelming success of both the AKA Shuffle and the Chi Sigma Omega First Annual Golf Tournament, we were able to fund program targets in the areas of Health, Economics, Education, the Arts, and Black Family.

Many of our community service projects planned and implemented as an interest group were expanded and continued in 2005 with renewed energy and vigor. The IVY Reading Akademy for example, a Saturday morning reading program for children in grades 3-5, sorors engaged in tutoring 35 children from two local elementary schools for 3 hours per session over a 16-week period. Realizing the effects that a down-turned economy was having on our local community, we participated in the Letter's Carriers Food Drive, joining in the effort with the United Postal Service to collect over 70.9 million packages of food to be distributed to the nation's homeless.

The chapter partnered with a local community service organization to provide Christmas gifts that included toys, clothing and books to 12 needy children through the 'giving tree' project. Our annual coat drive, the Martin Luther King, Jr. Day of Service Project, was a great success with sorors collecting hundreds of coats and various other outer wear for men, women and children that we distributed to a local shelter benefiting many needy families. Chapter members walked and registered participants in the annual National Multiple Sclerosis Society-Greater Illinois Chapter MS Walk. In addition to local programs, Chi Sigma Omega is pleased to submit an entry to Central Region for the national Young Author's Program initiative.

Chi Sigma Omega chapter members are approaching "Service to All Mankind" with unbridled enthusiasm. Future program activities include committing ourselves to participating in the eradication of Aids-HIV, developing a financial literacy program for youth, and serving as role models and mentors for young girls ages 12-18 through teen mentoring programs.

Through the years…Chi Sigma Omega members have focused on the business of the sorority by galvanizing the contributions of our Significant Sisters, Community Partners and Fundraising Patrons, in targeting resources toward high yielding initiatives. To highlight a few of these targeted efforts to date: The development of a scholarship program for local graduating seniors through our philanthropic arm, Spirited Pearls Foundation (est. 2007); facilitation of the T-Rose and Emerging Young Leaders mentoring programs for teen girls; instituting a financial literacy program; coordinating clothing and food drives for local pantries by expanding our Martin Luther King, Jr. Day of Service initiative; distributing school supplies to the children of incarcerated parents; delivering Christmas toys and presents to women and children in a battered women's shelter; initiating a voter registration drive effort at the Village of Bolingbrook annual community picnic; hosting a community baby shower for a Black family with quadruplets and providing community awareness regarding health-related & social justice issues at our annual Teen Summit.

Chi Sigma Omega's efforts in community programming and outreach have been recognized at the local, regional and international levels. At the local level, the chapter received the Leading Organization in the Community award from DuPage AME Church (2011), Outstanding Community Service award from St. John AME Church (2012) and was a finalist for the Bolingbrook Chamber of Commerce Best of Bolingbrook Business Award (2012). Regionally, Chi Sigma Omega chapter and individual members have received recognition for several awards, including: Overall Chapter Achievement for program execution (2007, 2009, and 2012), Outstanding Soror in Printing and Publications (Verena Briley-Hudson 2009), Basileus of the Year — Runner up (Marcia Banks 2009), Outstanding Chapter Website (2009), Overall Technology Achievement Award (2010), Award for Media Excellence (2010), Basileus of the Year (Marcia Banks 2010) and the President's Volunteer Service Award-by Barack Obama (2012). Notably, Chi Sigma Omega Chapter was the first Central Region overall winner of the Barbara A. McKinzie Award for Media Excellence. In 2010, both Chi Sigma Omega's Technology and Media Excellence award entries were selected to represent the region in the competition at the International Boule in St. Louis, MO. Additionally, at the international level, Chi Sigma Omega Chapter was recognized by the International Program Committee for execution of Platform III — Economic Growth of the Black Family (2009) and by the International Membership Committee for achieving at least 85% Retention and 10% Reclamation of chapter members (2009). Since inception, Chi Sigma Omega has instituted community service programs designed to address the prevailing needs of Bolingbrook and the surrounding communities and we are humbled by these numerous accolades for our efforts.

As Chi Sigma Omega achieved success as a chapter through programs and community outreach, the membership has answered the call to bring our collective and individual talents to the regional and international levels of the organization. At the regional level, the chapter performed philacter duties at the 71st Central Regional Conference in Indianapolis, Indiana (2005), served as event chair for the Tribute to Leaders and the Conference Gala dinners at the 75th Central Regional Conference in Schaumberg, IL (2009) and accepted the appointment as host chapter for the Clusters 1, 2 and 8 Fall Retreat in Bolingbrook, IL (2011). As a newer chapter, Chi Sigma Omega was honored to discover that the cluster retreat hosted in Bolingbrook enjoyed the highest conference attendance to date in Central Region history.   Nuhi Sigma Omega members engaged in leadership beyond the chapter level include; Chartering Basileus Emile Pendarvis-Murden, who served as the Central Region Development Officer during the Pamela Bates Porch administration. Also under that administration, Soror Glenda Blakemore was the Mental Health coordinator for Cluster 8 and chaired Central Region's Boule' Hospitality Committee (2010). Appointments under Central Regional Director Gisélé M. Casanova's administration include Centennial Basileus Marcia Banks, as chair of the Basilei Training Institute, Soror Monica Martin on the Central Region Protocol Committee, and Soror Glenda Blakemore to the Central Region Archives Committee. And most significantly, Soror E. JaNiece Bell was appointed as the Central Region representative to the International Program Committee. Chi Sigma Omega continues to build on this legacy of leadership in making preparation for the greatest challenge thus far, serving as lead hostess chapter, for the 80th Central Regional Conference in Chicago, Illinois in 2014.

Chi Sigma Omega Chapter, chartered with just thirty members, has grown to almost fifty members who continue to embrace the spirit of Alpha Kappa Alpha through sisterhood and service. As over 80% of chapter members are transplants and not native to the southwestern suburban Chicagoland area, being away from family has encouraged a special connection amongst members. In an effort to retain its membership, the chapter has created an extended family circle, through the common bond of service.

Chi Sigma Omega has also enjoyed the fruits of initiating new women into the sisterhood. In 2008, Chi Sigma Omega chapter conducted its first membership intake process and welcomed eight members into the sisterhood. Following that effort, six women were initiated during the 2010 membership recruitment activities. Amongst these fourteen women recruited by Chi Sigma Omega Chapter, one, Alyssia Benford, has already started blazing trails by being honored as a Woman of Power at the 75th Central Regional Conference.

Retention and recruitment have always been a hallmark of the sorority membership. In recent years, reclamation has also grown in significance to maintaining a vibrant membership. Chi Sigma Omega has reclaimed several pearls over the years, including Marva Brown, our first Golden Soror. Not only has the chapter grown in size, but has also grown in signature community programs and sorority leadership, evidenced by numerous program awards and chapter members serving in leadership roles throughout the international organization.

As Chi Sigma Omega Chapter (the 50th graduate chapter chartered in the Central Region) reaches her tenth anniversary, we reflect on the diverse fellowship of sincere and motivated members. Our membership not only celebrates the growth of the chapter in sisterhood, fostered by chapter efficiency in operations, but the steadfast commitment of each member to the founding principles of this service driven sorority. Moreover, Chi Sigma Omega chapter is proud to reflect on the commitment chapter members have made to training and leadership development by sending representatives to each cluster retreat, regional conference and Boule' since chartering. Chi Sigma Omega Chapter is on a great trajectory to reach the goal of serving as a role model for other new chapters entering this illustrious sisterhood. The lessons of the first ten years serve as a strong foundation for the evolution of a chapter not only significant in sisterhood and service, but a Chi Sigma Omega Chapter that is "SIGNIFICANT IN EVERY WAY."

CHI SIGMA OMEGA CHAPTER BASILEI

Emile L. Pendarvis-Murden	2004 – 2006
Marcia Morrow Banks	2007 – 2010
Glenda Lawrence Blakemore	2011 – 2012
Romelda Crosby Jordan	2013 – present

Chi Phi Omega

LAFAYETTE AND WEST LAFAYETTE, INDIANA
APRIL 7, 2005

Left to Right, Front Row: Pamella D. Shaw, Terri S. Jackson, Avione Y. Northcutt, Thomanisa J. Ash, Dorothy W. Buckhanan, Central Regional Director, Nicole Gale, Jamila R. Greene, Traci A. Graham. Back Row, Candiss Williams, Karla R. Smith, Aisha C. Reed, Stacy C. Curry, Naressa Cofield, Heather Smith, Johari N. Miller, Ja'Neair Perry, and Willette M. Crawford.

CHARTER MEMBERS

THOMANISA J. ASH	JOHARI N. MILLER
NARESSA COFIELD	AVIONE Y. NORTHCUTT
WILLETTE M. CRAWFORD	JA'NEAIR PERRY
STACY C. CURRY	AISHA C. REED
NICOLE GALE	PAMELLA D. SHAW
TRACI A. GRAHAM	HEATHER SMITH
JAMILA R. GREENE	KARLA R. SMITH
TERRI S. JACKSON	CANDISS WILLIAMS

In the fall of 2003, 14 Alpha Kappa Alpha women came together with the hopes of chartering a graduate chapter in the Greater Lafayette, Indiana community. The Lafayette area women of Alpha Kappa Alpha Sorority, Inc. held their first official meeting on September 26, 2003 in the basement of Second Baptist Church in Lafayette, IN. After sorors quelled their excitement and anticipation, the meeting was called to order by Soror Thomanisa Ash. Five women decided to become members of the Executive Board: President: Thomanisa Ash, Vice-President: Nicole Gale, Treasurer: Ja'Neair Perry, and Secretary: Naressa Cofield. There were 16 sorors in attendance (14 graduates and 2 undergraduates).

During this preliminary meeting a number of objectives and concerns were discussed. Among these goals discussed were acquiring the required number of interested members in order to charter a graduate chapter and gaining Regional Director Dorothy W. Buckhanan's approval. Many sorors expressed the need for a graduate chapter to oversee Epsilon Rho, Purdue University's undergraduate chapter. At the close of this first meeting, sorors left with the intentions of drafting the Bylaws and Constitution of the interest group and to brainstorm fundraising ideas.

Monthly meetings were held during the Fall of 2003 and Winter of 2003-2004. The women who initially met to discuss the possibility of chartering a graduate chapter later became the Lafayette Pearls interest group. During the October 2003 meeting, a dialogue ensued regarding the importance of having an official name. Subsequently and through a unanimous vote, these women became the Lafayette Polished P.E.A.R.L.S. Interest Group of Alpha Kappa Alpha Sorority, Inc. The acronym signifies: P: Perfection, E: Excellence, A: Allegiance, R: Radiance, L: Leadership, S: Styles. They began to enhance their communication with one another through a group list serve.

The interest group's first official meeting was held on March 2, 2004. The PEARLS at this point were: Thomanisa Ash, Naressa Cofield, Chasity Cole, Stacy Curry, Nicole Gale, Jamila Greene, Johari Miller, Avione Northcutt, Ja'Neair Perry, Aisha Reed, Pamella Shaw, Heather Smith, Karla Smith and Candiss Williams. In the dawn of a new academic year at Purdue in August 2004, three more sorors joined the interest group. These sorors were Willette Crawford, Traci Graham, and Terri Jackson. As an interest group, these Alpha Kappa Alpha women carried out the five targets presented under Supreme Basileus Linda M. White's "Spirit of AKA" program. Some of the many activities held during the group's first year include the following:

The Dr. Martin Luther King, Jr. Service Project, a voter registration drive, health walks, Second Baptist Church Annual Youth Fair, Gospel Fest, AKA Coat Day, breast cancer awareness activities, Buckle Up Day, Chat & Chew / Silent Auction, National Black Family Volunteer Day, World AIDS Day, the Young Authors Program, a prom dress drive, sisterly relations activities and many more.

One year and six months after their first meeting, these 16 hardworking sorors would soon become an official chapter of Alpha Kappa Alpha. On April 7, 2004 at high noon, the Lafayette Polished P.E.A.R.L.S. interest group became the Chi Phi Omega chapter of Alpha Kappa Alpha Sorority, Inc. during the 71st Regional Conference located at the Downtown Marriott Hotel in Indianapolis, Indiana. The official officers were inducted as follows: Basileus, Tomanisa Ash; Anti Basileus: Nicole' Gale; Grammateus: Naressa Cofield; Anti-Grammateus: Karla Smith; Tamiouchous: Candiss Williams; Pecunious Grammateus: Aisha Reed; Epistoleus: Willette Crawford; Parliamentarian: Stacy Curry; Hodegos: Ja'Neair Perry; Philacter: Jamila Greene; Chaplain: Heather Smith; *Ivy Leaf* Reporter: Terri Jackson; Members-at-Large: Stacy Curry and Johari Miller; Graduate Advisors: Pamella Shaw and Traci Graham; Historian: Pamella Shaw

The spirit of AKA was definitely in the room as the charter members of Chi Phi Omega pledged their lifelong commitment to Alpha Kappa Alpha Sorority, Inc. and Chi Phi Omega.

Chi Phi Omega Advises Epsilon Rho Chapter.

Chi Phi Omega Chapter Basilei

Thomanisa J. Noble-Ash	May 2005 (Chartering Basileus)
Nicole Gale	2005 – 2007
Candiss O. Williams	2008-2009
Lori M. Ward	2010-2011
Jennifer H. Dennis	2011-2012
Heather N. Smith	2013-present

PART V: THE NEW CENTURY

Chi Chi Omega Chapter

INDIANAPOLIS, INDIANA
MAY 21, 2005

CHARTER MEMBERS

CHASITY ADEWOPO
MAISHA ALBERT
NIQUELLE ALLEN
JOANNA ARCHIE
REQUETA BELL-WHITESIDE
TA'MELLA BOND
PAMELA BROADUS
ANIKA CALLOWAY
SANYA CEASAR
MONICA CRAIN-LOCKARD
ANIKA DAVIS
KIAHNA DAVIS
STACY DESADIER
YVETTE DUPREE
LINDA ENDERS
TONDA GAINES
TIFFANY GARNER
KRISTIN GIVENS
KRISTIN GRAHAM
RAIMEKA GRAHAM
ESTHER HARRINGTON
MICHELLE HAWKINS
ISOKE HOLLINGSWORTH

MALEKA JACKSON
AN JOU JOHNSON
Y'NESHA JOHNSON
SHELIA JONES
CHARLOTTE LEAVELL
ROCHELLE LEAVELL
LASHON MCCALL
MELISSA MCCOLLUM
SHERRON MOORE
CONNIE PASLEY-TAYLOR
LAUREN REDMOND
MAYA RHODES
DEBORAH RUSSELL
AYANA SMITH
CECELIA SMITH
JOLI TOWNSEND
LAWANDA WARD
EVONA WATSON
JENNENE WHITE
DIJEANA WILKS
YUWANIS WILLIAMS
BRIDGETTE WIMBLEDUFF
NATISSA WOODARD
STEPHANIE YOUNG

THE VISION FAIR

This 'vision fair' started as an inspiration of several general members of Alpha Kappa Alpha Sorority, Inc. in January 2003. Three sorors; Soror Kiahna Davis, Soror LaShon McCall, and Soror Sherron Moore, congruently had an idea to help birth a second chapter in Indianapolis. On February 6, 2003, Soror Kiahna Davis and LaShon McCall sat with Soror Dorothy Buchanan, 26th Central Region Director, after a Founder's Day luncheon in Champaign, IL. After expressing their desire for starting a new chapter in the Indianapolis metropolitan area, Soror Davis and Soror McCall left with an excitement about this new venture. During the conversation she noted that Soror Sherron Moore had contacted her a few days prior articulating the same desire of starting a new chapter. Soror Davis and Soror McCall soon got on the Ivy line and called on Soror Sherron Moore to aid in this venture.

After a brief conversation between Soror Davis and Soror Moore, the news went out to find other interested sorors in the Indianapolis area. Soror Candace Hasan and Soror Kimberly Grays joined the small group of Soror Davis, Soror McCall, and Soror Sherron, to make up the original organizers of this group. While this group was spreading the word, they were told two years prior, several sorors in the Indianapolis attempted a similar task. The organizers got in touch with many of those sorors and began the building process of an interest group.

Weekly meetings were held via teleconference and homes. Plans were underway to host a Reactivation and Sisterly Relations event for sorors interested in the possibility of a second chapter in the Indianapolis area.

The first Reactivation and Sisterly Relations meeting was held Saturday, March 15, 2003 at Nora Public Library in Indianapolis, IN. The event was attended by over 40 Sorors with 32 reactivating that day. Since the response was bigger than expected, another Reactivation and Sisterly Relations event was scheduled and held on Saturday, April 26, 2003 at Nora Public Library. The interested sorors then began to have monthly mass meetings on the third Saturday of each month.

Elections were held and Soror Kiahna Davis was elected the Interest Group President. The other officers included: Soror Raimeka Graham, Vice-President; Soror Joanna Archie, Secretary; Soror Kristin Graham, Treasurer; Soror Sherron Moore, *Ivy Leaf* Reporter.

On December 6, 2003, Emerging Pearls of Perfection was officially considered an interest group of Alpha Kappa Alpha Sorority, Inc. Emerging Pearls of Perfection was established to provide inactive and underactive Sorors of Alpha Kappa Alpha Sorority, Incorporated a vehicle through which each Soror can be a service all mankind. It is the belief of this collective body of Sorors that there are critical needs and issues to be identified and confronted through programming and activities that fulfill the mission of this group in underserved areas in Indianapolis, Indiana and surrounding counties.

Emerging Pearls of Perfectiion programs focus included their Annual HIV/AIDS Awareness Charity Ball in which funds were used for awareness and education among teens and youth. Other programs included National Volunteer Day at Blackburn House Projects, MLK, Jr. Day On Not Off, Senior Visitation Day, Partnership with Mentor Indiana with former first lady of Indiana Magggie Kernan, art show showcasing local artist talent, scholarship funds to graduating seniors, participation in Race for the Cure for Breast Cancer Awareness and Research, a summer youth literacy workshop in partnership with Indiana Young People's Department of the AME Church, various program partnerships with the Boys and Girls Club, The Salvation Army, and Guion Creek Elementary.

THE EMERGING PEARLS ARE PERFECTED-THE FIRST 12 MONTHS

On May 21, 2005, Emerging Pearls of Perfection became Chi Chi Omega Chapter of Indianapolis, IN with Kiahna Davis serving as the chapter's first Basileus. It is the second graduate chapter chartered in the city of Indianapolis. Forty-seven members of Emerging Pearls of Perfection became the chapter's charter members.

Chi Chi Omega hit the ground running as the newest pearl in Central Region. We kicked off 2006 creating signature chapter programs and service opportunities such as The F.L.Y Club (Financial Literate Youth), the Glass Slipper Project to promote self-esteem and awareness in which sorors donated new and gentle used formals so under-served high school girls could experience prom in style, and continued our partnership with Harcourt Elementary School through our Ivy Reading Akademy with over 15 students and 27 sorors serving as volunteers on a weekly basis. We continued our committed in the fight for increased awareness of the HIV/AIDS epidemic by sponsoring HIV/AIDS Awareness Charity Ball with this year's benefactor being the Damien Center, a not-for profit organization for domestic abuse and HIV/ AIDS outreach center.

As we continued to look for areas of service that had been under-represented, we begin tailoring our programs to foster two main focuses: provide community motivated service and create a very sisterly atmosphere for chapter growth. During our second year, we introduced the Emerging Black Professionals, an event which honored young African American Professionals through a social networking medium. Also, we began a program that focused on our chapter's commitment to encouraging strong Black Families within our community titled The Black Family Picnic.

TAKING STEPS TO SMARTER CHAPTER OPERATIONS

Beginning late 2006, Chi Chi Omega sought to grow and provide strategies to sustain the chapter into perpetuity, while encouraging out of the box approaches to conduct our business efficiently but with efficiency. The chapter immediately created its chapter website with a members-only section to house all important documents in order for sorors to have convenient and immediate access.

The membership and finance committee in 2007 reviewed the cost of membership and made a commitment to work to lower chapter membership dues each year. They succeeded by creating an on-going focus and strategy to increase membership through reactivation and created unique ways in which sorors could pay for their membership. In 2007 we introduced the Tiered Chapter Membership Dues Program to allow sorors to pick the level of financial participation they felt comfortable contributing toward. Our levels were Ivy (base-level) through Pearl (highest level). Our commitment was that at Pearl Level Membership, everything for the year was included in this fee therefore sorors did not have to feel as though each time we met they had to bring a checkbook. The motto was, "Pay at Pearls and Just Walk in…into everything."

During the next few years we would introduced online payments, payment coupon books, online management of account, document collaboration and storage, live remote viewing of chapter meetings and electronic reporting processes.

MEMBERSHIP: CLAIMING OUR LOST PEARLS

Chi Chi Omega has made a commitment since inception to approach membership with a different spin. We firmly believe diversity is the spice of our sisterhood. Being the second chapter formed in Indianapolis, we operate at a smaller scale, but our vow to make sisterly bonds with all we come in contact with that reaches far beyond our years in existence. Time and time again, sorors tell a story of randomly meeting a soror of Chi Chi Omega in the mall, at a meeting, riding down the street, to be greeted with a warm hug, sincere smile, and business card with our contact information and chapter meeting dates.

A visit to chapter meetings often compels sorors to join right away, feeling at "home" with Chi Chi Omega. Many Sorors are transplants into Indianapolis from other cities, often feeling lost and disconnected until reconnecting with sisters who embrace them immediately and encourage to become involved in committees and use their multiple skillsets to provide "service to all mankind" in the Circle City.

MEMBERSHIP: CULTIVATING NEW PEARLS

On November 18, 2007, Chi Chi Omega initiated its inaugural membership class of ten. These 10 women were Dr. Nneka Breaux, Chenille Ward, Monica Chaney, Jannet Foxworth, Monika Gillis, Flora Lewis, Judy Lewis, Tonya Naylor, Robyn Rucker, and Jiana Willis. They represent the fields of health care, science research and development, law, information technology, media, and fashion/merchandising.

On June 27, 2010, Chi Chi Omega welcomed its sophomore class of nine. The nine women initiated were Joy Carter-Hopkins, Ja'Neane Minor, Myesha Morrissette-Johnson, Marla Neal, Robin Owsley, Rhonda Stephens, Toyya Thomas-Jackson, Desiree Young, and LaShawna Young. Together, they represent the fields of recruiting, government, health care, business, and sports management.

On March 4, 2012, Chi Chi Omega initiated its third group of new members. These four women were Naomi Boone, Monica Durrett, LaNier Echols, and Janeille Johnson. They represent the fields of government, education, health care, and social work.

FUNDING: EMERGING PEARLS FOUNDATION, INC.

In 2007, Chi Chi Omega saw the need to establish a separate non-profit entity to garner more funding support through grants and the community to support scholarships and programs. In December 2007, through the state of Indiana, Emerging Pearls Foundation, Inc. was incorporated and the Board of Directors established with Aimee Laramore serving as its first President. The foundation holds its Annual Meeting in August of each year through an Awards Program honoring women in the Indianapolis area for their exemplary work in business and community. The foundation coins its Annual Meeting: Honor Her.

CELEBRATING OUR CENTENNIAL, CHI CHI OMEGA STYLE

Chi Chi Omega and the brothers of Iota Lambda Chapter of Alpha Phi Alpha Fraternity, Inc., co-hosted the '06 – '08 Legacy Scholarship Dinner and Ball on December 12, 2008. This formal event was held at the Indianapolis Downtown Marriott Hotel Ballroom and featured Hidden Beach recording artists Kindred The Family Soul. Proceeds from the gala and silent auction benefitted the Emerging Pearls Foundation, Inc. and Alphamen, Inc. Among those in attendance was the 27th Central Regional Director Pamela Bates Porch who included photos from the scholarship dinner in the Fall 2008 issue of "Centrally Speaking," the Central Region newsletter. This event was a great way to end our Centennial year.

SIGNATURE AND LEGACY PROGRAMS AND ACTIVITIES

Books & Breakfast with Santa — The idea has been a part of the fabric of Chi Chi Omega since 2005 when Sorors began thinking of a community based activity that would celebrate the child in each of us. Over the years, members of Chi Chi Omega became increasingly concerned over the achievement gap experienced by children of color, focusing on the most recent reports that featured insights about children who attend schools with the highest poverty percentages, the ongoing connection between morning nutrition and achievement, and intentionally wanting to make a difference beyond a one-day event. As the chapter grew and evolved, the concept behind "Books and Breakfast with Santa" evolved as well. This is a joint effort with Emerging Pearls Foundation, the Uplift Foundation and Lumina Foundation. This partnership has expanded the venue, onsite activities, give-a-way items and education infrastructure of the event. We are elated that families have been able to experience Winter Wonderland with literacy activities woven through every aspect of the event.

On-site reading for the duration of the day, age-appropriate reading materials, personalized assistance for the selection of books, pre-school activities for home-based play and free admission for all parents and adult care-givers has complimented the traditional activities that have defined holiday fun in the greater Indianapolis community.

Pearls Mentoring Program — In 2007, Chi Chi Omega recognized the growing need for mentorship in middle school-aged young ladies. Based on alarming trends amongst young girls, the chapter developed the PEARLS Mentoring Program. Members of the chapter served as one-on-one mentors, hosting and participating in service and leadership driven activities to individually build and reinforce core ethics and values. Additionally, monthly meetings were held to further instill educational lessons while fostering sisterly relations amongst the entire group of participants. Emphasis on financial literacy, self-esteem, character development, community service and etiquette in social settings and media were among the initial core areas of focus. To add to the impact of the program thru social and cultural exposure, the chapter also incorporated cultural excursions leading the girls to experience the African American History Museum in Cincinnati, OH, Freetown Village — an interactive African American History Museum in Indianapolis, IN and to Kentucky State University — Central Region's only Historically Black College.

In 2010, under the leadership of Soror Carolyn House Stewart, a new program was implemented — Emerging Young Leaders (EYL). Under the International Program theme: Global Leadership through Timeless Service, this program would lead Chi Chi Omega to incorporate 6th grade girls into the existing 7th & 8th grade group. Keeping with tradition of the PEARLS Mentoring Program, the 9-month club would culminate with a scholarship luncheon hosted by Emerging Pearls Foundation.

REGIONAL AWARDS

- 2010 Regional Conference Awards
- 1st Place Winners for Graduate Chapter Achievement: Platform II — Economic Keys to Success
- 1st Place Winners for Graduate Chapter Achievement: Platform III — Economic Growth of the Black Family
- 1st Place Winners for Assault on Illiteracy Graduate — Evelyn H. Roberts Award
- 1st Place Winners for Overall Chapter Achievement
- 1st Place Winners for Assault on Illiteracy
- 1st Place Winners for Chapter Scrapbook
- 1st Place Winners for Outstanding Chapter Website Award
- 2nd Place Winners for Chapter Program Exhibit
- 2nd Place Winners for Platform I — Non Traditional Entrepreneur
- 2nd Place Winners for Platform II — Economic Keys to Success
- 2nd Place Winners for Platform V — Health Resource Management & Economics
- EAF Silver Chapter Recognition
- 5 Hearts Reclaiming Sorors Award
- 2011 Regional Conference Awards
- 1st Place Winners for Chapter Scrapbook
- 2nd Place Winners for Chapter Program Exhibit
- Best of the Best for EAF Initiative
- 2012 Regional Conference Awards
- First Runner Up for Chapter Programs for Initiative I — Emerging Young Leaders
- First Runner Up for Chapter Programs for Initiative II — Health
- First Runner Up for Chapter Programs for Initiative III — Global Poverty
- First Runner Up for Chapter Programs for Initiative IV — Economic Security
- First Runner Up for Chapter Programs for Initiative V — Social Justice & Human Rights
- 1st Place Winners for Overall Chapter Programming
- 1st Place Winners for Chapter Program Exhibit
- 1st Place Winners for Chapter Scrapbook
- Record Attendance

CHI CHI OMEGA CHAPTER BASILEI

Kiahna Davis	2005 – 2007
Chasity Thompson	2008 – 2011
Bridgette Wimbleduff	2012 – 2013

Chi Omega Omega

Chicago, Illinois
June 18, 2005

First Row-L-R: Brandy Garris (cut off) Allison Shade, Rhonda Abdullah, Nichelle Bush, Tracey Cross Jones, Niquitta Berry, Kimi Ellen, Jane Stuart, Regional Director- Dorothy Buckhanan, Tamara D. Smith, Rita James, Jenine Wright, Tiffany Seay, Karla Owens Davis Charlotte Griffin (cut-off). 2nd Row- L-R: Lenita Gibson (cut-off) Antris Green, Paulette Grissett, Charise Westbrooks-Jones, Karla Hale, Tracey Richmond, Dawn Walker, Shawna Storey, Latoya Buchanan, Janice Wells and Angela Hamberlin. 3rd Row- L-R: Tara Reed, Sharon Ward, Natalie Harris, Gena Miller, Becky Harris, Karen Calloway, Dion Redfield, Orlett Pearson, Michelle Hoy-Watkins, Nicole Hasbrouck, Gail Hasbrouck, Dori Collins, Marisha Humphries, Onjalique Clark, Nona Austin, Monica Lane and Javonna Burton. 4th Row- L-R: Hope Tate, Fannieleah Brown, Melanie Brown, Nneka Thompson, Cheryl Morgan, Iris Gist Cochran, Zaa Zaax Brokemond, Stephanie Bradford, Wadeha Taylor, Nichele Woodson, Tondelaya Coger, Terri Buchanan, Dawn Smith, Michelle Chambers, Patricia Stern, Connie Hill, Davina Pulliam, Tannis Williamson and T. Marion Johnson. 5th Row-L-R: Marlyn Evans, Charlotte Hunt- Davis, Kimberly King, Tracey Simmons, Jeanene Tiffany Barrett, Lashawn Marsh, Tracie Clisby, Nicole Fuller, Mekia Hearn, Lisa Allen, Karla Hudson, Sheila Gailey Craig, Candase Lightfoot, Eboni Kelly Williams, Kelly Johnson, Bernita Thomas, Hanneke Hall and Samantha Joseph

RHONDA ABDULLAH	DIONNE DAY
PAMELA ADAMS	KIMI ELLEN
TRACI ADAMS	KELLY EVANS
LISA ALLEN	MARLYN EVANS
CHARMAINE APARA	FANNIELEAH FOOTE'-BROWN
NONA AUSTIN	NICOLLE FULLER
JEANENE (TIFFANY) BARRETT	SHELIA GAILEY-CRAIG
NIQUITTA BERRY	BRANDY GARRIS
STEPHANIE BRADFORD	DONNA GEORGE
ZAA ZAAX (SHAY) BROKEMOND	LENITA GIPSON
CHRISTINE BROWN	CHERYL GIST-WILLIAMS
MELANIE BROWN-OKOROH	ANTRIS GREEN
LATOYA BUCHANAN	CHARLOTTE GRIFFIN
TERRILYNN BUCHANAN	PAULETTE GRISSETT
JAVONNA BURTON	KAREN HALE
NICHELLE BUSH	HANNEKE HALL
KAREN CALLOWAY	ANGELA HAMBERLIN
MICHELLE CHAMBERS	BECKIE HARRIS
ONJALIQUE CLARK	NATALIE HARRIS
TRACIE CLISBY	GAIL HASBROUCK
IRIS GIST COCHRAN	NICOLE HASBROUCK
TONDELAYA COGER	MEKIA HEARNS
DORI COLLINS	CONNIE HILL
TRACEY CROSS-JONES	MICHELE HOY-WATKINS
KARLA OWENS DAVIS	KARLA HUDSON
MURIEL DAVIS LEE	MARISHA HUMPHRIES

CHARLOTTE HUNT-DAVIS
RITA JAMES
JANET JAMISON
KELLI JOHNSON
T. MARION JOHNSON
SAMANTHA JOSEPH
EBONI KELLY-WILLIAMS
KIMBERLY KING
MONICA LANE
CANDASE LIGHTFOOT
ANGELA MAHOME
LASHAWN MARSH
ADRIENNE MAY-RICH
TIFFANIE MCLEARY
GENA MILLER
MARIE MOORE
CHERYL MORGAN
SHELLY O'NEAL-BENSON
ORLETT PEARSON
DANA PHILLIPS-ASH
DAVINA PULLIAM
LINDA PITTS
DION REDFIELD
TARA REED
TRACEY RICHMOND

KIMBERLY SANDIFER
NATASHA SAWYER
TIFFANY SEAY
ALLISON SHADE
TRACEY SIMMONS
DAWN K. SMITH
TAMARA D. SMITH
PATRICIA STERN
SHAWNA STOREY
JANE STUART
MICHON STUTTLEY
HOPE TATE
WADEHA TAYLOR
BERNITA THOMAS
NNEKA THOMPSON
DAWN WALKER
SHARON WARD
JANICE WELLS
ETHELYN WESS
CHARISE WESTBROOKS-JONES
TONNETTE WILLIAMS
TANNIS WILLIAMSON
NICHELE WOODSON
JENINE WRIGHT

CHARTER MEMBERS

Chi Omega Omega Chapter has the privileged distinction of being the largest graduate chapter chartered in the wondrous history of Alpha Kappa Alpha Sorority, Incorporated. The efforts that culminated in that chartering began at a meeting in February 2002 when a group of seven sorors met to explore the idea of forming a new chapter in the Chicagoland area. Those sorors were Soror Rhonda Abdullah, Soror Niquitta Berry, Soror Charlotte Griffin, Soror Rita James, Soror Allison Shade, Soror Tamara Smith, and Soror Jenine Wright.

During the early meetings of the group the goals were established. At a meeting held on April 7, 2002, the group selected its officers and began discussion about possible locations for a new chapter. Soror Tamara Smith who has the original idea to establish a new chapter agreed to serve as president. The other original members also chose to uphold the duties of an office. At a subsequent meeting shortly thereafter, three committees were created including the Constitution & By-laws Committee, the Finance Committee, and the Programs Committee. In addition, possible names for the group were discussed including "Ladies of Tea Roses and Pearls" and "Ladies of Sheer Distinction." The members later agreed on the name "Imani Pearls," which held special meaning for the group as Imani is a Kwanzaa principle meaning faith.

At the first Executive Board meeting held on May 14, 2002, the selection of the service area for the planned chapter was considered. Bronzeville/Hyde Park was chosen based upon the statistical data presented, which indicated a need for services in those communities. Also in that meeting, guidelines were established for potential group members. It was determined that all Sorors who joined the group would be required to 1)attend 80% of the general body meetings, 2)participate in all community service activities, and 3)attend at least one Boule, Regional Conference or Cluster Meeting. In addition, the group agreed to create a handbook for presentation to the new Central Regional Director, Soror Dorothy Buckhanan articulating the interest to charter a new chapter in the city of Chicago.

Prior to being allowed to work as a group in the community, the focus of the group was recruitment. Receptions and other activities were held to recruit sorors including general members and sorors who were inactive. The members took care not to solicit sorors who were active in other chapters. The membership continued to gradually increase as inactive and general member sorors who visited meetings and other activities joined the group.

In April of 2003, the group received approval from the Regional Director to begin working in the community. The Group, eager to begin, held its first service project sponsored by the Health committee, on April 19, 2003 during Minority Cancer Awareness Week. Sorors distributed pamphlets on the various cancers that especially affect the African American community. The event was held at the Jewel Osco grocery store on 34th and King Drive in the Bronzeville neighborhood. The project was a success. From 2003 to 2005, the Group continued to organize various community service projects throughout the service area.

Chi Omega Omega Chartering Ceremony

The historic chartering of Chi Omega Omega Chapter was held on June 18, 2005 at the Millennium Knickerbocker Hotel in Chicago, at which time, Linda M. White was the Supreme Basileus for Alpha Kappa Alpha Sorority, Incorporated. Soror Dorothy Buckhanan, 26th Central Regional Director, and Soror Barbara A. McKinzie, First-Supreme Anti-Basileus, presided over the ceremony. Chapter Officers were installed and the first chapter meeting of Chi Omega Omega Chapter was held. At this first meeting, the chapter voted to nominate Soror Barbara A. McKinzie for the Carrie B. Preston Leadership Award. In addition, Soror Dorothy Buckhanan presented Soror Tamara Smith; Chi Omega Omega's chartering Basileus (President), with the official chapter books and documents. A reception and luncheon followed the meeting. The members of Chi Omega Omega Chapter hope to faithfully provide service to the Bronzeville and Englewood communities for years to come.

Chi Omega Omega is made up of a diverse group of women, including Life Members, Silver Star Sorors, and Golden Sorors. Chi Omega Omega is the home chapter of International Committee and Central Region Committee Chairmen and members. It is also the home of our very own Central Regional Director, Soror Giselé M. Casanova.

Major Chapter Events And Service Projects (2003-2012)

Y-ME RACE AGAINST BREAST CANCER — The second community service project of the group, also sponsored by the Health committee, was participation in the Y-me Breast cancer walk on May 11, 2003. The group walked to raise money for breast cancer research. The group continued its participation in this annual event on May 9, 2004.

KENWOOD ACADEMY COLLEGE FAIR — On May 20, 2003, sorors participated in the college fair by providing information on their various alma maters.

FEED-A-NEIGHBOR — On June 14, 2003, the Chicagoland General Members led by the Black Family committee participated in the in the Feed-A-Neighbor Program sponsored by Reverend Mitty Collier at the corner of 47th and Vincennes. During the event, the group helped to serve food to disadvantaged people in the community. The sorors were so moved by the event that they voted to continue quarterly participation. For the August event, Reverend Mitty Collier asked the group to focus on providing backpacks for children returning to school. Therefore, on August 16, 2003, the group donated and distributed book bags filled with school supplies to local residents. On December 20, 2003, the group endured cold weather to pass out clothing, hats, gloves, and food at the ABJ Community and Family Services Parking Lot on east 71st Street, in Chicago. This was a new location for the event. In January 2004, the group learned that the location of Feed-A-Neighbor had been permanently relocated to the ABJ lot, a site outside of the group's service area. The group wanting to continue its support of this worthwhile program agreed to continue participation until the end of the year. On August 14, 2004, the group again assisted with the special "Back to School" Feed-A-Neighbor serving food, clothing, and school supplies to the community. The group's final participation in the program was on December 11, 2004 with the serving of food and distribution of "bags of blessings" containing clothing items to the community. The group donated the gloves and other items.

CHICAGO CARES — On June 18, 2003, the group began its annual participation in Chicago Cares, a project also sponsored by the Black Family committee. The group was assigned to paint a mural on the wall at a public school. The following year, on June 24, 2004, the group participated by painting halls and classrooms. In addition, sorors painted murals and a map of the United States of America in the playground area or St. Helen School in Chicago. On June 13, 2005, just five days before being chartered, the group participated in Chicago Cares for the third consecutive year. The group was assigned to help improve Lorenz Brentano School on the northwest side of Chicago. The sorors and teen pearls helped by painting the gym and several classrooms.

IVY READING AKADEMY — The group began tutoring children at the Wabash Street YMCA using the Reading One-to-One Curriculum, which is recommended by the Alpha Kappa Alpha Reading Project. All of the sorors in the group were on the rotation schedule and participated as tutors.

ALPHA PHI ALPHA MARTIN LUTHER KING BREAKFAST — Sorors served as hostesses at the Ninth and Tenth Annual MLK Day Breakfast Fund Raisers sponsored by Iota Delta Lambda Chapter of Alpha Phi Alpha Fraternity on January 17, 2004 at the Harambee House in Chicago, Illinois and on January 15, 2005 at the Tinley Park Convention Center.

CAFÉ AKA — The group's first fundraiser was a poetry reading and live jazz performance held on September 25, 2003 in Chicago. The event was so popular that the group held its second Café AKA on September, 2004 and has continued to host this event every year at various venues in Chicago.

COAT AND BOOT DRIVE — On Saturday, November 15, 2003, in support of National Family Volunteer Day, sorors gathered at a Chicago firehouse and collected coats and boots for the homeless. Following the event, items were taken and donated to the Door of Hope Mission in Chicago.

20TH AND 21ST ANNUAL THANKSGIVING COMMUNITY DINNERS — On November 27, 2003 and November 25, 2004, many sorors took time away from their families to assist with serving Thanksgiving dinners to people in the community. The members served as hostesses, waitresses, servers, and clean up personnel as needed. The events were held at the Dawson Skills Institute.

ETA THEATRE EVENT — On Saturday, December 7, 2003, the group hosted its second fundraiser with a showing of "Every Night When the Sun Goes Down" at the ETA Theatre. A reception was held immediately following the show.

CHRISTMAS TOY GIVE-AWAY — On December 9, 2003 and December 7, 2004, sorors assisted with Alderman Dorothy Tillman's Annual Toy Giveaways by making donations and helping with toy distribution to nearly 1000 children in the community.

TEEN PEARL MENTORING PROGRAM — In March 2004, the Chicagoland General Members sent applications to teenage girls at King College Prep who were interested in increasing their awareness about the arts and enhancing their personal development. Fifteen high school sophomores and juniors were selected and assigned mentors. Workshops were held on art appreciation, self-esteem, fitness and health, dressing for success, etiquette, financial planning, and test-taking in addition to other topics. The young ladies were invited and encouraged to participate in some of the community service projects sponsored by the group.

ANNUAL MEMBERSHIP RETREAT — The group has benefited from two all day conferences. The first, held at the Oak Lawn Hilton in 2003, focused on leadership for those holding or interested in running for an office in the group. The second held on March 13, 2004, focused on sisterhood, protocol, and parliamentary procedure among other things. The exhibition step team made their debut at this event.

UNITED IN EXCELLENCE SCHOLARSHIP — In the spring of 2004, the group sent scholarship packets to high schools located in the Bronzeville and Englewood communities with the plan to award three college scholarships to high school students maintaining a "B" average. Due to a dearth of applications, the group awarded one high school senior with a five hundred dollar scholarship.

ANNUAL MOTHER'S DAY TEA — On May 8, 2004, the group held its first annual Mother's Day Tea. The event was held at the Hyatt Regency in Chicago, Illinois. The event was lovely and prompted inactive sorors who attended the event to join the group. On May 7, 2005, the second annual Mother's Day Tea was held at the Embassy Suites Hotel in Chicago. Over 400 tickets were sold. To date, the group continues to host this event every year at various downtown hotels in Chicago and sells over 500 tickets.

CELEBRATE OUR SENIORS — As a part of National Family Volunteer Day, the sorors decided to spend a day at a Senior Center entertaining and pampering the elderly. On Saturday, November 20, 2004, sorors along with the "teen pearls" held live performances and offered companionship to the seniors. Some of the residents were moved to tears.

In 2005, Chi Omega Omega created the Imani Pearls Community Development Foundation, its 501 (c)(3) non-profit organization. IPCDF was developed to serve as the fundraising and program arm of Chi Omega Omega Chapter of Alpha Kappa Alpha Sorority, Incorporated. The name "Imani" is from the Kwanzaa principle, "Faith." This faith drives IPCDF to continually service our communities with quality programming, volunteer projects and networking.

Chi Omega Omega may be a young chapter, but it's a chapter that has made incalculable contributions to the communities it serves and beyond. Chi Omega Omega/Imani Pearls Community Development Foundation has provided over $32,000.00 in scholarships to high school seniors and college undergraduates and donated over $43,000.00 in grants to community based organizations. Additionally, our chapter started our Educational Advancement Foundation (EAF) endowment in 2009 and we have donated $12,000.00 since then. We have also promoted health and financial awareness through our Annual Smart Fair and mentored both female and male students, as well as 6th — 8th grade girls.

We sponsor programs throughout the year that focus on youth, family and community and service several neighborhoods throughout the greater Chicagoland area. These areas include Bronzeville, Englewood, Hyde Park, Kenwood, and Washington Park.

MID-YEAR SCHOOL SUPPLY DRIVE — On February 3, 2005, the group donated a host of school supplies to 6th and 7th graders from economically stressed backgrounds at Altgeld School in Englewood.

CREATIVE ARTS AND LANGUAGE CONTEST — On February 18, 2005, the group hosted an essay and visual arts contest at Crispus Attucks School to promote literacy among lower and upper primary students. The contest theme was, "What would the world be like if I were president?" All of the students who participated received Certificates of Participation. Winners received trophies and gift certificates to Borders.

SUPPORTING SMALL LOCAL BUSINESS VENDORS (CHAPTER MEETINGS) — 2009-2012, Chi Omega Omega / IPCDF meet as a chapter 10 months out of the year to conduct business and promote service to all mankind. 8 out of the 10 monthly meetings, we invited a vendor/black-owned business to showcase there product(s) or services in order to encourage continued economic support.

IPCDF — ESP NEWSLETTERS — 2009 – 2010, IPCDF created a newsletter designed to encourage the support of local Chicago black-owned businesses. The newsletters were distributed at chapter meetings as well as electronically. Overall chapter members were impressed with the quality, layout and design. The document was a great promotional tool that highlighted and publicized our black owned businesses in which we could exercise our black buying power. Business owners were grateful for our support and used our newsletter in their shops.

VELVET ROPES — 2009 – 2012, IPCDF/COO created Velvet Rope Fridays as a stylish affair designed to provide individuals with a venue to socialize, network and share business ideas with other like minded entrepreneurial minds. If someone was looking for a great way to make new connections and cultivate new business, then Velvet Rope Fridays was an event to attend. Velvet Rope Fridays are highly attended by members along with their friends and are publicized manually, electronically, on Facebook, and Evite.

ANNUAL HEALTH AND ECONOMICS SMART FAIR — 2009 – 2012, each year, the foundation holds an annual health/economic fair. During the fair, a variety of resources are made available to community participants throughout the day: speakers discuss health topics relevant to the African American community, there are free health screenings, book bags with school supplies are given away, and workshops for families are held throughout the day. Additionally, there are games for children, health and financial vendors, and fitness and dance classes to take advantage of.

DIABETES AWARENESS PRESENTATION — 2010, this activity promoted diabetes awareness and provided helpful tips to the ninety-four members present at the chapter meeting. The Health Initiative Committee surveyed the chapter and foundation by asking members to stand if they fell into various categories at greater risk for diabetes. Many members were shocked to find that they had several risk factors for Type 2 diabetes.

Healthy cooking pamphlets were also passed out from the American Diabetes Association (Taste and See Recipes from the ADA's website and Healthy Soul Food recipe guide). Three blood glucose monitors were also donated and give away to three lucky winners!

PINK GOES RED FOR WOMEN — 2011 – 2012, The goal of this activity was to increase the awareness of heart disease. Members were asked to wear red and to take pictures in their red attire. All submitted photos were added to a collage that was put on display at a monthly chapter meeting.

Emerging Young Leaders (EYL): COLLEGE AND CAREER FAIR — 2011 – 2012, the Chapter provided EYL students with educational enrichment through a college and career fair. Girls were exposed to a variety of careers and informed of the education required for each profession. We also hosted a panel discussion on how to prepare for and choose a college. The girls then rotated to four different career workshops. Each workshop was based on a different career theme and was hosted by sorors who work in that particular area.

The themes included: 1. Law Enforcement (lawyers, police women); 2.Education & Social Services (professors, social workers); 3. Health & Wellness (nurses, pharmaceutical representatives, pharmacists); 4. Entrepreneurship (business owners). After the workshops, the girls participated in a panel discussion titled "College Readiness and Success." Sorors with careers in education and counseling participated on the panel.

GLOBAL POVERTY — COMMIT TO CHANGE — 2011–2012, through this activity, the Chapter raised funds for families living in poverty. In partnership with Heifer International, these funds give families a hand-up, empowering them to turn their lives of poverty into self-reliance and hope. Members were encouraged to clean out their purses and wallets of loose change and make a donation for a living gift to be purchased from the Heifer Project. This gift will be matched by IPCDF funds to make a difference in the lives of several families. As a result of the year-long collection of change, the items purchased were a sheep, a goat, a flock of chicks and a flock of geese. Members were made aware of how such a small amount of money makes a difference in the lives of those living in poverty. This fundraising event was held monthly at Chapter meetings. In addition, our foundation donated $1,600 to the Heifer International organization.

GLOBAL POVERTY — COMMUNITY GARDEN — 2011–2012, The purpose of this activity was to educate the female residents of the Maria Shelter about the sustainable environmental practices of gardening; to build skills in preparing, planting and maintaining a garden; and to promote healthy eating options. Residents also learned how hobbies, such as gardening, help reduce stress and had the opportunity to interact with positive female role models to help motivate their efforts to find permanent housing, employment and to build their support system.

SOCIAL JUSTICE AND HUMAN RIGHTS / GLOBAL POVERTY — RWANDA BOOK DRIVE/KINYANZA SECONDARY SCHOOL — 2011–2012, the goal of this activity was to donate books to adolescents at the Kinyanza Secondary School in Rwanda, Africa. Members both donated and collected books for children ages 8-16 years that focused on science, math, literature, English and social studies. More than 600 books were collected. The books were sorted according to course topic and academic levels and will be housed in the school's library. The school's library will be named after our chapter foundation, the Imani Pearls Community Development Foundation Library. In addition, our foundation has donated a little over $2500.00 to have furniture made for the library.

SOCIAL JUSTICE HUMAN RIGHTS — NEOPOLITAN LIGHTHOUSE DOMESTIC VIOLENCE SHELTER DONATION — 2011, the goal of this activity was to provide donations to the Neopolitan Lighthouse, a 25-bed shelter which offers services to women and children fleeing from abusive relationships 24-hours a day, 365 days of the year. The Social Justice and Human Rights initiative members led a clothing and toiletry drive for the women and children who have been rescued from domestic violence and reside at Neopolitan Lighthouse. More than 150 items were collected including soap, deodorant, shampoo, dental care products, clothing, and more.

SOCIAL JUSTICE HUMAN RIGHTS — Dreamcatcher Foundation — 2011–2012, In January 2011, we welcomed the co-founder Brenda Myers-Powell and a young survivor of human trafficking to our monthly chapter meeting to raise awareness of the issue of domestic human trafficking and prostitution for Anti-Human Trafficking Awareness month. In January, we did a large housewarming drive for a survivor of human trafficking and her daughter who moved into their first apartment together. In June and July 2011, we did a baby clothing/item drive for a baby born to a survivor of human trafficking and presented to the new mom in August 2011. In August 2012, we provided information at a table hosted by the Dream Catcher Foundation about domestic violence and human trafficking at the annual Smart Fair. In late August 2012, we teamed up with the Dream Catcher Foundation to walk in the annual Traffickfree 5k race and wore shirts in honor of the Dream Catcher survivors. In October 2012, SJHR invited Brenda to join our 3rd Thursday session with Teen Youth Alliance to discuss sex education. On November 16, 2012 our foundation held a joint event potluck between Dream Catcher and Traffickfree to raise awareness about Dream Catcher's efforts to help survivors.

Chi Omega Omega Advises Tau Mu Chapter.

Chapter Members Who Have Held International/National Office or Been Elected to the International/National Nominating Committee

Giselé M. Casanova	Central Regional Director	2010-2014
	Chairman, Nominating Committee	2006 – 2008
	Nominating Committee	2004 – 2006

Chi Omega Omega Chapter Basilei

Tamara D. Smith	2005 – 2006 (Chartering Basileus)
Jane L. Stuart	2007 – 2008
Tiffany V. Seay	2009 – 2010
Dawn K. Smith	2011 – 2012
Dion Redfield	2013 – 2014

Pamela Bates Porch

27th Central Regional Director
July 2006 – July 2010

Soror Pamela Bates Porch was elected the 27th Central Regional Director at the 72nd Central Regional Conference in Chicago, Illinois and installed at the 62nd Boule in Detroit, MI. Soror Porch directed the eight-state Central Region in programming activities focused on the international program theme "ESP" an "Extraordinary Service Program."

The theme of her tenure centered on: "Making the Difference: A New View of Leadership in Central Region: Teamwork, Integrity, Service and Vision."

Soror Pamela was initiated into Delta Beta Chapter at Southern Illinois University, Carbondale, Illinois. Soror Pamela believed in making the difference as an undergraduate and participated in all levels of service within the chapter. During the second year of her undergraduate year Soror Bates (Porch) returned home to her beloved Chicago and immediately transferred into Beta Chapter Citywide. There she served diligently as Membership Chairman, Program Chairman and eventually serving as the undergraduate chapter Basileus in 1974.

Her undergraduate experience was a positive one because of the mentorship of graduate Sorors in the sponsoring graduate chapter. Instilled early in her membership was the importance of active membership and making contributions through service and leading by example. During her undergraduate experience she believed in living up to the investment of those graduate Sorors who expected success not only within the sorority experience but transcending into all aspects of her life. It was their living examples of leadership that was the motivating examples of being a servant leader.

Upon graduation from Chicago State University Soror Porch received a Bachelor's of Education with a focus on Reading and Early Childhood Education. Soror Porch immediately went to work for the largest School District 299 and was employed by Chicago Public Schools.

Soror Porch believes in lifelong learning and became an Early Childhood Specialist and a Reading Coach.; Soror Porch made significant impact in the local community and served students and families at Caldwell Academy Elementary. While a brief time working for the Department of Early Childhood Education as a Specialist and then a Reading Coach with a responsibility for over 30 schools, impacting quality instruction and support for Early Childhood Education Teachers. As Soror Porch approached retirement she returned to her beloved Caldwell Academy until her retirement.

Soror Porch transferred into newly chartered Xi Nu Omega and served in all aspects of leadership. Soror Porch always believed in building strong chapters and served in numerous capacities and was known for her creative and innovative activities that nurtured current members as well as attracting new transferring members back to the chapter. Soror Porch became Program Chairman-Anti Basileus of Xi Nu Omega and developed a signature Xi Nu Omega Program that is currently in its 28th year serving the community.

During her tenure as Anti-Basileus her concentrated efforts to impact the community caused Soror Porch to Present Best Practice at the Regional Conference under then Dorothy Buckhanan

(Program Representative) which presented the opportunity to present at Boule as a best practices program.

Soror Porch was also instrumental with community revitalization with a partnership with the Harriet Harris WYCA. The Harris YWCA was an underutilized facility in the Woodlawn Community. During her tenure as Anti- Basileus Soror Porch cultivated a relationship with the Director Karen White and developed a partnership using the YWCA as the hub for all programs and meetings. Because of her commitment she was asked to be a part of the Advisory Board of Directors which concluded in 1999.

Soror Porch served as the 9th Basileus of Xi Nu Omega Chapter, serving for two terms during 1997-1998. During her tenure as Basileus she increased the chapter's presence on the Regional and International levels. She was identified as a trainer for Central Region and was responsible for all Graduate Advisor training in Central Region.

On the International level Soror Porch served the administrations of Norma Solomon White as the NPHC liaison representing Alpha Kappa Alpha Sorority, Inc.; served on the International Membership Committee designing the "Keeper of the Spirit" pin, campaign and logo under the Linda Marie White administration. During her tenure as Central Regional Director, 2006-2010, the journey of leadership continued. Striving to lead by compassionate service she added an additional Central C to the Region's already stellar list of attributes/adjectives, Caring.

Caring was the hallmark of Soror Porch's leadership. During trying times during the history of this sisterhood Soror Porch stressed the emphasis of being "IVY STRONG" in the midst of adversity and trial. The message of being productive and nurturing our sisterhood, allowed the region to weather the storms and stay productive, which is the strength of this region. Challenges bring strength of character and integrity.

Doing the work of the Regional Director was where she thrived and totally immersed herself during her tenure 2006-2010. Although she paved the way for chapters to be chartered including doing site visits meeting with university administrators; meeting with chapters; preparing for the chartering process to be presented to the Directorate; and packet review. She did not charter any new chapters during her tenure. This fact caused her to question "what would be my legacy during the four years of service? I had to come to the realization that is not the accolades of men but the service that we render." One must be cognizant that it is the personal sacrifice of each individual that will make the difference. If my theme was to Make the Difference, to be real and relevant it must be through the personal service of each individual.

It is that personal commitment that remained the focus to model as the leader for our members to follow and implement in chapters across Central Region. The question remains for the membership that brands this organization in Service to All Mankind can we stay the course in the midst of trial and inspire others not to give up? The test of faith had to become the substance and legacy of my service to the sorority. How we respond during a trial, is an important lesson that we modeled not only for the Region but for Alpha Kappa Alpha et al.

The excitement of helping our members become an informed membership was manifested through Clusters and Regional Conference's workshops and training.

During her tenure she met with Basilei Councils, Graduate Advisors, Undergraduates and Chapters. She was the guest speaker at many Founders' Day activities and Ecumenical Services. It is doing the work of service that is what our Sorors look to as the legacy and the success of leadership, whether it is at the chapter level, regional level or on the international level.

Also, during her tenure she shared the accomplishments of all of the chapters in Central Region. Central Region completed its Standard Evaluations ahead of schedule and was recognized by the International Standard's Committee during the 2009 Central Regional Conference. Additionally we strategized to minimize the cost of the evaluation of chapters by allowing chapters that were prepared to be evaluated to bring materials to Cluster meetings to be evaluated by the Standards Committee. "When you have a heart for your membership you cannot think singularly but with the total membership in mind."

The Celebration of the Centennial was one of the highlights of this administration. All over Central Region local chapters planned and implemented celebrations that were meaningful to the local communities where Alpha Kappa Alpha chapters' exists. This collective activity allowed for each state and cluster area to brand the activity with their unique creativity, meaning and imprint that is important to the local chapter and the services they provide in that community. Our celebration included the activities inclusive of the travelling Centennial Exhibit premiering in Milwaukee, Wisconsin Epsilon Kappa Omega Chapter and in St. Louis Missouri with Gamma Omega as host chapters.

Central Region under the direction of our musical director Soror Dolena Mack, asked the region for poems, and original musical submission, regional strolls that were collected to celebrate the individuality and uniqueness of the region as well as those commonalities that bring us together as a region. Soror Dolena Mack wrote an original Central Region song that is still being sung by members of Central Region.

Chapters prepared videos, oral histories, program celebrations, collaborations with other Pan Hellenic organizations, and monthly activities that led up to Founders' Day Celebration in Washington D.C and our return to our founding home during the Boule Celebration in Washington D.C.

The Porch View of Leadership, always focused on the local chapters in the region, celebrated their accomplishments and worked collectively to develop "IVY STRONG" chapters that make up the Confident, Competent, Caring and Capable Central Region.

"It was my distinct pleasure to serve an awesome region, along with the talented and caring women that make up the Central Region. This is the Region of my Alpha Kappa Alpha Sorority, Incorporated birth and the Confident, Competent, Caring and Capable awakening of my place in the historic Central Region History. "Soror Pamela Bates Porch is currently serving on the International Membership Committee, during the administration of Carolyn House Stewart, creating many of the icons and presentations that are presented by this international committee.

Giselé M. Casanova
28th Central Regional Director
July 2010 — July 2014

Soror Giselé M. Casanova is a charter member of Xi Zeta Chapter at Illinois Wesleyan University, Bloomington, Illinois where she served as Anti-Basileus and Dean of Pledges. She affiliated with Xi Nu Omega Chapter in Chicago, Illinois where she served in several offices including Basileus, Graduate Advisor to two undergraduate chapters, Parliamentarian, and Membership Chairman. Soror Casanova is currently a member of Chi Omega Omega Chapter in Chicago, Illinois. She is a Silver Star and a Life Member.

Professionally, Soror Casanova is a Licensed Clinical Psychologist and an Associate Professor of Psychology at Purdue University Calumet in Hammond, Indiana. She earned a Bachelor of Arts degree in Psychology from Illinois Wesleyan University, Bloomington, Illinois, where she graduated with honors. Soror Casanova pursued her graduate studies in psychology at Northern Illinois University in DeKalb, where she earned her Master's and Doctoral degrees in Clinical Psychology.

Soror Casanova has the distinct honor of being the first African American student to earn a Master's degree in Clinical Psychology and a Ph.D. in Clinical Psychology from Northern Illinois University's Graduate Program in Psychology. She is a Licensed Clinical Psychologist in the state of Illinois. She has a private practice and is an invited lecturer who presents seminars, workshops, and leads discussions on a variety of mental health topics. Soror Casanova is also a researcher who has published articles and books and presented papers in the areas of psychopathology, child abuse, family violence, and multicultural issues in psychology. Soror Casanova has received the "Outstanding Teacher" award at Purdue University Calumet in recognition of her accomplishments with actively and creatively engaging her students in the learning process. She has served as the Director of the Ethnic Studies Program, an instructor for the Upward Bound Program, and Faculty Research Mentor for students in the McNair Achievement Program at the university. Soror Casanova's support of campus TRIO Programs earned her the "TRIO's Director's Award." She is listed in the "International Who's Who of Professional and Business Women," "Whose Who Among American Teachers and Educators," "Whose Who Among African Americans," "Who's Who in America," and is the recipient of the "Black Pearl Award" for Education and the 'Woman of Achievement Award."

Soror Casanova is a member of Top Ladies of Distinction, Incorporated and is the chapter organizer for the Evergreen Park Chicago Chapter. She served as President, Top Teens Advisor and Financial Secretary. Soror Casanova is a native Chicagoan. She is the oldest of four siblings and has one daughter, Tatiyana.

Soror Casanova's record of service to Alpha Kappa Alpha includes conducting numerous workshops on the regional level, at Boules and at Leadership Seminars. She served as Cluster Retreat Chairman (1999), Undergraduate Round Up Chairman (2002), Chairman of Central Region's Awards Committee (2000-2002), Chairman of Central Region's Graduate Advisors' Training Institute (2002-2004) and Chairman of Central Region's Technology and AV Team (2002-2006). Soror Casanova was elected to serve as Central Region's Representative to the International Nominating Committee from

2004 to 2006. She was reelected to this position to serve from 2006 to 2008 and was appointed as Centennial Chairman of the International Nominating Committee. She also served as a member of the International Technology Committee (2008-2010).

Soror Casanova was elected 28th Central Regional Director at the 76th Central Regional Conference in Chicago, Illinois and installed at the 64th Boulé in St. Louis, Missouri. During Soror Casanova's tenure as Central Regional Director, the region grew to 90 chapters with 53 graduate chapters and 37 undergraduate chapters. She encouraged membership growth by chartering three undergraduate chapters: Tau Iota (Millikin University, Decatur, IL); Tau Mu (DePaul University, Chicago, IL); and Tau Rho (University of Southern Indiana, Evansville, IN) and one graduate chapter, Mu Delta Omega, Fort Knox, KY, that was originally chartered in 1978 and later dissolved due to lack of membership.

Soror Casanova is a strong supporter of our undergraduate sorors. During her tenure as Central Regional Director, she appointed undergraduates to every regional committee, appointed undergraduate Cluster Coordinators, and ensured that undergraduates (Leadership Fellows) served as workshop presenters at each Undergraduate Round Up. Through Soror Casanova's guidance and encouragement, Central Region had over one dozen Leadership Fellows and she spotlighted them on the Central Region website, in the Central Region newsletter and at each Central Regional Conference.

Soror Casanova presided over four record-breaking Central Regional Conferences where she utilized technology to increase the availability/accessibility of information. She introduced the first Central Region "app" for iPhones and Androids that gave real-time updates and information about the conference and its' events. Sorors could follow Central Regional Conference events, updates and information on Facebook and Twitter with live feeds available at the conference. The conference newsletters were published and accessible on the Central Region website and app and her Regional Director's "State of the Region" address was made live and available to members via the Central Region website immediately after her presentation at the first plenary session. Soror Casanova made available a "Cyber Café at Regional Conferences for sorors' convenience. Additional conference "firsts" introduced during Soror Casanova's tenure include: each conference Gala featured a "surprise" major, International R&B recording group as entertainment for the Gala party; the addition of "Undergraduate Hospitality" and "Honey-Do Hospitality" and organized activities; and the addition of the EAF Legacy Breakfast that featured a "live auction" to raise money for EAF. Soror Casanova believed in making a difference in the lives of the citizens in the community where each Central Regional Conference was held. Consequently, she ensured that an "off-site" service project was implemented in each conference community as a "kick-off" to the conference. Additionally, each Round Up and Cluster Retreat had a service project that was related to one of the sorority's program initiatives. As a result of Soror Casanova's appreciation of timeliness, all Central Regional Conference sessions and events started on time and ended ahead of time. Conference evaluations indicated that sorors described the conferences as "educational, sisterly, and fun."

Soror Casanova increased the usage of technology on a regional level as well. During her tenure, registration for all Undergraduate Round Ups, Cluster Retreats and Regional Conferences was available solely via the Central Region Online Registration Site. Important information from Corporate Office or from the Regional Director was sent to each member via a regional "e-blast." The Central Region website featured a "Members Only" password-secured section where important documents for sorors were posted. Soror Casanova introduced the Central Region "Online Store" as a means of selling conference items/paraphernalia to members.

Soror Casanova recognized the importance of supporting our Educational Advancement Foundation. During her term as Central Regional Director, the Haley, King, Beard Endowment Fund was capitalized in 2011 and the Giselé M. Casanova Endowment Fund was capitalized in 2013. At the 2011 Leadership Seminar EAF Luncheon, Central Region was presented an award for the "Greatest Amount of Contributions" among medium sized regions.

Soror Casanova's publications, as Central Regional Director, include 16 issues of the "Central

Solstice," the regional newsletter; four Central Regional Conference "Pictorial" newsletters; the 5th through 8th editions of Central Region's "Conference Planning Guide"; and she created the Undergraduate Round Up and Cluster Retreat "AV and Logistics Guide." Soror Casanova designed the first Central Region pin made and sold by the sorority's jeweler, 14 Karat Plus. In appreciation for the wonderful music that Central Region's "Ivy Notes" have provided to the region for upwards of 10 years, Soror Casanova requested that they record a CD of Central Region's songs. They did so and she presented the CD, entitled "The Ivy Notes: Songs Celebrating Our Sisterhood" as a gift to all 79th Central Regional Conference registrants.

Soror Cassanova also has the distinction of being the first Regionsal Director to have two chapters: Beta Chapter founded October 8, 1913 and Gamma Chapter founded February 12, 1914 (the first and second chapters established following the Incorporation and the second and third chapters in Alpha Kappa Alpha Sorority) to host "back-to-back" centennial celebrations during her tenure. In summary, Soror Casanova's service as Central Regional Director moved the region and its' members forward while continuing Central Region's legacy of being "Supreme in Sisterhood, Service and Leadership."

Tau Iota Chapter

Millikin University
Decatur, Illinois
April 17, 2011

Charter Members

NASHANA ALEXANDER	RUBYE COLEMAN
ARIELLE AUSTIN	KARA KNAZZE
TRENAE BATES	AUTUMN MORGAN
TIARA BRITTON	JORDAN MOXEY
BRITTANY BROWN	JOYCE RABY
KELSEY CARTER	RAVEN TOWNSEL
	GABRIELLE WILLIAMS

There have been several Alpha Kappa Alpha Sorority Incorporated interest groups on Milliken University campus dating back to the early 1980's. Though many were interested in earning membership into the sorority, a chapter was never established.

In 2004 Jean D. Reid, a charter member of the graduate chapter of Chi Xi Omega, Decatur, Illinois, began meeting with administration of Millikin University, and she continued to do so until just prior to her death. Realizing the value for Soror Jean's vision, Soror Melverta Wilkins continued to pursue a chapter on Millikin's campus. In the spring of 2010, Regional Director, Soror Pamela Porch began to meet with Millikin's administration.

During the summer of 2010, the new Central Regional Director, Soror Giselé M. Casanova began having conversations with Millikin University administration and in the fall permission was granted to pursue a chapter of Alpha Kappa Alpha Sorority on Millikin's campus.

In the spring of 2011 the very first Rush was held and the Millikin University Interest Group was established. On April 17, 2011 the Tau Iota Chapter was chartered. The chartering ceremony took place at Pilling Chapel, located on Millikin University's campus. In attendance was Central Region Director, Giselé M. Casanova, members of the Decatur Graduate Chapter, Chi Xi Omega and active

Sorors who personally knew members of the interest group chartering. Sorors Latrina Denson and Marquita Cunningham of the Chi Xi Omega were the Chartering Graduate Advisors.

The first officers of the Tau Iota Chapter were: Basileus — Autumn Morgan, Anti Basileus- Kara Knazze, Parliamentarian — Joyce Raby, Grammateus- Raven Townsel, Tamiouchos — Gabrielle Williams, Chaplin-Joyce Raby, Epistoleus — Jordan Moxey, *Ivy Leaf* Reporter — Kelsey Carter, Precunious Grammateus — Nashana Alexander, Hodegos-Kelsey Carter, Historian — Yasmine Scott, Philacter — Nashana Alexander, and Committee Chairmen: Standards — Yasmine Scott and Social Media C — Arielle Austin.

Major Chapter Events and Service Projects:

During the fall semester of 2011, Jeshauna Love, Stevene McGhee, Kara Knazze, and Gabrielle Williams joined hands to embark on the task of giving "Service to All Mankind." These Tau Omega Chapter members came together to assist the African American Cultural and Genealogical Museum of Illinois in Decatur to help coordinate and structure the facility's management and services.

These Sorors while assisting the museum gained insight on the history and artifacts in the museum. Some experiences included but were not limited to: creation of management hierarchy, placement of articles to better tell history as a story, etc. In the end, these women walked away with increased knowledge of their history as well as carrying out the promises they all vowed to do. In all, it was a joyous experience to be of service one opportunity at a time.

In the fall of 2011 Tau Iota hosted a campus wide event entitled Recycling Wars. The event involved getting dormitories on campus to recycle. The Office of Residence Life was included in the planning of this event and the Resident Assistances supported the event. The goal of the event was to inform people how easy it is to recycle even as a college student. The dorm with the most collected recyclables won a pancake breakfast cooked in there building by Tau Iota Chapter members. To show how effective recycling can be on Millikin University's campus, Tau Iota used the solar-powered recycling bins that have been placed around campus to dispose of the collected items. Over 2,000 recyclables were collected from the dormitories on campus!

Homelessness has many faces but can be defined as the lack of a permanent, safe and affordable place to live. The exact statistics on homelessness in America is difficult to determine, as the precise number of people who experience homelessness continues to change. Here in Decatur, Illinois, the rate of homelessness is nearly twice that of the statewide rate. In other words, this alarming epidemic of homelessness was happening right in our front yard.

On September 27, 2011, Alpha Kappa Alpha Sorority, Inc., Tau Iota Chapter sponsored a program entitled "Different Faces of Homelessness." This program was implemented not only to bring awareness of this social injustice to the campus community, but also sought to change the perception of what homelessness looks like. During the program, students and faculty were provided with a brochure highlighting the statistics of homelessness in our nation and, more specifically, our community.

We facilitated discussion by engagingly inquiring about their thoughts and opinions on the idea of being homeless. The discussion became more animated when particular questions were asked such as "Do you feel that it is one's own fault for being homeless?" After the discussion, there was a power point presentation portraying photographs and facts on individuals that are homeless, leaving many of those who attended very touched and emotional. The program was concluded by providing information on agencies and volunteer opportunities within our community. "Different Faces of Homelessness" sparked passion among students and faculty alike and started the discussion about a serious issue that is occurring in our area. It was truly engaging and fulfilled the purpose it was implemented to do.

Each October, the Decatur area puts together an annual food drive for different community servants. The food will fill the shelves of food pantries at Catholic Charities and The Salvation

Army, both of which have seen a greater need in recent months. Different organizations and companies are asked to participate and WSOY hosted this community service effort. Millikin University is invited to participate each year. In recent years, the Millikin University food drive committee set ambitious heights with 4,000 pounds plus in canned goods. Since chartering, the Tau Iota Chapter of Alpha Kappa Alpha Sorority, Inc. has made donations to be a part of this wonderful community service effort.

The Chapter members feel that it is always great to give back to the community because essentially we are a part of the community. For both years, since the Chapter's chartering, Tau Iota has donated the most canned food as an organization and have been acknowledged on campus for doing so. We are very proud of our accomplishments and strive to do bigger and better every year!

In November 2011, Alpha Kappa Alpha Sorority, Inc., Tau Iota Chapter volunteered at Webster-Cantrell Hall in Decatur, Illinois. The mission of Webster-Cantrell Hall is to serve children, youth and families in troubled circumstances. This agency provides for their physical, social, educational, and psychological needs through home and/or community based and residential programs. The professional services facilitate family preservation and the development of self-sufficient individuals. The vision of Webster-Cantrell Hall is that all children and youth, as a right, are nurtured, loved, and live in safe homes and communities. Our visit with Webster-Cantrell was actively engaging as we participated in games with the youth such as volleyball and basketball and capped the event with a dance competition.

Tau Iota Chapter in an effort to expose Millikin University's student body to African American women of elite status within corporate America and within the Decatur area created The Elite Women's Expo. The Expo included multiple women from the illustrious Alpha Kappa Alpha Sorority Inc., of course and from Decatur or near Decatur, IL. Their fields of work included medical practice, higher-level education, broadcast journalism and real estate. Others included women from the Decatur area whose work paths included law enforcement and entrepreneurs of businesses.

The Expo took place on Tuesday March 27, 2012 at 7pm. The students were introduced to the elite women and given an opportunity to observe each woman's exhibit in order to become familiar with the background of their career. A panel was also set up and the students had the opportunity to write questions that the panel members would answer. The student's questions, comments and/or concerns would be addressed anonymously in order for them to feel completely comfortable with voicing their thoughts.

The panel not only turned into a vital discuss on elements of success and work ethic, but it then became an inspirational heartfelt testimonial period in which each woman passionately spoke on their background and struggle to reach the status in which they are currently in. Connections were made, phone numbers were exchanged, and the ultimate goal of Millikin University students being impacted and learning from elite African American women was accomplished. The Elite Women's Expo will be held annually in March.

On September 22, 2012, Tau Iota in conjunction with the Macon County Department of Health Services held an interactive and informative Health Fair for the Millikin and Decatur communities to promote the importance of healthy living for youth. To do so, a Zumba instructor from the Decatur YMCA gave a physical dance based class; a CPR demo was provided by the Macon Health Department; and a healthy snack demo was given by the members of Tau Iota and DJ TAT from the local radio station HOT 105.5. He hosted the event with live music while spreading the importance of healthy living and eating. The Health Fair was held on Miller Quad on Millikin's campus during Millikin University's Fall Family Weekend in efforts to reach a greater community. At the end of the event, Tau Iota along with volunteers from the Decatur community surprised everyone by doing a flash mob dance of Beyoncé's "Let's Move," from Michelle Obama's Let's Move campaign.

Old Kings Orchard Community Center (OKO) is a neighborhood community center that has been open for 10 years in the inner city neighborhood of Decatur, IL. The community center holds an after school and summer program for children K-8th grade. They also help families in the area who are facing various hardships find resources such as jobs, food banks, and thrift shops, to better assist their family. In the summer of 2012, computers were donated to the center to further develop the technology skills of adults in the neighborhood such as resume building and job searching. These computers are also used by the kids from the summer and after school program for reading, math, science and the development of technological skills as well. On September 29, 2012 Tau Iota assisted in the setup of the new computer lab at OKO by painting and priming walls, doors, and window frames. The computer lab is up and running for the community and students to use.

To spread awareness of homelessness firsthand, Tau Iota members Arielle Austin and Jordan Moxey participated in Box City, a Millikin University event sponsored by the Human Services Department on November 9, 2012. During this event these brave women took on the life of a homeless person by living outside for a night in a box. Everyone brought canned good foods to put in the food pot for dinner, built homes out of used boxes, and gathered around a manmade fire to discuss the topic of "homelessness." The next morning they continued to be homeless and visited the American Refuge shelter for breakfast and another discussion to conclude the night. This event challenged the women to live outside of their normal element and really grasp a night of what homeless men, women and families may endure. It is our hopes to have the chapter at this event assisting and participating in the experience every year.

On October 24, 2012, Alpha Kappa Alpha Sorority Incorporated, Tau Iota Chapter, held an event based off of the ABC channel show "What Would You Do?" To address the Social Justice initiative, Tau Iota Chapter touched on stereotyping and the bullying that derives from it. Specifically, we focused on the mistreatment based on racial makeup, ability, and weight. These are all issues chosen because they are some of the issues that the Tau Iota chapter has personal connections to and was ecstatic about tackling. The conversation made during the event was insightful and meaningful; therefore, the discussion now is to make this program a yearly event. The Tau Iota chapter received a lot of the Greek community's support and expecting to make the program bigger each year to reach more of the community outside of Millikin's walls.

On February 26, 2012, tragedy struck Sanford, Florida. There was a shooting of an unarmed, teenaged, African American male. Trayvon Martin's story spread throughout the country as had the stories of his predecessors, Emmitt Till, Rodney King, and many others. Trayvon Martin became the face of injustice, especially to the African American community.

The City of Decatur had a Trayvon Martin rally where there were guest speakers and artists from all walks of life. Alpha Kappa Alpha Sorority Incorporated, Tau Iota chapter made sure to make an appearance to help get the message out that racial profiling and hate crimes occurs everywhere and affects everybody.

Flyers telling about racial profiling and hate crimes with help lines and a section on tips to follow if think you or someone you know is a victim of a hate crime were created and distributed at the rally. The only way to overcome is to become educated on the subject at hand.

The Tau Iota chapter of Alpha Kappa Alpha Sorority Inc. has not only been servants to homeless men, women, and children, but servants the homeless animals in our community. In the spring of 2012 we volunteered at Macon County Animal Shelter in Decatur, IL. The shelter serves to support the wellbeing of animals in the Decatur community. We were introduced to the animal shelter through an AmeriCorps Vista that specialized in community service. She thought that our bright spirits and positive attitudes would be a great confidence booster for the animals at the shelter. We saw this as an opportunity for us to be enablers for the homeless animals. The services that we provided at the shelter would help the animals' transition from living on the streets of Decatur to being a part of a loving family. Some of our services included training the dogs on how to walk properly on a leash, teaching them how to interact with other dogs, and guiding them on how to behave with adults and small children. What motivated us throughout our experience was the enthusiasm and sense of belonging we received from each animal. Although they can't talk, each animal has their own personality and it was our job to ensure they were able to express their individuality to their potential guardians. After our training was complete, we transported the animals to the local Pet Smart in hopes they would go home with a new family. Our experience at Macon County Animal Shelter gave us an opportunity to be advocates for a silent minority.

The "Read to Feed" program is a blanket program under Heifer International, which is designed to promote literacy among children in grades Preschool through eight in order to help end the world hunger problem. For the last two years, The Tau Iota Chapter of Alpha Kappa Sorority Incorporated partnered with the second grade classes at Dennis Elementary in Decatur, Illinois to help promote literary and fight hunger. The children were given one week and charged with reading as many books as they could. So far the students have read 782 books through our "Read to Feed" program. In a week during November 2011 the student's read 613 books, while this year during November 2012, 169 books were read throughout the classes. The class that read the most books received a visit from the women of Tau Iota and their Graduate Advisor; they were rewarded with a pizza party and they informed us of all of the books they read and their various plots.

Tau Iota Chapter Basilei

Autumn Morgan	April 2011 – April 2012 (Chartering Basileus)
Nashana Alexander	April 2012 – Present

Tau Mu Chapter

DEPAUL UNIVERSITY
CHICAGO, ILLINOIS
FEBRUARY 26, 2012

Left to Right: 1st Row: Yoko Ihaza, Venise Blow, Asia Delk, Alexis Hall, Giselé M. Casanova-Central Regional Director, Heather Jones, Alyssa Hernandez, Breanna Atwood, Channon Campbell; 2nd Row: Aasia Bullock, Camille Lester, Alyssa Barker, Christina Lewis, Mia Liggins, Erin Reed, Sarah Taylor Deaderick, Somalia Sadler, Courtney Sprewer, Arille Thompson, Kandace Thomas

CHARTER MEMBERS

BREANNA ATWOOD
ALYSSA BARKER
VENISE BLOW
AASIA BULLOCK
CHANNON CAMPBELL
ASIA DELK
ALEZIS HALL
ALYSSA HERNANDEZ
YOKO IHAZA

HEATHER JONES
CAMILLE LESTER
MIA LIGGINS
CHRISTINA LEWIS
ERIN REED
SOMALIA SADLER
COURTNEY SPREWER
SARAH TAYLOR DEADERICK
KANDACE THOMAS
ARIELLE THOMPSON

In April 2011, members of Chi Omega Omega Chapter's Graduate Advisors Council (GAC) met with DePaul University to discuss the possibility of chartering an AKA chapter at the university. Due to a new campus organization policy, the university no longer allowed/recognized City Chapters. This university action caused DePaul University to be removed from the Beta Chapter Charter. In order to honor the university's new policy, the GAC needed to insure that there was enough interest and probability to sustain a chapter before moving forward with a request to charter.

Throughout the Spring and Fall of 2011, GAC members continued to meet with university officials to discuss the feasibility of chartering a chapter. In addition, the GAC met with other Pan-Hellenic Council Organizations that were chartered on the campus to better understand the school climate pertaining to greek-letttered organizations. In October 2011, the GAC was permitted to conduct an information session at the DePaul Student Activities Center. The information session was attended by forty-eight young ladies who appeared eager to learn about the organization and a potential chartering. After conducting months of research, the GAC brought forth a recommendation to charter a chapter at DePaul University.

A Formal Rush was conducted by Chi Chi Omega's GAC on January 15, 2012. Thirty-eight young ladies submitted packets for membership consideration. Of the thirty-eight, only nineteen met the qualifications. The average cumulative and quarter GPA was 3.1 and 3.23 respectively. On February 26, 2012 nineteen DePaul University students were initiated into Alpha Kappa Alpha Sorority, Inc. were at, the DePaul Chartering Group with a total of 19 members.

The Initiation and Chartering Ceremony conducted by Central Regional Director, Soror Giselé M. Casanova took place at the Hyatt Regency Chicago. The ceremony was attended by 300 sorors including former and current Directorate members, Regional Officers and Committee Chairmen and local chapter members. Immediately following the Chartering Ceremony, the first chapter meeting for Tau Mu Chapter was conducted with Soror Giselé M. Casanova presiding. Elections were held for chapter officers. Members of the GAC served as tellers. The election results were as follows:

- Basileus — Arielle Thonpson
- Anti-Basileus — Channon Campbell
- Grammeteus — Mia Liggins
- Tamiochus — Alyssa Barker
- Pecunious Grammeteus — Somalia Sadler
- Hodegos — Courtney Sprewer
- Chaplin — Camille Lester
- *Ivy Leaf* Reporter — Kandace Thomas
- Parliamentarian — Sarah Taylor Deaderick
- Graduate Advisor — Tiffany V. Seay

Soror Giselé M. Casanova conducted the Installation of Officers ritual with the assistance of the Graduate Advisors Council. The Tau Mu Chartering Celebration Luncheon followed with over 330 participants including sorors, family, friends and DePaul University Officials.

Since its chartering, Tau Mu Chapter continues to make strides in service. Immediately following the chartering, a program calendar was created. The Program Committee instituted Pink Fridays which took place on the 4th Friday of each month. This staple event provided a consistent time and day where Tau Mu could raise awareness and implement projects connect with the Global Leadership through Timeless Service (GLTTS) Initiatives. In addition, Tau Mu Chapter was committed in developing partnerships with other DePaul based organizations. To date, Tau Mu Chapter has collaborated with Sigma Gamma Rho Sorority, Inc, Alpha Phi Alpha Fraternity, Inc, Kappa Alpha Psi Fraternity, Inc. and Sigma Lambda Gamma.

The remarkable and distinguished women of Tau Mu through hard-work, dedication and determination, are devoting themselves to building a groundbreaking chapter that aims to lift up the community in sisterhood and service.

Tau Mu Chapter Basilei

| Arielle Thompson | 2012 |
| Channon Campbell | 2013 |

Tau Rho Chapter

EVANSVILLE, INDIANA
APRIL 21, 2013

First Row (L-R): Briana Howard, Kali Hayes, Ariel Crenshaw, Central Regional Director Giselé Casanova, Chelsea Brown, Whitney Bowie, Tennille Baxton-Vaughn. Second Row (L-R): Alaisha Johnson-Rhone, Erica Langley, Kelsey Miller, Christina Pullings, Briony Towler, Sydney Watson

CHARTER MEMBERS

TENNILLE BAXTON-VAUGHN
WHITNEY BOWIE
CHELSEA BROWN
ARIEL CRENSHAW
KALI HAYES
BRIANA HOWARD

ALAISHA JOHNSON-RHONE
ERICA LANGLEY
KELSEY MILLER
CHRISTINA PULLINGS
BRIONY TOWLER
SYDNEY WATSON

Pamela Hopson, President of the local chapter of Alpha Kappa Alpha (ZZ) and Director of the University of Southern Indiana (USI) Multi-Cultural Center, caught the vision of the several undergraduate women on the USI campus interested in establishing a chapter. She was encouraged and supported by many of her Zeta Zeta Omega sorors who had been trying for more than 20 years to establish an undergraduate chapter on a local university campus. With untold persistence, continual discussions with interested undergraduate women, volumes of paperwork, and a tremendous amount of planning and coordination with Central Regional Director, Giselé Casanova and Pamela Hopson ushered in a dream — the formation of a group of 12 beautiful young women who would be initiated into Alpha Kappa Alpha Sorority and then charter members of Tau Rho Chapter.

After many training sessions directed by ZZ's Membership Chairman Jennifer Douglas and under the leadership of Regional Director Giselé Casanova, Supreme Basileus Carolyn House Stewart, and Zeta Zeta Omega Chapter Basileus Pamela Hopson, Tau Rho was chartered on April 21, 2013. Tau Rho became the first fraternal organization established by African Americans to be chartered on USI's campus.

The chartering of Tau Rho was an historic event and university officials welcomed Alpha Kappa Alpha with opened arms. In attendance at the celebration luncheon were Giselé Casanova Ph.D. and Nadine C. Bonds, current and former Central Regional Directors of Alpha Kappa Alpha Sorority, Inc., respectively; Linda L. M. Bennett, President of the University of Southern Indiana; Dr. Ronald Rochon, Provost of the University of Southern Indiana; David Stetter, Program Advisor of Fraternity/Sorority Life at USI, sorors of Zeta Zeta Omega Chapter, and many family members and friends. The formal luncheon, held in the Carter Hall ballroom, was catered and sponsored by USI. Twelve tables were elegantly decorated in pink and green for each new soror to receive her many gifts.

The charter members of Tau Rho included twelve dynamic and very accomplished young women:

Tennille Baxton-Vaughn — a senior majoring in Sociology, a recipient of the Duffus-Melvin Recognition Award in Sociology, member of the Dean's list, recipient of an Associate of Applied Science in Business Administration with a concentration in Marketing, a wife and mother.

Whitney Bowie — a junior majoring in Nursing, a member of the Dean's list, a volunteer with College Mentors for Kids program, chairman of the Student Alumni Association, and a volunteer with Peyton Manning Children's Hospital and St. Vincent Women's Hospital of Indianapolis.

Chelsea Brown — a junior majoring in Public Relations and Advertising with a minor in Nutrition, Vice President of the Public Relations Student Society of America organization, the oldest of six siblings and the first in her family to attend college.

Ariel Crenshaw — a junior majoring in Biology, recipient of an Associate Degree in Science from Lincoln Land Community College, a member of the Black Student Union, College Mentors for Kids, secretary of the Diversity Project, recipient of the Distinguished Sophomore Award and Phenomenal Woman Award.

Kali Hayes — a junior majoring in Nutrition and Wellness and a member of the USI Honor Roll.

Briana Howard — a junior majoring in Business Administration with a minor in Spanish, secretary of the Black Student Union.

Alaisha Johnson-Rhone — a junior majoring in Business Administration, a member of the Black Student Union, a member of the Executive Diversity Project, a Resident Assistant, intramural Supervisor at the USI Recreation Fitness and Wellness Center, a member of the USI University Women's Choir, Miss Teen Indiana 2012 with Elite USA Pageant System.

Erica Langley — a junior majoring in Psychology and a community volunteer.

Kelsey Miller — a sophomore majoring in Psychology with a minor in Sociology, Vice-President of the Activities Programming Board, College mentor at Glenwood Elementary, an Alpha Kappa Alpha Sorority legacy.

Christina Pullings — a junior majoring in Nursing, a transferee from Clark Atlanta University, a member of the Dean's list, a volunteer at the Day Spring Center, assistant general manager of College Mentors for Kids, a member of the Student Alumni Association.

Briony Towler — a sophomore majoring in Accounting, a member of the Student Government Association.

Sydney Watson — a junior majoring in Public Relation and Advertising, a member of College Mentors for Kids, Historian for the Black Student Union, an Alpha Kappa Alpha Sorority legacy.

The new officers included Christina Pullings as Basileus, Sydney Watson as Anti-Basileus, Briana Howard as Grammateus, Kelsey Miller as Anti-Grammateus, Alaisha Johnson-Rhone as Percunious Grammateus, Briony Towler as Tamiouchos, Whitney Bowie as Epistoleus, and Chelsea Brown as Ivy Leaf Reporter. Graduate Advisor Council members were Tijuanna Tolliver, Pamela Hopson, Edmonia Pringle, and Alisha Hopson.

In a very short time, during April and May 2013, the charter members of Tau Rho distinguished themselves with a great service project at the Evansville United Caring Shelter by preparing food to be served and donating baskets of toiletries to be given out to those in need. Continuing AKA's great tradition of bringing awareness to social ills, the newly chartered group participated in a campus march to end violence and to support the victims of the 2013 Boston Marathon Bombings. They demonstrated early a strong desire to live up to the ideals of Alpha Kappa Alpha and provide "Service to All Mankind."

Tau Rho Chapter Basilei

Christina Pullings   2013 – Present

Part VI

A Tradition of Service

A Tradition of Service

Through the years the sorors of Central Region have served Alpha Kappa Alpha Sorority and the community locally, regionally, nationally and internationally in various leadership roles. Eight Central Region sorors have received the sorority's Founders' Graduate Service Award for their outstanding record of service: Helen Cromer Cooper, Delta Chi Omega; Winona Lee Fletcher, Kappa Tau Omega; Constance Kinard Holland, Kappa Tau Omega; Johnetta Randolph Haley, Omicron Theta Omega, Nadine Bonds, Alpha Mu Omega, Loann J. Honesty King, Theta Omega; Peggy Lewis LeCompte, Delta Delta Omega; and Audrey Cooper-Stanton, Theta Omega.

Central Region can also take pride in the fact that the Ivy Leaf publication was created under the administration of Loraine Richardson Green, Beta; the sorority's coat of arms was designed by Phyllis Wheatley, Kappa; and music and words of the Ivy Hymn was written by Evangeline Harris Merriweather, Alpha Eta Omega. Constance Kinard Holland, Kappa Tau Omega drafted the incorporation papers for the Educational Advancement Foundation; Loann Julia Honesty King, Theta Omega was an Incorporator and the first Treasurer; Doris Parker, Alpha Mu Omega served as the first Executive Secretary; Marva Lee, Theta Omega served as Acting Executive Secretary; Deborah Dangerfield, Theta Omega served as Executive Secretary/Director (title was changed to Executive Director in 2007)and the current EAF Executive Director is also a member of Central Region: Barbara Sutton, Theta Omega.

A complete listing of the contributions of Central Region sorors throughout the sorority and region's history, sixty-five Boules, Leadership Seminars, other national and international meetings and the seventy-nine Central Regional Conferences would fill the pages of another history book.

Therefore, the author has chosen to include in this section, the names of Central Region sorors who have served as national/international officers; served on national/international committees; held positions with the Educational Advancement Foundation (EAF), and served as Central Region Cluster Coordinators.

Hardly is this list all inclusive and the author is certain that there are omissions. It is however, as complete as possible using the information submitted by chapters along with other sorority document sources.

Several of the national offices which Central Region sorors held were abolished and new positions created. The 48th Boule established the current size and composition of the Directorate in July 1978. This action abolished the offices of Supreme Anti-Grammateus, Financial Director, Graduate Member-at-Large, Editor-in-Chief of the Ivy Leaf and Undergraduate Program Advisor from the Directorate structure.

Also, this Boule dissolved the executive committee and the public relations committee and enlarged the constitution and program committees to include representation from each region. The establishment of national/international standing committees has undergone several changes as well and special national/international project committees and appointed positions have been created. All of which added to the enormity of this task.

Loraine Richardson Green
Supreme Basileus (2nd)
1919 – 1924

Through a life filled with firsts, Loraine Richardson Green made a lasting impression on all with whom she came in contact.

During a time when success was difficult for Blacks and women, Soror Green received her bachelor's degree in English, with honors in June 1918. She received the degree of A.M. in Sociology in 1919, being the first Black woman to receive the master's degree in that department at the University of Chicago. She was a former teacher and social worker and was the first Black woman offered a position by the charity Organization Society of Chicago.

Initiated into Beta Chapter in 1918, Loraine Green was elected chapter Basileus one year following her initiation. During her term as Basileus, she was elected Supreme Basileus.

She was a born speaker. Her voice could fill a room. During her term of office as Supreme Basileus she was responsible for the establishment of our present pin, crest, Ivy Leaf publication and National Founders Day Celebration.

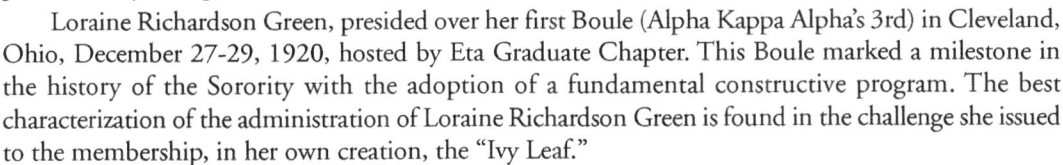

Loraine Richardson Green, presided over her first Boule (Alpha Kappa Alpha's 3rd) in Cleveland, Ohio, December 27-29, 1920, hosted by Eta Graduate Chapter. This Boule marked a milestone in the history of the Sorority with the adoption of a fundamental constructive program. The best characterization of the administration of Loraine Richardson Green is found in the challenge she issued to the membership, in her own creation, the "Ivy Leaf."

"In this era of mighty achievement, nationalization and unification of all interests into harmonious cooperating associations, the individual is submerged in the group, sacrificing personal interests for the common good. One of the first principles of far sighted men and women is to ally themselves with far-reaching powerful associations whose aims are to protect, foster and promote the common interests, purposes and ambitions. This is the function of the Alpha Kappa Alpha Sorority.

A national association cannot be successful unless it has a thorough and efficient organization—a government firmly and unselfishly administered by women of energy, ideal and ability. If the association wishes to bring about results, it must have a clearly defined purpose, with a promise of probability of results of such a substantial nature as to enlist the cooperation of practical women.

Given an efficient organization, a clearly defined purpose, and the inspiring ideals which promoted the founding of the Sorority, the Alpha Kappa Alpha can be a great practical help to her members, and a benefit to the community and to our group generally. We must perfect our national organization so that it is a manifestation of unity and concord. The day of awakening, reconstruction, reorganization, cooperation and coordination is at hand. If the AKA is to expand, we must strengthen and fortify the central government and at the same time come into closer contact with every chapter."

Through the years Soror Green made her career as a homemaker and civic worker. She served as a board member of the Urban League; on the state board of the League of Women Voters; and in 1935 she joined Jane Adams and the Women's International League for Peace and Freedom, and met with

Eleanor Roosevelt in an attempt to head off World War II. In 1958 she was the first Black person appointed to the Chicago Board of Education.

Her experience helped Theta Omega in its infancy, and in 1944 she served as General Chairperson when Theta Omega and Beta were hosts to the Silver Anniversary Boule in Chicago.

Soror Green became a Diamond Soror (75 years) in 1992. Alpha Kappa Alpha Sorority paid tribute to her major contributions to the sorority at the 55th Boule in New Orleans, Louisiana that same year.

On her 106th birthday, sorors throughout Alpha Kappa Alpha recognized her day through visits, gifts, cards and calls. These gestures of love and sisterliness would turn out to be the sorority's last opportunity to show Soror Green how much she meant to the sisterhood. Loraine Richardson Green became an Ivy Beyond the Wall on January 9, 1996. Her life epitomized her favorite quotation: "honor goes not to the swift, not to the strong, but to him who endures."

Maudelle Brown Bousfield

6TH SUPREME BASILEUS
1929 – 1931

Soror Maudelle Brown Bousfield was born and grew up in St. Louis, Missouri. She attended the University of Illinois where, after three years of study, she graduated with majors in two areas—mathematics and astronomy. She was the first Black woman to graduate from the University of Illinois. Her college record was excellent, and in 1965 she was recalled to her alma mater to be inducted into Phi Theta Kappa. She received the Master of Arts degree from the University of Chicago in 1931. From 1906 to 1914, Maudelle Brown taught in the high schools of East St. Louis, Illinois; Baltimore, Maryland; and St. Louis, Missouri. In 1914, she gave up teaching temporarily to marry Colonel Midian O. Bousfield, M.D., and subsequently became the mother of one daughter, Maudelle Bousfield Evans, a soror.

Resuming her teaching career in 1921, she taught mathematics at Wendell Phillips High School until 1926. Maudelle Brown Bousfield was the first Negro to become a principal of a high school in Chicago (Wendell Phillips High School).

During World War II, Mrs. Bousfield was a member of the Women's Advisory Committee of the War Manpower Commission. She was the vice-president of the Board of Trustees of Provident Hospital and from 1948 to 1962 was chairperson of the board of St. Edmund's Parochial School, which she had helped to organize. She was a member of the Mayor's Committee on Juvenile Delinquency and served for two years on the Ladies' Home Journal Political Progress Advisory Committee.

In her later years she earned another bachelor's degree (in music). After her retirement she wrote a weekly garden column for the Chicago Defender newspaper and hosted a very popular program for women, "Maudelle Bousfield Chats," on radio station WGES.

Soror Maudelle Brown Bousfield was initiated into Beta Chapter in 1921 and transferred to Theta Omega when it was chartered in 1922. In Theta Omega she held every office except Grammateus. From 1927-1929 she held the office of First Supreme Anti-Basileus and was elected the 6th Supreme Basileus in 1929.

She presided over the thirteenth Boule in Marshall, Texas, and was the speaker at the Public Meeting of the California Boule in 1932. Her subject, "Health," was an interesting forerunner of the Mississippi Health Project, which was established a few years later; Soror Bousfield served on the advisory committee for the project.

Some highlights of her administration included a drive to recruit inactive members, launching the project to print a sorority handbook, and developing a program of bond purchases by the sorority. She also served as chairperson of the committee from Theta Omega to examine the situation in Gamma Chapter relating to the efforts of the chapter to purchase a sorority house on the campus of the University of Illinois/Urbana.

Morality, scholarship, dependability, and service were the evaluation guideposts which Soror Bousfield always held for the membership of the sorority. Although she prized the examples of cooperation with other Greek-letter organizations, high scholarship was the primary goal toward which she would have the sorority strive. Maudelle Brown Bousfield became an Ivy Beyond the Wall on October 14, 1971.

On September 24, 2013, sorors from across the region joined Central Regional Director, Giselé M. Casanova, University of Illinois administrators, board members, faculty and staff for the dedication of the Maudelle Tanner Brown Bousfield Residence Hall on the campus of the University of Illinois at Urbana-Champaign.

This was the first residence hall built on the campus of the University bearing the name of an African American. This honor was given to Soror Bousfield for her many accomplishments throughout her stellar life and in recognition of her achievement as the first African American woman to graduate from the University. She graduated with honors in 1906 and was the only black woman on campus from 1903 to 1905.

Note: Information on Soror Maudelle Brown Bousfield was taken in part from "Alpha Kappa Alpha — Through The Years" (1908-1988) by Soror Marjorie H. Parker.

Maude Brown Porter

7TH SUPREME BASILEUS
1931 – 1933

Soror Maude Brown Porter was initiated in Alpha Chapter, Howard University in 1915 and served as Basileus of Alpha Chapter during the school year 1916-1917. She received her B.A. from Howard University in 1917, from Western Reserve in Cleveland. Ohio she earned a M.A. and a L.H.D., from Lane College in Jackson, TN.

Soror Brown was a charter member of Eta Omega, Louisville, KY and its first Basileus. She was also a member of Eta Omega when she was elected Supreme Basileus. Although the state of Kentucky was not a part of Central Region at the time of Soror Brown's election and did not become a part of the Region until 1956 Central Region claims her as its own.

Prior to her elected at the 1931 Cincinnati Boule, Maude Brown Porter served Alpha Kappa Alpha Sorority, Inc. as First Supreme Anti Basileus, Southern Regional Director, Chairman of the Nominating and Standards Committee, Chairman of the Regional Directors Council and a member of the Resolutions and Constitution Committee.

Professionally she taught Latin and English in the Central High School of Louisville and was appointed assistant principal in 1944 and served until 1960. Soror Brown worked with the Y.W.C. A. of Louisville for more than 20 years. Her other community and volunteer work included the Urban League, League of Women Voters and the Louisville Council of Church Women., She served as a charter member of the Louisville Pan-Hellenic Council and represented AKA as a Regional Director and National President of the National Pan-Hellenic Council. The Brown Memorial Christian Methodist Episcopal Church where her father was pastor was named in her honor. She was the wife of the Bishop H.P. Porter who presided over the Second Episcopal District.

As a Phi Beta Kappa member herself high scholastic achievement was paramount for Soror Porter. She fostered programs that enforced educational enrichment including the Vocational Guidance Project for High School students; annual scholarships for high school students and fellowships for graduate study. Soror Brown believed that members of the sorority should be more involved in programs and activities to help and educate others and less involved with social affairs. Soror Maude Brown Porter became an Ivy Beyond the Wall on January 4, 1960.

Linda Marie White

26TH SUPREME BASILEUS
JULY 2002 – JULY 2006

Central Region's own Linda Marie White was initiated in Alpha Pi Chapter, Clark College, in 1960 where she received her B.A. Degree in Political Science and was honored as the recipient of the Distinguished Alumna Award.

She received her M.A. Degree from the University of Chicago in 1969 and did graduate studies in systems analysis, Stanford University and Management Sciences, University of Michigan.

Soror White transferred to Theta Omega Chapter, Chicago, Illinois in 1964 where she served the chapter as Basileus, Anti-Basileus, Parliamentarian, Financial Secretary, Graduate Advisor and Anti-Grammateus. Soror White was an Incorporator and first president of the AKARAMA Foundation.

Prior to her election as Supreme Grammateus in 2002, Soror Linda served on the National Cleveland Job Corps Committee, as an International Protocol Liaison and co-authored "A Guide to Alpha Kappa Alpha Protocol." During her tenure as Supreme Grammateus she served as a member of the National Constitution and Bylaws Committee and Secretary for the Educational Advancement Foundation.

Professionally, she rose through the ranks of the Social Security Administration and in 1989 was appointed Area Director, Northern Ohio. The position she held until her retirement in 2002.

Soror White was the recipient of numerous community service and professional awards including 2003 History Makers, Spirit of Maynard Jackson Award, Social Security Regional Commissioner's Citation, Regional Supervisory Excellence Award and Regional Leadership Award

Elected First Supreme Basileus in 1998 at the 58th Boule in Chicago, Illinois, Soror Linda Marie White achieved Alpha Kappa Alpha's highest office when she was installed as the 26th Supreme Basileus of Alpha Kappa Alpha Sorority, Inc. at the 61st Boule.

Soror White adopted "The SPIRIT of Alpha Kappa Alpha" as the National Program theme for 2002-2006. The five targets included in the National Program were Education, The Black Family, Health, Economics, and the Arts. The Signature Program of her administration was the "The Ivy Reading AKAdemy." This reading initiative focused on early learning and mastery of basic reading skills of children by the end of third grade. All chapters were encouraged to implement a kindergarten through third grade after school reading initiative. Alpha Kappa Alpha received a $1.5 Million grant from the U.S. Department of Education to implement this one-on-one reading tutoring for children in grades K-3 in demonstration sites across the country. Through the efforts of the membership, improvement in reading skills of children across the country were documented.

Another major educational program was the Young Authors program where children were encouraged to write stories. Children who participate in this writing initiative had a chance to become a published author. The first publication of children's work was released at the 2004 Boule in Nashville, TN and the second set of publications was released in Detroit in July, 2006.

Alpha Kappa Alpha Sorority, under Soror White's leadership, also focused on the Black Family through programs such as the Presidential Freedom Scholarship; participation in the National Family Volunteer Day and the Martin Luther King, Jr's Day of Service. In the area of Health, chapters and members focued on awareness and educational activities related to cardiovascular health, Breast Cancer Awareness, HIV/AIDS, SIDS and many issues affecting children's health in partnership with the National Institute of Child Health and Human Development.

The Merrill Lynch "Investing Pays Off" Curriculum was used to promote economic awareness through Youth Financial Literacy Programs. During her tenure, members of Alpha Kappa Alpha gave over 3 million hours of service, benefiting 16 million people and contributed more than $20 million to communities.

Many technological advances were made during her administration. For the first time general members paid dues on line, chapters paid member per capital tax on line and members registered for conferences on line.

Central region will forever hold Central Region's own Soror Linda Marie White in high esteem because of her loyal service to Alpha Kappa Alpha Sorority, Inc. Soror White became an Ivy Beyond The Wall on February 26, 2010.

Barbara A. McKinzie

27TH SUPREME BASILEUS
JULY 2006 – JULY 2010

Soror Barbara A. McKinzie holds the distinction of being the only soror to serve Alpha Kappa Alpha Sorority, Inc. as Executive Director and Supreme Basileus of Alpha Kappa Alpha Sorority, Inc.

Soror McKinzie was a charter member and the 1st Basileus of Eta Pi Chapter (chartered 1973), East Central University in Ada, Oklahoma. On the Graduate level she served as Membership Chairperson of Alpha Chi Omega in Tulsa, Oklahoma; Tamiouchos of Beta Sigma Omega, Oklahoma City, Oklahoma; and Basileus, Anti-Basileus, and Tamiouchos of Theta Omega Chapter, Chicago, Illinois. She was a member of Theta Omega Chapter when she was elected Supreme Tamiouchos in 1998 and a member of Delta Lambda Omega Chapter, Shreveport, Louisiana when elected First Supreme Anti-Basileus at the 61st Boule in Orlando, Florida.

Soror McKinzie holds an MBA from Northwestern University's Kellogg School of Management and graduated cum laude from East Central University where she is a past recipient of the school's "Outstanding Graduate" Award.

Professionally, she is an entrepreneur and one of the most respected financial managers in the country with an impressive background in the financial industry. A Certified Public Account, she holds Investment Advisor licenses in most states.

Her professional awards and honors include: "Top 25 Outstanding Business Women of 2002" by the New York Network Journal; "International Who's Who of Professionals in the World," Midwest and Business edition, and "Outstanding Service Award" from the Illinois Certified Public Accountants Society.

In addition to the positions mentioned above, her sorority contributions include: Financial Advisor to the 20th and 21st Supreme Basilei, National Business Roundtable Chairperson, National Nominating and Program Committee and Strategic Planning Committee Chairperson, 1998-2002.

There is a special allegiance between Soror Barbara and Central Region. We proudly claim her as our own and celebrated her installation as the 27th Supreme Basileus.

"It's a New Day" was the rallying call of her programmatic thrust of "ESP" (Economics, Sisterhood and Partnerships). Her vision would spark an "Extraordinary Service Program" that yielded powerful results. More than 28 million individuals were impacted by the ESP platforms; chapter contributions exceeded 11 million with external contributions reaching in excess of 15 million; the first service initiative exclusively for undergraduates was initiated. Central Region's own Soror Loann J. Honesty King had the privilege of serving as the International Program Chairman.

During the 27th (Centennial) Supreme Basileus' administration in addition to the Execution of Successful Programs, the McKinzie administration Established Sustainable Partnerships and there was Excellence in Strategic Preservation. Alpha Kappa Alpha Sorority, Inc.'s assets in all funds grew to an unprecedented 50 million; the sorority became a founding member of the Smithsonian National

Museum of African American History and Culture with a million dollar donation and one million dollars was also donated to Howard University's Moorland-Spingarn Research Center.

Soror McKinzie was at the helm for Alpha Kappa Alpha's Centennial Year and history was made! Following a year of celebrations, one region at a time, more than 35,000 members, family and friends descended on Washington, D.C. to celebrate Alpha Kappa Alpha's 100th year of sisterhood and service. And the world knew of Alpha Kappa Alpha Sorority's heritage, service and achievements.

CENTRAL REGION SORORS WHO HAVE SERVED AS NATIONAL/INTERNATIONAL OFFICERS

CENTRAL REGIONAL DIRECTORS

1st	Pauline Kigh Reed	December 1919 – December 1922*
2nd	Fredericka Brown	December 1922 – December 1923*
3rd	Carolynne Payne	December 1923 – December 1925*
4th	Murray B. Atkins	December 1925 – December 1927*
5th	Althea M. Simmons	December 1927 – December 1930*
6th	Blanch Hayes Clark	December 1930 – December 1934*
7th	Alice McGhee Smart	December 1934 – December 1937*
8th	Arlene J. Washington	December 1937 – December 1940*
9th	Blanche L. Patterson Williams	December 1940 – December 1943*
10th	Maenell Hamlin Newsome	December 1943 – August 1946
11th	Lucille Wilkins	August 1946 – December 1950*
12th	Evelyn Roberts	December 1950 – December 1954*
13th	Maude L. Mann	December 1954 – August 1958*
14th	Annetta M. Lawson	August 1958 – December 1962*
15th	Lee Anna Shelburne	December 1962 – August 1966*
16th	Ordie Amelia Roberts	August 1966 – August 1970*
17th	Johnetta Randolph Haley	August 1970 – August 1974
18th	Gloria E. Smith Bond	August 1974 – July 1978*
19th	Peggy Jean Lewis LeCompte	July 1978 – July 1982
20th	Mable Evans Cason	July 1982 – July 1986*
21st	Loann Julia Honesty King	July 1986 – July 1990
22nd	Yvonne Perkins	July 1990 – July 1994
23rd	Martha Perine Beard	July 1994 – July 1997
24th	Peggy Lewis LeCompte	July 1997 – July 1998
25th	Nadine Celeste Bonds	July 1998 – July 2002
26th	Dorothy Wilson Buckhanan	July 2002 – July 2006
27th	Pamela Bates Porch	July 2006 – July 2010
28th	Giselé M. Casanova	July 2010 – July 2014

* Ivy Beyond the Wall

SUPREME BASILEUS

2nd	Loraine Richardson Green	1918 – 1923
6th	Maudelle Brown Bousfield	1929 – 1931
7th	Maude Brown Porter*	1931 – 1933
26th	Linda Marie White	2002 – 2006
27th	Barbara A. McKinzie**	2006 – 2010
29th	Dorothy Buckhanan Wilson	Installation 2014 Boule

CENTRAL REGION SORORS WHO HAVE SERVED AS NATIONAL/INTERNATIONAL OFFICERS
(CONTINUED)

FIRST SUPREME ANTI-BASILEUS

Zelma Watson	1925 – 1927
Maudelle Brown Bousfield	1927 – 1929
Maude Brown Porter*	1929 – 1931
	1937 – 1938
Lucile Robinson Wilkins	1934 – 1935
Linda Marie White	1998 – 2002
Barbara A. McKinzie**	2002 – 2006
Dorothy Buckhanan Wilson	2010 – 2014

*Eta Omega Chapter, Louisville, KY was not a part of Central Region at the time of Soror Porter's elections. She also served as Southeastern Regional Director.

**Barbara A. McKinzie was a member of South Central Region at the time of her election

SECOND SUPREME ANTI-BASILEUS

Betty Guess	1951 – 1952
Norma F. Carter	1952 – 1953
Frances E. Smith	1954 – 1956
Nan Arrington Peete	1958 – 1960

SUPREME GRAMMATEUS

Murray B. Atkins (Walls)	1922 – 1923
Irma Frazier Clarke	1939 – 1946
C. Elizabeth Johnson	1946 – 1949
Carolynn S. Blanton	1949 – 1951
Evelyn H. Roberts	1954 – 1958
Lauretta Naylor Thompson	1966 – 1970
Peggy Lewis LeCompte	1982 – 1986
Linda Marie White	1994 – 1998
Dorothy Wilson Buckhanan	2006 – 2010

SUPREME TAMIOUCHOS

Irma Frazier Clarke	1949 – 1953
Gladys Buffin Johnson	1954 – 1958
Helen Cromer Cooper	1966 – 1970
Loann J. Honesty King	1978 – 1982
Yvonne Perkins	1986 – 1990
Martha Levingston Perine Beard	1990 – 1994
Yvonne Perkins	1994 – 1998
Barbara A. McKinzie	1998 – 2002

SUPREME PARLIAMENTARIAN

Laura F. Fife *	1939 – 1941
Lucille B. Wilkins	1951 – 1953
Gladys Chapman Gordon	1954 – 1958
Helen Cromer Cooper	1970 – 1972
Johnetta Randolph Haley	1990 – 1994
Constance Kinard Holland	1994 – 1998

Beta Gamma Omega, Lexington KY was not a part of Central Region at the time of Soror Fife's election.

UNDERGRADUATE MEMBERS-AT-LARGE

Lillian C. Herndon	1954 – 1958
Erica S. Horton	2004 – 2006
Delta Springer Irby*	1978 – 1980
Anita L. McCollum*	1982 – 1984

Attending schools outside of Central Region when elected

INTERNATIONAL REGIONAL DIRECTOR
Nadine C. Bond 2002 – 2006

Following is a list of sorors who served in Directorate positions that were eliminated by the Boule:

Supreme Anti-Grammateus

Murray B. Atkins	1919 – 1921
Carolyn S. Blanton	1946 – 1949

Graduate Member-at-Large

Lauretta Naylor Thompson	1958 – 1962

Editor-in-Chief of the Ivy Leaf

Helen Kathleen Perry (1st)	1922 – 1923
C. Elizabeth Johnson	1937 – 1939
Althea Merchant Simmons	1935 – 1938
Robertann B. Cuthbert	1934 – 1935

Supreme Epistoleus

Phyllis Wheatley Waters	1919 – 1921
Alice McGhee Smart	1931 – 1935
Irma Frazier Clarke	1937 – 1939

Financial Director

Helen Cromer Cooper	1962 – 1964
Lauretta Naylor Thompson	1970 – 1974

Director of Publicity

Martha A. Horner	1927 – 1929

Undergraduate Program Advisor

Hazel R. Bolan	1954-1958

PART VI: A TRADITION OF SERVICE

National/International Standing Committees of Alpha Kappa Alpha Sorority, Inc. has been added, a few dissolved and their compositions have changed throughout the years. In addition, several special committees and appointments of sorors have been added for special purposes and dissolved when those purposes were accomplished.

In 1948, the Standing Committees of the sorority were: Advisory Committee on National Programs, Budget Committee, Housing, Boule Program, Standards, Publicity, Current Projects and Undergraduate Activities. By 1962, the Executive, Constitution, Nominating and Personnel Committees had been added and the Budget Committee became the Finance Committee. The Advisory Committee on National Programs became the Program Committee and the Publicity Committee became Public Relations. The Executive Committee was removed in 1978 and the Membership Committee was added. In 1977, the Cleveland Job Corps Committee was listed as a Standing Committee and remained until 1979.

In 1982 the Connection Committee was added as a Standing Committee and 1990 saw the addition of the following Standing Committees: Archives, Building and Properties and Honorary Members/Awards. In 2004 Technology was added as a Standing Committees; the Investment Committee was added in 2008; and the Graduate Advisors Certification Committee in 2010.

Central Region Sorors Who Have Served On National/International Committees

STANDING COMMITTEES
The Standing Committees are listed in the order of their establishment.

CONSTITUTION
Maquiba Ballentine
Diane Pillow Cargile
Helen Cromer Cooper — Chairman
Vera G. Davis
Glaydys Chapman Gordon
Ramona B. Griffin
Johnetta Randolph Haley — Chairman
V. Gale Greene Hardeman
Constance Kinard Holland — Chairman
Emily Johnson
Loann J. Honesty King
Akesha McClain
Paula Payne
Tralicia A. Powell
Susan M. Smith
Lauretta Naylor Thompson — Chairman
Ingrid Wider
Linda White, Secretary
Dorothy W. Buckhanan, Secretary
Tiffany Via
Jarnell Burks Craig, Resource
Kimberley Irene Egonmwan

FINANCE
Gloria Bond
Nadine C. Bonds
Helen Cromer Cooper — Chairman
Loann J. Honesty King — Chairman
Erica S. Horton
Nicole Jenkins
Barbara A. McKinzie — Chairman
Martha Levington Perine Beard — Chairman
Yvonne Perkins — Chairman
Lauretta Naylor Thompson — Chairman

PROGRAM
Dorothy W. Buckhanan
Rose Butler-Hayes
Zoearline Davis, Resource
Josephine Franklin
Clytee Gibbs
Constance Kinard Holland
Alfreda Keith Keller
Loann J. Honesty King — Chairman
Camilla Scott Tanner, Resource
Jacqulyn C. Shropshire
Marian J. Waring — Chairman
Cheryl Cole-Young — Chairman
E. JaNiece Bell

NOMINATING COMMITTEE (The Nominating Committee is an Elected Position)
Lavita Rose Anderson
Danette Anthony
Nadine Bonds
C. Louise Brown
Giselé M. Casanova — Chairman
Victoria Clark
M. Kathleen Coleman
Sherry Curry
Clarice Dreer Davis
Vivian Dreer

Valerie Epps
Pearlie Evans
Barbara Ann English
Yvonne Fluker
Clytee Gibbs
Marilyn Ghoston
Constance Kinard Holland — Chairman
Terrika Jarrett
Dayna Johnson
Susan Johnson
Loann J. Honesty King
Beatrice Lafferty Murphy — Chairman
Blanch Fisher Smith
Jerestler Thorpe
Evelyn Turner
Thea Rogers
Brandi M. Smith
Marian J. Waring
Cheryl Cole Young
Deborah A. Underwood
Evelyn Freeman Walker — Chairman

STANDARDS
Janis Brown
Dorothy Buckhanan
Mae R. Carr
Mary L. Chapman
Ernita R. Cooper
Elreta Dickinson
Johnetta Randolph Haley — Chairman
Leola Madison Travis — Chairman
Yvonne Perkins — Chairman
Hope D. Williams
Osie B. Davenport
Teri Denise Bascom
Yvonne Perkins — Chairman
Teri Denise Bascom

UNDERGRADUATE ACTIVITIES
Tomarra Adams
Kaweemah Bashir
Natalie Chavis
Chantel Hays Cason
Esther Cobb
Toya Corbett
Helena Davis
Erin Green
Erica Horton
Rosalyn Odom
Danielle McClain

Nichole C. Nicholson
Evelyn H. Roberts
Phyllis Smallwood
Leslie Williams
Osato Iyamu
Alendra R. Allen
Monique Brown
Kaydene DeSilva

PERSONNEL/HUMAN RESOURCES (1990)
Gloria Bond — Chairman
Jaunetha M. Cade
Deborah Hill Burroughs — Chairman
Lorraine Griffin Johnson
Nan E. McGhee — Chairman
Helen Cromer Cooper — Chairman
Martha Perine Beard — Chairman
Evelyn Freeman Walker — Chairman

MEMBERSHIP (1978)
G. Elretta Coates Blaine
Alana M. Broady — Chairman
Crystal J. Evans-Washington
Josephine Franklin
Constance Kinard Holland
Betty Jefferson
Cateena Joyce Johnson
Emily Dilworth Jones
Peggy Lewis LeCompte — Chairman
Pamela Bates Porch
Alfreda Keith Keller

CONNECTION (1982)
Anita Donaldson
Jenelle Elder-Green
Pearlie Evans
Betty Lee
Jacquelyn Heath Parker
Cheryl Cole Young
Denise Jackson
Frances G. Carroll
Kiahna W. Davis

BUILDING AND PROPERTIES (1990)
Alison Harris Alexander — Chairman
Mae R. Carr
Peggy Lewis LeCompte
Barbara McKinzie
Martha Levington Perine
Yvonne Perkins

PART VI: A TRADITION OF SERVICE

Carey B. Preston — Chairman
Pamela Bates Porch, Directorate Liaison
Phyllis L. McCune

ARCHIVES (1990)
Essie Blaylock
Adele Johnson Carpenter
Sheryl L. Clayton
Zelia Wiley Holloway
Bernyce Ware
Melody Easley Coleman
Annie R. Pope

HONORARY MEMBERS/AWARDS (1990)
(Honorary Members and Awards were separate committees prior to 1990)
Nadine Bonds
Mae Ruth Carr — Chairman
Stacie R. Collins
Johnetta Randolph Haley
Jamesanna Jones
June Mustiful
Mae Helen Smith
Staci R. Collins Jackson
Lyah Beth LeFlore

TECHNOLOGY (2004)
Brenda Ladipo — Chairman
M. Denise Thomas
Giselé M. Casanova
Tony Branch
Judith Daylie Armstead

GRADUATE ADVISORS CERTIFICATION (2010)
Margo S. Baines — Vice Chairman
Andrea V. Salone

CURRENT SPECIAL COMMITTEES
The Special Committees Are Listed In Alphabetical Order. Current Committees Are Listed First followed by Past Special Committees

Communications
Melody M. McDowell — Chairman
Staci R. Collins Jackson
Meredith Leigh Moore

Conference Planning
Maryam Brown
Deidra Y. A. Edwards
Judith Dayloe Armstead
Mary K. Palmore, Director, Medical Response Team

Diamond/Golden/Silver Sorors
Stella W. Harden
Jenelle Elder-Green

Economic Leadership through Service/International Leadership
Training for External Service
Carole L. Waiste
Bridget Robertson-Borum
Melanie C. Jones

Leadership Fellows
Leola Madison Travis
Audrey Cooper-Stanton — Chairman
Jamille Hall

Legacy Endowment Fund and Corporate Support
Lorraine Griffin Johnson

Protocol
Larnell Burks-Bagley, Liaison
Sheila Bonds
Alana Moss Broady, Liasion
Mae Ruth Carr — Special Liaison for Madame Leah Tutu
Kara Holloway
Marva J. Lee
Yvonne Perkins — Chairman
Linda M. White, Liasion
Francene Gilmer — Chairman (In South Eastern Region at Time of Appointment)
Angela Harper MaHome
DeborahUnderwood

Reinstatement Task Force
Theresa Sanders
Judith Daylie Armstead

Rituals
Shana N. Carpenter
Nadine C. Bonds

Strategic Planning
Barbara A. McKinzie — Chairman

APPOINTMENTS

CLUSTER COORDINATORS

With the formal approval of the appointment of Cluster Coordinators for each region by the Directorate, the 25th Central Regional Director, Nadine C. Bonds appointed Central Region's first Cluster Coordinators at the 66th Central Regional Conference in 2000.

2000 – 2002

Lora Jones — Chairman	Delta Delta Omega
Dororthy Buckhanan	Upsilon Mu Omega
Karen Haggerty	Theta Omega
Sheila Stuckey	Beta Upsilon Omega

2002 – 2006

Theresa Sanders — Chairman	Kappa Psi Omega
Alfreda Keith Keller	Theta Rho Omega
Jarnell Burks-Craig	Alpha Mu Omega
Martina Martin	Beta Gamma Omega
Minnie C. Perry	Gamma Omega

2006 – 2010

Cheryl Lewis Smith — Chairman	Omicron Sigma Omega
Vickie Brown	Delta Chi Omega
Lori Beamon	Epsilon Kappa Omega
Victoria Clark	Alpha Mu Omega
Rosalind Lowery	Nu Pi Omega
Alice Aldridge	Delta Delta Omega
Ramona Griffin	Beta Upsilon Omega
Cheryl Lewis Smith	Omicron Sigma
Jennifer Johnson	

2010 – 2014

Johnna Richmond — Chairman:	Phi Kappa Omega
Michele Lacy	Delta Chi Omega
Teresa Brown	Epsilon Kappa Omega
Sheila Bonds	Alpha Mu Omega
Rosalind Zanders Lowry	Nu Pi Omega
Pennie Denise Brown	Gamma Omega
Dana Branham	Beta Gamma Omega
Emma Kendrick	Omicron Sigma Omega

Undergraduate Cluster Coordinators were appointed by Soror Giselé Casanova, Central Regional Director in 2010.

2010-2011

Bree Smith	Omicron Alpha
Isioma Nwabuzor	Mu Beta
ShaDé Watson	Pi Lambda
Emmanuelle Baily-Greene	Epsilon Eta
Courtney Jones	Beta Epsilon
Angela Glore	Zeta Zeta
Elizabeth Harris	Nu Lambda

2011-2012

Bree Smith	Omicron Alpha
Isioma Nwabuzor	Mu Beta
ShaDé Watson	Pi Lambda
Kara Knazze	Tau Iota
Dalayna Jackson	Beta Delta
Jasmine Shadding	Beta Epsilon
Angela Glore	Zeta Zeta
Elizabeth Harris	Nu Lambda

2012-2013

Melissa Brown	Gamma Chi
Mercedes McKay	Mu Rho
ShaDé Watson	Pi Lambda
Ariel Austin	Tau Iota
Dalayna Jackson	Beta Delta
Jasmine Shadding	Beta Epsilon
Brittany Prather	Epsilon Zeta
Ge'Tina Williams	Nu Lambda

2013-2014

Ahriel Mullings	Pi Nu
Merone Melekin	Mu Rho
Taylor Gillespie	Beta Phi
Bria Purdiman	Gamma
Ashley Carriere	Delta Beta
Brittany Clayborne	Iota Sigma
Ashton Ray	Epsilon Zeta
Christina Jones	Zeta Iota

Past Special Appointments

Executive Assistant to the 27th Supreme Basileus
Erika V. Everett

Executive Assistant to the 26th Supreme Basileus
Essie Blaylock

*Financial Advisor to the
20th & 21st Supreme Basileus*
Barbara A. McKinzie

Central Region Heritage Chairman
Peggy Lewis LeCompte

Corporate Office Consultant
Loann J. Honesty King

Corporate Office Librarian
Essie T. Blaylock

Past Special Commitees

*Anti-Hazing Commission/Ad Hoc
Committee on Policy*
Peggy Lewis LeCompte — Chairman

Business Roundtable
Loann J. Honesty King
Barbara McKinzie — Chairman

Centennial Celebration
Nicole Thorne Jenkins
Melody M. McDowell
Linda M. White

Centennial Commission
Essie T. Blaylock
June Mustiful

Corporations Partnership/Marketing
Deidra Y.A. Edwards
Lorraine Griffin Johnson
Rita Wilson — Chairman

Evaluation
Jaunetha M. Cade
M. Katheleen Coleman
Josephine Franklin

Graduate Advisors Task Force
Winona L. Fletcher
Ramonda B. Griffin

Graduate Undergraduate Concerns
Janis Brown Thompson

Health
LaBertha Reddick Blair

Housing Foundation
Vallateen D. Abbington
Loann J. Honesty King, Treasurer
Barbara A. McKinzie, Treasurer
Yvonne Perkins, Treasurer
Martha Levingston Perine Beard, Treasurer

Ivy Reading Academy
Peggy J. Lubin, Director
Willie Gray, Site Coordinator

Job Corps (Former Standing Committee)
Mae R. Carr
Felice Dudley-Collins
Zoearline G. Davis
Johnetta Randolph Haley — Chairman
Ollie Mackey
Mildred Patterson
Janis Brown Thompson
Linda M. White

Life-Long Learning
Alma C. Powell

Long-Range Program Planning
Rosa A. Smith

Media Council
Barbara Pinder

NAACP
Susan Garr
Peggy LeCompte

NCNW
Claudette McFarland Winstead

*Program Subcommittee — Economic
Development*
Loann J. Honesty King — Chairman
Martha Levington Perine Beard

*Program Subcommittee
— Organizational Impact*
Elouise Gentry

Program Subcommittee — Renewal
Sheryl H. Clayton

*Publicity/Public Relations
(Former Standing Committee)*
Rochelle King Burch
Yvonne Perkins
Lauretta Naylor Thompson

Reactivation
M. Kathleen Coleman

Reading Experience/Commission
Carmelita Anson
Josephine Banks
M. Kathleen Coleman
Jesse Shaw
Mattie Williams

Risk Management
Alana Moss Broady

Self-Study Commission
Johnetta Randolph Haley

Sister Academics Institute
Gladys Beavers Lewis

Standards Evaluation Visitation Team
Alana Moss Broady
Mae Ruth Carr
Ernita R. Cooper
Audrey Cooper-Stanton
Johnetta Randolph Haley*
Constance Kinard Holland
Loann J. Honesty King
Barbara A. McKinzie
Hazel Moore
Henrietta Pelky
Ordie Roberts
LeAnna Selburne
Lauretta Naylor Thompson

SOC (Structure and Operations Commission)
Helen Cromer Cooper

Technology and Grantsmanship
Brenda Ladipo

UNCF
Mabel Evans Cason
Vivian Green

EDUCATIONAL ADVANCEMENT FOUNDATION

Doris Parker, (1st) Executive Secretary
Joycelyn Jordan, Former Executive Secretary
Marva J. Lee Acting Executive Secretary, Director-at-Large
Deborah Dangerfield, Executive Secretary/Director (Title Changed to Director in 2007),
Barbara Sutton, Executive Director (Current)
Erika V. Everett, Finance Manager

Constance Kinard Holland — Drafter of the Articles of Incorporation, Member-at-Large 1st elected Board of Directors
Loann J. Honesty King — Incorporator and 1st Treasurer
Peggy Lewis LeCompte — Secretary 1st elected Board of Directors
Challis M. Lowe — Member-at-Large 1st elected Board of Directors
Linda Marie White — President, First Vice-President, Third Vice President, Secretary
Barbara A, McKinzie — President, First Vice President, Third Vice President, Advisor
Dorothy Buckhanan Wilson — Secretary, First Vice President
Melanie C. Jones — Second Vice President
Martha Perine — Treasurer
Yvonne Perkins — Treasurer
Angela Okunsanya – Member-at-Large
Jarnell Burks Craig — Member-at-Large, Coordinator
Barbara A. McKinzie, Executive Director, Alpha Kappa Alpha Sorority, Inc.
Betty James, Executive Director, Alpha Kappa Alpha Sorority, Inc.
Deborah Dangerfield, Executive Director, Alpha Kappa Alpha Sorority, Inc.
Nicole Barrett, Acting Executive Director, Alpha Kappa Alpha Sorority, Inc.
Adrianna Braxton, EAF Youth Pac
Mable Evans Cason — Coordinator
Anita Donaldson — Coordinator
Cateena Johnson — Coordinator
Deborah Walton McCoy — Coordinator
Lorraine Griffin Johnson — Coordinator
Lorraine Griffin Jonson — Coordinator
Alfreda Keith Keller — Coordinator
Adrianna Braxton — EAF Youth Pac

The sorors of Competent Central Region are proud of their legacy of service. Greater laurels will be won and greater tasks begun as the region and the sorors who constitute it continue to render service to "All Mankind" and "Pass on the Torch."

Part VII

Regional Conferences

Central Regional Conferences

The holding of a Regional Conference was established at the thirteenth Boule of Alpha Kappa Alpha Sorority, Inc. in December 1930. Although the format of the regional conference has changed through the years, the purpose and focus of the conferences has remained consistent.

Regional Conferences have provided a forum for discussing social and civic issues; the sorority's involvement in programs of service; the dissemination of program information; instructional workshops on the sorority's documents, policies and procedures; leadership development; the recognition of individual and chapter achievements and providing the opportunity for fellowship. Guests at Central Regional Conferences have historically included many dignitaries from the sorority and from other walks of life. Each Regional Director and hostess chapter has brought their distinct style to carrying out the mission of the Central Regional Conference.

The first Central Regional Conference was held in Indianapolis, Indiana in 1931 with Alpha Mu Omega as the prime hostess chapter. Soror Blanche Hayes Clark was the presiding Regional Director.

At this time, there were nine chapters in Central Region, five Undergraduate Chapters and four Graduate Chapters: Beta, Gamma, Eta, Kappa, Tau, Gamma Omega, Theta Omega, Alpha Eta Omega and Alpha Mu Omega. There were forty-three sorors in attendance and approximately 100 recorded members in the region.

Eighty-Three years later, Central Region has grown to 90 Chapters fifty-three Graduate Chapters and thirty-seven Undergraduate Chapters with a region membership of more than 3,500 and attendance at Central Regional Conferences ranging from 1,500 – 2,000+ attendees.

Several document sources provided the information on Central's Regional Conferences. In the first and second editions information on these conferences was limited or no information could be located, especially for the earlier conferences. However, the availability of the Ivy Leaf Magazine Archives on the Alpha Kappa Alpha website was an invaluable resource for locating additional information. Nevertheless, there is still missing information and as in the past editions the author has attempted to report the available information in a consistent format with limited deviation.

REGIONAL AWARDS

The first Central Region award recognizing the most outstanding community work by a chapter was presented at the 6th Central Regional Conference in 1939. The award cup was named for the 8th Central Regional Director, Alice McGhee Smart. Gamma Omega Chapter, St. Louis, Missouri was the first recipient of the cup and Alpha Mu Omega, Indianapolis, Indiana received honorable mention.

In 1941 at the 8th Central Regional Conference Eta Chapter, University of Minnesota was the first undergraduate Chapter to receive the Alice McGhee Regional Award Cup.

Based on available information it was not until 1956 at the 22nd Central Regional Conference that achievement awards were presented to both a graduate and undergraduate chapter. The Graduate Achievement Award Cup was presented to Gamma Omega Chapter, St. Louis, Missouri and the Undergraduate Achievement Award Cup went to Beta Chapter, Chicago, Illinois.

In 1957 at the 23rd Central Regional Conference the first undergraduate scholarship awards were presented. The Arnetta Wallace Cup for the chapter with the highest scholastic average was awarded to Delta Beta, Southern Illinois University with Gamma Chapter, University of Illinois/Urbana, second, and Beta Zeta, Kentucky State College, third. The undergraduate soror with the highest scholastic average went to Verna Fowlkes, Tau, Indiana University/Bloomington; Rosalind Bishop, Beta Zeta, Kentucky State College, second; Kay Clark, Delta Beta, Southern Illinois University, third. The actual GPAs were not recorded.

Through the years, chapter achievement award categories have undergone several criteria changes including chapter size, composition (mixed, graduate or undergraduate) and undergraduate city or campus chapter. In addition, the naming of awards has been changed and award categories have been added including awards for individual soror accomplishments. In fact, the regional awards have grown from one award category in 1941 to 46 current award categories. Fourteen of the Graduate award categories are broken down according to chapter size and for Undergraduates by city or campus chapter, bringing the award total to 83. This total does not include runner-ups.

The awards for overall chapter achievement and recognition of undergraduates and undergraduate chapters' scholastic achievement have remained consistent. Therefore, awards for these categories are reported in this history with the addition of the Annetta M. Lawson Best Graduate Advisor Award established in 1968 and changed to Outstanding Graduate Advisor in 1992

Several notable chapter and individual awards named after Regional Directors and International/National Offices have been given through the years. Space restraints of this history would not permit the listing of the winners of these awards. However, for historical purposes following are the names of the current awards:

Peggy Lewis LeCompte Award – Outstanding Soror in Communications/Journalism (Graduate)
Gloria E. Bond Award – Membership Reactivation (Graduate)
Evelyn H. Roberts Award – Assault on Illiteracy (Graduate)
Gladys Gordon Award – Chapter Heritage (Graduate)
Lee Anna Shelburne Award – Chapter Program Exhibit (Graduate)
Pauline Kigh Reed Award – Chapter Scrapbook (Graduate)
Ordie Roberts Award – Attendance Greatest Percentage (Graduate)
Central Region Connection Award (Graduate)
Giselé M. Casanova Award – Leadership (Graduate)
Pamela Bates Porch Award – Outstanding Educator (Graduate)
Yvonne Perkins Award – Outstanding Basileus (Graduate)
Peggy Lewis LeCompte – Outstanding New Initiate (Graduate)
Dorothy Buckhanan Wilson – Outstanding Silver Soror
Dorothy Buckhanan Wilson – Outstanding Golden Soror
Nadine C. Bonds Award – Outstanding Soror Through The Years
Martha Perine Beard Award – Outstanding Soror of the Year
Irma F. Clark Award – Assault on Illiteracy (Undergraduate)
Peggy Lewis LeCompte Award - Outstanding Soror in Communications/Journalism (Undergraduate)
Helen Cromer Cooper Award – Chapter Program Exhibit (Undergraduate)
Maenell Newsome Award – Chapter Scrapbook (Undergraduate)
Johnetta Randolph Haley – Attendance Greatest Percentage (Undergraduate)
Gloria E. Bond Award – Membership Transfer (Undergraduate)
Yvonne Perkins Award – Connection (Undergraduate)
Giselé M. Casanova Award – Leadership (Undergraduate)
Pamela Bates Porch Award – Future Educator (Undergraduate)
Yvonne Perkins Award – Outstanding Basileus (Undergraduate)
Peggy Lewis LeCompte – Outstanding New Initiate (Undergraduate)
Martha Perine Beard Award – Outstanding Soror of the Year (Undergraduate)
Loann J. Honesty King Award – Undergraduate Service Volunteer/Leadership

PLEDGED TO REMEMBER: THE HISTORY OF CENTRAL REGION

Regional Conferences
A Pictorial View

*1st Central Regional Conference, May 23-24, 1931,
Indianapolis, Indiana*

*3rd Central Regional Conference, May 9-10, 1936,
Champaign, Illinois*

*8th Central Regional Conference, May 30 — June 1, 1941,
University of Minnesota*

*16th Central Regional Conference, April 28-30, 1950,
Samaritan Methodist Temple, St. Louis, Missouri*

*30th Central Regional Conference, April 10-12, 1964,
Statler Hilton Hotel, St. Louis, Missouri*

*38th Central Regional Conference, April 14-16, 1972,
Evansville, Indiana*

440 ALPHA KAPPA ALPHA SORORITY, INCORPORATED®

PART VII: REGIONAL CONFERENCES

47th Central Regional Conference, April 2-5, 1981, Radisson St. Paul, Minneapolis, Minnesota

61st Central Regional Conference, April 20-23, 1995, Hyatt Regency, at Union Station, St. Louis, Missouri

76th Central Regional Conference, 2010, Chicago, Illinois

1ST — MAY 23-24, 1931

Location:	Indianapolis, Indiana
Hostess Chapter:	Alpha Mu Omega
Attendance:	43
Conference Officers:	Hattie Jones, Frances Stout, Pauline Kigh Reed, Pauline Morton-Finney and Martha R. Honer
Regional Director:	Blanche Hayes
Region Membership Statistics:	9 chapters — 5 Undergraduate, 4 Graduate chapters Active Membership: Approximately 100

REGIONAL CONFERENCE NOTES:
Eight of the nine chapters in the region were represented at the conference: Alpha Eta Omega, Beta, Gamma, Kappa, Alpha Mu Omega, Tau, Gamma Omega and Theta Omega. The missing chapter was Eta, St. Paul Minnesota. Xi Graduate/Eta Omega, Louisville, Kentucky, had been chartered but was not among the states designated as a part of Central Region.

1932 — CONFERENCE NOT HELD: Soror Blanche Hayes, Central Regional Director, reported to the Boule "that a host chapter could not be found due to the small number of chapters and sorors in the region."

1933 — CONFERENCE NOT HELD: Alpha Kappa Alpha Sorority, Inc., held the 16th Boule in August 1933 in Chicago, Illinois. The sorors in Central Region anticipated that many of them would attend this Boule. In addition, Beta and Theta Omega Chapters were hosts for the Boule. For these reasons, the sorors in the region felt that a Central Regional Conference in the same year was not necessary.

2ND — JUNE 10-11, 1934

Location:	Poro College St. Louis, Missouri
Hostess Chapter:	Gamma Omega
Attendance:	35
Conference Chairman:	Ida Belle Lindsay
Regional Director:	Blanche Hayes
Region Membership Statistics:	10 Chapters — 6 Undergraduate, 4 Graduate Chapters Active Membership: Approximately 100

REGIONAL CONFERENCE NOTES:
In the words of the Central Regional Director, *"The conference was both enjoyable and profitable."* Twenty-five of the sorors attending were delegates representing five chapters outside the two in the city.

1935 — CONFERENCE NOT HELD: Soror Alice E. McGhee Smart, Central Regional Director, reported to the Boule that the region had only four graduate chapters which created the problem of finding a hostess for the conference. The chapters voted to donate the funds designated in 1934 for the 1935 regional conference to the Gamma House Project.

3RD — MAY 9-10, 1936

Location:	McKinley Foundation Champaign, Illinois

Hostess Chapter:	Gamma
Attendance:	44
Conference Theme:	*A.K.A. and the Community*
Conference Chairman:	Helen Payne
Regional Director:	Alice McGhee Smart
Region Membership Statistics:	10 Chapters — 6 Undergraduate, 4 Graduate Chapters
	Active Membership: Approximately 100

REGIONAL CONFERENCE NOTES:

Sorors attending the conference represented chapters in Indianapolis, St. Louis, Minneapolis/St.Paul and Chicago. A formal dance entitled, *"The Green Tea Pot,"* climaxed the Regional Conference activities.

4TH — MAY 22-23, 1937

Location:	Phyllis Wheatley Branch YWCA
	Indianapolis, Indiana
Hostess Chapter:	Alpha Mu Omega
Attendance:	Approximately 50
Conference Theme:	*Salutation to Dawn*
Conference Chairman:	Eugenia Asbury
Regional Director:	Alice McGhee Smart
Region Membership Statistics:	10 Chapters — 6 Undergraduate, 4 Graduate Chapters
	Active Membership: Approximately 100

REGIONAL CONFERENCE NOTES:

Approximately 50 sorors made the walls fairly ring as they sang a group of AKA songs to officially open the conference. Following chapter reports, the morning session adjourned for the luncheon. The afternoon session was a discussion of affairs pertinent to individual chapters and the region as a whole. The keynote, perhaps, was the common plea for a return to the old spirit of simplicity and camaraderie. A beautifully appointed banquet and dance climaxed a full day's activities. Sunday morning the sorors joined in morning worship and in a renewal of the spiritual bond of our great Sisterhood.

5TH — MAY 21-22, 1938

Location:	Second Baptist Church
	Terre Haute, Indiana
Hostess:	Alpha Eta Omega
Attendance:	55
Conference Theme:	*Working Together*
Conference Chairman:	Hattie Jones Edwards
Regional Director:	Arlene Jackson Washington
Region Membership Statistics:	10 Chapters — 6 Undergraduate, 4 Graduate Chapters
	Active Membership: Approximately 150

REGIONAL CONFERENCE NOTES:

The energetic work and cooperative spirit of the hostess sorors were apparent to the sorors in attendance at the 55th Central Regional Conference. During the afternoon session there was a discussion of chapter problems with the following topics: *Working Together, National Cooperation, The Sorority a Community Asset* and *Relatiionships of Sorors to Undergraduate Chapters to the Community*.

The closed banquet was held in the dining room of the Second Baptist Church. Soror Neimatilda Richie, Theta Omega offered a violin solo and Evangeline Harris, Alpha Eta Omega gave a vocal selection. The public meeting was held at the worship services Sunday morning with the inspiring sermon being delivered by Rev. B. C. Winchester. Sorors left the conference with the comforting assurance that Alpha Kappa Alpha womanhood is steadily achieving, widening horizons and lifting standards in various fields of endeavor.

6TH — MAY 27-28, 1939

Location:	Palais des Gardes
	Chicago, Illinois
Hostess Chapters:	Beta and Theta Omega
Attendance:	105
Conference Theme:	*College Failures: Their Cause and Probable Solutions*
Conference Chairman:	Anne Penny
Regional Director:	Arlene Jackson Washington
Region Membership Statistics:	10 Chapters — 6 Undergraduate, 4 Graduate Chapters
	Active Membership: Approximately 200

REGIONAL CONFERENCE NOTES:

Meetings were held at the Palais des Gardes, a recreational building operated by Negroes. One highlight of the meeting included a surprise visit by the Supreme Basileus, Margaret Davis Bowen, who delivered a brief but, inspiring message.

A "Handbook of Instructions" on the Sorority's Constitution was distributed to the chapters. *Soror Alice McGhee Smart, Immediate Past Central Regional Director, presented the first regional award cup, to be given each year to the chapter doing the most outstanding community work.* **Gamma Omega Chapter, St. Louis, Missouri was the first recipient of the cup and Alpha Mu Omega, Indianapolis, Indiana received honorable mention.**

Soror Washington in her report to the Boule, referred to the 1939 Central Regional Conference as the ninth. Had conferences been held in 1932, 1933 and 1935, this report would be accurate. However, the region did not hold conferences in those three years, making the 1939 Central Regional Conference the sixth conference convened.

7TH — APRIL 27-29, 1940

Location:	Pine Street Y.M.C.A.
	St. Louis, Missouri
Hostess Chapters:	Beta Delta and Gamma Omega
Attendance:	85
Conference Theme:	*The Increasing Awareness Of Our Social Responsibility*
Conference Chairman:	Bernice Mitchell
Regional Director:	Arlene Jackson Washington
Region Membership Statistics:	10 Chapters — 6 Undergraduate, 4 Graduate Chapters
	Active Membership: Approximately 200

REGIONAL CONFERENCE NOTES:

Soror Evelyn Roberts, Basileus of Beta Chapter welcomed the sorors during the opening session. Soror Washington, Central Regional Director responded to the greeting and formally seated the delegates.

Only three chapters of the region did not have delegates in attendance.

Reports of chapter activities were given by Tau, Beta, Alpha Mu Omega, Theta Omega, Alpha Eta Omega, Gamma Omega and Beta Delta. The afternoon session included reports on the Mississippi Health Project, Gamma House Project and National Council on Public Affairs.

The Conference made the following recommendation: that each chapter in the region affiliate with interracial groups, the NAACP and other civic groups in their locations; that a council on Public Affairs be established in each chapter; that an up-to-date file of all civil service examinations and information concerning elections and candidates be maintained; that each chapter boost all National projects; and that a public speaking bureau be maintained to boost worthwhile causes and that pledge cards be circulated for contributions for this project on Founders' Day.

Following a lively discussion centered on the conference theme the consensus was that AKA join hands with other organizations that are involved in correcting the terrible conditions under which many Negroes have to live. A resolution was also adopted to protest against the discriminatory policy of Butler University regarding admission to its Art College.

The highlight of the Banquet program was an address by Soror Ruth Word, entitled, *"Stock Taking Time in Alpha Kappa Alpha." Gamma Omega Chapter, St. Louis, Missouri was the recipient of the Alice McGhee Award Cup for the second year and Alpha Eta Omega, Terra Haute, Indiana received honorable mention.*

8TH — MAY 30-JUNE 1, 1941

Location:	Coffman Memorial Union University of Minnesota St. Paul, Minnesota
Hostess Chapter:	Eta
Attendance:	Not recorded but described as small
Conference Theme:	*Seeing and Securing National Defense through Organizational Cooperation*
Regional Director:	Blanche Patterson
Region Membership Statistics:	11 Chapters — 6 Undergraduate, 5 Graduate Chapters Active Membership: Approximately 225

REGIONAL CONFERENCE NOTES:

Sessions, banquets, dances, and artists' recitals were held at the newly constructed $2 million Coffman Memorial Union, described as matchless for beauty and convenience. Attendance at the conference was relatively small due to the lateness of the date and the distance of the locale. Yet, with all things considered, the small group of isolated sorors of Eta Chapter hosted their "coming out party" in the spirit of good fellowship and enthusiasm.

The attendees were delighted with the unique Ivy Leaves made of pewter as souvenirs. A special Sunday service was held at St. Peter's A.M.E. Church of Minneapolis, where Soror Stewart's husband the Reverend Carlyle F. Stewart was Pastor.

A round table discussion of undergraduate problems included the following questions:
1. Can we afford to sacrifice quality to quantity?
2. Are we developing sorors properly in the undergraduate chapters?
3. Is there a possibility that obligations to friends are influencing our selection of sorors more than consideration of qualifications?
4. Why are undergraduates reluctant to transfer to graduate chapters upon graduation?

Gamma Omega Chapter, St. Louis, Missouri was awarded the Graduate Cup and Eta Chapter, St. Paul, Minnesota, was the recipient of the Alice McGhee Regional Award Cup for ranking second out of twenty-two sorority groups on campus and hosting the Central Regional Conference with only eight members. Eta Chapter was the first undergraduate chapter to receive the Alice McGhee Award Cup.

9TH — APRIL 25-26, 1942

Location:	Wesley Foundation Trinity Church
	University of Illinois/Urbana
Hostess Chapter:	Gamma
Attendance:	79
Conference Theme:	*All for Defense and Defense for All*
Conference Chairman:	Mary Grace Jordan
Co-Chairman:	Lizzie Johnson
Regional Director:	Blanche Patterson
Region Membership Statistics:	11 Chapters — 6 Undergraduate,
	5 Graduate Chapters
	Active Membership: Approximately 225

REGIONAL CONFERENCE NOTES:

Dean Maria Leonard from the University of Illinois attended the opening session to bring greetings to the vistors. The afternoon session was marked by attention to undergraduate problems.

During the banquet program in the Illinois Union Building, guest speaker, Soror Marian Scott of Theta Omega Chapter told the sorors what the role of Alpha Kappa Alpha was in the "All for Defense, Defense for All" program. At the open meeting Sunday morning, held jointly with Kappa Alpha Psi, Soror Nathelia Bledsoe of Gamma Omega spoke on "Our Responsibility as College Women in the War Effort."

Gamma Kappa Omega Chapter, Carbondale, Illinois, gave the balance of the chapter's Gamma Loan Assessment to aid in paying off Tau Chapter's loan, a sum of $34.67. *Beta Chapter, Chicago, Illinois, was awarded the Alice McGhee Award Cup, making Beta Chapter the second Undergraduate Chapter to receive the award.*

10TH — NOVEMBER 13-14, 1943

Location:	Phyllis Wheatley Branch YWCA
	St. Louis, Missouri
Hostess Chapter:	Gamma Omega
Attendance:	79
Regional Director:	Blanche L. Patterson
Region Membership Statistics:	11 Chapters — 6 Undergraduate,
	5 Graduate Chapters
	Active Membership: Approximately 225

REGIONAL CONFERENCE NOTES:

Ten of the eleven chapters in the region sent representatives. The highlight of the conference was the public noon day luncheon in lieu of a formal banquet at which a panel discussion on Post War Reconstruction was held. Panel topics were as follows: Intercultural Relationships in the Community; Recreational Facilities; The Educational Pattern; On the Industrial Front; On the Political Front, and Propaganda or Control of Publicity via Press, Radio, and Screen.

Soror Essie Massey Riddle of New York, former member of Gamma Omega Chapter, and consultant to the National Nursing Council for War Service, gave a closing address on "Post-War Planning in Health."

PART VII: REGIONAL CONFERENCES

Beta Delta Chapter, St. Louis, Missouri, was awarded the Alice McGhee Award Cup for their volunteer work with the soldiers of Jefferson Barracks, Fort Leonard Wood, and Scott Field.

11TH — NOVEMBER 11-12, 1944

Location:	Phyllis Wheatley Branch YWCA
	Indianapolis, IN
Hostess Chapter:	Alpha Mu Omega and Kappa
Attendance:	Not Available
Regional Director:	Blanche L. Patterson
Region Membership Statistics:	12 Chapters — 6 Undergraduate,
	6 Graduate Chapters
	Active Membership: Approximately 250

REGIONAL CONFERENCE NOTES:

The local sororities and fraternities welcomed the sorors to Indianapolis. On Friday evening the members of Delta Sigma Theta were hostesses for a beautiful soirée followed by a cocktail party hosted by Kappa Alpha Psi; and on Saturday, afternoon Sigma Gamma Rho feted the sorors with a luncheon in Jordan Hall.

Special guests included Founder, Norma Boyd and Former Central Regional Director, Alice McGhee. During the afternoon session Soror Boyd spoke on the Non-Partisan Council and the National Health Project.

The hostess chapter entertained the sorors at a formal banquet on Saturday evening and the highlight of the evening was the presentation on behalf of the Boule of a "Mother's Pin" to Mrs. Cora Marshall Hardison, house mother to Gamma House since 1926. The main speaker for the evening was Soror Alice McGhee who had recently returned from an educational mission in Liberia. After the banquet the sorors went to the Walker Casino. A worship service was held on Sunday morning at the Bethel A.M.E. Church. Founder Boyd was the guest speaker and the service was followed by a reception.

1945 — CONFERENCE NOT HELD

The events of World War II precluded holding a Central Regional Conference in 1945. The Directorate also put regular operations of the sorority on hold. They canceled the Boule scheduled for 1942 and only the Directorate met during 1943.

The Boule did not meet again until February 1944. Meetings were held at the Bethesda Baptist Church in Chicago, Illinois, with Beta and Theta Omega Chapters as hostesses. At the 1944 Boule, because of the uncertainty of conditions as a result of World War II, the Directorate decided not to convene again until August 1946 and to appoint Regional Directors to carry on the work in the regions during this period. Soror Maenell Newsome was appointed Central Regional Director.

12TH — MAY 17-19, 1946

Location:	Indianapolis, Indiana
Hostess Chapters:	Tau, Alpha Mu Omega and Kappa
Attendance:	Not recorded
Conference Theme:	*One World Challenges Alpha Kappa Alpha*
Regional Director:	Maenell Hamlin Newsome
Region Membership Statistics:	13 Chapters — 6 Undergraduate,
	7 Graduate Chapters
	Active Membership: Approximately 250

REGIONAL CONFERENCE NOTES:

Although few sorors were in attendance, the discussions evolving around the Conference Theme made the sorors realize *"that a better world will not come merely because we wish very much for it, but will be made possible only by bold vision, intelligent planning, hard work and unfaltering faith."*

13TH — MAY 8-9, 1947

Location:	Chicago, Illinois
Hostess Chapter:	Theta Omega
Conference Theme:	*The Undergraduate — A Challenge to Alpha Kappa Alpha Sorority*
Conference Chairman:	Anne P. Clark
Regional Director:	Lucille B. Wilkins
Region Membership Statistics:	13 Chapters — 6 Undergraduate, 7 Graduate Chapters
	Membership: Approximately 250

The highlight of the morning session was an address by the guest of honor Supreme Basileus, Edna Over Gray. Reports were given on the Gamma House Project and Founder Norma Boyd gave reports on the Non Partisan Council on Public Affairs. The conference luncheon was hosted by Beta Chapter. Founder, Margaret Flagg Holmes attended the rededication banquet and Supreme Basileus Gray delivered remarks for the evening. The weekend of conference activities ended with a cocktail party and formal dance.

The Alice McGhee Achievement Cups were awarded to Beta, Chicago, IL and Alpha Mu Omega, Indianapolis, IN.

14TH — MAY, 1948

Location:	Southern Illinois University Carbondale, Illinois
Hostess Chapter:	Gamma Kappa Omega
Conference Theme:	*Strengthening Alpha Kappa Alpha From Within*
Regional Director:	Lucille B. Wilkins
Region Membership Statistics:	14 Chapters — 6 Undergraduate, 8 Graduate Chapters
	Active Membership: Approximately 250

REGIONAL CONFERENCE NOTES:

Four points were derived from the discussions around the conference theme at this Regional Conference: To strengthen Alpha Kappa Alpha from within, there must be coordinated responsibility; a closer association between the sorority and the community; a closer tie between the chapters and the Regional Director; and there should be a continual reevaluation of our projects and continued support from every chapter and from each soror in the region.

15TH — APRIL 29-30, 1949

Location:	Campbell Friendship House Gary, Indiana
Hostess Chapter:	Gamma Psi Omega
Attendance:	200
Conference Theme:	*Human Rights, Our Unfinished Business*
Regional Director:	Lucille B. Wilkins
Region Membership Statistics:	16 Chapters — 6 Undergraduate, 10 Graduate Chapters
	Membership:

REGIONAL CONFERENCE NOTES:

Thirty Basilei and Dean of Pledgees assembled on Friday night of the conference to discuss problems affecting their respective chapters. Following all visitors were honored with a cocktail party at the Delta House hosted by Delta Sigma Theta, Sigma Gamma Rho and Alpha Phi Alpha. Business sessions and workshops were held at the Campbell Friendship House. Soror Ida Scott delivered the formal banquet keynote address centered on the conference theme "Human Rights, Our Unfinished Business" particularly as it related to undergraduates. Soror Scott believed that human rights must be challenged from the point of view of every of every individual and must be championed wherever they are violated.

16TH — APRIL 28-30, 1950

Location:	Samaritan Methodist Temple St. Louis, Missouri
Hostess Chapter:	Gamma Omega
Attendance:	200
Regional Director:	Lucille B. Wilkins
Region Membership Statistics:	16 Chapters — 6 Undergraduate, 10 Graduate Chapters Active Membership

The 16th Central Regional Conference was one of the largest in the history of the organization. The official registration was 200. Fifteen chapters from Missouri, Illinois, Kentucky and Illinois were represented. The largest delegation was from Chicago, Beta and Theta Omega, with 57 attendees.

The conference officially opened on Friday, April 28 with a Basilei and Undergraduate Advisors Council meeting at Stowe Teachers College. Following the meeting fellowship activities were held at Achievement House and the Phyllis Wheatley Y.W.C.A.

A workshop panel was presented by undergraduates. Those participating were: Sorors Mary Lou Moore, Gamma; Orphah Shands, Beta; Dorothy Williams, Beta Epsilon; Josephine Davis, Beta Zeta; Shirley Lloyd, Kappa; and Anita Lyons, Beta Delta; with Betty Guess, Tau as Moderator. Four major areas were discussed: *Building a Sound Educational Program for Ivy Leaf Club Members*; *Blackballing, Cruelty and Paddling*; *Ways for Undergraduates to Raise Money*; and *Securing a Smooth Running Ivy Leaf Club With Proper Executive Administration*.

One of the major pieces of business was the conference going on record as being against the Mundt-Ferguson Bill because of the violations of the rights of free speech, press and assembly.

A closed formal banquet was held on Saturday evening. Beta and Theta Omega received the Achievement Cups for outstanding contributions to the community and the sorority. The conference closed on Sunday morning with a worshop service at Samaritan Methodist Temple.

17TH — APRIL 27-28, 1951

Location:	University of Minnesota Minneapolis, MN
Hostess Chapter:	Delta Phi Omega
Regional Director:	Evelyn Hoard Roberts
Region Membership Statistics:	18 Chapters — 6 Undergraduate, 12 Graduate Chapters Active Membership: Approximately 300

REGIONAL CONFERENCE NOTES:

The 17th Central Regional Conference was part of a Tri-Greek Conference with Omega Psi Phi and Kappa Alpha Psi fraternities. Each organization had separate agendas and business meetings. They came together for several social affairs.

18TH — APRIL 25-27, 1952

Location:	Kentucky State College
	Frankfort, Kentucky
Hostess Chapters:	Beta Upsilon Omega Chapter
Attendance:	92 Delegates
Conference Theme:	*Making Democracy Work—At Home and Abroad*
Regional Director:	Evelyn Hoard Roberts
Region Membership Statistics:	26 Chapters — 7 Undergraduate,
	19 Graduate Chapters
	Active Membership: Approximately 400

The hostess chapters executed an educational as well as an enjoyable experience. Soror Roberts, Central Regional Director convened a Basilei and Undergraduate Advisors' Conference on Friday afternoon followed by a soiree at McCullin Hall Lounge hosted by the Graduate Greeks of Frankfort. Kentucky State College President Dr. Rufus B. Atwood and Mr. Alexander Whitfield, President of the Pan Hellenic Council brought greetings at the opening session.

Four clinics were held in the afternoon: National Projects, The Ivy Leaf Club and Initiations, Evaluation; and Program Planning. Following the clinics the sorors reassembled to report.

A closed formal banquet was held on Saturday evening in the Underwood Cafeteria followed by a formal dance in the Bell Gymnasium to the music of the Kentucky State Collegians.

The public meeting was held on Sunday morning. Supreme Basileus, Soror Edna Over Gray was the main speaker and music for the event was furnished by the Kentucky State College Choir. Other special guests included two former Supreme Basilei, 7th Soror Maude Brown Porter, 13th Laura Lovelace; Soror Carolyn Blanton, Supreme Grammateus; and Soror Norma Carter, Second Anti-Basileus.

Alice McGhee Smart Graduate Achievement Cup
Beta Upsilon Omega, Frankfort, KY

Alice McGhee Smart Undergraduate Achievement Cup
Beta Chapter, City, Chicago, Illinois

19TH — MAY 8-10, 1953

Location:	Terre Haute, IN
Hostess Chapters:	Alpha Eta Omega, Alpha Mu Omega, Kappa and Tau
Conference Theme:	
Regional Director:	Evelyn Hoard Roberts
Region Membership Statistics:	28 Chapters — 9 Undergraduate,
	19 Graduate Chapters

Soror Evelyn Hoard Roberts convened the 19th Central Regional Conference. Regrettably, the only information that could be located for the conference was the date, location and hostess chapters. Beta Iota Chapter, Evansville College, Evansville, Indiana and Delta Beta Chapter, Southern Illinois University, Carbondale, Illinois would be chartered in 1951 and 1952 respectively bringing Central Region's total chapters to 28 — 9 Undergraduate and 19 Graduate Chapters.

20TH — APRIL 24-26, 1954

Location:	Congress Hotel
	Chicago, Illinois

PART VII: REGIONAL CONFERENCES

Hostess Chapters:	Beta, Delta Chi Omega and Theta Omega
Conference Theme:	*Equal Responsibility, The Challenge of Equal Opportunity*
Attendance:	183
Regional Director:	Evelyn Hoard Roberts
Region Membership Statistics:	28 Chapters — 11 Undergraduate, 17 Graduate Chapters
	Active Membership: Approximately 400

REGIONAL CONFERENCE NOTES

The Basilei and Graduate Advisors Council convened on Friday afternoon at the Washington Park Y.M.C.A. Following dinner the attendees assembled for workshops on the following topics: Business Procedures and Chapter Problems, National Programs, Improving Sorority Relations and Program Planning.

Soror Roberts convened the opening business session on Saturday morning. During the morning and afternoon sessions on Saturday several resolutions were adopted including a more effective implementation of ACHR programs and the establishment of more councils; and reemphasis on the substitution of "Help Week" for "Hell Week" in the conduct of probation and initiation activities. The region also reaffirmed its support of the Endowment Campaigm and pledged to encourage both inactive and active members to support over the next ten years.

The formal banquet and dance was held in the beautiful Gold Room of the hotel. Soror Roberts delivered the main address around the theme of the conference. Soror Etta Moten Barnett was guest soloist. Other special banquet guest included: Former Supreme Basileus Maude B. Porter, Carey M. Preston, Executive Secretary and Gladys Bufkin, Former Supreme Tamiouchos. On Sunday morning the conference concluded with a coffee sip at the National Headquarters.

21ST — APRIL 22-24, 1955

Location:	Southern Illinois University Carbondale, Illinois
Hostess Chapters:	Epsilon Lambda Omega, Zeta Zeta Omega, Beta Omega Omega, Beta Rho Omega, Delta Beta, Gamma Kappa Omega
Conference Theme:	*Strengthening Our Undergraduates For Future Leadership*
Regional Director:	Evelyn Hoard Roberts
Region Membership Statistics:	21 Chapters — 8 Undergraduate, 13 Graduate Chapters
	Active Membership: Approximately 400

REGIONAL CONFERENCE NOTES:

Highlights of the conference were the luncheon, Formal Banquet held in the Banquet Room of the University Cafeteria and the Semi Formal Dance was held in the Student Union Building.

On Friday night, the Alpha Phi Alpha Fraternity entertained the conference with a Moonlight Picnic at Giant City State Park. The Kappa Alpha Psi Fraternity entertained with a coffee Hour Sunday morning. Following the Coffee Hour, the Sorority worshipped at the Rockhill Missionary Baptist Church.*

*Taken from article in the June 1955 *Ivy Leaf* magazine.

22ND — APRIL 27-29, 1956

Location:	University of Illinois Urbana, Illinois
Hostess Chapters:	Gamma Psi Omega, Gamma, Epsilon Epsilon Omega

Attendance:	95
Conference Theme:	*Making Ideals Realities*
Regional Director:	Maude L. Mann
Region Membership Statistics:	28 Chapters — 9 Undergraduate, 17 Graduate and 2 Inactive (Beta Iota, Evansville College and Delta Phi Omega, St. Paul, Minnesota) Active Membership: 622 68 Undergraduates and 554 Graduates

REGIONAL CONFERENCE NOTES:

Soror Maude L. Mann set forth the purpose of this regional conference in her Regional Director's Report. *"Our task in meeting and planning together this weekend is to define specifically what our responsibilities are to our National program; to our undergraduate chapters; to one another as members of a great sisterhood; to discuss common problems; and to plan for improved organization within our constitutional framework."*

A Basilei and Graduate Advisors session was held on Friday evening. The 7th Supreme Basileus, Soror Maude Brown Porter delivered a stirring address at the formal banquet and the men of Alpha Phi Alpha and Kappa Alpha Psi Fraternities entertained the attendees with an "At Home" reception at their respective fraternity houses.

Special guests at the conference included: Soror Evelyn Roberts, Supreme Grammateus; Soror Gladys Buffin, Supreme Tamiouchos; Soror Gladys Gordon, Supreme Parliamentarian; Soror Helen Bolan, Undergraduate Program Advisor; and Soror Carey B. Preston, Executive Secretary.

This conference marked the first recorded indication that a decision had been made to separate undergraduate and graduate chapters in the award competition. Both an Undergraduate and Graduate Chapter were awarded the Achievement Cup.

Alice McGhee Smart Undergraduate Achievement Cup
Beta, Chicago, Illinois

Alice McGhee Smart Graduate Achievement Cup
Gamma Omega, St. Louis, Missouri

23RD — APRIL 26-28, 1957

Location:	Hotel Kingsway St. Louis, Missouri
Hostess Chapters:	Beta Delta, Delta Delta Omega and Gamma Omega
Attendance:	172
Conference Theme:	*The Role of Alpha Kappa Alpha Sorority In Times of Transition*
Regional Director:	Maude L. Mann
Region Membership Statistics:	28 Chapters — 10 Undergraduate, 18 Graduate Chapters Active Membership: 759 106 Undergraduates and 653 Graduates

REGIONAL CONFERENCE NOTES:

The year 1957 marked the first year that the region held a Central Regional Conference in a hotel. Soror Mann reported that *"our task in meeting and planning together this weekend is to define specifically, clarify, and discover means of carrying out our National Program; to face our responsibility to work together in harmony, both graduates and undergraduates, as members of a great sisterhood; to discuss common problems;*

and to plan for improved organization within our constitutional framework'" She also reported that the region had donated $2,197 to the National Projects Fund; $934.50 to the Lyle Endowment; and $4,444.86 to scholarship.

Undergraduate Achievement Cup

Winner:	Beta	City Chapter	Chicago, Illinois
Honorable Mention:	Gamma	University of Illinois/Urbana	

Alice McGhee Smart Graduate Achievement Cup

Winner:	Gamma Omega,	St. Louis, Missouri
Honorable Mention:	Theta Omega	Chicago, Illinois

24TH — APRIL 18-19, 1958

Location:	Henry Clay Hotel Louisville, Kentucky
Hostess Chapters:	Beta Epsilon, Beta Zeta, Eta Omega, Beta Gamma Omega and Beta Upsilon Omega
Conference Theme:	*Pride in the Past, Gratitude for the Present, Faith in the Future, Forward to a New Era of Service"*
Regional Director:	Maude L. Mann
Region Membership Statistics:	28 Chapters — 10 Undergraduate, 18 Graduate Chapters Active Membership: 759 106 Undergraduates and 653 Graduates

REGIONAL CONFERENCE NOTES:

The conference featured several unique ideas to honor chapter and soror donors to the Endowment Fund campaign. A large gold wheel was displayed during the luncheon and the names of $50.00 donors was printed on a pink and green ribbon and affixed to the wheel. Each donor also received a corsage and an engraved AKA bracelet.

Other features of the conference include a skit written by Soror Jean Chambers, Gamma Psi Omega and presented by Soror LaBertha Reddick, Gamma Omega. Featured speakers included Central Regional Director Maude L. Mann; 7th Supreme Basileus, Maude B. Porter; Former Central Regional Director Soror Evelyn Roberts; and Executive Secretary, Carrie B. Preston.

Central Regional Director, Maude L. Mann, Theta Omega Chapter, became an Ivy Beyond the Wall on December 5, 1958 eight months after convening the 24th Central Regional Conference.

Undergraduate Achievement Cup

Winner:	Beta	City Chapter	Chicago, Illinois

Alice McGhee Smart Graduate Achievement Cup

Winner:	Gamma Omega	St. Louis, Missouri

25th — SILVER ANNIVERSARY CONFERENCE — APRIL 17-19, 1959

Location:	Hotel Pfister Milwaukee, Wisconsin
Hostess Chapters:	Epsilon Kappa Omega, Delta Phi Omega and Eta
Conference Theme:	*Forgetting Not Tradition But Keeping Pace With The New Era*

Attendance:	116 (15 Undergraduates, 101 Graduates)
Regional Director:	Annetta Moten Lawson
Region Membership Statistics:	28 Chapters — 10 Undergraduate, 18 Graduate Chapters Active Membership: 444 59 Undergraduates, 385 Graduates

REGIONAL CONFERENCE NOTES:

The 25th Anniversary Central Regional Conference was a gala celebration. Epsilon Kappa Omega who had just been chartered ten years earlier and Eta Chapter rolled out the pink and green carpet with a silver lining.

Soror Lawson reported at Conference that the total active membership of the sorority as of January 1959 was 9,517. She further reported that Theta Omega Chapter, Chicago, Illinois, was the second largest chapter in the sorority with a membership of 187; Gamma Omega Chapter, St. Louis, Missouri, the fourth largest with a membership of 167, followed by Alpha Mu Omega, Indianapolis, Indiana, as the sixth largest chapter with a membership of 107.

A tribute to the immediate past Central Regional Director, Maude L. Mann, was conducted during the conference's Ivy Beyond the Wall Ceremony.

Undergraduate Achievement Cup
Beta Delta Chapter, St. Louis, Missouri

Alice McGhee Smart Graduate Achievement Cup
Gamma Omega, St. Louis, Missouri

26TH — APRIL 15-17, 1960

Location:	Sheraton-Lincoln Hotel Indianapolis, Indiana
Hostess Chapters:	Alpha Eta Omega, Alpha Mu Omega, Kappa, Tau
Conference Theme:	*New Directions for the Second Half Century*
Attendance:	155
Regional Director:	Annetta Moten Lawson
Region Membership Statistics:	30 Chapters — 10 Undergraduate, 20 Graduate Chapters Active Membership: 737 116 Undergraduates, 621 Graduates

REGIONAL CONFERENCE NOTES:

Events and activities of the 26th Central Regional Conference reached a crescendo at the closing banquet. Soror Marjorie Parker, Supreme Basileus, challenged the sorors to add the element of courage for effective action in the sixties, in her speech entitled: "Where Freedom Is Concerned — There Is No Such Thing as a Local Issue."

The Graduate Achievement Cup was not presented because the chairperson of the committee had not come to the conference nor was she able to be reached. Delegates recommended that Delta Beta Chapter evaluate graduate chapter achievements along with their Graduate Advisor and the Regional Director, and that the cup be forwarded to the winner with notice to all chapters. The recommendation passed.

Also, based on the previous year's Awards Committee recommendation merit certificates were presented to second and third place winners.

Undergraduate Achievement Cup

First Placer:	Beta Delta	St. Louis, Missouri
Second Place:	Beta	Chicago, Illinois
Third Place:	Beta Zeta	Kentucky State University

27TH — APRIL 14-15, 1961

Location:	Georgian Hotel Evanston, Illinois
Hostess Chapters:	Beta, Delta Chi Omega, Theta Omega
Attendance:	144 (27 Undergraduates, 115 Graduates, 2 Boule)
Conference Theme:	*The Undergraduate...Alpha Kappa Alpha's Investment In Strength*
Regional Director:	Annetta Moten Lawson
Region Membership Statistics:	30 Chapters — 10 Undergraduate, 20 Graduate Chapters Active Membership: 641 99 Undergraduates, 542 Graduates

REGIONAL CONFERENCE NOTES:

It was at this Central Regional Conference that the Evaluation's Committee made a recommendation to consider expanding the conference business to two days. Also, the Resolutions Committee presented a resolution to form a Graduate Advisor's Council. The resolution was accepted by the delegates.

Undergraduate Achievement Cup

First Place:	Beta Delta	St. Louis, Missouri
Second Place:	Beta	Chicago, Illinois
Third Place:	Beta Epsilon	University of Louisville

Alice McGhee Smart Graduate Achievement Cup

First Place:	Gamma Omega	St. Louis, Missouri
Second Place:	Alpha Mu Omega	Indianapolis, Indiana
Third Place:	Theta Omega	Chicago, Illinois

28TH — APRIL 13-14, 1962

Location:	McCurdy Hotel Evansville, Indiana
Hostess Chapters:	Epsilon Lambda Omega, Beta Omega Omega, Zeta Zeta Omega, Gamma Kappa Omega, Delta Beta, Beta Rho Omega
Attendance:	125 — 23 Undergraduates, 102 Graduates
Conference Theme:	*Assessing Our Strengths*
Regional Director:	Annetta Moten Lawson
Region Membership Statistics:	30 Chapters — 10 Undergraduate, 20 Graduate Chapters Active Membership: 641 99 Undergraduates, 542 Graduates

REGIONAL CONFERENCE NOTES:

Sorority workshops were held Friday evening for the first time. However, the Recommendations Committee reported that insufficient time was allotted for workshops to reach any conclusions regarding the new time.

Undergraduate Achievement Cup

First Place:	Beta Delta	St. Louis, Missouri
Second Place:	Beta	Chicago, Illinois
Third Place:	Delta Omicron	Northern Illinois University

Alice McGhee Smart Graduate Achievement Cup

First Place:	Theta Omega	Chicago, Illinois
Second Place:	Alpha Mu Omega	Indianapolis, Indiana
Third Place:	Gamma Omega	St. Louis, Missouri

29TH — APRIL 26-28, 1963

Location:	Hotel Gary
	Gary, Indiana
Hostess Chapters:	Gamma, Gamma Psi Omega, Epsilon Epsilon Omega, Eta Kappa Omega, Eta Mu Omega
Attendance:	195 — 31 Undergraduates, 164 Graduates
Conference Theme:	*Changing With the Changing Times: Moving Forward With Our Youth*
Conference Chairman:	YJean Chambers
Regional Director:	Lee Anna W. Shelburne
Region Membership Statistics:	30 Chapters — 10 Undergraduate, 2 Mixed, 18 Graduate Chapters
	Active Membership: 719
	99 Undergraduates, 542 Graduates

REGIONAL CONFERENCE NOTES:

In response to a national concern, a large portion of the conference was spent on undergraduate problems, specifically as they related to pledging. Sorors assembled discussed the issue of depledging and the national document "Implementing Changes Relating to Ivy Leaf Pledge Clubs" in workshops and open forum. Also, by this conference, the chapter scrapbook competition had evolved into a chapter exhibit competition.

Undergraduate Achievement Cup

First Place:	Beta Delta	St. Louis, Missouri
Second Place:	Beta	Chicago, Illinois
Third Place:	Beta Zeta	Kentucky State University

Alice McGhee Smart Graduate Achievement Cup

First Place (Tie):	Gamma Omega	St. Louis, Missouri
	Theta Omega	Chicago, Illinois
Second Place:	Alpha Mu Omega	Indianapolis, Indiana
Third Place:	Gamma Psi Omega	Gary, Indiana

30TH — APRIL 10-12, 1964

Location:	Statler Hilton Hotel
	St. Louis, Missouri
Hostess Chapters:	Gamma Omega, Beta Delta, Delta Delta Omega

Conference Theme:	*Changing With the Changing Times: Moving Forward With Our Youth*
Regional Director:	Lee Anna W. Shelburne
Region Membership Statistics:	31 Chapters — 10 Undergraduate, 2 Mixed, 19 Graduate Chapters

REGIONAL CONFERENCE NOTES:

A highlight of the conference was the public meeting on Friday evening. Former Supreme Basileus, Soror Margaret Davis Bowen was the guest speaker and delivered a timely message entitled: Youth: Preparation, Aspirations and Predictions. Music for the occasion was furnished by The Harris Teacher's College Interfraternity Singers and the Sumner Acappella Choir. A VIP reception following the meeting was sponsored by the Union Electric Company and featured the showing of the movie "The Golden Gift" the story of Grace Bumbry. While the VIP's including soecial Undergraduate Advisor, Soror Mary Chambers and National Finance Director, Helen Crommer Cooper and Graduate sorors were being entertained at the reception the Undergraduate Sorors were having a grand time in the Los Angeles and Dallas rooms of the hotel.

An elegant luncheon was held in the ballroom of the hotel and was enjoyed by the attendees and local dignitaries and citizenry. Supreme Basileus, Soror Julia Purnell was the closed banquet speaker. The banquet was followed by an "April in Paris Dance" and a card party.

New Central Region silver achievement cups donated by Soror Alice McGhee Smart were presented to Regional Director, Soror LeAnna Shelburne to be used by the region annually.

Alice McGhee Smart Undergraduate Achievement Cup

First Place:	Beta Delta	City Chapter, St. Louis, Missouri
Second Place:	Beta	City Chapter, Chicago, Illinois
Third Place:	Tau	IndianaUniversity/Bloomington

Alice McGhee Smart Graduate Achievement Cup

First Place:	Eta Omega	Louisville, Kentucky
Second Place:	Eta Kappa Omega	East Chicago, Indiana
Third Place:	Theta Omega	Chicago, Illinois

31ST — APRIL 2-3, 1965

Location:	Sheraton Hotel Louisville, Kentucky
Hostess Chapters:	Beta Epsilon, Beta Zeta, Eta Omega, Beta Gamma Omega, Beta Upsilon Omega
Attendance:	220 — 41 Undergraduates, 176 Graduates, 3 Boule members
Conference Theme:	*Advancement Through Knowledge and Action*
Conference Chairman:	Rosemary Bell
Co-Chairperson:	Charles Jones
Regional Director:	Lee Anna W. Shelburne
Region Membership Statistics:	30 Chapters — 10 Undergraduate, 4 Mixed, 16 Graduate Chapters Active Membership: 769 118 Undergraduates, 651 Graduates

REGIONAL CONFERENCE NOTES:

Several recommendations that were passed at the 31st Central Regional Conference would affect future regional conferences:

1. Local host chapters should secure outside impartial judges to judge exhibits;
2. A committee would be appointed to evaluate the Achievement Cup criteria;
3. The Regional Directors Council should consider a lower registration fee for undergraduate chapters;
4. The Basilei and Graduate Advisors Councils meet Friday evening of each Regional Conference; and
5. The composition of clusters for regional conferences was changed.

Undergraduate Achievement Cup

First Place:	Gamma	University of Illinois/Urbana
Second Place:	Tau	IndianaUniversity/Bloomington
Third Place:	Beta Zeta	Kentucky State University.

Alice McGhee Smart Graduate Achievement Cup

First Place:	Theta Omega	Chicago, Illinois
Second Place:	Gamma Omega	St. Louis, Missouri
Third Place:	Gamma Psi Omega	Gary, Indiana.

32ND — APRIL 22-23, 1966

Location:	Hilton Inn, Milwaukee, Wisconsin
Hostess Chapters:	Beta, Delta Phi Omega, Delta Omicron, Delta Chi Omega, Theta Omega, Epsilon Kappa Omega
Attendance:	184 — 20 Undergraduates, 164 Graduates
Conference Theme:	*Advancement through Knowledge and Action*
Conference Chairman:	Frances Strames
Conference Co-Chairmen:	Gloria Gliclor and Rochelle Burch
Regional Director:	Lee Anna W. Shelburne
Region Membership Statistics:	30 Chapters — 10 Undergraduate, 4 Mixed, 16 Graduate Chapters Active Membership: 829 119 Undergraduates, 709 Graduates

REGIONAL CONFERENCE NOTES:

Again, the format of the regional conference would be altered. A public meeting dinner was held on Friday evening of the conference. The criteria for chapter awards also underwent a change. Achievement Awards for graduate chapters would be awarded in two categories, based on chapter size: Class A—50 members and over and Class B—49 members and under. The Achievement Cup Evaluation Committee made several additional recommendations accepted for immediate implementation:

1. Additional achievement cups be donated or purchased for the first place winner in Class B;
2. Second and third place winners receive trophies;
3. All chapters receive a certificate of recognition for regional participation in the conference, from the Regional Director;
4. Appoint a regional committee to handle the solicitation and purchase of additional achievement cups, and in the ensuing years

PART VII: REGIONAL CONFERENCES

    5.   "The Annetta B. Wallace Cup" would be presented to the undergraduate chapter that maintains the highest scholastic average.

Former Supreme Basileus, Arnetta Wallace was the banquet speaker. The event was held in the dining room of the Allis Chambers Manufacturing Company

Alice McGee Smart Undergraduate Achievement Award
First Place:	Beta	Chicago, Illinois
Second Place:	Beta Delta	St. Louis, Missour
Third Place:	Beta Epsilon	Louisville, Kentucky

Alice McGee Smart Graduate Achievement Award Class A
(Membership 50 or more)
First Place:	Theta Omega	Chicago, Illinois
Second Place:	Eta Omega	Louisville, Kentucky
Third Place:	Gamma Omega	St. Louis, Missouri:

Graduate Achievement Award Class B (Membership 49 or less)
First Place:	Delta Chi Omega	Evanston, Illinois
Second Place:	Delta Delta Omega	East St. Louis, Illinois
Third Place:	Epsilon Kappa Omega	Milwaukee, Wisconsin

33RD — APRIL 21-23, 1967

Location:	Sheraton Lincoln Hotel
	Indianapolis, Indiana
Hostess Chapters:	Alpha Eta Omega, Alpha Mu Omega,
	Zeta Zeta Omega, Tau, Kappa
Attendance:	307 — 77 Undergraduates, 230 Graduates
Conference Theme:	*Alpha Kappa Alpha Embraces*
	The Challenges of the Sixties
Conference Chairman:	Hazel A. Moore
Conference Co-Chairmen:	Anna P. Stout and Ruby Woodson
Regional Director:	Ordie A. Roberts
Region Membership Statistics:	29 Chapters — 9 Undergraduate,
	20 Graduate Chapters

REGIONAL CONFERENCE NOTES:

Both a public meeting and sorority workshops were held on Friday evening. Time management of conference activities was a regional concern. In fact, the evaluation committee went as far as to recommend a suggested format for the next conference.

One highlight of the conference was the presentation of a model initiation, which was the first initiation held during a regional conference. Three pledges were initiated into Kappa Chapter, Butler College, Indianapolis, and one pledge as a general member.

The region awarded achievement awards in three new categories. Undergraduate chapters were divided into city and campus chapters, a mixed chapter category was included for Graduate chapters, and an award was given to the undergraduate soror with the highest grade point average. The award recipients were as follows:

Undergraduate Achievement Award to a City Chapter
First Place:	Beta	Chicago, Illinois

Second Place:	Beta Delta	St. Louis, Missouri
Third Place:	Beta Epsilon	Louisville, Kentucky

Undergraduate Achievement Award to a Campus Chapter
First Place:	Delta Omicron	Northern Illinois University
Second Place:	Gamma	University of Illinois/Urbana
Third Place:	Tau	University of Indiana

Chapter with the Highest Grade Point Average (Arnetta G. Wallace Cup)
First Place:	Delta Beta	Southern Illinois University
Second Place:	Gamma	University of Illinois/Urbana
Third Place:	Beta Zeta	Kentucky State College

Individual Soror Award for the Highest Individual Grade Point Average
Verna Fowlkes	Tau	Indiana University, Bloomington
Rosalind Bishop	Beta Zeta	Kentucky State College
Kay Clark	Delta Beta	Southern Illinois Universioty

Aactual GPA's were not recorded

Alice McGhee Smart Graduate Achievement Award Class A (Membership 50 or more)
First Place:	Gamma Omega	St. Louis, Missouri
Second Place:	Theta Omega	Chicago, Illinois
Third Place:	Alpha Mu Omega	Indianapolis, Indiana

Graduate Achievement Award Class B (Membership 49 or less)
First Place:	Delta Chi Omega	Evanston, Illinois
Second Place:	Gamma Psi Omega	Gary, Indiana
Third Place:	Beta Upsilon Omega	Frankfort, Kentucky

Graduate Achievement Award — Mixed Chapters
First Place:	Delta Delta Omega	East St. Louis, Illinois
Second Place:	Epsilon Kappa Omega	Milwaukee, Wisconsin
Third Place:	Beta Gamma Omega	Lexington, Kentucky

34TH — APRIL 19-21, 1968

Location:	Center for Continuing Education University of Notre Dame, South Bend, IN
Hostess Chapters:	Epsilon Epsilon Omega, Eta Nu Omega Eta Kappa Omega, Gamma Psi Omega, Gamma
Attendance:	198 — 36 Undergraduates, 162 Graduates
Conference Theme:	*Effective Service to Humanity . . . Alpha Kappa Alpha's Continuing Commitment*
Conference Chairman:	Ruby I. Jarrett
Regional Director:	Ordie A. Roberts
Region Membership Statistics:	29 Chapters — 9 Undergraduate, 20 Graduate Chapters Membership: 98 Undergraduates and 682 Graduates

REGIONAL CONFERENCE NOTES:

Delegates assembled at the 34th Central Regional Conference were duly impressed with the ambience of the executive decor of the general session meeting room. Some even commented that they felt they were deliberating at the United Nations.

Several regional achievement awards, at this point, were named for sorors. The Graduate Achievement Award for chapters with a membership of 50 or more maintained the name Alice McGhee Smart. Awards to chapters with memberships of 49 or less were named for Lucille B. Wilkins. The Achievement Award for Mixed Chapters was named for Ordie A. Roberts.

This regional conference would also mark the first Travel Grant Award—to the undergraduate soror with the highest cumulative scholastic average. The first recorded recipient of Central Region's Travel Grant Award was Alana Kathleen Moss, Beta Chapter, matriculating at Antioch College.

Another first in the awards category was the presentation of a plaque for the Annetta M. Lawson, Best Graduate Advisor. The first to receive this distinction was Soror Ruby Woodson, Graduate Advisor to Kappa Chapter, Butler College, and Soror Flora Chambliss, Graduate Advisor to Delta Beta, Southern Illinois University. In addition, the General Chapter Exhibit Award was named after Lee Ann Shelburne, the scrapbook award was reinstituted, and the Negro Heritage Award was added.

Undergraduate Achievement Award to a City Chapter
First Place:	Beta	Chicago, Illinois
Second Place:	Kappa	Indianapolis, Indiana
Third Place:	Beta Delta	St. Louis, Missouri

Undergraduate Achievement Award to a Campus Chapter
First Place:	Gamma	University of Illinois/Urbana
Second Place:	Beta Zeta	Kentucky State University
Third Place:	Tau	University of Indiana/Bloomington

Chapter with the Highest Grade Point Average (Arnetta G. Wallace Cup)
Kappa	Indianapolis, Indiana

Individual Soror Award for the Highest Individual Grade Point Average
Rosalyn Bishop (4.0)	Beta Zeta	Kentucky State University
Vernita Matellar (4.0)	Beta Zeta	Kentucky State University
Lea Williams (4.0)	Beta Zeta	Kentucky State University

Alice McGhee Smart Graduate Achievement Award (Membership 50 or more)
First Place:	Gamma Omega	St. Louis, Missouri
Second Place:	Alpha Mu Omega	Indianapolis, Indiana
Third Place:	Theta Omega	Chicago, Illinois

Lucille B. Wilkins Graduate Achievement Award (Membership 49 or less)
First Place:	Delta Chi Omega	Evanston, Illinois
Second Place:	Gamma Psi Omega	Gary, Indiana
Third Place:	Beta Upsilon Omega	Frankfort, Kentucky

Ordie A. Roberts Graduate Achievement Award — Mixed Chapters
First Place:	Delta Delta Omega	East St. Louis, Illinois
Second Place:	Epsilon Kappa Omega	Milwaukee; Wisconsin
Third Place:	Beta Gamma Omega	Lexington, Kentucky

35TH — APRIL 11-13, 1969

Location:	Sheraton-Jefferson Hotel St. Louis, Missouri
Hostess Chapters:	Beta Delta, Delta Beta, Gamma Omega, Delta Delta Omega, Epsilon Lambda Omega, Gamma Kappa Omega
Attendance:	333 — 85 Undergraduates, 248 Graduates
Conference Theme:	Effective Service to Humanity . . . Alpha Kappa Alpha's Continuing Commitment
Conference Chairman:	Mary S. Wrenn
Regional Director:	Ordie A. Roberts
Region Membership Statistics:	35 Chapters — 14 Undergraduate, 21 Graduate Chapters Active Membership: 901 214 Undergraduates, 687 Graduates

REGIONAL CONFERENCE NOTES:

A recommendation that a committee be appointed to study the composition of each hostess group and investigate the possibility of reassigning chapters had been proposed at the 34th Central Regional Conference in 1968. The committee reported at this conference that "a major redistribution of chapters to other hostess groups was a task that required intensive information and careful thought, and therefore was not easily accomplished at one Regional Conference planning meeting. The committee therefore suggested that the present system be maintained.

The Public meeting was a panel discussion of students, consultants, and representatives of the youth court regarding the role of young people in society. Other highlights included the Honorable William L. Clay, U.S. Representative as guest speaker at the conference luncheon and Supreme Basileus, Larzette G. Hale's address at the awards banquet.

Undergraduate Achievement Award to a City Chapter
First Place:	Beta	Chicago, Illinois
Second Place:	Beta Delta	St. Louis, Missouri

Undergraduate Achievement Award to a Campus Chapter
First Place:	Delta Omicron	Northern Illinois University
Second Place:	Gamma	University of Illinois/Urbana
Third Place:	Tau	University of Indiana/Bloomington
	Beta Zeta	Kentucky State University

Chapter with the Highest Grade Point Average (Arnetta G. Wallace Cup)
Beta Epsilon   University of Louisville

Individual Soror Award for the Highest Individual Grade Point Average
First Place:	Rosalyn Bishop, Beta Zeta	Kentucky State University
Second Place:	Carolyn Rogers, Delta Beta	Southern Illinois University
Third Place:	Cassandra Alfred, Beta	City Chapter, Chicago, Illinois

Annetta M. Lawson Best Graduate Advisor Award
Patricia D. Kelly — Advisor to Epsilon Iota, Southern Illinois University

Alice McGhee Smart Graduate Achievement Award (Membership 50 or more)
First Place:			Theta Omega			Chicago, Illinois
Second Place:			Alpha Mu Omega			Indianapolis, Indiana
Third Place:			Gamma Omega			St. Louis, Missouri

Lucille B. Wilkins Graduate Achievement Award (Membership 49 or less)
First Place:			Beta Upsilon Omega		Frankfort, Kentucky
Second Place:			Delta Chi Omega			Evanston, Illinois
Third Place:			Eta Omega			Louisville, Kentucky

Ordie A. Roberts Graduate Achievement Award — Mixed Chapters
First Place:			Delta Delta Omega		East St. Louis, Illinois
Second Place:			Epsilon Kappa Omega		Milwaukee; Wisconsin
Third Place:			Zeta Zeta Omega			Evansville, Indiana

36TH — APRIL 17-19, 1970

Location:	Phoenix Hotel
	Lexington, Kentucky
Hostess Chapters:	Eta Omega, Beta Upsilon Omega,
	Beta Zeta, Epsilon Zeta, Beta Epsilon,
	Beta Rho Omega, Beta Omega Omega
Conference Chairman:	Pauline Gould Gay
Regional Director:	Ordie A. Roberts
Region Membership Statistics:	38 Chapters — 17 Undergraduate,
	21 Graduate Chapters

A record of the proceedings for the 36th Central Regional Conference could not be located. The above information was obtained from other document sources.

37TH — APRIL 16-18, 1971

Location:	Sheraton Chicago Hotel
	Chicago, Illinois
Hostess Chapters:	Beta, Delta Omicron, Epsilon Delta,
	Gamma Chi, Theta Omega,
	Delta Phi Omega, Delta Chi Omega,
	Epsilon Kappa Omega,
Attendance:	404 — 160 Undergraduates,
	244 Graduates
Conference Theme:	*Greater Involvement — Alpha Kappa Alpha's Responsibility*
Conference Chairman:	Beatrice Murphy
Regional Director:	Johnetta Randolph Haley
Region Membership Statistics:	40 Chapters — 19 Undergraduate,
	21 Graduate Chapters
	Active Membership: 988
	321 Undergraduates, 667 Graduates

REGIONAL CONFERENCE NOTES:

The calendar of events for this regional conference took on a new look. In addition to the public meeting, the activities for Friday evening included a workshop for chapter officers, a VIP Dinner for Basilei, committee meetings and a mixer. Saturday's events included the first Undergraduate Rap Session. Sunday morning added "Ask Your Regional Director" and a city tour.

The awards presentation was highly organized with a new level of professionalism. Winners were designated as first place, second place and honorable mention. The Undergraduate Chapter Achievement Award for city chapters was named the Carolyn Blanton Cup and for campus chapters the Virginia M. Gilbert Cup. The Graduate Achievement Award for chapters with memberships of 50 or more reassumed its original name, Alice McGhee. *And the Mary E. Hill Community Service Award was added to the list of Undergraduate Awards—Beta Chapter, Chicago, Illinois was the first to receive this award.*

Carolyn Blanton Cup Undergraduate Achievement Award (City Chapter)
First Place:	Beta	Chicago, Illinois
Second Place:	Beta Epsilon	Louisville, Kentucky
Honorable Mention:	Beta Delta	St. Louis, Missouri

V. M. Gilbert Cup Undergraduate Achievement Award (Campus Chapters)
First Place:	Delta Omicron	Northern Illinois University
Second Place:	Gamma	University of Illinois/Urbana
Honorable Mention:	Epsilon Zeta	Western Kentucky University

Undergraduate Soror with Highest Scholastic Average
First Place:	Deborah Davis	Zeta Zeta	Murray State
Second Place:	Adrienne AshfordBeta	Chicago	
Honorable Mention:	Linda Patton	Beta Zeta	Kentucky State

Undergraduate Chapter with Highest Cumulative Average (Arnetta G. Wallace Cup)
First Place:	Epsilon Eta	Bradley University
Second Place:	Beta Zeta	Kentucky State University
Honorable Mention:	Beta	City Chapter — Chicago, IL

Annetta M. Lawson Best Graduate Advisor
Winnie Wilson — Advisor to Gamma Chapter, University of Illinois/Urbana

Lauretta Naylor Graduate Achievement Award (Membership 49 or less)
First Place:	Beta Upsilon Omega	Frankfort, Kentucky
Second Place:	Epsilon Kappa Omega	Milwaukee, Wisconsin
Honorable Mention:	Beta Gamma Omega	Lexington, Kentucky

Alice McGhee Smart Graduate Achievement Award (Membership 50 or more)
First Place:	Theta Omega	Chicago, Illinois
Second Place:	Alpha Mu Omega	Indianapolis, Indiana
Honorable Mention:	Gamma Omega	St. Louis, Missouri

The following recommendation would permanently change the tradition of passing on Regional Awards from one chapter to another. *"It is recommended that cups and plaques be purchased and engraved at the expense of the Regional Conference or individual chapters and that this is done annually. The winning chapters could then retain their cups or plaques, in other words, no traveling awards."*

38TH — APRIL 14-16, 1972

Location: Executive Inn
Evansville, Indiana

Hostess Chapters:	Kappa, Tau, Beta Phi, Epsilon Xi, Epsilon Rho, Alpha Eta Omega, Alpha Mu Omega, Zeta Zeta Omega
Attendance:	284 — 114 Undergraduates, 159 Graduates, 11 guests
Conference Theme:	*Greater Involvement! Alpha Kappa Alpha's Responsibility*
Conference Chairman:	Allouise J. Storey
Regional Director:	Johnetta Randolph Haley
Region Membership Statistics:	43 Chapters — 22 Undergraduate, 21 Graduate Chapters 1,093 Active Members 371 Undergraduates, 722 Graduates

REGIONAL CONFERENCE NOTES:

One of the many firsts of this regional conference was the singing of the Black National Anthem to open the first general session led by Delta Beta Chapter, Southern Illinois University. Also, under the leadership of Soror Haley, the Central Regional Conference would hold its first "Undergraduate Dress Out," and the Sunday morning Rededication Breakfast was born.

Carolyn Blanton Cup Undergraduate Achievement Award (City Chapter)
First Place:	Beta	Chicago, Illinois
Second Place:	Beta Delta	St. Louis, Missouri
Honorable Mention:	Epsilon Iota	Edwardsville, Indiana

V. M. Gilbert Cup Undergraduate Achievement Award (Campus Chapters)
First Place:	Zeta Zeta	Murray State University
Second Place:	Epsilon Zeta	Western Kentucky University
Honorable Mention:	Epsilon Rho	Purdue University

Loraine R. Green Undergraduate Soror with Highest Scholastic Average
Jocelyn Gouisha (3.42) Foreign Travel Grant Winner

Undergraduate Chapter with Highest Cumulative Average (Arnetta G. Wallace Cup)
Epsilon Iota (3.03)   City Chapter   Edwardsville, Indiana

Mary E. Hill Undergraduate Community Service Award
Gamma Chi — Northwestern University, Evanston, Illinois

Annetta M. Lawson Best Graduate Advisor
Joyce Berry — Advisor to Zeta Nu Chapter, Eastern Kentucky University

Lauretta Naylor Graduate Achievement Award (Membership 49 or less)
First Place:	Beta Upsilon Omega	Frankfort, Kentucky
Second Place:	Beta Gamma Omega	Lexington, Kentucky
Honorable Mention:	Beta Omega Omega	Paducah, Kentucky

Alice McGhee Smart Graduate Achievement Award (Membership 50 or more)
First Place:	Gamma Omega	St. Louis, Missouri
Second Place:	Theta Omega	Chicago, Illinois
Honorable Mention:	Delta Delta Omega	East St. Louis, Illinois

39TH — APRIL 12-15, 1973

Location:	Downtown Holiday Inn Gary, Indiana
Hostess Chapters:	Gamma Psi Omega, Zeta Phi, Epsilon Epsilon Omega, Gamma, Eta Kappa Omega, Eta Mu Omega, Theta Rho Omega, Epsilon Eta
Attendance:	401 — 163 Undergraduates, 10 Guests, 217 Graduates, 11 General Members
Conference Theme:	*Greater Involvement!* *Alpha Kappa Alpha's Responsibility*
Conference Chairman:	YJean S. Chambers
Regional Director:	Johnetta Randolph. Haley
Region Membership Statistics:	43 Chapters — 23 Undergraduate, 21 Graduate Chapters Active Members: 1,100 363 Undergraduates, 723 Graduates, 14 General Members

REGIONAL CONFERENCE NOTES:

The first Central Region Area Retreats were held in the fall of 1971. Soror Haley reported to the members assembled at this conference: "Again, I conducted five area retreats in September, October and November. All retreats with the exception of one were hosted by undergraduate chapters who showed exceptional maturity in carrying out their duties." Soror Haley also convened the first regional Basilei-Graduate Advisors Work Day.

Carolyn Blanton Cup Undergraduate Achievement Award (City Chapter)
First Place:	Beta Delta	St. Louis, Missouri
Second Place:	Beta Epsilon	Louisville, Kentucky
Honorable Mention:	Epsilon Iota	Edwardsville, Indiana

V. M. Gilbert Cup Undergraduate Achievement Award (Campus Chapters)
First Place:	Epsilon Rho	Purdue University
Second Place:	Epsilon Delta	University of Wisconsin
Honorable Mention:	Zeta Nu	Eastern Kentucky

Loraine R. Green Undergraduate Soror with Highest Scholastic Average
Mary Alexander (3.77)   Zeta Phi   Indiana University/Gary

Undergraduate Chapter with Highest Cumulative Average (Arnetta G. Wallace Cup)
Zeta Phi (2.9)   Indiana University   Northwest Gary, Indiana

Mary E. Hill Undergraduate Community Service Award
Epsilon Delta   University of Wisconsin   Madison, Wisconsin

Annetta M. Lawson Best Graduate Advisor
Barbara Penelton — Advisor to Epsilon Eta, Bradly University

Lauretta Naylor Graduate Achievement Award (Membership 49 or less)

First Place:	Epsilon Kappa Omega	Milwaukee, Wisconsin
Second Place (Tie):	Beta Omega Omega	Paducah, Kentucky
	Delta Chi Omega	Evanston, Illinois
Honorable Mention:	Beta Upsilon Omega	Frankfort, Kentucky

Alice McGhee Smart Graduate Achievement Award (Membership 50 or more)

First Place:	Gamma Omega	St. Louis, Missouri
Second Place:	Delta Delta Omega	East St. Louis, Illinois
Honorable Mention:	Gamma Psi Omega	Gary, Indiana

40TH — APRIL 19-20, 1974

Location:	Chase-Park Plaza Hotel St. Louis, Missouri
Hostess Chapters:	Epsilon Lambda Omega, Gamma Omega, Gamma Kappa Omega, Beta Delta, Delta Delta Omega, Delta Beta, Epsilon Iota
Attendance:	475 — 137, Undergraduates, 329 Graduates, 9 Guests
Conference Theme:	*Greater Involvement!* *Alpha Kappa Alpha's Responsibility*
Conference Chairman:	Marguerite S. Taylor
Co-Chairman:	Valla Abbington
Regional Director:	Johnetta Randolph Haley
Region Membership Statistics:	46 Chapters — 24 Undergraduate, 22 Graduate Chapters Active Members: 967 (Breakout not recorded)

REGIONAL CONFERENCE NOTES:

The city of St. Louis and the hostess chapters extended all attendees a warm and gracious welcome. The high esteem and respect held for the incumbent Central Regional Director was evident throughout the conference. Attendees enjoyed the special touches and pink and green hospitality. Many innovations to the region and the regional conference experienced during Soror Haley's tenure would remain as activities of the region and the regional conference.

Carolyn Blanton Cup Undergraduate Achievement Award (City Chapter)

First Place:	Epsilon Iota	Edwardsville, Indiana
Honorable Mention:	Beta	Chicago, Illinois

V. M. Gilbert Cup Undergraduate Achievement Award (Campus Chapters)

First Place:	Gamma	University of Illinois/Urbana
Honorable Mention:	Gamma Chi	Northwestern University

Loraine R. Green Undergraduate Soror with Highest Cumulative Scholastic Average — Foreign Travel Grant Winner
Enid Francis (2.667 on 3.0 scale) Beta Delta St. Louis, Missouri

Undergraduate Chapter With Highest Cumulative Average (Arnetta G. Wallace Cup)

First Place (tie):	Zeta Nu	Eastern Kentucky University
	Beta	City Chapter, Chicago, Illinois

Annetta M. Lawson Best Graduate Advisor
Wilma Battey — Advisor to Tau Chapter, Indiana University/Bloomington

Lauretta Naylor Graduate Achievement Award (Membership 49 or less)
First Place:	Theta Rho Omega	Markham, Illinois
Honorable Mention:	Beta Upsilon Omega	Frankfort, Kentucky

Alice McGhee Smart Graduate Achievement Award (Membership 50 or more)
First Place:	Theta Omega	Chicago, Illinois
Honorable Mention:	Gamma Omega	St. Louis, Missouri

41ST — APRIL 17-20, 1975

Location:	Marriott Inn Clarksville, Indiana
Hostess Chapters:	Beta Epsilon, Beta Zeta, Epsilon Zeta, Zeta Nu, Zeta Zeta, Eta Rho, Eta Omega, Beta Gamma Omega, Beta Rho Omega, Beta Omega Omega
Attendance:	395 — 133 Undergraduates, 249 Graduates, 6 Boule, 2 visitors and 5 Guests
Chairperson:	Leola E. Madison
Regional Director:	Gloria E. Bond
Region Membership Statistics:	50 Chapters — 27 Undergraduate, 23 Graduate Chapters Active Membership: 1,201 (Breakout not recorded)

REGIONAL CONFERENCE NOTES:
Due to the location, attendance at Soror Bond's first regional conference was relatively small. However, those sorors in attendance saw the business of the Central Regional Conference run like a well-oiled machine. The conference epitomized excellent time management. The Rules Committee met on Thursday evening and the VIP Dinner became the VIP Breakfast.

Carolyn Blanton Cup Undergraduate Achievement Award (City Chapter)
First Place:	Beta Epsilon	University of Louisville
Runner-up:	Epsilon Iota	Edwardsville, Indiana

V. M. Gilbert Cup Undergraduate Achievement Award (Campus Chapters)
First Place:	Tau	Indiana University
Runner-up:	Epsilon Rho	Purdue University

Loraine R. Green Undergraduate Soror With Highest Cumulative Scholastic Average
Carol Ladd	Tau	Indiana University

Undergraduate Chapter with Highest Cumulative Average (Arnetta G. Wallace Cup)
Epsilon Rho (4.0)	Purdue University	West Lafayette, Indiana

Mary E. Hill Undergraduate Community Service Award
Zeta Nu	Eastern Kentucky University	Richmond, Kentucky

Annetta M. Lawson Best Graduate Advisor
Winona Fletcher — Advisor to Beta Zeta Chapter, Kentucky State University

Lauretta Naylor Graduate Achievement Award (Membership 49 or less)
First Place: Beta Upsilon Omega   Frankfort, Kentucky
Runner-up: Epsilon Epsilon Omega   Urbana, Illinois

Alice McGhee Smart Graduate Achievement Award (Membership 50 or more)
First Place: Theta Omega   Chicago, Illinois
Runner-up: Alpha Mu Omega   Indianapolis, Indiana

42ND — APRIL 22-25, 1976

Location:	Hyatt Regency OHare
	Rosemont, Illinois
Hostess Chapters:	Beta, Gamma Chi, Iota Delta, Zeta Iota,
	Theta Omega, Delta Chi Omega,
	Delta Phi Omega, Epsilon Kappa Omega
Attendance:	413 — 142 Undergraduates, 255 Graduate,
	15 Guests and 1 visitor
Chairperson:	Dorothy Littlejohn Magett
Regional Director:	Gloria E. Bond
Region Membership Statistics:	52 Chapters — 28 Undergraduate,
	24 Graduate Chapters
	Active Members: 1,221 (Breakout not recorded)

REGIONAL CONFERENCE NOTES:

Soror Bernice Sumlin, Supreme Basileus, gave an overview of the sorority's national program. She reminded those present of the sorority's first AKA-NAACP DAY to be held in Chicago on May 14, 1976. Soror Sumlin also informed the membership that the sorority would present, for the first time, solid gold medallions to 50 year members of the sorority at the 47th Boule in New York City.

One primary issue at this Regional Conference was again the restructuring of the cluster system for hosting regional conferences. Soror Bond appointed a special committee of Past Regional Directors to review the current composition. Other interested sorors were also invited to join the committee.

Another first would be awards presented to chapters with the most members in attendance at the conference. Zeta Nu, Eastern Kentucky University, and Eta Mu Omega, South Bend, Indiana, were the first undergraduate and graduate chapters to receive this award. Also Eta Rho Chapter, Morehead State University, received the first award for the pledge line with the greatest increase in GPA above 2.5.

Carolyn Blanton Cup Undergraduate Achievement Award (City Chapter)
First Place: Beta Epsilon   University of Louisville
Runner-up: Epsilon Iota   City Chapter — East St. Louis, Illinois

V. M. Gilbert Cup Undergraduate Achievement Award (Campus Chapter)
First Place: Zeta Nu   Eastern Kentucky University
Runner-up: Gamma   University of Illinois/Champaign-Urbana

Loraine R. Green Undergraduate Soror with Highest Cumulative Scholastic Average
Deborah Jo Sports   Eta Rho   Morehead State University
Yvonne C. Day   Beta Phi   Ball State University

Mary E. Hill Undergraduate Community Service Award
Zeta Nu	Eastern Kentucky University	Richmond, Kentucky

Annetta M. Lawson Best Graduate Advisor
First Place: Zoearline Davis — Advisor to Beta Phi, Ball State University
Runner-up: Helen C. Cooper — Advisor to Iota Epsilon, Nat'l College of Education

Lauretta Naylor Graduate Achievement Award (Membership 49 or less)
First Place:	Beta Gamma Omega	Lexington, Kentucky
Runner-up:	Theta Rho Omega	Markham, Illinois

Alice McGhee Smart Graduate Achievement Award (Membership 50 or more)
First Place:	Theta Omega	Chicago, Illinois
Runner-up:	Delta Delta Omega	East St. Louis, Illinois

43RD — APRIL 22-24, 1977

Location:	Downtown Hilton Hotel
	Indianapolis, Indiana
Hostess Chapters:	Kappa, Tau, Zeta Zeta Omega, Beta Phi, Epsilon Xi, Iota Chi Omega, Alpha Eta Omega, Kappa Epsilon Omega, Alpha Mu Omega, Kappa Tau Omega
Attendance:	581 — 188 Undergraduates, 393 Graduates
Conference Theme:	*A Salute to Women: Past, Present, Future*
Conference Chairman:	Marilyn E. Strayhorn
Regional Director:	Gloria E. Bond
Region Membership Statistics:	55 Chapters — 28 Undergraduate, 27 Graduate Chapters
	Active Members: 1,433
	319 Undergraduates, 1,114 Graduates

REGIONAL CONFERENCE NOTES:

The Regional Ad Hoc Committee, appointed in 1976 to review the cluster structure for hosting regional conferences, presented a first draft of the suggested cluster composition to the body. The Committee reported that the final draft of the report would be presented at the 1978 Regional Conference. An added innovation to this regional conference was the "Honey Do" Farewell Continental Breakfast. "Honey Do" is the name given to husbands or significant others of sorors.

The formal awards banquet, "A Salute to Women: Past, Present, Future," was open to the public. Beautiful harp music was played by Soror Ivalue Patterson, Alpha Mu Omega Chapter as the elegantly attired sorors and guests entered the Royal Ballroom. The keynote address was delivered by Ms. Matcxia Ann Gillespie, Editor-in-Chief, Essence Magazine.

Prior to this Central Regional Conference only some chapter achievement awards were named in honor of sorors. It would be at this conference that all achievement awards would bear a soror's name except one, the Chapter Reading Exhibit. Following is a list of the conference awards and the sorors for whom they were named at this point in time.

UNDERGRADUATE AWARDS:
Helen C. Cooper	Undergraduate Chapter Program Exhibit
Maenell Newsome	Chapter Scrapbook
Gladys Gordon	Chapter Heritage Exhibit

Annetta G. Wallace   Undergraduate Chapter With Highest Scholastic Average
Loraine R. Green   Undergraduate Soror With Highest Cumulative Average
Carolyn Blanton   Chapter Achievement — City
V.M. Gilbert   Chapter Achievement — Campus
Annetta Lawson   Annetta M. Lawson Best Graduate Advisor
Johnetta R. Haley   Undergraduate Chapter With Most Sorors In Attendance

GRADUATE AWARDS:

Gladys Gordon   Chapter Heritage Exhibit
LeAnna Shelburne   Chapter Program Exhibit
Ordie A. Roberts   Alumna Chapter with the Most Sorors in Attendance
Lauretta Naylor Thompson Chapter Achievement (49 or less)
Alice McGhee Smart   Chapter Achievement (50 or more)

Carolyn Blanton Cup Undergraduate Achievement Award (City Chapter)
First Place: Beta   Chicago, Illinois
Runner-up: Kappa   Indianapolis, Indiana

V. M. Gilbert Cup Underfraduate Achievement Award (Campus Chapters)
First Place: Tau   Indiana University
Runner-up: Epsilon Rho   Purdue University

Loraine R. Green Award Undergraduate Soror with Highest Cumulative Average
First Place: Louise R. Cobb   Beta   (City) Chicago, Illinois
Runner-up: Linda Denise Holland   Epsilon Rho   Purdue University

Undergraduate Chapter with Highest Cumulative Average (Arnetta G. Wallace Cup)
First Place: Zeta Phi   Indiana University   NorthwestGary, Indiana
Runner-up: Kappa   City Chapter   Indianapolis, Indiana

Annetta M. Lawson Best Graduate Advisor
First Place: Zoearline Davis — Advisor to Beta Phi, Ball State University
Runner-up: Helen C. Cooper — Advisor to Iota Epsilon, Nat'l College of Education

Mary E. Hill Undergraduate Community Service Award
First Place: Kappa   City Chapter   Indianapolis, Indiana
Runner-up: Gamma Chi   Northwestern University   Evanston, Illinois

Lauretta Naylor Graduate Achievement Award (Membership 49 or less)
First Place: Beta Upsilon Omega   Frankfort, Kentucky
Runner-up: Theta Rho Omega   Markham, Illinois

Alice McGhee Smart Graduate Achievement Award (Membership 50 or more)
First Place: Theta Omega   Chicago, Illinois
Runner-up: Gamma Psi Omega   Gary, Indiana

44TH — APRIL 6-9, 1978

Location:	Sheraton-Homewood Inn Homewood, Illinois
Hostess Chapter(s)	Theta Rho Omega, Prime Hostess, Gamma, Epsilon Eta, Epsilon Epsilon Omega, Epsilon Rho, Zeta Phi, Eta Kappa Omega, Eta Alpha, Eta Mu Omega, Theta Omicron, Gamma Psi Omega,
Attendance:	716 (232 Undergraduates, 484 Graduates Largest attendance recorded to date.
Conference Theme:	*A Salute To Women: Past, Present & Future*
Conference Chairman:	Emma Jean Bakeman
Regional Director:	Gloria E. Bond
Region Membership Statistics:	60 Chapters 30 Undergraduate, 30 Graduate Active Members: 1,433 319 Undergraduates, 1,114 Graduates

REGIONAL CONFERENCE NOTES:

During this period, Supreme Basileus, Soror Bernice Sumlin, had appointed an Ad Hoc Committee on the realignment of regions. Soror Johnetta Haley, past Central Regional Director, represented Central Region on the committee. The committee's recommendations were presented at this conference; however, the Boule never took action on the report. One interesting note: If they had adopted the committee's recommendation, Central Region would have been divided into a central region composed of Illinois, Indiana, Wisconsin, Benton Harbor and St. Joseph Michigan, and a mid central region composed of Tennessee, Kentucky and West Virginia.

Closer to home, the Central Region's committee on the Realignment of Clusters for Regional Conferences presented three plans to the body. Soror Bond requested that action on the report be postponed until all chapters could review the recommendations. In response, the committee recommended that the plans be sent to every chapter and that a mail vote be taken.

A special moment at the Awards Banquet was the presentation of the first silver medallions to twenty-five-year members. Soror Bond presented the medallions following the Awards Committee Report. Soror Josephine Franklin, Theta Rho Omega Chapter concluded the presentations with a gift and a tribute to Soror Bond.

Carolyn Blanton Cup Undergraduate Achievement Award (City Chapter)
First Place:	Beta		Chicago, Illinois
Runner-up:	Epsilon Iota		Edwardsville, Indiana

V. M. Gilbert Cup Undergraduate Achievement Award (Campus Chapters)
First Place:	Zeta Iota		Western Illinois University
Runner-up:	Gamma Chi		Northwestern University

Loraine R. Green Award Undergraduate Soror with Highest Cumulative Average
First Place:	Louise R. Cobb	Beta	Chicago, Illinois
Runner-up:	Debra Jo Sports	Eta Rho	Morehead State University

Undergraduate Chapter with Highest Scholastic Average (Arnetta G. Wallace Cup)
First Place:	Beta Delta	Southern Illinois University
Runner-up:	Iota Sigma	University of Wisconsin/Milwaukee

Annetta M. Lawson Best Graduate Advisor
Emma S. Butler — Advisor to Zeta Nu, Eastern Kentucky University

Lauretta Naylor Graduate Achievement Award (Membership 49 or less)
First Place:	Lambda Mu Omega	Chicago, Illinois
Runner-up:	Kappa Epsilon Omega	Anderson, Indiana

Alice McGhee Smart Graduate Achievement Award (Membership 50 or more)
First Place:	Theta Omega	Chicago, Illinois
Runner-up:	Delta Delta Omega	East St. Louis, Illinois

45TH — APRIL 5-8, 1979

Location:	Breckenridge-Frontenac, Frontenac, Missouri
Hostess Chapters:	Delta Delta Omega, (Prime Hostess) Gamma Omega, Beta Delta Epsilon Lambda Omega, Delta Beta, Epsilon Iota, Gamma Kappa Omega, Eta Gamma
Attendance:	649 — 202 Undergraduates, 441 Graduates, 6 Guests
Conference Theme:	*Supreme in Service to All Mankind: A Call to Action*
Conference Chairman:	Mary L. Wrenn
Conference Co-Chairmen:	Gloria Abbington and Diana Logan
Regional Director:	Peggy Lewis LeCompte
Region Membership Statistics:	61 Chapters — 31 Undergraduate, 30 Graduate Active Members: 1,547 1,260 Graduate members, 287 Undergraduates

REGIONAL CONFERENCE NOTES:

Enter Soror Peggy Lewis LeCompte. *"I am proud and honored that I have been given the privilege and honor to serve Alpha Kappa Alpha. It is with love, humility, and appreciation and understanding of the expectations of you, my sorors, that I have approached the task of serving you."*

Many Regional Conference innovations of previous years were embellished under the leadership of Soror LeCompte. Thursday evening became an opportunity for *Rapping with the Regional Director*, followed by a Get Acquainted Cocktail Party.

The Ad Hoc Committee on Realignment of Clusters for Regional Conferences reported on the results of the mail vote. Only a third of the chapters in the region responded. This was of course, an insufficient number to decide. Therefore, a vote was taken at the conference on the three plans. The result of the vote was the adoption of Plan III to take effect in 1981. Plan III divided Central Region chapters into nine clusters; this cluster formation would stand until 1989. One recommendation of note made at this conference was that there are special seating at all dining functions for Golden Sorors.

State Comptroller Roland Burris was speaker for the Public Meeting and the sorors assembled at the Awards Banquet held onto every word delivered in the banquet address by Supreme Basileus, Soror Barbara K. Phillips. Following the inspirational address, the Awards Committee made their presentation. A one time Gloria E. Bond Regional Award was presented to Theta Omega and Beta Chapters, both of Chicago.

Special guests at the conference included Sorors Barbara Kinard Phillips, Supreme Basileus; Loraine Greene, 2nd Supreme Basileus, Loann Honesty King, Supreme Tamiouchos; Johnella Martin, Southeastern Regional Director, Deloris Gines, Mid-Western Regional Director, Gloria Smith, Great Lakes Regional Director; Anne Mitchem Davis, former Executive Director; Carey B. Preston, former Executive Director and former Central Regional Directors Annetta Lawson, Alice McGhee Smart, Lee Anna Shelbourne, Evelyn Roberts, Irma Clark, Pauline Kigh Reed, Ordie Roberts, Gloria Bond and former Central Regional International Officers — Gladys Bufkin Johnson, Helen Cromer Cooper, and C. Elizabeth Johnson.

Carolyn Blanton Cup Undergraduate Achievement Award (City Chapter)
First Place:	Beta	Chicago, Illinois
Runner-up:	Epsilon Iota	Edwardsville, Indiana

V. M. Gilbert Cup Undergraduate Achievement Awarde (Campus Chapters)
First Place:	Zeta Nu	Eastern Kentucky University
Runner-up:	Lambda Xi	University of Wisconsin

Loraine R. Green Undergraduate Soror with Highest Cumulative Average
First Place:	Annette Williams	Beta Zeta, Kentucky State
Runner-up:	Joyce Washington	Epsilon Xi, Indiana State

Undergraduate Chapter With Highest Scholastic Average (Arnetta G. Wallace Cup)
First Place:	Epsilon Xi	Indiana State University
Runner-up:	Mu Beta	Milwaukee, Wisconsin

Annetta M. Lawson Best Graduate Advisor
Linda McChristian — Advisor to Kappa Chapter, Butler College

Lauretta Naylor Thompson Graduate Achievement Award (Membership 49 or less)
First Place:	Lambda Alpha Omega	Western Suburbs/Chicago
Runner-up:	Gamma Kappa Omega	Carbondale

Alice McGhee Smart Graduate Achievement Award (Membership 50 or more)
First Place:	Theta Omega	Chicago, Illinois
Runner-up:	Delta Delta Omega	East St. Louis, Missouri

46TH — APRIL 10-13, 1980

Location:	Gault House
	Louisville, Kentucky
Hostess Chapters:	Eta Omega, Prime Hostess,
	Beta Gamma Omega, Beta Rho Omega, Beta Upsilon Omega, Beta Omega Omega, Mu Delta Omega, Epsilon Zeta, Beta Zeta, Zeta Zeta, Zeta Nu, Eta Rho and Iota Sigma
Attendance:	614 — 167 Undergraduates, 399 Graduates, 17 General Members, 31 Guests
Conference Theme:	*Supreme in Service to All Mankind: A Call to Action*
Conference Chairman:	Elizabeth Collins
Regional Director:	Peggy Lewis LeCompte
Region Membership Statistics:	63 Chapters — 32 Undergraduate, 31 Graduate Chapters
	Active Members: Data not recorded

REGIONAL CONFERENCE NOTES:

Patterned after the program symposiums at the Boule, Soror LeCompte introduced the Program Symposium to Central Region. The Program Committee's report was presented in this format at the Saturday morning general session.

During the Public Meeting forty-one members of the community received Community Service Awards for their contributions to mankind. 18th Supreme Basileus, Soror Mattelia Bennett Grays was the guest speaker.

First Supreme Anti-Basileus, Faye B. Bryant was the Banquet speaker. Other special guests at the conference included Sorors Barbara Kinard Phillips, Supreme Basileus; Loraine Green, 2nd Supreme Basileus, Loann Honesty King, SupremeTamiouchos; Johnella Martin, Southeastern Regional Director, Dorothy Johnson, South Central Regional Director; Earnestine Green, Executive Director; Deloris Gines, Mid-Western Regional Director, Gloria Smith, Great Lakes Regional Director; Anne Mitchem Davis, former Executive Director; Carey B. Preston, former Executive Director and former former Central Regional Directors Annetta Lawson, Alice McGhee Smart, Lee Anna Shelbourne, Evelyn Roberts, Irma Clark, Pauline Kigh Reed, Ordie Roberts, Gloria Bond and former Central Regional International Officers — Gladys Bufkin Johnson, Helen Cromer Cooper, and C. Elizabeth Johnson and Carolyn Thomas,

Carolyn Blanton Cup Undergraduate Achievement Award (City Chapter)
First Place: Beta   Chicago, Illinois
Runner-up: Epsilon Iota   Edwardsville, Indiana

V. M. Gilbert Cup Undergraduate Achievement Award (Campus Chapters)
First Place: Gamma Chi   Northwestern University
Runner-up: Gamma   University of Illinois/Urbana

Loraine R. Green Undergraduate Soror with Highest Cumulative Average Award
First Place: Annette Williams (3.68)   Beta Zeta   Kentucky State
Runner-up: Rhonda Barnes   (3.62)   Eta Rho   Morehead State

Undergraduate Chapter with Highest Scholastic Average (Arnetta G. Wallace)
First Place: Beta Zeta (2.84)   Kentucky State
Runner-up: Tau (2.599)   Indiana University

Annetta M. Lawson Best Graduate Advisor
Nadine Bonds — Advisor to Tau Chapter, Indiana University/Bloomington

Lauretta Naylor Thompson Graduate Achievement Award (Membership 49 or less)
First Place: Delta Chi Omega   Evanston, Illinois
Runner-up: Lambda Alpha Omega   Western Suburbs/Chicago

Alice McGhee Smart Graduate Achievement Award (Membership 50 or more)
First Place: Gamma Omega   St. Louis, Missouri
Runner-up: Delta Delta Omega   East St. Louis, Illinois

47TH — APRIL 2-5, 1981

Location:	St. Paul Radisson Minneapolis, Minnesota
Hostess Chapters:	Delta Phi Omega, Prime Hostess, Mu Rho, Mu Beta, Epsilon Kappa Omega, Kappa Psi Omega, Iota Delta, Epsilon Delta
Attendance:	427 — 99 Undergraduates, 313 Graduates, 15 Guest
Conference Theme:	*Influencing Decisions: A Design for Action in the 80's*
Conference Chairman:	Mable E. Cason
Regional Director:	Peggy Lewis LeCompte
Region Membership Statistics:	63 Chapters — 32 Undergraduate, 31 Graduate Active Members: 1,806

REGIONAL CONFERENCE NOTES:

In response to the concerns and problems experienced by undergraduate chapters, Soror LeCompte established the Undergraduate Roundup Committee as a logical extension of the Graduate Advisors Council. The first Roundup was scheduled and held in September 1981 in Edwardsville IL.

Also, the first Undergraduate Luncheon was held with Mu Rho, Iota Delta and Mu Beta as the luncheon chairpersons. The luncheon was beautifully executed and attended by a large number of both Graduate and Undergraduate Sorors.

During this conference the first Central Region flag designed by Soror Luereatha Griffin of Delta Delta Omega Chapter was presented and flown. Soror Margaret Bush Wilson, Esq., President of the NAACP Board of Directors was guest speaker for the Public Meeting. Soror Mattelia B. Grays, 18th Supreme Basileus was banquet speaker.

Carolyn Blanton Cup Undergraduate Achievement Award (City Chapters)
First Place:	Beta	Chicago, Illinois
Runner-up:	Epsilon Iota	East St. Louis, Illinois

V. M. Gilbert Cup Undergraduate Achievement Award (Campus Chapters)
First Place:	Tau	University of Indiana
Runner-up:	Epsilon Zeta	Western Kentucky University

Loraine R. Green Undergraduate Soror with Highest Cumulative Average
First Place:	Sandra Porter (3.54)	Beta Delta	St. Louis, Missouri
Runner-up:	Gloria Smith	Nu Lambda	Gary, Indiana

Undergraduate Chapter with Highest Scholastic Average (Arnetta G. Wallace)
First Place:	Nu Lambda	City Chapter	Gary, Indiana
Runner-up:	Epsilon Xi	Indiana State University	

Annetta M. Lawson Best Graduate Advisor
First Place:	Mary Bentley — Advisor to Tau, Indiana University/Bloomington
Runner-up	Adrianne Hayward — Advisor to Gamma Chi, Northwestern

Lauretta Naylor Thompson Graduate Achievement Award (Membership 49 or less)
First Place:	Kappa Tau Omega	Bloomington, IN
Runner-up:	Lambda Alpha Omega	Western Suburbs/Chicago

Alice McGhee Smart Graduate Achievement Award (Membership 50 or more)

First Place:	Gamma Psi Omega	Gary, Indiana
Runner-up:	Gamma Omega	St. Louis, Missouri

48TH — APRIL 1-4, 1982

Location:	Sheraton West Indianapolis, Indiana
Hostess Chapters:	Alpha Mu Omega Prime Hostess, Kappa, Alpha Eta Omega, Tau, Kappa Epsilon Omega, Epsilon Xi, Iota Chi Omega, Epsilon Rho, Kappa Tau Omega, Zeta Zeta Omega
Conference Theme:	*Influencing Decisions: A Design for Action in the 80's*
Attendance:	735 — 123 undergraduates; 594 graduates; 17 guests
Conference Chairman:	Yvonne Perkins
Regional Director:	Peggy Lewis LeCompte
Region Membership Statistics:	71 Chapters — 36 Undergraduate, 35 Graduate Chapters

REGIONAL CONFERENCE NOTES:

The Indianapolis conference afforded sorors the opportunity to experience many first. Among these were: the chartering of an undergraduate chapter, Xi Zeta, Illinois Wesleyan University, Bloomington, Illinois; the presentation of Soror Phyllis Waters portrait, the designer of the Coat of Arms, for display in the new headquarters; the perfect attendance of seven undergraduate chapters; the publishing of a daily newsletter "The Love Line"; the use of voting machines; the presentation of a Sisterhood Award and the display of a Regional Flag at sessions. Seven undergraduates chapter had perfect attendance at the conference.

The Public Meeting speaker was Dr. Lenore Col Alexander; Soror Julia Brogdon Purnell, 16th Supreme Basileus was banquet speaker. Special conference guests included Soror Delta Irby, former Undergraduate Member-at-Large, Anita Shelton, and Undergraduate Member-at-Large. Special guests at the conference included Sorors Loraine Greene, 2nd Supreme Basileus, Loann Honesty King, SupremeTamiouchos; Johnella Martin, Southeastern Regional Director, Deloris Gines, Mid-Western Regional Director, Gloria Smith, Great Lakes Regional Director; Anne Mitchem Davis, former Executive Director; Carey B. Preston, former Executive Director, Lauretta Naylor Thompson, former Supreme Grammateus, , Irma Clark, former Supreme Grammateus and Supreme Tamiouchos and former Central Regional Directors Maenell Newsome, Annetta Lawson, Alice McGhee Smart, Lee Anna Shelburne, Evelyn Roberts, Pauline Kigh Reed, Ordie Roberts, Gloria Bond and former Central Regional International Officers — Gladys Bufkin Johnson, Helen Cromer Cooper, and C. Elizabeth Johnson.

Note: A record of the award data could not be located.

49th — APRIL 14-17, 1983

Location:	Marriott — Century Center South Bend, Indiana
Hostess Chapters:	Nu Lambda, Gamma Psi Omega, Eta Kappa Omega, Theta Rho Omega, Lambda Tau Omega, Xi Eta Omega
Conference Theme:	*Our Diamond Jubilee Promise—Facets of Dynamic Power*
Attendance:	691 — 126 Undergraduates, 562 Graduates, 3 Guests

Conference Chairman:	Gloria E. Bond
Regional Director:	Mable Evans Cason
Region Membership Statistics:	71 Chapters — 36 Undergraduate, 35 Graduate Chapters

REGIONAL CONFERENCE NOTES:

Take a good thing and make it better. This statement best describes the Central Regional Conference format under the leadership of Mable Evans Cason. The first General Session was moved from Friday morning to after the Conference Luncheon. Time on Friday morning was given to committee meetings. The Regional Undergraduate Luncheon, started under Soror LeCompte in 1981, featured Undergraduate National Officers as main speakers. Soror Cason adopted the Gamma Omega Singers as Central Region's official performing group and they were featured in concert at her first Public Meeting.

Carolyn Blanton Cup Undergraduate Achievement Award (City Chapter)
First Place:	Beta	Chicago, Illinois
Runner-up:	Mu Rho	Minneapolis, Minnesota

V. M. Gilbert Cup Undergraduate Achievemnt Award (Campus Chapters)
First Place:	Gamma Chi	Northwestern University
Runner-up:	Delta Omicron	Northern Illinois University

Loraine R. Green Award Undergraduate Soror with Highest Cumulative Average
First Place:	Carolyn Booth (3.69)	Beta	City Chapter/Chicago
Runner-up:	Cherri Hursey (3.64)	Xi Kappa	Chicago State University

Undergraduate Chapter with Highest Scholastic Average (Arnetta G. Wallace Cup)
First Place:	Beta	City Chapter, Chicago, Illinois
Runner-up:	Xi Kappa	Chicago State University

Lauretta Naylor Thompson Graduate Achievemnt Award (Membership 49 or less)
First Place:	Lambda Mu Omega	Chicago, Illinois
Runner-up:	Lambda Alpha Omega	Western Suburbs/Chicago

Alice McGhee Smart Graduate Achievement Award (Membership 50 or more)
First Place:	Gamma Omega	St. Louis, Missouri
Runner-up:	Theta Omega	Chicago, Illinois

Annetta M. Lawson Best Graduate Advisor
First Place:	Pamela Rice — Advisor to Gamma Chi, Northwestern University
Runner-up	Barbara Travis — Advisor to Gamma Chi, Northwestern University

The Gloria E. Bond Award for the Undergraduate Chapter with the Most Transfers to an Alumna Chapter and for the Graduate Chapter with the Most Transfers from an Undergraduate Chapter was established at this conference. There were no entries for this award.

PART VII: REGIONAL CONFERENCES

50TH — GOLDEN ANNIVERSARY CONFERENCE

MARCH 29-APRIL 1, 1983

Location:	Hyatt Regency Chicago
	Chicago, Illinois
Hostess Chapters:	Theta Omega, Prime Hostess, Beta, Xi Kappa,
	Gamma Chi, Xi Epsilon,
	Delta Omicron, Xi Nu Omega,
	Lambda Alpha Omega, Lambda Nu Omega,
	Delta Chi Omega, Lambda Mu Omega
Attendance:	1,112 — 181 Undergraduates, 931 Graduates
Conference Theme:	*Our Diamond Jubilee Promise-*
	Facets of Dynamic Power
Conference Chairman:	Marva J. Lee
Regional Director:	Mable Evans Cason
Region Membership Statistics:	71 Chapters — 36 Undergraduate,
	35 Graduate Chapters
	Active Members: 2,322
	(Breakout not available)

REGIONAL CONFERENCE NOTES:

"Facets of Dynamic Power," exemplifies the activities of Central Region's Golden Anniversary Conference: Starting with the record-breaking attendance, paced by the sisterly hospitality of the hostess chapters, and moving with the cadence of the inspirational words of Soror Loraine Richardson Green, 2nd Supreme Basileus. The conference was driven by the power of the words of Chicago's Mayor Harold Washington and Supreme Basileus, Faye B. Bryant. From the elegant public banquet, studded with dignitaries, and concluding in unique form at the Rededication Breakfast with the presentation of the regional awards.

The Gloria E. Bond Award for the Undergraduate Chapter with the Most Transfers to an Alumna Chapter went to Gamma, University of Illinois/Champaign-Urbana. Theta Omega, Chicago, received the award for the Graduate Chapter with the Most Transfers from an Undergraduate Chapter. Also, the Regional Director presented the first awards for individual and chapter contributions to the Capital Improvement Project (CIP). The award for chapter contributions went to Delta Omicron, Northern Illinois University and Gamma Omega, St. Louis. The award for individual contributions went to Tau, University of Indiana, and Theta Omega, Chicago.

V. M. Gilbert Cup Undergraduate Achievement Award (Campus Chapters)
First Place: Gamma Chi   Northwestern University

Annetta M. Lawson Best Graduate Advisor
Sandra Hill — Advisor to Xi Epsilon, Kendall College, Evanston, Illinois

Loraine R. Green Undergraduate Soror with Highest Cumulative Average
First Place: Bethsheba Bullock (3.60) Xi Kappa   Chicago State University
Runner-up: Cherri Hursey (3.44)   Xi Kappa   Chicago State University

Undergraduate Chapter with Highest Scholastic Average (Arnetta G. Wallace Cup)
First Place: Xi Kappa   Chicago State University

Lauretta Naylor Thompson Graduate Achievement Award
(Membership 49 or less)
First Place: Delta Chi Omega Evanston, Illinois
Runner-up: Lambda Mu Omega Chicago, Illinois

Alice McGhee Smart Graduate Achievement Award
(Membership 50 or more)
First Place: Lambda Alpha Omega Western Suburbs,/Chicago
Runner-up: Theta Omega Chicago, Illinois

51ST — APRIL 4-7, 1985

Location:	The Chancellor Hotel and Convention Center Champaign, Illinois
Hostess Chapters:	Epsilon Epsilon Omega, Prime Hostess, Eta Gamma, Eta Alpha, Xi Eta, Theta Omicron, Lambda Psi, Nu Pi Omega Omicron Delta Omega, Nu Omicron Omega
Attendance:	484 — 92 Undergraduates, 379 Graduates, 13 Guests
Conference Theme:	*Energizing for the 21st Century*
Conference Chairman:	Patricia McKinney Lewis
Regional Director:	Mable Evans Cason
Region Membership Statistics:	75 Chapters — 36 Undergraduate, 39 Graduate Chapters

REGIONAL CONFERENCE NOTES:
Only five of thirty-six undergraduate chapters and ten of thirty-nine graduate Chapters submitted reports to the Regional Awards Committee. In addition, there were no entries in several award categories.

Loraine R. Green Undergraduate Soror with Highest Cumulative Average
First Place: Cynthia Wilburn Iota Sigma University of Kentucky/Lexington

Undergraduate Chapter with Highest Scholastic Average (Arnetta G. Wallace Cup)
First Place: Iota Sigma University of Kentucky/Lexington

Annetta Lawson Best Graduate Advisor Award
First Place: Pamela Watson — Advisor to Gamma Chi, Northwestern University

Lauretta Naylor Thompson Graduate Achievement Award (Membership 49 or less)
First Place: Lambda Alpha Omega Western Suburbs/Chicago
Runner-up: Delta Chi Omega Evanston, Illinois

Alice McGhee Smart Graduate Achievement Award (Membership 50 or more)
First Place: Theta Omega Chicago, Illinois
Runner-up: Gamma Omega St. Louis, Missouri

PART VII: REGIONAL CONFERENCES

52ND — APRIL 10-13, 1986

Location:	Hyatt Regency Lexington
	Lexington, Kentucky
Hostess Chapters:	Beta Gamma Omega, Beta Omega Omega,
	Beta Upsilon Omega, Beta Rho Omega,
	Eta Omega, Mu Delta Omega,
	Omicron Sigma Omega, Beta Epsilon,
	Beta Zeta, Epsilon Zeta, Eta Rho,
	Iota Sigma, Zeta Nu, Zeta Zeta
Attendance:	725 — 147 Undergraduates, 578 Graduates
Conference Theme:	*Energizing for the 21st Century*
Conference Chairman:	Teresa Louismas
Regional Director:	Mable Evans Cason
	Peggy Lewis LeCompte
Region Membership Statistics:	77 Chapters — 36 Undergraduate,
	41 Graduate Chapters
	1,811 Active Members

REGIONAL CONFERENCE NOTES:

Soror Mable Evans Cason laid the groundwork for her last Regional Conference as Central Regional Director. Soror Cason's trademarks: love, graciousness and sisterly cooperation, allowed Soror LeCompte to carry the conference to a successful conclusion.

Again, the response by chapters to the Regional Awards Committee was poor. Only six of thirty-six undergraduate chapters and eighteen of forty graduate chapters reported.

Added to the list of awards were the Peggy LeCompte Award for Outstanding Undergraduate Soror in Communications or Journalism Leadership and the Per Capita Award (first chapter to pay per capita). Soror Victoria Clark, Alpha Mu Omega was the first recipient of this award. Epsilon Delta, Nu Sigma and Epsilon Xi shared the honors for the first chapters to pay per capita tax.

V. M. Gilbert Cup Undergraduate Achievement Award (Campus Chapters)
First Place: Gamma Chi   Northwestern University

Loraine R. Green Undergraduate Soror with Highest Cumulative Average
First Place: Crystal J. Evans (3.63)   Xi Kappa   Chicago State University
Runner-up: Kaweemah M. Bashie (3.42) Xi Kappa   Chicago State University

Undergraduate Chapter with Highest Scholastic Average (Arnetta G. Wallace Cup)
First Place: Iota Sigma (2.89)   University of Kentucky/Lexington

Annetta Lawson Best Graduate Advisor Award
Cheryl Cole Young — Advisor to Beta Delta City Chapter, St. Louis, Missouri

Lauretta Naylor Thompson Graduate Achievement Award (Membership 49 or less)
First Place: Omicron Theta Omega   St. Louis, Missouri
Runner-up: Delta Chi Omega   Evanston, Illinois

Alice McGhee Smart Graduate Achievement Award (Membership 50 or more)
First Place: Theta Omega   Chicago, Illinois
Runner-up: Lambda Alpha Omega   West Suburbs/Chicago

53RD — APRIL 9-12, 1987

Location:	Marc Plaza Hotel Milwaukee, Wisconsin
Hostess Chapters:	Epsilon Kappa Omega, Prime Hostess, Delta Phi Omega, Kappa Psi Omega, Pi Gamma Omega, Epsilon Delta, Iota Delta, Mu Beta, Mu Rho
Attendance:	798 — 115 Undergraduates, 673, Graduates, 10 Guests
Conference Theme:	*Service with A Global Perspective*
Conference Co-Chairmen:	Frances Jefferson and Mildred Pollard
Regional Director:	Loann J. Honesty King
Region Membership Statistics:	78 Active Chapters — 36 Undergraduate, 42 Graduate Chapters 2,120 Active Members 122 Undergraduates, 1,998 Graduates

REGIONAL CONFERENCE NOTES:

Anticipation was high and so were the expectations of the sorors attending the 53rd Central Regional Conference. They were not disappointed. The conference flowed from one innovation to the next: imported-hand made bags from Nairobi as the conference kit, a chapter roll call, the public meeting's Black Arts Showcase, a video awards presentation and remarks by the Reverend Jesse Lewis Jackson at the awards banquet, and a Palm Sunday worship service at the Rededication Breakfast.

Sorors assembled at the Ivy Beyond the Wall Ceremony paid tribute to Past Central Regional Director Annetta Moten Lawson. She became an Ivy Beyond the Wall on December 8, 1986.

The previous year's Regional Awards Committee made fifteen recommendations. These recommendations were implemented by the 53rd Central Regional Conference Awards Committee. Including a the addition of a third category for the Graduate Achievement Award for chapters with 25 or less members named after former Central Regional Director, Mabel Evans Cason.

Two new awards were presented at the conference. The Lee Anna Shelburne Award to the graduate chapter that best manifests the national program targets went to Lambda Alpha Omega, Western Suburbs/Chicago, First Place and Theta Omega, Chicago, Runner-up. The Connection Award was given in the name of the current Central Regional Director to the chapter that best exemplifies the purpose of the National Connection Committee. The first recipients of this award were Omicron Theta Omega, St. Louis, First Place and Eta Mu Omega, South Bend, Runner-up. First, Second and Third Place awards were also presented to the winners of the Undergraduate Step-Out.

Carolyn Blanton Cup Undergraduate Achievement Award (City Chapter)
First Place: Kappa   Indianapolis, Indiana
Runner-up: Beta Delta   St. Louis, Missouri

V. M. Gilbert Cup Undergraduate Achievement Award (Campus Chapters)
First Place: Epsilon Delta   University of Wisconsin/Madison
Runner-up: Xi Kappa   Chicago State University

Loraine R. Green Undergraduate Soror with Highest Cumulative Average
Winner: Frances Wilkerson   Epsilon Delta   University of Wisconsin/Madison

Undergraduate Chapter with Highest Scholastic Average (Arnetta G. Wallace Cup)
First Place: Iota Delta   University of Wisconsin/Milwaukee

Annetta Lawson Best Graduate Advisor Award
First Place: Comella Smith — Advisor to Xi Kappa, Chicago state University
Runner-up: Pam Hammond McDavid — Advisor to Eta Gamma, Eastern Illinois

Mabel Evans Cason Graduate Achievement Award (Membership 25 or less)
First Place: Theta Rho Omega Markham, Illinois
Runner-up: Eta Mu Omega South Bend, Indiana

Lauretta Naylor Thompson Graduate Achievement Award (Membership 49 or less)
First Place: Omicron Theta Omega St. Louis, Missouri
Runner-up: Delta Chi Omega Evanston, Illinois

Alice McGhee Smart Graduate Achievement Award (Membership 50 or more)
First Place: Lambda Alpha Omega West Suburbs/Chicago
Runner-up: Gamma Omega St. Louis, Missouri

54TH — APRIL 21-24, 1988

Location:	Clarion Hotel, St. Louis, Missouri
Hostess Chapters:	Gamma Omega, Prime Hostess, Gamma Kappa Omega, Delta Delta Omega, Epsilon Lambda Omega, Omicron Eta Omega, Omicron Theta Omega, Beta Delta, Delta Beta, Epsilon Iota
Attendance:	1,081 -151 Undergraduates, 912 Graduates, 18 Guest
Conference Theme:	*Service with A Global Perspective*
Conference Co-Chairmen:	Irene F. Schell and Sara I. Scroggins
Regional Director:	Loann J. Honesty King
Region Membership Statistics:	78 Chapters — 36 Undergraduate, 42 Graduate Chapters, 2,269 Active Members

REGIONAL CONFERENCE NOTES:

The hostess chapters left no stone unturned in ensuring that the attendees at the conference experienced St. Louis hospitality in pink and green style. Highlights of the 54th Central Regional Conference included the public meeting featuring the East St. Louis Lincoln High School Jazz Band performing Alpha Kappa Alpha through the Years in Music held at the Harris-Stowe State College; the sorors dressed in nautical attire at the AKA Port of Call Luncheon and enjoyed the motivational words of Soror Patricia Russell McCloud at the Undergraduate Luncheon.

Supreme Basileus Soror Janet Jones Ballard enlivened the sorors with her remarks at the conference awards banquet which took on a Hollywood Academy Awards ambience with the regional awards presentation being moderated by Sorors Janice Huff, KSDK TV — Channel 5 and Sharon Stevens, KTVI TV — Channel 2.

The inspirational words of First Supreme Anti-Basileus Mary Shy Scott, followed by the video presentation of "Soror to Soror: A Conversation with Loraine Richardson Green," at the Rededication Breakfast brought a fitting conclusion to the conference.

Carolyn Blanton Cup Undergraduate Achievement Award (City Chapter)
First Place: Beta Chicago, Illinois

V. M. Gilbert Cup Undergraduate Achievement Award (Campus Chapters)
First Place: Epsilon Rho Purdue University
Runner-up: Epsilon Delta University of Wisconsin/Madison

Loraine R. Green Undergraduate Soror with Highest Cumulative Average
Frances Wilkerson Epsilon Delta (3.7) University of Wisconsin/Madison

Arnetta G. Wallace Undergraduate Chapter with Highest Scholastic Average
First Place: Beta (3.2) City Chapter/Chicago

Mable Evans Cason Graduate Achievement Award (Membership 25 or less)
First Place: Eta Mu Omega South Bend, Indiana

Lauretta Naylor Thompson Graduate Achievement Award (Membership 26 to 50)
First Place: Omicron Theta Omega St. Louis, Missouri

Alice McGhee Smart Graduate Achievement Award (Membership 51 and above)
First Place: Lambda Alpha Omega West Suburbs/Chicago

Annetta Lawson Best Graduate Advisor
First Place: Ludella Harris — Advisor to Gamma Chapter, University of Illinois
Runner-up: Kathy Thornton — Advisor to Delta Omicron, Northern Illinois

55TH — APRIL 6-9, 1989

Location:	Grand Wayne Convention Center
	Fort Wayne, Indiana
Hostess Chapters:	Iota Chi Omega, Prime Hostess, Kappa, Tau, Beta Phi, Epsilon Xi, Epsilon Rho, Alpha Eta Omega, Omicron Phi Omega, Kappa Epsilon Omega, Kappa Tau Omega,
Attendance:	866 — 150 Undergraduates, 716 Graduates
Conference Theme:	*Supreme In Service — Reaching Out To Touch Mankind*
Conference Chairman:	Ella M. Green
Conference Co-Chairmen:	Nadine C. Bonds and Juanita Bedenbaugh
Regional Director:	Loann J. Honesty King
Region Membership Statistics:	79 Chapters — 37 Undergraduate, 42 Graduate Chapters
	2,747 Active Members — 416 Undergraduates, 1,873 Graduates, 254 Boule, 204 Life

REGIONAL CONFERENCE NOTES:

The 55th Central Regional Conference Luncheon was a very special occasion. The luncheon program was a tribute to Soror Loraine Richardson Green, the second Supreme Basileus of Alpha Kappa Alpha Sorority, Inc., entitled "Our Most Fragrant Rose." Another special event was the joint formal dance with Kappa Alpha Psi Fraternity.

The conference presented Chapter Achievement Awards for outstanding Project Implementation in the International Program Strands. For consistency, the author has cited only the winners in the categories previously listed. Also, campus and city undergraduate chapters would compete in the same category for overall chapter achievement.

Carolyn Blanton/Virginia Gilbert
Undergraduate Overall Chapter Program Achievement
Winner: Omicron Alpha   College Consortium   Northwest Suburban Illinois

Loraine R. Green Undergraduate Soror with Highest Cumulative Average
Winner: Leslie Clemmens

Arnetta G. Wallace Undergraduate Chapter with Highest Scholastic Average
Winner: Iota Sigma (3.19)   University of Kentucky/Lexington

Annetta M. Lawson Best Graduate Advisor
Not recorded

Mable Evans Cason Overall Chapter Program Achievement (Membership up to 25)
Winner: Pi Lambda Omega   East Jefferson County, Kentucky

Lauretta Naylor Thompson Overall Chapter Program Achievement (Membership 26-50)
Winner: Theta Rho Omega   Markham, Illinois

Alice McGhee Smart Overall Chapter Program Achievement (Membership 51 and above)
Winner: ambda Alpha Omega   West Suburbs/Chicago

56TH — APRIL 19-22, 1990

Location:	Hyatt Regency Hotel Oak Brook, Illinois
Hostess Chapters:	Lambda Alpha Omega, Prime Hostess, Delta Chi Omega, Theta Omega, Lambda Mu Omega, Nu Omega, Beta, Gamma Chi, Xi Epsilon, Omicron Alpha
Attendance:	1,083 — 178 Undergraduates, 877 Graduates, 28 General Members
Conference Theme:	*Alpha Kappa Alpha's Image...A Reflection of Our Standards*
Conference Chairman:	Patricia White Bauldrick
Conference Co-Chairperson:	Rose Thompson
Regional Director:	Loann J. Honesty King
Region Membership Statistics:	80 Chapters — 37 Undergraduate, 43 Graduate Chapters 2,612 Active Members 487 Undergraduates, 2,125 Graduates

REGIONAL CONFERENCE NOTES:

Two major changes in the regional conference format were made at this conference. For the first time the public meeting took the form of a public luncheon. The motivational words of Les Brown mesmerized those attending. The traditional undergraduate luncheon was replaced by an "Evening with the Undergraduates" that included a buffet dinner, followed by a step-out and a party. An elegant champaign-reception was the surroundings for Soror King's thank you to the sorors for their support during her tenure.

The banquet awards presentation included a video production highlighting the achievements of the sorors for whom the region awards are named. Unfortunately, the conference minutes did not record the recipients of the achievement awards.

57TH — APRIL 4-6, 1991

Location:	Concourse Hotel Madison, Wisconsin
Hostess Chapters:	Kappa Psi Omega, Prime Hostess, Delta Phi Omega, Mu Beta, Epsilon Kappa Omega, Lambda Nu Omega, Mu Rho Pi Gamma Omega, Eta Omega, Omicron Xi, Epsilon Delta, Iota Delta, Lambda Xi,
Registration:	869 — 133 Undergraduates, 736 Graduates
Conference Theme:	*Supreme in Service Reaching Out To Touch Mankind*
Conference Chairmans:	Theresa Sanders and Betty Reneau Rowe
Regional Director:	Yvonne Perkins
Region Membership Statistics:	81 Chapters — 38 Undergraduate, 43 Graduate Chapters 2,612 Active Members 418 Undergraduates, 2,194 Graduates

REGIONAL CONFERENCE NOTES:

Soror Peggy Lewis LeCompte described Soror Perkins as "A Soror of Strength and Service," in her introduction of the Central Regional Director. In this same introduction, Soror Yvonne Perkins was described as being a woman who is practical, patient, persistent, proficient, pragmatic, professional, progressive, and who had push and pull. Soror Perkins' tenure as Central Regional Director proved the accuracy of this description.

New additions to the regional conference format were "A Tribute to Leaders," hosted by the Regional Director and a Mentoring Breakfast for Undergraduates. Soror Mary Shy Scott, Supreme Basileus, in her address at the Public Meeting stated "There is a sweet, sweet spirit in this place. There is a sweet expression on each face and I truly believe that it should be called Alpha Kappa Alpha."

Two additional awards were added to the list of Regional Conference Awards: The Loann J. Honesty King Leadership Award, awarded to Stephanie Crayton, Kappa Chapter, and runner-up Karen McCurtis, Mu Beta; and the Yvonne Perkins Outstanding Basileus of the Year Award, awarded to Anita Harmon, Theta Rho Omega, and runner-up Shirley Phillips, Lambda Tau Omega.

Carolyn Blanton/Virginia Gilbert Undergraduate Overall Chapter Program Achievement

Winner:	Gamma Chi	Northwestern University
Runner-up:	Mu Beta	Marquette University

Loraine R. Green Undergraduate with Highest Cumulative Average

Winner:	Donica Glass (3.74)	Xi Kappa	Chicago State University
Runners-up:	Monica Scott (3.67)	Lambda Psi	Lewis University
	Wendi Thomas (3.59)	Kappa	City Chapter-Indianapolis

Arnetta G. Wallace Undergraduate Chapter with Highest Scholastic Average

Winner:	Beta	(3.0)	City Chapter-Chicago, Illinois

Runner-up: Lambda Xi (2.91) University of Wisconsin/Whitewater

Annetta Lawson Best Graduate Advisor Award
Michele McClure — Advisor to Kappa, City Chapter, Indianapolis, Indiana

Mable Evans Cason Overall Chapter Program Achievement (Membership up to 25)
Winner: Pi Lambda Omega East Jefferson County, Kentucky
Runner-up: Omicron Phi Omega Kokomo, Indiana

Lauretta Naylor Thompson Overall Chapter Program Achievement (Membership 26-50)
Winner: Theta Rho Omega Markham, Illinois
Runner-up: Lambda Tau Omega South Suburbs/Chicago

Alice McGhee Smart Overall Chapter Program Achievement (Membership 51 and above)
Winner: Gamma Omega St. Louis, Missouri
Runner-up: Theta Omega Chicago, Illinois

58TH — APRIL 9-12, 1992

Location:	Executive Inn Hotel, Evansville, Indiana
Hostess Chapters:	Zeta Zeta Omega, Beta Rho Omega, Beta Omega Omega, Omicron Sigma Omega, Epsilon Zeta, Zeta Zeta
Registration:	888 — 196 Undergraduates, 692 Graduates
Conference Theme:	*Sisterhood: Rising Above the Ordinary*
Conference Co-Chairmen:	Cateena Johnson and Frankye Calloway
Regional Director:	Yvonne Perkins
Region Membership Statistics:	83 Chapters — 39 Undergraduate, 44 Graduate Chapters, 2,775 Active Members, 456 Undergraduates, 2,319 Graduates

REGIONAL CONFERENCE NOTES:

Bev Smith, hostess of the Black Entertainment Network Television (BET) popular prime time talk show "Our Voices" was the public meeting speaker. Golden Sorors and Silver Stars were honored at the Pink Ladies' Conference Luncheon. First Supreme Anti-Basileus Soror Eva Evans captivated the sorors with her remarks at the conference banquet.

Recipients of achievement awards were not recorded in the conference minutes for the 58th Central Regional Conference. However, the 59th Central Regional Conference awards information which follows once again separates undergraduate city and campus chapters in the overall program achievement competition which suggests that a decision was made at this conference to do so.

59TH — APRIL 22-25, 1993

Location:	Pere Marquette, Peoria, Illinois
Hostess Chapters:	Nu Pi Omega, Eta Gamma, Nu Omicron Omega, Epsilon Eta, Omicron Delta Omega, Eta Alpha, Epsilon Epsilon Omega, Gamma,

Registration:	935 — 188 Undergraduates, 747 Graduates
Conference Theme:	*The Spirit Within*
Conference Chairmans:	Joyce Banks and Rose Hulum
Regional Director:	Yvonne Perkins
Region Membership Statistics:	81 Chapters — 37 Undergraduate, 44 Graduate Chapters
	2,853 Active Members
	376 Undergraduates, 2,477 Graduates

REGIONAL CONFERENCE NOTES:

The Public Meeting featured a salute to trailblazers in state government. The Honorable Pamela Carter, Indiana Attorney General and the Honorable Roland Burris, Illinois Attorney General were the featured speakers.

The Conference Luncheon included a special tribute to new Golden Sorors and Silver Stars. Chapters' Soror of the Year were also recognized.

Soror Mary Shy Scott, Supreme Basileus, was the Rededication Breakfast speaker. Graduate Advisor Training was conducted and more than 24 workshops were offered. Soror Sheila Kyles, Undergraduate Member-at-Large, was the special guest of the undergraduates at their luncheon.

Virgina Gilbert Overall Chapter Program Achievement (Campus Chapters)
Winner:	Pi Lambda	DePauw University

Carolyn Blanton Overall Chapter Program Achievement (City Chapters)
Winner	Beta Epsilon	Louisville, Kentucky
Runner-Up	Beta	Chicago, Illinois

Loraine R. Green Undergraduate Soror with Highest Cumulative Average Award
Winner:	Lorenda Betts (3.71)	Zeta Nu Eastern Kentucky University
Runner-up	Dionne Moore (3.702)	Beta Phi Ball State University

Annetta G. Wallace Undergraduate Chapter with Highest Cumulative Average
Winners (tie):	Beta Phi (2.991)	Ball State University
	Omicron Alpha (2.991)	West Surburban Chicago
Runner-Up	Pi Nu	Northeastern University

Annetta M. Lawson Outstanding Graduate Advisor
Winner:	Deborah Underwood — Beta, City Chapter, Chicago, Illinois
Runner-up:	Valeria Jones — Xi Kappa — Chicago State University

Mabel Evans Cason Overall Chapter Program Achievement (membership 25 or less)
Winner:	Pi Lambda Omega	Jeffersontown, Kentucky
Runner-up:	Omicron Phi Omega	Kokomo, Indiana

Lauretta Naylor Thompson Overall Chapter Program Achievement (membership 26-75)
Winner:	Lambda Tau Omega	South Suburban Chicago
Runners-up:	Theta Rho Omega	Markham, Illinois
	Lambda Mu Omega	Chicago, Illinois

Alice McGhee Smart Overall Chapter Program Achievement (membership 76-125)
Winner:	Epsilon Kappa Omega	Milwaukee, Wisconsin

Runner-up: Gamma Psi Omega Gary, Indiana

Loann J. Honesty King Overall Chapter Program Achievement (membership 126 and above)
Winner: Theta Omega Chicago, Illinois
Runner-up: Gamma Omega St. Louis, Missouri

60TH — APRIL 7-10, 1994

Location:	Radisson Hotel
	Merrillville, Indiana
Hostess Chapters:	Gamma Psi Omega, Prime Hostess,
	Lambda Psi, Nu Lambda, Eta Kappa Omega,
	Eta Mu Omega, Theta Rho Omega,
	Lambda Tau Omega,
	Sigma Phi Omega
Registration:	946 — 211 Undergraduates, 735 Graduates
Conference Theme:	*Soaring to New Heights — Addressing the Crisis of '90's*
Conference Chairmans:	Janice E. Culver and Millicent W. Ross
Regional Director:	Yvonne Perkins
Region Membership Statistics:	81 Chapters -37 Undergraduate,
	44 Graduate Chapters
	2,862 Active Members
	517 Undergraduates, 2,345 Graduates

REGIONAL CONFERENCE NOTES:

Commitment and involvement was the tone set by the opening session greetings of the 2nd Supreme Basileus, Soror Loraine Richardson Green and reinforced by Second Supreme Anti Basileus, Soror Berna Rhodes special guest of the undergraduates and speaker at the Undergraduate Luncheon.

The Conference Luncheon included a special tribute to new Golden Sorors and Silver Stars. Chapters' Soror of the Year were also recognized. Entertainment was provided by the nationally acclaimed Joel Hall Dancers of Chicago.

The Public Meeting was an evening of "Art and Jazz," and featured a salute to African American Artist and Honorary Member Soror Jan Spivey Gilchrist. The Awards Banquet was followed by a variety of activities for the attendees' enjoyment including a dance for the undergraduates, an evening of fun activity in several rooms and a Freddie Jackson concert.

Soror Faye B. Bryant, Former Supreme Basileus, was the Rededication Breakfast speaker. Graduate Advisor Training was conducted and more than 18 workshops were offered. A record of the award recipients could not be located.

61ST — APRIL 20-23, 1995

Location:	Hyatt Regency at Union Station
	St. Louis, Missouri
Hostess Chapters:	Omicron Theta Omega, Prime Hostess,
	Gamma Omega, Delta Delta Omega,
	Gamma Kappa Omega,
	Omicron Eta Omega,
	Epsilon Lambda Omega,
	Epsilon Iota, Nu Sigma, Delta Beta
Registration:	1,084 — 183 Undergraduates, 901 Graduates

Conference Theme:	*Building the Future: Alpha Kappa Alpha Strategy — Making the Net Work*
Conference Chairman:	Hazel Mallory
Conference Co-Chairperson:	Elaine Flipping
Regional Director:	Martha Levingston Perine
Region Membership Statistics:	81 Chapters — 32 active Undergraduate, 2 inactive, 43 Graduate and 1 inactive 2,192 Active Members — 280 Undergraduates, 1,712 Graduates, 200 General Members

REGIONAL CONFERENCE NOTES:

The city of St. Louis opened their arms and extended the Pink and Green welcome mat for the sorors of Central Region and St. Louis's own Soror Perine for her first regional conference. The conference truly embraced the theme Building the Future: Alpha Kappa Alpha Strategy Making the Net Work.

Sorors overwhelmingly rated every aspect of the conference as excellent or above Average. Conference highlights included a Tribute to Leaders Dinner; Business Roundtable, AKA BEST Training session; Graduate Advisors Breakfast; public meeting with a keynote address by the Honorable William I. Clay, U.S. Congressman, and a conference luncheon honoring Golden Sorors

An additional highlight was another first for Central Region. In Soror Perine's words: "Sorors, many of you thought that the Supremes was a trio from the 1960's but, in actuality the Supremes represent the three sorors from Central Region who serve on the Directorate in the roles of Supreme Grammateus (Linda M. White), Supreme Tamiouchos (Yvonne Perkins), and Supreme Parliamentarian (Constance Holland). And we are happy to have all three in attendance with us at this conference."

Virgina Gilbert Overall Chapter Program Achievement (Campus Chapter)
Winner:	Beta Epsilon	University of Louisville
Runner-up:	Mu Beta	Marquette University

Carolyn Blanton Overall Chapter Program Achievement (City Chapter)
Winner:	Omicron Alpha	Illinois Western Suburbs

Loraine R. Green Undergraduate Soror with Highest Cumulative Average Award
Winner:	Paula Barnes	Beta Epsilon	University of Louisville
Runner-up:	Tracey Bush	Beta Zeta	Kentucky State

Annetta G. Wallace Undergraduate Chapter with the Highest Cumulative Average
Winner:	Mu Beta (3.146)	Marquette University
Runner-up:	Beta Zeta (2.997)	Kentucky State University

Annetta M. Lawson Outstanding Graduate Advisor
Winner:	Pamela Porch — Advisor to Pi Nu Chapter, Northeastern Illinois
Runner-up:	Joyce King-McIver — Advisor to Mu Beta, Marquette University

Mabel Evans Cason Overall Chapter Program Achievement (membership 25 or less)
Winner:	Omicron Delta Omega	Normal, Illinois
Runner-up:	Beta Beta Omega	Paducah, Kentucky

Lauretta Naylor Thompson Overall Chapter Program Achievement (membership 26-75)
Winner:	Delta Chi Omega	Evanston, Illinois
Runner-up:	Theta Rho Omega	Markham, Illinois

Alice McGhee Smart Overall Chapter Program Achievement (membership 76-125)
Winner: Epsilon KappaOmega Milwaukee, Wisconsin
Runner-up: Delta Delta Omega East St. Louis, Illinois

Loann J. Honesty King Overall Chapter Program Achievement (membership 126 and above)
Winner: Theta Omega Chapter Chicago, Illinois
Runner-up: Gamma Omega Chapter St. Louis, Missouri

62ND — APRIL 25-28, 1996

Location:	Galt House East Hotel
	Louisville, Kentucky
Hostess Chapters:	Eta Omega, Prime Hostess,
	Beta Gamma Omega, Beta Upsilon Omega
	Mu Delta Omega, Pi Lambda Omega,
	Beta Epsilon, Beta Zeta
Registration:	1,093 -164 Undergraduates,
	878 Graduates, 51 guest
Conference Theme:	Building the Future: Alpha Kappa Alpha Strategy
	— Making the Net Work
Conference Chairman:	Sara C. McPherson
Conference Co-Chairperson:	Barbara W. Stringer
Regional Director:	Martha Levingston Perine
Region Membership Statistics:	82 Chapters (30 active Undergraduate,
	4 inactive, 4 suspended chapters,
	43 Graduate and 1 inactive chapter
	1,744 Active Members
	130 Undergraduates, 1,614 Graduates

REGIONAL CONFERENCE NOTES:

The hostess chapters "the Bluegrass Connection" captured the aura of the Kentucky Derby in their execution of the 62nd Central Regional. Several of the conference activities featured a Derby Theme beginning with the welcoming reception. "A Call to the Post" and ending with the "Run for the Roses" Awards Banquet. Speakers for the conference included Eva Evans, Supreme Basileus at the Public Meeting; Soror Norma Solomon White, First Supreme Anti-Basileus spoke at the Rededication Ceremony and Soror Lesa R. Woodson, Second Supreme Anti-Basileus spoke at the Undergraduate Luncheon.

The 62nd Central Regional Conference adopted a resolution that the 62nd Central Regional Conference be dedicated to the memory of Soror Loraine Richardson Green, 2nd Supreme Basileus of Alpha Kappa Alpha. The conference was a fitting tribute.

Virginia Gilbert Overall Chapter Program Achievement (Campus Chapter)
Winner: Iota Delta University of Wisconsin
Runner-up: Pi Nu Northeastern Illinois University

Carolyn Blanton Overall Chapter Program Achievement (City Chapter)
NO ENTRY

Loraine R. Green Undergraduate Soror with Highest Cumulative Average Award
Winner: Victoria N. Afari (4.0) Xi Epsilon National Lewis University

Undergraduate Chapter with the Highest Cumulative Average
Winner: Lambda Psi (2.95)   Lewis University

Annetta M. Lawson Outstanding Graduate Advisor
Winner: Vivian Mays — Advisor to Iota Delta, University of Wisconsin
Runner-up: Pamela Bates Porch — Advisor to Pi Nu, Northeastern University

Mabel Evans Cason Overall Chapter Program Achievement (membership 25 or less)
Winner: Lambda Nu Omega   Waukegan, Illinois
Runner-up: Theta Rho Omega   Markham, Illinois

Lauretta Naylor Thompson Overall Chapter Program Achievement (membership 26-75))
Winner: Lambda Tau Omega   Park Forest, Illinois
Runner-up: Delta Delta Omega   East St. Louis, Illinois

Alice McGhee Smart Overall Chapter Program Achievement (membership 76-125)
Winner: Epsilon KappaOmega   Milwaukee, Wisconsin
Runner-up: Xi Nu Omega   Chicago, Illinois

Loann J. Honesty King Overall Chapter Program Achievement Membership (126 and above)
Winner: Theta Omega Chapter   Chicago, Illinois
Runner-up: Gamma Omega Chapter   St. Louis, Missouri

63RD — APRIL 3 - 6, 1997

Location:	Chicago Marriott Hotel Chicago, IL
Hostess Chapters:	Delta Chi Omega, Prime Hostesses, Lambda Alpha Omega, Lambda Mu Omega, Tau Gamma Omega, Theta Omega, Xi Nu Omega, Beta, Delta Omicron, Omicron Alpha, Pi Nu, Xi Epsilon and Xi Kappa
Registration:	1,382 (196 Undergraduate, 1,153 Graduate, 33 guest)
Conference Theme:	Building the Future: Alpha Kappa Alpha Strategy Making the Net Work
Conference Chairman:	Jamilla Pitts
Co-Chairperson:	Yendis Gibson-King
Regional Director:	Martha Levingston Perine
Region Membership Statistics:	83 Chapters — 29 active Undergraduate, 5 inactive, 4 suspended, 43 active Graduate and 1 inactive chapter

REGIONAL CONFERENCE NOTES:

The 63rd Central Conference was truly a memorial experience. The weekend was filled with activities highlighting the talents of Central Regional sorors. Sorors were entertained through verse, song and music throughout the luncheons, sessions and social activities. Soror Eva Evans, Supreme Basileus and Soror Norma Solomon White, First Supreme Anti-Basileus brought greetings at the Public Meeting and Soror Daria Ibn Tamas, Second Supreme Anti-Basileus spoke at the Undergraduate Luncheon.

Througout the conference the sisterly warmth of Central Region was displayed as the sorors of Alpha Kappa Alpha Sorority, Inc. paid tribute to Cenntral Regional Director, Soror Martha Perine for her administration as Central Regional Director and extended well wishes and on her new position with the Federal Reserve Bank.

Virginia Gilbert Overall Chapter Program Achievement (Campus Chapter)
Winner: Iota Delta University of Wisconsin
Runner-up: Pi Lambda DePauw University

Carolyn Blanton Overall Chapter Program Achievement (City Chapter)
Winner: Beta Chicago, Illinois
Runner-up Kappa Indianapolis, Indiana

Loraine R. Green Undergraduate Soror with Highest Cumulative Average Award
Winner: June Early (4.0) Pi Nu Northeastern Illinois University

Annetta G. Wallace Undergraduate Chapter with the Highest Cumulative Average
Winner: Beta Delta (3.08) City Chapter St. Louis, Missouri

Lauretta Naylor Thompson Overall Chapter Program Achievement (membership 26-75)
Winner: Xi Nu Omega Chapter Chicago, Illinois
Runner-up: Chapter Joliet, Illinois

Alice McGhee Smart Overall Chapter Program Achievement (membership 76-125)
Winner: Lambda Tau Omega Park Forest, Illinois
Runner-up: Delta Delta Omega East St. Louis, Illinois

Loann J. Honesty King Overall Chapter Program Achievement Membership (126 and above)
Winner: Gamma Omega Chapter St. Louis, Missouri
Runner-up: Theta Omega Chapter Chicago, Illinois

Annetta M. Lawson Outstanding Graduate Advisor
Winner: Lavana Davis — Advisor to Pi Lambda, DePauw University
Runner-up: Kimberly Black — Advisor to Epsilon Rho, Purdue University

64TH — APRIL 23-26, 1998

Location: The Westin
Indianapolis, Indiana
Hostess Chapters: Alpha Mu Omega, Prime Hostess, Alpha Eta Omega, Iota Chi Omega, Kappa Epsilon Omega, Kappa Tau Omega, Omicron Phi Omega, Beta Phi, Kappa, Epsilon Xi, Epsilon Rho, Pi Lambda, and Tau
Registration: 1,244 (273 Undergraduate, 902 Graduate, 35 General and 34 guest)
Conference Theme: *Energizing...Strategizing...Organizing... Mobilizing ... To Make the Net Work!*
Conference Chairman: Nadine C. Bonds
Co-Chairpersons: Sherry E. Curry and Nichole Nicholson
Regional Director: Peggy Lewis LeCompte
Region Membership Statistics: 86 Chapters — 33 active Undergraduate, 4 inactive, 3 suspended, 45 active Graduate and 1 inactive chapter
1,902 Active Members
221 Undergraduates, 1,681 Graduates

REGIONAL CONFERENCE NOTES:

Soror Peggy Lewis LeCompte who had once again been called upon to lead Central Region, did not miss a step in the planning and execution of the the 64TH Central Regional Conference.

Returning to the site of the 48th Central Regional Conference over which she presided the sorors in attendance where once again met with the pink and green hospitality of the hostess chapters. The conference innovations introduced by Soror LeCompte during her tenure were effectively merged with the format of the conference instituted by Soror Perine. Several sorority and community dignitaries were highlighted at the conference including: Alexine Clement Jackson, National President, YWCA of the USA, speaker at the public meeting; Toya Corbett, Undergraduate Member-at-Large , Undergraduate Luncheon speaker and Former Supreme Basileus, Barbara Kinnard Phillips at the Rededication Breakfast.

Thelma Mothershed Wair of the Little Rock Nine was honored at the conference a and a resolution was adopted in memoriam to Soror Lee Anna Shelburne, Past Central Regional Director who became an Ivy Beyond the Wall earlier that year.

Virgina Gilbert Overall Chapter Program Achievemen (Campus Chapter)
Winner: Tau   Indiana University/Bloomington

Carolyn Blanton Overall Chapter Program Achievemen (City Chapter)
Winner: Kappa   Indianapolis, Indiana

Loraine R. Green Undergraduate Soror with Highest Cumulative Average Award
Winner: Kaliha White (3.727)   Mu Beta Marquette University

Annetta G. Wallace Undergraduate Chapter with the Highest Cumulative Average
Winner: Mu Beta (3.3)   Marquette University
Runner-up: Gamma Chi (3.0)   Northwestern University

Annetta M. Lawson Outstanding Graduate Advisor
Winner: Danielle Porch, Advisor to Delta Omicron, Northern Illinois
Runner-up: Loretta Davis, Advisor to Pi Lambda, DePauw University

Mabel E. Cason Overall Chapter Program Achievement (membership 0-25)
Winner: Xi Eta Omega   Moline, Illinois
Runner-up: Kappa Psi Omega   Madison, Wisconsin

Lauretta Naylor Thompson Overall Chapter Program Achievement (membership 26-75)
Winner: Xi Nu Omega   Chicago, Illinois
Runner-up: Delta Chi Omega   Evanston, Illinois

Alice McGhee Smart Overall Chapter Program Achievement (membership 76-125)
Winner: Upsilon Mu Omega   Milwaukee, Wisconsin
Runner-up: Lambda Tau Omega   Park Forrest, Illinois

Loann J. Honesty King Overall Chapter Program Achievement Membership (126 and above)
Winner: Theta Omega   Chicago, Illinois
Runner-up: Gamma Omega   St. Louis, Missouri

PART VII: REGIONAL CONFERENCES

65TH — APRIL 8-11, 1999

Location:	Hyatt Regency Minneapolis, MN
Hostess Chapters:	Delta Phi Omega, Mu Rho — Prime Hostesses, Epsilon Kappa Omega, Kappa Psi Omega, Lambda Nu Omega, Pi Gamma Omega, Upsilon Mu Omega, Xi Eta Omega, Epsilon Delta, Iota Delta, Lambda Xi, Mu Beta, and Omicron Xi
Registration:	1,142 — 193 Undergraduates 949 Graduates
Conference Theme:	*Blazing New Trails*
Conference Chairman:	Peggy Mezille
Co-Chairpersons:	Joanne Bluford and Kyra Turpin
Regional Director:	Nadine C. Bonds
Region Membership Statistics:	86 Chapters — 33 active Undergraduate, 4 inactive, 3 suspended chapters 45 active Graduate and 1 inactive chapter 2,986 Active Members 263 Undergraduates, 2,164 Graduates, 559 General Members

REGIONAL CONFERENCE NOTES:

Minneapolis and the hostess chapters welcomed the conference participants in true AKA style. One of the special highlights of the conference was the Public Meeting Speaker, Dominque Dawes, US Olympic Gymnast and Gold Medal Winner.

Soror Bond initiated Vendor Appreciation (vendors provided continental breakfast and lunch) at this conference and a special award for *Overall Alumnae Chapter Achievement was presented to Upsilon Mu Omega, Milwaukee, Wisconsin with runner-up going to Xi Nu Omega, Chicago, Illinois*

Virgina Gilbert/Carolyn Blanton Overall Chapter Program Achievement
Winner:	Epsilon Rho	Purdue University
Runner-up:	Pi Lambda	DePauw University

Loraine R. Green Undergraduate Soror with Highest Cumulative Average Award
Winner:	Tiffany Gordan (3.65)	Delta Omicron	Northern Illinois
Runner-up:	Shavonda Irwin (3.41)	Epsilon Zeta	Western Kentucky

Annetta G. Wallace Undergraduate Chapter with the Highest Cumulative Average
Winner:	Beta Delta (3.146)	City Chapter, St. Louis, Missouri
Runner-up:	Epsilon Zeta (2.913)	Western Kentucky University

Annetta M. Lawson Outstanding Graduate Advisor
Winner:	Nanette Casaonva, Advisor to Delta Omicron, Northern Illinois
Runner-up:	Adrienne Upchurch, Advisor to Pi Nu, Northeastern Illinois

Mabel E. Cason Overall Chapter Program Achievement (membership 0-25)
Winner:	Omicron Delta Omega	Bloomington/Normal, Illinois

Lauretta Naylor Thompson Overall Chapter Program Achievement (membership 26-75)
Winner: Theta Rho Omega   Markham, Ilinois
Runner-up: Lambda Alpha Omega   Western Suburbs, Chicago

Alice McGhee Smart Overall Chapter Program Achievement (membership 76-125)
Winner: Delta Delta Omega   East St. Louis, Illinois

Loann J. Honesty King Overall Chapter Program Achievement Membership (126 and above)
Winner: Theta Omega   Chicago, Illinois
Runner-up: Gamma Omega   St. Louis, Missouri

66TH — APRIL 6-9, 2000

Location:	Regal Riverfront Hotel, St. Louis, Missouri
Hostess Chapters:	Delta Delta Omega, Epsilon Iota, Prime Hostesses, Gamma Omega, Gamma Kappa Omega, Epsilon Lambda Omega, Omicron Eta Omega, Omicron Theta Omega, Upsilon Phi Omega, Delta Beta, Beta Delta
Registration:	1.423 — 219 Undergraduates, 1,204 Graduates
Conference Theme:	*Blazing New Trails*
Conference Chairman:	Kathy Walker
Conference Co-Chairmen:	Lora Jones and Nicole Jenkins
Regional Director:	Nadine C. Bonds
Region Membership Statistics:	3.419 — 507 Undergraduates, 2,906 Graduates, 6 General members

REGIONAL CONFERENCE NOTES:

The 66th Regional Confrence was originally scheduled to be held at the Adams Mark Hotel in St. Louis, MO, but was moved to the Regal Riverfront hotel due to discrimination allegations against the Adam's Mark Hotel. The Regal Riverfront comped all of the needed VIP suites for conference; St. Louis Visitor and Convention Bureau sponsored $25,000 cash to keep conference in St. Louis and co-sponsored Regional Hospitality and reception at 2000 Boule.

Other highlights of the conference included the implemention of a website developed by undergraduate Soror Iona Montgomery, Kappa Chapter. And the appointment of the Region's first Cluster Coordinators: Soror Dorothy Buckhanan, Upsilon Mu Omega; Soror Lora Jones, Delta Delta Omega; Soror Karen Haggerty, Theta Omega and Soror Sheila Stuckey, Beta Upsilon Omega.

In addition, the initial training of Central Region's Leadership Team, Soror Ernita R. Cooper, Chairman, was conducted by Soror Mattelia Grays, 18th Supreme Basileus and Chairman of the International Leadership Development Task Force.

Virgina Gilbert Overall Chapter Program Achievement (Campus Chapter)
Winner: Tau Chapter   Indiana University

Carolyn Blanton Overall Chapter Program Achievement (City Chapter)
Winner: Nu Lambda Chapter   Gary, Indiana

Loraine R. Green Undergraduate Soror with Highest Cumulative Average Award
Winner   Olivia Williams (3.86)   Beta Delta   Harris Stowe College
Runner-up: Holly Marie Hall (3.72)   Iota Sigma   University of Kentucky

Annetta G. Wallace Undergraduate Chapter with the Highest Cumulative Average
Winner: Kappa (3.1) City Chapter, Indianapolis, Indiana
Runner-up: Gamma Chi (3.0) Northwestern University
Runner-up: Beta Delta (3.0) City Chapter, St. Louis, Missouri

Annetta M. Lawson Outstanding Graduate Advisor
Winner: Victoria Clark — Advisor to Tau, Indiana University/Bloomington
Runner-up: Peggye Mezile — Advisor to Mu Rho, University of Minnesota

Lauretta Naylor Thompson Overall Chapter Program Achievement (membership 26-74)
Winner: Upsilon Mu Omega Chapter Milwaukee, Wisconsin

Alice McGhee Smart Overall Chapter Program Achievement (membership 75-125)
Winner: Lambda Tau Omega Park Forest, Illinois
Runner-up: Xi Nu Omega Chapter Chicago, Illinois

Loann J. Honesty King Overall Chapter Program Achievement (Membership 126 and above)
Winner: Gamma Omega Chapter St. Louis, Missouri
Runner-up: Theta Omega Chapter Chicago, Illinois

67TH — APRIL 19-22, 2001

Location:	Crowne Plaza, Springfield, IL
Hostess Chapters:	Nu Omicron Omega, Eta Epsilon, Prime Hostesses, Epsilon Epsilon Omega, Omicron Delta Omega, Pi Nu Omega
Registration:	1,225 — 247 Undergraduates, 978 Graduates
Conference Theme:	Blazing New Trails
Conference General Chairperson:	Edna Shanklin
Conference Co-Chairmen:	Marian Goza, Falisha McGhee
Regional Director:	Nadine C. Bonds
Region Membership Statistics:	3,597 Active Members, 437 Undergraduates, 3,160 Graduates

REGIONAL CONFERENCE NOTES

In the tradition of Alpha Kappa Alpha Sorority, Inc. and Central Region recognition of leadership took front stage at the 67th Central Regional Conference. The first Central Region Leadership Institute was conducted and covered modules 1 thru 7 of the new Leadership Development Process Manual.

The second Basilei Training Institute and Graduate Advisors Institute were conducted. Certificates were presented to the participants by the institute coordinators, Soror Audrey Cooper-Stanton and Soror Pamela Porch respectively.

Supreme Basileus, Soror Norma Solomon White announced Central Region's winner of the Norma Solomon White Leadership Award: Soror Brandon Johnson, Iota Sigma Chapter at the University of Kentucky. Soror Brandon received an all expenses paid trip to the Leadership Seminar in San Juan Puerto Rico.

In recognition of her dedicated service as Executive Director to Alpha Kappa Alpha Sorority, Inc., Soror Carey B. Preston was honored in memoriam. And the 67th Central Regional Conference also resolved that the Central Region of Alpha Kappa Alpha Sorority, Inc. commend the United States Postal Service for honoring Roy Wilkens and the 23 other outstanding African Americans through the Black Heritage Series Postal Stamps.

Virginia Gilbert Overall Chapter Program Achievement (Campus Chapter)
Winner:	Pi Nu	Northeastern University
Runner-up:	Epsilon Rho	Purdue University

Gladys Bufkin Johnson Overall Chapter Program Achievement (Campus Chapter 20+)
Winner:	Iota Sigma	University of Kentucky

Carolyn Blanton Overall Chapter Program Achievement (City Chapter)
Winner:	Beta Delta	City Chapter, St. Louis, Missouri

Loraine R. Green Undergraduate Soror with the Highest Cumulative Average
Winner:	Monica Akins (3.66)	Delta Beta	Southern Illinois University
Runner-up:	Jahahn Coleman (3.58)	Kappa	City Chapter, Indianapolis, IN

Arnetta G. Wallace Undergraduate Chapter with Highest Scholastic Average
Winner:	Kappa	2.829	Butler University

Annetta M. Lawson Outstanding Graduate Advisor
Winner:	Yendis Gibson King — Advisor to Gamma Chi, Northwestern University
Runner-up:	Adrienne Upchurch — Advisor to Pi Nu, Northeastern Illinois

Mable Evans Cason Overall Chapter Program Achievement (membership up to 25)
Winner:	Omicron Delta Omega	Bloomington, Illinois

Lauretta Naylor Thompson Overall Chapter Program Achievement (membership 26-74)
Winner:	Delta Chi Omega	Evanston, Illinois

Alice McGhee Smart Overall Chapter Program Achievement (membership 75-125)
Winner:	Lambda Tau Omega	Matteson, Illinois
Runner-up:	Upsilon Mu Omega	Milwaukee, Wisconsin

Loann J. Honesty King Overall Chapter Program Achievement (membership 126 and above)
Winner:	Theta Omega	Chicago, Illinois
Runner-up:	Alpha Mu Omega	Indianapolis, Indiana

68TH — APRIL 11-14, 2002

Location:	Hyatt McCormick Chicago, Illinois
Hostess Chapters:	Lambda Tau Omega, Theta Rho Omega, Prime Hostesses, Gamma Psi Omega, Eta Kappa Omega, Eta Mu Omega, , Sigma Phi Omega, Phi Epsilon Omega, Phi Kappa Omega, Nu Lambda, Epsilon Rho, Zeta Iota, and Lambda Psi
Registration:	1,660 — 255 Undergraduates, 1,405 Graduates

Conference Theme: *Blazing New Trails*
Conference Chairman: Sonya Bowen
Conference Co-Chairmen: Mary Palmore and Dakita Jones
Regional Director: Nadine C. Bonds
Region Membership Statistics: 3,468 — 431 Undergraduates,
3,037 Graduates

REGIONAL CONFERENCE NOTES:

Based on the results of a survey regarding the judging of Regional Conference awards and in an attempt to improve the judging process and maintain a high level of integrity and fairness external judges were used for the first time to judge one phase of chapter program awards.

Other highlights included the book signing of "A Legacy Supreme" by Supreme Basileus Soror Norma Solomon White and the 18th Supreme Basileus, Soror Mattelia Grays.

The 68th Central Regional Conference was a celebratory occasion beginning with the presentation by Central Regional Director, Soror Nadine C. Bonds of a beautiful golden pin to each of the Former Central Regional Directors and the newly elected 26th Central Regional Director.

The awards banquet provided the occasion in story book splendor for the sorors of Central Region to pay tribute to outgoing Central Regional Director, Soror Nadine C. Bonds for her service to the region.

Virginia Gilbert Overall Chapter Program Achievement (Campus Chapter)
Winner: Epsilon Xi Indiana State University
Runner-up Epsilon Rho Purdue University

Carolyn Blanton Overall Chapter Program Achievement (City Chapter)
Winner: Omicron Xi Milwaukee, Wisconsin
Runner-up: Kappa Indianapolis, Indiana

Loraine R. Green Undergraduate Soror with the Highest Cumulative Average
Winner Kimberly Troutman (3.74) Mount Mary College
Runner-up: Terri McMillan (3.72) Washington University

Arnetta G. Wallace Undergraduate Chapter with the Highest Cumulative Average
Winner: Xi Kappa (3.1) Chicago State University
Runner-up: Beta Delta (3.06) City Chapter, St. Louis, Missouri

Annetta M. Lawson Outstanding Graduate Advisor
Winner: Tamara Smith, former Advisor to Lambda Psi,
Runner-up: Kathleen Coleman, Epsilon Kappa Omega, Advisor to Omicron Xi

Mabel E. Cason Overall Chapter Program Achievement (membership up to 25)
Winner: Nu Omicron Omega Springfield, Illinois

Lauretta Naylor Thompson Overall Chapter Program Achievement (membership 26-74)
Winner: Upsilon Mu Omega Milwaukee, Wisconsin
Runner-up: Omicron Delta Omega Bloomington, Illinois

Alice McGhee Smart Overall Chapter Program Achievement Membership 75-125
Winner: Epsilon Kappa Omega Milwaukee, Wisconsin
Runner-up: Xi Nu Omega Chicago, Illinois

Loann J. Honesty King Overall Chapter Program Achievement (membership 126 and above)

Winner: Gamma Omega — St. Louis, Missouri
Runner-up: Theta Omega — Chicago, Illinois

69TH — APRIL 11-14, 2003

Location:	Galt House Hotel, Louisville, Kentucky
Hostess Chapters:	Pi Lambda Omega, Prime Hostess, Beta Gamma Omega, Beta Epsilon Omega, Eta Omega, Beta Omega Omega, Beta Rho Omega, Omicron Sigma Omega, Beta Epsilon, Eta Rho, Iota Sigma, Epsilon Zeta and Zeta Zeta
Registration:	1,315 (1,157 Graduates, 113 Undergraduates, 45 guests)
Conference Theme:	*The Spirit of Alpha Kappa Alpha — Continuing the Tradition in Derby City*
Conference Chairman:	Antoinette Davis-Jones
Conference Co-Chairmen:	Denise Jackson, Jan Brown-Thompson and Maquiba Ballentine
Regional Director:	Dorothy W. Buckhanan
Region Membership Statistics:	84 Chapters — 32 Undergraduate Chapters (1 suspended, 3 inactive) 48 Active Graduate chapters 3,279 Active members: 351 Undergraduates, 2,928 Graduates

REGIONAL CONFERENCE NOTES:

The conference opened with a Community Outreach Project (Health Fair), partnering with local agencies to provide free screenings and critical health care information, to over 500 Louisville residents.

Soror Linda White — 26th Supreme Basileus — reported on the progress of her initiatives under the "Spirit of AKA" program banner and updated members on the California litigation situation. She also answered questions about the fees requested from chapters for liability insurance.

The issue of Cluster re-alignment came up at the regional conference. Soror Buckhanan appointed a special committee, chaired by Soror Audrey Cooper-Stanton, to review the issue and bring back recommendations in 2004.

Other Conference highlights included the presentation of Central Region's Living Legacy Award to honorary Soror Nichelle Nichols (Lt. Uhura of Star Trek fame).

Conference innovations included introduction of a Legacy Breakfast and Parade; the Welcome Reception Spirit Night Chapter Stroll; Recognition of Central Region Scholars at the Undergraduate Luncheon and a hat luncheon. The first recipents of the new awards named in honor of Dorothy W. Buckhanan were Soror Audrey Cooper-Stanton (Theta Omega Chapter) and Soror Josephine Franklin (Theta Rho Omega Chapter).

The 69th Regional Conference Steering Committee made a generous contribution to the Educational Advancement Foundation in support of the Dorothy Buckhanan Endowment Fund for Students in Business. Upsilon Mu Omega Chapter (Milwaukee) and the 68th Central Regional Conference initially established this fund in 2002.

The 69th Central Regional Conference was indeed a very special one to Soror Buckhanan — it was well attended, it was the first of her administration and it marked her 25th year in Alpha Kappa Alpha.

Virginia Gilbert Overall Chapter Program Achievement (Campus Chapter)
Winner: Lambda Pi   DePauw University
Runner-up   Beta Phi   Ball State University

Carolyn Blanton Overall Chapter Program Achievement (City Chapter)
Winner: Beta   Chicago, Illinois
Runner-up: Nu Lambda   Gary, Indiana

Loraine R. Green Undergraduate Soror with the Highest Cumulative Average
Winner: Tameka Miles   Epsilon Zeta   Western Kentucky University
Runner-up: Andrienne Holloway Gamma Chi   Northwestern University

Annetta G. Wallace Undergraduate Chapter with the Highest Cumulative Average
Winner: Beta Delta   City Chapter   St. Louis, Missouri
Runner-up: Gamma Chi   Northwestern University

Annetta M. Lawson Outstanding Graduate Advisor
Winner: Tamara Johnson — Advior to Epsilon Xi, Indiana State University
Runner-up: Ernita Cooper — Beta, City Chapter, Chicago, Illinois

Mabel E. Cason Overall Chapter Program Achievement (membership up to 25)
Winner: Alpha Eta Omega   Terre Haute, Indiana

Lauretta Naylor Thompson Overall Chapter Program Achievement (membership 26-74)
Winner: Tau Gamma Omega   Oak Park, Illinois
Runner-up: Omicron Delta Omega Bloomington/Normal, Illinois

Alice McGhee Smart Overall Chapter Program Achievement (membership 75-125)
Winner: Lambda Tau Omega   South Suburban, Illinois
Runner-up: Lambda Mu Omega   Chicago, Illinois

Loann J. Honesty King Overall Chapter Program Achievement (membership 126 and above)
Winner (tie):   Epsilon Kappa Omega Milwaukee, Wisconsin
                 Gamma Omega   St. Louis, Missouri
Runner-up: Lambda Alpha Omega Western Suburban, Illinois

70TH — APRIL 15-18, 2004

Location:	Four Points Sheraton Airport Hotel Milwaukee, WI
Hostess Chapters:	Upsilon Mu Omega, Prime Hostess, Delta Phi Omega, Epsilon Kappa Omega, Kappa Psi Omega, Lambda Nu Omega, Pi Gamma Omega, Xi Eta Omega, Iota Delta, Lambda Xi, Mu Beta, Mu Rho, Omicron Xi, Ad Sigma Gamma
Registration:	1,552 (162 Undergraduates, 1,340 Graduates, 50 guests)
Conference Theme:	*The Spirit of Alpha Kappa Alpha —Soaring Through Service*
Conference Chairman:	Deidra Y.A. Edwards
Conference Co-Chairmen:	Michele McKnight, Margaret Rogers and Erica Horton

Regional Director: Dorothy W. Buckhanan
Region Membership Statistics: 84 Chapters — 48 Graduates
36 Undergraduates Chapters
(3 suspended and 3 inactive)
3,236 Active Members
363 Undergraduates, 2,873 Graduates

REGIONAL CONFERENCE NOTES:

The 70th Central Regional Conference featured no line registration, many special touches from Cluster II and unprecedented hospitality. The Community Outreach Project for this conference was a K-3 book collection drive for Milwaukee area students. Central sorors donated 5,000 books to local agencies. The school district acknowledged this effort as one of the largest of its kind to date. The region was also recognized for donating nearly 3,000 books to Nashville area schools as part of the 2004 Boule book collection drive.

The men of Kappa Alpha Psi were also present in Milwaukee on that same weekend, at their Regional Conference. The Kappa Regional Executive Team joined the sorority's VIP Dinner guests for a joint reception.

The second Central Region Living Legacy Award was presented to Milwaukee's first African American Mayor — the Honorable Marvin Pratt (honey-do). In addition, the Spirit of AKA Award was presented to the first and only Alpha Kappa Alpha soror ever elected to the Wisconsin State Assembly — Representative Lena Taylor of Upsilon Mu Omega Chapter-Milwaukee.

Because of unique space challenges, the traditional banquet was replaced with a Gala consisting of three themed, elegant, venues in 3 different ballrooms (Jazz, R&B, and Step). Sorors came attired in all shades and styles of leather.

The other "new event" was the Golden Soror Reception. Golden Sorors were treated to a high tea, entertainment and special mementos in recognition of this milestone.

Other conference high points included establishment of the Central Region EAF Endowment Fund. It was also announced that Central Region was the only region to achieve 100% participation by all chapters Central Region was the only region to have all states sponsor an AKA Day at the Capitol event.

The Young Author Award Winners (from Theta Omega and Lambda Mu Omega Chapters) were presented at the public meeting and Epsilon Kappa Omega Chapter was recognized as the regional Ivy AKAdemy Winner. This chapter went on to receive the National Award at the Nashville Boule.

Virginia Gilbert Overall Chapter Program Achievement (Campus Chapter)
Winner: Beta Phi Ball State University Muncie, Indiana

Carolyn Blanton Overall Chapter Program Achievement (City Chapter)
Winner: Omicron Xi Milwaukee, Wisconsin
Runner-up: Beta Chicago, Illinois

Loraine R. Green Undergraduate Soror with the Highest Cumulative Average
Winner: Alexia Gist (3.85) Xi Kappa Chicago State University
Runner-up: Kelly Preston (3.69) Beta City Chapter, Chicago, IL

Arnetta G. Wallace Undergraduate Chapter with the Highest Cumulative Average
Winner: Xi Kappa (3.47) Chicago State University
Runner-up: Gamma (2.99) University of Illinois/Urbana

Annetta M. Lawson Outstanding Graduate Advisor
Winner: Ernita Cooper Beta City Chapter Chicago, Illinois
Runner-up: Cyhthia Mitchell Xi Kappa Chicago State University

Mabel Evans Cason Overall Chapter Program Achievement (membership up to 25)
NO ENTRY

Lauretta Naylor Thompson Overall Chapter Program Achievement (membership 26-74)
Winner: Theta Rho Omega   Markham, Illinois

Alice McGhee Smart Overall Chapter Program Achievement (membership 75-125)
Winner: Lambda Alpha Omega   Western Suburban, Chicago

Loann J. Honesty King Overall Chapter Program Achievement (membership 126 and above)
Winner: Gamma Omega   St. Louis, Missouri

71ST — APRIL 7 – 10, 2005

Location:	Marriott Downtown Indianapolis, Indiana
Hostess Chapters:	Alpha Mu Omega.Prime Hostess, Alpha Eta Omega, Iota Chi Omega, Kappa Epsilon Omega, Kappa Tau Omega, Omicron Phi Omega, Kappa Tau, Epsilon Xi, Pi Lambda
Attendance:	1,584 — 1,336 graduates, 191 undergraduates, 57 guests
Chairperson:	Marian C. McKinnie
Regional Director:	Dorothy W. Buckhanan
Region Membership Statistics:	86 Chapters — 36 Undergraduate (4 Suspended and 3 Inactive), 50 Graduate 3,325 Active Members 327 Undergraduates, 2.998 Graduates

REGIONAL CONFERENCE NOTES:

The 71st Central Regional Conference convened under the theme "The Spirit of Alpha Kappa Alpha — Celebrating Sisterhood and Service in Circle City." The conference was dedicated to 20th Central Regional Director — Soror Mabel Cason, who became an Ivy Beyond the Wall in 2004.

This conference convened on a high note, with the chartering of a new graduate chapter: Chi Phi Omega of West Lafayette, Indiana. Our 500 sorors and community residents participated in the Community Outreach Event which focused on the Ivy Reading AKAdemy Project.

The Cluster Realignment Committee reported on its findings, as commissioned in 2003 and indicated that Clusters would remain structured as is. Other business items included approving a motion that regional conferences will be hosted by the same clusters no more than once every four years.

Other conference highlights included: The introduction of an EAF Jazz/Blues Brunch; continuation of the Conference Gala with an Indy Sports Theme; an off-site excursion to the famed Madame C. J. Walker Theater and a special Golden Soror reception.

Conference special guests included: Soror Muriel Lyle Smith, granddaughter of Founder Soror Ethel Hedgeman Lyle and Rev. Landrum Shields, son of Founder Soror Johanna Berry Shields. Three new diamond sorors were inducted (a region record), including former Central Regional Director, Soror Maenell Newsome, who resides in the host city of Indianapolis.

For the second consecutive year, the region achieved 100% EAF chapter participation and the Buckhanan and Linda White EAF Endowments were fully capitalized. In addition, Central Region was recognized for being one of two regions to host AKA Day at the Capitol in all states.

Virginia Gilbert Overall Chapter Program Achievement (Campus Chapter)

Winner:	Pi Nu	Northeastern Illinois University	Chicago, Illinois
Runner Up:	Pi Lambda	DePauw University	Greencastle, Inidiana

Loraine R. Green Undergraduate Soror with the Highest Cumulative Average
Winner:	Maria Clark	(3.7)	Lambda Psi, Lewis University
Runner-up:	Alexia Gist	(3.67)	Xi Kappa, Chicago State University

Arnetta G. Wallace Undergraduate Chapter with the Highest Cumulative Average
Winner:	Xi Kappa (3.33)	Chicago, Illinois
Runner-up:	Beta Delta (3.11)	St. Louis, Missouri

Annetta M. Lawson Outstanding Graduate Advisor
Winner:	Latrice E. Eggleston — Pi Nu, Northeastern Illinois University
Runner-up:	Cynthia Mitchell Dunbar — Xi Kappa, Chicago State University

Lauretta Naylor Thompson Overall Chapter Program Achievement (membership 26-74)
Winner:	Lambda Tau Omega	Matteson, Illinois
Runner-up:	Lambda Mu Omega	Chicago, Illinois

Alice McGhee Smart Overall Chapter Program Achievement (membership 75-125)
Winner:	Epsilon Kappa Omega	Milwaukee, Wisconsin
Runner-up:	Lambda Alpha Omega	Chicago, Illinois

Loann J. Honesty King Overall Chapter Program Achievement (membership 126 and above)
Winner:	Gamma Omega	St. Louis, Missouri
Runner-up:	Xi Nu Omega	Chicago, Illinois

72ND — APRIL 12 — 15, 2006

Location:	Hyatt Regency Hotel Chicago, Illinois
Hostess Chapters:	Theta Omega (Prime Hostess), Chi Alpha Omega, Delta Chi Omega, Lambda Alpha Omega, Lambda Mu Omega, Tau Gamma Omega, Chi Omega Omega, Xi Nu Omega, Beta, Gamma Chi, Pi Nu, Omicron Alpha, Sigma Eta, Xi Kappa
Attendance:	1,750
Chairperson:	Audrey Cooper-Stanton
Co-Chairperson:	Dorretta Evans Parker, Amethyst D. Moore
Regional Director:	Dorothy W. Buckhanan
Region Membership Statistics:	89 Chapters — 36 Undergraduate (4 suspended, 1 inactive) 53 Graduate 3,659 Active Members 351 Undergraduates, 3,308 Graduates

REGIONAL CONFERENCE NOTES:

The 72nd Central Regional Conference was the second largest Regional Conference at the time with 1,750 registered. Several noteworthy events took place during the conference: Generated and donated $10,000 to Gift of Hope for organ and tissue research and held an on-site educational initiative to register more African American donors; Unveiled the second edition of The History of Central Region — *Pledged to Remember* with a book signing featuring author, Loann J. Honesty King; Hosted an EAF Jazz and Blues Breakfast to recognize chapters that support Alpha Kappa Alpha Educational Advancement Foundation; Presented the Regions' Living Legend Award to then U.S. State Senator Barack Obama and Mrs. Michelle Obama.

Other honorees at the Public Meeting included Mr. John Johnson — Ebony Magazine, Ms. Desiree Rogers and the Honorable Emil Jones Jr.; and recognized young authors, outstanding undergraduates and chapter members who supported the work of the "SPIRIT" administration under the leadership of Central's own 26th Supreme Basileus, Soror Linda Marie White.

The conference celebrated four years of strong programming across the region; strong membership growth; and creative, high quality, well-attended regional conferences.

Virginia Gilbert Award Chapter Overall Chapter Achievement (Campus Chapter)
Winner: Pi Nu Chapter Northeastern Illinois University — Chicago, Illinois
Runner-up: Pi Lambda Chapter — DePauw University — Greencastle, Indiana

Carolyn Blanton Overall Chapter Achievement Award (City Chapter)
Winner: Beta Delta — St. Louis, Missouri

Loraine R. Green Undergraduate Soror with the Highest Cumulative Average
Winner: Teresa Walker Iota Sigma Chapter (3.76) Lexington, Kentucky
Runner-Up: Autherine Ikanine Epsilon Delta Chapter (3.60) Madison, Wisconsin

Arnetta G. Wallace Undergraduate Chapter with the Highest Cumulative Average
Winner: Beta Delta (3.11) St. Louis, Missouri
Runner-Up: Epsilon Delta (3.00) Madison, Wisconsin

Outstanding Graduate Advisor — Annetta Lawson Award
Winner: Latrice E. Eggleston Pi Nu Chapter Northeastern IL University of Chicago, IL
Runner-Up: Mariatu Abdullah Pi Lambda Chapter DePauw University Greencastle, IN

Mabel E. Cason Overall Chapter Program Achievement (membership 25 or less)
Winner: Nu Omicron Omega — Springfield, IL **Runner-up:** Kappa Psi Omega — Madison, WI

Lauretta Naylor Thompson Overall Chapter Program Achievement (membership 26-75)
Winner: Lambda Tau Omega — Matteson, IL
Runner-up: Lambda Mu Omega — Chicago, IL

Alice McGhee Smart Overall Chapter Program Achievement (membership 76-125)
Winner: Lambda Alpha Omega — Naperville, IL
Runner-Up: Chi Omega Omega — Chicago, IL

Loann Honesty King Overall Chapter Program Achievement (membership 126 or more)
Winner: Gamma Omega — St. Louis, Missouri
Runner-Up: Xi Nu Omega — Chicago, Illinois

73RD — MAY 24-27, 2007

Location:	Crowne Plaza Hotel Springfield, Illinois
Hostess Chapters:	Nu Omicron Omega, *Prime Hostess Chapter*, Epsilon Eta, Epsilon Epsilon Omega, Omicron Delta Omega, Nu Pi Omega, Chi Xi Omega
Registration:	892 (Graduates 809, Undergraduate 73, Guests 10) Note: Opening Session Report (1,400 Reported to Directorate)

Conference Theme:	*Sisterhood and Service- Planning for the Future the ESP Way*
Conference Chairman:	Edna Shanklin
Conference Co-Chairmen:	Belinda Carr, Muriel Bondurant, Tiara Davidson
Regional Director:	Pamela Bates Porch
Region Membership Statistics:	89 Chapters — 36 Undergraduate (4 suspended, 1 inactive) 53 Graduate (1 inactive) 3,791 Active Members 432 Undergraduate, 3,359 Graduate

REGIONAL CONFERENCE NOTES:

Highlights of this Conference included a Community Outreach Event focused on sorors health and living a healthy Lifestyle; Training Institutes; Legacy Luncheon—Norma Solomon White Keynote Speaker; Undergraduate Luncheon: "Every Soror is a Pearl" Soror Ranika Sanchez 2nd Supreme Anti-Basileus—Speaker; Central Region Hall of Fame and Honoring Central Region She'Roes Outstanding Service; Parade of Chapters featuring the Chapter Banners given from the Central Region Conference to each Chapter; and the Central Region Step Show and Undergraduate Dance.

Virginia Gilbert Award Chapter Overall Chapter Achievement (Campus Chapter)
Winner: Delta Omicron Chapter   Northern Illinois University

Carolyn Blanton Overall Chapter Achievement Award (City Chapter)
No Entry

Loraine R. Green Undergraduate Soror with the Highest Cumulative Average
Winner: Teresa Walker (3.86)   Iota Sigma   University of Kentucky (Lexington)
Runner-up: Janaya Tucker (3.8)   Delta Beta   Southern Illinois University

Arnetta G. Wallace Undergraduate Chapter with the Highest Cumulative Average
Winner: Nu Lambda (3.11)   City Chapter, Gary, Indiana
Runner-up: (Tie)   Iota Sigma (3.10)   University of Kentucky (Lexington)
                   Beta Delta (3.10)   City Chapter, St. Louis, Missouri

Annetta M. Lawson Outstanding Graduate Advisor
Winner: Sheila Bonds, Advisor to Kappa, Butler University
Runner-up: Nadine DeJohnette, Delta Omicron, Northern Illinois University

Mabel E. Cason Overall Chapter Program Achievement (membership 25 or less)
No Entries

Lauretta Naylor Thompson Overall Chapter Program Achievement (membership 26-75)
Winner: Chi Sigma Omega   Bolingbrook, Illinois

Alice McGhee Smart Overall Chapter Program Achievement (membership 76-125)
Winner: Lambda Tau Omega   Far South Suburban Chicago, Illinois

Loann Honesty King Overall Chapter Program Achievement (membership 126 or more)
Winner: Theta Omega Chapter   Chicago, Illinois

74TH — APRIL 10 — 13, 2008

Location:	Grand Renaissance Hotel — St. Louis, MO
Hostess Chapters:	Omicron Eta Omega, *Prime Hostess Chapter*, Delta Delta Omega, Omicron Theta Omega, Upsilon Phi Omega,

PART VII: REGIONAL CONFERENCES

	Epsilon Lambda Omega, Gamma Kappa Omega, Beta Delta, Delta Beta, Epsilon Iota
Registration:	863 (Graduates 795, Undergraduate 62, Guests 6) Note: Opening Session Report
Conference Theme:	*Expecting Sensational Possibilities of Service*
Conference Chairman:	Melanie Chambers
Conference Co-Chairmen:	Wanda Jackson, Veronica Stacker
Regional Director:	Pamela Bates Porch
Region Membership Statistics:	89 Chapters — 36 Undergraduate (3 suspended, 2 inactive) 53 Graduate (1 inactive) 3,929 Active Members 377 Undergraduate, 3,552 Graduate

REGIONAL CONFERENCE NOTES:

The Conference Chairman Soror(s) Melanie Chambers, Wanda Jackson and Veronica Stacker were commended on their leadership and support during the planning and implementation of the vision of the Centennial Regional Conference. This Conference introduced for the first time a flawless Electronic Registration Process. The registration committee did a yeoman's job in education and delivery of a seamless registration process. They also focused on personal customer service with the personal touch of service all the way to resolution of any conflicts. Sorors Pamela Westbrooks –Hodge and Soror Jettie Bryant and their committee brought Central Region into the Electronic Age.

Other highlights included a Centennial Walk with a local football celebrity and a brisk walk around the hotel, with Sorors joining in along the way. Sorors were treated to a centennial bracelet and received a Centennial Central Region charm designed by the Central Regional Director. The 2008 Class of Unsung Sheroes was inducted into the Central Region Hall of Fame.

The Tribute to Leaders Dinner thanked the chapter Basilei and Graduate Advisors for their Service to the Regional and their chapters. Each member received an AKA pin.

The conference started with an electronic video welcome from the Regional Director and Greeks from the St. Louis Pan –Hellenic Council bringing greetings to the members of Central Region. Central Region's Scholars and Leadership Fellows were acknowledged and saluted and for academic excellence two undergraduates achieve with the highest GPA's were selected for the Post Boule Tour.

In addition: a Historic Reflection of Soror Ethel Hedgeman Lyle and the contribution of the St. Louis area in the expansion of Alpha Kappa Alpha Sorority. The Sunday Rededication activity included Soror Pamela Bates Porch as the speaker. The activity concluded with a video reflection from our members, reflecting on highlights of their stay in St. Louis. It was a wonderful keepsake of the conference. The entertainment was Freddie Jackson and a Graduate Greek Step Show.

Virginia Gilbert Overall Chapter Program Achievement (Campus Chapter)
No Entry

Carolyn Blanton Overall Chapter Program Achievement (City Chapter)
Not Recorded

Loraine R. Green Undergraduate Soror with the Highest Cumulative Average
Winner: Dericka Canada (3.88)   Beta Epsilon   University of Louisville
Runner Up: Marsha Ashley (3.81)   Iota Sigma   University of Kentucky (Lexington)

Arnetta G. Wallace Undergraduate Chapter with the Highest Cumulative Average
Winner: Epsilon Zeta (3.51)   Western Kentucky, University
Runner Up: Beta Delta (3.47) City Chapter   St. Louis, Missouri

Annetta M. Lawson Outstanding Graduate Advisor
Winner: Essie Kelly, Advisor to Beta, City Chapter, Chicago, Illinois
Runner Up: Kimberly Beck, Advisor to Beta Delta, City Chapter, Chicago, Illinois

Mabel Evans Cason Overall Chapter Program Achievement (membership up to 25)
Winner: Kappa Psi Omega   Madison, Wisconsin

Lauretta Naylor Thompson Overall Chapter Program Achievement (membership 26-74)
Winner: Theta Rho Omega   Markham, Illinois

Alice McGhee Smart Overall Chapter Program Achievement (membership 75-125)
Winner: Lambda Tau Omega   Far South Suburban, Chicago

Loann J. Honesty King Overall Chapter Program Achievement (membership 126 and above)
Winner: Theta Omega   Chicago, Illinois

75TH — APRIL 16-19, 2009

Location:	Renaissance Schaumburg Hotel and Convention Center Schaumburg, Illinois
Hostess Chapters:	Phi Epsilon Omega: Prime Hostess Chapter Insert Names of other chapters (Cluster VIII
Registration:	No Record
Conference Theme:	*An Engaged Sisterhood Standing on a Legacy of Promise*
Conference Chairman:	Dr. Bakhia Madison-Phi Epsilon Omega
Conference Co-Chairmen:	Johnna Richmond—Phi Kappa Omega
Regional Director:	Pamela Bates Porch
Region Membership Statistics:	89 Chapters — 36 Undergraduate (3 inactive, 1 pending dissolution) 53 Graduate (1 inactive) 3,857 Active Members 306 Undergraduates, 3,551 Graduates

REGIONAL CONFERENCE NOTES:

The Steering Committee under the Leadership of Soror(s) Dr. Bakhia Madison — Phi Epsilon Omega and Soror Johanna Richmond- Phi Kappa Omega and the Sorors of Cluster VIII are to be commended for the implementation of the 76th Central Regional Conference.

The highlight of this conference was the conference vendor fair which took place prior to the opening of the conference. Conference participants were treated to healthy living, specialty items for Soror growth, and Specialty Teas by Carol Mosely Braun (former Senator from Illinois).

Members attend pre-conference training opportunities: Graduate Advisors Training Level 1 and 2, Basilei Institutes, Tribute to Leaders Dinner, Legacy Breakfast, EAF Breakfast, and Workshops offered by ESP administration chairman and committees.

Virginia Gilbert Overall Chapter Program Achievement (Campus Chapter)
No Entry

Carolyn Blanton Overall Chapter Program Achievement (City Chapter)
Winner: Beta Delta   City Chapter St. Louis, MO

Loraine R. Green Undergraduate Soror with the Highest Cumulative Average
Winner: Dericka Canada (3.884)   Beta Epsilon   University of Louisville
Runner-Up: Erica Lyles (3.771)   Beta Delta   City Chapter St. Louis, MO

Arnetta G. Wallace Undergraduate Chapter with the Highest Cumulative Average
Winner:	Beta Zeta	3.312	Kentucky State
Runner-Up:	Sigma Gamma	3.245	Lake Forrest College

Annetta M. Lawson Outstanding Graduate Advisor
Winner:	Kimberly Beck	Beta Delta	City Chapter St. Louis, Missouri

Mabel Evans Cason Overall Chapter Program Achievement (membership up to 25)
Winner:	Chi Sigma Omega	Bolingbrook, Illinois
Runner-Up:	Kappa Psi Omega	Madison, Wisconsin

Lauretta Naylor Thompson Overall Chapter Program Achievement (membership 26-74)
Winner:	Theta Rho Omega	Markham, Illinois

Alice McGhee Smart Overall Chapter Program Achievement (membership 75-125)
Winner:	Lambda Alpha Omega	Western Suburban, Chicago, Illinois
Runner-Up	Lambda Mu Omega	Chicago, Illinois

Loann J. Honesty King Overall Chapter Program Achievement (membership 126 and above)
Winner:	Gamma Omega	St. Louis, Missouri
Runner-Up	Theta Omega	Chicago, Illinois

76TH — MARCH 25 — 28, 2010

Location:	Marriott Chicago Chicago, Illinois
Hostess Chapters:	Xi Nu Omega, *Prime Hostess*, Theta Omega, Delta Chi Omega, Lambda Alpha Omega, Lambda Mu Omega, Tau Gamma Omega, Chi Alpha Omega, Chi Omega Omega
Registration:	No Record
Conference Theme:	*A New Century of Leadership: An Encouraged Sisterhood Preparing for the Future*
Conference Chairman:	Phyllis McCune — Xi Nu Omega Chapter
Conference Co-Chairmen:	Jasmyne Portee—Delta Omicron Chapter
Regional Director	Pamela Bates Porch
Region Membership Statistics:	89 Chapters — 36 Undergraduate (4 inactive, 1 suspended, 1 pending dissolution), 53 Graduate (1 inactive) 3,678 Active Members 306 Undergraduates, 3,372 Graduates

REGIONAL CONFERENCE NOTES:

The conference opened with a parade of state flags. Welcoming reception and service project collecting items toiletries and items for senior citizens. In addition local vendors in the service community partnering with local agencies to provide free screenings and critical health care information, to over 500 Louisville residents.

Soror Barbara A. McKinzie — 27th Supreme Basileus — reported on the progress of her initiatives under the "Extraordinary Service Program" banner and updated members on the State of the Sorority.

Soror Pamela Bates Porch was recognized by the Supreme Basileus for her service to the region. Soror Deborah Dangerfield Executive Director brought forth the Corporate Office report and Soror Barbara Sutton gave the Educational Advancement Foundation report and initiated a giving campaign during the plenary session. The Ivy Notes performed and were requested to perform at the Boule. Soror Porch acknowledged the administrative team and their support.

The Evening Gala was held in multiple ballrooms with various types of entertainment. The Regional Director was escorted by her Grandson Master Robert Andre Spicer Jr. Young Mister Spicer also introduced the Regional Director and started the festivities by the first dance with the Regional Director Soror Pamela Bates Porch.

Virginia Gilbert Overall Chapter Program Achievement (Campus Chapter)
Winner:	Pi Lambda	DePauw University	Greencastle, Indiana
Runner-Up:	Pi Nu	Northeastern Illinois University	Chicago, Illinois

Carolyn Blanton Overall Chapter Program Achievement (City Chapter)
Winner:	Beta Delta	City Chapter St. Louis, MO

Loraine R. Green Undergraduate Soror with the Highest Cumulative Average
Winner:	Kaydene Desilvia (3.894)	Omicron Alpha	Dominican University
Runner-Up:	Andriene Anderson (3.799)	Tau	Indiana University

Arnetta G. Wallace Undergraduate Chapter with the Highest Cumulative Average
Winner:	Pi Nu Chapter (3.372)	Northeastern Illinois University	Chicago, IL
Runner-Up:	Epsilon Zeta (3.302)	Western Kentucky University	Bowling Green, KY

Annetta M. Lawson Outstanding Graduate Advisor
Winner:	Ersa Austin	Epsilon Zeta	Western Kentucky University
Runner-Up:	Phyllis Weir	Tau	Indiana University

Mabel Evans Cason Overall Chapter Program Achievement (membership up to 25)
No Entry

Lauretta Naylor Thompson Overall Chapter Program Achievement (membership 26-74)
Winner:	Chi Chi Omega	Indianapolis, Indiana
Runner-Up:	Upsilon Mu Omega	Milwaukee, Wisconsin

Alice McGhee Smart Overall Chapter Program Achievement (membership 75-125)
Winner:	Lambda Alpha Omega	Western Suburban, Chicago, Illinois

Loann J. Honesty King Overall Chapter Program Achievement (membership 126 and above)
Winner:	Gamma Omega	St. Louis, Missouri
Runner-Up	Chi Omega Omega	Chicago, Illinois

77TH — MARCH 31- APRIL 3, 2011

Location:	The Lexington Convention Center
	Hilton Lexington Downtown
	Hyatt Regency Lexington
	Lexington, Kentucky
Hostess Chapters:	Beta Gamma Omega, *Prime Hostess*, Eta Omega, Beta Rho Omega, Beta Upsilon Omega, Beta Omega Omega, Omicron Sigma Omega, Pi Lambda Omega, Beta Epsilon, Beta Zeta, Epsilon Zeta, Zeta Nu, Zeta Zeta, Eta Rho, Iota Sigma, Sigma Eta
Registration:	1,445: 1,312 Graduates, 133 Undergraduates
Conference Theme:	*Celebrating the Legacy of Alpha Kappa Alpha: Timeless Sisterhood, Service & Leadership*
Conference Chairman:	Dana S. Branham

Conference Co-Chairmen:	Bridgett Rice and Aleidra Allen
Regional Director:	Giselé M. Casanova, Ph.D.
Regional Membership Statistics	87 Chapters — 35 Undergraduate, 52 Graduate
	3,813 Active Members
	332 Undergraduates, 3,481 Graduates

REGIONAL CONFERENCE NOTES:

The 77th Central Regional Conference kicked off with the first-ever "off-site" service project. The project involved sorors volunteering their time at the Lexington, Kentucky "Salvation Army Emergency Shelter." Sorors prepared and served lunch to community citizens. Sorors also assisted with cleaning the shelter and sorting clothes in the Clothing Bank. Two additional service projects included sorors donating over 600 pairs of shoes for Soles4Souls, Inc. and 200 new and gently used wigs that were donated to the Lexington branch of the American Cancer Society's Patient Service Room.

Another conference "first" was the introduction of "Undergraduate Hospitality" on the Friday of the conference, immediately following the second plenary session. Undergraduate sorors from across the region were able to mix, mingle, and network while enjoying refreshments. One hundred and eight Central Region undergraduate sorors, who attained a cumulative G.P.A. of 3.0 or higher, were recognized as "Central Region Scholars" at the Undergraduate Luncheon. Central Region's 2010 Winter Leadership Fellows were spotlighted during the second plenary session and were seated on the dais.

During the Public Meeting, awards were presented to the following Program Initiatives and Program Partners: Emerging Young Leaders — Soror Lillian Bland, Beta Gamma Omega Chapter; American Cancer Society — Mrs. Kerri Buchanan, Community Representative; Kentucky Public Health HIV — Ms. Michele McCrary, Disease Investigative Specialist; and Department for Public Health — Ms. A. Medina Tipton, Surveillance Coordinator — HIV/AIDS Branch, Kentucky Department for Public Health.

During the Conference Luncheon, Soror Gladevelle Bell, was honored as a new Diamond Soror with 75 years of service. Eleven "new" Golden and 29 "new" Silver Sorors were also honored. Saturday's Pre-Gala Cocktail hour was hosted by the men of Alpha Phi Alpha Fraternity, Incorporated. The conference Gala featured another "first" for Central Region. The "surprise" entertainment was a performance by international R&B recording group "Midnight Star."

Virginia Gilbert Overall Chapter Program Achievement (Campus Chapter, 19 members or fewer)
Winner: Pi Lambda DePauw University Greencastle, Indiana

Gladys Bufkin Johnson Overall Chapter Program Achievement
(Campus Chapter, 20 or more members)
Winner: Tau Indiana University Bloomington, Indiana

Carolyn Blanton Overall Chapter Program Achievement (City Chapter)
Winner: Beta Chicago, Illinois

Lorraine R. Green Undergraduate Soror with the Highest Cumulative Average
Winner: Marcella Moore (3.88) Beta Epsilon City Chapter, Louisville, Kentucky
Runner-up: Kaydene DeSilva (3.86) Omicron Alpha City Chapter, Northwest Suburban, Illinois

Arnetta G. Wallace Undergraduate Chapter with the Highest Cumulative Average
Winner: Epsilon Delta (3.36) University of Wisconsin Madison
Runner-up: Beta Epsilon (3.23) City Chapter, Louisville, Kentucky

Annetta M. Lawson Outstanding Graduate Advisor
Winner: Patricia Smith (Xi Nu Omega), Advisor to Delta Omicron, Northern Illinois University
Runner-up: Katasha Butler (Alpha Mu Omega), Advisor to Pi Lanbda, DePauw University

Mabel E. Cason Overall Chapter Program Achievement (25 members or fewer)
Winner: Alpha Eta Omega Terre Haute, Indiana

Lauretta Naylor Thompson Overall Chapter Program Achievement (26-75 members)
Winner: Lambda Tau Omega Far South Suburban Chicago, Illinois

Alice McGhee Smart Overall Chapter Program Achievement (76-125 members)
Winner: Chi Omega Omega Chicago, Illinois

Loann Honesty King Overall Chapter Program Achievement (126 members or more)
Winner: Alpha Mu Omega Indianapolis, Indiana
Runner-up: Xi Nu Omega Chicago Heights, Illinois

78TH — APRIL 26-29, 2012

Location:	The Monona Terrace Community Convention Center, Hilton Madison Monona Terrace Hotel, Madison Concourse Hotel Governor's Club Madison, Wisconsin
Hostess Chapters:	Kappa Psi Omega, Prime Hostess, Epsilon Kappa Omega, Delta Phi Omega, Lambda Nu Omega, Pi Gamma Omega, Upsilon Mu Omega, Xi Eta Omega, Epsilon Delta, Lambda Xi, Mu Beta, Mu Rho
Registration:	1,440: 1,247 Graduates, 193 Undergraduates
Conference Theme:	*Strengthening Our Commitment to Timeless Sisterhood, Service and Leadership*
Conference Chairman:	Theresa Sanders
Conference Co-Chairmen:	Frances Huntley-Cooper, Teresa Brown, and Tiffany Jones
Regional Director:	Giselé M. Casanova, Ph.D.
Regional Membership Statistics:	3,876 — 3,514 Graduates, 362 Undergraduates (89 Chapters: 52 Graduate and 37 Undergraduate)

REGIONAL CONFERENCE NOTES:

The 78th Central Regional Conference kicked off with the "off-site" service project. The project involved sorors volunteering their time at the Second Harvest Food Bank of

Southern Wisconsin. Sorors volunteered a total of 60 hours and processed 3,820 pounds of food, equivalent to 3,183 meals. Additionally, Central Region collected donations of adult undergarments, disposable diapers, slippers for adults and children, toiletries, hair care products, and phone cards that were presented to the Domestic Abuse Intervention Service (DAIS) of Madison and chapters made monetary donations of over $400.00 to DAIS. The region hosted a "Youth Summit," the Saturday morning of the conference that was sponsored by State Farm. Madison area youth, 12-18 years of age, were treated to a hot breakfast before participating in a series of three interactive workshops that included: Distracted Driving; Top Teen Issues of Today: Parenting Issues, Bullying & Social Media; and Teenager Economics: How to Earn the Money You Deserve. Participants were given a certificate and giveaways donated by State Farm.

One hundred and seventy-six Central Region undergraduate sorors, who attained a cumulative G.P.A. of 3.0 or higher, were recognized as "Central Region Scholars" at the Undergraduate Luncheon. Central Region's 2011 summer and Winter Leadership Fellows were spotlighted during the second plenary session and were seated on the dais.

During the public meeting, awards were presented to the following program initiatives and program partners: Ms. Cora E. White, CEO, Partner in Foster Care; Ms. Emily Sanders, Community Manager, Group Health Cooperative; and Mr. Michael Johnson, CEO, Boys and Girls Club of Dane County. Ms. Andrea L. Neely, Regional Development Director, UNCF, Indianapolis Region, made a special presentation to Central Region in recognition and appreciation of "Distinguished Service" on behalf of UNCF and to Alpha Mu Omega Chapter for being the chapter in Central Region identified as the largest contributor to UNCF.

The EAF Legacy Breakfast, a new event for the conference, featured a lively "hat auction" to raise money for EAF scholarships. During the Conference Luncheon, Soror Fannie Frazier Hicklin, was honored as a new Diamond Soror with 75 years of service. Twenty-six new Golden and 48 new Silver Sorors were also honored. The conference Gala once again featured surprise entertainment which was a performance by international R&B recording group The SOS Band.

Gladys Bufkin Johnson Overall Chapter Program Achievement
(Campus Chapter, 20 or more members)
Winner: Tau Indiana University   Bloomington, Indiana

Lorraine R. Green Undergraduate Soror with the Highest Cumulative Average
Winner: Marcella Moore (3.90)   Beta Epsilon City Chapter, Louisville, KY
Runner-up: Kaydene DeSilva (3.89)   Omicron Alpha City Chapter, Northwest Suburban, IL

Arnetta G. Wallace Undergraduate Chapter with the Highest Cumulative Average
Winner: Eta Rho (3.49)   Moorehead State University
Zeta Zeta (3.49)   Murray State University
Runner-up: Beta Epsilon (3.45)   City Chapter, Louisville, Kentucky

Annetta M. Lawson Outstanding Graduate Advisor
Winner: Lisa Bennett (Alpha Mu Omega), Advisor to Pi Lambda, DePauw University
Runner-up: Debra Hill (Delta Chi Omega), Advisor to Gamma Chi, Northwestern University

Lauretta Naylor Thompson Overall Chapter Program Achievement (26-75 members)
Winner: Chi Sigma Omega   Bolingbrook, Illinois
Runner-up: Beta Gamma Omega   Lexington, Kentucky

Alice McGhee Smart Overall Chapter Program Achievement (76-125 members)
Winner: Chi Chi Omega   Indianapolis, Indiana

Loann Honesty King Overall Chapter Program Achievement (126 members or more)
Winner: Xi Nu Omega   Chicago Heights, Illinois
Runner-up: Alpha Mu Omega   Indianapolis, Indiana

79TH — APRIL 4-7, 2013

Location: The Indianapolis Marriott Downtown Hotel, the Westin Indianapolis Hotel, and the Indianapolis Convention Center Indianapolis, Indiana

Hostess Chapters: Alpha Mu Omega, *Prime Hostess*, Alpha Eta Omega, Chi Chi Omega, Zeta Zeta Omega, Iota Chi Omega, Omicron Phi Omega, Chi Phi Omega, Beta Phi, Kappa, Tau, Epsilon Rho, Pi Lambda

Registration:	1,891: 1,718 Graduates, 173 Undergraduates
Conference Theme:	*A Supreme Sisterhood Providing Timeless Service and Leadership in a Global Society*
Conference Chairman:	Kiahna W. Davis
Conference Co-Chairmen:	Anika R. Allen, Victoria L. Clark, and Kelli S. Bennett
Regional Director:	Giselé M. Casanova, Ph.D.
Regional Membership Statistics:	3,887 — 3,509 Graduates, 378 Undergraduates (90 Chapters: 53 Graduate and 37 Undergraduate)

REGIONAL CONFERENCE NOTES:

On Friday, March 22, 2013, the conference kick off event, a Youth Summit, was held at the Charles A. Tindley Accelerated School, Indianapolis, IN. One hundred sixty-two students participated in the Summit that was sponsored by State Farm. Representatives presented workshops on Distracted Driving and Financial Literacy. Students were treated to a pizza lunch, door prizes, and other giveaways. On Thursday, April 4, 2013, the off-site service project was conducted. Central Region Sorors volunteered at the Girl Scout Camp Dellwood by helping to clean and prepare the grounds for spring and summer campers. The region also made a $2,500.00 donation to the Girl Scout Camp. Central Region Chapters made generous donations of school supplies and gift cards to "Use What You Got" prison ministry that benefitted children of incarcerated parents. A total of 21, 137 school supply items were donated as well as $520.00 in gift cards. Central Region partnered with the Indiana Coalition Against Domestic Violence (ICADV) and the Indianapolis Recorder to bring the production "Breaking the Silence" to the historic Madame C. J. Walker Theatre. This production was free to the public and combined film, photography, and dance to depict societal ills of domestic violence, bullying, and human trafficking. Service providers were also on hand to answer questions and assist those in need. Central Region was proud to make a $3,300.00 donation to the ICADV.

The first Central Regional Conference "app" was introduced, as well as the first "Cybercafé." One hundred twenty-three Central Region undergraduate sorors, who attained a cumulative G.P.A. of 3.0 or higher, were recognized as "Central Region Scholars" at the Undergraduate Luncheon. Central Region's 2012 Summer and Winter Leadership Fellows were spotlighted during the second plenary session and were seated on the dais.

During the public meeting, awards were presented to the following program initiatives and program partners: Ms. Betty Perry, Founder/Director, Metropolitan Youth Orchestra; Ms. Diana Maxam and Ms. Deborah Oatts, National Association of Women Business Owners; and Ms. Cindy Lanane, Indiana Coalition Against Domestic Violence. This year, once again, the EAF Legacy Breakfast featured a live auction. In addition to hats, designer bags were also auctioned off.

During the conference luncheon, Soror Doris Evans Russell, was honored as a new Diamond Soror with 75 years of service. Twenty-one new Golden and 50 new Silver Sorors were also honored. The surprise entertainment for the conference gala was international R&B recording group Zapp. Sorors and guests danced the night away while enjoying the group's high-energy performance.

Gladys Bufkin Johnson Overall Chapter Program Achievement (Campus Chapter, 20 or more members)
Winner: Tau Indiana University Bloomington, Indiana

Lorraine R. Green Undergraduate Soror with the Highest Cumulative Average
Winner: Marissa Lyles (3.940) Epsilon Rho Purdue University, West Lafayette, Indiana
Runner-up: Teya Everett (3.832) Beta Zeta Kentucky State University Frankfort, Kentucky

Arnetta G. Wallace Undergraduate Chapter with the Highest Cumulative Average
Winner: Pi Nu (3.53) Northeastern Illinois University
Runner-up: Epsilon Rho (3.51) Purdue University

Annetta M. Lawson Outstanding Graduate Advisor
Winner: Constance Turner Burkes (Theta Omega), Advisor to Beta, Chicago City-wide Chapter
Runner-up: Jerrie Hayes (Alpha Mu Omega), Advisor to Tau, Indiana University

Alice McGhee Smart Overall Chapter Program Achievement (76-125 members)
Winner: Lambda Alpha Omega Western Suburbs Chicago, Illinois
Runner-up: Lambda Tau Omega Far South Suburban Chicago, Illinois

Loann Honesty King Overall Chapter Program Achievement (126 members or more)
Winner: Xi Nu Omega Chicago Heights, Illinois
Runner-up: Alpha Mu Omega Indianapolis, Indiana

80TH — MARCH 27-30, 2014

Location:	The Hyatt Regency Chicago Hotel Chicago, Illinois
Hostess Chapters:	Chi Sigma Omega, Prime Hostess, Lambda Omega, Gamma Psi Omega, Eta Kappa Omega, Eta Mu Omega, Theta Rho Omega, , Sigma Phi Omega, Phi Epsilon Omega, Phi Kappa Omega, Nu Lambda
Registration:	Anticipated: 2,200
Conference Theme:	*A Supreme Legacy of Timeless Sisterhood, Service and Leadership*
Conference Chairman:	Marcia Banks
Conference Co-Chairmen:	Glenda Blakemore, Ge'Tina Williams and Melissa Brown
Regional Director:	Giselé M. Casanova, Ph.D.
Regional Membership Statistics:	3,887 — 3,509 Graduates, 378 Undergraduates (90 Chapters: 53 Graduate and 37 Undergraduate) [at the time of publication]

REGIONAL CONFERENCE NOTES:

While planning has begun for the 80th Central Regional Conference, it will not have occurred during the publication of this 3rd edition of the Central Region History Book. It is anticipated that the book will be available for distribution at the conference. The 80th Central Regional Conference will include an off-site service project that is tentatively scheduled to occur at the Greater Chicago Food Depository. The "Youth Summit" will be held at a Chicago Public School. The Central Regional Conference "app" will be utilized again to communicate important information to attendees. Honey-Do Hospitality and activities will be introduced at the conference and Gala attendees will again be treated to a concert performance by a surprise International R & B band.

Chapter Listing

CHAPTER NAME/LOCATION   CHARTER DATE

Beta ....October 8, 1913
City Chapter/Chicago, IL

Gamma ....February 12, 1914
University of Illinois
Champagne-Urbana

Kappa ....February 20, 1920
Butler College
Indianapolis, Indiana

Mu Graduate/Gamma Omega ....December 2, 1920
St. Louis, Missouri

Xi Graduate/Eta Omega 1921/May 6, 1922
Louisville, Kentucky

Theta Omega ....November 5, 1922
Chicago, Illinois

Eta ....December 12, 1922 – 1964*
University of Minnesota
St. Paul, Minnesota

Lambda Omega ....December 15, 1922 – 1928*
Indianapolis, Indiana

Tau ....December 16, 1922
Indiana University
Bloomington, Indiana

Alpha Eta Omega ....June 16, 1928
Terre Haute, Indiana

Alpha Mu Omega ....February 16, 1929
Indianapolis, Indiana

Beta Delta ....November 12, 1932
City Chapter
St. Louis, Missouri

Beta Zeta ....February 25, 1933
Kentucky State College
Frankfort, Kentucky

Beta Epsilon ....November 6, 1933
University of Louisville
Louisville, Kentucky

Beta Gamma Omega ....March 30, 1934
Lexington, Kentucky

Beta Rho Omega ....February 14, 1937
Hopkinsville, Kentucky

Beta Upsilon Omega ....March 6, 1938
Frankfort, Kentucky

Beta Omega Omega ....February 18, 1939
Paducah, Kentucky

Gamma Kappa Omega ....March 15, 1941
Carbondale, Illinois

Gamma Psi Omega ....October 28, 1944
Gary, Indiana

Delta Delta Omega ....May 25, 1946
East St. Louis, Illinois

Delta Phi Omega ....April 17, 1948
Minneapolis/St. Paul, Minnesota

Delta Chi Omega ....June 25, 1048
Evanston, Illinois

Epsilon Epsilon Omega ....April 9, 1949
Champaign, Illinois

Epsilon Kappa Omega ....May 11, 1949
Milwaukee, Wisconsin

Epsilon Lambda Omega ....May 28, 1950
Cairo, Illinois

Beta Iota ....June 2, 1951 – July 1982*
Evansville College
Evansville, Indiana

Delta Beta Chapter ....April 19, 1952
Southern Illinois University
Carbondale, Illinois

Zeta Zeta Omega Chapter ....March 13, 1954
Evansville, Indiana

Delta Omicron .... May 22, 1960
Northern Illinois University
Normal, Illinois

Eta Kappa Omega .... February 20, 1960
East Chicago, Indiana

Eta Mu Omega .... March 26, 1960
South Bend, Indiana

Epsilon Delta .... May 18, 1968
University of Wisconsin
Madison, Wisconsin

Theta Rho Omega .... November 17, 1968
Markham, Illinois

Epsilon Zeta .... November 22, 1968
Western Kentucky University
Bowling Green, Kentucky

Gamma Chi .... December 1, 1968
Northwestern University
Evanston, Illinois

Epsilon Eta .... December 14, 1968
Bradley University
Peoria, Illinois

Epsilon Iota .... May 30, 1969
Southern Illinois University

Beta Phi .... November 14, 1969
Ball State University
Muncie, Indiana

Epsilon Xi .... December 6, 1969
Indiana State University
Terre Haute, Indiana

Epsilon Rho Chapter .... December 13, 1969
Purdue University
West Lafayette, Indiana

Zeta Zeta .... January 9, 1971
Murray State University
Murray, Kentucky

Zeta Iota ....February 20, 1971
Western Illinois University
Macomb, Illinois

Zeta Nu Chapter ....April 25, 1971
Eastern Kentucky University
Richmond, Kentucky

Zeta Phi ....December 12, 1971
Indiana University — Northwest Campus
Gary, Indiana

Eta Alpha ....March 4, 1972 – July 2002*
Illinois State University
Normal, Illinois

Eta Gamma ....October 28, 1972 – July 2000*
Eastern Illinois University
Charleston, Illinois

Eta Rho ....April 29, 1973
Morehead State University
Morehead, Kentucky

Iota Chi Omega ....December 15, 1973
Fort Wayne, Indiana

Theta Omicron ....January 20, 1974 – July 1992*
Eureka College
Eureka, Illinois

Kappa Epsilon Omega ....May 25, 1974 – July 2010*
Anderson, Indiana

Iota Delta ....July 21, 1974
University of Wisconsin
Milwaukee, Wisconsin

Iota Epsilon ....September 28, 1974 – July 1982*
National College of Education
Evanston, Illinois

Iota Sigma ....May 5, 1975
University of Kentucky
Lexington, Kentucky

Kappa Mu Chapter ....April 5, 1975
Joliet, Illinois

Kappa Tau Omega ....April 10, 1976
Bloomington, Indiana

Kappa Psi Omega ....May 15, 1976
Madison, Wisconsin

Lambda Alpha Omega ....May 29, 1976
Western Suburban — Chicago, Illinois

Lambda Xi ....May 14, 1977
University of Wisconsin
White Water, Wisconsin

Lambda Mu Omega...March 5, 1977
Chicago, Illinois

Lambda Nu Omega ....May 27, 1977
Lake County, Illinois

Lambda Psi..February 19, 1978
Lewis University
Lockport, Illinois

Lambda Tau Omega...February 26, 1978
Far South Suburban Chicago, Illinois

Mu Beta...March 4, 1978
Marquette University
Milwaukee, Wisconsin

Mu Delta Omega ....June 3, 1978
Fort Knox, Kentucky

Mu Rho...March 25, 1979
University of Minnesota
Minneapolis/St. Paul, Minnesota

Nu Lambda..May 4, 1980
City Chapter
Gary, Indiana

Nu Omicron Omega..December 13, 1980
Springfield, Bloomington, Decatur, Illinois

Nu Pi Omega...December 14, 1980
Peoria, Illinois

Nu Sigma ....March 22, 1981 – July 2002*
Southeast Missouri State University
Cape Girardea, Missouri

Xi Epsilon...December 12, 1981 – July 2000*
National-Kendall Colleges
Evanston, Illinois

Xi Zeta ....April 1, 1982 – July 1992*
Illinois Wesleyan University
Bloomington, Illinois

Xi Eta Omega ....May 15, 1982
Moline, Illinois

Xi Nu Omega ....July 9, 1982
Chicago Heights, Illinois

Xi Kappa..July 10, 1982
Chicago State University
Chicago, Illinois

Omicron Delta Omega ....March 24, 1984
Bloomington/Normal, Illinois

Omicron Eta Omega...May 26, 1994
University City, Missouri

Omicron Theta Omega...May 27, 1984
St. Louis, Missouri

Omicron Sigma Omega ....March 31, 1985
Bowling Green, Kentucky

Omicron Phi Omega...May 18, 1985
Kokomo, Indiana

Pi Gamma Omega...January 25, 1986
Rockford, Illinois

Omicron Alpha ....April 20, 1986
College Consortium
North West Suburban Illinois

Pi Lambda Omega ....June 28, 1986
Eastern Jefferson County, Kentucky

Omicron Xi...December 3, 1988
City Chapter
Milwaukee, Wisconsin

Sigma Phi Omega ....June 21, 1990
Gary, Indiana

Pi Lambda ....March 23, 1991
DePauw University
Greencastle, Indiana

Tau Gamma Omega..November 2, 1991
Oak Park, Illinois

Pi Nu ....March 21, 1992
Northeastern Illinois University
Chicago, Illinois

Rho Lambda..April 30, 1995 – July 2010*
Indiana Institute of Technology
Fort Wayne, Indiana

Upsilon Mu Omega ....March 29, 1997
Milwaukee, Wisconsin

Upsilon Phi Omega...January 31, 1998
Edwardsville, Illinois

Phi Epsilon Omega ....January 23, 1999
Chicago, Illinois

Phi Kappa Omega...January 8, 2000
Evergreen Park, Illinois

Sigma Gamma..April 9, 2000
Lake Forrest College
Lake Forrest, Illinois

Sigma Eta..April 22, 2001
Northern Kentucky University
  Highland Heights, Kentucky

Chi Alpha Omega ....April 14, 2002
Schaumburg, Illinois

Chi Xi Omega...January 10, 2004
Decatur, Illinois

Chi Sigma Omega..December 5, 2004
Bolingbrook, Illinois

Chi Phi Omega..April 7, 2005
Lafayette-West Lafayette, Indiana

Chi Chi Omega ....May 21, 2005
Indianapolis, Indiana

Chi Omega Omega ....June 18, 2005
Chicago, Illinois

Tau Iota...April 17, 2011
Millikin University
Decatur, Illinois

Tau Mu ....February 26, 2012
DePaul University
Chicago, Illinois

Tau Rho ....April 21, 2013
University Southern Indiana
Evansville, Indiana

Dissolution date

Selected Resources

The following list includes the resources consulted in the preparation of *The History of Central Region "Pledged to Remember" – A Tradition of Timeless Service*

Davis, Kenneth C. *Don't Know Much About History: Everything You Need to Know about American History but Never Learned.* New York: Avon Books, 1991

Franklin, John Hope. *From Slavery to Freedom: A History of Negro Americans* (5th Edition). New York: Knopf, 1980.

Grossman, James B, Keating, Ann Durkin, Reiff, Janice I. The Encyclopedia of Chicago, Chicago and London: The University of Chicago Press, 2004

Wesley, Charles H. *The History of Alpha Phi Alpha a Development in College Life* (9th edition). Washinbgton, D.C.: Foundation, 1959

Our Glorious Century, Pleasantville, New York/Montreal: Reader's Digest Association, Inc., 1994.

Our Lives & Times – An Illustrated History, North Dighton, MA: World Publications Group, Inc., 2003.

The Black Chicago Renaissance / Edited by Darlene Clark Hine and John McCluskey, Jr., Urbvana, Chicago and Springfield: University of Illinois Press, 2012

King, Loann J. Honesty. *The History of Central Region Pledged to Remember*, Chicago: Range Publishing Company, 1957

King, Loann J. Honesty. *The History of Central Region Pledged to Remember*, 2nd edition. Oak Park, IL: Range Publishing Company, 2006

Parker, Marjorie H. *Alpha Kappa Alpha Sorority 1908 – 1958*. Chicago: Alpha Kappa Alpha Sorority, Inc., 1958.

Parker, Marjorie H. *Alpha Kappa Alpha: Sixty Years of Service*. Chicago: Alpha Kappa Alpha Sorority, Inc., 1966.

Parker, Marjorie H. *Alpha Kappa Alpha: In the Eye of the Beholder*. Washington D.C.: Alpha Kappa Alpha Sorority, Inc., 1979.

Parker, Marjorie H. *Alpha Kappa Alpha: Through the Years*. Chicago: Alpha Kappa Alpha Sorority, Inc., Mobium Press, 1990.

Parker, Marjorie H. *Past is Prologue: The History of Alpha Kappa Alpha*. Chicago: Alpha Kappa Alpha Sorority, Inc., 1999.

McNealey, Earnestine Green. *Pearls of Service, The Legacy of America's first Black Sorority, Alpha Kappa Alpha,* Chicago, Illinois: Alpha Kappa Alpha Sorority, Inc., 2006

McNealey, Earnestine Green. *The Pearls of Alpha Kappa Alpha, A History of America's first Black Sorority, Alpha Kappa Alpha*. Chicago, Illinois: Alpha Kappa Alpha Sorority, Incorporated®, 2010

Alpha Kappa Alpha Sorority, Incorporated®, *Ivy Leaf Magazine*:
    December 1933 Issue — Page3
    March 1932 Issue — Page 16, 23, 29
    Volume 29, Issue 3 September 1951 — Page 14
    Volume 32, Issue 3 September 1954 — Page 13
    Volume 45, Issue 2 May/June 1969 1954 — Page 25
    Volume 45, Issue 4, November/December 1969 — Page 13
    Volume 48, Issue 2, May 1972 — Page 43
    Volume 58, Issue 1 Spring 1981 — Page 60
    Volume 58, Issue 2 Summer 1981 Page — 43
    Volume 59, Issue 3 Fall 1982 — Page 51
    Volume 61, Issue 2 Summer 1984 — Page 50
    Volume 63, Issue 1 Spring 1986 — Page 27
    Volume 73, Issue 1 Spring 1995 — Page 57

Alpha Kappa Alpha Sorority, Incorporated® Central Regional Conferences Minutes

ELECTRONIC RESOURCES:

Wikipedia, the Free Encyclopedia. The History of African Americans in Chicago,
    http://en.w.kipedia.org/wiki/history_of_African_Americans_in_Chicago, Modified February 19, 2014

Encyclopedia of Chicago. Manning, Christopher, African Americans,
    http://www.encyclopedia.chicagohistory.org/pages/27.html

Chicago Public Library Digital Collection, Chicago Defender Newspaper,
    http://www.chipublic.org/cplbooksmovies/research/database_atoz.php

University Archives — The University of Chicago Library,
    https://www.libuchicago.edu/e/webexhibits

Index

A

Adams, Jane — i, 313, 417
Adopt-a-Highway — 223, 314, 358, 359
Adopt-a-School — 39, 192
African American Heritage Series — xiv, 127, 191, 209, 219, 498
African American History — 81, 82, 212, 216, 245, 247, 262, 359, 361, 362, 374, 390, 425
African American Male — *See Black Male.*
AKA Coat Day — 19, 23, 31, 94, 143, 164, 260, 321, 349, 364, 386
AKA Day at the Capital — 210, 223, 283, 309, 336, 341
AKAdemy — 21 41 50 74 82 95 96 103 120 135 136 156 167 168 203 213 216 246 263-265, 278, 289, 297, 305, 308, 320, 336, 349, 354, 359, 361, 362, 378, 383, 388, 395, 422, 502, 503
Alpha Eta Omega Chapter — x, xvi, 55, **57-60**, 63, 90, 170, 240, 327, 416, 438, 442, 443, 444-445, 450, 454, 459, 465, 470, 484, 493, 501, 503, 511, 513, 516
Alpha Mu Omega Chapter — x, xvii, xviii, 19, 55, 58, **61-64**, 76, 90, 138, 170, 173, 196, 206, 293, 325, 327, 328, 346, 416, 432, 438, 442, 443-445, 447, 448, 450, 454-456, 459-461, 463-465, 469, 470, 477, 481, 493, 498, 503, 511-513, 515, 516
Alpha Phi Alpha, Fraternity — 2, 14, 49, 88, 130, 131, 143, 223, 288, 236, 390, 395, 411, 449, 451, 452, 511, 524
ACHR — xiv, 107, 127, 451
American Red Cross — 6, 7, 58, 103, 109, 167, 237, 248, 264, 265, 278, 279, 309, 319, 335, 344

B

Barnett, Eta Moten — 54, 63, 72, **138**, 176
Beard, Martha Levingston Perine — ix, xvi, xvii, 27, 28, 196, 241, 335, **337-338**, 426, 428-430, 343, 345, 439, 490-492, 494
Beautillion — 73, 78, 142, 219
Beta Chapter — i, xv, 3, **5-10**, 20, 29, 36, 37, 42, 107, 137, 160, 311, 312, 399, 404, 410, 417, 419, 438, 444, 446, 448, 450, 454, 461, 464, 473, 517
Beta Delta Chapter — xi, 21, 27, 56, **65-67**, 90, 101, 126, 128, 433, 444, 445, 447, 449, 452, 454, 455-457, 459-462, 464-467, 472, 473, 476, 481-483, 493, 495-499, 501, 504, 505, 507, 509, 516
Beta Epsilon Chapter — xi, 30, 33, 56, **70-71**, 150, 337, 338, 433, 449, 453, 455, 457, 459, 460, 462-464, 466, 468-469, 481, 488, 490-491, 500, 509-511, 513, 517
Beta Gamma Omega — x, 56, **72-75**, 181, 428, 432, 453, 457, 460, 461, 464-465, 470, 474, 481, 491, 500, 510, 511, 513-517
Beta Iota Chapter — 129, 134, 135, 136, 450, 452, 517
Beta Omega Omega Chapter — x, 79, **84-85**, 451, 455, 463, 465, 467, 468, 470, 481, 487, 500, 517
Beta Phi Chapter — xi, 63, 151, **165-168**, 193, 433, 465, 469-471, 484, 488, 493, 501, 502, 514, 518
Beta Rho Omega Chapter — x, **77-78**, 158, 287, 288, 455, 463, 468, 474, 481, 487, 500, 510, 517
Beta Upsilon Omega Chapter — x, 68, 79, **80-83**, 432, 450, 453, 457, 460, 461, 463, 464, 465, 467-469, 471, 481, 491, 496, 510, 517
Beta Zeta Chapter — xi, 56, **68-69**, 240, 438, 449, 453, 455-458, 460-464, 468-469, 474-475, 481, 490-491, 509-510, 514, 516
BGLOs — 48, 65, 103, 113, 126, 131,

INDEX

162, 203, 269, 320, 329-330, 335
Black Dollar Day — 73, 136, 147, 156, 216, 274, 279, 297, 309, 319, 341
Black Family — 21, 23, 27, 31, 33, 40, 41, 48, 50, 74, 103-104, 157, 171, 219-220, 228-229, 231, 258, 265, 284, 300, 314, 315, 320, 329, 332, 335, 348, 354, 358, 359, 363, 364, 373, 376, 382-383, 386, 389, 391, 394, 395, 422, 423
Black History — *See African American History.*
Black Male — 25, 32, 48, 59, 78, 97, 219, 245, 248, 408
Blazing New Trails — 14, 206, 354, 495, 496, 497, 499
Bonds, Nadine C. — xvi, xvii, 62-64, 171, 212, 248, 327, 328, **346**, 347, 348, 357, 369, 373, 374, 412, 416, 426, 428, 429, 431, 432, 439, 475, 484, 493, 495-497, 499,
Bousfield, Maudelle Brown — xvi, 6, 8, 9, 35, 42, **419-420**, 427
Breast Cancer — 8, 31, 49, 71, 74, 88, 94-95, 97, 117, 143-145, 148, 189, 206, 220, 235, 265, 269, 289-290, 309, 313, 320, 322-323, 335, 349, 364, 367, 373, 386, 388, 394, 423
Brown, Frederika — 4
Buckhanan, Dorothy W. — ii, ix, xvi, 26, 121, 213, 290, 306, 340, 341-342, .55-356, **378**, 380, 381-382, 385, 392-394, 399, 426-427, 429, 430, 435, 439, 496, 500, 502-504,
Burke, Beulah Elizabeth — xv, 3, 5, 11

C

Cason, Mabel Evans — xvi, 110, 117, 170, 240, 260, **271-272**, 273, 275, 280, 398
Casanova, Giselé — ii, ix, xvi, xvii, 26, 59, 98, 99, 233, 243, 255, 267, 307, 308, 312, 334, 335, 255, 356, 384, 394, **402-404**, 405, 412, 420, 426, 429, 430, 431, 433, 439, 510, 512, 514, 515

Centennial — i, xvii, 8, 23, 25, 35, 42, 59, 66, 96-97, 113, 176, 209, 290, 321, 325, 351, 355, 364, 384, 390, 401, 403-404, 424-425, 434, 507
Centennial Traveling Exhibit — xvii, 25, 325, 355, 464
Chi Alpha Omega Chapter — xi, 346, 372, 374, **375-377**, 504, 509, 522
Chi Chi Omega Chapter — xi, 379, **387-391**, 411, 513, 522
Chi Omega Omega Chapter — x, xi, 356, 379, **392-398**, 402, 410, 505, 509, 511, 523
Chi Phi Omega Chapter — xi, 379, **385-386**, 503, 514, 522
Chi Sigma Omega Chapter — xi, 354, 356, 379, **381-384**, 507, 509, 513, 515, 522
Chi Xi Omega Chapter — xi, 379, 380, **405-406**, 506
College Fair — 22, 193, 216, 228, 375, 394
College Tours — 22, 32, 229
Connection — 31, 120, 154, 156, 248, 260, 266, 271, 276, 282, 284-285, 315, 320, 325, 341, 359, 362, 367, 429, 439, 482, 491
Cotillion — 22, 30, 62, 101-102, 118-119, 148, 203, 213, 229, 236, 248, 278, 288, 298, 350, 361

D

Debutant Cotillion — *See Cotillion.*
Delta Beta Chapter — xi, 87, 89, 123, **130-133**, 240, 399, 433, 438, 450-451, 454-455, 460-461, 462, 464, 467, 473, 483, 489, 496, 498, 507, 517
Delta Chi Omega Chapter — x, 37, **111-114**, 450
Delta Delta Omega Chapter — x, xvii, xviii, 86, 90, **100-106**, 163, 176, 239, 284, 355, 452, 476, 491
Delta Omicron Chapter — xii, 37, 38, 42, 138, **139-141**, 261, 262, 267, 456, 458, 460, 462-464, 478, 479, 484, 492, 494, 495, 509, 511, 518

Delta Phi Omega Chapter — x, 37, 107, **108-110**, 271, 327, 354, 449, 453, 458, 463, 469, 476, 482, 486, 495, 501, 512, 517

Delta Sigma Theta Sorority — 74, 88, 98, 131, 148, 282, 288, 323, 477, 479,

Divine Nine — *See National Pan-Hellenic Council.*

E

EAF — i, x, xiv, xvi, xvii, xviii, 6, 8, 12, 25, 26, 62, 96, 104, 120, 140, 196, 198, 206, 212, 213, 232, 240, 260, 264, 265, 269, 278, 295, 311, 321, 325, 326, 328, 338, 346, 350, 354, 356, 376, 378, 379, 391, 396, 403, 416, 422, 435, 500, 502, 503, 504, 505, 509, 510, 513, 514

Ebony Fashion Show — 72, 88, 92, 93, 95, 109, 142, 223, 244, 245

Economic Development — i, xiv, xvii, 39, 40, 93, 196, 213, 311, 317, 318, 338

Economics — 7, 27, 41, 50, 87, 104, 140, 220, 229, 231, 265, 271, 314, 315, 329, 332, 333, 337, 349, 354, 373, 378, 382, 391, 397, 422, 424, 512

Educational Advancement Foundation — *See EAF.*

Emerging Young Leaders — xiv, 32, 42, 51, 78, 82, 89, 98, 105, 135, 136, 144, 145, 210, 223, 230, 231, 232, 246, 259, 267, 290, 298, 299, 308, 309, 323, 333, 341, 344, 349, 356, 365, 366, 375, 383, 390, 391, 397, 511

Endowment — 26, 58, 62, 107, 119, 127, 251, 265, 297, 311, 321, 325, 326, 346, 350, 356, 376, 378, 396, 403, 431, 451, 453, 500, 502, 504

Endowment Fund — 58, 107, 119, 127, 265, 297, 311, 321, 325, 326, 346, 350, 356, 378, 403, 431, 453, 500, 502

Epsilon Delta Chapter — xii, 120, 151, **152**, 209, 210, 463, 466, 476, 481, 482, 484, 495, 505, 511, 512, 518

Epsilon Epsilon Omega Chapter — x, xi, 14, 107, **115-117**, 451, 456, 460, 466, 472, 480, 487, 497, 506, 517

Epsilon Eta Chapter — xii, 151, **162**, 251, 464, 466, 472, 487, 506, 518

Epsilon Iota Chapter — xii, 101, 105, 151, **163-164**, 344, 462, 465, 466, 467, 468, 469, 472, 473, 474, 475, 476, 483, 489, 496, 507, 518

Epsilon Kappa Omega Chapter — x, xvii, 37, 107, **118-121**, 152, 218, 219, 234, 313, 314, 355, 378, 401, 432, 453, 458, 459, 460, 461, 463, 464, 467, 469, 476, 482, 486, 488, 495, 499, 500, 501, 502, 504, 517

Epsilon Lambda Omega Chapter — x, 107, **122-123**, 130, 451, 455, 467, 473, 489, 496, 507, 517

Epsilon Rho Chapter — xii, 63, 95, 99, 145, **173-175**, 182, 320, 324, 385, 386, 465, 466, 468, 471, 472, 477, 484, 493, 498, 499, 514, 518

Epsilon Xi Chapter — xii, 57, 59, 63, 151, **169-172**, 346, 465, 470, 474, 476, 477, 481, 484, 493, 499, 503, 518

Epsilon Zeta Chapter — xii, 77, 151, **158-159**, 291, 433, 463, 464, 465, 468, 474, 476, 481, 487, 495, 500, 501, 510, 518

ESP — 23, 25, 42, 50, 51, 97, 104, 144, 230, 260, 321, 354, 396, 424, 506, 509

Eta Alpha Chapter — **184**, 274, 472, 480, 487, 519

Eta Chapter — x, 4, **45**, 55, 90, 110, 162, 242, 251, 438, 445, 446, 454

Eta Gamma Chapter — xii, 101, 105, 151, **163-164**, 344, 462, 464, 466, 467, 468, 469, 472, 473, 474, 476, 483, 489, 496, 507, 518

Eta Kappa Omega Chapter — x, 93, 94, 97, 138, **142-145**, 182, 323, 456, 457, 460, 466, 477, 489, 498, 515, 518

Eta Mu Omega Chapter — x, 138, **146-149**, 154, 198, 456, 466, 469, 472, 482, 483, 489, 498, 519

Eta Rho Chapter — xii, 72, **186-187**, 468, 469, 472, 474, 475, 481, 500, 510, 513, 519

Expo — 103, 189, 192, 193, 229, 264, 266, 298, 300, 349, 364, 376, 407

Extraordinary Service Program — 96, 161, 354, 399, 424, 510

EYL — *See Emerging Young Leaders.*

F

Facets of Dynamic Power — 271, 477, 479

Fashionetta — 14, 21, 22, 25, 30, 92, 93, 100, 101, 102, 104, 108, 116, 127, 142, 189, 212, 213, 248, 257, 258, 278, 297, 298, 299, 305, 342

Financial Literacy — 81, 113, 284, 378, 423, 514

Food Pantry — 21, 23, 144, 210, 267, 269, 370

Founders' Day — xvi, 6, 26, 30, 46, 58, 60, 73, 88, 90, 94, 95, 102, 103, 105, 113, 118, 155, 183, 210, 217, 244, 259, 261, 263, 273, 290, 307, 316, 318, 319, 335, 344, 350, 358, 359, 361, 363, 364, 366, 400, 401, 417, 445

G

Gamma Chapter — xv, 3, 4, **11-15**, 20, 56, 76, 115, 117, 151, 362, 419, 438, 464, 484

Gamma Chi Chapter — xi, 113, 151, **160-161**, 240, 355, 356, 433, 463, 465, 467, 469, 471, 472, 475, 476, 478, 479, 480, 481, 485, 486, 494, 496, 501, 504, 513, 518

Gamma House — 12, 13, 14, 76, 79, 107, 115, 151, 442, 445, 447, 448

Gamma Kappa Omega Chapter — x, 86, **87-89**, 130, 446, 448, 451, 455, 462, 473, 474, 483, 489, 496, 507, 517

Gamma Psi Omega Chapter — x, 63, **91-99**, 142, 182, 244, 245, 246, 293, 323, 355, 448, 451, 453, 456, 458, 460, 461, 466, 467, 471, 472, 477, 478, 479, 498, 515, 517

Global Leadership Through Timeless Service — 51, 89, 98, 105, 230, 349, 411

GLTTS — *See Global Leadership Through Timeless Service.*

Green, Loraine Richardson — ix, xv, xvi, xviii, 3, 5, 6, 8, 9, 20, 29, 35, 38, 42, 45, 47, 196, 215, 222, 244, 292, 311, 325, 416, **417-418**, 427, 465, 466, 468, 469, 471, 472, 474, 475, 476, 478, 479, 480, 481, 482, 483, 484, 485, 486, 488, 489, 490, 491, 493, 494, 495, 496, 498, 499, 501, 502, 505, 506, 508, 509

H

Habitat For Humanity — 81, 96, 156, 276, 290, 309, 323

Haley, Johnetta Randolph — xvi, xvii, 26, 27, 28, 38, 100, 164, **176-177**, 182, 186, 188, 191, 196, 198, 272, 280, 283, 284, 285, 286, 344, 281, 355, 416, 426, 428, 429, 430, 431, 434, 435, 439, 463, 465, 466, 467, 471, 472

Harris, Evangeline — xvi, 57, 59, 60, 416, 444

Hayes Clark, Blanche — xv, xvi, 27, 28, 65, 438, 442

HBCU — 21, 22, 40, 93, 103, 212, 228, 229, 230, 278, 289, 297, 329, 305, 390

Health Fair — 21, 22, 23, 31, 40, 41, 42, 78, 81, 82, 93, 103, 148, 167, 189, 203, 209, 216, 278, 289, 295, 364, 376, 407, 500

Hedgeman, Ethel — *See Lyle, Hedgeman Ethel.*

Historical Black Colleges — *See HBCU.*

HIV/AIDS — 8, 31, 49, 50, 66, 81, 82, 94, 206, 220, 230, 243, 246, 248, 264, 269, 309, 314, 319, 320, 335, 376, 383, 386, 388, 423, 511

Howard University — xiii, xiv, xv, 2, 3, 29, 54, 96, 97, 136, 138, 166, 196, 364, 421, 425

I

Iota Chi Omega Chapter — x, **188-189**, 470, 477, 484, 493, 503, 519

Iota Delta Chapter — xii, 120, **194**, 314, 395, 469, 476, 482, 486, 491, 492, 493, 495, 501, 519

Iota Epsilon Chapter — **200**, 470, 471, 519

Iota Sigma Chapter — xii, 72, **201**, 433, 472, 474, 480, 481, 485, 496, 497, 498, 500, 505, 510, 519

Ivy Reading Academy — *See below.*

Ivy Reading AKAdemy — 41, 50, 74, 95, 96, 120, 135, 136, 213, 284, 297, 305, 320, 332, 336, 349, 354, 378, 383, 388, 395, 422, 434, 503

J

Job Corps — xiv, 7, 58, 62, 126, 127, 152, 154, 156, 176, 177, 206, 212, 216, 228, 235, 269, 329, 335, 422, 429, 434

K

Kappa Alpha Psi Fraternity — 32, 130, 131, 132, 189, 223, 230, 288, 289, 346, 411, 446, 447, 449, 451, 452, 484, 502

Kappa Chapter — 3, 4, 14, **18-19**, 29, 55, 62, 76, 173, 325, 459, 474, 486, 496

Kappa Epsilon Omega Chapter — **191-193**, 473, 477, 484, 493, 519

Kappa Mu Omega Chapter — x, **202-204**, 225, 432, 472, 480, 489, 493, 498, 515, 519

Kappa Psi Omega Chapter — xi, **208-210**, 432, 476, 486, 494, 495, 501, 505, 508, 509, 512, 520

Kappa Tau Omega Chapter — xi, xvii, xviii, 58, 196, **205-207**, 327, 416, 470, 476, 477, 484, 493, 503, 520

King, Loann Julia Honesty — i, ii, ix, xvii, xviii, 7, 8, 9, 26, 37, 38, 39, 43, 44, 81, 96, 189, 196, 212, 296, 297, **311-312**, 313, 316, 317, 327, 338, 354, 355, 416, 424, 426, 429, 430, 434, 435, 439, 473, 475, 477, 482, 483, 484, 485, 486, 489, 491, 492, 493, 494, 496, 497, 498, 500, 501, 503, 504, 505, 507, 508, 509, 511, 513, 515, 524

King, Jr., Martin Luther — xiv, 31, 39, 42, 62, 66, 73, 74, 78, 85, 88, 104, 105, 113, 117, 126, 127, 143, 166, 173, 189, 216, 223, 231, 265, 266, 290, 293, 295, 305, 308, 314, 321, 322, 326, 336, 341, 349, 363, 364, 367, 374, 383, 386, 388, 395, 423

L

Lambda Alpha Omega Chapter — xi, **211-214**, 302, 367, 474, 475, 476, 478, 479, 480, 481, 482, 483, 484, 485, 492, 496, 501, 503, 504, 505, 507, 509, 515, 520

Lambda Mu Omega Chapter — xi, **215-217**, 268, 269, 473, 478, 479, 480, 485, 488, 492, 501, 502, 504, 505, 509, 520

Lambda Nu Omega Chapter — xi, **222-224**, 369, 479, 486, 492, 495, 501, 512, 520

Lambda Omega — 4, 18, **46**, 55, 61, 496, 516

Lambda Psi Chapter — xii, 203, **225-226**, 480, 486, 489, 492, 498, 499, 504, 520

Lambda Tau Omega Chapter — xi, **227-233**, 361, 486, 487, 488, 489, 492, 493, 494, 497, 498, 501, 504, 505, 508, 511, 515, 520

Lambda Xi Chapter — xii, 120, **218-221**, 240, 474, 486, 495, 501, 512, 520

Lawson, Annetta M. — xvi, 15, 62, 63, **138**, 146, 245, 426, 439, 454, 455, 461, 462, 464, 465, 466, 468, 469, 471, 473, 474, 475, 476, 477, 478,

479, 480, 481, 482, 483, 484, 485, 487, 488, 490, 492, 493, 494, 495, 497, 498, 499, 501, 503, 504, 505, 506, 508, 509, 511, 513, 515

Leadership Training — 156, 207, 212, 362, 363, 367, 375

League of Women Voters — 24, 31, 279, 417, 421

LeCompte, Peggy Lewis — xvi, xvii, xviii, 58, 97, 102, 105, 106, 150, 183, 196, 212, 234, **239-241**, 247, 250, 253, 255, 256, 257, 261, 262, 263, 267, 268, 272, 343, 355, 416, 426, 427, 430, 434, 435, 439, 473, 474, 475, 476, 477, 478, 481, 486, 493, 494

Literacy Programs — 21, 22, 23, 25, 50, 51, 59, 81, 95, 96, 97, 98, 103, 113, 122, 143, 156, 212, 213, 230, 264, 284, 305, 309, 335, 366, 368, 383, 388, 390, 391, 396, 409, 423, 439, 514

Little Miss AKA — 30, 82, 85, 155, 171

Lyle, Ethel Hedgeman — ii, xiii, 2, 3, 11, 22, 24, 58, 65, 97, 127, 282, 283, 504, 507

M

March of Dimes — 72, 74, 102, 117, 156, 192, 237, 262, 263

McKinzie, Barbara A. — xvi, xvii, 39, 40, 41, 43, 44, 96, 155, 196, 197, 321, 348, 349, 354, 355, 382, 394, **424-425**, 427, 428, 429, 430, 431, 434, 435, 510

Mississippi Health Project — 36, 56, 62, 119, 419, 445

MLK Day of Service — 31, 66, 85, 88, 96, 105, 113, 117, 246, 265, 266, 290, 305, 314, 336, 341, 349, 365, 367, 374, 383, 423

Moten, Etta — 54, 72, 176, 451

Mu Beta Chapter — xii, 120, **234-235**, 433, 474, 476, 482, 486, 490, 494, 495, 501, 512, 520

Mu Delta Omega Chapter — xi, **236-238**, 356, 403, 474, 481, 520

Mu Graduate/Gamma Omega — x, xv, 3, 4, 14, **20-28**, 516

Mu Rho Chapter — xii, 110, 239, **242-243**, 433, 476, 478, 482, 486, 495, 497, 501, 512, 520

N

NAACP — *See below.*

National Association for the Advancement of Colored People — xiv, 2, 6, 7, 17, 24, 27, 31, 36, 58, 72, 78, 85, 88, 101, 102, 116, 135, 143, 154, 166, 192, 193, 206, 209, 211, 212, 213, 216, 225, 240, 248, 269, 277, 278, 288, 290, 294, 309, 319, 320, 321, 322, 341, 344, 346, 434, 445, 469, 476

National Bone Marrow Registry — xiv, 341

National Council of Negro Women — 17, 74, 212, 269, 300, 309

National Non-Partisan Council — 36, 107, 447

National Pan-Hellenic Council — 49, 50, 132, 167, 168, 237, 267, 300, 336, 362, 365, 369, 400

National Reading Seminars — xvii, 38

NCNW — 36, 300, 309, 434

Newsome, Maenell Hamlin — xvi, 62, 63, **90**, 91, 99, 146, 169, 327, 426, 439, 447, 470, 477, 504

NPHC — *See National Pan-Hellenic Council.*

Nu Lambda Chapter — xii, 97, 99, 239, **244-246**, 433, 476, 477, 489, 496, 498, 501

Nu Omicron Omega Chapter — xi, 239, **247-249**, 273, 380, 480, 487, 497, 499, 505, 506, 520

Nu Pi Omega Chapter — xi, 239, **250-252**, 432, 480, 487, 506, 520

Nu Sigma Chapter — xv, 123, 239, **253**, 481, 489, 520

O

Omega Psi Phi Fraternity — 274, 288, 320, 322, 449
Omicron Alpha Chapter — xii, 213, 214, 240, **302**, 433, 485, 488, 490, 492, 504, 511, 513, 521
Omicron Delta Omega Chapter — xi, **273-274**, 480, 487, 490, 495, 497, 498, 499, 501, 506, 521
Omicron Eta Omega Chapter — xi, **275-279**, 344, 354, 483, 489, 496, 507, 521
Omicron Phi Omega Chapter — xi, **292-295**, 487, 488, 493, 513, 521
Omicron Sigma Omega Chapter — xi, 77, **287-291**, 432, 481, 487, 500, 510, 521
Omicron Theta Omega Chapter — xi, xvii, 176, **280-286**, **344**, 416, 481, 482, 483, 484, 489, 496, 507, 521
Omicron Xi Chapter — xii, 120, 311, **313-315**, 486, 495, 499, 501, 502, 521
On Track — 58, 156, 229, 332, 333, 349

P

Patterson, Blanche Williams — 27, 90, 445, 446
Payne, Carolynne — xvi, 4, 426
Perkins, Yvonne — ix, xvi, xvii, 31, 62, 63, 64, 155, 196, 245, **325-326**, 327, 328, 332, 334, 338, 426, 428, 429, 430, 431, 434, 435, 439, 477, 486, 487, 488, 490
Phi Beta Sigma Fraternity — 131, 167, 288, 361
Phi Epsilon Omega Chapter — xi, 346, **347-351**, 364, 498, 508, 515, 522
Phi Kappa Omega Chapter — xi, 346, 350, **357-368**, 432, 498, 508, 515, 522
Pi Gamma Omega Chapter — xi, 209, **296-301**, 482, 486, 495, 501, 521
Pi Lambda Chapter — xi, xii, 63, **327-330**, 433, 485, 487, 488, 491, 493, 494, 495, 500, 503, 504, 505, 510, 511, 513, 521
Pi Lambda Omega Chapter — xi, **303-310**, 485, 487, 488, 491, 500, 510, 521
Pi Nu Chapter — xii, 264, 267, 311, 326, **334-336**, 433, 488, 490, 491, 492, 493, 495, 497, 498, 504, 505, 514, 522
PIMS — 21, 40, 264, 265, 369
Political Action — 93, 248, 271, 282
Porch, Pamela Bates — xvi, 42, 132, 212, 266, 267, 293, 300, 322, 365, 384, 390, **399-401**, 405, 426, 430, 431, 439, 490, 492, 494, 497, 506, 507-510,
Porter, Maude Brown — xvi, 29, 33, 61, 80, 84, **421**, 427, 450, 452
Poverty — 24, 51, 58, 59, 71, 105, 181, 186, 231, 232, 238, 285, 309, 333, 366, 390, 391, 397
Preston, Carey B. — xvii, 13, 38, 102, 126, 127, 177, 361, 362, 394, 431, 451, 452, 453, 473, 475, 477, 498, 502

Q

Quander, Nellie — xiii, xv, 2, 3

R

Reading Is Fundamental — 103, 116, 135, 136
Reed, Pauline Kigh — xv, xvi, xvii, 3, **17**, 36, 42, 43, 426, 439, 442, 474, 475, 477
Rho Lambda Chapter — 338, **339**, 522
RIF — *See above.*
Roberts, Evelyn — xvi, 58, **128**, 130, 134, 426, 444, 452, 453, 474, 475, 477
Roberts, Ordie Amelia — xvi, 13, 14, 37, 43, 101, **151**, 154, 162, 163, 170, 173, 222, 426, 435, 439, 459, 460, 461, 462, 463, 471, 474, 475, 477
Roosevelt, Eleanor — 14, 17, 120, 126, 418

S

Shelburne, Lee Anna — xvi, 33, 58, 101, **150**, 163, 426, 439, 456, 457, 458, 461, 471, 477, 494

Shelters — 19, 31, 74, 82, 94, 104, 122, 143, 147, 175, 209, 216, 237, 238, 246, 274, 279, 290, 317, 320, 322, 331, 335, 358, 360, 362, 383, 397, 398, 408, 409, 413, 510

Sickle Cell Anemia — xiv, 37, 49, 62, 78, 95, 101, 119, 122, 126, 127, 154, 164, 168, 212, 246, 262, 264, 269, 271, 317, 318, 335, 350, 359, 362, 364

SIDS — 88, 140, 164, 220, 265, 320, 423

Sigma Eta Chapter — xii, 33, 346, **371**, 504, 510, 522

Sigma Gamma Chapter — xii, 74, 131, 224, 346, **369-370**, 411, 447, 449, 501, 509, 522

Sigma Gamma Rho Sorority — 74, 131, 411, 447, 449

Sigma Phi Omega Chapter — xi, 94, 97, **316-324**, 489, 498, 521

Smart, Alice McGhee — xvi, xvii, 9, 12, 14, 27, **76**, 406, 426, 428, 430, 438, 442, 443, 444, 445, 446, 447, 448, 450, 452, 453, 454, 455, 456, 457, 458, 460, 461, 463, 464, 465, 467, 468, 470, 471, 473, 474, 475, 477, 478, 480, 481, 483, 484, 485, 487, 488, 491, 492, 493, 494, 496, 497, 498, 499, 501, 503, 504, 505, 507, 508, 509, 511, 513, 515

Smith Bond, Gloria E. — xvi, xvii, 148, 149, 183, 196, **198-199**, 202, 203, 205, 206, 208, 212, 219, 222, 225, 227, 234, 429, 430, 474, 475, 477

SPIRIT — 41, 89, 95, 229, 276, 349, 354, 361, 422, 505

T

Tau Chapter — 4, 12, **47-51**, 205, 206, 207, 446, 468, 475, 496

Tau Gamma Omega Chapter — xi, 326, **331-333**, 361, 492, 501, 504, 509, 522

Tau Iota — x, xii, 403, **405-409**, 433, 523

Tau Mu — xii, 398, 403, **410-411**, 523

Tau Rho — xii, 136, 380, 403, **412-413**, 423

Tax Freedom — 95, 194, 246, 314

Teen Conference — 89, 258

Teen Pearls — 42, 395, 396

Test Preparation — 229, 263, 289

Theta Omega Chapter — i, x, xi, xvii, xviii, 4, 6, 7, 8, 12, 14, 17, **35-44**, 55, 107, 137, 151, 154, 176, 196, 197, 198, 212, 215, 311, 327, 354, 355, 356, 361, 416, 418, 419, 422, 424, 432, 438, 442, 444, 445, 446, 447, 448, 449, 450, 453, 454, 455, 456, 457, 458, 459, 460, 461, 463, 464, 465, 468, 469, 470, 471, 473, 474, 478, 479, 480, 481, 482, 483, 484, 487, 489, 491, 492, 493, 494, 496, 497, 498, 500, 502, 504, 507, 508, 509, 515, 516

Theta Omicron Chapter — **190**, 480, 519

Theta Rho Omega Chapter — x, 147, 151, **153-157**, 355, 361, 432, 466, 468, 470, 471, 472, 477, 485, 486, 487, 488, 489, 490, 492, 496, 498, 500, 503, 508, 509, 515, 518

Tutoring — 21, 23, 31, 38, 40, 81, 84, 93, 108, 116, 154, 156, 167, 171, 203, 216, 228, 229, 245, 251, 264, 289, 294, 320, 332, 349, 361, 383, 395, 422

U

UNICEF — 171, 219, 245, 263

Upsilon Mu Omega Chapter — xi, 338, **340-342**, 378, 432, 494, 495, 496, 497, 498, 499, 500, 501, 502, 512, 522

Upsilon Phi Omega Chapter — xi, 240, **343-345**, 496, 507, 522

Urban League — 6, 17, 24, 31, 36, 72, 97, 126, 147, 168, 192, 193, 212, 213, 241, 248, 251, 269, 309, 323, 417, 421

Vocational Guidance Program — 7, 8, 21, 35, 36, 37, 84, 90, 112, 271, 421

Voter Registration — 7, 8, 31, 38, 39, 42, 78, 81, 103, 116, 135, 148, 156, 196, 209, 216, 274, 275, 279, 282, 290, 367, 374, 383, 386

W

Walk-A-Thon — 23, 39, 81, 98, 143, 144, 220, 269, 358, 359, 362, 364

Washington, Arlene — 43, **79**, 112, 443, 444

Waters, Phyllis — xvii, 3, 29, 46, 47, 61, 62, 63, 477

White, Linda Marie — xvi, xvii, 26, 38, 40, 41, 42, 43, 44, 95, 155, 196, 197, 325, 338, 346, 354, 363, 378, 386, 394, 400, **422-423**, 427, 431, 434, 435, 490, 505

Wilkins, Lucille — xvi, 9, 108, 111, 426

Wilson, Dororthy Buckhanan — ii, ix, xvi, 26, 121, 213, 290, 306, 340, 341, 342, 355, 356, **378-379**, 380, 381, 382, 385, 392, 393, 394, 399, 426, 427, 429, 430, 435, 496, 500, 502, 503, 504

X

Xi Epsilon Chapter — 113, 239, **254**, 479, 485, 491, 492, 521

Xi Eta Omega Chapter — xi, 239, **256-260**, 477, 494, 495, 501, 512, 521

Xi Graduate/Eta Omega — 4, **29-34**, 442, 516

Xi Kappa Chapter — xii, 217, 239, **268-270**, 478, 479, 481, 482, 483, 486, 488, 492, 499, 502, 503, 504, 521

Xi Nu Omega Chapter — xi, 140, 212, 319, **261-267**, 334, 335, 336, 356, 399, 400, 402, 479, 492, 493, 494, 495, 497, 500, 504, 506, 509, 511, 512, 513, 515, 521

Xi Zeta Chapter — 239, **255**, 274, 402, 477, 521

Y

YMCA — 22, 72, 112, 159, 309, 344, 348, 349, 395, 407

Y-Me — 349, 394

YWCA — 4, 6, 23, 36, 58, 93, 95, 135, 136, 138, 148, 192, 216, 263, 264, 265, 276, 278, 282, 335, 400, 443, 446, 447, 494

Z

Zeta Iota Chapter — xii, **179**, 240, 249, 350, 351, 433, 469, 472, 498, 519

Zeta Nu Chapter — xii, 72, **180-181**, 465, 466, 467, 468, 469, 470, 473, 474, 481, 488, 510, 519

Zeta Phi Beta Sorority — 74, 88, 131, 288

Zeta Phi Chapter — xii, 92, 99, **182-183**, 466, 471, 472, 519

Zeta Zeta Chapter — x, xii, 85, **178**, 433, 464, 465, 468, 474, 481, 487, 513, 517

Zeta Zeta Omega Chapter — x, 57, **134-136**, 412, 451, 455, 459, 463, 465, 470, 487, 513, 517